Praise for Tim Cook

"Cook has written what will surely be the definitive history of the Canadian Army in the First World War." —*Edmonton Journal*

"*Shock Troops* never lets us forget that when the barrage lifted and the whistles blew, everything rested on the shoulders of the men about to clamber over the top." —*The Globe and Mail*

"If you want to know more about the Canadian experience in the Great War, these books are a fine resource—exhaustively researched and yet vividly accessible." —*The Star Phoenix* (Saskatoon)

"Tim Cook knows more about WWI than you ever will." —*National Post*

"Compelling narrative … [Cook's] easy-going style, interesting personal stories and attention to detail engage the reader." —*Ottawa Sun*

"Gripping history." —*The Gazette* (Montreal)

"Military scholar John Keegan described how military history ought to be written— 'rigorously but vigorously, with emotional passion but intellectual dispassion' … [and] *Shock Troops* and its predecessor, *At the Sharp End*, reach this lofty standard. They will remain essential reading for historians and anyone interested in the Canadian Expeditionary Force for years to come." —*Guelph Mercury*

Praise for *At The Sharp End*
Canadians Fighting the Great War, 1914–1916, Volume One

Winner of the J.W. Dafoe Book Prize and the Ottawa Book Award
Nominated for the British Columbia Award for Canadian Non-Fiction

"An authoritative and brightly written narrative." —*The Gazette* (Montreal)

"Cook has produced an impeccably researched and immensely readable account of the Great War. The mark of a good historian is finding new ways to tell a tale we thought we knew, and Cook has that quality in spades." —*The Globe and Mail*

"Exhaustively researched and written with great narrative momentum, *At the Sharp End* creates an unforgettable canvas of Canada's men at war." —*Hill Times* (Ottawa)

"Cook's First World War history arrives with a difference ... it is the common foot soldier that drives the narrative ... [A] magnificent and accessible history of the Great War." —*Sun-Times* (Owen Sound)

"Provides an intimate look at the Canadian men who fought in World War One ... An engrossing, moving experience." —*London Free Press*

"*At the Sharp End* is a landmark work of military scholarship and gripping narrative ... Featuring never-before-published photographs, letters, diaries, and maps, the book recounts ... the Great War through soldiers' moving eyewitness accounts." —*Scene* magazine (London, Ontario)

PENGUIN CANADA

SHOCK TROOPS

TIM COOK is the curator of the South African and First World War galleries at the Canadian War Museum, as well as an adjunct research professor at Carleton University. He is the author of *No Place to Run* and *Clio's Warriors* as well as *At the Sharp End: Canadians Fighting the Great War, 1914–1916, Volume One*, which won the the 2007 J.W. Dafoe Prize and the 2008 Ottawa Book Award for Non-Fiction. He lives in Ottawa with his family.

Also by Tim Cook

No Place to Run

Clio's Warriors

At the Sharp End: Canadians Fighting the Great War,
1914–1916, Volume One

TIM COOK

SHOCK TROOPS

CANADIANS FIGHTING THE GREAT WAR, 1917–1918

VOLUME TWO

PENGUIN
CANADA

PENGUIN CANADA

Published by the Penguin Group

Penguin Group (Canada), 90 Eglinton Avenue East, Suite 700, Toronto, Ontario, Canada M4P 2Y3
(a division of Pearson Canada Inc.)

Penguin Group (USA) Inc., 375 Hudson Street, New York, New York 10014, U.S.A.
Penguin Books Ltd, 80 Strand, London WC2R 0RL, England
Penguin Ireland, 25 St Stephen's Green, Dublin 2, Ireland (a division of Penguin Books Ltd)
Penguin Group (Australia), 250 Camberwell Road, Camberwell, Victoria 3124, Australia (a division of Pearson Australia Group Pty Ltd)
Penguin Books India Pvt Ltd, 11 Community Centre, Panchsheel Park, New Delhi – 110 017, India
Penguin Group (NZ), 67 Apollo Drive, Rosedale, North Shore 0745, Auckland, New Zealand (a division of Pearson New Zealand Ltd)
Penguin Books (South Africa) (Pty) Ltd, 24 Sturdee Avenue, Rosebank, Johannesburg 2196, South Africa

Penguin Books Ltd, Registered Offices: 80 Strand, London WC2R 0RL, England

First published in Viking Canada hardcover by Penguin Group (Canada), a division of Pearson Canada Inc., 2008
Published in this edition, 2009

1 2 3 4 5 6 7 8 9 10   (CR)

LIBRARY AND ARCHIVES CANADA CATALOGUING IN PUBLICATION

Cook, Tim, 1971-
Shock troops : Canadians fighting the Great
War, 1917-1918 / Tim Cook.

"Volume Two".
Continues: At the sharp end : Canadians fighting the
Great War, 1914-1916.
Includes bibliographical references and index.
ISBN 978-0-14-305593-8

1. Canada. Canadian Army—History—World War, 1914-1918.
2. Canada. Canadian Army. Canadian Corps—History. 3. World
War, 1914-1918—Campaigns—Western Front. 4. World
War, 1914-1918—Canada. I. Title.

D547.C2C557 2009   ~~940.4'1271~~   C2009-902755-0

Visit the Penguin Group (Canada) website at **www.penguin.ca**

Special and corporate bulk purchase rates available; please see
www.penguin.ca/corporatesales or call 1-800-810-3104, ext. 477 or 474

For Sarah, Chloe, Emma, and Piper-Paige

Contents

SHOCK TROOPS

"I am going to be a little morbid this afternoon and tell you something of No Man's Land—that strip of land, varying from forty yards to eight hundred in width, lying between our front trench and the Germans," wrote thirty-two-year-old Corporal Harry Coombs to his brother in July 1915. He was recovering from a gunshot wound he'd suffered to his arm while serving on the Western Front. Coombs had left Peace River Crossing and enlisted in Edmonton in the first month of the war, and he would spend much of the next four years serving in the trenches, rising to the rank of captain, winning the Military Cross for gallantry, and receiving two additional injuries in battle, including multiple wounds from grenade fragments and another gunshot wound to the left thigh and hand, resulting in the loss of several fingers.

"I think I am safe." Coombs continued. "There is not a square yard of No Man's Land which is not saturated with the blood of either friend or foe. Thousands of tons of death-dealing missives have passed over it. If the blades of grass could talk … [they] could tell of the dying agonies of wounded men—some from loss of blood which a friendly hand could have stopped if possible to reach them, others from starvation, others possibly by their own hands when the pain was unbearable."

Into the abyss went Harry and his brother, or at least insofar as the former surveyor tried to portray their destination in his letter home:

It is one o'clock in the morning. A little late to start out but Fritz will probably not be watching so close for us at that hour. As the sky darkens after being illuminated by a star shell, (there is no moon) we run up a ladder and drop over the parapet, immediately falling flat in the long grain as another star shell goes up. We are under cover from view but not from fire. As the sky darkens again, we pick our way through our barbed wire. If we get entangled in it we are gone. We get through without being seen. The stench is awful. Then we start crawling through the long grass towards Fritz's trenches. As the lights go up we drop into a shell hole, which are as thick as holes in a sponge. Or if caught suddenly just lie motionless with our faces buried in the grass roots. A white face is easily seen. In this way we have gone a few yards. The stench right here is much worse. The sky darkens and I prepare to crawl again but the man's boots in front of me do not move. I whisper "go on".... Then I realize it is a dead man's boots I have been watching. I crawl around him and again the star shell breaks. I am level with the dead man and his bloated face, black and shiny with his eyes wide open and large, staring at me. I am calloused to these things by now. If the stench is not too bad I try to get his identity disc and any papers he may have so that the folks at home can get away from that "missing" uncertainty. We go on. We crawl over rifles, bandoliers and other equipment. Maybe we pass an arm or a leg. We pass more bodies—some our own, some the enemy. Finally we come to the trip-wires—entanglements about six inches off the ground and with the wire forming triangles that hold one hard and fast if one gets a boot into them. If we are particularly bold we may work through the trip-wire and then through the higher entanglements right up to the enemy's parapet. Then we pull out the safety pins and pitch in our hand grenades.... Into another shell crater we pitch. They hold us there until daylight comes. Then we must "stick it" all day. When night comes again we manage to work back. Dangerous! Very. But not much more than sticking back in the trenches with the shells breaking all around you and if you "go out" you do so without a fighting chance.[1]

NO MAN'S LAND perfectly symbolized the futility of the Great War on the Western Front. Only the rotting dead could hold this blasted landscape. Front-line soldiers on the edge of this unreal world had to pass through death's territory before they could even meet the enemy, let alone punch through to the green fields beyond.

Each time the Allies or the Germans pushed into No Man's Land through a large-scale attack or, as Coombs related, a small-scale raid, they realized that unless they could somehow annihilate the enemy, or destroy his will to fight, even a successful offensive would likely result only in driving the enemy back to a new position and create a new dead zone between the opposing armies. No Man's Land could never be won, much like the war itself, which seemed never to end.

No Man's Land seemed to disappear by day, as front-line soldiers lived their troglodytic existence, crouching in their underground trench systems that stretched along 700 kilometres of the Western Front, from Switzerland to the North Sea. This trench system had been formed in the first months of the war as the manoeuvring armies had run face-first into machine-gun and small-arms bullets, as well as experiencing the horrific effects of shrapnel or shards from high explosive shells. Soldiers found cover within the earth, and they rarely emerged while at the front. Operations that sent the troops over the top resulted in heavy destruction of the exposed forces that advanced over open ground, negotiating around craters, looking for openings in the entanglements of barbed wire, and all the while being fired upon by defenders who were better protected and knew from which direction the enemy came. The failure of the attackers was not due to a lack of courage or discipline but to the inability of their weapons to dislodge or kill the defenders. No army had enough heavy guns to pound enemy fortifications and there were never enough shells to clear the barbed wire. Most of the attacks on the Western Front in the first two years of the war had resulted in shattering losses, and no matter the exertions or sacrifice, that ribbon of destruction that separated and buttressed the two opposing armies always remained.

Despite the grim odds facing the infantry, many of these civilian-soldiers were, like Coombs, willing to risk life and limb for a "fighting chance." The men who formed the Great War's armies actively sought new ways to endure, survive, and fight in this brutal environment. And perhaps one day they might reclaim No Man's Land (thus destroying the buffer with the enemy), send the German armies reeling, and return to their loved ones.

"THE CANADIANS," wrote British prime minister David Lloyd George, "played a part of such distinction [during the 1916 Battle of the Somme] that thenceforward they were marked out as storm troops; for the remainder of the war they were brought along to head the assault in one great battle after another. Whenever the Germans found the Canadian Corps coming into the line they prepared for the worst."[2] The label nicely sums up the reputation of the Canadian Corps in the Great War. When British forces were often portrayed as floundering in the mud, the Canadian elite shock troops were thrown into battle in the last two years of the war to deliver victory time and time again.

Although Lloyd George knew well the fighting capabilities of the Canadians, the fact that he was fighting his own war of reputations in the 1930s should not be discounted. It was during this time that he penned his multi-volume memoirs, in which he took few prisoners among the British high command.[3] The prime minister's bitter attacks on the generals—those dead and alive—and his perception of the futile war effort on the Western Front were supported by his portrayal of the tough Dominion soldiers as shock troops, especially in relation to British soldiers who never had a chance since they were lions supposedly led by donkeys. But the Canadians had not always been so successful, having stumbled at times during the first two years on the Western Front as the four divisions grappled with learning the art of warfighting.[4] Absorbing the hard-won tactical lessons had been a slow and painful process.

The Canadians had arrived on the Western Front in February 1915, having luckily missed the killing battles of 1914. But almost immediately, the raw and untried Canadian Division had been ordered to the Ypres salient, where they faced the previously unknown terror of lethal chlorine gas at the Second Battle of Ypres in April 1915. Here, the Canadians exhibited bulldog tenacity as they confronted overwhelming German forces, were outgunned, were often abandoned by their Allied comrades. The four days of nearly continuous fighting was the Canadians' baptism of fire, and they made a name for themselves. They also paid a terrible price, sustaining 6,000 casualties. Ragged and torn, the division, having lost a third of its strength in the defence of Ypres, would fight a month later at Festubert. This was one of the worst debacles of the entire war for the Canadians, as they repeatedly charged over open ground, with little artillery support and in the face of concentrated German fire. A week of futile attacks had left another 2,605 Canadians on their way to hospitals or buried in shallow graves.

THE WESTERN FRONT

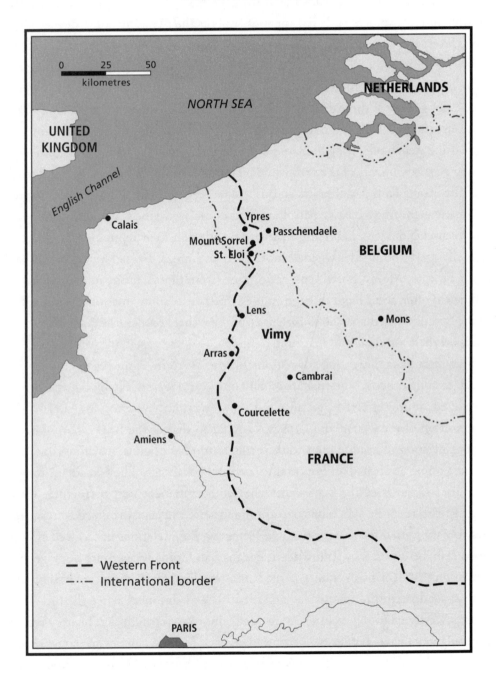

- 0 25 50
- kilometres

NORTH SEA

NETHERLANDS

UNITED
KINGDOM

English Channel

BELGIUM

Calais

Ypres
Passchendaele
Mount Sorrel
St. Eloi

Lens
Vimy

Mons

Arras

Cambrai

Courcelette

Amiens

FRANCE

- – – Western Front
- –·–· International border

PARIS

The Canadians learned what the British, French, and other Allied armies had already come to understand: the maw of war on the Western Front opened very wide. From the summer of 1915, and for almost a year, the Canadian Division, which would be joined by the 2nd and 3rd Divisions to form the Canadian Corps at the end of the year (the 4th Division would join in 1916), was engaged in holding the long lines of dirty ditches that had become their homes. Unyielding mud, flies, rats, and lice; cold and dampness in the winter, heat and thirst in the summer; the wafting stench of rotting flesh and body odour; and bad food and boredom were among the tiny horrors of the war, while major ones of shells, bullets, gas, and mortars killed Canadians day after day in this strange siege warfare. Pushing back against the steady hemorrhage, active patrolling, and raiding gave the Canadians temporary control over No Man's Land and further strengthened their reputation as elite soldiers. By 1916, both sides wielded more guns and more shells. The Canadian battles at St. Eloi, Mount Sorrel, and the Somme were titanic affairs in which victory and defeat often went hand in hand in the same battle, sometimes on the same day. At the cost of more than 35,000 casualties in these three battles, the Canadians consolidated their reputation as fearsome fighters.

The Canadians, like other formations on the Western Front, went through an active learning process. They paid for their failures and victories in blood, and slowly developed more effective tactics and new weapon systems. By 1916, the composition of the Canadian Corps was similar to that of the British corps—from the organization of headquarters to their rough number of guns, machine guns, and support units, but it had an important structural advantage. The Canadians fought together for much of the war within the semi-permanent corps structure: while other British corps had divisions pass through them, the Canadians stayed together, allowing the varied formations to forge strong working relationships as well as pool resources where necessary. But while the Canadian Corps was a more homogenous formation than its British counterparts, it also benefited from important lessons that were disseminated throughout the larger British Expeditionary Force (BEF).

The Western Front left little room for glamorous warfighting. There were no sweeping manoeuvre battles, no deception plans to force the enemy to retreat or risk being enveloped. On a continuous front that was now deepening to several kilometres, the fighting was brutal, plunge-ahead warfare. Armies were forced to batter their way forward. But the Canadians responded to this environment with a fighting system that was in fact glamorous in its intensity and intricacy, as it focused on set-piece engagements (intensely planned operations that aimed to achieve limited objectives rather than hoped-for yet unobtainable breakthroughs), robust combat units, and an understanding that the command-and-control problems that plagued all forces could be successfully addressed only through decentralization and faith in junior officers and front-line soldiers. Good commanders and aggressive soldiers employed and refined their battlefield tactics throughout 1917 and 1918, during which time the Canadians never lost another set-piece battle, punched far above their weight as a combat formation, and earned respect as an elite shock force.

ANY HISTORIAN studying the Great War must be humbled by the scope of the conflict. The world war affected tens of millions of people around the globe. More than 50,000 French-language books on the Great War are listed in the National Library in Paris; likely three or four times more are in English libraries in North America, Britain, and other Commonwealth countries.[5] Even to focus on Canada alone, and its fighting forces on the Western Front, requires that the historian stare down ninety years of historiography as laid out in thousands of books and academic articles. The sheer number of archival files available would require several lifetimes to read. And the history of battle is particularly hard to write. It is as much about the clash of arms and the cries of men as it is about the silences missing from the record. Most of the struggles endured in the war will never be known, having been buried with the participants and decision makers who didn't survive the battles. But this book is based on over a decade's study of tens of thousands of pages of official and private documents, including letters, diaries, memoirs, and less traditional forms of documentation, such as artifacts, postcards, photographs, works of art, and countless types of archival ephemera. An understanding of the complexity of battle can be achieved only by consulting these multiple sources of information—not to mention walking the battlefields to explore the very ground upon which the soldiers fought. Having read almost every book published in Canada on the war, and hundreds by international scholars, I am only too aware that even a two-volume history can present just a fraction of the nation's experience in the Great War. But the role of the historian is to both chronicle and make sense of the past through recourse to limited surviving evidence. By building the story upon the rich scholarship that has come before, and further supporting it with deep investigations into the archival records, I hope to present a new view of the Canadian Corps' battles in the Great War. As in *At the Sharp End*, the volume that precedes and is meant to be read in conjunction with this one, the focus here is on the Canadian Corps, Canada's land army on the Western Front. Over 100,000 strong by 1917, it was a superb force, recognized by Allies and enemy alike as a formidable fighting formation. The "creation of the Canadian Corps was the greatest thing Canada had ever done" up to that point in its history, wrote famed historian C.P. Stacey.[6] The vast majority of Canadian soldiers served with the Canadian Corps, which was part of the overall Canadian Expeditionary Force (CEF), and those Canadians who served outside of the corps—in the Canadian Cavalry Brigade, forestry and railway units, the Siberian

These Canadian sentries guard a portion of the trench system on the Western Front. The determined look on the face of the soldier in the middle of the photograph suggests that he and his comrades will live up to the Canadian Corps' reputation as shock troops.

Expeditionary Force, for example—will find a voice here only when they interact with the corps.

Pound for pound, the Canadian Corps was the most renowned formation on the Western Front. Never before, and never again, would Canada field a force that outperformed all other armies in terms of combat effectiveness. "The British they are good soldiers but the Canadians they are madmen," one captured German officer supposedly remarked, as recounted by Alexander Lightbourn, a prewar law student before enlisting in the 4th Canadian Mounted Rifles. "I tell you it makes a fellow proud of his country to hear that sort of thing."[7] Indeed, the Canadians were elite soldiers, but it must be remembered that the Canadian Corps fought as part of the BEF and was ably supported by the Imperial forces' staff officers, artillery, and supplies and logistics. The Canadians nevertheless developed a methodical system of waging war that overcame the stalemate on the Western Front, and that is the focus of much of this book.

ALTHOUGH THE CONTINUOUS TRENCH SYSTEM of the Western Front was rarely broken until the last months of the war, soldiers were always looking for new ways to survive and to eventually break the deadlock. Weapons, doctrine, and organization all evolved to create a more flexible, efficient, and robust attack system, which relied on set-piece battles and innovative tactics at the sharp end. While ongoing modifications were made to the Canadian way of war—primarily in terms of learning to fight with an increased tempo, with less time to plan for operations, and with newly introduced organizations, doctrines, and weapons—many of the lessons of battle would be processed over the winter months of 1916, the transformative period for Canadians fighting in the final two years of the Great War. But the struggles in 1917 and 1918 would be far more intense and costly, and would require battle-hardened organizations, leaders, and troops to deliver victory. Canada met those requirements.

The CEF's shock troops comprised nearly as many foreign-born soldiers as Canadians—primarily British, but also American and other members of what we now call the Commonwealth countries—but all fought under the Maple Leaf. One such soldier, Private George Bell, an American printer from Detroit, had enlisted in

September 1914 and fought for much of the war in the trenches until his demobilization in 1919. Bell wrote of his view in the front lines: "Field Marshals and generals see the war in terms of armies, corps, and divisions; a private sees it in terms of sections, squads, occupants of his own dugouts.... The historian sees the reasons that prompt a general to order that a certain position be taken; the private sees the dead and dying, men blown to pieces and horribly mutilated, attempting to carry out that order."[8] In this book, I have tried, as the historian, to present the battle from the view of both the generals and the privates, but if the emphasis is weighted to those at the sharp end—men like George Bell and the tens of thousands of his comrades—it is because it was they who would ultimately deliver the hammer-blow victories in the coming two years. And while the blasted ruins of No Man's Land remained a chimera beyond the grasp of the attacking forces, in 1917 and 1918 it would increasingly be owned by the Canadian Corps, which spearheaded the Allied grinding push to victory.

CHAPTER 1

DYING TO SURVIVE

The Battlefield Specialists on the Western Front

The Battle of the Somme had degenerated into an attritional slaughter almost unparalleled in the history of warfare. More than one million casualties were inflicted on both sides in the see-saw battles. Tens of thousands were buried where they fell, along with millions of unexploded shells. These farmers' fields would for decades produce only a winter's harvest of corpses that were seasonally disgorged to the surface by frost. The Canadians limped off the Somme at the end of 1916, moving north to the quiet Artois region. The corps left behind some 8,000 dead, and another 16,000 wounded had been sent to hospitals at the rear. Georges Vanier wrote to his mother that he "barely recognized" his 22nd Battalion after the Somme. "I miss the cheery faces of those who had been with us from the start and who gave up their lives at Courcelette."[1]

Every Canadian infantry battalion was in the same desperate situation: long-service veterans realized that they were alone, their friends having been killed or maimed and replaced by new recruits, who had then been replaced by other men, who had in turn been replaced by more men. Some veterans had lost so many buddies that they refused to make friends with the green troops until they had survived at least a few weeks in the trenches. Others found themselves viewing life, death, and survival with new eyes. Tom Johnson, who had joined the 102nd Battalion after the terrible Somme casualties, wrote of his feelings in the trenches:

The Canadians fought on the Somme from September to November 1916 and suffered 24,000 casualties. The catastrophic losses forced the Canadian Corps to re-examine its warfighting tactics, doctrine, and weapons.

I may have my head blown off tomorrow, but I am not worrying about that nearly so much as whether I shall have a good dinner, and on time. The particular jam I shall have is of more consequence to me than the number of German prisoners taken. If by any chance the dining room doors are not opened exactly as the clock strikes twelve, I shall feel so irritated that I shall complain bitterly about the whole government conduct of the war. That will effect [sic] me far more than the loss of a battle.[2]

It was the simple pleasures that sustained the men—good billets out of the line, letters, food, cigarettes, and rum—although not the latter for Johnson, who was deeply against alcohol. In the winter of 1916–1917, he was in the minority on this score. Most soldiers who had spent any time at the front had hardened considerably, the furnace of the Somme having blasted a great many of the civilian niceties from recent recruits.

The Canadians were an army of civilian-soldiers. While tens of thousands had militia experience, these combat soldiers were straddling a strange world. "I am beginning to feel that I have always been in the army," wrote twenty-two-year-old Gunner Charles Pearce to his father on August 21, 1915, the one-year anniversary of his service in the forces. "I feel as though I have lived two lives for I have seen as much in one year here as I had in all my life before."[3] He would never return to that old life, dying on August 24, 1916, in an aircraft accident, after being granted his wish to leave the ground forces to enlist in the British flying services.

FROM THE STEEL HELMETS tilted on their heads to their muddy boots and trousers joined by the war's signature puttees, everything the Canadian soldier owned had to be worn, or stored, either in the small haversack on his pack or hung from his webbing. Ammunition, grenades, a respirator worn in a bag on the chest when in the alert position, a waterproof groundsheet, a detachable shovel, water bottle, mess tin, extra clothes (especially socks), bayonet, and a host of other gear kept the infantryman in the line a self-sufficient fighting machine. A soldier carried at least sixty pounds of kit, and more when laden with extra ammunition; Sergeant Garnet Dobbs of the 21st Battalion, in a letter to his sister, Millie, in Toronto, complained: "I don't know just what a soldier's full kit weighs but after carrying it for about half an hour, it will weigh several hundred pounds."[4]

Canadian soldiers had fought tenaciously on the Somme. Lance Corporal Armine Norris, a machine-gunner who survived the grim battle of 1916 but not the war, believed that the Canadians now had "two or three things—a record, traditions, some recognized heroes, and some dead chums, and oh! we're proud of the battalion and the division—our division and our corps." Even if his men were weary and wary of the high command—and he firmly believed "it is the soldier's privilege to grouse"—he reminded his mother, "These are the same kind of men who, with eyes wide open, entered hell to die for people and a country that had never done anything very special for them."[5] He was proud of them and of what they had endured.

Both the Allies and the Central Powers—consisting primarily of Germany, Austria-Hungary, and the Ottoman Empire—needed a break from the killing. "The endeavours of the year 1916 had been too much," wrote a German general. "The vigour of the troops had weakened under the enormous fire of the artillery and by our losses. On the Western Front, we were totally exhausted."[6] Lord Lansdowne, a member of the British cabinet, wrote an unpopular memo to his colleagues on November 13, 1916: "No one for a moment believes that we are going to lose this war, but what is our chance of winning it in such a manner, and within such limits of time, as will enable us to beat our enemy to the ground and impose upon him the kind of terms which we so freely discuss?"[7] Lansdowne was condemned as a coward, as few could imagine seeking peace in the all-out war that raged around the globe. But all knew that it would be won or lost on the Western Front.

After the Somme, few Canadian operations were planned for at least a couple of weeks as both sides licked their wounds and tried to incorporate new troops into their battered regiments. "The part of the line we are in now can be best described to a Canadian as 'apple pie,' after our experiences since early last March," wrote Major William Coleman of the 4th Canadian Mounted Rifles. Coleman had performed with uncommon bravery on the Somme, and had been awarded a Military Cross for virtually saving his company from annihilation.[8] The new front in the Artois region was indeed apple pie in comparison to the unending slaughter of the Somme, but the mud and freezing slush were new burdens for the infantry. Major W.H. Hewgill noted in his diary:

> Trenches in a very bad condition owing to last nights [sic] rain. Have never seen them worse in such a short time. Bosche walk [a trench] had 4 to 5 feet of water in it and several deep dugouts were filled to the brim. The water was coming in torrents and trenches were tumbling in all along the line. We had every available man at work on repair work and at the pumps. Have a party out tonight trying to run a drain through so as to carry the water off to the Bosche lines.[9]

A new soldier at the front, Herbert Burrell of the 1st Canadian Mounted Rifles, a forty-six-year-old cartoonist who had worked for *Punch* magazine in England and who held a master's degree from Cambridge in pure mathematics and music, was equally dismayed: "We are like the rats which infest the trenches burrowing in the ground; sleeping by day; grovelling in the mud at night. Mud in your bed; in your mess tin; on your food. We seldom wash. No water to spare. One marvels at the cheerfulness of the boys who have been out here a long time."[10] Even though much of the 1916–1917 winter was spent fighting the weather rather than the Germans, there was still iron in these fighting troops. The 10th Battalion issued orders: "All positions will be held at all costs, no matter what the nature of the enemy attacks."[11]

Over Christmas, the mud turned to concrete when the temperature dropped. It was one of the coldest winters in decades. Soldiers wrapped themselves in layer upon layer of clothing. Sandbags were slipped over the feet and extra socks were wrapped around the hands. Leather jerkins, vests without arms, were worn on the outside of the bundle of clothes but underneath the greatcoats. The jerkins rarely came off, as they were warm, looked good, and fetched a high price on the black market operating behind the lines between civilians and other units. The kilted units were the hardest pressed, especially with their distinctive kilts picking up mud in the pleats and cutting the back of frozen legs. But trousers were viewed with disdain by these soldiers, and most Highland units refused to break with tradition.

Victor Wheeler remembered that his 50th Battalion had been so shattered in the Somme fighting that morale was low over the winter. In the coming months, a liberal supply of fortifying rum helped to ease nerves, becoming an "essential part of Johnny Canuck's daily ration."[12] For the men at the sharp end, it was hard to avoid brooding about the losses and the seemingly endless war, although some found that dark humour helped them to endure. "They say the first seven years are the worst and after that we won't mind it very much, so 'cheer up,'" wrote a joking Herbert Clemens, a former druggist from St. Thomas, Ontario, serving with No. 10 Stationary Hospital, to his parents.[13]

Sir Julian Byng was the Canadian Corps commander from May 1916 to June 1917. Byng was the single most important figure of guidance for the Canadians as they progressed towards maturity as a fighting force.

Lieutenant General Sir Julian Byng, the Canadian Corps commander, did not have seven years to wait. Since his arrival at the end of May 1916, his corps had been involved in almost constant warfighting: first at Mount Sorrel in June and then on the Somme as of September. Now, with the shambles of the Somme in the corps' wake, he ordered a systematic analysis into its structure and operations.[14] Byng wanted to know where the Canadians had failed and how their attack doctrine could be improved. Despite his reputation as a "cheerfully unintellectual cavalryman" and his disarming nickname "Bungo," Byng had a deeply analytical mind for the challenges of fighting on the Western Front. He understood that his soldiers needed to improve to survive.[15]

Responding to their much respected leader, the Canadians went back to the classroom. Studies were conducted at every level of command, via boards of inquiry, interviews of survivors, and analyses of field reports. Pre-battle preparation, the interaction of supporting arms, the usefulness of equipment in battle, necessary improvements to tactics, reasons why communication had failed: all of these subjects were queried and probed in the attempt to build upon success and prevent failure. This exchange of ideas within the corps was also supported by lessons that were circulating throughout the larger BEF, which was undergoing its own gut-wrenching analysis. Brigadier General C.D. Baker-Carr, who was responsible for setting up the British machine-gun school in 1915, remarked on the difficulty of processing the lessons of war at this time when it was crucial that every lesson be processed:

> The chief trouble at GHQ [general headquarters] was that there was no one there who had time to listen to any new idea. Everybody was so busy writing "Passed to you," "Noted and returned," or "For your information," etc. etc. on piles and piles of "jackets" that no one had a moment to consider any proposal for altering the existing condition of affairs.[16]

With changes needed to organization and administration, unit structures and sizes, tactics and doctrines, weapons and control, and almost everything that pertained to the warfighting or administration of the war effort, it was difficult to know where to focus or begin. The smaller but self-contained Canadian Corps appears to have been more efficient in targeting its weaknesses in order to effect change, and could also rely on broader British support. The period after the Somme would be the key pivotal moment for the corps, marking its transformation into a professional force.

CANADIAN CORPS, 1917

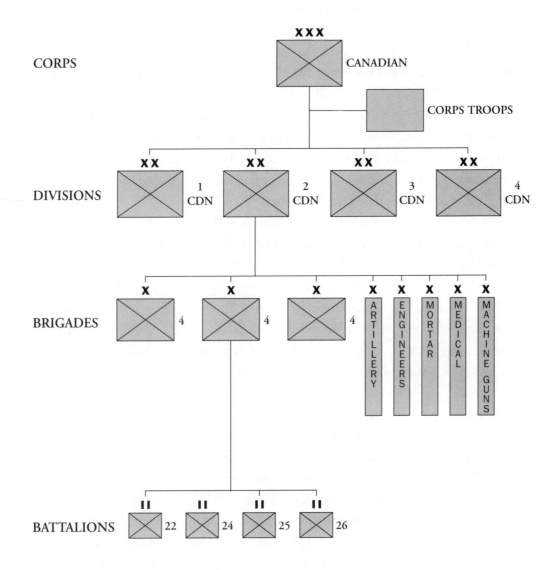

The Canadian Corps was the centrepiece of the Canadian war effort. At four divisions strong, it hovered between 85,000 and 100,000 soldiers, although it would grow in strength in the last two years of the war. Commanded by the experienced British general Byng, the corps had four divisions, each composed of about 19,000 men. A division was the smallest self-contained battle formation in the BEF that controlled assets beyond those of the infantry. While the infantry made up the largest component of the division—containing three infantry brigades of four battalions, each of about 1,000 at full strength (or 12,000 infanteers in total)—they were supported by formations of artillery, engineers, machine guns, trench mortars, divisional trains that transported war materiel, field ambulances, signallers, and headquarters. The corps had additional units and formations, including heavy siege batteries, labour units, and army service corps, which contributed several thousand additional men to form the corps' total strength.

Sir Julian Byng had begun to put his stamp on his Canadian Corps, and first turned to assessing those officers who had survived the Somme battles. Many had simply burned out from the unceasing stress and the shock of having lost so many good men under their command. Officers were found wanting and sent back to England to assume less demanding roles. Garnet Hughes—son of Sir Sam Hughes, the minister of militia and defence—and his uncle, William St. Pierre Hughes, were deemed unfit. But it was not easy to manoeuvre them out of command. William was sent back to Canada, but Garnet was given command of the 5th Division, which was training in England at the time; he would never command troops in France again, however, as his division was eventually broken up for reinforcements. Byng removed or transferred fifteen of the forty-eight battalion commanders and two of the twelve brigadiers.[17] The cheerful cavalry commander had steel in him.

In addition to making way for new men by clearing away the old, Byng sent his most trusted subordinates on a mission to the British and French armies in an attempt to harness the lessons they had distilled from the Somme. Major General Arthur Currie, commander of the 1st Division, would lead one mission. Currie had already proven himself to be the best divisional commander, but he had not been flawless. He had made questionable decisions at the April 1915 Second Battle of Ypres, and had been unable to convince his superiors of their folly in ordering a frontal assault at Festubert a month later. While he had distinguished himself during the trench warfare phase of 1915–1916 and had been responsible for the methodical counterattack at Mount Sorrel in June 1916, his division had fared only middling on the Somme, where his forces, like most Allied ones, had been stopped and then shattered by German wire and machine guns. Currie had exhibited few flashes of inspiration, but he was desperate to find a solution to the stalemate of the trenches and to save his men's lives. He was willing to embrace new warfighting methods, displaying an open-mindedness that Byng had spotted early.

Byng had faith in the forty-one-year-old major general and had given Currie time to mature as a battlefield commander. The two appeared an odd couple. Byng was soldierly, experienced, a friend to royalty, and informal to the point of returning salutes by a slight lifting of the shoulders with hands still in pants pockets. In contrast, Currie believed in a sharp salute, a formality that he enforced among his men—and even among British troops that crossed his path. This preference seemed to contradict the Canadian reputation for carefree ways, often embodied in their refusal to salute superiors. It may be that the major general was overcompensating for his own somewhat unsoldierly appearance. Currie was tall, at six foot two and a half inches, but heavy, even lumpy, with his uniform rarely fitting well on his pear-shaped body. Too often his belt looked like it was pulled up to his chest. He even refused to wear a moustache, thus being the only general in the BEF who faced the war with a clean upper lip. Was he afraid of drawing attention to his weak chin? But if Currie was unorthodox in appearance, he had a sharp mind, worked hard at preparing his soldiers for battle, and though he never had the gift of conversing lightly with the men, he cared for them deeply.

In early January, Currie visited the French near Verdun. That horrible battle had ground to a halt months earlier in November after France and Germany had suffered some 700,000 casualties. With both armies bled white, the campaign provided many lessons in the art of killing. The Canadian party visited the battlefield and talked to senior officers. Currie absorbed the best and worst from the French, as well as talking about such lessons with his British counterparts. His resulting detailed report helped Byng and the senior officers of the Canadian Corps develop ideas and solutions to problems, some of which had already been identified in the corps-wide study of previous months. Perhaps the most important lesson, from Currie's perspective, was that the French were ahead of the British and Canadians in decentralizing the command structure, a reorganization that empowered soldiers to make their own choices according to changing battlefield circumstances and also allowed troops to spread out, as they were not required to group around only a few commanders. In this formation, the men were harder to hit, covered more ground, and could exploit success on their own limited fronts. To assist these small combat formations in surviving on the battlefield, where they often had no communication with rear guns and mortars, the French had already begun to increase the firepower at the sharp end by issuing the infantry with light machine guns. Currie took note, calling for "self-reliant and self-sufficient units."[18]

But Currie was no patsy, and he compared the stories of successful operations or tactics he heard from the French generals with the significantly different accounts

This rare photograph shows unidentified infantrymen—likely French soldiers—advancing across the shattered battlefield in October 1916. Note the infantry who can be seen among the craters in the centre of the photograph and the shellfire exploding over the enemy trench in the upper portion of the image. The Canadians sought to emulate the French infantry tactics based on the advance of smaller combat units in diffused formations rather than long lines of soldiers moving forward in unison.

more junior French officers often related to him in confidence. For example, the generals talked about the importance of training troops for the assault, by such means as providing accurate maps, walking the men through mock-up battlefields, not wearing out the infantry with labour jobs of building trenches or roads, and ultimately ensuring that they had time to prepare for battle. These were indeed important practices to follow, but junior officers often noted that while this was the theory, rarely did it equate with practice.[19] The need to rest the infantry was an important lesson learned, and despite manpower shortages in the Canadian Corps, Currie tried his best to let pioneers and labour battalions do more of the pick-and-shovel work to free the infantry to train and fight. The poor bloody infantry were never fully liberated from hated fatigues, but their lot at the front improved in the final two years of the war.

After returning from his tour, Currie gathered together his ideas and codified the lessons he had learned, which he communicated to the officers and men of the corps in a series of lectures. He was Byng's chief instructor and had clearly been tapped as his successor. But it fell to the corps commander to process Currie's recommendations, and to his headquarters to standardize them in a new series of training and doctrinal lessons that were disseminated throughout the corps. Because the Canadian Corps had a semi-permanent structure—with the Canadians almost always training and fighting together and then relieving other Canadian units—a well-formed sense of unity and purpose prevailed in the corps. Canadians understood one another, often knew their counterparts in their division or other divisions from prewar life in Canada or from serving in the First Contingent, and would come to know each other better in the various divisional and corps training schools that were established from 1916 onward to impart lessons and bring senior and junior officers together. The Canadians were extremely effective as they fought together "under a corps commander whom they could trust, and whose methods and abilities they knew and understood," wrote E.L.M. Burns, a junior officer who would later rise to command one of the two Canadian corps in the Second World War.[20] While it is important to note that the Canadian Corps was not a tight-knit family of 85,000 men all working in unison, and that it suffered from its share of petty jealousies, weak leaders, and ambivalent enlisted men, the corps structure was strong and sufficiently flexible to allow for divisions to instigate their own training but also to benefit from the overall corps doctrine that pulled the best from British and French analyses.

The lessons the Canadians learned in the crucible of the Somme, and those drawn from other armies, were fused into a new doctrine and then employed within the Canadian Corps. The dense infantry tactics of advancing in lines and, later, in several waves, had to be re-evaluated. Though tactical reforms had begun before the Somme, they had seldom been implemented on the battlefield. Instead, officers had tried to exert control over the chaos by centralizing command. Within the 1,000-man infantry battalion, the four infantry companies were the primary formations for manoeuvre on the battlefield. Each company contained four platoons about forty-five to fifty men strong, and largely composed of riflemen. In earlier battles, company and platoon commanders had tried to corral their men, but this became a nearly impossible task once the firing started in earnest. Attempts to do so only resulted in destroying any chance for individuals to succeed through their own bravery and initiative. With soldiers spread out on the battlefield and cohesion disintegrating under the fall of enemy shells and sweeping machine-gun fire that sent soldiers scrambling to the mud for cover, the failure to communicate among the officers and men in a unit, and then from unit to unit, and from front to rear, had been a significant problem on the Somme, as well as during the previous two years of fighting. When the infantry were sent into battle, the commanders in the rear often had no idea what was happening in the front lines. Their desperate waiting was broken only as the first casualties and prisoners streamed to the rear. By then, it was often too late to order ammunition and reinforcements forward to reinforce success or support endangered forces. Towards the end of the Somme campaign, forward artillery observers had begun to provide those at the rear with important information about the apparent success and failure of an infantry advance, but this process was hindered by fragile communication systems based on easily cut telephone wires and even more rudimentary flag or semaphore signalling. The communication problem would never be solved during the war, though the infantry commanders worked on it and made improvements through new technology and the further decentralization of their infantry formations. The soldiers at the front were given the training to lead themselves in battle; no longer did they have to wait

INFANTRY BATTALION, 1917

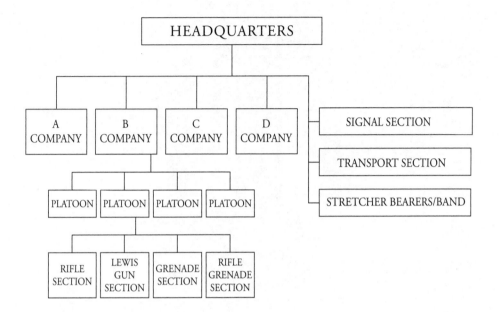

for orders that never arrived because of telephone lines severed or runners killed.

If rear commanders could not control their troops, then command would need to be devolved to more junior officers. The answer was to reshape the doctrine and provide more leadership and flexibility among junior officers and senior non-commissioned officers (NCOs). The rank and file who formed the four sections of about a dozen men each, who were grouped into a platoon, had to be empowered and allowed to fight their own battles. "It is not too much to say that this is the Platoon Commander's war," observed Brigadier General Percy P. de B. Radcliffe, Byng's trusted chief of staff, at the end of December 1916.[21] The platoon was the "largest unit that, under modern conditions, [could] be directly controlled and manoeuvred under fire by one man."[22] Success was in the hands of those at the front; they must keep going forward and carry out their mission-orientated goals. Throughout this training process, Byng simulated accurate battlefield conditions: as

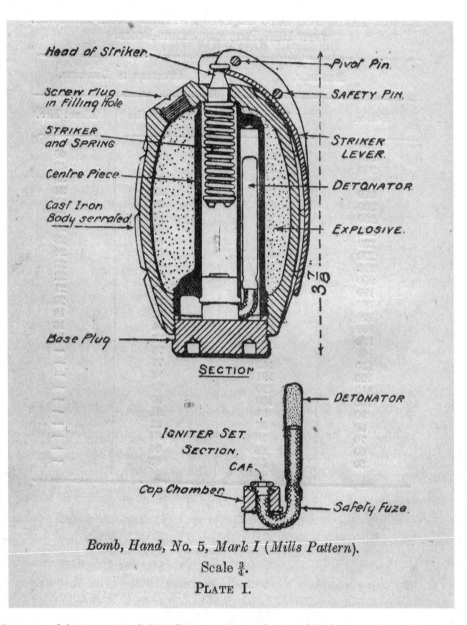

Head of Striker.
Screw Plug in Filling Hole
Striker and Spring
Centre Piece
Cast Iron Body serrated
Base Plug

Pivot Pin.
SAFETY PIN.
STRIKER LEVER.
DETONATOR.
EXPLOSIVE.

$3\frac{7}{8}$"

SECTION

IGNITER SET. SECTION.

DETONATOR
CAP
Cap Chamber
Safety Fuze.

Bomb, Hand, No. 5, Mark I (Mills Pattern).
Scale ¾.
PLATE I.

Diagram of the No. 5, Mark I (Mills pattern) grenade, one of the best British and Dominion grenades of the war. Grenades were a popular weapon among trench warriors, as they allowed attackers to toss grenades from behind cover and clear enemy positions, and thus to suffer less exposure to fire. This grenade, often referred to as the "Mills bomb," had a small explosive charge that detonated five seconds after the safety pin was released and the grenade thrown. The explosion sent the serrated cast-iron pieces whirling over a wide radius; it was extremely deadly to a radius of 3 to 5 metres, and could cause injury far beyond that in open terrain.

training operations continued, the senior officers were removed as "casualties," with the responsibilities devolving to the next level of command. In the end, it was often a corporal or a sergeant who was left to carry out the final fighting phase of an operation or the process of consolidation.

While many of these lessons had been practised before the war, they had been forgotten in the wartime attempt to fuse the infantry and the artillery together into a fearsome offensive weapon.[23] This combination was still crucial, as shells were needed to destroy enemy positions. But now commanders realized that the infantry had to have the power to manoeuvre within the creeping barrage, or to fight their way forward should the foot soldiers be held up by unsuppressed strongpoints and have their creeping barrage "march off," leaving them vulnerable. The new type of training showed the corps commander's faith in his men, and it encouraged the infantry to think about their role on the battlefield and the need for individual action and initiative rather than strict Pavlovian obedience. Byng needed lions, not salivating dogs.

The massive set-piece battles of the Somme had proven costly, especially when the artillery had been unable to clear wire or defences. Simply adding more guns and men, as had often been the approach on the Somme, was not the answer. Neither was decentralizing command an uncomplicated solution, however. Brave groups of infantrymen, charging forward on the battlefield, might find ways around enemy positions, but they would not last long if they were armed only with the Lee-Enfield rifle and bayonet, and a few Lewis machine guns.

The grenade had proven its worth since its reintroduction during 1915 trench fighting, but grenade specialists were not part of the platoon, being instead grouped at the company level. This concentration resulted in a stronger centralized bombing group, but it left the infantry in the fighting platoons lacking these bombers except when they were formally attached to an ad hoc battle group. While the riflemen and grenadiers trained together to achieve their missions, and were to protect one another in battle, the fighting formation would have been more cohesive if the two groups had served together permanently in the same platoon. Soldiers and survivors from units that live, train, and fight together always forge tighter bonds and usually exhibit more resilient combat motivation.

A similar reorganization had occurred with the heavy machine-gun units, which had been pulled from positions of permanent attachment to infantry battalions to

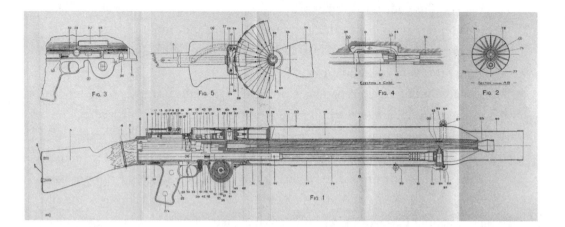

NUMBERED LIST OF PARTS

1. Butt Plate.
2. Butt Plate Screws.
3. Buttstock.
4. Butt Tang Screw.
5. Butt Tang.
7. Butt Catch.
8. Back Sight Bed Spring.
9. Back Sight Bed Spring Screw.
10. Butt Catch Spring.
11. Back Sight Bed.
13. Body Cover.
14. Back Sight Leaf.
20. Back Sight Slide.
21. Ejector.
22. Pistol Grip Side Pieces.
23. Back Sight Axis Pin Washer.
24. Back Sight Axis Pin.
26. Body.
27. Feed Pawl Spring.
28. Right Stop Pawl.
29. Left Stop Pawl.
30. Trigger.
31. Feed Arm Actuating Stud.
31x. Feed Arm Actuating Stud Boss.

32. Safety R. and L.
33. Trigger Axis Pin.
34. Feed Arm.
35. Feed Pawl.
36. Feed Pawl Spring.
37. Bolt.
38. Cocking Handle.
39. Pistol Grip.
40. Cartridge Guide Spring.
41. Sear Spring.
42. Sear Spring Box.
43. Magazine Pan.
44. Ejector Cover.
45. Extractors (2).
46. Gear Stop.
47. Striker Fixing Pin.
48. Gear Stop Pin.
49. Gear Stop Spring.
50. Striker.
51. Cartridge Spacer Ring.
52. Gear.
53. Return Spring Casing.
54. Magazine Top Plate Rivets (6).
55. Return Spring.
56. Tension Screw.
57. Return Spring Collet.
58. Return Spring Centre.

59. Return Spring Rivets.
60. Magazine Latch Spring.
61. Pinion Casing.
62. Magazine Latch.
63. Centre Key.
65. Gear Casing Hinge Pin.
66. Feed Arm Latch.
67. Magazine Top Plate.
68. Body Locking Pin.
69. Space Ring Rivets (5).
70. Interior Separators (25).
71. Radiator Casing, Rear, Locking Piece.
72. Rack.
74. Radiator Casing, Rear.
75. Piston Connecting Pin.
76. Barrel.
77. Gas Cylinder.
78. Radiator (Aluminium).
79. Piston.
80. Gas Regulator Key Stud.
81. Gas Regulator Key.
82. Gas Chamber.
83. Barrel Band.
84. Gas Regulator.

85. Clamp Ring.
86. Front Sight.
87. Clamp Ring Positioning Screw.
88. Clamp Ring Screw.
89. Barrel Mouthpiece.
90. Radiator Casing, Front.
91. Sear.
92. Hand Grip.
93. Oil Well.
94. Oil Well Cap.
95. Oil Brush.
96. Spade Grip Butt Tang.
116. Back Sight Elevating Screw.
117. Back Sight Elevating Screw Head.
118. Back Sight Elevating Screw Head Pin.
119. Back Sight Elevating Screw Head Spring.
120. Sear Axis Pin.
121. Butt Catch Pin.
136. Barrel Mouthpiece Spanner.
137. Magazine Filling Handle.

The Lewis light machine gun, introduced in 1915, was an essential weapon during infantry assaults against enemy positions and when holding ground. The two-man Lewis-gun crew— a firer and an ammunition loader—could be augmented by two or three more ammunition carriers. The team had to keep the 137 parts of the weapon clean in the filth of the trenches.

be grouped in specialist companies. Even though these machine-gunners, firing their Vickers guns, had been parcelled out to support infantry battalions in battle, they were often not in the right place at the right time, and the Canadians on the Somme had been unable to match the German machine guns with suppressing fire. The need for greater fire support was met by pushing Lewis guns forward to pin down the enemy, but this also made machine-gunners, as part of the first waves, more susceptible to heavy casualties. In addition to the machine-gunners, rifle grenades were crucial in providing firepower to clear trenches or fortified positions, and with a range of up to 200 metres, they put much-needed striking power in the hands of those at the sharp end.

The rifle grenade provided much-needed firepower to the infantry, who could project their grenades up to 200 metres. The rifle was fired in a reverse position, with the base grounded, much like a mortar.

One of the hard lessons learned on the Somme was that specialists had to be brought back into the platoon, as they were an essential complement to the riflemen. The platoon was acknowledged as the most important tactical unit for the infantry arm, and the corps' new appreciation of firepower transformed the infantryman into a technician of battle. Instead of hiving off specialists from the platoon—an approach that had often denuded the battalion of its most aggressive and elite men—the specialist positions were incorporated back into the platoon to make it a self-contained, if small, battle group composed of four sections: riflemen, rifle grenadiers, bombers, and Lewis machine-gunners. By December 1916, the Canadians formalized the four supporting parts of the infantry platoon, even though it took a few months for all units to fall into line.

There were similar reforms throughout the wider BEF, and many doctrinal changes were codified in pamphlets such as *SS143, Instructions for the Training of Platoons for Offensive Action*, and *SS144, The Normal Formation for the Attack*. The Canadians continued to profit from this sharing of ideas, but also from carrying out their own internal analysis. Infantry tactics were evolving. The infantry could not go forward in evenly spaced lines as they had done in the past. These linear tactics had been implemented for discipline and control over new recruits drawn from civil society. But the chaos of battle made it increasingly hard to keep soldiers in straight lines, and they made good targets for scythe-like machine-gun fire. Instead, the platoons were to advance in less formal lines, leaving greater space between troops. Battalions would employ two companies in the advance, and a third was to follow them as a "mopping-up" force in an echeloned position to the rear, although battalions had leeway to alter this formation depending on terrain or enemy disposition. The attackers still advanced in waves, but they were now formed in broken, disjointed lines that were supported by follow-on forces advancing in diamond-shaped formations. These support units could react quickly to defenders by using parts of the diamond to pin down strongpoints with fire while units on the diamond's flanks worked forward to take the enemy from the side or rear. This increased flexibility had its own problems—particularly since it often left units with open flanks or sticking their necks out to be cut off—but it was an essential tactical evolution and would be a key ingredient in the battles of the war's final two years.

On the Somme, once the infantry had survived the firestorm of No Man's Land, weaved through the barbed wire, and captured a battered trench, the problem had been in holding the position. The consolidation of gains with weakened forces that were low on ammunition and struggling to fend off counterattacks always left the attackers-turned-defenders in a desperate fight for survival. Elaborate pre-planned machine-gun and artillery barrages that brought fire down on predetermined positions over which the Germans were predicted to pass had bought time for the infantry in the latter stages of the Somme. So, too, did the rushing of reserves forward, though these troops were often caught in the enemy's counter-barrage and torn to shreds. Having denser forces advance closer together in bounds was seen as a possible solution, but it risked more men being slaughtered if an attack was held up in crossing No Man's Land. There were no easy solutions, and each new tactic

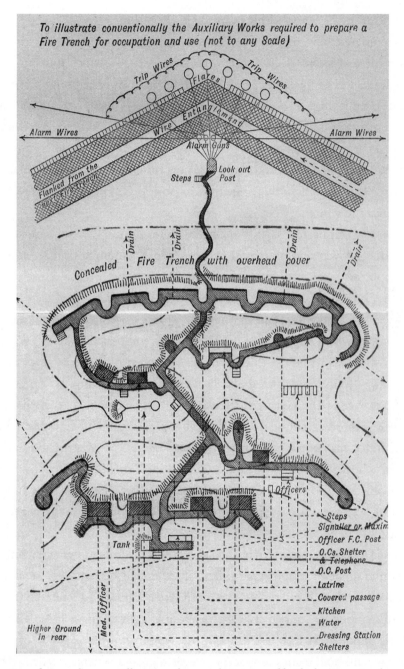

To illustrate conventionally the Auxiliary Works required to prepare a Fire Trench for occupation and use (not to any Scale)

This diagram of a trench system illustrates the complex system of barbed-wire entanglements, forward listening posts, and fire and support trenches that created a defence-in-depth, built with the aim of slowing and then destroying enemy attacks. By 1917, these underground cities stretched back to over a kilometre in depth and housed hundreds of thousands of soldiers.

was paid for in the blood of previous failed operations.

Byng ordered new methods of advancing through bounds, in which the first waves went to ground after a certain distance, usually after capturing a front-line trench, and succeeding waves passed through them, each grabbing more enemy territory. Typically, these bounds could consist of three or four waves, each with its own reinforcements and follow-on forces. The method required intense training as units tended to get mixed up—and even to shoot one another in the confusion—but it did allow for the later waves to hold the new outer crust, while the first waves had more time to consolidate their newly won positions. These reforms were practised all through the winter.

At the core of this new assault doctrine was the concept of the limited attack. The Somme had proven that no matter the weight of the bombardment, or its length or innovation, no breakthrough could be achieved through these conventional attack methods. Enemy machine-gunners survived, new defensive tactics were used (involving either digging deeper into the ground or thinning out the front, but always holding it in depth), and reinforcements could always be thrown against the attacker, who was weaker with each metre advanced into enemy lines, as he moved further away from his logistical and artillery support. In the first three years of the war, the power of the German defensive outmatched that of the Allied offensive. However, if there would be no breakthrough, victory might be achieved through a limited attack, also known as a "bite and hold" operation. Massing the artillery would allow for a heavy rupture of the enemy front lines, enabling the infantry to advance to their objectives. Having "bitten," the infantry would now dig in to hold the front instead of overextending their push by attempting to continue further forward into the maze of enemy trench systems. The latter approach had to be avoided, as past experience had proven that driving too deeply left the increasingly vulnerable infantry at the outer range of supporting artillery shellfire and susceptible to enemy counterattacks. While these limited bites were often successful, this tactical approach to battle, within a more restrained strategy, would make for a long war in which the Allies had little opportunity to break through the Western Front.

For bite and hold tactics to work, however, a greater synergy needed to be in place between the infantry and artillery. The Somme had epitomized the industrial war, with all nations reorganizing their heavy industries to spit out shells by the millions.

The infantry on both sides were subjected to limb- and mind-shattering bombardments. One Canadian gunner described a barrage: "It resembled a great curtain of smoke, flickering with light from the shrapnel air-bursts of the field guns, like myriads of giant fire-flies flashing through and through it. Great geysers of earth continually sprouted up, as the shells from the heavy guns and howitzers plunged in and lashed out with a roar of explosion."[24] The weight of fire tore through the ground defences like a hot rake, but the enemy defenders, aware that remaining on the firing line was akin to suicide, took refuge in deep dugouts that could withstand all but the most direct hits from heavy howitzers. Towards the end of the Somme campaign, the gunners experimented with new tactics that sought to suppress fire instead of attempting to annihilate the enemy. It was essential to keep the enemy in his dugouts long enough for the infantry to cross the killing zone of No Man's Land. Previous tactics had relied on an artillery bombardment that laid a terrific weight of shells on enemy strongpoints but then jumped to the next position. This was effective in smashing defences and defenders, but not all of them.[25] When the barrage jumped off to the next objective, the defenders rose from their dugouts and shot down the infantry still struggling through No Man's Land.

Learning from these failures, and the occasional success, gunners now fired a creeping barrage—a wall of fire that moved forward over the enemy lines slowly and in shorter leaps. The infantry were to "lean into the barrage" for protection. The barrage would usually rest on an enemy position for a few minutes, and then jump forward in 90-metre lifts. The infantry would follow it, aware that if they were slowed down by the enemy opposition, they would be left defenceless in No Man's Land as their wall of protection crept away. Arthur Bonar of Princess Patricia's Canadian Light Infantry (PPCLI) described how the creeping barrage worked:

> The infantry advance in long waves, the first wave keeping forty yards behind the barrage or as near as it is comfortable. When the barrage lifts the waves of men jump forward a given distance, keeping close to the barrage until it lifts again, when the same tactics are repeated. The concentrated drumfire from artillery and machine-guns keeps the enemy in his deep dugouts. When the barrage lifts he hasn't time to come out of his subterranean galleries to work his machine-guns before our infantry are on top of him.[26]

The creeping barrage was a vast improvement over the destructive tactics of earlier years: in 1916, these involved the artillery trying to shatter the enemy's defences with massive firepower (which never succeeded in fully destroying all positions), and before that, in 1915, the approach was for gunners to fire on the enemy line and then cease when the infantry attacked in order to avoid friendly fire incidents—but the cessation left the infantry in No Man's Land completely vulnerable to unimpeded enemy fire. Now, in 1917, instead of gunfire preceding movement, firepower was combined with movement, and the enormous proliferation of guns and shells meant that destructive bombardments and other complex fireplans, such as targeting enemy batteries, could be used in conjunction with creeping barrages.

Andrew McNaughton was one of the pre-eminent gunners of the war. He applied the principles he mastered as a prewar professor of engineering to improving the ability of gunners to locate and destroy enemy artillery in counter-battery work. This photograph from 1919 shows McNaughton as a brigadier general, and his postwar career would be spectacular as he rose to become chief of the general staff of the Canadian armed services and later served as commander of the First Canadian Army during the Second World War.

Yet, having several hundred guns firing in unison on the same target and then moving forward at the same pace along broken terrain, with worn-out guns, faulty shells, and disruptive enemy fire, usually meant that no operation was without shells dropping short and killing Canadians. As well, the new tactics afforded little flexibility: communication between front and rear was so rudimentary that once a barrage started, it could not be called off or brought back across the field to deal with obstinate defenders. Even when the barrage worked effectively, it was dangerous to the Canadian infantry marching behind it. Though Bonar described soldiers staying within 35 metres of the barrage, this was dangerously close, and the infantry generally moved within 75 to 130 metres of the barrage, although they closed that gap in extraordinary circumstances. Even though there were countless examples of "friendly fire," or "drop-shorts"—as infanteers innocuously called their own shells that dismembered and maimed those at the front—the infantry accepted this burden if it meant suppressing enemy small-arms fire that did even more damage to their advancing ranks. The creeping barrage showed promising results in neutralizing enemy fire, especially towards the end of the Somme battles. Too often, even when the barrage succeeded, barbed wire remained uncleared because of faulty fuses and dud shells. Furthermore, first-wave troops and follow-on forces always remained vulnerable to enemy counter-barrage fire, which made any support of an attack costly since supplies and reinforcements always had to travel over open ground.

Along with the need to twin the infantry and artillery into an efficient battle system, the killing power of artillery could not be denied after the Somme. Battles had succeeded when the gunners had saturated the front, cleared obstacles, killed the enemy, and kept the survivors deep in their protective dugouts. But even with the emergence of the creeping barrage, too often the enemy gunners had struck a terrible blow against most operations with their counter-barrages. This had been unavoidable on the Somme, since the massive pre-battle bombardments—prefaced by a telltale logistical buildup of hundreds of thousands of shells in multiple ammunition dumps that could not be fully camouflaged—were a clear indication to the enemy of what sector an attack would likely target, resulting in the movement of additional defenders and guns to that area to ensure that a breakthrough would not occur. Even the time of the operation could be predicted as the increased tempo of artillery fire indicated an attack would soon commence. When the Allied bombardment began, the German gunners fired their own barrage behind the attackers' moving wall of shells in order to catch the advancing infantry in the open. The Canadians realized that somehow the enemy guns had to be located, targeted, and destroyed.

The senior Canadian gunner was Major General E.W.B. Morrison. A prewar militia officer and former editor of the *Ottawa Citizen* newspaper, Morrison had served in the South African War with the Canadian gunners. "Dinky" Morrison was an inspiring leader, and his personal motto was "Kill Boche."[27] Though Morrison exhibited little brilliance and was more inclined towards rushing guns into battle, much of the credit for the successful close cooperation between artillery and infantry must go to him, and his strength in recognizing talent in subordinates such as Lieutenant Colonel Andrew McNaughton.

Though Morrison's expertise as an old-school gunner was valuable, Byng turned to one of the new breed to help revitalize gunnery work in the corps. The twenty-nine-year-old McNaughton had a scientific mind and had been an engineering professor at McGill University before the war. He had proven himself in battle since the desperate fighting at Ypres, and had been noted by both Morrison and Byng for his dash, flair, and scientific approach to warfighting. His reputation for being a soldier's soldier was strengthened by his often sitting down with his men and sharing a cold can of bully beef. His housing of Tony, a pet lion, for some time in his headquarters to startle visiting British officers was a devil-may-care sang-froid that went over well with the rank and file.

Early in 1917, Byng appointed the young McNaughton counter-battery officer at corps headquarters. McNaughton's passion and expertise in embracing science to improve the Canadians' gunnery tactics had been acknowledged early in the war, and he was now given free reign to devise a gunnery system that would enable the Canadians to more efficiently knock out enemy batteries, sometimes located 5 to 7 kilometres behind enemy lines, camouflaged in gun pits, and often positioned in dead ground that could not be observed. It was a monumental challenge.

Like Currie, McNaughton visited the French to learn from their experiences at Verdun. While Currie had been impressed by their artillery tactics, McNaughton was disappointed to find that despite having survived the bloodbath of the 1916 battles, the French had not codified their lessons into any sort of doctrine. Since their forces lacked a unified system, artillery tactics differed among armies, corps, and divisions. In fact, McNaughton later observed that the key lesson he learned from the French was "what not to do" in organizing an efficient artillery service.[28] More important and useful was McNaughton's discussion with British artillery officers, especially Colonel A.G. Haig of the V British Corps—a cousin of Sir Douglas. While many of the British gunners were hidebound and unwilling to accept the intrusion of science into the realm of gunnery, A.G. Haig was an innovative forward-thinker. McNaughton left their meeting with the confidence to fully embrace new principles such as flash-spotting and sound-ranging to locate enemy guns. McNaughton even invited a number of British scientists, including a few Nobel Prize winners and specialists in meteorology, to share their findings with the Canadian Corps. When McNaughton made these "boffins"—as the soldiers called scientists—comfortable at his new counter-battery headquarters, and treated them with the respect they did not always receive within the larger BEF, they were happy to share their ideas on how to improve upon some of the emerging scientific gunnery principles.

Through these consultations, McNaughton gained a better understanding of how artillery could be effective in supporting the infantry arm. By embracing the principles of scientific gunnery, McNaughton aimed to "exploit gun power to the limit for the purpose of saving the lives of our infantry."[29] With the creeping barrage accepted and ever improving, the Canadians now turned their attention to the question of how to target enemy guns.

McNaughton's Canadian Counter-Battery Office (CCBO) was a central headquarters that gathered intelligence and processed information on the enemy to help the Canadian gunners suppress and paralyze enemy batteries. Aerial reconnaissance from the Royal Flying Corps was of great assistance. The spotting of new battery positions, spent casings, and other telltale enemy tracks from the sky were sent back to headquarters through letter drops and primitive wireless radio technology. The crew of one- and two-seater planes, the latter with a pilot and an observer who also acted as a gunner, risked their lives to photograph the front. While slow-moving observatory aircraft were forced to fly at predictable heights, and were vulnerable targets for enemy fighters, they remained an essential intelligence asset.

"The observers take enormous risks and seldom get any glory," recounted Canadian air ace Billy Bishop. "It's no child's play to circle above the German artillery batteries for half an hour or more, with your machine tossing about in air tortured by exploding shells and black shrapnel puffballs coming nearer and nearer to you like ever-extending fingertips of some giant hand of death."[30] Although the work of the observers was less glamorous than that of the scouts or fighter pilots, who often garnered the glory of engaging in aerial dogfights and in running up the number of "kills," the observer aircraft played an integral role in coordinating the land battle on the Western Front.

McNaughton, with the full support of his senior commanders, encouraged gunners to acquire additional scientific skills. Daily meteorological reports were sent out to all brigades and batteries. Wind, rain, and weather pressure could throw off the flight of a shell by dozens of metres over several kilometres. While some gunners wondered at how deeply the boffins would intrude into their work, there was no point in collecting information about and analyzing enemy artillery locations if the gunners missed their targets because they failed to account for weather conditions. The wear on gun barrels was also factored into targeting the enemy since most guns had been fired long beyond their lifespan. Rapid fire over prolonged periods melted the barrel, and the nose would turn up slightly, thereby impeding accuracy.[31] Acknowledging these constraints did not always translate into success, but such a recognition helped to lessen the factors that had interfered with the gunners' attempts to hit their targets during the previous two years.

Flash-spotting was eagerly embraced by McNaughton. The tactic involved observers dug-in on high ground, surveying the enemy lines. At least three posts were needed, usually spread out along a 6,000- to 10,000-metre front. When an enemy gunner was spotted by aircraft or advanced observers, the flash-spotters were advised by telephone to turn their attention to that area behind the enemy lines. After studying the flash of the gun, the designated observers would hit a key that was connected to a lamp at headquarters. From the position of the observers, and by triangulating their estimates, those back at headquarters could locate enemy gunners with high precision.

Sound-ranging was an equally complicated process. Listeners sat 2 kilometres behind the line, equipped with microphones. Well ahead of these positions, additional microphoned posts were manned. As long as not more than one shell was being fired per second, on hearing the blast of an enemy gun, the sound-detecting soldier at the forward listening post pressed a key that started an oscillograph, an instrument that recorded on audio-film the sound of the shell in flight, as it reached each microphone. The time-intervals between the microphones allowed the CCBO staff at headquarters to analyze the shell's speed and trajectory and, if conditions were optimal, to pinpoint enemy guns to within 25 metres of their location. However, atmospheric pressure, fluctuating temperature, and strong winds could reduce the measurability of the soundwaves.[32]

The need for artillery to respond to emergency infantry SOS calls was also worked on by both the counter-battery guns and the regular heavy guns of the Canadian Corps. By 1917, gunners were comfortable "shooting from the map." Trench maps at a large scale of 1:10,000, made from aerial photographs, were cut into squares and pasted to wooden boards, and target sheets were then superimposed on the map to allow gunners to fire without ever seeing their targets. Forward observers had the same maps in the front lines, and they could convey information about targets to the rear, to effect immediate destruction.

The CCBO's greatest strength was its ability to gather, analyze, and process intelligence.[33] Experienced intelligence officers studied the aerial photographs, looking for telltale signs of camouflaged enemy batteries. These estimates were combined with other forms of intelligence obtained from forward observers and from infantry battle patrols that snatched prisoners in the hope of extracting information. The intelligence was built up to create a target list that would either be acted upon immediately or, to surprise the enemy, kept for later use when a target could be destroyed before a raid or battle. While none of these intelligence techniques delivered victory on its own, especially since bad weather interfered heavily, McNaughton was fashioning a system with which enemy guns could be located and destroyed, which was essential to saving the lives of the Canadian infantry.

THE CANADIANS learned from the Somme, but not all units processed the lessons at the same rate. This was a top-down process devolving from officers such as Currie and McNaughton, as well as a bottom-up evolution within units, originating in particular with surviving officers who had been through the Somme—first-hand witnesses to the fact that those at the sharp end needed to find better ways to survive. The blood curve of battle was long and difficult, with lessons learned, lost, implemented, and forgotten. No singularly upward curve towards steady enlightenment could be followed, as the Germans were also evolving, and therefore rendering some lessons redundant. The Canadians staggered along, drawing on the lessons imparted by the British, as well as on their own painful experiences. While the corps was moving along its difficult road to professionalism, changes were also occurring among the civilian high command in Canada and in England.

CHAPTER 2

FROM AMATEURS TO PROFESSIONALS

Taking Control of the Canadian War Effort

Sam Hughes, Canada's minister of militia and defence, was "mentally unbalanced with the low cunning and cleverness often associated with the insane," or so believed Joseph Flavelle, chairman of the Imperial Munitions Board, the agency responsible for coordinating the manufacture of the millions of Canadian shells made by 1916.[1] A whirlwind of a man, Hughes raced from patriotic speeches to military march pasts. The minister was in his glory as he strutted about, shouting orders, demanding answers, appointing friends to positions of power, and demoting those in whom he had lost faith. Although he made enemies at every turn, Hughes was Canada's war leader, at least for a time. The fiery Hughes not only cut through red tape, but he never allowed much tape to be strung anywhere—for that would have implied a bureaucracy of some kind, structured by rules and regulations. His office in Ottawa was besieged by patronage-seekers and businessmen looking to profit from the enormous Canadian war machine. Flattery and good Conservative connections usually resulted in their securing some sort of contract or command appointment; but a sign might as well have been hung above the door: "Liberals need not apply." Of course, this was how much of politics was carried out at the beginning of the twentieth century. It was not, however, the way to prosecute a major war.

In the first two years of the war, the nearly autocratic power Hughes wielded as Canada's war minister helped to streamline and stimulate the incredible transformation taking place in Canadian society as it shifted from economic depression to war economy. His knighthood was well warranted and Hughes's constant improvisations had often succeeded within the vacuum of guidance on how to run a major war. There had been scandals, of course, including those related to poorly made Canadian equipment, boots that dissolved in the mud, even the ridiculous MacAdams shovel. More serious ones revolved around the problem-riddled Ross rifle, the inefficient shell committee, and kickback schemes. These failures began to accumulate and detract from Hughes's earlier ad hoc achievements.

By 1916, cracks had begun to show in Hughes's administration. His inopportune outbursts often made him an easy figure for the Liberal opposition to attack. Sir Sam didn't care, but his colleagues did. He began to alienate his few friends, and his scandals, blatant patronage appointments, and bullheadedness left him increasingly vulnerable. Although Canadian prime minister Sir Robert Borden did not know what to do with Hughes—as his warnings and cautions never seemed to be absorbed by his excitable minister—he did recognize the value of Hughes's intense commitment to the war effort.[2] Hughes worked diligently for the Canadian soldier, although, in hindsight, not always in his best interest. Some of his colleagues and many vocal critics were not so generous. The governor general, the Duke of Connaught, described the war minister as little more than a "conceited lunatic."[3] Hughes was a frenzy of activity, but like all frenzies, his could not last forever. Despite the minister's unbridled passion, he became more erratic, his outbursts more difficult to ignore. While Hughes had been Borden's bulldog who barked at the British to remember Canadian sensibilities, it became increasingly clear that he was not the type of man Borden needed to direct the long-term mobilization of the nation.

Hughes's system was showing the strain of two years of war and, by late 1915, it was breaking in places. Borden had already pulled essential war projects from him, including the all-important production of shells, which he gave to the efficient Joseph Flavelle, a millionaire meat-packing businessman, who reorganized the nationwide project under the auspices of the Imperial Munitions Board. Military matters overseas were just as bad. At one point, seven competing commanders were overseeing and influencing parts of the CEF in England—fighting among themselves for control and influence. Borden demanded that Hughes reform this Byzantine administrative structure. Some of these men, including Lord Beaverbrook and J.W. Carson, were powerful intriguers who often outmanoeuvred or simply ignored the comparatively simple military men. Beaverbrook and Carson had the war minister's ear, and that was what mattered in the politically riven, patronage-driven overseas administration. The British War Office watched this colonial chaos with a puzzled eye, and was not anxious to step in, especially since it much preferred to deal with Beaverbrook or Carson than with the mercurial minister himself.

Yet an increasingly deafening chorus of angry letters and communiqués was making its way to Borden by the beginning of 1916—missives that spoke to the confused nature of Hughes's overseas administration. Borden again ordered Hughes to sort it out. However, in Hughes's customary manner, when he arrived in England in March 1916, he promptly ignored Borden's orders and established his own friends in a governing militia council. But the improvisation that had worked so well for Hughes in 1914 and much of 1915 was no longer fit for the increasingly professional forces of 1916. With more than 100,000 troops training in England, and almost as many in the field, the Canadians needed to become more efficient. The militia council met only twice and was an absolute failure, with its members absent or bickering among themselves as they continued to claw for control over the Canadian forces.

Borden had always given Hughes room to manoeuvre in the war. He was a force to be reckoned with. But Hughes had grown increasingly unstable: shouting, threatening, and cajoling one minute, tearful and conciliatory the next. Borden later wrote in his postwar memoirs that Hughes had committed "countless indiscretions," had "absurd vanities," an "erratic temperament," and a "lack of systematic administrative capacity." Reflecting on these characteristics, Borden observed that "on matters which touch his insane egotism, he is quite unbalanced. On all other matters he is able and sometimes brilliant."[4]

The normally patient prime minister had had enough. He quashed Hughes's attempt to reform the militia council and established an overseas ministry at the end of October 1916, which became operational on December 5. It was an extraordinary agency, with a Canadian cabinet minister sitting in another country, and it would be responsible for the administration of the overseas Canadian forces. George Perley, an old friend of Borden who was at the time high commissioner for Canada in the United Kingdom—and one of Hughes's many political enemies—would head the new Ministry of Overseas Military Forces of Canada (OMFC).[5]

This Hughes found unacceptable, as it would mark the end of much of his influence. He also argued that with Perley in power, "Our gallant boys at the Front [will] be placed in danger—not from the enemy but from improper management behind them."[6] Offering platitudes about the "perfect harmony" of his administrating units, Hughes was proving again that he was more delusional than dependable.[7] Not surprisingly, the prime minister refused to be persuaded. A further unbalanced letter from Hughes to Borden in early November 1916 accused the prime minister of lying to him and, in so many words, conspiring against him. Borden reacted with uncharacteristic decisiveness, demanding the war minister's resignation. Hughes was gone in a matter of days. But he did not disappear. Sitting in a back-bench position, an aura of anger emanating from him, he remained an expert on Canada's part in the war, attacking the government, the opposition, the generals, and anyone else in his way. He was no longer a force, but he remained a thorn in almost everyone's side.

A.E. KEMP was asked to run the war ministry. Kemp had served his party well over the years, and his rotund body proved he had lived the good life as a result of a number of successful Toronto business ventures. He began to reorganize the Department of Militia in Ottawa; overseas, Sir George Perley was burdened with righting Hughes's wrongs. A millionaire anglophile from Quebec, Perley was considered by many as more British than the British themselves. Perley was less than pleased to give up his cushy position as high commissioner (which allowed him to hobnob with the upper crust of British society) in favour of untangling Hughes's empire of fratricidal politics. But Perley had a hard edge to him, which he had often shown as party whip and in quashing a number of back-bench revolts against Borden in the past; Borden was pleading with him to organize matters, and Perley would not let down his friend and party leader.

Perley immediately sorted out the command structure in England. One of Hughes's cronies, "special representative" Colonel J.W. Carson was out, and few regretted his loss since he was so closely linked to the former war minister. Beaverbrook's powers were also minimized, although he was too well connected and too powerful to be cut out entirely, and he would continue to support the CEF through his publicity and historical agency, the Canadian War Records Office.[8] A few of Hughes's other appointees were initially slated for the chopping block, but they had proven themselves useful, diligent, and, in a few cases, indispensable, so they were spared. A major controversy over the handling of wounded Canadians, resulting from a Hughes-ordered investigation that condemned the Canadian Army Medical Corps, was artfully dealt with by Perley, who well understood the delicate business of stamping out corruption and not allowing a workable system to degenerate into chaos.[9] Most important, the overseas forces needed a strong, proven military leader to corral the various Canadian commands and reorganize the training system. Either Currie or Turner, as the two senior divisional commanders, would be pulled back from the front to become chief of the general staff.

After both generals were interviewed for the position, Currie was intrigued but ultimately unwilling to accept the role, believing that the post was fraught with difficulties because of the propensity of politicians to interfere in command decisions.[10] Turner was no more willing to take up the mantle, believing that by giving up a field command he would never be considered for Sir Julian Byng's position when the British general was promoted to take an army, as many expected he would.[11] Yet Turner also had a weaker operational record, and it was unlikely that the British would ever have given him command of the prestigious corps.

Turner's performance as a senior officer is difficult to unravel. He had clearly failed as a brigadier at Second Ypres in April 1915. But that was an utterly chaotic battle, and he and his staff were wholly inexperienced. Moreover, the other senior commanders—generals Alderson and Currie—had fared little better. A month later, at Festubert, Turner had shown moral courage in attempting to call off a fruitless frontal attack, even though he had been overruled by higher authorities. More damaging in the eyes of his seniors was the image of Turner's 2nd Division as lax in discipline, as evidenced by the higher rate of trench foot among his troops in the winter of 1915. Even worse, the Battle of St. Eloi in April 1916 was a terrible failure, and one that reflected badly on Turner and his division. Although many of the problems at St. Eloi were inherited from the British division that the Canadians had been forced to relieve early—as well as being exacerbated by almost unspeakable battlefield conditions—ultimately, Turner was responsible for the failure. He would surely have been fired from a British division for his role in the defeat. Often overlooked, however, is his admirable defence of his junior officers and his refusal to serve up scapegoats as was required to satisfy his superior officers. After the St. Eloi debacle, his division was redeemed on the Somme by their role in the victory at Courcelette, one of the true highlights of the entire campaign.

Turner's physical and moral bravery were never called into question. He was fearless, and his protestations to senior officers about inadequate support or poorly conceived plans proved his moral courage. On those issues he cannot be faulted. Unfortunately, though, Turner is often compared to Currie, and always unfavourably.[12] Where Turner far outperformed Currie, however, was in his inspirational style of command. D.E. Macintyre, who began the war as a lieutenant of the scouting section in the 28th Battalion and ended it as a senior staff officer, described the men's admiration for Turner: The general came down "to see me [after a successful raid] and he was very nice. We all like him immensely, no fuss or frills, just as human as anybody. He thanked me for my work and congratulated me on my promotion, all the while with his two hands, one on each of my shoulders…. Every time he speaks to a man he makes a friend."[13] Currie rarely excited such admiration in his men. As popular as Turner was, however, Currie's attention to planning and his active mind distinguished him in the eyes of his superiors. And no matter how generously one assesses Turner's command on the Somme, his earlier failures cannot be excused on the basis of inexperience. Yet one is tempted to believe that he would likely have emerged a better general if he had been afforded the five months that Currie had to prepare his division for its attack on Vimy Ridge in April 1917, which made so many names and reputations in the Canadian Corps.

But Turner's time as a fighting general was up, and he reluctantly took the prestigious position in England as chief of the general staff. He performed extremely well in the role, with his no-nonsense approach, managerial skills, battlefield experience, and his desire to shed many of the patronage chains, placing him in good stead with the Canadians and the British. At the time, overseas minister George

Perley promised Turner that he would keep his seniority and be considered for the Canadian Corps when Byng vacated command of it. This would later create conflict between Currie and Turner, who always had an uneasy relationship. The slightly paranoid Currie wrongly believed that the South African War hero was scheming against him. He wasn't, and after Currie became corps commander, Turner supported him to the best of his abilities.

Situated at Argyll House, London, Perley's new ministry, the OMFC, brought together the various Canadian agencies and organizations under one structure. Equally important was the new-found impetus for Canada to control its own troops. English Canadians' fierce support of the war was based on a proud sense of the country's place in the British Empire, but also—for many—on a nascent Canadian nationalism. Yet the Canadian government had entered the war wielding almost no control over its forces. In August 1914, Sam Hughes had stood up in the House of Commons and revealed: "We have nothing whatever to say as to the destination of the troops once they cross the water."[14] In fact, Canadian recruits were attested as Imperial troops, no different from other forces recruited throughout the Empire. And while the British kept the Canadian force together as a fighting unit, the Canadians remained subject to all Imperial regulations. No one seemed to mind this power structure at the start of the war.

But the Canadian government had demanded the right to pay for the cost of fielding the CEF. In the heady patriotism of 1914, this was seen as part of the Dominion's contribution to the war effort. Later, after much haggling over what was owed to Whitehall, the Canadians were less eager to hand the necessary hundreds of millions of dollars over to the British, especially with Canada's economy sinking under debt. However, by paying for the Canadian forces, Sir Robert Borden had retained some leverage over them. This control was little exercised in the first three years of the war, but the tension between imperialism and nationalism that emerged in Canada in the decades before the war was reflected in the nation's force overseas. As the Canadian troops gained confidence, a sense of their own distinctiveness in relation to their British cousins emerged. Canadians in the trenches and at home took pride in a separate, identifiable status and reputation for Canadian troops. Borden felt it too, believing that if his countrymen were being called on to make the blood sacrifice for the Empire, then he, as their representative, needed to exert greater influence on the direction of the war. This would prove difficult, as the British were anxious for the involvement of the Dominion's men, but not for the nation's voice in directing the war effort. Borden nevertheless instructed Perley to begin the process of regaining control over the Canadian overseas troops.

With the establishment of the overseas ministry, Canada now had a structure to implement some of the changes that would generate greater Canadian control over the war effort. The bluster and amateurism of Hughes had been replaced by the diplomatic manoeuvres of Perley, supported by his champion, Turner. While the overseas ministry acquired a reputation for "insensitivity, inefficiency, and confusion," such epithets would aptly describe most civilian command headquarters in military organizations.[15] The ministry had its problems—as would any department established in the panic of war and only a few months old—but it was an important step forward for Canada in exerting autonomous control over its forces. By the end of the war, the Canadians were no longer Imperial troops but part of an overseas Canadian militia.

BY THE TIME of Perley's appointment in late 1916, tens of thousands of Canadians had already crossed the Atlantic, evading the dreaded U-boats that tried to intercept the destroyer-protected convoys, and had begun to train in England. While Salisbury Plain, used for training in the early stages of the war, was legendary for its viscous, porridge-like mud, subsequent Canadian troops were sent to a number of centres throughout southeast England. Shorncliffe was the primary training camp by mid-1915. It was a massive camp of stone barracks, wooden huts, and tents. Georges Vanier noted that beyond the camp's fences, it was surrounded by "fields of lush green where hundreds of sheep were grazing."[16] Shorncliffe was a rustic, idyllic environment in which to prepare for war, and its location a mere four miles from the sea allowed for a warm and peaceful escape for soldiers on leave.

Successive waves of new trainees meant that by the autumn of 1916, Canadians were established in other camps, such as Bramshott, Crowborough, Hastings, New Shoreham, Seaford, and Witley—all within close proximity of Aldershot, where the Imperials instructed most of their troops. Throughout southeastern England, an array of Canadian training divisions, reserve battalions, and brigades were honing their fighting skills. As more battalions arrived from Canada, they were put into training camps, but also broken up to become reinforcements. Of the first hundred battalions to cross the Atlantic, less than half went to Europe to serve in one of the four infantry divisions. The rest, and almost all the other battalions—those numbered from 101 to 258—were broken up and used as reinforcements.

In Canada, prominent local citizens had been asked to raise battalions from their communities. The idea of chums and co-workers fighting together appealed, and had brought many men into the ranks. Other specialist battalions had been raised: sportsmen, Highland, Scandinavian, temperance groups, bantams (men under five feet tall), and even a Methodist unit had been rounded up. But overseas, these units were shattered. Men who had enlisted and trained together in Canada, forging bonds of friendship and camaraderie, were now scattered to the four corners of the CEF. This was perceived as nothing short of a betrayal, especially by the officers who had been asked to use their influence to raise these units in Canada. Though most soldiers got over their disappointment, they rarely forgot their old units. Letters home to loved ones constantly referred to the mates they had enlisted with, even though they were spread throughout various units. This dismantling of battalions had the unintentional advantage, however, of creating bonds among units.

By the end of 1916, over 135,000 Canadians were training in camps in England, waiting to reinforce the forces on the continent, which numbered some 108,000, most of whom were in the Canadian Corps.[17] The camps were surrounded by picturesque countryside and friendly English folk who, though acknowledging the sacrifice of Canadians in coming to assist them, also profited handsomely from catering to the better-paid Dominion troops. There were more than a few misconceptions about the wild men from Canada. "Who are you blokes?" a young boy asked Gunner Frank Ferguson and his mates. "We're Canadians," one of the chaps answered. "Strike me pink, Cannydians, and you're white!" exclaimed the boy. "I suppose he shared the popular idea that all Canadians were redskins," Ferguson commented in his diary.[18] Private Willard Melvin informed his father after returning from a trip to Edinburgh that he was treated extremely well by the people there: "A Canadian up here is something of a curio, you can hear the people on the street saying, 'There's a Canadian,' like I was strange animal of some kind!"[19] Melvin would survive the war and return to his parents in Halifax, although he suffered multiple gunshot wounds, including one to the face, while serving as a sergeant in the PPCLI. Twenty-one-year-old Sapper H.J. Elliot, on his first trip overseas, wrote to his family with some pleasure, "The people around here have great ideas of Canada. They imagined we were all wild savages or cowboys that lived in tents, and forests were everywhere, and no farm land."[20] No matter what the English thought of the Canadians, most often there was a friendly relationship among the two nations' citizens. More than a few of the English would have been surprised to find that almost half of this foreign Dominion army had been born in the United Kingdom.

OVER 152,000 of the total recruits for the CEF had previous military experience, mostly with the militia, but this was a new type of war.[21] Even though the Canadian forces drew heavily on bankers and bakers, factory workers and farmers, many had

These Canucks sit relaxed, revealing with their toothy smiles and varying physiques that the Canadian Corps was not simply composed of giants from the colony of snow and ice. The fit and runty, the old and young: all served together. The average Canadian soldier was a little over twenty-six years old, and he could not have stood taller than five and a half feet.

previously handled a rifle and understood basic military drill. But the new training program in England was a shock for most men. Prewar teacher and railway mail clerk Herbert Bolster wrote only half jokingly to a friend about his transition from civilian to army life:

> Once I was young and handsome and laid claim to an intelligence which permitted me to hold intercourse with beings fashioned just a little lower than angels. I was almost human in my action and tastes. I was said by some to possess a "temperament" (whatever that may be). I claimed a little originality and considered myself someone. I washed twice or three times a day. And wore clothes which might have been said to fit—but behold me now—I am become a portion of Canada's gift to the Empire. I am a full private in the army—My number is 12606 and on parade the sergt. says, "Number 4 correct that slope!! What the H— do you mean tryin' to wear your rifle like a necktie!" I have not even a name. How have the mighty fallen![22]

But there was method to the annoyance, prattle, and harassment. Soldiers had to learn to react instinctively to commands. The mind might shut down, but the body would go forward.

Practice trenches were dug, fought over, and recaptured in mock battles. Rifle training was important. "This musketry course is to make better shots out of the new army," wrote Private J.W. McClung. "Anything [that] will make better murderers of us is welcomed with open arms by the officials."[23] The new recruits moved from rifle practice to open warfare training. Private John Saywell described how the infantry trained to close with the enemy:

> Yesterday in the morning we tried our battle practice, had overcoats and packs on and were issued with 20 rds at the 650 yards mark, doubled to 600 yds, flopped down in all the mud and slush on our stomachs, fired 3 rounds, doubled to 500: down again and more rds, then same procedure at the 400 yds [where] we fixed bayonets. Then on to the 300, 3 more rds, then 200, 3 more here with the warning of gas. We put on our helmets, then ran on to 100, it was simply pouring and our eye pieces were covered with water and mist. Could not see anything. Here we got 5 rds rapid fire, couldn't see blessed

targets—so fired in the general direction, mud and water on the bolt of our rifles made it almost impossible to eject cartridges so some of them had to use their heel then we ran forward 40 yds and bayoneted the sandbags.[24]

Saywell's account noted how, at this juncture, the infantry were building up fire while advancing to the point where they could drive home the bayonet. Later training would integrate the infantry with machine guns offering key fire support, and provide instruction in how to move in steady advances behind artillery barrages.

The ever-present shovel was introduced, or reintroduced, to all men. Digging became a part of the sweaty infantry's day. Bayonet practice remained popular among instructors who tried to make new recruits more "offensive." Stabbing a bag of hay repeatedly while instructors demanded more blood lust, accepting the need to gouge eyeballs with thumbs, or learning how best to disembowel the enemy by the turn of a wrist reminded more than a few men of their own weak stomachs.[25]

Although bayonet usage remained an important part of training, especially as it helped men handle themselves in close combat, the experience of 1915 trench fighting had proven that it was more advantageous not to engage in hand-to-hand fighting if it could be avoided. Grenades were popular as they allowed soldiers to kill from afar and avoid plunging seventeen inches of steel into another man's belly. The innocuous-looking egg-shaped weapon was given to new recruits, who weighed the one-pound metal explosive in their hands and learned its intricacies. "It was amusing to see the different fellows handling the lit bombs," wrote Lieutenant Armine Norris. "Some just shut their eyes and chucked them wildly."[26] Others waited too long, nearly having the grenades go off in their hands. Alert instructors kept an eye on all nervous men, and more than a few gave their lives as grenades bounced off practice parapets or fell out of trembling hands to land at the soldiers' feet.

Officers received different training, of course. In the hierarchy of the army, the officers were always differentiated from the men, and it would do no good for anyone's confidence—either the officers' or the men's—to have a commissioned man stumble around failing to march in step or figure out how to read a map in front of his men. Technical and tactical skills—signalling, military law, tactical appreciation, trench-building—were taught in special officer training schools, but so too were leadership qualities emphasized. Officers were instructed to be firm but fair. The popular memory of the war is one in which draconian discipline was exercised. And it is indeed true that the rules and regulations were in place to support the hierarchy, and the punishments that were issued often reinforced discipline rather than supporting justice. However, officers were told they needed to master more than the "iron hand" of discipline: these new leaders were instructed to care for their men as a father might care for his family. This could be absolutely foreign to a twenty-year-old university student turned lieutenant, but the privilege of command brought its own burdens.

IN DECEMBER 1915, Currie had written to authorities in England that the training was "d—d rotten and the men responsible ... should be told so in no unmistakable terms."[27] Inefficiency in getting reinforcements to the front was evident in all camps; but in June of 1916, one report noted that of the nearly 20,000 Canadians at Shorncliffe, only 11,560 were available for training, the rest engaged in odd jobs, including more than 1,200 in brass and bugle bands.[28] When Byng had sent urgent cables to England for these troops to be converted to fighting men, a nonchalant Hughes had cabled back that he should "Stand firm." This was obviously unhelpful.[29] Byng would have to deal with fewer inane comments after Hughes's removal, but the training system had to be improved.

Functioning as a much-needed central authority, Turner employed his experience gained on the Western Front's battlefields to organize a new training system based on territorial units. The regions in Canada, and their recruiting depots and centres, would now have corresponding units in England, as opposed to the numbered battalions. As well, volunteers would now be sent over from Canada in drafts rather than full battalions, which reduced the agony of seeing these surrogate families broken up. These regional reserve battalions were also linked to fighting units in the CEF, a connection that allowed for men from a particular province to be sent to battalions containing soldiers from that province. Although men from all provinces could be found in most battalions, this was an attempt to create a link from firing line, through England, back to Canada. Experience proved that infantry battalions with dedicated feeder units containing regional pools of men had a greater impetus to send officers on a rotational basis from front to rear, in order to provide up-to-date tactical and battlefield information to new recruits in England.[30]

One of Turner's most successful accomplishments was the development of more specialized training for men and officers through the standardization of the varied types of training that were taking place throughout the Canadian camps.[31] At the tactical level, Turner organized a standard syllabus. The training program for a new infantry recruit was fourteen weeks, during which all manner of trench warfare lessons were imparted. Units coming from Canada, where some had been training for months, were usually assessed and placed between their first and third week of the training syllabus after arrival.[32] Many Canadians were aggrieved at having to engage in another long period of training, feeling that the British were lording their experience over the colonials. This was sometimes true, but most units coming from Canada were woefully unprepared for the new warfare. The multi-decorated Major David Corrigall of the 20th Battalion remembered his unit's officers grappling with the issue of gas warfare while in Canada. Their tactical solution was, upon viewing a gas cloud, to command the men to restrain their breathing for ninety seconds, during which they were to advance at a jog from their trenches to a position some 200 metres to the flank. The unit practised this for two or three days, attempting to outrun imaginary gas clouds while not breathing.[33] The approach was absurd, but was probably a response typical of men desperate to find solutions to problems they could not yet comprehend. So, while Canadians were angry to find that they would have to start their instruction over again, they soon realized that the training in England was far more realistic than that carried out an ocean away. "We learned more the first week of our actual training in England than we did from November to April in Canada," testified Alexander McClintock.[34]

Nonetheless, the monotony of the work grated on men anxious for the fight; Private Donald Fraser of the 31st Battalion concluded, "Our training was decidedly amateurish and impractical. It consisted mainly of route marches and alignment movements. Our musketry course amounted to nothing; we had only half an idea about the handling of bombs. We were perfectly ignorant regarding rifle grenades."[35] Fraser's condemnation should be accepted with some caveats, as he was at this point looking back on his training experience from the shattering effects of the trenches, and he had been there since September 1915. A year and a half later, the training was more proficient and relevant to surviving on the Western Front. Yet there has never been a means to match training to actual combat in any war ever fought. In the first two years of the war, the Canadians no doubt spent too long building perfect trenches with proper 90-degree angles, or in route marches intended to toughen them up, but they had also practised small-unit tactics of advancing in controlled bounds and using the terrain effectively to set up fields of fire to advance on the enemy.[36] However, the Western Front and its multitude of machine guns demanded more.

Soldiers might wait for weeks or months after they finished their basic training before there was a need for them on the Western Front. Many muttered that they were killing time when they should have been killing the Hun. But after the terrible casualties of the Somme, it was clear that units needed a steady stream of reinforcements to keep them up to strength, and it did not take long before the wastage of the trenches forced commanding officers to request more men. The training brigades sent reinforcements in penny-packets during quiet times or in vast contingents consisting of several hundreds after a big push. Regardless of the pace, Canadians continued to be fed into the machine.

THE LIKABLE LIBERAL PRIME MINISTER Herbert Asquith had carried the British into the war in 1914, but he seemed wholly unprepared for the emotional rigour required to fully prosecute the ensuing death struggle. He lacked drive and energy, and found solace in the bottle. When his government fell in December 1916, Asquith was replaced by the fiery David Lloyd George, known by some as the Welsh Wizard. Lloyd George had made his mark as a tough, unionist scrapper who had supported and fought for the common man. He had blown through the decrepit British war industries and reformed them to adequately feed the guns and armies on the Western Front. He did the same as prime minister, revitalizing a weary people who had seen too much blood.

The prime minister believed a large part of the problem in the British war effort was his commanders at the front. Lloyd George commenced a protracted battle with his own generals, most prominently the despised General Douglas Haig, whom the wizard felt was an incompetent dullard. To help manoeuvre against his generals,

Lloyd George incorporated the Dominion leaders into the war effort in order to strengthen civilian control. However, his promises to Borden and others of a more influential role in decision making never materialized during the war, and their influence remained more symbolic than literal. While the British prime minister still kept a small, select committee to guide the war effort, Dominion representatives such as Borden had a greater understanding of the difficulties on the battlefield through more open lines of communication with British politicians, and from the essential military-related information passed on by army commanders in the field. While wartime advancements were limited, Borden was able to ensure an important agreement at the 1917 Imperial War Conference through Resolution IX, which stated that the relationship between Britain and the dominions would be renegotiated after the war, with most of the principle politicians assuming it would mean greater autonomy for the dominions within the Empire. Obtaining such assurances was only possible because of the enormous sacrifices of the men of the Dominion troops and those at home who continued to support the war effort.

The professionalization and increased control of its forces in England was another sign that Canada was preparing itself for a long war. Such changes were also an indication that Canadian politicians and soldiers were shedding their amateur ways. Equally important, they signalled a growing belief that Canadians could direct and guide their own national destiny. The steps to nationhood are measured in short shuffles and long bounds: the establishment of the Ministry of Overseas Military Forces of Canada may indeed have been mundane and administrative, but it marked an essential change in Canadian politicians and a large leap forward to greater national autonomy.

CHAPTER 3

RAIDING—THE LABORATORY OF BATTLE

January—April 1917

As new tactics and doctrines were hammered out behind the lines, much of the real testing was carried out by individual battalions, sub-units, and individual infantrymen at the front. By raiding and patrolling, the Canadians experimented with new battle theories and tactics, while gaining experience in the planning and carrying out of operations. With so few large-scale engagements taking place, it was the trench patrol and raid that became the laboratory of battle.

In late 1915 and early 1916, much of the raiding originated episodically from the battalion or brigade headquarters. By the last half of the year, however, the raiding became more systemic and an essential component of the Canadian approach to fighting on the Western Front. All along No Man's Land, battalions sent out patrols to gather intelligence and create a forward defence. Raiding was more dangerous, and focused on attacking the Germans in their trenches. The enemy would receive no respite; every sector would be pushed and prodded, its forces set on edge from constant pressure.

As both sides engaged in trench warfare, dirty tricks of every sort were used: the Germans were known to booby-trap potential souvenirs in No Man's Land, even attaching explosives to corpses. The Canadians responded by reaching into their own black bag of nasty tricks. Lieutenant Louis Keene of the machine-gun corps recounted how his men lured in some of the enemy after realizing the Germans liked

This sketch by H.J. Mowat captures a small group of Canadians setting off on a trench raid. The full moon would have made for a dangerously well-lit No Man's Land, so that most Canadian raiders would have left behind their backpacks and possibly even their helmets, choosing instead more shapeless clothing and masks in order to blend into the environment and better stalk their prey.

Allied bully beef. They began to throw over cans of beef into the enemy lines. "Throw one over ... sounds like shuffling and getting out of the way are heard in the enemy trench. Fritz thinks it's going to go off [as a grenade]. Pause, and throw another. Fritz not so suspicious this time. Keep on throwing until happy voices from enemy trenches shout, 'More! Give us more!' Then lob over as many hand grenades as you can pile into that part of the trench and tell them to share those too."[1] Attrition was not just a balance sheet of straight numbers—it also included the wearing down of the enemy's morale and his will to continue fighting.

The Canadians had rightly acquired a fierce reputation from their successful raiding, and were acknowledged innovators and experts in the dark art. From November 1916 to the end of March 1917, the Canadian Corps launched sixty raids, forty-eight of which managed to enter the German trenches. Some 338 prisoners were taken and the Canadians were justifiably proud of their aggressive manner.[2] But there was also competition among Canadian units to pull off larger and more dangerous raids for the biggest bag of prisoners or the most destruction wrought on the enemy. With raids going off every couple of nights, and some of them ballooning to involve several hundred men, the crucial element of surprise—the greatest ally of the raider—was slowly eroded.[3] In the absence of surprise, a raid was little more than a frontal attack on the enemy's prepared defences.

ONE OF THE MOST SUCCESSFUL RAIDS of the war was against a series of German trenches northeast of Calonne on the night of January 17, 1917. The enemy lines ran through the core of the coal mining district of Lens, and were strongly fortified. The 2nd Division's 4th Brigade orchestrated the miniature set-piece battle that would throw some 860 specially trained troops against the enemy lines. The bulk of the raiders came from the 20th and 21st Battalions, who were supported by engineers and machine-gun units. With several weeks to prepare for the operation, the attacking troops broke down into five units and went over practice grounds behind the lines. The leaders were hard trench warriors who had seen considerable combat on the Western Front. Methodical gunfire targeted barbed-wire obstacles. As the zero hour approached, sectional leaders and NCOs took to patrolling No Man's Land to familiarize themselves with the ground.[4] The raiders were confident and ready.

The five storming parties were organized into separate battle groups, equipped with riflemen, bombers, wire-cutters and, in the second wave, Lewis gunners. Preparations to deal with obstacles were incorporated into the assault, with each unit carrying large canvas-covered boards to lay on barbed wire and allow for their entry into and exit from trenches. Combat engineers were embedded in each party. They would enter the enemy trenches after the infantry had cleared a section and then set mobile charges and gun-cotton to collapse dugouts and strongpoints. Some of these "bunker bombs" contained phosphorous grenades attached to a gallon of gasoline and rigged with 10 kilograms of ammonal. Weighed down with these deadly charges, most men must have been looking to drop them quickly. And that was the nature of the raid: a smash-and-grab operation where the raiders limited themselves to forty-five minutes in order to create the greatest amount of damage and confusion, and then left before the enemy had a chance to regroup and counterattack.

At 4 A.M. the raiders were given a hot meal and then moved to the front lines. The attack would go in at 7:45 A.M., in the morning's grey light. The Germans had been conditioned to expect night attacks, and so after a tense night, the defenders would have stood down and gone about their usual mundane trench duties. In the stillness of the morning, two batteries of 18-pounders and 4.5-inch howitzers opened up a creeping barrage on the enemy front line at 7:45 A.M., and the raiders, now unencumbered from all but essential equipment, raced across the snow-covered No Man's Land. A smokescreen covered some of the assaulters, but so too did a diversionary mine explosion on the flank and supporting fire on the other flank. Confused defenders raced away from the attack.

Within five minutes, the raiders had crossed the killing zone, passed through barbed wire, and begun dropping into the enemy trenches. Meeting little resistance, bombers cleared a few strongpoints, after which bayonet men led the charge laterally through trenches and then down communication trenches. Behind them came the engineers, who set their charges and blew in dugouts, emplacements, and stores of ammunition.

The company majors set up command positions that relayed information back along land-line telephones and signals. These positions also allowed forward observers for the artillery to call down accurate artillery fire on obstinate enemy positions blocking the advance through the trenches.[5] German defenders, harried and scared, attempted to avoid battle or capture by leaving the trenches and running to the rear, but Lewis gunners anticipated such tactics and mowed them down over open ground. In other positions, terrified defenders refused to leave the safety of their dugouts, even with the Canadians shouting at them to surrender. Most were entombed alive as dugouts collapsed around them. One engineer described his demolition work: "You come to a dugout—light the fuse—drop the charge in—run like hell—look over your shoulder and see the dugout come out the door."[6] Raiders had little time to ponder the morality of war or the nature of terrified soldiers huddled together in the gloom of a deep dugout screaming for mercy. In other cases, lone Canadian privates began to march back a dozen or more disarmed prisoners.

As scheduled, forty-five minutes after the operation started (or "Z plus forty-five" in the army's parlance) Canadian officers set off green rockets to signal the retreat. The raiders had done some severe damage but had stayed too long; several units had to disengage themselves in a fighting retreat. The German counter-barrage had also increased in intensity, even if it was scattering shrapnel all over the front—unclear as to where the main Canadian thrust was driving into their lines. Covering parties laid down fire to protect retreating troops, and heavy machine guns fired an interdictory barrage on known enemy communication trenches to cordon off the front. Tens of thousands of shells and 327,000 rounds of small-arms ammunition were unleashed in only a few hours; the raid became known throughout the Canadian Corps as the "Million-Dollar Scrap" since that was the rumoured price of the armaments fired.[7] Behind the artillery and machine-gun barrage, Canadians dashed back across No Man's Land. One engineer blasted the chains of a heavy German MG-08 machine gun, which had been secured so it could not easily be turned around and used against the Germans, and dragged it across No Man's Land under enemy fire. The 21st Battalion hurried 100 prisoners out of the German trenches, and scores of other enemy soldiers had been killed.[8] Forty dugouts were destroyed, three ammunition dumps blown up, and a large portion of the front left in disarray.

The Canadians came out of the Calonne raid the victor, but they had still suffered not inconsequential casualties. Forty men were killed, most of whom had been caught in the initial charge by small-arms fire, and another 135 were wounded. All of the soldiers in the raid had been hand-picked, and therefore were likely the best and most aggressive. Their loss would have been keenly felt throughout the battalion. Still, the raid was considered an important victory and a morale-raising event. Idle chat and gossip about the successful raid passed up and down the line. Byng was particularly proud of Burstall's division, taking delight in personally handing out medals to distinguished raiders. The general ordered that the lessons learned from the raid be circulated and presented to other units so that all the Canadians could master "any new form of 'Boche Killing.'"[9] The effective planning and preparation for the raid was highlighted, as was the dangerous, if ultimately successful, surprise daylight timing of the attack. The Calonne raid confirmed that Canadians were mastering the essential lessons of the Somme. "The ease and regularity with which

This illustration shows the danger soldiers would face in a trench raid as they inched across No Man's Land, navigating around craters, corpses, rats, and barbed wire, and under the periodic glare of illuminating flares. Once the raiders closed with the enemy, they unleashed a surprise attack, aiming to hit hard and fast and then return to the safety of their own lines before the Germans recovered and struck back.

we carry out our smaller operations seems to augur well for the larger one that will be undertaken later on," wrote Lieutenant Maurice Pope.[10] Most Canadians agreed with Pope. However, though Byng's trusted subordinate, Arthur Currie, recognized the importance of raids in providing essential battle skills for his troops, he also knew that the casualties sustained in these missions were taking out the best men. When he raised his concerns with Byng, the senior corps commander chided him for being too cautious, commenting that perhaps his veteran division was "losing its go."[11] Currie was not convinced, but he respected Byng's experience and did not raise the issue again.

By the winter of 1916–1917, raiding had begun to spiral out of control, with battalions or brigades feeling pressure from higher formations to show their aggression by launching a continuous series of raids. Brigadier Victor Odlum of the 11th Brigade, who had helped to pioneer raiding in the Canadian Corps, informed his men in early January 1917: "I desire the attitude of this Brigade to become more aggressive."[12] Similar orders were issued to all infantry battalions throughout the corps. Rewards, reputations, revenge, and pride drove units onward, with a competitive attitude developing among units to put up the best scores. But increasingly reckless behaviour meant that raids began to lose the advantage of surprise. The growing competitiveness was detrimental to effectiveness as operations were rushed and plans poorly conceived.

IN FEBRUARY 1917, the most junior of the four divisions planned the biggest Canadian Corps raid to date. It would be launched against the commanding heights of Vimy Ridge, an objective that the Canadians had been given as part of the forthcoming joint British–French offensive in April. The slopes of Vimy were a graveyard, with thousands of corpses from previous offensives offering macabre testimony to the tenacity of the German defenders who held the ground and had spent over two years fortifying it. Ringed with barbed wire and a fortified series of interlocking machine-gun nests, the ridge extended 7 kilometres and held a commanding view of the Allied lines. Major General David Watson ordered his troops to have a practice run at the position in a massive 1,700-man raid scheduled for late February.

Watson had performed well at Ypres, but his brigade had also been involved in the debacle at St. Eloi. Unlike Turner, who refused to serve up his junior officers after this failed battle, Watson had no problem with firing a number of battalion commanders. After the St. Eloi affair, Watson received command of the 4th Division. He owed the promotion to his good battlefield record but also to his friendship with Sam Hughes. The machinations of the war minister and his confidant, Lord Beaverbrook, cleared the way of competitors in England for Watson's appointment.[13] But Watson was strong-willed, and after he received the division, he cut ties with Hughes, especially after the minister's firing. This rejection left Hughes in a fury, but it helped Watson avoid the back-channel communiqués for which Hughes was infamous. Watson's division had performed well on the Somme, but it had fought as part of a British corps and therefore Byng had not got to know him or his staff very well. As the most inexperienced divisional commander, Watson realized that Byng was keeping a close eye on him and felt the pressure to perform. He aimed to outdo all the other Canadian divisions by launching the largest raid of the war.

While the 2nd Division's raid at Calonne had been a success partially because of its unusual daylight timing, Watson and his trusted Imperial staff officer, Colonel Edmund Ironside, planned an even more elaborate surprise for the enemy at Vimy. The imposing six-foot-four, red-haired Ironside spoke half a dozen languages and understood another half a dozen more, and was "supremely self-confident, forceful and opinionated."[14] Nicknamed "Tiny," he brought years of experience to help ease the young division through its Western Front trial by fire. But neither he nor Watson showed much common sense in planning the coming operation. Instead of a crushing artillery bombardment, the division would rely on lethal chlorine gas to surprise and choke the enemy into submission.

The Canadians had had a special hatred of poison gas since they had been its first victim at the Second Battle of Ypres in April 1915. But despite being ravaged by the chemical horrors, they had not broken. The quick development of respirators and the slow evolution of instruction in how to survive on the battlefield ensured by the end of 1915 that gas would not be a war-winning weapon. But it was nonetheless a terrifying one. Those afflicted were left gasping for breath through corrupted lungs; men turned green and then black as they coughed up gluey mucous and blood. Though conventional weapons were in fact deadlier than gas, in that they caused more fatalities, the invisible nature of chemicals that swirled and saturated the very place where soldiers made their homes left the men in a state of anxiety. For service-men who had, before the war, seen the horrifying effects of tuberculosis—the white death that claimed thousands—this seemed to be a new incarnation of that same damnation.

By the time they entered the 1916 Battle of Verdun, both the French and the Germans had perfected chemical artillery shells that could be dropped into positions behind the front. While the payload was less dense than the massive gas clouds of 1915, there was also less worry about the clouds turning and blowing back on friendly troops because of the vagaries of wind and weather. The gas-mongers also responded by developing more lethal chemical agents, including phosgene, which was many times deadlier than chorine, and nearly invisible and odourless.

Along with these evolutions in artillery gas tactics, the British continued to use gas clouds, which were now released by special gas companies of the Royal Engineers.[15] Although they were distrusted and disliked by the infantry, these engi-neers were tasked with overseeing the transportation of large metal canisters filled with gas into the front lines, setting them up in prepared pits and releasing them at the appropriate moment to allow for a gas cloud to form and drift over the enemy lines. The infantry were particularly unimpressed because it was they who were called on to carry the heavy canisters to the front and it was they who usually received the angry retaliation from the enemy's artillery after the specialists had retreated to the rear.

The gas specialists were shunned by soldiers throughout the BEF for their nefar-ious and seemingly uncontrollable chemical agents that polluted the battlefield. Moreover, the infantry had little experience in training with gas. The Canadians, for instance, had never attempted to send an infantry assault in behind a gas cloud, for the most part because the British and Germans had tried this tactic earlier in the war and had failed miserably, with the death clouds turning on the attacking troops and gassing thousands. However, on January 31, 1917, the Germans released a dense, daylight gas cloud against lax French troops, with the devastating result of 500 dead and 1,900 wounded.[16] A series of panicky directives passed through the Allied armies, demanding that officers highlight the importance of an anti-gas doctrine. The event also revealed the deadly effect of gas in surprise attacks.

HILL 145, the highest point on Vimy Ridge, held a commanding view over the Canadian lines. It was the raiders' objective, but was just about the last place against which gas should have been used. The gas specialists would need a strong wind to blow the gas cloud up the ridge, and without a powerful gale, the chemical cloud, which was heavier than air, would sink into the low-lying trenches, shell holes, and dugouts, leaving a polluted battlefield over which the Canadians would have to attack.

Watson and his staff clearly did not understand the limitations of gas. Moreover, while elements from four battalions had been training behind the lines, going over similar terrain and studying aerial photographs, they could not, of course, incorporate the use of gas into their training. Nor was an attempt made even to train with smoke, to at least stimulate the bewildering effects of keeping pace with a massive noxious cloud. Senior commanders simply had very little understanding of this weapon, and hoped that any release of gas against the enemy would emulate the terrible and terrifying effect of the first gassing at Second Ypres, or the more recent attack against the French.

"It was said that fifteen tons of gas was to be sent over to strike terror into the black heart of the enemy," wrote Joseph Hayes of the 85th Battalion. "The first wave was to be of deadly poisonous gas that would kill every living thing in its path: while the second would corrode all metal substances and destroy guns of every description. When complete, all our men would have to do would be to walk into the enemy trenches, throw out their dead bodies and take possession."[17] Another trench raider, Alex Jack of the 54th Battalion, remembered hearing that the gas was a new type that would render the enemy's rifles "useless" through instant corrosion.[18] Such assumptions must have sounded fanciful to some of the long-service veterans, but constant rumours percolated along the front with regard to new, lethal gases. Gas was a frightening, almost mystical weapon that was little understood and much feared. The infantry might have understandably placed faith in their gas to clear the enemy trenches, but one must question the senior officers, whose job it was to know the workings of the weapon systems that they planned to use to support their men in battle.

Although poor weather conditions required that the operation be postponed several times, Watson and Ironside were anxious to proceed with the gas raid. However, at least two of the four battalion commanders argued that the operation was impractical. Lieutenant Colonel A.H.G. Kemball was commander of the 54th Battalion. Having served in the British army since 1880, before retiring to Canada, he had re-enlisted at the age of fifty-four at the start of the war and been given command of the battalion. On the Somme, he had led his boys from the front, winning a Distinguished Service Order (DSO) for the attack and capture of Desire Trench. Here at Vimy, however, facing no less daunting a position, he objected strenuously to his senior officer, Brigadier General Victor Odlum, commander of the 11th Brigade, arguing that because of the unpredictable wind, the raid should be postponed and more artillery fire brought to bear on the German lines. The commander of the 75th Battalion, Lieutenant Colonel Sam Beckett, who had raised his unit in Mississauga, was no less concerned, informing the same high command that not only was the surprise attack no longer a secret, due to postponements, but that his troops had no training in manoeuvring with gas. Aware that two of his experienced and decorated battalion commanders had serious misgivings about the plan, Odlum, himself a long-service veteran and accomplished planner of raids, questioned his orders by writing to, and then visiting in person, divisional headquarters, where he argued strenuously with Ironside. He questioned how his men were to get across No Man's Land before the enemy barrage opened up if the gas failed to silence the enemy troops.[19] Despite this important concern, Ironside refused to entertain the idea of further postponement, as too much planning and hope were riding on the raid.

With the front-line soldiers' objections overruled, the attack formations moved to the front to prepare for the assault in the last days of February. Both Kemball and Beckett refused to send their men into the questionable battle unless they themselves led from the front. In the end, two experienced battalion commanders, who had scouted the area and seen the formidable defences their men were up against, were ignored by their superiors, who instead relied on an untested super-weapon to overcome defenders who had spent two years fortifying their position.

AS THE 1,700 RAIDERS lay in the cold mud, nerves taut, waiting in anticipation for the chemical clouds to be released, they cursed the weather, the Germans, and the gas specialists as the wind remained too light or blew in the wrong direction to allow for a gas release. The frustration began to mount as the intricate raid was postponed again and again, eventually resulting in a two-day delay. Staff officers began to wonder if the surprise of both the raid and the use of gas had been lost; officers and men at the front knew for certain that it had, as the defenders of the German 261st Infantry Regiment of the 79th Reserve Division, consisting of three battalions of about 1,000 men each, shouted taunts to the Canadians to come over the top whenever they were ready, as they were waiting for them with open arms.[20]

In addition to the psychological pressure the men suffered as a result of the repeated postponements, the waiting also took its toll physically: the Germans laid down heavy searching artillery bombardments along the Canadian front and the 12th Brigade reported three killed and twenty-two wounded by stray shelling alone.[21] The Canadians were learning the hard way that employing infantry and gas together in an attack was a dangerous proposition, a lesson underscored when several additional infantrymen were gassed by canisters breached by shellfire. Still, the plan remained unchanged and the raiders were to follow behind the second of two gas clouds sent into the German trenches. It was the second gas cloud that was to seal the Germans' fate, as it was intended to catch many of the defenders unprepared, exhausted, and lethargic as a result of their ordeal with the first cloud less than forty minutes earlier.

At last the wait ended when the British gas specialists indicated that the proper wind strength was present on the last night of February 1917.[22] At 5 A.M. on March 1, the special companies' gas sergeants—wearing red, white, and green brassards to indicate to the Canadian infantry who they were—released 1,038 cylinders of White Star (chlorine and phosgene) gas into a stiff breeze of 14 kilometres per hour, which carried it quickly into the German lines.[23] Unfortunately for the Canadians, the German defenders, who wore efficient gas respirators, had recently been issued new orders on how to combat gas cloud releases: "As soon as the alarm is given ... Our artillery will fire into the gas cloud and on the hostile trenches."[24] True to orders, the German counter-barrage fell on the Canadian lines and immediately punctured several canisters holding phosgene for the second wave release, thus gassing groups of Canadians. Amidst uncontrollable hacking and retching, the infantry waited for the second gas cloud to be released.[25]

Messages sent back to the 4th Division headquarters by forward observers noted that the Germans, adopting the new gas defence, immediately fired red SOS flares and kept their rifle fire "fairly regular" until the gas had moved past their lines.[26] The use of gas had brought the Germans out of their dugouts, and because the artillery fire from Canadian guns was "not sufficiently concentrated and caused no slackening of enemy fire," that was where they remained—in position and manning their fortified trenches.[27] Lieutenant Zeller of the 7th Company, 262 Reserve Regiment, wrote of the gas: "In the front line, gas casualties were practically zero, but the relieving troops from the 5th Company, who were underway, suffered worse."[28]

The raiders were to go into No Man's Land at 5:40 A.M., forty minutes after a second discharge of gas. But minutes before the second gas cloud was to be released, the wind direction changed, and so the cloud release was cancelled. In the 12th Brigade's sector, however, the message was not received and, when the gas was released there, it slowly moved up the ridge only to stop and reverse, floating back towards the Canadian lines, eventually drifting directly towards the waiting soldiers of the 11th Brigade on the left.[29] Private Maurice Bracewell remembered with terror the grey gas seeping back into the Canadian lines: "Our front lines got all the gas, the front trenches were saturated with it."[30] Although the gas casualties suffered by Canadians were not recorded amidst the confusion, they were probably not heavy since most men were equipped with the very effective small box respirator, and they had time to don it before the death mist reached them. However, because the gas was very dense, the raiding parties in this sector, most from the 73rd Battalion, were forced to leave their trenches. They suffered additional casualties from shell and bullet as they proceeded overland until they found their assembly points.[31]

Mistakenly assuming that the second gas attack had blown through the German ranks, one officer of the 50th Battalion, whose unit was acting as a reserve on the flank of the 75th Battalion, dangerously poked his head up to watch the spectacle of the gas cloud and, he believed, his brothers in arms that would soon be advancing calmly behind it. Instead, when he looked across the 250 metres of No Man's Land, just minutes before the first wave of 75th Battalion men were to go over, he was shocked to see the Germans tightly packed in their trenches, bayoneted rifles aimed at the Canadian lines.[32] The Canadian raiders, already committed to battle and spurred on by their earlier raiding success, persevered in the hope that the Germans had been sufficiently overcome by the first wave of gas. They had not.

AT ZERO HOUR, the Canadians went over the bags and were met by withering fire. The two battalion commanders were killed while leading their men in the charge: Kemball, of the 54th Battalion, was riddled with bullets as he searched for an opening through uncut barbed wire, his body caught on the spooled rolls like some macabre scarecrow; Sam Beckett, of the 75th, was shot through the heart by a sniper during the aborted advance. Because it was expected that the gas would silence the enemy, white flags had been set up to mark the gaps in the wire. These now drew the Canadians into natural killing zones as German machine-gunners aimed at these hard-to-miss targets. The Germans had even mined a few of the pathways so that lead infantrymen had their feet and legs blown off.[33] In less than five minutes, the 54th Battalion alone lost its commanding officer, all four company commanders, and close to 190 men, remembered Sergeant Major Alex Jack.[34]

The futile assault degenerated into a charnel house, but throughout it the Canadians displayed their reputation for dogged tenacity. It was a grim time, nonetheless, as friends and companions who had survived the horrors of the Somme were cut down in swaths. Caught on some wire in No Man's Land, Signaller Stanley Baker turned to his partner for help, only to see a bullet shatter his skull and have brain matter and blood splattered over him.[35] Still the Canadians rushed on, advancing through craters and over fallen comrades. Jack Quinnell, like the rest of the Canadians caught within the barrage of metal, advanced on the enemy line in bounds, from crater to crater. Dropping into a hole already occupied by one of his officers, the man turned to him and shouted, "I'm going to make a run for it; you can do what you like." He rose and stumbled off, only to be promptly taken down by a bullet.[36] The wild dash across No Man's Land that day was the last for many Canadians, as enemy fire, poison gas, and even Canadian artillery shells falling short left bodies strewn over the battlefield.

Added to the confusion resulting from the deaths of key senior commanding officers, gas cloud vapours clung to shell holes in No Man's Land, so that the attackers had to advance through their own lethal agent. To further hamper the raiders, the Germans fired gas shells into the Canadian assembly trenches, forcing the raiders to wear their respirators, which left them short of breath and almost blind as they ran through the dawn light, desperately searching for gaps in the wire as bullets and shells rained down.[37] Those that found their way through quickly discarded the ladders they had been issued, as it was apparent that the German trenches were not filled with chlorine and phosgene. They switched to the grenades and bayonets more appropriate for the vicious trench fighting that was soon to ensue.

Despite this frontal assault into uncut wire, machine-gun fire, and alert troops, a group of Canadians crashed through the enemy front line, clearing a 450-metre section of the German trench in hand-to-hand fighting. However, the Canadians were unable to reinforce the raiders in the enemy trenches because it was nearly impossible to get more troops forward over the fireswept battlefield, and because the raid was planned as a "hit and run" operation. The surviving Canadians, jumbled together from the four battalions, were forced into a running battle within the German trenches. Soon they were cut off from their own lines by German counterattacks. A successful breakout by the raiders back to their lines was made possible only by the brave rear-guard action of several officers who sacrificed themselves in holding off surging German attackers, which allowed dozens of men to escape. As one trench warrior remembered, "We had very heavy casualties, especially among the officers."[38]

The retreat back across No Man's Land was equally deadly as the enemy swept the battlefield with flanking fire. Wounded soldiers had nowhere to go and crawled to shell holes for safety. Here, they often fell victim to their own gas, which had pooled in the mucky depressions. Stuck in a crater while the Germans sniped at anything that moved, Stanley Baker watched the men in his large hole being killed one by one as exposed heads and backs were picked off by sharpshooters. Employing one of the Canadian corpses for cover, he used his helmet to dig a shallow trench through the mud to reach another hole in the rear. The lingering gases made him vomit uncontrollably, but he finally wormed his way back to the Canadian line later that night, heaving and retching as he crawled for his life.[39]

ALL THROUGH THE NIGHT, Canadians dragged themselves back into their trenches, their chlorine-tarnished brass buttons just as noticeable as their ashen faces and bluish lips, and the rattle of breath through constricted lungs audible to the sentries. The slow strangulation by gas meant that many who did not quickly escape their shell holes never regained the strength to leave their informal graves. Those who were not suffocated by their own gas cried out piteously all night, their voices rising and falling in shrieks and moans, but always carrying over the battlefield. One final tragedy occurred when several wounded men were trapped in a series of shell holes near the Canadian lines by German snipers who fired at them every time they tried to move. An officer in the Canadian front lines saw the trapped men and called down an artillery barrage on the German positions to give some cover. The shells screamed down, but once again the fire was short and many of those wounded men were annihilated by Canadian shells before the guns were frantically called off.[40]

Although the danger of snipers and stray shells remained, many of the Canadians who escaped could not stand leaving their companions behind, and several slipped over their own parapet to locate victims and drag them into the lines. Dozens who were not saved were later found in gas-infected shell holes covered in yellowish bile as they discharged pints of liquid from their corrupted lungs until they suffocated. One German officer noted, "We came across the dead Canadians, who were indeed very numerous. In fact all the shell holes were filled with the dead."[41] For those survivors who did not succumb to the chemicals, the gurgling of their companions' last breaths was a memory that haunted them for the rest of their lives.

The next morning revealed the horrifying aftermath of the raid. A ghastly carpet of Canadian corpses covered much of the battlefield. It was so disturbing that a German officer rose above his parapet with a white flag and walked into No Man's Land, where he offered the Canadians a respite in the fighting to collect their wounded and dead. In an act of compassion, several Germans also helped to gather a number of the slain, which they deposited near the Canadian lines. The hostilities continued on the morning of March 3, at the prearranged time of 8:15 A.M.[42] After the last of the wounded and missing were accounted for, the full extent of the disaster became known: the four attacking battalions had suffered 687 casualties—a 43 percent casualty rate.[43] Those men who were not too numb with exhaustion or suffering from the lingering effects of gas began to question the validity of the raid. The war diary of the 54th Battalion critically remarked that the "first discharge of gas apparently had no effect on the enemy," but more important, the question arises as to why Watson and Ironside would have thought that chemical warfare would have acted any differently.[44] Both the Canadians and Germans were equipped with very good gas masks by this point in the war, which made the use of canistered gas almost useless unless employed against poorly trained or surprised opponents. The distance of 175 to 250 metres between the lines meant that the enemy had several minutes before the gas reached them. That was certainly enough time to don respirators, especially if they were alert to the possible use of gas. Further, the series of delays, when combined with German intelligence gathered from raids and simple observation, had eliminated the surprise factor. It is clear, however, that both Ironside and Watson were unwilling to call off the long-awaited raid. They had succumbed to that strange act of delusion that occurs when people realize the odds are stacked against them but nonetheless throw caution to the wind. In this case, they and their men were blown away by the storm.

THE GERMANS DUG-IN around Vimy had repulsed another attack against their heights. But they were not complacent, as it was also clear that the Canadian Corps, which was spread out before the German observers, was preparing for another larger operation. Did they wonder if the Canadian reputation, forged in the big battles and trench raids of 1915–1916, had been exaggerated? If so, in five weeks' time, on April 9, 1917, the Canadians would show that it had not. During the Battle of Vimy Ridge, the Canadians would not behave like blind cattle mounting the slaughterhouse ramp as the men of the 4th Division did on March 1; the men at the sharp end from all four divisions were to be thinking, acting soldiers whose commanders relied on the ever-refined doctrine of infantry battalions leaning into massive forward-moving artillery barrages rather than following a nebulous gas cloud. No one wanted to repeat the gas raid, which was, in the words of Lieutenant Howard Green of the 54th Battalion, little more than "a proper slaughter."[45]

CHAPTER 4

BUNGO AND THE BYNG BOYS

Preparing for the Vimy Battle

Easter Sunday night & we go over the top tomorrow morn at 5:30. I guess a fellow has more sensations & feelings in this short night than in his whole life. I fixed up all my bombs, 15 in all, cleaned rifle, bayonet and ammunition & then sat down. Some fellows are singing songs sacred & otherwise. I have read of the boys who were first over at the Somme & Neuve Chapelle. I bet none ever went over at a place with the formidable name Vimy. The French won & lost it, so did the Imperials & now the Canadians are after it. If we win, well & good. Should we not it will not be through lack of preparation. Of course he has it all mined but even if we go up, there are plenty more to come. One fellow has tried to start "Just before the battle Mother." It was a failure. Any other kind of a song gets an ovation, but each of us is trying to hide the real state of his mind. I know how much I am thinking about Mother, Dad and all the kids; The sooner I can get back the better & the more I do to help end it, the better.[1]

So wrote Private Jack McClung of the PPCLI, who left the University of Alberta at the age of eighteen to enlist in December 1915. Now nineteen, he had been serving at the front for nearly a year and would continue to fight with his battalion, eventually rising to the rank of lieutenant. Although this would be McClung's first battle, he had been on the Western Front long enough to know that Vimy was an imposing position, strongly fortified, and that the Canadians could very well be driven back with crippling losses. But before pitting flesh against steel, the Canucks prepared for the battle for several months.

AFTER THESE MONTHS of aggressive raiding, training, and preparation, the Canadians were to tackle Vimy Ridge. The Canadian operation, which would include all four of the divisions attacking together for the first time, was part of a larger British and French offensive. But the Dominion force drew the most formidable part of the entire German defensive system in the British sector, and perhaps along the whole of the Western Front. The Allies had thrice tried to take the ridge, and each time the operation had been reduced to a bloody shambles. Although the last French attack in the autumn of 1915 had moved the Allied lines forward, thereby eating into the German buffer zone of trenches in front of the ridge, few must have thought the Canucks had a chance against such a fortress. Members of the French general staff, upon hearing of the order for Canada to take the ridge, could barely hide their contempt, predicting that the Dominion troops would certainly fail.[2] But there was no turning back. Byng's corps was part of a larger Allied offensive, and the plan had been finalized months earlier.

At the Chantilly Conference in November 1916, the French and British commanders-in-chief, Joseph Joffre and Sir Douglas Haig, had agreed to launch a coordinated attack in 1917. Nor were these plans upset when Joffre, the hero of the Marne but also the commander during the terrible bloodletting in the first two and a half years of the war, was replaced the next month by a dynamic, confident, handsome general, Robert Nivelle. The new commander had made his name at Verdun as the general responsible for recapturing a number of lost forts through highly successful attacks—sharp assaults behind massive artillery barrages—that had given new confidence to the French *poilus* after their continuous disappointments and bloody setbacks since the start of the war. Yet Nivelle had also run up the butcher's bill, though this was overlooked by most politicians and propagandists.

The ambitious French general promised a solution to the stalemate, stating, "I can assure you that victory is certain."[3] And like a dying patient, France's politicians listened to his quackery. He promised no more Verduns and then promptly planned a major offensive that looked a lot like another titanic battle. Nivelle's plan was to destroy the Germans in the Chemin des Dames, a large salient that extended north from Soissons to Arras. He would cut off the enemy's head that was jutting forward, and then thrust through the German lines and force them into a full retreat. In its promised breakthrough behind a heavy artillery barrage, the plan was not dissimilar to Haig's on the Somme.

With his impeccable English, Nivelle convinced British prime minister David Lloyd George of his plan. Nivelle promised that his forces would do the bulk of the fighting, but it was his charm that persuaded the British prime minister, who, quite shockingly, placed the British forces at his disposal. It was a blow to Haig, but was not very surprising since Lloyd George despised his field commander, whom he blamed for the enormous casualties of the previous year. Haig kicked hard in his attempts to reverse the subservient position—claiming he "would rather be tried by Court Martial than betray the Army by agreeing to its being placed under the French"—but he was nonetheless ordered to support Nivelle's pie-in-the-sky plan.[4]

The French would carry the weight of the assault. However, the British armies were to attack a week earlier and draw German reserves to the north. Haig did not like this one bit, noting rightly that it exposed the British army to "heavy losses with the possibility of no showy successes."[5] Haig acknowledged the importance of supporting his ally, but it was no envious position for the British to "willingly play second role to the French."[6] As part of this strategic diversion, the Canadian Corps would participate in the British offensive, their target being the linchpin at Vimy Ridge.

Yet the Germans were not obliging. The French planning for the operation was atrocious, with all pretences at secrecy lost months before the battle. Operational orders were found circulating in London, and the Germans could easily have guessed the location of the offensive—if they had not already captured other orders during a series of raids against French troops who had, in an appalling display of poor discipline, brought the war plans and orders into the front lines. Instead of ordering his troops to fight to the death, as they had in the past, the German high command, led by generals Paul von Hindenburg and Erich Ludendorff, hurried the final construction of a new reserve position, known as the Hindenburg Line. In March,

Hindenburg and Ludendorff ordered the evacuation of the salient that Nivelle hoped to attack and destroy. Willing to trade blasted land for a more secure position, the Germans applied a "scorched earth" policy, destroying roads, bridges, and railways. Unlike the Allies, who had a fixation on the sanctity of ground—evidenced by their need to recapture occupied terrain and their unwillingness, except in extraordinary circumstances, to give up more of it—the Germans had pulled off a brilliant retreat, shortening their line by pulling back and reducing the need to hold salients and irregular parts of the front. This retreat added thirteen divisions and fifty heavy batteries to the strategic reserve, which could be rushed to backstop vulnerable parts of the line when the Allied forces finally attacked.

General Nivelle appeared untroubled by this inconvenience, even though his armies would now have to struggle through the newly emptied wasteland. In fact, some crowed that the Germans had been forced to give up twenty times the ground that had been won during the four months of the Battle of the Somme. Surely rot had set in, even if the Allies now had no chance of mounting a surprise attack to crush the previously extended German forces. Rot there was, but all of it unfortunately in the French plan for an offensive; when the attack came, Nivelle's forces were smashed as they struggled forward through the kill zone that stretched for kilometres. To the north, though, the Canadians faced far different terrain.

VIMY RIDGE, known informally as "the shield of Arras," appeared as a low-lying, blue-grey promontory, running along a 7-kilometre northwest–southeast axis. Located 3 kilometres northeast of Arras, one of the most important logistical hubs in France, the ridge commanded the entire region. The highest point on the ridge was Hill 145, site of the disastrous gas raid of March 1, 1917, and further to the northwest lay another high ground, the Pimple. Both positions allowed the Germans to look into the Canadian lines and down the ridge, which gradually ran into the Douai plain to the southeast.

Moving in from the west, the Canadians had to advance up the gradual incline of the shell-pocked ridge that became increasingly steep; on the far eastern side, behind the German lines that were situated on the western slope and the top of the ridge line, there was a clear view of the Douai plain, which was largely untouched by the ravages of war. This geography offered the Germans both inherent advantages and disadvantages, though the former outweighed the latter. The advantages consisted of forcing the Allies to advance up the open, muddy, cratered western slope, which provided a natural killing ground from the perspective of the dug-in defenders on the ridge. As well, the Germans could bring their artillery and ammunition very close to the front without fear of direct observation since it was nearly impossible to see most of the enemy positions over the ridge without aerial support. The lone disadvantage of their position was the steepness of the drop on the eastern side, which meant that the ridge could not be held in depth and would be very hard to recapture or reinforce if it was lost during a defensive battle.

The ridge had fallen to the Germans in October 1914, and the French had failed to recover it with their six-division attack in December 1914. In the summer of 1915, another French assault was more successful, but it was ultimately crushed by a series of counterattacks, resulting in a loss of more than a 100,000 men. French commander Ferdinand Foch admitted that his troops could not prevail by "mere force of numbers."[7] In September 1915, the Allies attacked a third time and nearly captured the fortress. But they were repulsed again, sustaining 40,000 casualties. In all, some 300,000 German, French, and British troops had been killed or maimed in the see-saw battles for Vimy.[8] Canadian infantryman Sergeant R.G. Kentner was right to describe the ridge's western slope as an "immense graveyard."[9]

In the years since these French attacks, the Germans had fortified the imposing ridge with deep dugouts of concrete, as well as reinforced ancient caves to withstand all but the most direct hits from high explosive shells, laying rows of barbed wire, and, as always, expertly situating their machine-gun posts to spray the front in overlapping fields of fire. German doctrine emphasized that it was not possible "in a defensive action, to paralyze the whole of the attacking artillery, or to prevent the exposure of a considerable portion of our position to preparatory bombardment by the enemy." But German gunners were instructed that: "The attacking infantry, however, is always vulnerable, and every means of defence should be employed which can reach and annihilate it…. The object of artillery barrage fire is to break up a carefully prepared attack by the infantry, by subjecting the latter to fire … in the assembly trenches at the moment that attack is launched."[10] The Canadians had experienced this devastating shellfire on the Somme, and well recognized that it some-how had to be smothered. But few easy solutions were at hand. The Vimy position was so strong in fact that Nivelle, the French commander-in-chief, did not believe that the Canadians could take the ridge and recommended that the British start their offen-sive further to the south.[11] Haig thought otherwise, and Nivelle did not press the point, having his own battle to worry about and not being particularly interested in whether the Canadians left behind thousands of corpses in the already grim abattoir that formed the ridge's western slope, as long as they tied up German forces.

From atop the ridge, the Germans had all the advantages. In holding the high ground, the enemy observers could direct plunging shellfire onto the forward corps zone, a tactic that, according to Byng's chief of staff, Percy Radcliffe, "denied the use of the road to us by daylight."[12] Opposite the Canadians were three German divi-sions: the 1st Bavarian Reserve Division (straddling the 1st Canadian Division's front), the 79th Prussian Reserve Division (covering the sector that stretched from the Canadians' 2nd to 4th Divisions), and the 16th Bavarian Infantry Division (which was holding the Pimple, to the north of the ridge). German divisions were smaller than their Canadian equivalents, but were still a powerful striking force at about 12,000 men each. Within the divisions were three regiments, each containing three battalions. While the regiments were smaller than a Canadian infantry brigade the battalions were approximately the same size, at around 900 men.[13]

Five regiments of German infantry were dug in along the the complex defensive grid that ran like a steel spine along Vimy Ridge, with two more regiments of the 16th Bavarian Infantry Division to the north on the Pimple. General of the Infantry Ritter Karl von Fasbender, a sixty-five-year-old decorated veteran whose career stretched back to the Franco-Prussian War of 1870–1871, was in command of the Vimy sector. The general had situated his five regiments in depth, so that there were five battalions in the front lines, five in reserve, and five more in the rear area, about a two-hour march from the front, which was an ideal position for counterattacking against any force that might break into his lines. The ten battalions on the front or reserve lines were also supported by machine-gun, artillery, and logistical units that made up several thousand additional defenders. The primary German position ran along the crest of the ridge and consisted of three trench lines. The second position was located at the foot of the eastern slope and was not very useful in providing a strongpoint from which to regain the ridge should it be lost.

Despite the narrow depth of the position—which ranged on average from 700 to 1,000 metres in front of, on top of, and behind the ridge itself, although deeper on the 1st and 2nd Division's fronts—the heavy MG-08 and the lighter German machine gun, the MG-08/15, added firepower to the defensive groups that were often formed around these weapons, of which there were twenty-four to a battalion.[14] Battalion commanders had access to two light mortars, while the divisional commanders controlled the artillery. The *frontsoldaten* was equipped with his Mauser rifle, as well as being issued a number of "potato-mashers"—the German *Stielhandgranate*, a hand bomb that could be thrown further than the Allied grenades because of its long wooden handle but that also had less fragmentation effect and therefore was less deadly as an anti-personnel weapon. In all, some 8,000 German defenders manned the ridge, supported by heavy firepower and situated in strong defences. These advantages aside, since the position was not held in significant depth, if the Canadians could strike hard and fast, they might take and hold the ridge before counterattacks could be launched to throw them back into the shattered landscape.

THE CANADIANS HAD LEARNED from the French failures that numbers alone would not prevail. Guns, shells, and men were essential, but so too was detailed training to prepare the Canadians for battle. "Our fights are won or lost before we go into them," declared Brigadier Victor Odlum.[15] He was overstating the case, but adequate preparation did give the infantry a fighting chance against the deeply fortified positions.

Stockpiling ammunition, digging gun pits, building new roads, and establishing underground subways to allow the infantry to move close to the jumping-off points without losing men to stray enemy artillery fire—all these preparatory measures saved lives. Dozens of deep caves pocketed the rear areas, providing additional cover. But the Canadian Corps was a vast organization, and much of the work carried out by the men who formed it was done under fire, especially in Zouave Valley—a key logistical staging area to the west of Vimy. Harry Bond, a law student from Vancouver before enlisting, recounted hurrying through a trench in Zouave Valley and stumbling across half a dozen intact severed hands, still wrapped around the handles of metal water cans. After poking around in horrified fascination, he surmised that a heavy shell had landed near a number of men carrying the metal-handled cans, and the "concussion had been great enough to sever their hands." In an understatement worthy of the phlegmatic trench soldiers, Bond noted more than forty years after the war, "I remember that, that impressed me."[16]

The logistical planning that sustained the Canadians verged on the unbelievable. The corps' daily consumption of water alone was an incredible 600,000 gallons, which was pumped through 70 kilometres of pipeline to various reservoirs along the front.[17] An estimated 1,800 vehicles passed nightly through Mont St. Eloi, a key logistical town, returning to rear areas before dawn.[18] Horse and mule teams braved the steady barrage of intercession fire that the Germans laid down on the lines of communication. "Our wretched, emaciated, starving, shivering horses died under the lash as we were forced by swearing, raving provost marshals [military police] to flog them into starting heavy loads of shells," recounted a saddened Stephen Beames of the Canadian Field Artillery.[19] Drivers led their mud-splattered friends through the slop, past the bodies of rotting horses, and steadily forward into the darkness. Montrealer Paul Metivier, who enlisted at age 16 and was one of the last surviving veterans of the war when he passed away at 104, recounted towards the end of his life his memory of the terrible mud that was deep enough "to swallow a man."[20] In the fight for survival, horses were worked to death, and the men of the 15th Battalion were shocked to stumble across a field where more than a hundred horses had been "mercifully killed" after "having been worked into such exhaustion that they were beyond taking their oats."[21] No one had yet got around to burying their wet carcasses.

Vast armies of engineers, labour units, tunnelling companies, and infantrymen toiled furiously through the night while bathed in the glow of flares. The soft and slimy chalk came apart easily, but the thousands of tonnes of tailings all had to be dragged or carried out of caves, dugouts, and trenches, which added to the back-breaking work. A severe setback occurred in March, when an early thaw caused many of the trenches to cave in. Again, the army turned to the infantry. Lessons learned from the Somme had led to the infantry being relieved of much of this

The logistical preparation before the Battle of Vimy Ridge played an integral role in supporting the troops at the sharp end. But the roads and conditions behind the lines were so bad that horses and mules had to be mercy-killed by the hundreds as they were worked to death.

manual labour, but the enormous challenge posed in the preparatory phase meant that the high command again placed this burden on the fighting men.

An efficient logistical system was essential to winning the battle, but victory would hinge on the infantry, who were instructed over and over again, through the use of models and courses built from aerial photographs to simulate the battlefield. General Currie of the 1st Division ordered the construction of a full-size practice course in which every known enemy trench and machine-gun nest, as well as suspected enemy position, was represented.[22] Other divisions had their own intense training regimes. All commanders, from the corps to battalion level, agreed that the infantry were to capture key geographical features, rather than more nebulous targets shown on a map. On the battlefield, lines drawn on a map—for instance, positions marked as 300 or 400 metres east of a certain trench or redoubt—often disappeared under the weight of gunfire, but key trench systems or pill boxes were not so easily destroyed and could therefore be identified by the soldier even in the smoke and fire of battle. Day after day, the troops walked through their courses, studying the battlefield and practising the advance of 90 metres every three minutes to keep pace with the creeping barrage.

After the terrible casualties suffered on the Somme, Canadian command also realized the necessity for junior officers and NCOs to lead their men forward into battle when senior officers were knocked out. Each man had to know his role on the field. Byng involved himself personally in overseeing the training, consulting closely with his subordinates. Following the doctrinal changes of the post-Somme training, 40,000 maps were issued to the troops, thus reducing the high command's traditional monopoly on information and empowering the fighting men to understand where their objectives were and the best ways to get there. "In the last sector which the 1st Canadian Division held," wrote Currie, "my G.S.O. 1 and I had to be content with the same map."[23] Almost no one else in the division had access to a map. Now, with the new proliferation of cartographic guides, Byng ordered his spearhead forces to exploit weakness and move around areas of resistance, and to always push forward, which they could do as the maps gave them some idea of where they were going. He instructed that

> In the event of any Division or Brigade being held up, the units on the flanks will on no account check their advance, but will form defensive flanks in that direction and press forward themselves as to envelop the strong point or centre of resistance which is preventing the advance. With this object in view reserves will be pushed in behind those portions of the line that are successful rather than those that are held up.[24]

In short, into each man was drilled the dictum, "Should your officers be knocked out, it is up to you to improvise and fight forward." Practice sessions attempted to incorporate the confusion of battle, with officers being told they had been killed and junior men being ordered to take over. This devolution of authority continued until privates were leading the assault. The training fostered confidence: "We had time to learn about Vimy Ridge," wrote one soldier new to the front.[25]

Confidence was also encouraged by units' strength and health. Unlike the Somme, where battalions usually were down to 600 or 700 men even before an attack, the Canadian Corps before Vimy was up to full strength. The battalions of the 1st, 2nd, and 3rd Divisions were even over-strength, at 1,100 men; each division also had an extra (thirteenth) battalion, while the 4th Division, even after the disastrous March 1 raid, had units at full strength of 1,000. The total strength of the Canadian Corps was 97,184, of which some 56,494 infantry were in the four Canadian divisions and another 11,554 were available in the British 5th Division, which was attached to the Canadian Corps and fought effectively within its operational envelope, proving that the British training was not very different from that of the Canadians.[26]

Byng and the senior officers had faith in the Canadian infantry, and the men believed in themselves and their leaders. The Canadians even began to call themselves "The Byng Boys," after the popular musical theatre comedy *The Bing Boys*— the nickname no doubt a reflection of their commander's beloved status. This pervasive faith throughout the corps was also due to the advanced training methods and the evolution in infantry tactics since the Somme; these had created specialist positions and added firepower to the men at the sharp end. With a new organization among the infantry that favoured decentralized command, and the embedding of specialist units back into the platoon to create a more balanced and effective fighting force of grenadiers, rifle grenadiers, Lewis-gun teams, and riflemen, those on the front lines had an improved chance of battling their way through areas of resistance.

The infantry first trained to operate at the section level, then practised how the four sections would fight in a platoon-level attack, and then how the four platoons would push forward to a company-level objective. The aim of this training was to instruct the infantry platoons to knock out strongpoints, especially machine-gun positions, by pinning them down with fire and then attacking them from the flank.[27] Brigadier W.A. Griesbach of the 1st Brigade, an experienced commander, warned his troops that using wave tactics against enemy strongpoints would be disastrous: "As long as an enemy machine gun is firing, it is clear that our people cannot advance in any sort of formation, and they must instead advance in short bounds or by stealth."[28]

While these infantry tactics were important, the foot soldiers would have no chance without the support of an artillery barrage. The barrage to be used at Vimy had been planned by the artillery staff, but Major Alan Brooke, staff officer Royal

Artillery, was its chief architect. At thirty-three, Brooke was young but experienced, having organized many of the Canadian barrages on the Somme and studied the success and failure of the French at Verdun.[29] One of Currie's close friends and his aide-de-camp, Wilfrid Bovey, remarked "'Brookie' had a mind like a tabulating machine."[30] This talent would put him in good stead when he rose to the position of chief of the imperial general staff during the Second World War, but at this point he needed it to keep track of the enormous resources at the disposal of the corps.

Brooke's job was exceedingly difficult because of the inherent advantages afforded the enemy by Vimy's imposing ridge. The Canadian fire plan had to provide for the destruction of enemy fortifications and the suppression of enemy gunfire, as well as reserving enough guns for the all-important creeping barrage—the protective screen for the infantry that would tear up the enemy defences. The divisional artillery consisted of 480 18-pounders, 138 4.5-inch howitzers, 96 2-inch trench mortars, and 24 massive 9.45-inch trench mortars. All had been manhandled, dragged, and winched into gun pits in a rough semi-circle around Vimy Ridge, arranged in depth from light field guns to the massive siege guns in the rear.[31] In addition to these divisional guns, corps headquarters controlled another 14 heavy- and 24 medium-siege gun batteries (with all batteries now raised from 4 to 6 guns), plus assorted other mortars, for a total of 245 heavy guns to stoke the forthcoming firestorm. Another 132 guns were on British I Corps' front, to the north of the Canadian lines, and many of these artillery pieces were directed at Vimy Ridge as added support for the primary assault.[32] In all, there was one heavy gun for every 18 metres of frontage and one field gun for every 9 metres, equating to three times the Allied firepower on the Somme for the all-important heavy guns, and double the power of the field guns.[33]

The preliminary bombardment by about half the batteries began on March 20 and lasted for thirteen punishing days. Over 200,000 18-pounder shells would be fired, as well as 143,000 larger-calibre shells.[34] The bombardment focused on enemy fortifications, barbed wire, and lines of communication. One by one, the enemy's positions were destroyed, the constant bombardment making it nearly suicidal for the Germans to repair their defences. "My dugout is four metres under the ground, but yet is not quite safe from the British who bombard us like the very devil," wrote one Bavarian defender. "Men are constantly being killed or wounded."[35] Another

German lamented in a captured document: "Tommy uses his ammunition as if it were grains of sand."[36] It would get worse. A week before the scheduled Canadian infantry advance on the morning of April 9, the full weight of the guns opened up on the enemy positions, pulverizing the front with nearly 2,500 tonnes of ammunition every day. "The losses of soldiers and materiel visibly multiplied at the beginning of April," wrote Generalleutnant Alfred Dieterich, commander of the 79th Reserve Infantry Brigade, which was the administrative headquarters linking the 79th Reserve Infantry Division headquarters to the three divisional regiments, the 261st, 262nd, and 263rd Regiments, whose battalions were situated along the 4th, 3rd, and 2nd Canadian divisional fronts.[37]

Even with 1.6 million shells allotted to the corps to destroy enemy trenches and fortifications, the Canadians' task would be daunting.[38] Intelligence officers estimated that there were some 34,000 metres of enemy fire trenches, 15,000 metres of communication trenches, and 9,100 metres of barbed wire.[39] Canadian night patrollers and aerial observers anxiously tracked the enemy's replacement of wire: older, rusted wire was brown, while new wire had a tinted blue sheen. Even after weeks of bombardment, there was still a lot of blue-sheen wire. But for the men at the front, the success of the artillery bombardment was encouraging and raised morale. Few expected they would encounter conditions similar to those on the Somme, where the infantry had gone over the top only to run into mountains of intact barbed wire. "Our guns were working hard all day, terrible fire," observed fifty-three-year-old Captain Edouard Leprohon of the 14th Battalion. "There cannot be much of the Hun lines left."[40]

The availability of guns, the skill of the gunners, and the type of fuses had all improved since the Somme battles six months earlier. The 106 "instantaneous" fuse was a vital addition to the gunner's craft, and Byng used his influence to secure some of these still-rare fuses. At the Somme, many of the shells had failed to explode, or had only exploded once they were embedded in the ground. The 106 allowed a high explosive shell to explode instantaneously on contact with the wire, thereby creating a deadlier and more effective burst at the point of impact—where it was most needed to cut wire. The fuse proved to be extremely successful and resulted in shells leaving fewer craters in the ground.[41]

While softening up the Vimy defences was crucial, the enemy's guns also had to be silenced. McNaughton and his counter-battery staff relied on intelligence, unremitting study, and scientific principles to locate, target, and destroy enemy gunners—or reduce their effectiveness in supporting their troops in battle.[42] Many of these targets were located by the aerial formations newly attached to the Canadian Corps. While the artillery mulched the Vimy battlefield, an intense air battle was raging above the ridge. The Germans had recently changed their tactics, and were flying in larger formations, scattering the Allied flyers before them. No. 16 Squadron, Royal Flying Corps—its planes flying with two streamers on each right rear strut to identify them as friendly craft—and No. 1 Kite Balloon Company provided the essential air observatory role for the Canadian ground forces.

The importance of aerial photography to the artillery in directing their guns meant that command of the air was sought by both sides. There were vicious engagements almost every hour of the day in the lead-up to the battle. The "knights of the sky" swooped and manoeuvred for advantageous position. Baron Manfred von Richthofen, better known as the "Red Baron," and his all-scarlet Flying Circus of Albatross were skilled and deadly adversaries. From the ground, William Antliff recounted in a letter home the day before the Vimy battle: "There has been a lot of aerial activity on both sides lately and Fritzy seems to have a plane which puts it all over our men. It is called the Red Devil and simply plays rings around our best machines."[43] Desperate for flyers, the British were sending new pilots into the sky who had just graduated from their training. In this aerial maelstrom, the average life expectancy of a new pilot was about eleven days. April 1917 was known as Bloody April, and was the worst part of the war for Allied flyers, with the Allies losing 245 aircraft in comparison to the Germans' 66.[44] But despite the danger, the planes had to go up to meet the enemy to ensure that the German observation planes did not have unhindered access to the Allied forces' build-up on the ground. The flyers often sold their lives dearly to ensure that the ground forces had a fighting chance against the entrenched enemy.

Isolated German guns and batteries were the primary targets of the pre-battle artillery assault, as the larger groupings of guns were to be neutralized on the day of battle with crash bombardments of high explosives, shrapnel, and poison gas. McNaughton's counter-battery groups were extremely successful, locating eighty-three percent of the eighty-nine guns and mortars manned by the enemy's 79th Reserve

Division before the battle, knocking out dozens of them in the process and disabling another forty-seven after zero hour on April 9.[45] The gunners had learned the hard lesson of the Western Front: they held the heavy responsibility not only for destroying enemy fortifications and supplying a complicated creeping barrage, but also for suppressing the gunfire aimed at their infantry as it advanced in the open after zero hour.

THE SOMETIMES HAPHAZARD PLANNING that went into fighting on the Somme was now gone: officers and men alike realized that victory could be achieved only if every detail was observed. Experienced divisional commanders and brigadiers knew the keys to success. The twelve infantry brigadiers had all been tested in battle. The best of them, Archibald Macdonell, William Griesbach, Frederick Loomis, Victor Odlum, and J.H. MacBrien, would not only shape their brigades and the battalions that formed them, but would act as a conduit for the dissemination and forging of the Canadian Corps' attack doctrine. As the senior divisional commanders were killed or promoted, these brigadiers would fill the ranks of the major generals in the last two years of the war. By April 1917, most of the divisional and brigade commanders had between nine and eleven months of battlefield experience behind them, and knew their comrades, their superiors, and their juniors.[46]

The engineers were an equally important arm of support for the corps in battle. William Lindsay, the chief engineer of the corps, controlled much of the labour manpower, which he employed to build and sustain the infrastructure behind the lines and even in the trenches. Although he had a Friar Tuck build—short in stature and wide in girth—he commanded respect. Both Byng, and later Currie, would rely heavily on the chief engineer, and the chain-smoking Lindsay was a constant presence in the corps headquarters. He was not a man with whom to trifle, or with whom to come up short, as he had high expectations, but he afforded his subordinates full independence and responsibility and they rarely failed him. "More than anyone else it was he who created the new engineer organization which played such an important and effective part in the last year of the war," wrote Currie. He was an "outstanding engineer and soldier."[47]

With all of this activity behind the Canadian lines, especially the massive stockpiling of thousands of rounds of ammunition, the Germans could observe that an attack was imminent.[48] Overlooking the Canadian trench system, enemy gunners fired to disrupt preparations and kill the infantry who were beginning to concentrate at the front.[49] Sergeant Walter Draycot, an experienced intelligence scout for the PPCLI, noted, "The enemy, far from being asleep, had nearly as accurate a description of our trenches as we had; how they were held, and of what strength in men, whether they were in good condition or otherwise, what new work was going on.… These facts I discovered by taking a map from a prisoner after a successful raid by our troops."[50] Such detailed information in the hands of the enemy worried Draycot and the corps' high command.

The only way to escape such observation was by going deeper into the ground. Hundreds if not thousands of lives were saved by burrowing the infantry forward in trenches eight to ten feet deep, labour that required permanent work parties of a hundred men for each trench, who would rebuild it after enemy bombardments. These communication trenches extended some 2,500 metres, and all supplies moved back and forth along them in the months prior to the battle. Signs were placed throughout the underground trenches and rear areas, helping to direct the men. One of the more memorable ones warned: "For Fuck's sake, don't Fuck about here … signed D. Haig, Field-Marshal."[51] The high command was not amused when they were informed of the irreverent sign, but thousands of Allied soldiers had no doubt smiled and grimly pushed forward past its written warning, realizing that staying still or fucking about anywhere near the front would attract shell and sniper fire.[52]

Another geographical form of protection, and one far deeper than the communication trenches, was the system of underground tunnels that offered shelter from shells and from prying Teutonic eyes. Thirteen tunnels, some running over a kilometre in length, had been carved out of the earth and chalk over the winter.[53] Although they were tall enough to accommodate a standing man, this was not the place for the claustrophobic. Located at least 6 metres beneath the earth, the labyrinthine galleries and passages, ill-lit by electric lights strung along the rough walls, contained latrines, command posts, ammunition dumps, and medical stations. They also allowed for the running of telephone lines from front to rear, which vastly improved the ability of the commanders to influence the battle. Before the tunnels were built, enemy fire had continually severed communications, leaving 500 men a night engaged in cable-burying work.[54] In the days before the assault on

Vimy, these underground cities housed thousands of men in their damp khaki-wool uniforms, fear oozing as if liquid from their pores, while the dull thud of shellfire resounded through the walls day and night.

IT WAS WORSE ON THE OTHER SIDE of No Man's Land. Shell after shell slammed into the German positions, rocking the earth, sending gut-wrenching reverberations through the deep dugouts. Enemy forward positions were cut off from the rear so that no food could get through to the front. A German brigadier noted that his starving men were forced to gather food and water from the dead on the battlefield, and from "gas- and feces-contaminated shell holes."[55] Men were buried alive or killed by the concussion of shells. Exhausted, drawn, and shell-shocked, the German defenders were further harassed by the changing tempo of Canadian barrages that slowed, stopped, and started furiously again. Each time the shelling stopped, the defenders were forced to rush up from their dugouts in case the barrage was a

These Canadian gunners at Vimy Ridge contributed to the Germans' Week of Suffering. The Canadians deluged the German fortress on the ridge with some 1.6 million shells, which shattered kilometres of trenches and barbed wire but left intact some formidable positions that could not be obliterated out of existence. The infantry would have to assault these in order to capture their final objectives.

precursor to an infantry assault. So tired were they of the seemingly unending bombardment that many hoped for something, anything, that would offer relief from this cruel war of waiting. The seven days before the battle became known by the Germans as the Week of Suffering.

The Germans rarely strayed from their fixed defences and were decidedly uneasy about running into prowling Canadians in No Man's Land. Aggressive raiding parties that now involved several hundred men and concentrated bombardments destroyed German trenches and dugouts. Patrols were sent out every night to check the wire; daring Allied officers even coated themselves in mud and crept out during daylight hours. One of the high command's main goals was to find enemy mine shafts and destroy them with mobile charges and ammonal tubes. In the months preceding the battle, the raiders successfully shut down the German mining and counter-mining operations, allowing the Canadians to control the war underground.[56]

Byng also ordered that prisoners be taken in order to determine the state of enemy intelligence. The Canadians were fighting for facts. German sentries could be heard along the front, coughing and hacking in the cold, and occasionally they were grabbed or dispatched. But it was not easy to capture enemy troops who were on high alert. A few failed attempts by the 1st Division to bring back a prisoner elicited a scathing order from Currie to Brigadier General W.A. Griesbach of the 1st Brigade:

> My orders regarding the capture of a German prisoner are evidently not clearly understood. I want a prisoner, not for curiosity sake, not to see what he looks like. I want to get from him information that will be of some use to us in preparation for the forthcoming operation.... I want you to tell your Battalion Commanders that, if they are not successful tonight, you will order raids at three hour intervals until they are successful. Tell them I want results and I want them now.[57]

Griesbach ordered his battalions to send out patrols all night and, should that fail, to continue even into daylight hours, which amounted to a veritable death sentence. Currie was against the use of raiding simply to give his soldiers battlefield experience—or to "bloody them," in the parlance of the times—but when he needed a prisoner, he demanded one. After an intense series of raids, Currie and Byng got their prisoners—fortunately for the men of the 1st Brigade, before they were forced to resort to round-the-clock operations.

George Hancox of the PPCLI recounted the story of one battle patrol that captured a German officer. "We know all about your plans," gloated the prisoner. "You might get to the top of Vimy Ridge but I'll tell you this, you'll be able to take all the Canadians [who make it to the ridge] back to Canada in a row-boat."[58] With the Germans having repulsed every attack thrown against them in the last two years, including the Canadians' gas raid of March 1, 1917, the taunt hit home.

CHAPTER 5

"YOU LIVE LIKE PIGS, AND YOU KILL LIKE PIGS"

The 1st Canadian Division

The ninth day of April 1917 was miserable. Sleet, rain, and snow drove down in the early hours as tense Canadian infantrymen huddled in their start lines, their breath forming in the air in front of them. Those lucky ones in the underground tunnels were drier but had to contend with the smell of urine, body odour, and fear. Hundreds of men carved their names or regimental crests into the sweating chalk walls, a mute testimony to their place on this earth. The front-line infantry dealt with parched mouths, hearts beating heavily in chests, their sweat forming and then freezing. Thousands more did not fit in the tunnels, and were forced to creep out into the newly dug jumping-off trenches, many of which were filled knee-deep with icy slush and mud. Groundsheets were cinched around their necks, reducing the bite of the wind. All along the front, fidgety men had to be watched to ensure that they did not smoke and give away the position in the darkness. Veterans went through their pre-battle rituals while new men tried to look calmer than they were. Most told themselves no bullet had their name on it.

The day before and throughout the night, Allied artillery shells had crashed down on the enemy lines. Thundering explosions filled the air, and reverberations passed along the tunnels and trenches while the smell of cordite wafted over the battlefield. These sonic blasts eventually brought a numbness to the mind, and it became impossible to distinguish the sound of one shell from another within the continuous rhythmic pounding. A German account presented the dazzling and deafening barrage from atop the ridge:

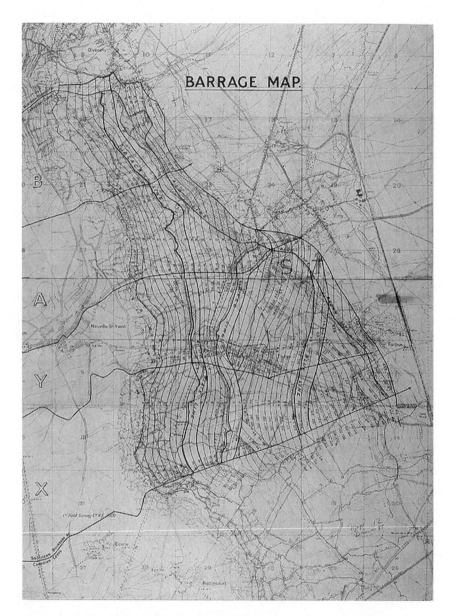

Canadian artillery barrage map for the April 9, 1917, Battle of Vimy Ridge. Note the scheduled lifts as the timed creeping barrage rakes over the battlefield from west to east (left to right). The four objectives, the Black, Red, Blue, and Brown Lines, can be seen on this map. The process of keeping such barrages uniform over broken ground was extremely complicated, but the Allied gunners proved up to the task at Vimy, and the enormous weight of shellfire supported the Canadian Corps' "shock and awe" operation.

THE BATTLE OF VIMY RIDGE: APRIL 9 TO 12, 1917

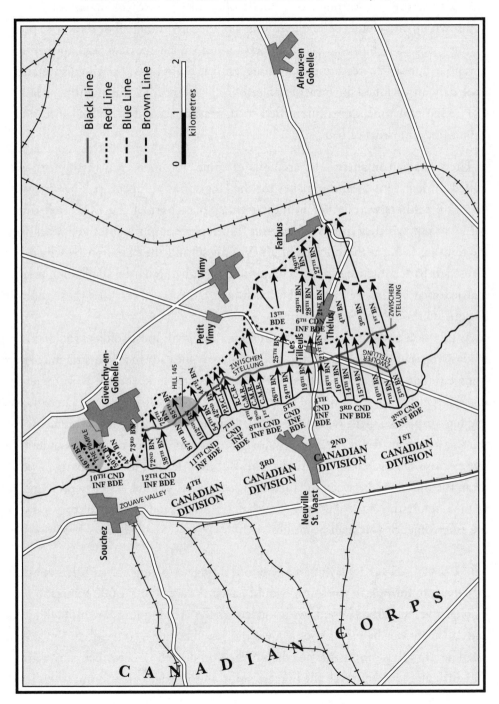

What the eye sees through the clouds of smoke is a sea of masses of earth thrown up and clouds of smoke rolling along.... [A]mong all of these are spitting fuses, slow burning gas shells, exploding trench mortars, and the white vapour appears to consume everything until it obliterates the whole spectacle of dancing madness in impenetrable fog. How long did this nightmare last? The sense of time seems intensified so that every second is divided into one hundred moments of fear.[1]

The Canadian infantry, 21 battalions of some 600 men each in the first wave waited in their tunnels and trenches for the "big show" to open up. The remaining battalion soldiers were either headquarters staff or part of the LOB (left out of battle) group, which accounted for about fifteen percent of the force kept back from the fighting to form the nucleus of a new unit should the battalion be wiped out. Those left back sometimes pushed hard to be included in battle; single men relieved married men, noting awkwardly, but with heartfelt earnestness, that they would be less missed should the worst happen.

As the thousands of Canadians waited for the signal, most soldiers took comfort in knowing their role in the battle. The infantry would advance in a straightforward frontal assault, moving 90 metres every three minutes to keep pace with the creeping barrage that would soon light the dark skies like sheet lightning. The shrapnel and high explosive shells would spew their lead balls and jagged shell fragments forward in a rain of steel. One can only imagine the taut nerves of soldiers ordered to stay as close as possible to this maelstrom. But their leaning into the barrage would mean the difference between the infantry's success and failure. As General Byng had warned before the battle, "Chaps, you shall go over exactly like a railroad train, on the exact time, or you shall be annihilated."[2]

THE CANADIAN LINES lay at an angle to the ridge, creating an irregular front: the 1st Division, furthest to the south, would have to move across 4,000 metres to reach its objectives at Farbus Wood, with aspects of the attack going downhill. The 2nd and 3rd Divisions had steeper objectives but less distance to travel than the veteran 1st. The 4th Division, furthest to the north, would need to claw their way through 700 difficult metres to reach the highest point on the ridge, the summit of Hill 145.

The objectives for each of the four divisions were divided into coloured lines: only two for the 4th and 3rd Divisions on the left (the Black and Red), but four for the 1st and 2nd Divisions (Black, Red, Blue, and Brown). The Black Line included the enemy crater posts, his observation line, and his front-line defences, which extended back about 600 metres. It ran along part of the Zwolfe Graben trench on the right, the powerful Zwischen Stellung trench in the centre, and to the west of Les Tilleuls on the left, where it snaked along the crest of Hill 145. On the right, the 1st Division's front was lightly held, but it became progressively more fortified to the east. The Red Line ran along the Zwischen Stellung on the right because the German trench bent back on the 1st Division's front, weaving along below the ridge's crest until it broke back to the west and met the Black Line on the left flank. It ranged from 400 to 1,000 metres beyond the Black Line and was the final objective for the 3rd and 4th Divisions on the left. The Blue Line was located an additional 1,100 metres beyond the Red Line. It incorporated the fortified village of Thelus, Hill 140, and most of the Bois du Goulot, and was riven with trenches and belts of barbed wire. Finally, the Brown Line lay furthest to the east, extending about 4,000 metres from the 1st Division's start lines. It included more reserve trenches and woods, and wire entanglements 50 metres deep in places. The entire front was mouse-holed with caves, tunnels, concrete machine-gun positions, fire trenches, and deep and elaborate dugouts.

Vimy was the fortress that everyone had feared it would be. Although many considered that it could not be captured at all, it certainly could not be taken in one fell swoop. Byng ordered that units would attack and overrun positions, and then fresh forces would push through them. The Black Line was to be captured thirty-five minutes after the zero hour of 5:30 A.M. Then a pause of forty minutes would allow the troops to dig in as new units passed through to continue the push. The Red Line was to fall only twenty minutes after the pause ended. Another long break of two hours and thirty minutes would allow the infantry and artillery to pull back the hammer and unleash it again at 9:35 A.M. on the 1st and 2nd Division's front, where the spearhead infantry would capture the Blue Line in seventy-five minutes. Finally, after another ninety-six-minute interruption, the last advance would be launched at 12:26 P.M., capturing the Brown Line at 1:18 P.M., seven hours and forty-eight minutes after the zero hour.[3] An active defence of patrols and outposts, backed by new trench lines, would aim to stave off the enemy's expected counterattacks. The battle was set to go off like clockwork, and once the barrage started it could not be changed or called off, as commanders lacked the ability to communicate with the hundreds of gun batteries and thousands of infantrymen.

Just outside of the Canadian boundary, on the far left, was the Pimple—an enemy-held position. This blemish on the landscape, along with Hill 145 to the south, allowed the Germans to fire into the Canadian lines of communications. The two German positions could also set up a crossfire to destroy any attack caught in between them. The Pimple would have to be taken, but the British troops initially assigned to conquer it were too weak in strength, and so it was decided that it would not be attacked until the ridge fell to the main Canadian assault. That was a risky proposition, especially since, as on the Somme, all units had to succeed together or thrusting forces would take it in the neck as they jutted deep into enemy lines.

SOME 15,000 INFANTRYMEN prepared for battle all along the front, with another 12,000 or so in support. The gunners slowly reduced fire as the 5:30 A.M. zero hour loomed, in the hope of lulling the Germans into a sense of passivity as they might assume this signalled some relief from the shelling. During the Week of Suffering, the Germans had cowered for safety in their deep dugouts, deprived of water, food, and sleep: few were now inclined to run up dugout stairs every time the bombardment paused. A reprieve was greeted with weary acknowledgment—perhaps some food might finally make its way forward and men might get a few hours of sleep before the next round of aerial tormenting.

Sergeant John MacGregor, a Scottish Canadian from Powell River, British Columbia, who would win the Distinguished Conduct Medal (DCM) at Vimy, recounted a pre-battle moment with his comrades: "Most of my section had been with me at the Somme; we were fatalists; if we were going to stop one, so be it. But one man was just in from Shorncliffe and looked as though he was about to cry.... He called out, 'What's that noise?' and some of the men laughed. They laughed because the guns had stopped. That was the noise he'd heard. Silence. It only lasted a few seconds, but it was more frightening than the guns."[4]

At 5:30 A.M., the Allied barrage exploded the silence. Nine hundred and eighty-three guns and mortars, manned by Canadian, British, and a few other Allied gunners, crashed down on the German positions. Unmoving, standing barrages fell on identified strongpoints, while counter-battery fire harassed enemy batteries and targets of opportunity. The creeping barrage moved off after three minutes, with each gun firing three rounds a minute on the German front lines; the barrage crept forward in 90-metre lifts, as the guns slowly reduced their fire to two rounds per minute. Some 400 metres beyond the 18-pounder creeping barrage, 150 heavy machine guns laid down saturation fire blindly across the zone. The machine guns, wrote gunner Stephen Beames—a First Contingent man who had already survived taking a piece of shrapnel through his head—"chatter[ed] away like the devil's sewing machine."[5]

With their lives depending on it, the infantry followed the creeping barrage that was chewing its way through the enemy trenches, steamrolling the front, barbed wire, and defenders. With tens of thousands of shells and hundreds of thousands of bullets whirling over top in an almost solid wall of shrieking steel, many simply put their heads down, hunched over, and advanced forward, as if pushing through a hailstorm. The infantry were to "hug their barrage," getting to within 60 metres, in order to make the final rush when the shells lifted off to their next objective.[6] Those in the first waves needed to close the gap in the three minutes that the barrage remained still, or risk having the wall of fire move off, thereby losing its protective sweep and allowing the surviving enemy to rise from his dugouts and gun them down in the open. Cozying up to the barrage took nerves of steel, but most Canadians realized it was far worse for the enemy on the receiving end.

Commanding the veteran 1st Division was Major General Arthur Currie, who ordered an initial push with the six battalions of the 2nd and 3rd Brigades. Once the first two lines were captured, three fresh battalions of the 1st Brigade were to bound through them and capture Farbus Wood, a hiding place for German artillery pieces. The remaining battalions of the three Brigades were held in reserve; they would be fed into the battle in the final phase to overcome the last strongpoints and hold the captured ground against expected enemy counterattacks.

On Currie's front, the 2nd Brigade attacked with the 5th Battalion on the right, the 7th in the centre, and the 10th on the far left. The 5th Battalion surged forward behind the barrage, overrunning the first line and sustaining few losses. A good part of the unit's success was attributed to the commanding officer's decision to send many of the lead platoons into No Man's Land before zero hour to close with the enemy. This gave the infantry the jump on crossing the kill zone, as well as helping them to avoid the devastating counter-barrage that would come crashing down on Allied front lines once the German SOS flares alerted their guns to the operation.

Forward German outposts barely fired a shot in response before they were overrun by the 2nd Brigade. "Nothing could equal the scene of destruction and desola-

The western face of Vimy Ridge was pitted with trenches, barbed wire, concrete pillboxes, and craters. Montreal Crater, shown here after the battle, was one of the largest on the ridge.

tion wrought by the terrific concentration of our gunfire and by the fury of the infantry attack," wrote Gunner Donald Stuart Macpherson, who would be awarded the Military Medal for his bravery during the battle.[7] The infantry advanced into the darkness fringed with fire, passing around the torn barbed wire and thousands of shell craters. The intense pre-battle training kept the men moving forward, even if the reality was far from the easy glide that had been practised behind the lines and in the absence of shellfire and small-arms fire. The first and second lines fell quickly, but the third defensive line, some 1,100 metres beyond and alerted to the attack by emergency flares, recovered from the shock. The German fire was sporadic and desultory, but Canadians fell by the dozens, and then the hundreds. Every step forward seemed to leave a man behind, wounded or dead.

While the enemy artillery was largely silenced by counter-battery fire, German machine guns were delivering devastating bursts of fire. A screen of them had remained untouched by the barrage, and several were outside of the battalion's objectives, making them hard to knock out since if the 5th crossed over into its neighbour's sector, friendly fire incidents became likely as the infantry were trained to shoot anyone in front them. Despite their fear of being slaughtered by their own comrades, under unrepressed fire the options available to the 5th were either to retreat or push forward. The battalion chose the latter, rushing into and clearing the positions with bombs, bayonets, Lewis guns, and rifle fire, before returning to their sector. The enemy gunners caused many of the estimated 350 casualties among the 5th Battalion during the course of the battle, but they were wiped out by the relentless advance of the infantry. "Casualties among [Canadian] officers and NCOs were extremely heavy," recounted one report, "but at no time were there wanting natural leaders to carry the work forward with speed to success."[8]

After-battle reports acknowledged the ferocity of the defenders, noting, "both machine gunners and snipers appeared to be picked men" who, in most cases, fought "till the last."[9] The enemy's deep dugouts continued to hold many Germans who were waiting for the firestorm to pass over them. If conquering soldiers' orders to surrender and emerge without weapons were not quickly followed, mopping-up parties cleared dugouts with grenades. Yet the rules of combat were not always followed, especially when the Canadian Tommies could look back over the battlefield and see the twisted shapes of what had been their friends. In the face of such horrors, they were not always eager to take prisoners. However, since there were not enough Allied stretcher-bearers to clear the battlefield (even though each battalion's allotment had been augmented to 100), grim-faced Canadians ordered German prisoners to assist in carrying the wounded back to Allied lines.[10] Weighing the hard options of possibly being killed by their own artillery fire while transporting the wounded or being executed by Canadians on the spot, it is unlikely that any refused.

In the centre, the 7th Battalion had encountered heavy resistance and pushed forward. On the left of the brigade front, the 10th Battalion was also forced to make its advance into heavy small-arms fire. The Calgarians and other Westerners who formed the bulk of the 10th Battalion included ten newly arrived Japanese Canadians. They all moved forward in four tight waves, supported by mopping-up parties, in order to quickly get beyond the expected enemy counter-barrage. "When we reached the German lines we hardly recognized them," wrote one infantryman. "The ground between the trenches was so pitted with shell-holes that it resembled a gigantic honeycomb."[11] But there were still many fierce battles with rifles, bombs, and bayonets before German resistance collapsed.

The 2nd Brigade units were on their first objectives within thirty-five minutes of zero hour, and on all final objectives by 9:30 A.M., including the strongpoint of Zwischen Stellung, a trench that ran through many battalion sector fronts. The 2nd Canadian Machine Gun Company, wielding eight Vickers machine guns, had assisted the infantry by pushing forward and offering direct fire, while also laying down indirect fire over the front.[12] By the end of the day, the eight guns, along with eight more British guns, had fired 110,000 rounds of ammunition.[13] Under this protective rain of steel, the Canadians traded small-arms fire with German troops throughout the day.

On the 3rd Brigade's front, the 15th Battalion benefited from the 10th's having clawed their way forward through German defences after bursting forth from the protection of Douai Tunnel. One infantryman noted that the barrage was like a "lawn mower" in the way it tore up the enemy lines. Although some short shelling occurred, an artillery forward observer embedded in the infantry battalion was able to call off the shelling quickly.[14] But the Canadians fought hard against isolated strongpoints, and some sixty Highlanders of the 15th Battalion had been killed by 10 A.M., with more to die of their wounds later in the day.[15]

On the 15th Battalion's left, the 14th Battalion stormed forward but had to overcome four machine-gun nests, which were firing to the last bullet. The infantry, pinned down by enemy fire, were able to move forward only by working as a team: Lewis gunners laid down a protective screen that forced the Germans to remain in their trenches. Two enemy gun crews were wiped out by grenades while the other two were annihilated by individual men: Lieutenant B.F. Davidson, who shot a crew dead with his revolver as they desperately tried to swing the Maxim gun to shoot him down, and Sergeant Major J.F. Hurley, who "unassisted, bayoneted the crew of three men and captured the gun."[16] The way was open for the Canadians to drive into the German lines, but harsh fighting continued all along the slushy ridge. Lance Corporal Archie McWade, a lacrosse champion from Havelock, Ontario, ruthlessly remarked that the infantry had the dirtiest jobs on the face of the earth: "You live like pigs, and you kill like pigs."[17]

Several bayonet charges effectively cleared dug-in positions, and the 14th was assisted by accurate artillery fire that laid down important screening barrages. The fighting at the sharp end was chaotic. "In action a man is dazed, his senses are benumbed," wrote one Canadian soldier. "Everything he does is automatic, he actually doesn't know what is happening."[18] It was no clearer for the officers in the rear. Communication was cut early in the battle, and a number of men tasked with signalling back to the artillery with flags were killed or wounded. Brave runners kept the lines of communication open, racing back through the shell craters, stumbling over hidden barbed wire, falling into smoking holes, evading searching small-arms and artillery fire. Runners who survived on the Western Front for any length of time developed a sixth sense for when to dart from hole to hole and when to dive for cover as the roar or whine of artillery shells slammed into the battered earth. The front-line units, largely isolated from those in the rear, were fighting for their lives. By the end of the battle, the 14th Battalion had suffered 287 casualties to their 701-strong unit, almost double the number sustained by the 15th Battalion on their right.[19]

On the far left of the brigade front, the 16th Battalion was chewed up by enemy fire. The two lead companies, advancing side by side with mopping-up units behind them, were taking terrible casualties from machine guns that survived the crushing barrage along the forward crust, as well as from units in hardened rear positions that were saturating the slopes with direct and indirect fire. These units were firing from behind specially built steel loopholes in their trench system that provided nearly perfect protection and were almost impossible to see amidst the smoke, shell bursts, and confusion of battle.

In several spots, the infantry could not see their tormentors—only the results of the gunners' deadly work. Each time a man gingerly put up his head to search the front, bullets sent it back down quickly. But cautious study of the battlefield suggested that a suspicious-looking mouldy haystack contained at least one machine-gun crew. Fire and movement was again the key to advancing. An accurate rifle grenade eventually made a direct hit that allowed the infantry to continue driving up the ridge. At other times, the enemy was overcome through sheer personal bravery. Private W.J. Milne, a young Scot from Moose Jaw, and his section were caught in the open by machine-gun fire. His mates lying dead around him, Milne crawled through the slush and mud, bullets whipping over his head as he drew closer to the enemy nest. With a series of grenades, he put the crew out of action, allowing the advance to continue. He knocked out a second machine-gun nest single-handedly and was awarded the Victoria Cross for his valour. Sadly, he never saw it, as he collected a wooden cross the same day. He was one of the 16th Battalion's 333 casualties during the battle.[20]

Behind the two lead units, which steadily lost their momentum as men were killed, wounded, or went to ground and stayed there, two mopping-up companies helped to clear points of resistance. Small groups of defenders lay doggo in dugouts or craters as the Canadians overran their positions. They often had little chance and generally surrendered to whomever they could find on the battlefield. But some of the most courageous defenders fought to the end, assaulting lead units from behind or presenting a strong obstacle for follow-on forces. The attackers ground them out one at a time in costly and often brutal battles.

But these breakwaters of defenders could not slow the waves of Canadian forces. Currie's men pressed on to the first two objectives. They began to consolidate, and the 1st Brigade in reserve moved forward to continue driving the enemy back on his heels, aiming to capture the Blue and Brown Lines, the last two lines of resistance. Having watched as their divisional companions advanced ahead of them, the assault formations of the 1st Brigade—from the 1st, 3rd, and 4th Battalions—waited anxiously for their turn. Had the first waves failed? Would they in turn be ordered forward into the face of machine guns, past the bodies of their mangled comrades, without proper artillery support? The three battalions went forward shortly after the zero-hour bombardment went off, but they spent the first two hours simply advancing over the battlefield, marching to the new front, often getting mixed up with the mopping-up units that continued to clear strongpoints that had been missed by other attacking units.

Advancing in waves, the men of the 1st Brigade had to travel over and around hundreds of bodies, both Canadian and German, before they closed with the enemy. Private William Green of the 4th Battalion, newly arrived at the front, remembered marching over the entrails and bloody bodies of Germans ripped "open right from the head down." At the designated points, they picked up their barrage and began to advance behind it, hugging it as closely as possible "to miss the return barrage the Germans threw at us."[21] Green was nearly killed when a dud shell slashed through the air, barely missing him but tearing off the head of a machine-gunner a few metres away. The gunner's body staggered forward several steps, with blood pumping into the air out of the jagged gap where his head had been. Green kept marching, but saw in a backward glance that the same beheading shell had also ripped the leg off a man who had been behind the machine-gunner. For Green and his companions, it was unclear whether the first phase had been a success, but it had certainly not been a Somme-like annihilation.

The Blue Line—the Canadians' third objective—was captured after some light fighting, and involved infantry sections snuffing out untouched machine-gun or rifle positions with Lewis guns and rifle grenades. The 4th Battalion, attacking on the left, was "played over" to their objectives by pipers from the 16th Battalion in a show of divisional solidarity. But this was no parade. After the Canadians consolidated the Blue Line, another massive creeping barrage erupted at 12:26 P.M., which the 3rd and 4th Battalions followed into the strongly held German trenches on the final Brown Line, while the 1st Battalion remained dug-in behind them.

In the assault on the Brown Line, fierce fighting brought the 1st Brigade into the heart of the enemy positions, where they established Vickers and Lewis machine-gun posts to fire on the retreating enemy—both infantry and moving horse-drawn wagons. While enemy morale among troops on this part of the front was described as "poor" in the brigade's official documents, pockets of resistance fought to the bitter end.[22] The Canadians sent battle patrols to assess enemy strength, and a defensive flank was turned south to protect against an attack coming across the British front. The Canadians had lost touch with the 51st British Division, which was struggling to close the gap and overcome uncut barbed wire—a dangerous situation which, if exploited by the Germans, could enable them to drive a wedge between the two formations. Ultimately, they were not able to do so, but for the next two days the 1st Canadian Division's right flank was exposed to enemy fire. By the end of the day on April 9, the men of the 1st Division could look up the ridge from their unique position behind enemy lines and watch the fierce fighting that was being carried out by their countrymen. They did so in the company of close to 2,500 of their divisional comrades strewn behind them over the 4,000-metre advance: mangled corpses and the writhing wounded. Such was the price of victory on the Western Front.

CHAPTER 6

"EVEN IF ONE MAN [IS] LEFT ALIVE THE OBJECTIVE MUST BE TAKEN AND HELD"

The 2nd Canadian Division

"All one could do was trust to luck and the guidance of the good Lord," remembered eighteen-year-old Private Neville Tompkins of New Brunswick's 26th Battalion.

> I took the view that the other fellow might get it, but not me....We arrived at our jumping-off trenches at around 4:30 A.M., with the barrage scheduled for 5:30 A.M. Just prior to the opening of the barrage, which was the heaviest of the war to date, I heard an explosion in the trench-bay next to mine, and later learned that my good friend Ned Mullaly from Newfoundland, in hitching up his equipment, had in some manner loosened a pin of one of the grenades in the bag he was carrying on his back, with the result that the grenade exploded and he was killed instantly. This, I believe, was the first casualty of our company in the attack.[1]

Hundreds more would follow in the Battle of Vimy: men killed charging forward valiantly while others were killed by strange and terrible twists of fate. Tompkins would survive the battle, and the war.

When the 2nd Division had lost its respected commander, Richard Turner, to the chief of staff position in England in December 1916, Byng had replaced him with

Major General Harry Burstall. The experienced forty-seven-year-old soldier from Quebec City, who had graduated from Staff College and had distinguished himself as commander of the Royal Canadian Artillery since the start of the war, was a good choice for command. Despite an inherent shyness not usually associated with generals bringing twenty-five years of experience to the job, Burstall was a professional who was greatly respected by his men.[2] He would lead the 2nd Division, comprising the 4th, 5th, and 6th Infantry Brigades, through the final two years of the war.

"The sector of the 2nd Canadian Division ... is likely to have the heaviest fighting," believed Sir Julian Byng.[3] While Burstall's division did not have as great a distance to cover as the 1st Division on its right, its frontage was irregular and more difficult for the gunners to accommodate with their artillery barrage. The front started narrowly, at 1,300 metres, but expanded in width as the infantry advanced deeper into the enemy positions, to a final approximate width of 2,000 metres. As well, it curled to the right, so it was far less uniform than a straightforward advance would be, with the left section advancing 2,200 metres and the right having to push 2,700 metres into the enemy lines. Further, this uneven distancing of the sector made it not only more difficult for the gunners to target and destroy the barbed wire in order to keep the creeping barrage uniform, but also more likely for infantry units to drift into other sectors, possibly failing to take out enemy strongpoints that could later cause destruction to follow-on forces.

To compensate for the possibility of enemy defences remaining unscathed, Burstall ordered a thick assault of four battalions forward in the initial attack against the Black Line and the battered hamlet of Les Tilleuls. Another group of battalions would pass through this initial force to capture the second position, the Red Line. Further on, the fortified villages of Thelus and Farbus, all far from the start line, would be tough nuts to crack, even though they had been bombarded mercilessly with siege guns during the week before the battle, including the super-heavy 12-inch and 15-inch guns that fired shells weighing over 850 pounds to an astonishing distance of 27 kilometres.[4] Byng's earlier assessment was not just lip service, and he placed all of the corps' eight tanks and the 13th British Brigade at Burstall's disposal to support his attack. The tanks proved uniformly useless, getting bogged down in the mud and craters, but the 13th Brigade would perform well in the third and fourth phases of the battle. In all, more than half of Burstall's divisional infantry would cycle through the attack behind 46 artillery lifts during an 8-hour period. They would be supported by 183 field guns, 102 heavy machine guns, and 9 additional batteries of 54 medium- and heavy-siege guns. Though the first positions were to be captured in minutes, the entire battle would go on until at least mid-afternoon.

On the far right, the 4th Brigade's rum-warmed 18th and 19th Battalions, each about 600 strong, grimly pushed forward in four waves at 5:30 A.M., passing through the cratered mush and around dozens of mine craters. The first line fell easily, though the advance of the 19th Battalion was temporarily held up at Balloon Trench before the defenders were ultimately annihilated. While the supporting artillery fire on this portion of the front had wreaked havoc on the enemy trenches, isolated outposts and strongpoints had remained untouched. They were methodically knocked out, but the defenders fought hard. The German brigadier for the sector observed, "Where German guns and machine guns were still firing, the attack was stopped, and the dead piled high. Where ammunition and grenades ran out or muddy machine guns gave up the job, they fought with bayonets."[5] The advance to the first line, the Black Line to the Canadians (Zwischen Stellung to the Germans), was tougher, and a series of machine guns held up the attack just short of Les Tilleuls.

Sometimes these positions were knocked out by volleys of rifle grenades and concentrated rifle and Lewis-gun fire, while at other times success came down to men sacrificing themselves to draw fire and allow their companions to clear the positions with bullets and cold steel. Lance Sergeant Ellis Sifton of the 18th Battalion, a former farmer who was born in Wallacetown, Ontario, found his men pinned down and slowly being sniped by small-arms fire. With no way to manoeuvre around the defenders, Sifton charged the German trench, shot down the defenders and kept going. Emptying his rifle into the enemy, he then used his bayonet, killing every German. His men caught up with the blood-splattered lance sergeant and helped him secure the rest of the trench. As they were consolidating the positions, however, Sifton was shot by one of the dying Germans. He did not live to find out that he had been awarded the Victoria Cross. The 18th and 19th continued to push to their

Black Line objective, ultimately taking it and digging in. The operation had cost the 18th Battalion 166 in dead and wounded, and the 19th had lost 209, but the numbers would have been much higher if not for the bravery of men like Sifton, and countless others whose deeds went unrecorded.[6]

At 6:45 A.M., the 21st Battalion passed through the 18th and 19th, rushing on behind their creeping barrage to the Red Line, the second objective of the day, which ran along the front just before Thelus. Past the wounded and the chilling sight of rifles sticking out the ground to act as markers for the stretcher-bearers who would follow, the Canadians pushed forward. Twenty-two-year-old Lieutenant J.E. Johnson, leading a small party of several riflemen, came across a cave of Germans, tossed in a few Mills bombs, and went in firing. He came face to face with 105 enemy troops, all armed. Both sides stared in shock, but Johnson bluffed his way through the encounter, claiming to have more men up above. After disarming the enemy, Johnson led them up. The German prisoners were not pleased to find the small party that greeted them outside. The Red Line fell to the 21st Battalion, even though the battalion had lost a third of its strength.

To the left of the 4th Brigade's initial assault carried out by the 18th and 19th Battalions, the 5th Brigade's 24th and 26th Battalions had also made good progress behind the barrage, and had captured the Black Line. Mopping-up forces tossed grenades into every dugout or tunnel they could find. A steady stream of prisoners passed through the lines moving west, and the Canadians pushed east up the ridge.

After a pause to allow follow-on forces to reach their jumping-off positions, the creeping barrage crashed down again at 6:45 A.M. towards the Red Line objectives. The men of the 25th were piped over the top, even though the skirl of sounds was drowned in the barrage. Along with the 21st Battalion to the south, they passed through the consolidating forces. The Haligonians who formed the majority of the 25th had been told by their commanding officer that "even if one man was left alive the objective must be taken and held."[7]

The artillery bombardment had cleared most of the wire and the German trench was reduced to an "outline" of what it had once been.[8] The two battalions captured Les Tilleuls, Turko-Graben trench, and the Red Line, along with 400 prisoners, 8 machine guns, and a pair of 77mm field guns. By 7:15 A.M., the 25th and 21st had dug in, but in the less than two hours since the kick-off, and in only about thirty minutes of sustained combat, the battalions had lost 253 and 215 men each.[9]

The Iron Sixth from Western Canada had drawn the final leg of the battle, which included taking several strong positions of machine guns and field guns in the Bois de la Ville. All advantage of surprise had been lost at this point, and the Germans were now fighting for their lives. Lieutenant Colonel A.H Bell's 31st Battalion was ordered to capture Thelus by passing through the 21st Battalion. The men assembled under the fall of enemy and friendly shells, with dozens being killed or maimed as they tried to form up their sections.

Three companies pushed forward in a cold rain that alternately turned to snow and back to rain again. While facing this driving storm, they also advanced behind the leaping walls of the creeping barrage, at times closing to within 50 dangerous metres of the wall of fire. The barrage rolled over the battlefield like a hot rake tearing up everything in its path: "Buildings were demolished, trenches obliterated and wire smashed to atoms," noted the 31st Battalion's official report. "There was hardly an inch of ground that did not bear witness to the tremendous effect of our guns."[10] Most of the German defenders were killed or too stunned to continue fighting. Yet there were strongpoints, several of which held out even after they were surrounded, in the desperate hope of being relieved by counterattacking troops. One German described the fighting:

> One man after another fell or was rendered unfit for combat and one machine gun after another was destroyed. In the face of an overwhelming grenade attack, the last defenders were pushed into the "*Felsenkeller*," where the fighting continued for the only undestroyed entrance. Two soldiers with rifles and hand grenades held a fearless guard. A waiting comrade would immediately replace whichever entrance guard fell or was wounded. But the numbers that were still able to fight continued to dwindle.[11]

Eventually the Canadians forced their way through the dugout entrance, bombing the lead Germans to death before the survivors surrendered.

The 31st dug trenches in the muck to the east of what was left of Thelus at around 10:20 A.M., and mopping-up units of the 31st and 28th Battalions snuffed out the remaining German resistance. Claude Craig, an infantryman with the 28th who would survive the war but die at the age of thirty-two of a stroke thought to be brought on by his wartime injuries, wrote in his diary that after passing over the top that morning, "The rest of the day is all a haze as I don't remember anything very distinctly but have just a very few vivid pictures of it. One was a war correspondent taking a picture and another was when I climbed up over the ruins of a house and fell over a dead man."[12] Other soldiers focused instead on the immediacy of their grumbling stomachs and parched throats. "[We had] little food or water except what the Hun had left behind," observed Lieutenant Ralph Lewis; but other lucky units overran dugouts filled with wine and beer.[13] These prizes were shared after the treasure hunters drank their fill; for those not privy to the booty, petrol-tasting water was brought into the line later in the day.

The 27th and 29th swept past the now burned-out shell of Thelus, and through to the Blue and Brown Lines beyond it. On the Canadians' left, the 13th British Brigade fought resiliently and both forces thrust deep. They were supported by light artillery field batteries—known as "silent batteries" since they had not fired at zero hour—that had raced forward at the start of the battle to more ably support the troops who were now out of range of most of the lighter Canadian guns. This was a good idea in theory, but many of the guns were never brought into combat since they could not keep up with the infantry, and when they did finally unlimber and fire off a few shells they did not know where the enemy was located on the empty battlefield. The infantry had luckily not needed these guns as they moved rapidly, capturing some 250 prisoners, including the commander of the 3rd Bavarian Reserve Regiment and his staff, thereby decapitating the unit.[14] The Winnipeggers of the 27th Battalion wanted to ensure that they got the glory, and some of their men had brought pots of green paint along on the advance. As the 250 prisoners walked to the rear, each had the unit's designation, a rectangle with a circle above it, painted on his back.

"The first German I saw was spread-eagled against the parados, or back wall, of his trench, arms flung out as though crucified. Where his head had been was a red pulp like a crushed strawberry," observed Major D.E. Macintyre. "Many of the dead lay as though sleeping, without a mark of disfigurement … but others were

Canadian infantrymen from the 2nd Division advance up Vimy Ridge, passing a knocked-out British tank and a slain comrade. Some Canadian units encountered fierce opposition on their sector of the front, while others rarely saw the enemy, except for the dead or those trying to surrender.

disembowelled or with limbs shattered and clothing torn from their bodies by the blast of high explosives. The water in the shell holes was stained blood red."[15] Most of the German defenders were killed, routed, or captured, but the enemy responded to the Canadian advance by deluging much of the front with chemical shells, forcing the attackers to don their respirators—which protected against the lethal chemicals but left the wearer nearly suffocating from lack of oxygen. As the soldiers slowed to a crawl, choking and coughing inside their respirators, a few noticed that the cloud was composed of tear gas rather than a more lethal variety, so the men tucked their respirators away and continued to advance. They overran German artillery gunners who were surprised at the speed of the attack. Though some of the German 77mm field guns continued to fire over open sights at a range of 50 metres, others began to limber up and retreat. Few escaped, especially when the Canadians charged over open ground. "Fritz lambasted us right till we got right up to him," remembered W.J. Sheppard. "They threw their hands up and said, 'Mercy,

Comrade,' but I don't think they got much mercy."[16] The enemy was buried under the advance, and the 27th and 29th, as well as the 1st Battalion, Royal West Kent Regiment, and the 2nd Battalion, King's Own Scottish Borderers, were on the Brown Line by about 2:15 P.M., which they indicated to headquarters by firing three white rockets.

Throughout the rest of the day, enemy snipers made undertaking any movement over land difficult and accounted for many of the killed and wounded during the operation. But the exposed Canadians and British troops dug in, consolidated the line, and spent the day pulling back to less exposed positions while setting up interlocking fields of fire. Engineering units began to create strongpoints behind the lines that were completely enclosed by wire and capable of holding off enemy attacks on all sides. Having got to the eastern edge of the Bois de la Ville, the 2nd Division was not going to be driven out.

WITH THE GROUND REDUCED to a churned-up, glutinous mess, enemy dugouts became important points for new forces moving to the front. All of the Canucks who saw these dugouts marvelled at their deep construction in comparison to the Allied ones now to the rear. More satisfying, along the front, trained specialists turned around captured enemy machine guns and artillery pieces and fired them into the backs of the retreating German forces. This use of enemy weaponry was important since many of the Canadian guns were mired in the mud along the shattered roads on the western slope, their horses and mules straining to pull the hunks of steel through the glue.[17] However, these specialist gunners quickly realized that the Germans well knew the location of their own guns, and when the Canadians opened up fire against them, crash bombardments soon landed on these sites.[18] Most of the specialists prudently retreated from the marked gun positions.

Lance Corporal Donald Fraser, a machine-gunner attached to the 27th Battalion and a two-year veteran of the war, pushed his way to the front, past splayed bodies and scared prisoners, to set up a forward defence on the reverse slope of Vimy. The Canadian lines were blasted all day, and the strain was terrible as they waited for the whiplash counterattacks. "One poor fellow, a big chap, was crying like a baby with shellshock," wrote Fraser. "His nerves and control were absolutely gone," and he was sent to the rear.[19] A few German counterattacks appeared to be forming up, but these were smashed by supporting artillery and machine-gun fire before they could do any damage to the Canadians.

By the end of the day, most of the ridge was in Canadian hands. The 1st and 2nd Divisions suffered about 2,500 casualties each, and the units in the first four brigades had received a far higher proportion of losses than the two that passed through them.[20] It had been a great day for the two senior divisions, but the operation had been terribly costly. "Wounded men sprawled everywhere in the slime, in the shell holes, in the mine craters, some screaming to the skies, some lying silently, some begging for help, some struggling to keep from drowning in [water-filled] craters," recounted one eyewitness.[21] Medical Officer Andrew Macphail noted that in battles up to this point in the war, the ratio of light (walking wounded) to serious (stretcher case) casualties was about three to one; at Vimy, it was nearly one to one, meaning that the wounded required greater care, and more victims were likely to suffer fatal or maiming injuries.[22] Not only was the fighting at Vimy of the most brutal nature, pitting men against men in hand-to-hand combat, it was also far more lethal than anything the Canadians had encountered in the last two years.

Captain Claude Williams, a machine-gun officer in the 2nd Division who led his men over the top on April 9, remembered watching his fellow soldiers lurching forward through the churned-up ground, pulling their legs out of the gluey slop, shrapnel falling around them to sizzle in the mud. Smoke and explosions shrouded much of the battlefield. Lethal gases poisoned the air. Some men wore their bug-eyed respirators, wheezing through the filter; others left them hanging around the neck until they encountered strong concentrations of chemicals, choosing to advance rather than play it safe by encumbering themselves with the near-suffocating, if life-saving, devices. The dead and dying lay on the battlefield, but many of the injured had dragged themselves into shell craters to escape further wounds from the indiscriminate, whirling metal. Williams passed one man in a deep crater, who was mumbling and crying out, "Water! Water!" He stopped to offer assistance, but recoiled in horror after seeing that the top of the man's head had been blown off, exposing his brains, and that the glazed look of the man's eyes indicated he could not survive the terrible wound.[23] Such nightmarish scenes made it hard for most of the Canadians engaged at the sharp end of the historic battle to realize that Vimy was a victory, let alone a nation-building event. Slathered in mud and the substance of slaughter, the fighting men found the advance on Vimy Ridge little more than a brutal drive for survival.

CHAPTER 7

"THERE BEFORE US, FRIGHTFULLY CLOSE, WAS THE EDGE OF HELL"

The 3rd Canadian Division

Moving up the line, passing by the little white crosses in cemeteries dotting the approach to the Vimy battlefield, William Breckenridge of the 42nd Battalion, a former bookkeeper from Sherbrooke, Quebec, thought, "Can the Canadians drive Fritzie from Vimy Ridge after the French and British have failed?" After studying the objective, and the history of previous Allied operations, he remarked coolly that "the task was almost impossible." But with characteristic Canadian determination that was echoed by thousands on April 9, he remarked, "At least we could try."[1]

The 3rd Division was commanded by Louis Lipsett, who had replaced Malcolm Mercer after he was killed at the Battle of Mount Sorrel in June 1916. Lipsett was a Welsh-born British professional soldier who had come to Canada before the war to instruct the Canadian army. He exuded confidence and rose from the level of battalion commander at Second Ypres, where he was among the best on the battlefield, to brigadier, to his current position of major general. At each level of command, he inspired his men and thoroughly processed the rigours of the ever-changing tactics and technology. While he could be difficult and did not suffer fools, he had the common touch with the rank and file. His propensity to patrol through the front lines at night, challenging sentries and junior officers to identify key features of the front, was much commented upon by men, who were often surprised to see a major general anywhere close to the forward trench. The 3rd Division had improved since its trial-by-fire engagement in June, and much of the credit went to Lipsett and his commanders, who engaged in sustained training.[2]

Lipsett's division attacked along the same frontage as the 2nd Division, but had closer objectives—less than two-thirds the distance on the right and less than half on the left. However, the ridge was steeper here than on the 1st or 2nd Division's front, and the men faced the same criss-cross of trenches, machine-gun nests, and strongpoints that marked the rest of the front. While the entire ridge was cratered, a number of enormous craters on Lipsett's front were considered almost impassable. To move past these obstacles, some 10 to 15 metres deep, the infantry would need to go around them, but it was feared that the enemy might find ways to survive the bombardment by taking cover in the craters and then harass units on the flanks. These craters were therefore pounded with concentrated artillery fire and the infantry were instructed to advance along the lips of the saucers, making sure to bomb any inhabitants. It would be hard to tell if any Germans were in the huge holes, as they were full of mud, water, and corpses.[3]

Lipsett decided to pack in six battalions of the 7th and 8th Brigades to crash the German positions: the first, the Black Line, on top of the ridge; the second, the Red Line, on the reverse slope. It was an all or nothing rush. On the right of the divisional frontage, the 8th Brigade, commanded by Brigadier J.H. Elmsley, and consisting of the 1st, 2nd, and 4th Canadian Mounted Rifles (CMR), swept up the ridge behind the moving bounds of the creeping barrage at 5:30 A.M. Additional trench mortar fire was called down on parts of the front to clear wire, and No. 4 Special Brigade, Royal Engineers, fired thermite shells onto the support line from their 4-inch Stokes mortars. The Royal Engineers usually projected gas, but the thermite burned white hot, transforming the shell and contents into a mass of molten steel.[4]

The 1st CMR advanced on the right, the four companies leapfrogging each other as they pushed forward through snow and sleet. The German artillery, which had been pounded by British and Canadian guns in the counter-barrage, opened up slowly, firing a few shells at five minutes after zero hour, but then expanded in intensity after a few more minutes. However, due to the quick advance, most of the

A Canadian trench mortar team sets up their 9.45-inch mortar in the firing position during the Battle of Vimy Ridge. This mortar fired an enormous shell known by the soldiers as a "flying pig," and is located in a dugout to offer better protection against counter-battery fire.

shells landed behind the infantry as it swept forward. The first company, D, was quickly on its objectives, and all of the enemy's front-line outpost defenders were "either killed or taken prisoner." The other three companies passed through D, each dropping off and digging in when objectives were captured. The survivors of the companies established machine-gun positions on the forward lips of craters, building up additional firepower for their fellow battalion mates, who were tasked with continuing the push up the ridge, flowing around deep, water-filled craters and the slain. The barrage had made the trenches "unrecognizable," but the infantry still encountered pockets of fierce resistance.[5] Though these were crushed under the weight of the infantry's firepower, each position took time to destroy, leaving the infantry in the open, exposed to searching enemy fire. The attack began to break down, and confusion reigned. As Private Herbert Burrell penned in his diary after the battle, "There was a curious feeling of bewilderment and helplessness and a stifling smell of powder and smoke. A lack of leadership was evident and neither officers nor men seemed to know exactly where they were intended to go. Companies and platoons got mixed up with other companies," and elements of the 5th Brigade's troops—from the 2nd Division's front—had lost direction and were attacking into the 1st CMR's lines.[6]

The last two companies, A and B, had to travel the furthest over unprotected ground, and as they advanced over the cratered battlefield, a German barrage caught them in the open. The two companies were down to sixty men within two hours of starting the operation, and the first two companies, C and D, were ordered to send forward reinforcements to hold the front.[7] Having taken and consolidated the trenches, the 1st CMR withstood enemy bombardments and snipers; the assault, which was deemed a success at all levels, still cost the 1st CMR 365 dead, wounded, and missing in action.[8]

Those figures can be hard to grasp, but Herbert Burrell, who operated as a stretcher-bearer at the front, offered some insight into the face of battle he saw as he dodged shells and crawled from crater to crater looking for the wounded who had likely pulled themselves into the shallow pits for protection. "My first case was a man I found suffering from fright more than anything else. He was a big husky looking chap and I told him to get up and come along." The older Burrell pushed the younger soldier forward, and then moved off in search of the dead and dying, whom he quickly found:

> My [first] casualty was a lad of the 2nd C.M.R. who had a bad wound, being shot through the right lung. Then I attended to a man who had his left hand shot off at the wrist and the member was just hanging by a thread or two and his eye was also injured. Poor fellow he was in great agony but set a splendid example in his stoical endurance. He begged for a cigarette and wanted to know my name. It now commenced to snow and rain and was bitterly cold, adding immensely to the sufferings of the wounded and the difficult of atteng. [sic] to them.

Burrell then crawled over to another man, whom he had known back in Winnipeg:

> He was badly wounded by a shell in the left leg and was almost dead with cold. I let him have my coat and ground sheet. There was no stretcher or stretcher

bearers in sight for some two hours after the action started. I was at a loss to know what to do for the suffering, but on looking round the trenches I found a German stretcher with a dead German on it, who had apparently lain there for some days; so I lobbed him out, took the stretcher and got some men to help me get my cases into a Fritz dugout which was warm.

Burrell left to dress more men, one of whom was a "fine young fellow of the 2nd C.M.R. Vancouver contingent," who had been

shot through the temple and otherwise badly injured, breathing steadily, but unconscious. Put two shell dressings on him and looked in vain for stretcher bearers. Later in the morning I went back to him. He was still alive but weaker. I beckoned some stretcher bearers coming over the hill and when they arrived they refused to take him as they thought he was too poor and there were other cases who were more likely to live. I think he could have been saved if attended to earlier—awful, awful, and he was left to die!"[9]

Burrell spent the rest of the day trying to save the wounded, collaring German prisoners to carry out the maimed, and comforting those beyond all care.

The 2nd CMR, in the middle of the brigade assault, attacked with three companies, hoping to push forward most of their infantry before the enemy counter-barrage came crashing down behind them. The fourth company would stay further back unless it was needed to shore up the attack. C.S. Burgess of the 2nd CMR had felt that the pre-battle training was "very foolish" and repetitive, but now it gave him confidence as he was caught within machine-gun and artillery fire, a cacophony of sounds that left him almost deaf, and a terrain that had been chewed up by the creeping barrage.[10] The training and discipline also emphasized the importance of continually pushing forward. During the advance, Burgess witnessed one of his mates who, when a high explosive shell landed at his feet and buried itself in the mud, was blown dozens of feet in the air, his helmet, rifle, boots, and kit pin-wheeling to the ground. Amazingly, the dazed soldier picked himself up, checked his body for wounds, and—in front of Burgess's disbelieving eyes—grabbed his helmet and rifle, and kept advancing.

Private M.E. Parsons, also of the 2nd CMR, noted, "Once the show started every man was his own general." Not feeling as confident as those words, he attached him-self to an experienced sergeant and his subsection of men. During the advance up the ridge, they encountered eight Germans: "They gave us a bad time and we gave them a bad time, but it ended up that Sergeant Swanby and I were the only two alive."[11] Swanby was knocked out by friendly fire shortly after that engagement, leav-ing Parsons as the only man from that small battle group to reach the final objective.

On another part of the 2nd CMR's narrow front, Sergeant John MacGregor—or "Jock," as his men called him—urged his men forward. Gus Sivertz, a twenty-year-old who served with his brother, Henry, and who would win the Military Medal three times before he was killed at the end of the war, described the action:

> When the barrage started, Sergeant John MacGregor cried out, "What urr we waitin furr?" and climbing out of his shelter, started forward roaring, "Follow me, boys. Follow me." And follow him we did … Bullets whined, thudded and pinged through our ranks and grenades boomed, splattering mud and shrap-nel. Lucky for us, the blowing snow hindered the snipers. Jock led us up the slopes behind, and sometimes in, the creeping artillery barrage, zigzagging and leaping from cater to hillock to crater but always forward. He was nearing our objective when Hun machine guns rata-tat-tatted at his platoon. Yelling at us to lie low, Jock charged the machine gun nest, killed the crew, and captured the gun. He saved many of our lives that day.[12]

MacGregor would win the DCM for his actions and be promoted from the ranks. Later in the war, he would be awarded the Military Cross for bravery, and would fin-ish the war wearing the Empire's highest award, the Victoria Cross.

Within ninety minutes, the strongest part of the German line, La Folie Farm, had fallen to the Canadians. It had been reduced to a pile of rubble. The 2nd CMR dug in, but were forced to endure heavy shelling and German airplanes sweeping their lines, firing their machine guns with impunity. Yet neither these assaults, nor a snowstorm the next day—which was particularly difficult since most troops had left their greatcoats behind—could dislodge the determined soldiers from their position. At roll call several days later, after being relieved, the men of the 2nd CMR would find out that they had entered the assault with 687 and been reduced to 367.[13]

On the left of the 8th Brigade's front, the 4th CMR's four companies advanced individually in successive waves, each of which was about 150 strong and divided between two forward platoons and a mopping-up formation. The 4th CMR's objectives were located nearly 1.5 kilometres past La Folie Farm. While the German barrage was quick to respond on this front—with some shells falling ninety seconds after the assault began—the Canadians pushed on. Lieutenant Gregory Clark, a five-foot-two former journalist with the *Toronto Star*, and now commander of the 4th CMR's 15 Platoon, described the experience of advancing behind the barrage:

> In one sense, it was a beautiful sight. It was still quite dark. Sleet was falling. There before us, frightfully close, was the edge of hell. It blazed, flashed and flickered, the bursting shells; and white and colored flares were fired frantically by a distracted enemy. And the flashing, flickering lights showed an infernal wall of twisting, boiling smoke and flame, against which stood out the distorted silhouettes of men advancing into it.[14]

Forward Clark's unit went, in a measured walk behind the creeping barrage that was tearing up the enemy lines. Enormous craters gaped all around them; barbed wire had been torn apart; dead Germans lay splayed out in grisly poses of death. All horrors were passed in the steady march up the ridge. The iron discipline of the troops took over. Every three minutes they halted, lay down, and waited for the barrage to jump another 90 metres. They followed the artillery for more than a dozen 90-metre jumps, and each time they lay tense under the fire. Canadian shells were falling short into their own lines, and enemy shells exploded in the mud. Occasionally, the sound of the heavy German MG-08 could be heard firing above the din, but Clark's platoon encountered no Germans except those prisoners fleeing back towards Allied lines, hands in the air.

But men were killed all around Clark, as bullets and shrapnel whirled over the battlefield. For thirty-five minutes, they continued this advance until they hit the main enemy reserve trench. Here, the artillery barrage paused for forty-five minutes, playing all over the enemy lines, but allowing straggler units to catch up. There was not much for the infantry to do, and so they dug in to the craters, smoked cigarettes, and relieved heavy bladders. There were no Germans to be seen, as the entire front continued to be obscured by the hurtling artillery shells.

During this wait, Clark and a small group of men were in a crater, studying the front, eyeing their watches to know when to move off again. As Clark tried to shout to his batman, an enemy shell landed in the bottom of the crater—putting paid to the superstition among soldiers that a shell never landed in the same hole twice. In Clark's words, it "blew us all in the air, smashing the cigarette case Sgt. Windsor had in his hand, cutting Bertrand's rifle in two at the breech and heaving us in all directions." Stunned and shaken, Clark's small group patted frantically at arms and legs, making sure everything was still attached. Almost miraculously, no one was hurt.

After checking on his platoon, Clark heard the change in the sound of the barrage, and off it went again, like some fiery rake tearing through the enemy lines. Clark scrambled forward, slithering over the muddy ground, and off they pushed, following the barrage. By 7:05 A.M., they were on their final objectives, with neither Clark nor any of his men having fired a single shot. This was not the case for other platoons in his company, nor for the other twenty first-wave battalions attacking across the Vimy front, but it had been a strange battle thus far for 15 Platoon of the 4th CMRs. Yet it was far from over.

Most of the 4th CMR's lead platoons had overrun Zwischen Stellung trench and were on their final objectives by a few minutes after 7 A.M. Many soldiers reported a curious phenomenon of advancing up the ridge through shell craters the colour of blood. At first, it was thought that hidden corpses were polluting the water, but too many shell craters were crimson. The mystery remained unsolved, although Captain S.G. Bennett, a 4th CMR veteran, thought the men's perception may have been in part warped by the stress of the battle.[15]

Taking their objectives had been fairly easy for the men of the 4th, but they paid for holding them, being shelled and sniped at and losing a steady flow of men who had been established in strongpoints centred around seven machine guns. Following a forward reconnaissance by their experienced lieutenant colonel, H.D.L. Gordon, he asked for and received permission to pull back the line.[16] But the battalion still remained in danger. Lieutenant Gregory Clark, who would win the Military Cross for his gallantry at Vimy, was coordinating the defence of a key position. Throughout the day, his platoon and several others kept up a firefight with Germans who were dug in on the western slope below them. Artillery fire had also begun to slam into the ridge—both the enemy's and Canadian shells firing short. In the early afternoon, Clark's friend and fellow officer, Lieutenant W.G. Butson, was about 20 metres from Clark, trying to organize his men into rifle pits, when he fell to the ground. Clark raced over to help him and saw, to his horror, that a bullet had passed right through his head, ripping out both of his eyes. Clark nearly vomited at the sight. He cradled his friend in his arms and held his hand as he cried out deliriously for his mother. Clark did not have a lot of time to comfort Butson, who was taken by stretcher-bearers to the rear, where he did not survive, and Clark returned to organizing the defence, establishing a Lewis machine-gun perimeter.

For the 8th Brigade, the rest of the day was spent digging in and dodging enemy shells. A few desultory enemy counterattacks were mounted down the line, but Canadian gunners, directed by their forward observers on the hill with the infantry,

Following their "bite and hold" operation, the Canadians had bitten off Vimy Ridge from the enemy lines by April 10, but the high command expected that holding the position would be equally difficult. This photograph illustrates Canadian Vickers machine-gun teams establishing themselves in shallow gun pits in order to sweep the front against enemy counterattacks.

called down punishing fire. Several German planes flew low over the hill, sweeping it with machine-gun fire, but no sustained attack was attempted. Brigadier Elmsley reported that, over four days of fighting, his brigade lost 34 officers and 993 men, most of them on April 9.[17]

THE THREE BATTALIONS of the 7th Brigade, the Royal Canadian Regiment (RCR), the PPCLI, and the 42nd Battalion, had made deep advances into the enemy lines, after having poured forth from Grange Tunnel and the surrounding trenches. Massed artillery and machine-gun fire over their heads pinned down many of the defenders, allowing the infantry to overrun them. The barrage was effective in most spots, but all soldiers were wary of the storm of shells. The infantry drove on, and often through unspeakable conditions in which only automatic, learned actions could keep a soldier moving. "We have our flank in the air and are suffering from enfilade fire in newly dug trenches," wrote Major Agar Adamson.[18] Snipers and machine-gunners on both sides picked off stray troops in their muddy holes that passed for trenches. Carrying parties were bringing forward barbed wire and sandbags, as well as collecting tools and ammunition that had been dropped by the infantry in the initial assault, but they too were targets for enemy gunners. Brave men sacrificed themselves to unroll barbed wire as snipers fired at them: A.A. Bonar, who survived the chaotic battle, remembered seeing one poor fellow who "lay bent over his roll of wire, dead, with a large hole through his head."[19] The blood pouring from his body quickly stained the new snow that had begun to fall.

On the far left of the divisional front, the 42nd Battalion was harassed by fire coming from Hill 145, the highest section of the ridge, which was holding out against several assaults by the 4th Division. German forward observers on Hill 145 also called down plunging howitzer fire into the Canadian lines. The fragile nature of the battle, which dictated that the success or failure of the advance could rest on units fighting on the flanks, meant that the 42nd Battalion was in trouble. By 8:30 A.M., while the rest of the 3rd Division's front was being consolidated, the Highlanders of the 42nd Battalion were taking withering punishment. The 7th Brigade's commanding officer, Archibald Macdonell, known affectionately by his men as Batty Mac, was made aware of the situation by runner, and ordered that the 42nd pull back to create a more secure defensive flank. Throughout the day, the Highlanders, reinforced by a company from the 52nd Battalion, engaged enemy snipers in rifle fire. By the end of the battle, only one rifleman from the sniping section of the 42nd Battalion, H.J. Pearce, remained unwounded, although he had accounted for several of the enemy.

The Germans were even more savaged in the fighting. The surviving officers of the 263rd Reserve Regiment of the 79th Reserve Division noted that only one man of the 1st Battalion, which was holding the front lines, returned to the rear areas on April 9. The lone survivor recounted how the German machine guns on the flanks caught many of the attacking Canadians in the open before they were put out of action by artillery fire.[20] But the Canadian advance had been irresistible. Infantry platoons, firing on and pinning the enemy down, and then destroying strongpoints from the flanks, allowed the Canadians to punch deep into the defenders' lines. By noon, most of the 3rd Division's units were on the Red Line and waiting for the counterattack. The 3rd Division's front was firming up, but on their left the Germans were massacring the 4th Division.

CHAPTER 8

"WE WILL TAKE IT OR NEVER COME BACK"

The 4th Canadian Division

The 4th Division had the shortest but steepest objective as they attacked on the left of the Canadian Corps line. Their front was dominated by the heights of Hill 145, which held a commanding view of the northern ridge and all the troops moving across the Souchez and Zouave valleys. The German commander of this sector, Lieutenant Colonel Wilhelm von Goerne of the 261st Prussian Infantry Regiment, had ordered four protective lines to ring the top of the hill, and deep dugouts had been built into the reverse side of the ridge, making them very hard to destroy with gunfire. Goerne had walked the ridge several times, personally situating machine guns to sweep every avenue of approach. This was the citadel atop fortress Vimy.

While Hill 145 anchored the ridge, supporting it to the north was the other German-held high point, the Pimple. Although this position was about 25 metres lower than Hill 145, it still overlooked the Canadian advance. Defenders on the Pimple, situated in trenches that ran perpendicular to Hill 145, could be expected to pour heavy fire into the flanks of the Canadian forces. Despite this imposing location, Byng decided to leave the Pimple objective outside of the scope of the Canadian attack, and to screen it off with smoke and poison gas. Division commander Major General David Watson and his staff objected to this screen, but Byng felt he did not have enough troops to spread out the attack to include the Pimple. Even without the added threat of the Pimple, of all the terrain at Vimy, that on the

4th Division's front worked most strongly in the enemy's favour, and gave them every conceivable advantage.

Brigadier Victor Odlum's 11th Brigade was to take Hill 145 with three battalions, while Brigadier J.H. MacBrien's 12th Brigade was to drive forward on the left, providing a strong shoulder. MacBrien, who would become Canada's chief of staff after the war, ordered the 38th, 73rd, and 72nd Battalions to consolidate the left of the corps attack and punch through to the southwest corner of Givenchy-en-Gohelle, beyond the crest of the ridge. At zero hour, mines were blown along the front, leaving gaping holes in the German lines, and the infantry advanced behind the lifting barrage fire. But the mud was glutinous, sucking the infantry down. Many of the attackers went forward in socks, as boots were pulled from their feet, leaving them stepping gingerly over torn barbed wire and sizzling shrapnel. While the force quickly overran the enemy front lines, these were only lightly held. Moving towards the second and final line, the spearhead formations ran into deeper mud and water-filled shell holes coloured copper with old blood, which slowed the progress of the advance.

Despite the masking cloud of gas and smoke intended to shield the advancing Canadians from view, enfilading fire from Hill 145 and the Pimple added to the maelstrom as the attackers closed on the highest points of the ridge. The front was entirely pocketed with craters, many 3 to 4.5 metres deep. Canadian soldiers slithered over the battlefield, stumbling and pushing forward, blown left and right by the concussion of closely exploding shells. Some of the advancing infantry were lifted from their feet by the blasts and found themselves driven into the deep craters. Trapped in these sinkholes, men could not climb out because of the slimy walls, scrambling up only to fall back into the scummy water, which was filled with old and new corpses. As soldiers up above pushed around these enormous holes, they could hear the pleading voices of men screaming for help. They were ordered not to stop.

Casualties from artillery and small-arms fire began to mount as forces were caught in a crossfire. One of the junior officers, Lieutenant Desmond Vicars of the 72nd Battalion, a twenty-year-old former teacher, advanced through the artillery fire with the remains of his platoon, cleaning out dugouts and capturing two machine guns and two teams of *Minenwerfers* (mortars). Vicars was awarded the DSO, but was badly wounded with a gunshot wound through his stomach a month later, ending his war. Vicars and his men drove off a series of counterattacks, but the operation had stalled. The 72nd dug in about 300 metres short of Givenchy. Much of the force had been left to engage the defenders of the Pimple, but of the 262 officers and men in the attack, a shocking 202, or seventy-seven percent, were killed or wounded.[1]

The Ottawa-raised 38th Battalion attacked along the slope of Hill 145, on the right of the 72nd, in four waves, 562 men strong in total. The craters were so bad in places that the infantry were unable to keep up with their barrage, which soon moved off without them, stranding them in the open. Accounts were heard of wounded men being hit, rolling into shell holes for cover and drowning in these watery graves.[2] The acrid smell of smoke and fumes mixed with the cries of the wounded and steaming blood in the snow. Many of the German positions were overrun, but other areas were avoided as troops flowed around them, anxious not to lose their proximity to the barrage. The follow-on companies experienced tough fighting with bombs and bayonets against these German pockets of resistance, which refused to give up despite being surrounded. But they were slowly reduced through a series of grim battles in which quarter was rarely asked for or given.

Most of the Canadian formations disintegrated under the fire and in the featureless terrain. Privates lost their officers, and leaders soon found that they were alone as their men had gone to ground and stayed there. At one point in the battle, Captain T.W. MacDowell of the 38th Battalion, in charge of a company of more than 150 men, was left with only two subordinates. Together, his small battle group knocked out two machine-gun positions, killing and capturing the prisoners. Confusion reigned over the battlefield, and MacDowell eventually found some of his men. He sent a message back to battalion headquarters about two hours into the battle:

> The mud is very bad and our machine guns are filled with mud. I have about 15 near here and can see others around and am getting them in here slowly…. The runner with your message for 'A' Company has just come in and says he cannot find any of the Company officers. I don't know where my Officers or men are but am getting them together. There is not an NCO here. I have one machine gunner here but he has lost his cocking piece off the gun and the gun is covered with mud. The men's rifles are a mass of mud, but they are cleaning them.

MacDowell noted further that, on coming across a German dugout, he and his small party captured seventy-five prisoners. He sent them back to the rear in batches of twelve, "so they could not see how few we were. I am afraid few of them got back as I caught one German shooting one of our men after he had given himself up. He did not last long—and so I am afraid we could not take any back except a few who were good dodgers." He finished: "I cannot give an estimate of our casualties but believe they are severe…. I can see the 72nd men on our left. The 78th have gone through after we reached here. The barrage was good but the men did not keep close to it enough and held back," and they had therefore been shot up badly.[3] The twenty-six-year-old Captain MacDowell, who already wore the DSO, would win the Victoria Cross for his leadership and bravery in the battle, and specifically for the capture of the German prisoners who vastly outnumbered his small party. But even the monumentally brave could succumb to the terrible stress at the front; within a few months of Vimy, MacDowell broke down from shell shock, his career as a front-line officer over.

Despite this expert leadership and the tenacity of the rank and file at the sharp end, their task was no stroll up the ridge behind the all-consuming barrage. German machine guns were raking the front, and MacBrien's reserve battalion, the 78th from Winnipeg, passed through the ragged line established by the 72nd and 38th Battalions, one hard metre after another. Their objective was located 1,200 metres from the start line. Almost immediately, the Canadians were assaulted by fire on three sides. D.G. Anderson, a scout leading his company forward, remembered, "Snipers were picking us off."[4] No mercy was shown, with even runners and stretcher-bearers cut down in the open. Lieutenant Stewart Scott recounted that confusion reigned on the battlefield: "Where my sergeant was I couldn't tell you, where my company commander was I don't know, and he certainly didn't know where I was."[5] As Scott tried to find his men, he was shot in the head by a sniper, but his helmet saved him by deflecting the bullet, which ran around the brim. The defenders at Hill 145 and the Pimple had stopped the Canadians' attack cold. The 46th Battalion, from the 10th Brigade, was thrown into the line to protect against counterattacks, but the only way the 12th Brigade could move forward was if Hill 145 fell.

THE BATTERED 11TH BRIGADE had been tasked with overtaking the hardest objective at Vimy: Hill 145. To succeed, Brigadier Victor Odlum's brigade had to pass through four lines of defences. Odlum had already proven himself an aggressive general and a firm believer in trench raiding, but even he did not like the odds here. He ordered the 102nd and 87th Battalions to make the initial assault, but he knew that he needed the full weight of his infantry up front if his force was to punch through the defences. The 54th and 75th would advance closely behind the front waves, with all four moving as one. The barrage was good, but the infantry were held up by heavy small-arms fire. By 7:40 A.M., the 102nd's command headquarters noted laconically that "things were not going well."[6] All officers in the attack were killed or wounded. A German officer noted of his comrades: "They fought like men possessed."[7] Soon, members of the 261st Prussian Reserve Infantry Regiment testified that the Canadian "corpses accumulate and form small hills of khaki" in front of the slopes.[8]

Sergeant D.S. Georgson, holder of a Military Medal for his bravery during the Battle of the Somme, was defending a key strongpoint with a small group of men, but most of the infantry had gone to ground and, in the face of nearly uninterrupted fire, stayed there. Moreover, responding to uneven advances along the front, the Germans were counterattacking, trying to find the weak points and seams in the defence. The 54th, which had passed through the 102nd, had its flanks unguarded, or "in the air," which meant it could be attacked from several directions. The battalion was forced to pull back after several probing enemy raids. Canadian artillery attempted to help by harassing these attackers, but because of the ragged front the gunners proceeded with caution, often firing behind the German front lines, catching reinforcing enemy troops but doing little to suppress the heavy fire at the front. By the end of the day, 116 of the 54th's men had been killed and 104 wounded: 220 of the 350 who had gone over the top. The 102nd were even worse off, with 122 killed, 189 wounded, and 27 missing.[9] Most of the missing were never found. As one trench soldier warned his mother: "If you ever get word that I'm missing, just make up your mind I'm gone.... I think you need not hope against hope, as usually one is never found, and I realize it only prolongs the agony if one is waiting for the word that never comes."[10] The missing remained in a purgatory: neither living nor dead, simply gone.

The 87th Battalion's (Canadian Grenadier Guards) assault also collapsed. During the pre-battle bombardment, parts of the enemy's trenches on this front had been abandoned. In planning the operation, brigade headquarters ordered that the Canadian artillery barrage skip over these trenches, as they were unoccupied by the Germans and would make for an undamaged command centre. This was a grave error. Air photographs taken on April 7 revealed that barbed wire had been replaced in front of the trench. Despite this evidence of reoccupation, however, this sector was not added to the artillery's target list. In the chaos of the lead-up to the battle, the target appears to have been simply overlooked. The 87th Battalion paid for the error.[11] When the Grenadiers went over the top, they found that the strong enemy trench running only about 100 metres had been left unscathed, and that it was now packed with defenders who had gravitated there during the barrage.[12] The lead company of Grenadiers was nearly annihilated in only a few minutes, and sixty percent of its men lay dead and wounded within metres of the start line. This was the Somme all over again. The 75th Battalion was to support the 87th, but the battalion's first waves were so unnerved by the 87th's slaughter and the enemy's unsuppressed fire that most did not leave their trenches. One can hardly condemn men for balking at committing suicide—especially a unit like the 75th, whose members had been so callously treated by their superior officers during the March 1, 1917, raid. Those few platoons that did go over the top went forward in short bounds and were cut to ribbons, especially after the barrage moved off without the infantry. Odlum's attack had been reduced to a bloody shambles, his men left searching desperately for cover while under fire on the slopes of Vimy.

HILL 145 WAS THE LINCHPIN to the German defence. It had to fall. General David Watson turned to an unlikely unit: the 85th Highlanders from Nova Scotia, who had recently arrived in France. A raw formation that had been handed shovels instead of rifles, they did not even have kilts yet, something that rankled the men deeply—more so when their new comrades teased the "trousered" Highlanders. While assault units had been training or resting for the operation, the men of the 85th had been involved in work parties every night in the period leading up to the battle, building roads and consolidating positions, bringing forward ammunition and clearing the wounded. No one expected them to go into battle—least of all the men themselves. But with his forward battalions carved up by heavy German fire, and even attacked from behind in places when the enemy emerged from their over-run trenches, a desperate Watson threw the Highlanders into the line at mid-after-noon on April 9.

Rushed to the front, the lead companies spread out in the hastily dug jumping-off trenches, which were under fire and filled with exhausted and wounded men of the 87th. Bayonets were fixed, and soldiers waited for the prerequisite barrage at 6 P.M. As tension mounted, the unit's medical officer, Joseph Hayes, noted that despite his "cheerful and encouraging words," all realized the operation was a "des-perate one and that there was a chance that few if any might return." Captain Percival Anderson, who commanded one of the companies and would later die at Passchendaele, gave a short speech, spiced with more than a few Cape Breton exple-tives; he finished by vowing, "We will take it or never come back."[13]

Unbeknownst to the assaulting companies, however, the brigade's commanding officer had called off the artillery barrage, fearing that the gunners could not lay it down accurately without killing his own troops.[14] But he had not been able to get word to the two forward companies in time, as the runners were floundering in the mud or had been caught by one of the many death-dealing weapons that pervaded the battle space.

Spread out along winding trenches, the two lead assault companies waited in silence. Tension mounted; muscles in shoulders and backs felt like iron. Officers stared at their wristwatches: one minute, thirty seconds, fifteen seconds, five sec-onds. But instead of the enormous barrage at zero hour, the Highlanders were greeted only with silence, and the company commanders were faced with a horrible decision. It was with searching eyes that the men looked at each other. Ten, fifteen, twenty seconds ticked away in silence. At thirty seconds, the tension was broken with a battle cry, and the Nova Scotians went over the top. Firing on the run, they surprised most of the Germans, whose Pavlovian training had drilled them in the idea that a barrage signalled an attack. They knew that no one in their right mind attacked without the protection of a barrage. But no one mentioned that to the Nova Scotians.

Three machine guns and more than a hundred Germans were overrun as the Easterners of the 85th shot and stabbed their way forward. The Germans recovered quickly, though, and soon machine-gun and rifle bullets tore through the Canadian ranks. But the Highlanders did not stop, crashing through the German lines, clearing positions at the end of their bayonets. This mad charge over hundreds of metres of open ground, with bullets flying around them, must be considered one of the most daring Canadian attacks in the entire war.[15] The 85th captured most of Hill 145, but parts on the eastern slope remained in German hands.

The Germans tried to counterattack Hill 145 immediately, hoping to take advantage of the confusion that invariably reigns after any attack. But small groups of defenders banded together, Lee-Enfields and Lewis guns at the ready. Organizing a defensive position under such conditions was not easy. Yet because the enemy forces were also disorganized, it took time for them to regroup. Fierce firefights continued all day, and several counterattacks were dealt with by small-arms fire and shellfire. Sergeant Walter Draycot of the PPCLI had little sympathy for the enemy who had bombarded the Canadian lines for months from atop the ridge, and these counterattacks were torn apart before they even got started: "The agony suffered by the enemy [would be partial] atonement for their [earlier] murderous shellfire."[16]

THE CANADIANS HAD CAPTURED most of Vimy Ridge, except for the upper summit on the 12th Brigade's front and parts of the eastern slope. With the 11th Brigade shattered, Watson ordered Brigadier General Edward Hilliam, commander of the 10th Brigade, to orchestrate the capture of the final objectives. The 44th and 50th Battalions were sent in, but they were forced to show an open flank to the German defenders dug in along the Pimple. The divisional artillery tried to protect the Canadian battalions by masking the Pimple with gas and smoke, but that worked only partially. With communications severed along the front, artillery ammunition piles largely spent, and the torn-up ground slowing movement, the operation did not go off until 3:15 P.M. on April 10.

Although Watson knew that the Pimple had to be taken out, as defenders on it were harassing his front and it could be used as a counterattack position, he first needed to capture the rest of Vimy Ridge still in enemy hands. A heavy and methodical creeping barrage allowed the 10th Brigade's two battalions to claw their way forward to drive the Germans from the eastern slopes, leaving the Pimple out of the mix for the moment. The 44th took their objectives, but the 50th Battalion were held up by machine-gun fire from dug-in defenders, in front and again from the Pimple. All around him, remembered Victor Wheeler of the 50th Battalion, men "were being impaled like grotesque scarecrows on rusty concertina wire, splashed into water-filled craters, scattered over the lower slope of the Hill in gruesome fragments."[17] The attack looked like it was about to be defeated, but once again it fell to a few individuals to tip the balance. John Pattison, a forty-two-year-old British-born engineer from Calgary, single-handedly advanced on a machine-gun post, working his way forward via shell holes. He moved to within 30 metres and then stood up and tossed three accurate grenades; he followed his grenades by charging with his bayonet, killing all the Germans before his men arrived. From there, the 50th Battalion pushed forward, clearing the rest of the ridge. Pattison learned that he had been recommended for the Victoria Cross but did not survive the war to wear it; he was killed six weeks later on the Douai plain.

Now, on April 10, all along the front the exhausted and battered Canadians were greeted by a glorious sight: the open fields of the Douai plain that stretched out before them to the east. As Lieutenant Stanley Edgett remarked to his parents, "I don't suppose any one who has not been out here can begin to imagine what [we] have endured."[18] But the Canadians were not done; they had to capture one more position. Hill 145 remained the key high point on Vimy Ridge, but defenders on the Pimple could still rain fire down on the Canadians, as the 4th Division had found out the hard way on April 9. The ridge would not be safe with this hill still in German hands, and Canadian intelligence detected that an elite Prussian guard formation, the 5th Guard Grenadier Regiment, had been sent to hold the heavily defended position that was riven with mazes of trenches, deep dugouts, and interlocking tunnels. Byng and Watson ordered the assault before the position could be more fortified.

The Vimy battle required further sacrifice from the men of the 44th and 50th. Having captured the final positions on Hill 145, the Westerners were now ordered to attack the Pimple. Both battalions had been cut up, with the 50th having lost more than 200 men and officers only days before, so they were reinforced by two companies from the 46th Battalion.[19] The operation was to go in at 5 A.M. on April 12, supported by the fire from about 100 field guns. These gunners could not offer an overwhelming bombardment, but it would be thickened up by machine-gunners firing from Hill 145. Still, the defences of the Pimple were formidable, and the dugouts and pillboxes had been hardened—having been interwoven in many spots with concrete and steel. The Germans also enjoyed good fields of fire since the Canadians would have to attack over open ground and up a gently rising slope.

Assault troops from the 44th, 46th, and 50th Battalions were awakened around 2 A.M. by the opening bombardment, and fed hot soup, biscuits, and rum to fortify them for the coming battle. Many men preferred the burning sensation of rum to the cold, empty feeling that gnawed away in their bellies. Extra ammunition and grenades were handed out. Greatcoats were left behind: better to shiver for a few hours than to be burdened by extra kit during the mad scramble. But this would be no easy advance. D.M. Marshall of the 44th Battalion recounted that the "mud was so bad that you couldn't stand still in any place. You'd have to move or you'd sink."[20]

German flares bathing the front in a ghostly white light only added to the strange battlefield that looked more like the moon than a hill. As the freezing Canadians huddled in their muddy jumping-off trenches, veterans could at least approve of the fact that the snow was blowing into the eyes of the German defenders. "What agonizing moments are these just before the barrage opens up! ... huddled figures, waiting, quietly, anxiously, in the mud and snow for the beginning of what to some meant death, to others affliction, and to others hours of suffering, of weariness beyond description," wrote Sergeant R.G. Kentner of the 46th Battalion before the battle—which would be his first.

The Canadians surged forward at zero hour. Kentner noted, "I was surprised to find that I was not afraid, that I only went doggedly forward ... the barrage appeared to steady us."[21] But all around him his companions were being shot down. On the far left of the front, the 46th Battalion's two companies came under heavy Mauser rifle fire and suffered about 100 casualties in simply crossing No Man's Land. The creeping barrage was lost to the infantry early in the battle, as the mud—thigh- to waist-deep in places—stuck the men fast, reducing their movement to about 100 metres every fifteen minutes.[22] Although at least one German defender described the supporting barrage as "insanely violent," the situation did not appear like this to the Canadians, some of whom were literally stuck to the ground in places, forced to watch the battle raging around them but still vulnerable to enemy fire.[23]

The central thrust of the attack was better supported by the artillery, but the Prussians and Canadians were often reduced to hand-to-hand fighting. At one point, two groups met in No Man's Land as the Prussians charged the Canadians. The Canadians eventually prevailed in the ferocious struggle, and within an hour, they had taken the position. According to the 50th Battalion's official records, a great many of the "enemy were bombed and bayoneted."[24] Victor Wheeler noted that as his battalion overran German positions, prisoners began to emerge from their honeycomb underground dugouts "unarmed and nervously trudging toward our advancing line, hoping to be taken alive. Many of them were not. The number of men required to herd them back to the P.O.W. cages could not be spared. Our men were still falling at twice the rate of the enemy's casualties, and the job of highest priority, capturing the Pimple, was becoming the task of fewer and fewer of us."[25] But the Germans had been defeated again, driven from the last point from which they could threaten the Canadian-held ridge.

"I went over the Pimple yesterday," wrote Byng in a special letter to his wife—special because it is the only one written to his wife during the war that is known to exist. "It is a sight: the dead are rather ghastly but a feat of arms that will stand for ever. Poor old Prussian Guard. WHAT a mouthful to swallow being beaten to hell by what they called "untrained Colonial levies."[26]

CHAPTER 9

A VICTORY TOO COSTLY?

The Bloodiest Battle in
Canadian Military History

"It was Canada's day," wrote Sergeant Walter Draycot of the PPCLI, who would be shot in the eye, gassed, and shell shocked during the course of the war.[1] The Canadian capture of Vimy was more than just a battlefield victory that had driven the Germans from their fortress and ensured that the British had a position of observation over the Douai plain. Because all four Canadian divisions attacked together and all regions of Canada were present in the battle, Vimy became a symbol of what Canadians could do together—a symbol that epitomized the sacrifice of the young Dominion. In 1922, the French government ceded Vimy Ridge and the surrounding land to Canada in perpetuity to honour the country's sacrifice on behalf of France during the war. Though it was the collective sacrifice and deeds of all Canadians during the war years—both those at the front and those on the home front—that eventually won Canada's full independence from Britain, the Vimy Memorial, which was unveiled in 1936, remains one of the most visible and evocative symbols of Canadian nationhood.

Though heady myths and symbols infuse the memory of Vimy Ridge, it is important to remember the grim reality at the front in April 1917. Vimy is often portrayed as an artillery battle, with the guns shredding the enemy defences as the infantry simply advanced to victory. The counter-battery fire was equally devastating: of the 89 enemy guns, only 17 remained active at the end of April 9.[2] The artillery shellfire was, without a doubt, essential in allowing the infantry to advance. Indeed, as William Antliff of the No. 9 Canadian Field Ambulance put it, "The boys can't praise our barrage too much and every inch of the ground is chewed up."[3] One Canadian infantry staff officer even went so far as to write in his diary, "It is no wonder the Germans couldn't hold us for our artillery work had been terrible, everything smashed to pieces. We had broken their hearts first and there was no fight left in them."[4] While this was true along parts of the front, and more than 4,000 prisoners were captured, the battle the Canadians faced at the sharp end was in most sectors nothing short of brutal, and there was a lot of fight left in the defenders.[5] Though success could not have been achieved without the guns, the firepower did not translate to victory on its own. German troops survived the barrage in every sector of the front. It fell to the Canadian infantry to pin the enemy down with machine-gun fire, snipe him with rifles, tear him apart with grenades, and spear him with bayonets.

The Canadians' intense training and pre-battle preparation had paid dividends. Driver Cyril Brown, from Port Hope, Ontario, felt that the pre-battle training had so well prepared him for the front that he felt he knew every trench and crater he might encounter, as well as "a lot of rats by their first names."[6] The new platoon organization had also shown its value: junior officers and NCOs led from the front, and when they were wounded, new leaders took their place on the battlefield. There were certainly cases of men going to ground after their officers were killed and wounded, and then staying there in a relatively safer shell hole, but more often the ground-pounders found ways to reorganize themselves, bring sufficient firepower to bear on strongpoints, and then snuff them out. And it was often done one position at a time—one after another, in relentless combat.

Some divisional sectors had less daunting objectives than others, but countless acts of bravery were required for all the isolated infantry sections and platoons to drive forward. The 4th Division had the most imposing obstacle to surmount, but casualty statistics indicate that the fighting on the 1st and 2nd Divisions' fronts was even more costly, for the intensity of fighting in these sectors and the length of the advance required more infantry battalions to be crossing the killing ground over a longer period of time. During the four-day battle, the Canadian Corps as a whole suffered 3,598 killed and another 7,000 wounded. A.F. Brayman of the

50th Battalion, who was wounded by shellfire during the battle, resulting in a fractured elbow and the loss of three fingers on his left hand, wrote:

> From the very first minute of the attack we came under murderous and hellish fire from the machine guns.... we lost about 30 per cent of the fighting forces before we got into his green line of trenches and then went into hand-to-hand fighting.... As we looked back up that ridge in the early dawn we witnessed a scene never to be forgotten. The entire face of the hill was covered with German green and Canadian khaki. Men lay out there in that blood-soaked field, some dead, some dying.[7]

The more than 10,500 casualties were spread over only four days of battle, with 7,707 occurring on April 9 and the early part of April 10, thereby making the fighting at Vimy far more intense and costly than the slaughter on the Somme. The

This memorial to the fallen of the 2nd Division is one of several Canadian unit memorials constructed after the battle to mark the sacrifice at Vimy Ridge. During the battle, 3,598 Canadians were killed and more than 7,000 were wounded, making it the costliest victory in Canadian military history.

Somme had accounted for 24,000 casualties over three months.[8] April 9, 1917, was the single bloodiest day of the entire war for the Canadian Corps, and bloodiest in all of Canadian military history: worse than Beaumont Hamel on July 1, 1916, worse than Dieppe on August 19, 1942, worse than D-Day on June 6, 1944; in fact, worse than all three combined. The high casualty rate does not detract from the victory, but it is worth remembering that the sober work of the Canadian infantry in the days following the capture of the ridge was often made up of scouring the battlefield for their fallen comrades, sewing them in their blankets, and burying them in mass graves.

THE CANADIANS NOW HELD a commanding view of the enemy lines from atop the ridge. Even with the enemy on the run, however, it was not possible to exploit their advantage without artillery support, which was mired at the bottom of the western slope. With the ground shell-pitted, shattered, and reduced to thigh-deep muck in places, there would be few guns and little ammunition brought up the ridge for at least a day or two. Horses and men strained through the slime to pull the guns up the now boggy and cratered slope, and they did so under fire from German gun teams on the Douai plain, who realized the importance of harassing the enemy artillery in order to purchase time for their own disorganized forces.

Despite the temporary Canadian vulnerability, the Germans were in a worse position, and they knew it. The German Sixth Army high command had badly misread the operational situation at Vimy, believing wrongly that its forces on the ridge could hold out for days—at least long enough to bring several divisions of counter-attacking forces forward from their rest positions more than 20 kilometres to the rear. It had been a grave oversight to not keep the forces closer to the front, but the German high command believed its troops dug-in on Vimy could not be knocked from their fortress, and, although this consideration is often overlooked by historians, divisions cannot simply be quartered out in the middle of a plain for long and hope to keep their combat effectiveness. These reserve divisions were therefore spread out across a number of villages and towns far from the ridge. While a heavy and rapid counterattack might have turned the tide against the Canadians, few armchair generals have accounted for how these forces would have advanced up the steep eastern slope of the ridge when the Canadians were prepared to respond to this exact operation. And, without playing guessing games, the only hard evidence available reveals that the Canadians summarily destroyed a series of piecemeal attacks that the Germans did indeed launch on April 9 and 10. When these failed, the Germans rightly retreated several kilometres from the ridge and out of shellfire range. They dug in to their new reserve position, the Drocourt-Quéant Line, which tied two deep and powerful trenches together. The Canadians would be forced to capture this position, but not until a year and half later.

While the Germans had been soundly defeated and pushed off a key position, the Battle of Vimy Ridge did not change the strategic picture of the war—though it was a blow to the Germans, who had always defended strongly on the Western Front. General Ludendorff, whose fifty-second birthday was celebrated on April 9, wrote of the larger Arras offensive: "I had looked forward to the expected offensive with confidence and was now deeply depressed."[9] It was the Canadians who had been primarily responsible for blowing out his candles. As always, however, the Germans recovered quickly, though there were some pessimists: Crown Prince Rupprecht wrote in his diary, after realizing that Vimy could not be recaptured, "Is there any sense in continuing the war?"[10]

Despite the Crown Prince's despairing entry, from the German perspective there was much sense in continuing the war, especially since the stunning Canadian victory was part of a larger Allied offensive that had failed badly. The British component of that offensive had started well, with the deepest advance of the war to date having been made on April 9, but it had broken down quickly. The friction of battle, ongoing challenges of communication, and a stiffening reaction by the Germans to the shock of the battle militated against the British putting together a string of victories in the following days. Succeeding attacks bogged down, and the initial success ground to a near halt in a hail of gunfire. Of all the British offensives during the war, the 159,000 casualties during the thirty-nine days of Arras fighting, from April 9 to May 17, produced the highest average daily casualty rate—more than any other major battle—and worse, for example, than the daily casualty rate of the longer Somme battles during the previous fall.[11] Despite the terrible losses, Haig felt the need to push the offensive "much longer than he wanted to," according to Fourth Army commander Sir Henry Rawlinson, "in order to help the French out of a hole."[12] Such was the nature of coalition warfare, but even the initial success offered few tangible trophies other than the gobbling up of a few more kilometres of French territory, and certainly nothing like the Canadians' triumph on Vimy Ridge.

It was worse for the French. So fruitless were the attacks of the brave *poilus* to the south, which yielded more than 117,000 casualties in the first eight days of fighting (rising to 187,000 by the end of the campaign), that a large portion of the French army mutinied in the next month.[13] German forces suffered nearly the same number of casualties, admitting to 163,000, but Nivelle had promised so much and delivered so little that no one paid attention to the equally terrible German losses. After fighting with all they had to regain vast tracts of the motherland, the French soldiers had reached their limit. Sixty-eight French divisions—almost equalling the size of the entire BEF—were unsuitable for service, with many on the verge of collapse. They had been asked once too often to risk their lives in useless and costly offensives, and they refused to partake in further callous battles. While the mutineers did not want to lose the war, and continued to hold the line, they refused to attack. Order was eventually restored by the new French army commander, Henri Pétain, who provided both the carrot and the stick in the form of more leave on the one hand, and the execution of twenty-seven ring leaders on the other.[14] But the French force, callously used over the last two and half years, would need time to recover, and its generals wisely kept it from major engagements for almost a year, with Pétain promising his troops that they would wait for the Americans to help share the burden.

THE CANADIAN VICTORY at Vimy stood out against these failures. The French called it Canada's Easter gift to the Allies. British newspapers were no less praiseworthy, and many were in line with the sentiments of King George V, who intoned: "Canada will be proud that the taking of the coveted Vimy Ridge has fallen to the lot of her troops."[15] The Canadians had solidified their reputation as dogged fighters on the Somme, but here at Vimy they had redeemed the defeat of the larger Allied offensive. Yet it should be recognized, as many Canadians did at the time, that the British had ably supported the Canadians. The battle could not have been won without the Empire's logistical and artillery support, not to mention one of its brigades attacking on the 2nd Division's front. The victorious Canadian commander, Sir Julian Byng, paid a high tribute to Sir Henry Horne, commander of the British First Army, when he remarked: "Horne has been more than helpful and backed me up in everything."[16] In our elevation of the Battle of Vimy Ridge to the status of icon and our reverence for it as a milestone along Canada's slow march to nationhood, we must still remember the full support of the British in logistics, in gunfire, and in fighting on the ridge.

Though the significance of the victory at Vimy for the larger war effort is clear, its vital importance to the maturation process of the Canadians in particular should not be underestimated. Vimy would be the turning point in the war for the Canadian Corps: the point where it moved from an amateur to a professional warfighting force. After Vimy, remembered E.S. Russenholt, "there was a feeling that we had mastered this job and that we were the finest troops on earth."[17] Captain Georges Vanier of the 22nd Battalion wrote to his mother: "The morale of our troops is magnificent. We cannot lose."[18] Such elevated levels of pride and confidence were powerful and necessary motivators for soldiers who would be called on to fight for another year and a half. From Vimy onward, the Canadians never lost another set-piece or major engagement, delivering victory after victory, and often against the most formidable of defensive positions. By war's end, the Canadian Corps had fully earned their reputation as shock troops. And though the corps made up only about one twentieth of the entire BEF before Vimy (although one fifteenth of the fighting divisions), here, and later, they always hit above their weight.[19]

For those Canadians at the sharp end, Vimy was a bittersweet victory, recognized as important at the time but also as a trophy that had been won at a heavy cost. Sergeant Percy Willmot, who fought at Vimy until wounded in the leg, and who later died of complications from his wound, recounted his experience of the battle emotionally to his cousin: "As the guns spoke, over the bags they went, men of C.B. [Cape Breton] sons of NS [Nova Scotia] & NB [New Brunswick]—FC's [French Canadians] and westerners—all Canucks…. So far it was the most decisive, the most spectacular and the most important victory on this front since the Marne and Canada may well be proud of the achievement."[20] Samuel Honey, who was promoted from the ranks and would be awarded a chest full of medals, told his parents, "I came through the thickest of it unscratched. Perhaps, at some future time, I may be able to tell of some of the things I saw and how I felt, but not now."[21] Words also seemed inadequate to describe the postbattle task of brothers Fred and Lewis Campbell, both from the 58th Battalion, who, despite their exhaustion, trudged over the battlefield, turning over corpse after corpse, looking for one another.[22] Their relief at finding each other safe must have been staggering.

Canada, of course, was not born at Vimy, and had been a country for fifty years. But nations, and especially young ones, need symbols. The victory at Vimy had been achieved by all four Canadian divisions, which drew men from across the country. It had been accomplished against what many considered to be nearly insurmountable odds—and while the stronger British and French forces had failed on the flanks. This failure alone has appealed to many Canadian nationalists, wallowing over the decades in feelings of colonial inferiority to the parent countries. Vimy was a success that Canada could call its own, even though many of the gunners, logistical units, and even an infantry brigade were British. But in the nation's memory, Vimy is actively constructed as a Canadian battle; it remains an important symbolic signpost in Canadian history—and it should be. It was the first major Allied victory of the war on the Western Front, in which the Canadians captured more ground, more prisoners, and more guns than any previous operation, all of which had been done against the heaviest of odds.

But again it is worth returning to the poor bloody infantry, who had been called on and succeeded in delivering victory. On Vimy, they could look out over the green acres of the Douai plain beyond, relatively untouched by war. Behind them lay the wastage of battle. Ahead was victory, but only after another twenty months of grinding, attritional warfare. To men who lacked the gift of seeing into the future, even from their victorious position atop Vimy Ridge the war looked as if it might go on for twenty more years.

CHAPTER 10

"DO YOUR DUTY AND FIGHT TO THE FINISH"

The Battles of Arleux and Fresnoy, April 28 to May 8, 1917

"This is getting to be an awful war, I'm beginning to fear that it is going to last longer than even I had figured on still a lot can happen yet befor[e] next Oct, by the time this war is past History, it will be different than other war[s], instead of asking [a] cripple how he got it, they'll ask a sound man when they see one, how he missed it."[1] Such was the heartfelt and despondent observation John Macfie expressed to his sister after recovering from a wound suffered at Vimy. He would lose one nineteen-year-old brother in the war, but his other sibling, Roy, survived.

From the heights of Vimy Ridge, the Canadians surveyed the German forces on the Douai plain. Through the use of binoculars and quick instructions to gunners in the rear who were employing the same map grid references, the Canadian forward observers directed the fall of artillery shells that pounded the enemy front lines laid out before them. The Germans retreated to the east and established a new trench system, organized in depth, with outposts and first and second lines of defence to absorb and dissipate further offensives. The German defenders at Vimy had been unable to do this, but now they were holding a looser front, largely based on machine-gun strongpoints. The new German doctrine afforded more flexibility to the soldiers at the front; in Ludendorff's words, no longer must the infantryman tell himself, "Here I must stand or fall."[2] Standing firm in places and yielding in others, the infantry had more authority to fight their own battles in response to the circumstances at the front.

Just as the Allies were decentralizing their command-and-control structure, so too were the Germans. They were also thinning out the front lines, creating fewer targets for the now crushing artillery bombardments that preceded and accompanied all Allied operations. This forward outpost line—in fact, a series of trenches and connected shell hole defences—could be sacrificed, but only after making the attackers pay for their massed attacks. Upon giving over this ground to the attackers, counterattacking forces would push back, behind artillery barrages that pounded the lost lines but also masked the front, thereby cutting off the now weakened attackers-turned-defenders from reinforcements and supplies, as they struggled against the rising tide of German attacks. Because these counterattacking forces were often 5 or 6 kilometres behind the lines, the defenders had some time to prepare for the onslaught and soon also learned to organize killing artillery bombardments or chemical barrages to reduce the enemy's hitting power. The see-saw of battles continued over the wasteland of farmers' fields now tilled with thousands of tons of steel.

With the Germans out of range of the Canadian guns, which negated the advantage of attacking from atop Vimy, Byng's corps fortified and wired their positions. New reinforcements were integrated into the now ragged units. "I had several narrow escapes but thank God I'm yet safe," wrote Private John Ellis of the 2nd Battalion to his dear wife in the aftermath of the battle. "I do hope & pray it will soon be all over as I don't want to see anything like it again."[3] It would soon be over for Ellis, who would be killed within a month of writing that post-Vimy letter.

AROUND MID-APRIL, lead Canadian units edged their way down the eastern slope of Vimy, passing over the now shattered road systems and through heavy clouds of chemical agents. The Germans fired thousands of gas shells to harass the Canadians, but also against the essential horses and mules that were straining to pull the heavy guns over the mulched land. "Horses sank up to their bellies in the soft ground," recounted twenty-seven-year-old Courtney Tower from Arabella, Saskatchewan, who was bringing up supplies to the front lines.[4] E.P.S. Allen was an officer with the 116th Battalion, the newest unit to be added to the Canadian Corps' order of battle when it replaced the 60th Battalion, which had been so badly cut up after the Somme that it had to be disbanded. Allen recounted the conditions under which his formation carried out their labour: "Every variety of 'hate,' large and small ... was thrown at that road blocked with mule transports, guns, ambulances, and working parties."[5] It was slow progress, and Byng was forced to devote thousands of men every night to rebuilding the logistical lines.

As ever, though, the Canadian infantry were out in front of the army, patrolling in darkness, probing enemy lines for weaknesses. Dozens of minor, chaotic night battles took place as the Canadians slowly snuffed out the forward outposts. During this advance, which included all four Canadian divisions, it was gratifying for the Canadians to march past abandoned guns and charred stockpiles of ammunition that had been left behind in the German haste to evacuate the front. Thousands of shells had not been damaged, however, and the Canadian gunners, as they had at Vimy, turned captured German pieces against their former owners, bombarding the enemy lines with their own shells. During the next two weeks, no large-scale operations were carried out, but the Canadians continued to move forward, aware that they would soon run into German resistance.

General Haig ordered another phase in the Arras offensive, which would become the Second Battle of the Scarpe on April 23, 1917. The Canadians, however, did not take part in that attack. In five days of harsh fighting, The British Third Army advanced on a front of some 13.7 kilometres, and drove over 2 kilometres into enemy lines, but much of this progress was through the lightly held outpost zone. Cut up here by long-range fire, British forces were stopped by massed barbed wire within the main battle zone that had not been cleared by shellfire. A lack of attention to detail pervaded the command and staff of the Third Army, and clearly the forward divisions, which when patrolling the front, either did not recognize the danger, did not have the courage to ask for more time for the wire to be cut, or were ignored by their superiors. Often it was a combination of all three. The British attacks were costly failures that resulted in another 10,000 casualties.[6]

In accordance with his policy of wearing out the enemy, Haig ordered a new phase of the offensive for April 28, pushing forward in the hope of redeeming some victory in the wake of the now floundering Nivelle offensive.[7] The Canadians would take part in a limited four-battalion attack against Arleux-en-Gohelle, which was 1,000 metres to the west of Fresnoy. The positions of Fresnoy and Arleux were well protected by barbed wire, reverse slope trenches, and strongpoints buried and camouflaged within the villages. The killing ground over which the Canadians would have to approach was flat and devoid of much natural cover, and the attackers would find no easy way to advance on the enemy stronghold that was held by the 111th Infantry Division.

Brigadier Frederick Loomis, one of Currie's trusted officers and friends, would lead the attack with three battalions from his 2nd Brigade. The 8th, 10th, and 5th Battalions would assault the trench system, supported by the 25th Battalion to the far north. The narrow front was only 2,400 metres, but it still presented a challenge for only four battalions. Each battalion was to attack with three companies forward; a company consisted of two or three of the available platoons, each of which was about thirty-five to forty men strong. This meant that each platoon had a 140-metre width of front to cover, and needed to push forward to a depth of between 900 and 1,200 metres. It was a lot of terrain to overrun, with the rolling nature of the ground and the thousands of craters that pitted the area offering many places for German defenders to find coverage.

Training in rain and ever-present tendrils of poison gas, Loomis's brigade had rehearsed offensive operations during the week before the battle. As at Vimy, the attackers practised advancing behind a creeping barrage, which would steamroll over the enemy lines. One hundred and eight field guns, howitzers, and siege guns, as well as another forty-six heavy machine guns, would support the infantry.[8] The siege batteries fired some 4,437 rounds on a 1,300-metre front located just before the village.[9] With the bombardment came a creeping barrage, but the limited nature of the objectives meant it would make only two lifts before landing on Arleux, so the infantry would have to cross the battlefield in six minutes or be left without this protective wall. Barbed wire and machine-gun nests were expected to slow the advance, but no one knew by how much time. However, reports a day before the operation noted worriedly that wire remained in many sectors, and appeared to be "a very serious obstacle."[10]

Equally troubling was the recognition that German counterattacking forces in Fresnoy would be almost immediately unleashed against the weary Canadians should they capture Arleux. German doctrine declared, "The defence in a battle is to cause the attacking force to fight itself to a standstill and use up its resources of men, while the defenders conserve their own strength."[11] Through the application of firepower, the attackers would be worn down in the initial assault and during the consolidation phase. Then a rapid counterattack would drive through the attackers-turned-defenders, routing them, and recapturing the lost territory.

To protect against this, an elaborate Canadian artillery plan called for divisional and corps guns to assist both in the creeping barrage and in defeating the counter-attack. Interdictory fire would fall between the two villages, thereby creating a devastating wall of shells and machine-gun bullets. While there were not enough shells to fire for long because of logistical constraints and temporary shell shortages, the barrage would buy precious time for the Canadians to dig in and reverse the trenches (by building new parapets on the back walls) in order to engage enemy counterattacking forces.[12] Lewis guns would provide the first line of defence, as would heavier Vickers machine guns and mortars that could saturate the battle zone with fire. Sacrificial forward outposts were to be established to slow enemy attacks. If the infantry were to survive in their isolated trenches, they needed to be self-sufficient battle groups, as the German counter-barrage would likely trap them in the wrecked, captured trenches for hours. The 8th Battalion alone hauled some 40,000 rounds of ammunition, 140 boxes of No. 5 Mills bombs, and 184 boxes of Stokes mortar rounds into forward ammunition dumps, which would be carried further ahead by succeeding waves of troops.[13] As preparation went ahead for the battle, and the artillery was finalizing complicated fireplans, the Canadians were lacking good intelligence on the enemy. Aerial photographs seemed to indicate the existence of fortified cellars and deep trenches, but the one bit of solid information they had was that the Germans were "holding the front with an unusually large number of machine guns."[14]

THE ASSAULT TROOPS moved into the line on April 26. It wasn't much of a line, however. The forward units had dug like demons every night to expand shell craters

THE BATTLE OF ARLEUX: APRIL 28, 1917

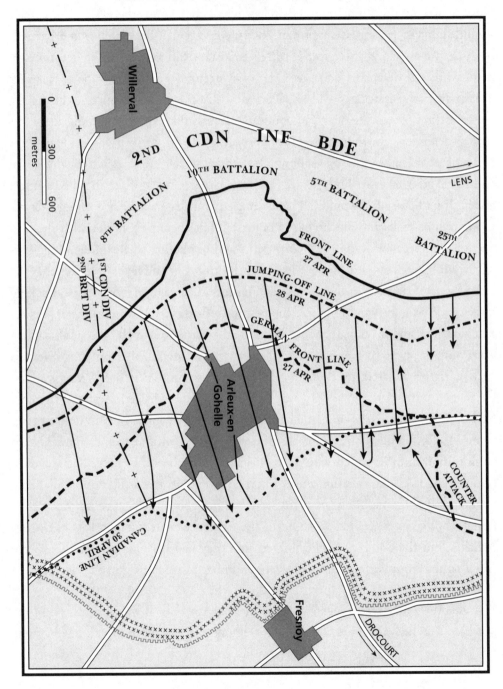

into slit trenches and then, finally, into a rough and shallow trench, but the result was nothing like the semi-permanent trenches of the previous three years. Fortunately, the spearhead troops did not plan to stay there long. They needed to cross No Man's Land quickly in order to avoid the enemy counter-barrage, and all three battalions began digging new assembly positions that ate forward into No Man's Land, in order to close the distance with Arleux. At two feet wide and three feet deep, these jumping-off trenches offered only temporary protection and left their occupants vulnerable to shellfire. But by the end of the second night, in time for the predawn kickoff on April 28, the 10th Battalion had moved to within 200 metres of the German front line; the 8th Battalion, which had further to go, pushed their jumping-off trench to within 500 metres of their objectives. Isolated and hugging the dirt, forward units were dangerously close to the creeping barrage, which would rain down 100 metres in front of the enemy trench. But every metre taken before the battle meant one fewer that had to be captured while German MG-08s swept the killing zone.

The Little Black Devils, as the men of the 8th Battalion called themselves, put three companies forward: C, B, and D, arranged from left to right. Each had some 500 metres of battlefield to cover. They crept into the line under cover of darkness at 11 P.M., and were ready in their jumping-off positions an hour before the barrage. Then they stared into the abyss and waited for "the stunt" to begin.

When the barrage went off at 4:25 A.M. in a crash of fire and smoke, the Canadians surged forward. Eyes that had been straining into the darkness were dazzled by the lightning fire dropping down with a nearly continuous rumble. As in a firestorm tearing through a dry forest, the air was supercharged, heated, and swirling. The shellfire tore up the enemy lines and was reported by the 8th Battalion as being "quite satisfactory," but in comparison to the Vimy barrage, the "intensity was very disappointing."[15] The 1st Brigade advanced, bayonets at the ready. Despite the barrage that obscured the world of darkness on the near horizon, dozens of Canadians were caught by sweeping machine-gun fire as they marched over a low rise that the Germans had established as a perfect killing ground. The Canadians regrouped and pushed on behind their own firepower.

Fuelled by adrenaline, fear, and bravery, the Fighting Tenth, to the north of the Little Black Devils, pushed through outpost positions and then into Arleux. Rifle and Lewis-gun fire pinned down German strongpoints, while grenadiers tossed lethal bombs. Holes were blown in the German line, and then the troops infiltrated through, pushing deeper, allowing secondary forces to mop up nests that refused to surrender. As the 8th Battalion tended to its sector in the southern part of the village, the 10th did the same in the north, moving from house to house, clearing the enemy who resolutely held his ground. In the northwest corner of the village, two German machine-gun crews survived the barrage and held out against several attacks. Private Frank McMackin, a twenty-year-old farmer from Moncton, New Brunswick, finally grabbed a Lewis gun that had been dropped when its owner had been shot. McMackin fired pan after pan of ammunition in a machine-gun duel with the Germans. When the Lewis gun jammed, he grabbed a rifle and kept firing, buying enough time for flanking units to get close enough to bomb the German crews to death. McMackin would be awarded the Military Medal for his bravery.[16]

The battles were chaotic, but this worked in favour of the Canadians, who were actually outnumbered but were able to concentrate their force at key spots. The Germans did not know where the attackers were coming from, and how many of them were swarming in the rubble-filled streets. Soon, German morale crumbled under the assault, and their forces were streaming from Arleux a little before 6 A.M. Canadian outposts were established, and officers moved from one exposed position to the next in an attempt to ensure that flanks were covered and all parts of the ground swept by fire. Harsh orders noted that SOS barrages might catch some of the Canadians in the forward outpost zone, but that their sacrifice was for the greater good of the operation.[17] Those Canadians in the forward sacrificial posts— where their role was to slow the enemy and take a toll on him, but where they would also surely be overrun by any large-scale attack—knew that their only hope of survival in the expected intense fighting to come was to dig down and become temporarily one with the earth, to avoid becoming permanently one with it.

BEHIND THE NEW OUTPOST DEFENCE, the wounded crawled to the rear, passed by reinforcements moving forward, who were often weighed down like bent-over Christmas trees, with bombs, sandbags, and ammunition hanging off their straps and webbing. Stretcher-bearers worked miracles, binding wounds, offering morphine and an encouraging word. German prisoners were conscripted to carry men; they obliged, knowing that they would have a greater chance of surviving the harrowing trip to the rear, especially as they weaved around the nervous follow-on forces, which would be readying themselves to confront the Germans in the smoke, haze, and confusion of the battlefield. Of the 10th Battalion's 301 casualties, 103 were killed (numbers roughly equal to those for the 5th and 8th Battalions). The dead lay sprawled where they fell, or wherever they crawled to perish.[18] Some died quickly; others lingered in agony, writhing in pain from gut wounds or shattered femurs. After the battle, burial parties searched for the fallen, removing identity discs and personal effects. Bodies and body parts were collected and buried in shallow graves, with a sprinkling of quicklime added to deaden the smell and prevent disease. Later, they would be disinterred and moved to proper cemeteries. Now, however, it made for grim work, often carried out by exhausted men, but few complained. These men had been friends and companions.

The brigade headquarters had little idea as to the success of the operation along the three-battalion front, but at 5:15 A.M., German SOS rockets indicated that their forces were retreating through their own barrage, and an hour later most of the Canadian battalions reported being on their objectives. Supporting parties from the 7th Battalion were released to brave the storm of fire, carrying essential ammunition, water, and rum into the lines to ensure that the now ragged attacking battalions could hold the front. It is surprising that Brigadier Loomis did not wish to bring reinforcements into the line, but perhaps the narrow frontage precluded this overloading, which would only have created more targets for German shells, especially during daylight hours. Runners, wireless communication, pigeons, and telephone lines (when they were not cut) soon kept him apprised of the unfolding battle.

The 8th and 10th Battalions' fronts received no German counterattacks. All through the night, flares were fired from the Canadian lines, their ghostly radiance lighting the battlefield, floating downward with a hiss before snuffing out and returning the front to darkness. A few jittery but alert sentries thought they saw the enemy forming up in the Fresnoy woods, but sudden and heavy SOS retaliatory fire from the Canadian guns silenced these operations, whether real or imaginary.[19] And despite the absence of enemy attacks, machine-gun batteries laid down harassing interdictory fire all night on identified roads and crossroads.[20]

On the 5th Battalion's front, the Germans massed for a counterattack at 8:30 P.M., and again at 4 A.M. on April 29. Both attacks were spotted by the Canadian sentries, who fired SOS flares; the Canadian gunners responded, deluging the enemy's front and destroying both forces before they had a chance to attack. The 5th Battalion pulled back their line on the left, where the Germans had set up several machine guns, and the divisional guns bombarded the front with high explosives.[21] Having softened up the German defences, the 25th Battalion, on the far left, attacked and captured the position that they had failed to seize earlier in the day. With Canadian firepower poised to be unleashed on additional counterattacks, the German divisional commander of the 111th Division cancelled further attempts to retake Arleux. His three battalions in the line had been severely mauled, with the front-line battalion of the 73rd Regiment reporting more than 400 missing and countless more wounded.[22] The Germans surveyed the battlefield and pulled their line back to Fresnoy.

THE CANADIANS HAD ACHIEVED success in an otherwise dismal offensive. Most of the British divisions involved on April 28 had been shot to pieces. A sombre observation by the 34th British Division concluded that, unlike in the offensive on April 9, the troops had not been afforded sufficient time to prepare for the battle. Green troops had replaced combat veterans knocked out in previous fighting, and their inexperience led to confusion on the battlefield, especially in the assessment of enemy strongpoints.[23] Other British divisions suffered similar challenges. The set-piece battle of April 9 had offered success but had failed to move from the break-in to the breakout phase of fighting, eventually grinding to a halt under the weight of German fire and a stiffening defence. Two and half weeks later, with the Germans aware of the Allied offensive, the

British army's new phase of battle had been shattered in a firestorm.

In contrast, the Canadian Corps had regrouped and absorbed the terrible blood-letting from Vimy. New men had been integrated into the efficient system, and the sharp-end units, ably supported by their gunner and machine-gunner comrades, seem to have suffered little degradation to their striking power. After the Vimy victory, the hard-fought success at Arleux further cemented the Canadians' reputation as shock troops. The British official historian, Cyril Falls, wrote that the Arleux battle "was only a local success, but at this stage of the battle even local successes were hard enough to win, and it must be accounted a fine feat of arms."[24] A proud General Currie described how one captured German officer had thought the Canadians "must be a special assaulting division—they wouldn't believe that we are the same division which put them off Vimy Ridge and are still at it."[25] And though the Arleux operation had cost them 1,255 casualties, for a successful Great War operation this was a seemingly acceptable blood sacrifice—from the high command's perspective, of course.[26]

Sir Douglas Haig felt compelled to keep pushing the Arras offensive, despite the apparent failure of his own forces and that of the French to the south. Any reduction of pressure on the Western Front, he believed, would allow the Germans to prepare plans against the Russians or Italians, as well as the French, who were in a desperate situation with their mutinies. The wearing-out battles had to go on, to ensure that the Allied coalition was not smashed. While Haig continued to plan for an offensive in the Flanders region, which he would indeed launch in the summer, he ordered another offensive against Oppy-Méricourt and Fresnes-Boiry, which were parts of the fortified Drocourt-Quéant Line. These engagements were known, for the First and Third Armies, as the Third Battle of the Scarpe, and for the Fifth Army, as the Battle of Bullecourt. Despite these grandiose names, the offensive had few objectives other than the goal of straightening the line, and Haig ordered three armies to attack on a front of 22 kilometres.

As part of this large offensive, Sir Julian Byng's corps was ordered to capture the hamlet of Fresnoy, which had become an important anchor on the German Oppy-Méricourt Line. Fresnoy had remained largely undamaged during the recent fighting, and its red-roofed houses were a beacon to the Canadians who were dug in around the now ruined village of Arleux. The objectives ranged from a mere 500 to 700 metres away, but the enemy had laid rows of barbed wire and fortified numerous strongpoints along the front. The entire position was defended by the 25th Reserve Regiment, and dominated by German guns that swept the front from their high ground to the northeast.

Byng ordered the 1st Brigade to lead the main assault, supported by two battalions of the 6th Brigade that would provide a strong flank attack to the north. With the Canadians clearly massing for an assault, and with patrols more active at night, there would be no surprise—a situation that prevailed all along the British line. In the hope of supporting the infantry at the sharp end, Haig's headquarters ordered a dangerous night operation, which pleased few of the generals. It suited the situation on the Canadian front, however, where the attack was on a limited objective. The Canadians did not have far to go, and if they could get there under an almost full moon, lives would be saved. More important, Byng had the luxury of pulling together not only the 1st and 2nd Divisions' guns, but also the 3rd Division's, the corps' heavy guns, and additional British artillery formations. Although the planning was rushed, Byng refused to let his Canadians attack without a screen of protective fire.

Brigadier William Griesbach would coordinate the attack. His 2nd Battalion would drive through Fresnoy, with the 1st and 3rd Battalions on the flank. In the days before the assault, he ordered that practice trenches be built to give the troops an opportunity to move over ground similar to what they would encounter on the battlefield. The rushed operation allowed only a few practice runs, but it offered important guidance to the men who would soon be doing this with earth-shattering explosions erupting all around them, in terrain where the ground would be rearranged by the weight of shellfire.

The main problem the Canadians faced was the building of their jumping-off trenches. The Germans knew where the attackers' front line was located, so it would be pulverized within minutes of the Canadian barrage opening, which signalled their assault. While the Canadians had been successful in pushing their jumping-off trenches deep into No Man's Land for the Arleux operation, they found this nearly impossible to do now because a full moon left the front lit up

THE BATTLE OF FRESNOY: MAY 3, 1917

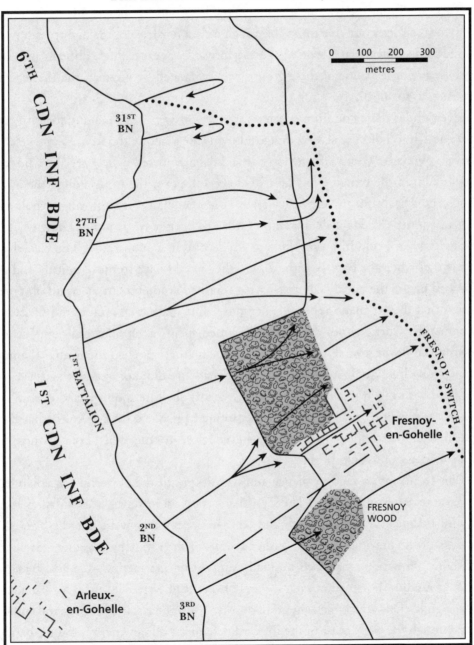

6TH CDN INF BDE

31ST BN

27TH BN

1ST BATTALION

1ST CDN INF BDE

2ND BN

3RD BN

Arleux-en-Gohelle

0   100   200   300
metres

FRESNOY SWITCH

Fresnoy-en-Gohelle

FRESNOY WOOD

almost as if it were daytime. As well, the hard, solid chalk that made up the ground between the front lines was nearly impenetrable, leaving desperate infantrymen digging for their lives but able to push through only a few feet. In the nights leading up to the battle, moving large working parties forward was exceedingly difficult and dangerous, and at least one of these groups was decimated by German fire that caught the men in the open.

Even under these conditions, some jumping-off trenches were dug forward, but not enough to hold the several thousand men spread along the front. Vimy veteran Private William Woods of the 1st Battalion remembered a new recruit who was beside him in the trench a few hours before going over the top. Though the battle would be a "baptism in very heavy style," the new man was surprisingly cool, asking a bemused Woods if the battalion "attacked every day! 'I do not know what he thought when I told him that this was my second in 7 months.'"[27] The Canadians knew that when the barrage came down, they would have to move quickly and get forward before the enemy counter-barrage crashed among them. Forward observers noted that the Germans appeared "nervous," anticipating an attack, and divisional commander Currie wrote that he and his men spent "a very anxious night" as the enemy laid down several artillery bombardments that searched the front.[28] Though their front lines took a pounding, the Canadians did not reveal themselves or respond with much retaliatory fire, so the enemy shellfire soon quieted down. The Germans remained on high alert, and captured prisoners later revealed that their intelligence had anticipated the day—even close to the exact hour—when the Canadian assault would begin.[29]

The front was covered in silence and darkness until the powerful Canadian barrage came down at 3:45 A.M. The Canadians attacked in waves, with infantry companies rushing forward to catch the barrage. The waves were not the rigid line attacks of the previous year, but rather groups of men moving together, advancing in looser formations that used mutually supporting fire tactics—the goal being to gain ground in short rushes even if parts of the front were held up. The Canadians made good their attack, getting away quickly from their start trenches and punching through the weak crust of the forward defenders, but an enemy counter-barrage fell behind the Canadian lines within a minute of their guns opening up. This cut the first-wave units off from their reinforcements, although it was a stationary bombardment and did not sweep through the Canadians moving forward and exposed in No Man's Land. There would be no retreat and no chance to receive reinforcements for several hours.

The village of Fresnoy was easily located as the Canadians used the burning Fresnoy Wood to the south as a beacon. But the attackers had to move quickly. The lead companies had 120 seconds to cross 90 metres, after which the barrage would jump to the next position, resting there for six minutes. Although the Germans had laid down a heavy concentration of machine-gun fire, the darkness offered cover to the Canadians, even when many platoons were forced to mill about in the wire, desperately searching for gaps. Attesting to the men's desire to get out of the kill zone, the second and third waves bunched up, creating some confusion as units became mixed up with each other. Nothing was neat under fire. Within the darkness, dust, and enemy fire, section leaders were the catalysts on the battlefield: "It was only because of the fact that NCOs handled their sections in a cool manner that the opposition was finally disposed of," testified Brigadier Griesbach.[30] Despite a gap that formed between the 1st and 6th Brigades to the north, which the Germans exploited by sending forward machine-gunners, Fresnoy fell to the Canadians after a few hours of heavy fighting.

MAJOR KARL WEATHERBE of the 6th Field Company, Canadian Engineers, who was coordinating wiring parties to help consolidate the position, observed, "Walking cases reported desperate resistance on the enemy's part and much uncut wire…. It was evident our advance was stubbornly contested."[31] Although they lost the village and surrounding area, the Germans made two determined counterattacks during the daylight hours of May 3. The first was broken up by SOS artillery fire, the second, launched by elements of the 4th Guard Division and 185th Infantry Division, was stopped cold by Canadian riflemen and machine-gunners firing from a distance of 400 metres. The 1st Brigade's after-battle report noted, "the Lewis gun was the most valuable weapon in the front lines."[32] The machine-gunners were especially useful since the artillery fire was erratic and several guns were firing short, and shells as large as 9.2 inches fell into the Canadian lines all day long. But the front was held, despite the bombardment coming from both sides. Captain Edouard Leprohen of the 22nd Battalion, then in a support position to the north of the line, recounted in his diary: "Shelled all day by the Hun. No one in the BN [battalion] has been under worse fire."[33] Leprohen had not experienced the Somme, but there was no doubt that the enemy shellfire at Fresnoy was intense.

The Canadian attack bit deep into enemy lines but left both flanks in the air. Runners carrying water, rum, rations, and ammunition braved the interdiction fire. This support was essential to holding the front: the spear was there, but the shaft was needed to drive it home. Private William Woods remembered the agony of thirst as he and his surviving mates held the trenches under a heavy bombardment with no drinking water. Two underage boys, who had been pulled out of the line before the battle because of their age, were taken back to battalion headquarters, but someone had ordered them forward through the barrage to carry water to the lead troops. Woods remembered seeing one of the boys coming from the rear through a

Canadians in a support trench near Arleux. This support trench has only recently been dug, as it contains no sandbags and does not appear to have a connecting communication trench leading to the rear. These trenches, manned by Canadian infantrymen, were essential in holding back the German counterattack during the battle.

haze of smoke, poison gas, and shrapnel, stumbling over the broken ground with two cans of water slung over his shoulder.[34] The crying boy told Woods that his friend had been killed on the way in. Though food, water, and rum were essential for morale, many casualties were incurred in the transport of these supplies forward over the open ground. In the opposite direction, prisoners and walking wounded moved to the rear, and many were killed in the indiscriminate firestorm. If they survived, they were stopped and questioned, often providing essential information as to enemy locations and where SOS artillery fire might be allocated. Throughout the day, Currie pushed forward several machine-gun units to assist in holding the front.

The Canadians had suffered 1,259 casualties in taking and holding Fresnoy, with 1,080 of them coming from the 1st Brigade alone. But the Germans admitted to at least that many, and 500 of their men had been taken prisoner.[35] "Our boys gained their objective," wrote Gunner Bert Walker, who operated a gun in support of the infantry, "but they paid pretty dearly for it."[36] However, the battle was not yet over. The Germans would not relinquish the key position without a fight, and over the next few days they deluged the Canadian lines with an enormous weight of fire. At least 100,000 shells rained down, and the Canadian Corps' gunners were overwhelmed since the barrage had a high composition of poison gas. Gunner Wilfred Kerr remembered the German artillery retaliation that was directed on "our poor infantry, chiefly in the form of shrapnel bursts high in the air which seemed in the distance like a thick cloud of flies."[37] Gagging and choking in the gas barrage, the defenders dug in and waited for an attack as shrapnel whirled around them, embedding in flesh or sizzling red hot in the slushy mud.

Private Donald Fraser, a machine-gunner with the 31st Battalion on the northern flank, recounted how one German gun was perfectly ranged on their trench system. All day long, the cursed gunners fired shells, moving up and down the trench. It was so methodical that the infantry could predict the fire, with sections of men bunching up and running down the trenches, trying to stay ahead of the artillery fire. It made for a chaotic, terrifying situation. "We were completely at the mercy of the artillery.... The suspense was unnerving," wrote Fraser.[38] Adding to the terror were the swooping enemy aircraft that bombed the trenches and village and then raked the front with machine-gun fire.

Despite mounting casualties, the Canadians would not break. The tension was agonizing, however, and Private Deward Barnes of the 19th Battalion, experiencing his first battle, responded in his diary, "my eyes must have been half out of my head from excitement."[39] After days of heavy fire, and in a drenching rainstorm, the Germans launched an attack at 4 A.M. on May 8. Despite the jamming of many mud-clogged rifles and Lewis guns, the dug-in Canadian infantrymen fired directly into the enemy attack. Hundreds were cut down, but the Germans made it to the Canadian trenches, where desperate infantrymen engaged in fierce hand-to-hand combat. Barnes remembered his officer telling his now depleted section, "Boys, we are done, do your duty and fight to the finish."[40] This they did, and even though Germans overran their trenches, they kept fighting. The bodies began to pile up, but by the end of the day, the Germans were driven back to their lines.

In the village of Fresnoy, however, the 1st Brigade had already handed the position over to British troops and moved into reserve. Under the overwhelming weight of fire and fighting forces, the understrength British garrison was overcome and nearly annihilated to a man. Even though the British were aware of an impending attack—as the enemy build-up in guns, shells, and troops was impossible to misconstrue—poor planning and confusion in the British high command resulted in a delay in unleashing a counterattack that, if mounted immediately, might have knocked the three German regiments from the 5th Bavarian Division out of the village and surrounding area. Instead, the Germans had a day to prepare for the counterattack, and when the British operation was ordered at 2:30 A.M. on May 9, the assault floundered in confusion and heavy enemy defensive fire. Fresnoy was lost, and the front was pulled back to the east of Arleux.

It was a hard blow to the British troops, who appeared to have folded where the Canadians had stood strong. This assessment was unfair, though, considering the weight of fire the Germans had brought to bear on the position, but the confusion in the divisional high command was inexcusable. This disorder proved again that while the Canadians and British had both benefited from the lessons of the Somme and the recasting of the attack doctrine in the winter of 1916–1917, the lessons had not been processed evenly throughout the BEF. With victories at Vimy, Arleux, and now Fresnoy under their belts, the Canadians had more than proven that they were elite troops. Sir Henry Horne, commander of the British First Army, cabled to Currie after the battle that his 1st Division was "the pride and wonder of the British Army."[41]

Yet the Canadian Corps had been savagely cut up during the first five months of trench warfare in 1917 and especially in the three big battles at Vimy, Arleux, and Fresnoy. A shocking total of 9,904 had been killed, 135 made prisoners of war, and another 17,187 wounded. Almost all of these casualties had been sustained by the infantry: some 27,000 out of the approximately 45,000 infantrymen in the forty-eight fighting battalions had been lost.[42] The harsh nature of the fighting also resulted in the deaths-to-wounded ratio being far higher and more costly than in previous battles. The infantry had suffered more than fifty percent of their total casualties since the beginning of 1917. It would be hard to replace these men. Combat veterans who had, to use the American Civil War phrase, "seen the elephant" for over two years, were wearing out. And back in Canada, the number of enlistees had dwindled away to almost none.

Coming on the heels of Vimy, the Arleux and Fresnoy operations had reinforced the value of Byng's set-piece battles composed of limited attacks. Major General Arthur Currie declared, "The greatest lesson to be learned from these operations is this: if the lessons of the War have been thoroughly mastered, if the Artillery preparation and support is good; if our Intelligence is properly appreciated; there is no position that cannot be wrestled from the enemy by well-disciplined, well-trained and well-led troops attacking on a sound plan."[43] He was right, and though the British had troops equally as tough as the Canadians, their failures in battle can be attributed to a lack of adequate preparation. This emphasis on preparation became the hallmark of the Canadian Corps' approach to battle. It created a framework to assist the infantry in conquering the enemy by ensuring the proper marshalling of artillery and logistical support, but it did not lock the infantry into a straitjacket. No preconceived plan survived contact with the enemy, and the Canadians understood this. While the infantry would have the support they needed, often they had to figure out how to fight their way forward when they were staring down the muzzles of Maxim machine guns. Despite the victory at Fresnoy, Lieutenant Stanley Edgett was right to note on May 8, 1917, that the "Hun is putting up a tough fight here." He joked to his brother, "It looks like another winter in the trenches unless I get a nice wound, or contract some contagious disease."[44] Edgett would remain on the Western Front forever. He was killed by a shell two days after writing this last letter home.

HAIG SHOULD HAVE BEEN dismayed by the limited gains and terrible losses suffered by his forces during the Arras offensive and its aftermath, but instead he resolutely relied on divine providence and saw the way forward by launching bigger and heavier attacks. But not on this front. Haig abandoned the Arras sector, which returned to a condition of static warfare, and turned his sights towards the Flanders region around Passchendaele. The attacks there would prove far more costly, equally fruitless, and would nearly destroy the morale of the stoic British Tommy.

CHAPTER 11

"GOOD TO BE BACK IN CIVILIZATION"

Blighty, the Temporary Respite

"I never looked forward to a holiday so eagerly in my life," wrote Sergeant George Ormsby to his wife. "The chance even for a week will make a new man of me."[1] Private Charles Pearce observed to his father that the men talked constantly of leave, and when they got it, they swore they would "go crazy" in the big city. He, too, had "an awful sick feeling" of growing anticipation, as he yearned to be away from the front. In case his father thought he might celebrate too much, however, Pearce promised that he would stay with relatives.[2] But the holidays were few and far between. One trench newspaper produced by the soldiers satirized the policy of leave:

> Privates pray for one
> Corporals crawl for one
> Sergeants scheme for one
> Officers often get one.[3]

Officers received roughly four leave passes a year, in comparison to only one for an enlisted man, which allowed for a mere ten to fourteen days. It was a constant bone of contention between the ranks and officers.

When leave came through, it was like Christmas. A master list was kept by the soldiers' headquarters unit, and a steady trickle of men were given their leave throughout the year. But there were a lot of men in a battalion, and a soldier's turn

Returning from "up the line," these mud-splattered and exhausted Canadian infantrymen have earned their temporary rest in the rear area. The soldier in the centre manages a smile for the camera, while the rest of his comrades have little time for the official photographer.

usually did not come up before he had served at least a year at the front. As casualties removed names from the list, long-service veterans moved closer to the top. If a battalion was close to full strength, more men could go on leave; if it was weakened or to be used in a forthcoming battle, the leave passes dried up, or even stopped entirely, as was the case in the summer of 1916, prior to the Somme. Collective enforcement of discipline against a battalion could result in a stoppage of leave. This much-reviled punishment was found to be effective in combating the epidemic of trench foot over the winter months, and it impelled men to keep an eye on their comrades in the platoon or section. Individually, those who had committed offences dropped to the bottom of the list. So important was leave from the front that men risked their lives for it. It was not uncommon for a commanding officer to offer leave as a reward for pulling off a dangerous trench raid. The leave policy was a complex part of the informal hierarchy of power that reinforced officers' ability to command.

The desperation of waiting for leave plagued all men. Superstitions sprang up around the lists: "I had been first on the Battery leave list ever since all leaves were cancelled last March," remembered nineteen-year-old William Ogilvie. "It is not an enviable spot to be in. There was a superstition among the troops that it was bad luck to be first on the leave list for too long. Too many soldiers about to go on leave had been killed and while everyone craved their leave, no one relished being first for very long before they could get away. It seemed like tempting fate."[4] Other stories— likely apocryphal, although recounted with relish, and always when a man who was going on leave was within earshot—told of unlucky soldiers getting their leave and being killed on the way to the rear or while packing their gear. Whether the tales were true or not, most soldiers did not waste time at the front when their ticket was punched. Close friends might wish the departing man best of luck, or perhaps ask him to look up a relative for them, while others only looked on with sullen jealousy.

At headquarters, a soldier received his pay—and sometimes even a new uniform, depending on the rags he wore. Most men handed over their rifles but kept their haversacks and respirators. The required forms and passes were filled out and carefully tucked away, and a medical exam was performed to ensure that the soldier carried no communicable diseases. A final shower at the baths helped to wipe away some of the war grime. Then it was a train ride to the coast, where the men were greeted by the inevitable questions and examinations by military police looking for deserters or contraband material such as ammunition, bombs, or uncensored letters. The first two of these were usually left behind, but the last were smuggled for mates in the field, and posted on civilian ground to avoid tampering by military censors.

SINCE THE CANADIANS had strong links to England, Scotland, or Ireland through blood or culture, most soldiers spent their leave there. The United Kingdom was known as "Blighty," soldiers' slang derived from the Hindustani word for "home." For those without family ties, "There was one magnet, and one only—London," wrote Captain George Gibson.[5] "It was the largest, the best, the wickedest, the most beautiful and the ugliest city that many of us had even seen, or ever will see," recounted Hugh Kay of the 43rd Battery, Canadian Field Artillery.[6]

"It seems good to be back in civilization," wrote Gunner Harvie Stewart.[7] Yet arrival in London, surrounded by tens of thousands of milling civilians, was initially disorientating. Scarred battlefields, the constant boom of the guns, and ambulances racing to the rear were replaced with monumental buildings, the laughter of children, and reckless trucks. "The streets are very dark at night ... traffic is really dangerous," wrote Lieutenant Clifford Wells while on leave, and only months before he was killed in battle.[8] Future Canadian prime minister Lester B. Pearson's military career ended before it really got started when he stepped in front of a bus during an enforced blackout. But soldiers got their bearings soon, helped along by civilians or one of the thousands of Allied soldiers who swarmed the city.

"London is quite a large place, just a mite bigger than Summerside," wrote a wide-eyed David O'Leary from Prince Edward Island.[9] For young men who had farmed all their life or lived in one of the many small towns dotting the Canadian landscape, a visit to London, the world's metropolis, was a glorious treat. These soldier-tourists took in all the attractions, from Buckingham Palace to St. Paul's Cathedral, as well as popular theatre shows or local parks.[10] Cards, knick-knacks, and souvenirs were purchased for themselves and loved ones: birthdays and anniversaries had of necessity been missed while the men were in the field, and leave offered the opportunity to catch up with some gifts. But despite their efforts to live life to the fullest during their short leave and take in all London had to offer, soldiers still found its scope overwhelming. As Bill Hutchinson from Dorchester, New Brunswick, noted to his mother, "I was on the go from morning till night every day, and then only saw a small part of the city."[11] Expressing the thoughts of many Canadian soldiers before and after him, Captain William E.L. Coleman, who had twice been awarded the Military Cross for bravery, wrote to his wife, Dell, "I would not want to live here unless I had lots of money, but one can spend a very pleasant holiday."[12]

Dapper in their uniforms, soldiers also went in search of photographers. For men who were away from home for years on end, these representations were essential for bridging the gap between the battlefield and the home front. While on leave, thousands of Canadians were photographed in professional studios. These snaps—mute black-and-white testimonies to their service—were sent back home and became visual treasures to loved ones left behind.

While everything in London was expensive, most Canadians were better off than their Imperial comrades. Canadian troops were known by scowling British Tommies as the "fuckin' five bobbers," as they received almost five times the pay of their British counterparts. Flush with cash, the men made binge-eating or -drinking the order of the day. Canadians could reside in expensive hotels until the money ran out, when they would move to one of the many cheaper soldiers' hostels, of which there were at least five devoted to the Canadians. They went to music halls or plays, ate in good restaurants, and stood drinks for their mates in the pubs. "Lots of money is spent foolishly," wrote Captain Maurice Pope. Yet "one toughs it a good deal in the trenches and when the best is to be had for asking, one is inclined to do himself well."[13]

Life in the metropolis also offered a chance to meet soldiers from the other Allied armies. "On the sidewalks were continual processions of khaki uniforms, to be identified by their badges and hats," remarked Gunner Wilfred Kerr.[14] They crammed into the same shows, museums, and bars. Sergeant Harold Mason recounted his experience in a YMCA drop-in canteen where he wrote a letter home: "Across the table are a Canadian artilleryman, a Gordon Highlander, and a U.S. Marine. Beside me is a Canadian infantryman, and to my left an Australian and New Zealander."[15]

Canadians generally developed good relations with the Scottish soldiers, but they held an uneasy and grudging admiration for the Australians. The men of both nations took pleasure in strutting behind their reputations. "Canadians and Australians always seemed to antagonize one another," wrote Captain Herbert McBride, an American serving in the CEF. "Many a bitter and bloody fight has been staged back of the lines between detachments of the two factions when they happened to meet."[16] The two dominion forces were similar in size, filled with volunteers, and had a reputation as hard-as-nails soldiers: when they met, neither side backed down. The high command soon learned not to billet them near each other behind the lines in Europe, and to let the military police sort them out in England.

Canadians on leave did their best to meet the local population—particularly women. The colonials from the outer reaches of the Empire were popular with the opposite sex. Given their willingness to spend money, Canadian soldiers had no problem finding companionship. Though more than a few women were disappointed to find that not all Canadians were bronze-skinned warriors, even the runty soldiers found a good time. Morality texts such as the YMCA's *Facts for Fighters* warned against interaction with women: "Kissing and 'spooning' before engagement are not only unwise, but dangerous. Dangerous, hygienically, mentally, and morally."[17] But the moxy of young men who lived for months only inches from death's door lent itself to relationships—and even quick marriages. "It appears 'wounded, Blighty, marriage' is becoming a popular pastime with our fellows," penned a bemused Private Donald Fraser in his diary.[18]

Other soldiers avoided London's tourist attractions and were simply aching to see their families. Thousands of women and children had sailed across the Atlantic to set up temporary homes in England in order to be near their soldier-husbands. With the battlefield only a day's train ride away, soldiers could come back to England to see their families. As well, mail could reach them more quickly, as it only had to travel to Blighty in comparison to a minimum of two weeks to Canada. In England, Canadian women and children often kept busy with patriotic work or caring for wounded soldiers. Hundreds worked as nurses in Canadian hospitals established in England, while others volunteered with the Red Cross. Lady Perley, the wife of the Canadian overseas minister, played a critical role in devoting time, energy, and money to care for soldiers on leave or recovering from wounds. Other prominent Canadian women—such as Lady Drummond, who lost her beloved son, Guy, early in the war—ensured that a steady supply of comforts, including toilet articles, food, fruit, tobacco, games, and books, were sent to soldiers at the front, and that a number of leisure centres like the famous Beaver Hut were established to provide a safe environment for soldiers on leave.

Since many Canadian soldiers' families had relocated to the United Kingdom, when these soldiers went on leave, they were simply returning home. However, as such relocation was an expensive luxury, these sojourning families usually came from the upper-middle class; the poor, in contrast, had to wait for years before they might see a loved one again. Private Herbert Cooke, a working-class older soldier in his mid-thirties, was able to bring his wife and children across, but only because they could stay with his parents. When he arrived in Cirencester on his first leave, he recounted how uplifting it was "to meet my wife and boys at the station.... I spent a relaxing ten days at home and packed wife and boys up ready to go to Canada."[19]

It is not clear why Cooke's family went back to Canada, but by 1915 the British government was placing pressure on all Canadians to dissuade them from crossing the Atlantic. Shortages of food and Zeppelin attacks meant that Canadian families were not always welcome. Further, as a result of safety concerns, from 1916 onwards the Canadian government urged women not to go overseas, except for very serious reasons or for purposes of organized patriotic work.

ALTHOUGH SOME SOLDIERS were lucky enough to have such cozy homes and families waiting for them in England, since almost eighty percent of those in the CEF were unmarried, most soldiers could not look forward to such comforts. Temporarily wealthy soldiers on leave soon got into trouble with prostitutes. "A fellow meets all kinds of new temptations at almost every turn in the soldiering game," recounted one young soldier.[20] Another, Private Percy McClare, who had enlisted at age seventeen and would not survive the war, described a specific temptation in a letter to his father:

> The worst of London is the girls that run around the streets there.... They will come up to you, that is, after nine o'clock, and they will take you by the arm and want you to go home with you [sic] and stay all night with them. I have not had much experience with them, but it is an awful temtation [sic] when they act like that. An awful lot of fellow that go to London come back in bad shape and are sent to the V.D. hospitals.[21]

William Antliff recounted his sadness and shame at finding that his fellow Canadians were being riddled with disease while on leave. But he believed venereal disease

> will always prevail where there is an army living away from civilization for months at a time and from the good influence of home life perhaps for years.... The brutalizing influence of militarism tends to lower the best of men. Add to this the absence of church life, home life, wives, mothers and sweethearts and the wonder isn't that so many fall but that any go straight at all.[22]

The military, too, was worried about the seeming epidemic of prostitutes who flooded to the big cities to service the soldiers. The high command tried to dissuade

Canadians as best as it could, through either appeals to righteous living or fear-mongering about potential diseases. Soldiers who contracted venereal diseases were a significant drain on the forces, as they had to be pulled from the front lines and held in specialized hospitals where nurses were not allowed to work because of the "unclean" patients. Each diseased man needed at least a month to recuperate.[23] The Canadian high command finally broke down and issued contraceptives towards the end of the war. Fines were levied, leave was withheld, and more severe punishments threatened if soldiers hid their afflictions. For a short time, the military even went so far as to maliciously contact wives about a husband's disease, but after several suicides, this policy was aborted. However, many wives discovered that their husbands had been unfaithful when their separation allowance (paid by the government and with money put aside by soldiers) failed to arrive, as afflicted men received reduced pay, and eventually no pay, during the period of their recovery.

English women were "snakes from hell with fire in their mouth all over," wrote Francis Maheux, an Ottawa Valley logger, to his wife, Angelique, a full-blooded Odawa, after listening to his chaplain.[24] But it was a long war, and Maheux, like thousands of others, could not resist temptation: he was later diagnosed with a venereal disease. The Canadians had one of the highest venereal disease rates in all the BEF. At the epidemic's most troubling point, 28.7 percent of the men were reported to be infected; by the end of the war, some 15.8 percent of overseas enlisted men had contracted some form of venereal disease, and this remained almost six times the figure of that experienced by British troops.[25] There can be no doubt that more of the British Tommies went home to their wives on leave, but it is hard to explain such high rates among the Canadians—except to suggest that they likely resulted from a combination of better pay and distance from family, rather than from the heightened randiness and recklessness that was surely prevalent in most soldiers. That said, a prewar estimate in the respected Canadian medical journal *Canada Lancet* may provide an important answer: in 1907, it was estimated that a similar portion of the Dominion's adult population—15 percent—was infected with syphilis.[26]

"I am not going to promise to be any little angel because it is no use and I don't want you to think that I am one," wrote Warren Hendershott to his parents. "I am a boy the same as the rest of the fellows and am behaving myself better than the majority and maybe not quite as well as the 'stay at home' few we have here.... There are a lot more temptations in this country than there were at home."[27] It was hard for soldiers to turn their backs on women and alcohol after spending months within death's constant grasp. What was the use of denying simple pleasures when one's life might span only a few more weeks?

DESPITE THE LAVISH EXPERIENCES the big city offered, many soldiers on leave instead found peace in a good meal, a warm bed, and one of London's many parks. The tens of thousands of Canadians staying with family in the United Kingdom, or with a mate's relatives, or sometimes even with generous civilians who would put enlisted men up in their houses free of charge, underwent an important process of recivilization after being long hardened by their barren existence at the front.

All soldiers on vacation—whether those who lived hard or those who simply relaxed for two weeks—felt the spectre of the front hovering over them. It was impossible to leave the war on the Western Front fully behind, and the shock of moving from front to rear could be intensely jarring. Corporal John Harold Becker recounted that after months of hard ground and mud, his first night in a bed resulted in a long and heavy slumber. But the war was never very far from his mind, and Becker was troubled all night by the "sound of guns" in his head and the "call for stretcher-bearers."[28] Roy Macfie of the 1st Battalion declared, "It is just as well they don't let us away very often. It is so hard coming back it spoils it all, I didn't know how used I was to it till I got away and saw what civilian life was like again."[29]

Fourteen days in Blighty sped by quickly. On the last one, men dutifully kissed their loved ones goodbye, shook hands with new mates, and boarded their ships and trains for the front. More than a few grabbed a couple of extra days and were charged with being absent without leave. Some produced stories of being lost or detained through no fault of their own; clever ones invented stories about being forced to stand at attention for "God Save The King," and, being a loyal soldier, refusing to dishonour the monarch rather than worry about some connection to a ship or train, which they had then missed. Officers could see right through these excuses, but innovative stories brought grudging admiration and sometimes even a commuted sentence. More often, however, the soldier had to forfeit a week's pay or suffer minor field punishment. Most took it without complaint.

Leave remained an essential component of the soldiers' well-being and morale, even if it was awarded far too infrequently. But for most men, their short vacations back to "civilization" served to remind them that too soon they would again be within the sound and the reach of the guns. Major George McFarland summed up his feelings well: "I realized bitterly the truth of the old saying that the man who is most in need of leave is the man who has just had it."[30]

CHAPTER 12

"SING ME TO SLEEP
WHERE BULLETS FALL"

Soldiers' Culture

"The human body was never called upon to endure more than was suffered by our men in the trenches," wrote Arthur Currie. The brutal conditions "taxed endurance, health and powers of resistance to the utmost."[1] But within this strange subterranean world of mud and death, of rats and lice, of terror and shells, the soldiers refused to give up hope. Letters connected soldiers to their loved ones at home and were essential in keeping up morale. Men also turned to one another for help in surviving the psychological strain of the industrial battlefield, but many demanded more from their troglodytic existence than mere survival. These soldiers felt impelled to create a culture that reflected their unique experiences in the trenches. This culture helped to distinguish servicemen from civilians at home, which strengthened the relationships forged in the trenches and assisted soldiers in coping with and making sense of the war.

Soldiers relied heavily on those at home to support and sustain them emotionally. Almost every man had left behind loved ones—a wife, children, friends, parents— and the constant passage of communication between front and rear kept soldiers apprised of events in Canada. Although army discipline, comradeship, and the small pleasures of rum or cigarettes were important in building and sustaining morale, soldiers also depended on the home front for reassurance and comfort.

This soldier stares longingly at a picture of his sweetheart, or a woman he fancies.
The photograph serves as a stark reminder of the hundreds of thousands of
Canadians who were separated from loved ones while serving overseas.

Frequent care packages of treats, clothing, and supplies told trench-dwellers they had not been forgotten by those back home. Letters were even more important. "I am dreadfully homesick and I am longing to be home with you and the children again," wrote Sergeant George Ormsby to his wife from the trenches. "Every time I go to sleep I dream that the war is over and that I am back again home. For comfort I read your letters and look at your pictures and I can tell you they are a great comfort to me."[2] An estimated eighty-five million letters passed back and forth across the Atlantic, bringing comfort to both the soldiers and those left behind.[3] Lawrence Rogers, who enlisted at a nearly ancient thirty-seven years of age, and who had a wife and two children in Canada, wrote home with reassuring words: "I miss you and the kiddies every minute of the day."[4] Unlike Ormsby, who would survive the war with shrapnel in his back and return home to British Columbia, where he would take up fruit farming and sire a third child, Rogers would never see his family again, as he was killed in the muck of Passchendaele.

In the trenches, the mail came up almost every day. When a call went out that a carrier had arrived, men crowded around him. "It is … pathetic to see those who are not lucky turning away sometimes with tears in their eyes," remembered one trench warrior.[5] A constant stream of correspondence was kept with family members, friends, girlfriends, neighbours, and countless others at home, who in turn wrote or sent along gifts. "Write often because letters are very welcome. The next two months are the worst of the whole year in the trenches so I will need letters to keep my spirits up," wrote Basil Morris to his sister, Grace.[6] Basil was killed later in the war while flying with the Royal Flying Corps, having spent many months pestering senior officers to transfer him out of the infantry. While he never returned, his letters lived on.

Servicemen ached to provide emotional support to their wives, many of whom had been abandoned in the rush for King and country. These women were now running a farm, business, or a household on their own. Soldiers also tried to impart loving words to their children, who would be growing up without a fatherly presence in the home. And there was always the need for a gentle word to a mother or father. The letters contained much bravado in the hope of downplaying the danger of life in the trenches. Lieutenant Clifford Wells kept up a steady correspondence with his mother, but his letters to her were guarded, as he was anxious not to mention "anything which is liable to cause unnecessary worry."[7] But most soldiers periodically dropped the mask in their letters, recounting almost all aspects of their war experience, from the terror to the sorrow, from the stress of war to the joys of new friendships.

Servicemen were warned not to impart any military information in letters for fear of assisting the enemy, and all letters were censored, first within the regiment by an officer, and then sometimes at headquarters. Some men followed the rules rigidly, but most played fast and loose with content that the army considered to be off limits. Private John Ellis got creative by trying to devise a complex code with his sweetheart, but later gave it up when neither of them could remember how to decipher it. He did his best to explain it in one letter:

Now darling I have a code figured out so that I can give you a lot of news without being censored…. I'll try & explain it to you. The code works on my [service] number 675928. You start reading my letter & you take the 6th word (not including "My Own Darling Kitty") now from that you take the first letter.

Then from the 6th word you'll count 7, then take the first letter of that word. Then from that count 5 words & take the first letter again & so on till you have the whole number then start over again all through the letter. Now if you see one kiss only at the end of the letter look for something & pick out the letters as I explained, if I put 2 kisses instead of taking the letter take the whole word…. Do you understand me dearest?[8]

Few soldiers went to such lengths to avoid the censor, although some took delight in testing the system. Alwyn Bramley-Moore would occasionally insert sentences in his letters about certain officers to see if his censoring superiors were paying attention. Private Ronald Main's parents, from Amherst, Nova Scotia, found that his letter had not only been censored by an officer, but that the censor had also included a note: "It has been my unpleasant duty to Sinsor [sic] letters today but it is good to come across letters like this. As my wife comes from Amherst, NS, it made me think a few serious thoughts. We are in a rather serious and warm spot here and I sincerely trust your boy will pull through OK."[9] On the whole, most officers found the task of censoring tedious and distasteful, although it could sometimes be useful for gauging the men's morale.

Notwithstanding the diligence of the censors, resourceful soldiers found ways to post letters containing sensitive information. One method was to hand them over to a friend going on leave, who smuggled them back to Blighty and then mailed them through normal postal routes. Or soldiers simply took their chances, hoping—often rightly—that exhausted officers overwhelmed by reading fifty letters at one go would not read every one closely, or that they were simply not concerned with applying the black marker unless a soldier's message dealt directly with military matters such as a unit's location in the field. The *frontsoldaten* were not above writing their true feelings, which could include warnings to their younger siblings about the dangers of the front. Samuel Honey suggested in one letter that, should his brother George enlist, he would be well advised to look for a "bomb-proof" job in the rear: "But if he wants the hardest biscuits and the toughest bully beef, the most unpleasant place to sleep and the fewest blankets, let him be satisfied to plug along as an ordinary private in the ranks."[10]

Another way for soldiers to get letters home unread by censors was by using the special green envelope they were usually issued once a week, the contents of which were not censored by their officers—although the envelopes were periodically opened at various general headquarters in France or England. Alfred Baggs wrote to his wife in a regular letter that he would soon have access to a green envelope, which he would use to "write my Dear Wife more personally than I've been able to for a long time now."[11] So important were these envelopes that allowed for the expression of true feelings that they became, as Gunner Wilfred Kerr noted, "commodities of a substantial traffic."[12]

But it was always hard to find time to write: putting pen to paper meant making a choice between precious relaxation or sleep and clawing through the inertia to find words for the sometimes indescribable. However, disciplined men kept up a steady correspondence no matter their fatigue, as most realized the importance of keeping those at home informed of their struggle. The soldiers had another option, too: they could fire off a "whiz-bang" field service card. Named after the small-calibre field-gun shells that often arrived without warning, these bizarre and impersonal postcards would be "destroyed," it was warned, if soldiers added to or deviated from the text on the card. The card contained prewritten messages, and soldiers struck off those that did not apply to them, with most opting to keep the message: "I am quite well." Although the whiz-bangs contained little personal information, they provided an indication to a worried family that a soldier was still alive. They also offered a less taxing method of correspondence for men at the front—especially the more than half who had less than a grade-six education and to whom writing did not come easily.

Much remained unsaid. "I have seen sights in the bloodstained trenches of Flanders that I will never forget," wrote Elmer Bowness, a twenty-one-year-old former carpenter from Prince Edward Island, to his family. "If the people at home could see the real horrors of the battle-field [,] they would be worried to death."[13] Bowness made the probably wise decision to leave his description at that, and to spare those at home from the troubling details of such horrors. The gap between firing line and home front could not be covered in a once-a-week 500-word letter. Nonetheless, soldiers often tried to put their feelings down on paper. They might mask them behind dark humour or an ironic phrase, but real and affecting aspects of the war were caught on paper. Many letters were even published in local newspapers. They contained vivid accounts of the horrible effects of poison gas that rotted out men's lungs or the sadness of seeing old friends killed off. Those at home received a steady stream of letters from the front, and many contained word-pictures portraying the hell of the trenches.[14]

AFTER WRITING HOME, men could laze about, dreaming of the day the war might end. "Après la guerre," or, as the soldiers liked to refer to it, "la gare"—writing it thus and pronouncing it as "car" in order to deliberately bastardize the French—remained an important point of conversation. Although the war defined the soldiers' lives, they did not want it to be the only thing in their reality. Reuniting with loved ones was a cherished goal, but many demanded more—especially young men with only a dead-end job to go back to at home. A life in a quiet house or an opportunity to stake out a farm in the west did not always meet these heightened expectations, but such dreams got many men through the long days and longer nights at the front.

Of course, lying about in a trench daydreaming was a pretty good way to attract an officer's attention and be ordered on work duty. Experienced men therefore pushed their way into the hidden reaches of the dugouts, perhaps past a game of cards or even a mate trying to develop illegal photographs using his glass negatives and chemicals. In the gloom, soldiers might relieve their pent-up sexual urges with a secret look at postcards of coy-looking, scantily-clad women, and then a quick pull. The cave's darkness could also allow for precious sleep. Subsisting on only a few hours of shut-eye a day for four or five days straight left men chronically sleep-deprived, walking around in a perpetual daze, bodies aching at every joint, heads pounding. But the trenches were their home, at least temporarily, and they learned how to not only survive, but to go beyond that to create their own culture.

While there was almost nothing alive on the empty battlefield, below ground teemed an active, bustling city. Grousing and grumbling were a popular pastime. Complaints about food, discipline, and almost anything else were uttered—from the mildly caustic to an almost reverential litany of profanity. For soldiers blowing off steam, there was always someone to listen or to contribute their own thoughts on any matter.

"Rumours are not hard to find in army life," wrote Stanley Rutledge.[15] They passed through the trenches with lightning speed and "experts" seemed to know all about upcoming offensives, the state of the enemy's morale, where the division might be moved to next, and—the favourite of all men—whether leave might be extended to the troops or, perhaps, even increased in frequency. Engaging with rumours was one way for soldiers to construct meaning in their bizarre world. *The Listening Post*, one of the most popular Canadian trench newspapers, a journal published by the soldiers for the soldiers, addressed the widespread promulgation of rumours.

> In an army which is dependent on the London papers a day or two old for exact knowledge of what is happening on its own particular front, it is inevitable that rumours of all sorts should travel from unit to unit, and grow increasingly grotesque until they break down from the sheer overweight of untruth. Rumours are generally born in the brain of some person whose occupation leaves him sufficient time to concoct and spread a tissue of half-truths, sufficiently highly coloured to appeal to troops whose one and everlasting hope is change.[16]

These exchangeable and malleable stories revealed fears, hopes, and desires, and provided a way to pass the time as soldiers picked lice from their clothes or rested on the firestep fighting boredom instead of the enemy. Even if most soldiers understood the inherent inaccuracy of rumours, they listened intently, passed them on, and waited for the next one that might help to make sense of their trench experience, or at least manage the unknowable in times of never-ending stress. "It is a notable fact," wrote one soldier, "that although one may be convinced of the utter falsity of a rumour, that does not usually prevent one from passing it along."[17]

Some rumours had been passed around so many times that veterans laughed them off in a show of swagger. But even grizzled soldiers could listen avidly to particularly appealing rumours, wishing them to be true. One of the most enduring rumours, based upon a seemingly fervid mass hallucination, centred on the small

British regular army during their desperate retreat from Mons in the opening month of the war. Pressed by overwhelming German forces and retreating day after gruelling day, the soldiers began to circulate a legend about angels having saved the army.[18] Armoured knights or shimmering angels (depending on the version of the rumour) had swooped down from the heavens and blocked the German armies from closing with the British troops. In another version, ethereal bowmen fired on the Germans, forcing them back—a story no doubt influenced by the British army's retreat past the medieval battlefield of Agincourt. These saviour angels and knights became instant legends, fuelled by soldiers' desire to view the war as a crusade. A bestselling book by wartime journalist Arthur Machen kept the story alive, even after the author publicly admitted his story had no grounding in fact. Countless anxious Britishers, grappling with private fears for loved ones or nation, chastised Machen for recanting, assuring him he was wrong! The powerful story of the angels of Mons continued to spread as rumour throughout the war.[19] Stanley Rutledge observed that the tale circulated among the Canadians, too, even though no Canadians were at Mons. "It was told in semi-poetic language. And then we all hoped it had really happened. Glad to believe, you know, in such a manifestation of righteous judgment." Even when it was revealed that the story was a fabrication, Rutledge noted, "there are many who will not disbelieve the vision."[20]

In a war in which the British Empire forces were depicted as literally on the side of the angels, and the evil Hun portrayed as raping and burning his way across Europe, a particularly sick rumour gained currency among troops and civilians. It was said in hushed tones that the British naval blockade had choked Germany of fats necessary for the war effort, and that, accordingly, the callous German high command had responded by transporting their own soldiers' corpses back to an unknown factory to render them into nitroglycerine, or even tallow for candles.[21] In a letter home, Canadian infantryman Herbert Clemens remarked—in jest, but also demonstrating the influence of the story—that his recently enlisted brother would have a chance "of getting a whack at those beastly body-boiling Sausage Eaters."[22] While many of the men may have scoffed at such extreme characterizations of the enemy, as well as at the validity of the "corpse factory," others may have felt uneasy. The effectiveness of the Royal Navy blockade in systematically starving Germany of raw materials, mixed with the seemingly brutal nature of the German *Kultur* that had unleashed submarine warfare, aerial bombardment, and poison gas, reinforced the possibility of the Hun's wanton disregard for life, and the depths to which he would sink to win the war. The fraudulence of the corpse factory legend was not exposed until nearly a decade after the war ended, when John Charteris, who had been Haig's senior intelligence officer, let it slip that the British had planted the story and encouraged the spread of the rumour.[23]

Those men who were tired of listening to rumours and gossip might turn to reading. Newspapers from home and magazines such as *Maclean's* and *Punch* were readily available in the front lines, brought up through the mail or in care packages. Many soldiers used the media to stay connected to their families and communities back in Canada, but scoffed at the hyper-patriotic, soothsaying journalists who were continually predicting how the next big push would finally topple the supposedly rotten German army. But such jingoistic papers had their uses, especially during the daily visit to the latrine.

Outraged or bemused by what they read, soldiers began to produce their own trench newspapers. Despite the difficulties of putting together a newspaper with almost no resources, and the constant danger of losing key editors and writers in battle, soldiers turned publishers to "preserve a record of their thoughts and experiences, both for themselves and for history."[24] In a war where almost everything was foisted on them by some higher ranking officer, the papers were their own. The journals' content—supplied by the soldiers themselves—was something that rang true, unlike the civilian rags awash in hopeful predictions and demonizations of the enemy.

When the idea caught on, soldiers found editors within their ranks and began to produce newspapers on a periodic basis, when time and resources allowed. Editors cajoled, pleaded, and harassed the men for content. Some efforts lasted for only a handful of issues while select others had a much longer life: *The Listening Post*, the 7th Battalion's publication, had a three-year run and a circulation of almost 20,000 copies, both at the front and at home. This example was unusual, however, and most of the papers had press runs of less than 1,000, which was not insignificant since they were usually run off on small presses smuggled into the lines or rear areas, and printed on paper that was purchased, borrowed, or stolen.

Publishers solicited soldiers for poems, jokes, satirical observations, trench doggerel, and cartoons. The 14th Battalion's *R.M.R. Growler* claimed, "As the name will suggest, our columns are open to every grouch in the Battalion, and a growl on any subject, whether the grievance be either real or fancied, will be joyfully received and have immediate insertion."[25] These soldiers' products were infused with humour, irony, and irreverence. Writing about *The Twentieth Gazette*, Major D.J. Corrigall provided some insight into how the two non-commissioned officer-editors approached the content:

> They developed quite a news instinct, and made the publication popular by being bold enough to take a sly dig at the Commanding Officer, to feign respect for majors, to treat captains with cynicism, to be distressingly sarcastic about subalterns, to be openly insulting about sergeants, to be abusive about corporals, but wise enough to be extremely polite about privates.[26]

The newspapers could be subversive, and provided a forum for soldiers to air grievances in a safe environment. *The Brazier*, the journal of the 16th Battalion, and later the entire 3rd Brigade, had a section—like most papers—where soldiers could demand to know certain things: the first issue, for example, included complaints about the rum ration and why the soldiers could not be trusted to drink it without doing so in the presence of an officer. But there were other gripes. For example, "Why have no decorations been bestowed on the rank and file of No. 3 Coy.? What ho! Festubert!" was a reminder that the issuing of gallantry awards could be contentious, as the rank and file of the mentioned company wished to remind the high command of their sacrifice during the May 1915 Battle of Festubert. As well, one reader cheekily inquired about "How to get a transfer to the Pay and Record Office, London." And the aggravating issue of the unfair leave policy led to a direct question that could not be ignored: "Why does the Tommy not have as much leave as the officer?"[27] One of the harshest condemnations from the rank and file was published in *Dead Horse Corner Gazette*, the paper of the 4th Battalion, which demanded to know "whether the officer of a certain Canadian battalion who ordered one of his men to pick up scraps of paper from the top of a communication trench in broad daylight attended the man's funeral?"[28] Papers allowed for these grievances to be heard by the officers in a safe context, and it showed the rank and file that they were not alone in their grumbling. The inclusion of such questions and comments from the men also reinforced the authenticity of the journal as being for the soldiers and not for the officers. In turn, officers allowed subversive newspapers to be published because it seemed wiser than clamping down on the men and letting their anger fester.

But the newspapers were not simply a vehicle for airing complaints: they were a forum in which soldiers expressed themselves in a variety of ways. Poetry remained one of the most popular forms of expression. The experience of the Great War was being captured by the prolific pens of British war poets such as Wilfrid Owen and Siegfied Sassoon, and Canadians including John McCrae and Canon Frederick Scott, but countless others also tried their hand at finding words and rhyming couplets to make sense of the war. One simple yet moving poem from *The Brazier* spoke of the loss of comrades:

> There were nine of us camped at West Down South,
> And nine of us crossed to France,
> And we grew to savvy each others gaits,
> When all of a sudden we fouled the fates,
> And the only one left of all my mates
> Is me, by the grace of Chance.[29]

There was also unpublished poetry written by soldiers to loved ones left behind. Gunner Robert Hale wrote to his girl, Alice:

> Remember me is all I ask
> But if remembrance proves a task
> Forget me.[30]

Cartoons were another popular form of expression, and were often published within the papers. The drawings by Captain Bruce Bairnsfather, a British officer and cartoonist, who depicted the sad-sack experience of weary trench soldiers, struck a chord with most Allied soldiers—their appeal crossing national boundaries. Lieutenant Clifford Wells wrote home that Bairnsfather's cartoons "are wonderfully true to life, and very popular out here."[31] Another infantryman, Sergeant Samuel Honey, told his parents that the cartoons "depict incidents and situations at the front in a humourous light, but yet with a great deal of grim reality underlying the humour."[32] Influenced by Bairnsfather, many Canadian soldiers tried their own hand at drawing, and like their mentor, the Canadian servicemen often took pride in portraying themselves as unheroic and insubordinate.

COOK: " What's wrong, chum, shell-shock ? "
BILL: " No, back off leave."

A dark cartoon from the pages of The Listening Post, *the most widely distributed Canadian trench newspaper. The trench newspapers and cartoons broached sensitive topics—often through humour—and here Corporal Hugh Farmer, one of the most prolific Canadian cartoonists of the war, makes light of shell shock and the difficulty of returning from leave.*

AS AN ISOLATED TRIBE, the trench soldiers developed their own dialect, with new words and meanings. Captain R.J. Manion observed that many of the words in the trenches resembled a new form of communication, as the language drew on English, French, and approved facial gestures.[33] "No bon" was a common expression for something that was "no good," a play on the French. Other choice usage included "compree" and "napoo" to signify death, the latter drawn from "il n'y en a plus" ("there is no more"). For good fun, the names of French and Belgian cities were changed to suit the English tongue: Albert became "Bert," Ypres was spat out as "Wipers."

But the soldiers' dialect was composed of more than bastardized French. New words helped to express the uniqueness of the trench experience. A soldier was not killed; instead, he "went west." Attacking the enemy was called "going over the top" or "hitting the bags." "Cooties" were lice, and a "coffin nail" a cigarette. All the deadly weapons of war, including the myriad shells and mortars, were renamed in a nonchalant display of taking the piss out of death: "pineapples," "rum jars," "toffee apples," "flying pigs," "Jack Johnsons," "Black Marthas," "fish tails," and "whizbangs" were all terms easily understood by trench soldiers.

Of course, one of the most common words of the trench was the multi-functional "fuck," which could be a noun, verb, adverb, adjective, and almost any other part of speech. Its employment by a grizzled old hand in a litany of vulgarities could impress even the most hardened soldier. Its frequent use was a shock to men raised in strict homes. One can only imagine what Harold Innis—who would become one of Canada's most famous historians after the war—thought of this ceaseless swearing when he already wrote worriedly in his diary about the temptations of "beer and rum and electric pianos."[34] And Private William Ogilvie, a seventeen-year-old mule driver from Lakefield, Ontario, testified to his own naivety: "I was amazed at the cursing, the extravagant use of the four letter word seldom heard in our quiet village. I, whose swearing propensities generally ran to such inoffensive outbursts as, "God all fishhooks," or "gosh, golly," or an occasional "darn" or "damn," was now treated to round after round of obscene language."[35]

Although the ubiquitous four-letter word remained a constant in this masculine society, other phrases and parts of the lexicon changed rapidly. "A new word appears from no one knows where and is adopted for a season on every possible occasion," wrote Sergeant Leonard Gould, a journalist who had enlisted at the age of thirty-nine. "Some words had a long life, such as 'odd.' Food became the 'odd bite'; a written message 'the odd chit'; sleep was 'the odd wink,' and so on."[36] Despite these passing linguistic flights of fancy, some words endured, becoming absorbed into the lexicon of the English language. We still use "chat," "shell shocked," "ace," "No Man's Land," "bat out of hell," "trench coat," "over the top," and countless other Great War phrases, many of which originated in the trenches or found common usage therein.

These new words and vulgarities fed directly into the soldiers' songs. Trench ballads and songs were sung with relish in the front lines, in the rear, and while on the march. These songs were rough badges of identity. With time on their hands, soldiers in the dugouts and trenches drew upon their prewar civilian culture and struck up a song. Soloists or "leaders of unecclesiastical choirs" sang from the heart, belly, or somewhere below that.[37]

Lyrics about such topics as the allure of the French farmer's daughter or a lack of alcohol appealed to men who had little chance of satisfying either of these urges. Songs such as "Oh, It's a Lovely War," "I Don't Want to Join the Army," and "Far, Far from Wipers" had subversive, anti-heroic and anti-military themes, and to civilians or enemy soldiers they might imply that rot had set into the British and Dominion armies. This was far from the case, however, and such songs were simply another form of communication using satire and parody. Soldiers' songs were most often based on recognized civilian melodies or hymns. Yet these civilian tunes were appropriated and became the soldiers' own, and the melodies of the songs would be augmented with new lyrics that better reflected the soldiers' culture. "We're Here Because" was sung to the melody of "Auld Lang Syne":

We're here
Because
We're here
Because
We're here
Because we're here.

Of course the soldiers loved this song because there were many days when they were not quite sure why and what they were doing in the trenches. Or if they did know why they were fighting, then it was simply fun to complain.

The lyrics of another popular song, "Far, Far from Wipers," sung to the tune of "Sing Me to Sleep," a sentimental ballad from the period, had a similar bent:

Sing me to sleep where bullets fall;
Let me forget the war and all.
Damp is my dugout, cold are my feet,
Nothing but bully and biscuits to eat.
Sing me to sleep where bombs explode
And shrapnel shells are à-la-mode.
Over the sandbags you find,
Corpses in front of you, corpses behind.

Far, far from Ypres I long to be,
Where German snipers cannot pot me.
Think of me crouching where the worms creep,
Waiting for someone to sing me to sleep.

Sing me to sleep in some old shed;
The rats are running around my head.
Stretched out on my waterproof,
Dodging the raindrops through the roof.
Sing me to sleep where the camp fires glow,
When nights are cold and spirits are low,
Dreaming of home and days in the West,
Somebody's overseas boot on my chest.

Far from the star-shells I long to be,
Lights of old London I'd rather see;
Think of me crouching where the worms creep,
Waiting for someone to sing me to sleep.

A fan of the song, R.E.N. Jones noted that this "parody [is] much circulated over here. It absolutely reflects the impression and feelings of the men, and officers as well, in my opinion."[38] Singing allowed soldiers to cope with the stress of war. If a sergeant cheated you out of your rum, you had to deal with it. If the mud was nearly impassable, you still had to find a way around. The absurdity, weariness, and exasperation of war remained favourite topics for singers, who did not suffer silently. The songs changed over time, as jesters added new and often dirty verses, slights, and personal abuse that resonated within the soldiers' community. The lyrics "We are Fred Karno's army," referring to the popular British music hall entertainer, were changed to "We are Sam Hughes's army," and followed by, "No bloody good are we; / We cannot shoot, / We cannot fight; / What bloody good are we?" The infantry, it was clear, could poke fun at themselves. Rival units, civilians, even abusive sergeants all became victims of the singers, especially if their names could somehow rhyme with "bastard" or "tart." "Behind the Lines" took a melodic shot at authority, bomb-proofers to the rear, and those who urged on the infantry without sharing in the danger:

> We've got a sergeant-major,
> Who's never seen a gun;
> He's mentioned in dispatches
> For drinking privates' rum;
> And when he sees old Jerry,
> You should see the bugger run
> Miles and miles and miles behind the lines!

While many songs were aimed at figures of authority or at the worst aspects of army discipline, some songs were simply crude. These were the testosterone-driven ones that were often sung on the march, with a strong sun beating down, and 10 kilometres to go before a rest. "Mademoiselle from Armentières" had hundreds of verses, many of which were extremely smutty. Perhaps the worst offender was "Three German Officers," which was also known as "Inky-Dinky Parlez-Vous":

> Three German officers crossed the Rhine, parlez-vous
> Three German officers crossed the Rhine, parlez-vous

Three German officers crossed the Rhine
To fuck the women and drink the wine,
Inky-Dinky parlez-vous

They came to the door of a wayside inn, parlez-vous

…
Pissed on the mat and walked right in,
Inky-Dinky parlez-vous

"Oh landlord have you a daughter fair?" parlez-vous
"With lily-white tits and golden hair?" parlez-vous
…
Inky-Dinky parlez-vous

"My only daughter's far too young," parlez-vous
"To be fucked by you, you bastard Hun," parlez-vous
…
Inky-Dinky parlez-vous

"Oh father dear I'm not too young," parlez-vous
"I've just been fucked by the blacksmith's son," parlez-vous
…
Inky-Dinky parlez-vous …[39]

There were countless versions of this song, few of which could be sung in polite company.

Although many of the songs were crude and rough, the roster of favourites contained a surprising number of sentimental and religious hymns. Victor Wheeler of the 50th Battalion recounted the sadness he and his fellow survivors felt after a costly battle. One of his mates sang "Roses of Picardy," a sentimental ballad that few would associate with battle-hardened warriors. "We implored him, 'Sing it again, Cross. Please sing it once more.' Seeming to realize how much that song meant to us, Cross sang many encores—until every hardened soldier, recumbent around the sides of the low mud-whitewashed walls of the high pitched roof, was in tears."[40] These songs played an important role in the soldiers' culture, both in allowing men to remember their past lives as civilians and in helping them to process the reality of their new one as soldiers.

SOLDIERS REFUSED to be victims. They railed against the war and its terrible cruelty. These were brothers and fathers, sons and uncles, who were desperate to return one day to their loved ones. While in the trenches, these same soldiers relied heavily on those they had left behind. Letters to and from home were an essential lifeline that helped to keep the soldiers sane and motivated. Yet the soldiers needed more, and so within their subterranean cities a new culture emerged. This underground culture remained an essential part of the Great War experience, providing the men with a way to make sense of their world and find meaning in its ruthlessness. Without these emotional and constructive outlets, many more men would have succumbed to the brutal psychological stress of enduring ceaseless slaughter. "There was a philosophy of 'gruesome humour' that allowed men to mock death," wrote British war journalist Philip Gibbs.[41] Indeed, medical officer R.J. Manion remembered being shocked by how the trench soldiers scoffed at their suffering, but he later learned that this stoicism was part of the combat soldiers' coping mechanism. One long-serving veteran of the trenches told him the night before a big push: "You know, Doc, the main objection I have to death is that it is so damned permanent."[42] He was killed the next day. But others took his place, and they in turn found ways to endure on the Western Front.

CHAPTER 13

"CAMARADERIE OF THE DAMNED"

Rewards, Combat Motivation, and Sick Grins

"I am pretty fit myself, except that I simply cannot sleep since my shaking; that will no doubt wear off when I get away from the din for a bit," wrote E.P. Blake, a Canadian who fought as part of a tank crew. Blake had survived the harrowing experience of being in a tank on the Somme, and recounted that "boxed up like that under intensely heavy shellfire of all kinds … [it was] worse than anything I have ever felt before." His nerves had been pushed to the limit when a high explosive shell had landed among the group of men he was with while on work patrol. Several of his comrades were killed outright while he was blown off his feet, his tunic ripped open from the blast and his shirt shredded. Blake had, in his words, a "miraculous escape." The next night, a shell landed only a few metres away, again blowing him off his feet, and rendering him unconscious as his limp body flew through the air to land in a ditch. After that, Blake's hands were wracked with tremors, he suffered headaches, and he could not sleep. He noted rather calmly, however, that "the infantry must have escapes like that two or three times a day." Most did not, but he was probably more accurate in stating, "It is the man of iron nerves and will who scores out here."[1]

A soldier started as a new recruit, unsure of himself and his place in the unit. If he survived the first couple of months, he learned essential tricks for survival: how to recognize the sound of shells in flight, when to drop into a dugout, how to move effectively through No Man's Land, and a host of other means of staying alive. Stray shells and eagle-eyed snipers still took the lives of experienced and inexperienced men, but the longer a soldier served, the better chance he had of surviving many of the trials of the war. Though the men could find some reassurance in this likelihood, they nonetheless saw comrades killed and maimed every day, and the randomness of the deaths only added to the soldiers' propensity towards fatalism. At the front, the only thing that was certain was the certainty of death. And amidst death's unfathomable patterns, the chance of surviving steadily decreased: near misses, being buried alive, and other horrors began to wear on a man, who could only wonder how many lives he had left before a whirling bit of metal would claim him.

Within this insane world, almost everyone experienced fear. The quickening of the pulse; the cold sweat; the chattering teeth; the weakness in the legs; the parched, dry throat: the physical effects of fear on the battlefield were nearly impossible to control. "I take no stock in the man who says he never was frightened in battle," wrote hard-nosed Private George Bell, who served nearly the entire war at the front. "He is either a freak or a blooming liar—more likely the latter."[2] It was almost physically impossible not to shake or tremble during an artillery bombardment or as the gas alarms rang out down the line, jerking men from their sleep.

"It took far more courage to wait in a trench and take shelling or dodge *Minenwerfers* than it did to go out over the top and risk getting shot down," wrote Private E.W. Russell.[3] While a soldier who went forward was at greater risk of being killed, the man who waited in his trench had no chance to strike back at his tormentors. Prolonged fear and stress manifested themselves in physical ways as the body became imprinted with stories of the war. Hair began to fall out or turn white. Tremors, shakes, and twitches were common. Thomas Johnston of the 5th CMR wrote to his sweetheart in his home town of Peterborough, after nineteen months at the front: "I feel and look a lot older than when I left. I feel quite middle aged in fact."[4] He was thirty.

Endurance was the key to surviving at the front. Yet even hard men walked the razor's edge between sanity and madness. Studies of U.S. soldiers in the Second World War found that after thirty-five days of uninterrupted combat, ninety-eight percent manifested psychiatric disturbances and progressively frequent breakdowns.[5] Combat infantryman Robert Graves estimated that it took an officer about three weeks at the front to know his way around and avoid being a danger to himself. He was at his sharpest from three weeks to about six months; after that, "he was still more or less all right, but by nine or ten months, unless he had been given a few weeks' rest on a technical course, or in hospital, he usually became a drag on the other company officers. After a year or fifteen months he was often worse than useless."[6] How then could the armies remain coherent fighting forces at the front, where units and men had fought for months, even years? The answer lay in factors such as morale, leadership, discipline, soldiers' agency, and a belief in the cause, which helped the civilian-soldiers to withstand the terrible strain at the front.

MORALE HAS ALWAYS BEEN an essential factor in war, feeding the willingness to serve, obey orders, and fight. As the spirit of a group of individuals and units—how they view their tasks, leaders, the war effort, and their lot in life—morale has to be sustained and nurtured over time, and is as necessary to winning battles as effective equipment or competent leaders. Napoleon's dictum of war held that the importance ratio of moral to physical force was three to one.[7] Though the complexity of human agency obviously cannot be reduced to a math equation, this perspective suggests that a breakdown in combat motivation and morale could leave seemingly efficient, well-equipped armies disintegrating into broken formations, easily routed by forces of far inferior numbers. Units suffering from low morale soon lost the will to fight, as the powerful desire for self-preservation overpowered all other actions. Wars have been lost for less.

Working against such collapse, morale bound groups of soldiers together. Camaraderie was an essential part of the glue. Brigadier William Griesbach, much loved by his men, wrote astutely: "Men do not soldier, fight and die for a dollar ten a day. Sentiment after all is the only thing for which men will suffer and die."[8] A man needed to have a sense of belonging to a new family, as well as belief and pride in his unit, if he hoped to endure at the front. Like the soldiers of old who refused to let a regimental standard fall, most Canadians took great pride in their fighting formation, as it was their new family. In this war of industrial might, where soldiers looked and felt like cogs in the machine, they knew they would be supported by their mates through the difficult times or, if the worst should happen, remembered by them in death.

A soldier soon learned that only the man who stood next to him in the line, who scratched at the lice and suffered through the seemingly endless indignities and miseries of life at the front, could be relied upon. Men were pushed beyond the limits of what they thought they could withstand because they could depend on their mates. "We were all scared ... but there was a job to do and you had to do it. The thing to do was to try and hide it from the others and not let fellows know you're scared," explained Sergeant James Page of the 42nd Battalion.[9] Cyril Searle, an underage soldier with the 18th Battalion, believed that it was mates who "maintained your morale and kept you going."[10] With so much privation at the front, soldiers needed to band together to survive: to cook meals together, to share warmth, to watch each other's back. "The way we overcome difficulties is three or four of us pal together," wrote Joseph Monaghan of the PPCLI.[11] As officer James Pedley observed, it was the "camaraderie of the damned."[12]

Mateship was important, but this did not always equal friendship. "Most of my companions in France were savages," wrote Lieutenant Harold Baldwin. "Common, little people who proved a far greater trial than the real horror."[13] Coningsby Dawson, an Oxford-educated officer, was perhaps in a miserable mood when he similarly described the ranks as composed of "coarse men, foul-mouthed men—men whose best act in life is their manner in saying good-bye to it."[14] Although most soldiers likely did not feel the same as Baldwin or Dawson, strife, anger, and resentment among men in a section, platoon, or company was not uncommon. But soldiers learned to live with it, since their lives were often in the hands of others and, moreover, most men found their comrades to be good mates as well as reliable warriors. Sergeant Harold Baldwin from Saskatchewan—not to be confused with the lieutenant described above, and in fact one of five Harold Baldwins in the CEF!— felt that "the greatest privilege ever accorded an ordinary mortal like myself was that of serving with that devil-may-care crowd of lads who sang and chaffed and swore their way from exile in western Canada to their graves in France and Flanders."[15]

The importance of camaraderie and community in maintaining trench warriors' morale cannot be overemphasized. The fraternity among men was the key factor in keeping soldiers motivated and willing to sacrifice when called upon by their seniors. But these ties were not the men's only source of motivation.[16]

"TO BECOME A LEADER, you must show your superiority, and not hide it. You must mix with your men, talk with them, congratulate them on their successes, call them by their names.... Don't foolishly throw your lives away, and don't foolishly throw your men's lives away. Live men are going to win this war, not dead ones."[17] So read a series of instructions to junior officers in Canadian training documents. Soldiers fought for one another in battle, but they fought more effectively for inspirational leaders. While the popular memory of the war derides the generals who lived comfortably in their chateaux miles behind the lines, the junior officers of the battalion, the lieutenants, captains, and majors, were the men who orchestrated the fighting from the sharp end.

Officers automatically received the privilege of command, but they had to earn respect from those they led. Martinets were despised, but so too were soft men. Sergeant W.P. Doolan of the 21st Battalion, who served two and a half years at the front and was awarded the Military Medal before he was knocked out with a shrapnel wound to his head, advised that if an officer was not a "good disciplinarian, he would lose the respect of the men."[18] The rank and file wanted leaders. Officers also had to share the dangers with their men. In the middle of a firefight, officers—like all men—were tested. Private Donald Fraser remembered the sinking feeling of dread when he watched his captain panic, running around like a terrified mare when they were first under fire: "Our estimation of our officers sank to zero and it was a lesson to us that in future it is best to rely on your own wits and do not expect too much from those senior to you."[19] And an embittered Stephen Beames, who respected some of his commanders, observed boldly: "I hated officers far more than I did the enemy. The enemy was a circumstance like the weather. A bad officer was a very personal objective for pent up hatred. A good officer could get our respect and admiration if he was man enough, but he had to be all man."[20] Echoing Beames, George Magee of the 43rd Battery offered a scathing account of some of his officers who were unwilling to shoulder the burden of danger, but expressed profound respect for an older officer, "Chuck" Lawrence, who "wouldn't ask anyone to do what he was afraid to tackle himself."[21]

Good leaders were paternalistic, and ensured that food and lodging were always available.[22] William Antliff of No. 9 Field Ambulance wrote of how, over the course of the war, the officers better understood their role in managing the lives of the men. By joking with the rank and file and playing sports with them, the officers created a "remarkable spirit of camaraderie."[23] The Western Front was no easy place to live, but the infantry's leaders—lieutenants, captains, and majors—aimed to relieve some of the trials for their men. Captain Percy Bell, a thirty-year-old physician from Winnipeg, Manitoba, concluded that "The men only demand that their officers should take a genuine interest in their progress and welfare—this being assured they will trust him through thick and thin."[24] Private Leo LeBoutillier described his relief when his ragged 24th Battalion stumbled off the Somme: "We were met by our officers who couldn't do enough for the men. Fires were burning to dry our clothes and rum and hot tea was handed around."[25] It was the little things that mattered. Not much more could be done, as often the officers suffered along with the men: they faced the same bad food, the same weather, the same rats and lice, the same dangers from shellfire or snipers. They may have had drier dugouts and batmen to cook their meals, but such luxuries were tempered by unyielding administrative work and the heavy weight of responsibility for the lives of others.

The NCOs were just as important as the officers in motivating the rank and file. After the successful battles of Vimy, Arleux, and Fresnoy, Major General Arthur Currie wrote: "Napoleon used to say 'there are no bad battalions there are only bad officers.' We have an equally wise saying 'The backbone of our army is the Non-Commissioned Officers'. The high casualties amongst the officers and NCOs proves they were true leaders. They had trained their men, and on the day of battle they led them."[26] The NCOs, corporals and sergeants, were most closely associated with the rank and file. They were the middlemen between privates and officers, much like the foremen in a large company mitigate between management and workers. The NCOs accepted orders, passed them on to the men, dealt with their grumbles, and even kept officers in line through gentle prodding or more forceful urging. Long-service NCOs were an essential conduit, and officers who did not heed their expertise or who undermined their authority would only weaken combat effectiveness in the section, platoon, or company.[27]

As the war progressed, a firm policy was followed of promoting men from the ranks to fill the holes above them left by battle losses. By mid-1917, almost all those promoted to junior officer positions were senior NCOs—solid sergeants and hard corporals who had proven themselves in battle. After a while, as one promoted sergeant quipped, the officers' mess began to resemble "the old Sergeants' Mess gone wrong."[28] Having risen from the ranks, the NCOs did not easily forget the trials of those at the lowest end of the chain of command. There were poor NCOs and officers by the bush load, no doubt, but the good ones, the ones who had an impact on morale, were recognized as such by the men. These leaders were the glue that kept fighting units together and pushing ahead. The junior officers and NCOs, in the mind of Private E.W. Russell and his mates, ensured that units in the Canadian Corps were "ably led and that the well being of the rank and file received any consideration possible."[29]

OFFICERS TRIED TO INSPIRE men through their actions and paternalistic behaviour, but when these attempts failed—or in conjunction with such methods—they could always fall back on army discipline. Discipline was defined by the army in its doctrine for junior officers as

> the instruction of obedience and self-sacrifice for the good of the community—as opposed to the personal inclination of the individual and the spirit of self-preservation. It is discipline that makes the difference between a mob of men which is unmanageable and powerless, and an organized army.... It is discipline which enables you to stick it in a tight place—when the officers are down and you are getting shelled to pieces. It is discipline that is going to win this war—and nothing else."[30]

The coercive influence of discipline kept many men in line far beyond their breaking point. And this same adherence to discipline was used during training to mould the soldiers into effective fighting forces. Hour upon hour of following orders to the very letter ensured that in battle discipline would take over and men would carry out actions as directed, enabling them to conquer fear. Sometimes this meant accepting without question the need to rush a machine-gun nest to draw enemy fire, allowing grenadiers to advance and attack from the flank. Discipline taught that the sacrifice of a few might save the group. The army did not want zombies, but men had to know how to act under terrible times of stress and against the logic of self-preservation. Battle drill was mindless and frustrating for many men, but it provided an anchor in the storm of battle.

Everything was different at the front. Officers soon learned that their authority—which they had been instructed was the key element in ensuring the hierarchical army—did not work unless those at the bottom accepted their rule. In the Allied forces, there was a belief that since Canada was less class-driven than Britain, Canadians did not show the same deference to superiors as the British rank and file did. This idea was certainly debatable, and there was still a strong hierarchy in the Canadian Corps, but the different approach to discipline in the corps was frequently flaunted in letters and postcards from Canadians at the front, and became a part of the Dominion soldiers' identity. A contemporary journalist who was embedded with the Canadian forces for part of the war described the Dominion view of discipline:

> Canada's first contingent has been described as a mob of amateur soldiers passionately inspired to give their all for a great cause. Discipline was lax, the officers unproved, and though the stuff was there, it took time to transmute it into the perfect fighting machine it became. Take the simple matter of saluting. To men of democratic birth and habit of mind, saluting had in it something of kow-tow—to the young officer it seemed an insult to his men, the tried comrades of his civil life, and they in turn might resent the implication of a social distinction that had no existence in fact. And so, for long, saluting was a perfunctory affair.[31]

Private E.W. Russell also believed the Canadians had a "light hearted response to rules and regulations." Instead of "silent obedience, it was not unusual to hear remarks concerning authority which in the Home Forces [Imperials] might have been regarded as insubordinate." Despite these marks of distinctiveness, orders were always carried out, even if under much grumbling. Often the Canadians found new ways to approach problems. "I think the western pioneering spirit was responsible for this so that in the ultimate the end justified the means," wrote Russell, who also thought this often led to "appreciable success on some important occasions."[32] He was likely right, but the Canadians from 1916 onwards were far different from those in the First Contingent. Haig meant it when he remarked in 1918 that the Canadians are "really fine disciplined soldiers now and so smart and clean."[33] The victories in the last two years of the war came through a disciplined approach to fighting, not through soldiers behaving as cowboy-voyageurs shooting up the Wild Western Front.

The Canadians' improved sense of self-control helped soldiers steady themselves in the hurricane of battle. And when discipline failed, there was always the threat of punishment: from minor stoppages in pay or forced labour to more brutal examples of the army's power, such as field punishment number 1, which involved strapping the condemned to a post or wagon for two hours and allowing the flies and lice to go to work on him, or the ultimate threat, death by firing squad. The punishments handed out to the men tended to have little uniformity across the corps, and the sentence almost always depended on the level of discipline within a battalion or unit. If the commanding officer or his superiors felt it was low, then a stiff punishment might be applied to a soldier; if it was relatively high, a soldier could get off with little more than a slap on the wrist.

Officers' authority to hand out punishments was important in reminding the rank and file of the hierarchical nature of the army; but equally crucial was a commanding officer's innate understanding of when to look the other way and let an old hand off with a verbal dressing-down and an ill-concealed smile. Sometimes more serious issues of soldiers' misbehaviour were treated informally, and within the battalion. Private Deward Barnes wrote laconically, if perhaps sympathetically, of how "one night, all the men on the outpost next to us ran away and left their post, every man of them. Sergeant Scott was too good to report it. They got frightened."[34] Barnes tacitly agreed with Scott that some issues, even ones as serious as abandoning one's post—which could result in the death penalty—should be dealt with informally. But not all units or men felt this way. A more unnerving example of a senior-ranking soldier taking a punishable matter into his own hands was recounted by Signaller Thomas Rowlett of the 25th Battalion, a fisherman from Centreville, Nova Scotia. Rowlett witnessed a private tell his sergeant to "go to H[ell]" when he was ordered to expose himself to enemy fire in an attempt to find a break in the line. After the private refused a second order, "the sgt. picked up a rifle and put a shell in the barrel and put the barrel to Campbell's head and said you will either get up or die right here."[35] The insolent man made his choice and went to find the break in the line.

Throughout the war, power in the corps was continually negotiated between the leaders and the led, and many Canadians felt that their army allowed for greater leeway in this regard than the Imperial forces.[36] "Thank the Lord we belong to an army in which we can look the officers in the eye and talk to them and about them without being court-martialed," wrote one ranker. "Sometimes we hate them all, usually at reveille and at parade times, and then a man is apt to hate himself as well. Sometimes we are agreed that they are not half bad but, as a rule, when we sit around the dugout fires, we feel sorry for them because they are forced to put up with another's society and cannot chum with the rank and file."[37]

Edward Hilliam, as a battalion commander and then brigadier, noted to officers that "firmness and kindness will ensure the confidence of all ranks.... Do not allow at any time any one to bully or unnecessarily worry your men."[38] This humane approach to command, discipline, and combat revealed that soldiers at the front were far from disillusioned, passive, broken men. The rank and file needed to be treated with respect or they would push back against the system, and often against their own officers. Even the lowest private had a sense of his own agency. If men felt they were being treated unfairly, or that the unwritten contract that underpinned the relationship between leaders and the led was being abused or broken, they reacted. Resistance came in many forms: grousing was common; unflattering rumours were spread about officers; and songs were replete with references of being cheated of leave or rum by seniors.

Will Bird recounted one anecdote of a soldier's cheeky and somewhat threatening response to an officer:

Paddy Flynn went on parade one morning with a 'kitchen mark' of black across the arm of his tunic. He discovered it at the last moment, when there was no time to remove it. Along came the officer. 'And who,' he demanded with heavy sarcasm, 'are you in mourning for?' 'For yirsif, sir,' came Paddy's surprising answer. 'I dreamt last night that you were killed badly, and it was so rale that I put on me black before I was thinkin'' He spoke so earnestly that the officer paled and said no more to him.[39]

This was one of many saucy tales of "old soldiers"—a term of rough endearment for long-service men who often found ways into and out of trouble—turning the tables on their officers, but there were other darker stories that circulated of hated officers who were shot in the back while going over the top in battle: more dead soldiers in a war that had already claimed millions. No such murders have in fact been documented, but the rumours were strong enough to perhaps dissuade some officers from exerting the full might of their command.

Soldiers found a myriad of other ways to push back against their superiors. When the rank and file felt cheated or forced to stifle discontent towards discipline and threats that were held over their heads, they reacted by malingering, finding ways out of their duties, slowing down to the point of being useless, embracing feigned patrols, or establishing live-and-let-live systems with the enemy, rather than engaging in more obvious forms of resistance such as mutiny, which had to be crushed by the army to ensure that the rot of dissent did not spread.

By the mid-point in the war, however, the authority to exercise initiative had passed down the hierarchy, and all troops were encouraged to think and act independently on the battlefield to achieve their missions. Such a doctrinal change made for better soldiers, but it also meant that the military's traditional draconian discipline had to be mitigated. Good officers learned to manage these challenges, and the fact that the British and Dominion armies were among the very few that went through the meat grinder of fighting without succumbing to massive breakdown in the form of mutiny is telling. In 1917, the Russian morale cracked as a result of terrible casualties and even worse leadership, and their fighting forces broke under the strain; the Italians would run away that same year at the Battle of Caporetto; the French mutinied, too; and even the much-vaunted German army was in ruins by the end of the war. In the end, relationships among officers, NCOs, and men were a significant key to victory. The Canadian Corps, and other formations in the BEF, were not run solely by means of fear, punishment, and discipline: soldiers in the trenches and in battle had to agree to follow their leaders, and those officers would generally get the best results from men who trusted and were inspired by them. The junior officers had the most difficult job in the army. As one Canadian combat veteran from the rank and file remarked: "They were an odd lot, those officers, but they died in front of their men."[40]

COMBAT MOTIVATION was formed of a constellation of important factors. The simple pleasures in the life of the soldier were paramount in supporting morale and the men's willingness to endure privations. If they felt they were not being cared for, they would find ways to shirk their duty. The steady rotation from front to rear, the receipt of letters and care packages from home, and the hope that there might eventually be a "bomb-proof" job for long-service veterans were all helpful in forging and maintaining morale.

The crucial significance of rum to the trench soldier bears repeating. Private George Bell recounted that "When a good stiff 'tot' of rum began working, it served to buck up the spirits of those wavering."[41] Tea was almost as important, particularly for the teetotallers; George Eyles of the 15th Battalion swore by it: "You could do without anything else but you couldn't do without tea."[42] Smoking and cigarettes remained another simple pleasure for almost everyone in the trenches. "The trench is filled with the blue gray smoke of thousands of cigarettes, lighted, puffed once, thrown away," wrote Private Harold Peat. "It soothes our nerves. It gives us something to do with our hands. It takes our mind off the impending clash."[43] This soothing of nerves, achieved either immediately through the aid of nicotine and rum, or over the longer term by reading and rereading letters from home or dreaming of eventual relief, helped to recharge the steadily dwindling batteries of men in sustained combat.

These daily means of relief could also be augmented by less common rewards. Periodic leave was a coveted prize that kept men disciplined and hungry for more in the line, as those who failed to follow the rules could be punished by its loss. Rotation through the trenches was essential in relieving the strain on soldiers, and units that felt they had been left in the firing line too long grumbled loudly, with prolonged isolation at the front eventually affecting combat motivation. This rotation was an obvious means by which soldiers could escape the trenches. Alexander Bain recounted the tension after marching out of the hell of gas, shells, and hand-to-hand fighting at Hill 70:

> For about two weeks after our arrival at this camp, a great many of the boys had to report sick and quite a few had to go to hospital, among whom my old comrade, Fred Flaherty, was one. I felt very miserable myself for a week or so. This was due to the great nervous strain which we had undergone in the last battle. I was low spirited, could not sleep at nights, and suffered considerably with pains in my legs.... I just felt that I never could go up into the line again, or bear the sound of a shell. Thank goodness we were out of the sound of them here.[44]

Bain recovered, although he and all men knew they would again return to the firing line.

Gallantry medals were also a means of acknowledging extraordinary valour on the battlefield, and were perhaps the ultimate tangible reward for soldiers. As part of the British Empire, Canadians were awarded Imperial medals for their service, with all soldiers receiving the British War Medal 1914–1920 and the Allied Victory Medal 1914–1919, and a few units receiving the 1914–1915 Star, reserved for those who served in a theatre of war before December 31, 1915. But there were also gallantry awards for those who performed uncommon bravery and sacrifice. In 1914, the decorations available to soldiers were limited: the coveted Victoria Cross for all ranks, the lesser Mentioned in Despatches and Distinguished Service Order for officers, and the Distinguished Conduct Medal for other ranks and non-commissioned officers. But the list of such awards would be added to as hundreds of thousands joined the ranks to fight on several continents.

The highest ranking medal was the Victoria Cross, the most recognized medal in the Empire, and perhaps the world. It was established in 1856 during the Crimean War. A simple bronze cross inscribed with "For Valour," those receiving it became instant heroes, both among contemporaries and for all time. Eight Canadians had been awarded the Victoria Cross while serving with British forces in the nineteenth century or during the South African War, but the terrible struggle of the Great War created far more opportunities for gallantry, and gallant death. Of the total 94 Victoria Crosses awarded to Canadians over the last 150 years, 70 went to Canadians in the Great War. The honour remained exceedingly rare and was the mark of heroics, although it—and all awards—were sometimes bestowed inconsistently.[45]

An application for a Victoria Cross required thorough support from commanding officers. Recommendations for the prestigious award went up the chain of command and could be rejected or downgraded to a lesser award, and often were. By late 1916, the army was changing the eligibility requirements for the medal, and explicitly ordered that Victoria Crosses could not be awarded to men who rescued comrades trapped under fire in No Man's Land, unless the recipient was a stretcher-bearer.[46] By the last two years of the war, the Victoria Cross was given most frequently for warlike actions, particularly for knocking out dreaded machine-gun nests that often resulted in the death of the soldier.

As the war progressed, the British authorities found they needed a more robust gallantry award system to meet the heroic demands of millions of British and Dominion soldiers in uniform. The significant medals included the Distinguished Service Order (DSO), Military Cross (MC), Distinguished Conduct Medal (DCM), and the Military Medal (MM). If a man was awarded a second gallantry award, he received a bar to add to his medal, which was worn on the ribbon.

The Distinguished Service Order—a gold cross covered in white enamel and edged in gold—was awarded for meritorious or distinguished service in the war, and after January 1, 1917, it could be awarded only to those serving under fire. Awarded 857 times during the war to Canadians, it was reserved for officers, and usually those at or above the rank of lieutenant colonel, for gallantry just short of the Victoria Cross. The Military Cross, established in December 1915 to complement the DSO, was available only to junior officers below the rank of captain (acting majors too), and also to warrant officers, a senior NCO rank. The Military Cross was a silver Imperial Cross with the Royal Cypher of the reigning sovereign in the centre. The MC was awarded to 3,195 Canadians during the Great War, including 294 who received it twice, and a rare 16 who were honoured three times.[47]

Enlisted men and NCOs were eligible for other medals. "For Distinguished Conduct in the Field," was the reverse imprint on the Distinguished Conduct Medal. Awarded to NCOs and the rank and file, it was the second-highest award for gallantry in action for all ranks, next only to the Victoria Cross. The DCM was the first award created to fill the demand to recognize heroes of the Crimean War, and the first Canadian received the honour of wearing the crimson ribbon with its dark blue central stripe during the South African War. During the Great War, 1,947 Canadians received the DCM, 36 received the DCM and Bar, and one, Company Sergeant Major George Soles, received the DCM with Second Bar. For those deeds that did not reach the standard of the DCM, the Military Medal was available. First introduced in March 1916, the silver medal reads, "For Bravery in the Field," and 12,345 were issued during the Great War, as well as 875 First and Second Bars. Many officers wore Military Medals on their chest, which revealed their rise from the non-commissioned ranks.[48]

These Imperial awards linked the Canadians to the Empire's forces, as was true for other Dominion and colonial forces. There was some movement in mid-1916 to create a Canadian order, as part of the gradual process of Canadianization. In fact, this made its way up to Sir Sam Hughes, but the ludicrously titled, "The Order of the Beaver and Maple Leaf," thankfully never made it out of the committee stage after Hughes resigned.[49]

While medals remain a mark of extraordinary service, they were not always viewed as such by the hardened soldiers. Cases occurred of officers endangering others to put themselves in dangerous situations where they might be recognized with a medal. The rank and file, who likely would not have received the same recognition, thought meanly of such selfish actions. The Germans even had a particularly appropriate word for the practice: "throat envy," referring to the desire to win an Iron Cross, which was worn around the neck. Canadians had their own quips, including their advice that men who went searching for Military Crosses usually ended up with wooden ones. Official records suggest that within the Canadian

Corps there was an acknowledgment that officers had been known to put others at risk in "attempting to win honours for the sake of honours themselves."[50]

Some soldiers were positively scathing in their assessment of the gallantry awards. "Medals are given out at the front and we have learned to attach little or no importance to a military medal & not much more to the military cross," wrote William Antliff, who (perhaps ironically) would later be awarded the Military Medal.[51] The annual awards issued twice a year, on the King's birthday and the New Year's Honours List, were not given for specific incidents but for general good service, and sometimes to soldiers not even in contact with the enemy. H.W. MacPherson wrote, "A big list of honors DSOs and MCs is out. I'm afraid they are rather spoiling the MC by giving it for all sorts of things. The O.C. Divisional Baths got it! Why not a K.C.B. [knighthood]? It's rather hard luck on men who have really won it." The soldiers who "really won it," in his mind, were those who did so at the sharp end.[52]

Not only did the less deserving sometimes receive awards, but so too did many brave men whose accomplishments on the battlefield had previously been overlooked. Major Agar Adamson admitted to this: "It is a most trying and difficult matter to pick out any one when they all did so well, and then to write a separate account of each act."[53] To be recognized with an award meant first battling the enemy, then the bureaucracy. An officer had to witness the brave deed and then take the time to write it into a recommendation. Depending on the officer's literary skills, a deserving action might not impress senior officers, while one less distinguished might make its way up the chain of command because of literary rather than battlefield prowess. In the last year of the war, corps headquarters even recommended that units find an officer "specifically gifted in regard to writing up recommendations."[54] In battles where units were decimated, there might be no officer left from the action to write the necessary recommendations. William Griesbach was always forward-thinking, and while serving as a battalion commander he encouraged other ranks "to come forward with statements as to deserving cases."[55] This democratization of the gallantry award likely encouraged its acceptance among the men and augmented its value as a combat motivator. Some units took great pride in garnering awards, and therefore never missed an opportunity to nominate men, while others were more haphazard in their recommendations, echoing Adamson's statement that it was difficult to note extraordinary gallantry among men who were almost all doing their jobs, which inherently involved unbelievable bravery. Richard Turner, while writing as a brigadier after the Second Battle of Ypres, jotted in his dairy: "A long list of officers and men have been recommended for honours—some will be left out. C'est la fortune de la guerre."[56]

There was no doubt a contradiction in the soldiers' perspective on medal winners. While the men sneered at the bomb-proofers who received their medals "with the ration bags," as the saying went, those who earned them at the front were held in high esteem. Living Victoria Cross winners were so rare that the men could not help but be awed by them. Other medal winners were equally respected if they had earned the awards in battle. Lieutenant Stanley Edgett, who served with the 60th and 87th Battalions, was proud to tell his mother: "… my sergeant is a brave chap. He won the D.C.M. at Hill 60 up at Ypres."[57]

Winners of gallantry awards almost always downplayed them among their mates, often acknowledging that others could have received the same medals for similar brave deeds. Donald Fraser of the 31st Battalion remarked bitterly: "Decorations have become so much of a joke that the recipient, conscious that he has done nothing, often remarks when questioned by his 'pals' what did he do: 'Oh, I guess I was first at the rations!' as if to signify that the Quartermaster dealt them out. Failing which he may answer quizzically, after pondering the matter over, 'Blest if I know.'"[58] No doubt such nonchalance was rooted in hard men's embarrassment by the "gongs" bestowed on them from men in the rear who did not share their danger. Lieutenant Allen Oliver's letter to his mother shortly before his death in battle, suggesting that she might be pleased that he had been awarded the Military Cross, conveyed his conflicted feelings about the award: "Your son is therefore a hero in a moderate sort of way, at least to outsiders."[59]

Despite this ambivalence, and even anger, towards what seemed the increasingly prolific handing out of gallantry awards, the medals were still extremely rare. The 14th Battalion, the Royal Montreal Regiment, makes an interesting case study in this regard. The battalion served from 1914 to 1919—for a total of 1,721 days. During that time, 6,270 men passed through the battalion, sustaining 4,469 casualties.[60] This shocking sacrifice of more than two-thirds of the battalion's men was similar to the loss suffered by other Canadian front-line infantry battalions. Fighting in almost every major Canadian battle, the 14th Battalion accrued the following medals:

- 2   Victoria Crosses
- 1   Distinguished Service Order with Bar
- 6   Distinguished Service Orders
- 4   Military Crosses with Bar
- 33   Military Crosses
- 2   Distinguished Conduct Medals with Bar
- 40   Distinguished Conduct Medals
- 1   Military Medal and two Bars
- 23   Military Medals with Bar
- 156 Military Medals[61]

In addition, a number of officers and NCOs received official Mentioned in Despatches, and several foreign decorations were bestowed on men for liaising with other national units, such as those belonging to the French or Belgian armies, or for being at the right place at the right time. However, the awards the unit received exclusively for gallantry numbered just 268 separate medals, with 30 men counted twice or more. These totals suggest that only 4 out of 100 men ever received a gallantry decoration, while 71 out of 100 could expect to be wounded or killed. These ratios provide stark evidence that despite serving honourably and in horrific conditions, most soldiers would never receive a gallantry medal.

Although medals were sometimes viewed cynically, over the decades they have become the primary means of distinguishing bravery on the battlefield. Often they did, and the citations for many medal winners indeed speak for the actions they represent. An award given for single-handedly charging a machine-gun nest over open, broken ground in order to draw fire away from one's vulnerable companions should never be derided. But perhaps Albert West summed it up best after being awarded the Military Medal: "All the medal I want is a consciousness of duty done and my only souvenir, a whole skin."[62]

GIVEN ALL OF THE COMPLEX FACTORS depended upon to augment morale and inculcate combat motivation in soldiers, it can often be forgotten that many men wanted to fight the Germans. This is not to highlight an inherent warring nature in the Canadians, but instead to underscore their genuine belief in the cause of defeating what they perceived to be a tyrannical enemy. Charles Pearce, a gunner who later served with the British flying services, wrote a year before his death: "I hope mother does not worry Dad, but I am afraid she does but when you think of the murders committed by the Germans you cannot help feeling that no hardship is too great."[63] Similarly, George Ormsby wrote to his wife: "Keep up courage Dear and don't be afraid, and if it should happen that I do go under, I trust you will be proud that I have had the courage to get out and fight against such a domineering race. Should Germany win this war then may God help Canada—in fact the whole world."[64] While such sentiments of the trench soldiers might have served as a tonic to soothe worried loved ones, or even to convince themselves of the righteousness of their actions and sacrifices, one cannot help but be struck by William Antliff's frank appraisal:

> The newspaper-talk about the cheerfulness & devil may care spirit of the Tommy under shell fire is pure bunkum but in spite of this I would sooner a thousand times die and lick the Boche than live under the Prussian tyranny. This isn't any high-minded noble sacrifice principle but a matter of absolute existence. It is only by every man doing his bit we can win but we are going to win because we can't afford to lose.[65]

While many men had patriotic beliefs blasted from them in the trenches, and many more hated the trials of trench warfare and the equally distasteful experience of submission to control in the hierarchical forces, Canadians in the twenty-first century should not lose sight of those who believed fully in the necessity of the sacrifice. Such men did not fold easily in the face of the terrible carnage of the battlefield.

Any analysis of fighting troops must also account for men who were tough to the core. They knew hardship and they learned to push through it. "Believe me if the civvies had to put up with a tenth of what the Tommys do there would be a revolution in every country of Europe," wrote an exasperated William Antliff. But, his upper lip stiffened, he finished quickly with, "Enough of this grousing."[66] The civvies, too, proved resilient, but few had to endure what the Great War front-line soldier faced. Iron men were needed for an iron war.

Opposing armies of millions or more would never be fully destroyed on the battlefields. The slow grind of attritional warfare would wear down the adversary by killing and maiming his troops, but also by breaking him psychologically. If attrition of German men and morale was the aim of the British, it was also acknowledged that their own forces had to be protected against this strain. One of the great marvels of the war is how long the civilian-soldiers held out in the trenches. Suffering from frustration towards their inability to break through the enemy trench system, and bitterness towards the futility of friends lost, the British and Dominion troops never gave up, never succumbed to revolution, never refused to see the war through to the end. This dogged perseverance was the key to victory, probably more so than the introduction of new weapon systems or interventions by the high command. It was the extraordinary tenacity and phlegmatic endurance of the trench soldier that made the difference between victory and defeat.

But irrespective of a battle's result, the Canadians always paid in blood. Private Donald Fraser described his machine-gun company's desperate advance into Lens during the Battle of Hill 70 on August 21, 1917. Their path was straight into the German guns, and experienced men like Fraser knew that such fighting would be brutal.

> We had about a mile to go. The trench, an old German one, was wide and not very deep, badly knocked about by shell fire and in parts full of broken strands of wire which proved troublesome. Snipers were busy. Shells were either whizzing past us or dropping all around, miraculously missing us.... I was a little in the rear of Ladd when a shell roared by Ladd missing him by the barest inch and crashed into the foot of the side of the trench—a dud. Ladd pulled in his stomach as if to dodge it and slowly turned around revealing the whitest face I ever saw in my life. He tried to grin, but it was a very, very sickly-looking grin.[67]

Survival on the Western Front was about measuring life and death in inches; playing hand after hand in a game of long odds; and realizing that there no way to defend against death except with the sickest of grins.

CHAPTER 14

SUPERNATURAL BATTLEFIELDS

The Dead and the Undead on the Western Front

Death in the trenches came with little warning. There was no dodging one's fate, no way to sidestep a shell or avoid a sniper's bullet. In addition to the important role played by comrades, officers, and a reward system in supporting the morale of soldiers, most men also found ways to cope by turning to a belief system. The Canadian Corps was an army that very much embraced divine agency and protection. Fred Robinson wrote of his belief in God to decide his fate:

> The fire of the opposing artilleries assumes such violence as to practically carry everything before it, one wonders how Human beings can live in such a Hell of fire and flame nothing else can live there. I have seen men with their clothes blown half off them but still unhurt and determined to carry on. I have myself been buried no less than five times during one bombardment of about four hours duration and at one time had the experience of being completely buried by one shell and literally blown clear out again by another without sustaining so much as one scratch. It is such happenings as these which make fatalists of the majority of us, by that I mean that we believe God holds our destinies in His hands and will seal our fate in His own time.[1]

Others, such as infantryman Frank Maheux, believed that a higher power would see them through the terrible fighting: "I do believe God will preserve me again when

I go back to the trenches."[2] But many soldiers were far more irreverent: Conn Smythe, for instance—who would later found the Toronto Maple Leafs hockey team—simply referred to God, with wonderful trench-warrior nonchalance, as "The Man Upstairs,"[3] while John MacGregor of the 16th Battalion, a Victoria Cross winner, credited his survival to his "Friend."[4] Many men would have shared the sentiments of Tom Spear, who survived the war and lived past the age of 100: "In my breast pocket, right next to my paybook, I carried a small Bible. I read it every day and I honoured it. The verses gave me a lot of confidence and security—and, believe me, I needed both."[5]

While many soldiers resented church parades and fire-and-brimstone speeches by the military chaplains—with Sergeant L.M. Gould going so far as to call the church parades the "grimmest and ghastliest of Service jokes ... provocative of more blasphemy and discontent than any active operation"—countless soldiers took solace in organized religion.[6] Some of the padres were viewed as positively heroic, such as the star poet and fearless Canon Frederick Scott, who was always in the front-line trenches with his flock. "The chaplain who does his turn in the line with the men," wrote Canadian infantryman Harold Innis, "who goes through the battle with them, has won a large place in the hearts of his men."[7] Conversely, those padres who were less inclined to move within range of the guns were openly derided by combat soldiers.

Religion mattered to the fighting men: on attestation forms, 30.9 percent identified themselves as Anglican, 22.9 percent as Catholic, 21.1 as Presbyterian, and 13.6 per cent as Methodist, with many other faiths represented.[8] But despite the important role of organized religion in helping soldiers cope or make sense of the war, one wonders how many men agreed with infantryman Herbert Burrell, who admitted: "One cannot enter into the spirit of the service when the guns are vomiting death and destruction all around."[9]

Many soldiers were mystified as to why God let the slaughter continue. When shells landed next to men but failed to explode, it appeared that some higher power had protected them; but why had their friend, who was just as worthy, been taken? Religion did not seem to offer the guidance that it once had, leaving many soldiers disillusioned and yearning for answers.[10] There may indeed have been "no atheists in foxholes," as the Second World War phrase went, but in the strange subterranean killing ditches of the Western Front, soldiers often turned to other means of coping psychologically, sometimes relying on them in conjunction with religion, sometimes using them as a replacement for it.

"WAR ITSELF and the conditions which surrounded our daily lives, the possibility of death at any moment and the need of dying as decently as might be, bred in us a kind of medieval paganism which substituted picturesque symbols or legends, partly of our own creating, for the cut-and-dried 'mother's knee' business which had sufficed our souls in less spacious days," wrote Sergeant Ralf Sheldon-Williams, a farmer who had enlisted in Victoria, British Columbia, at the age of forty. "We had, in short, reverted, because of and as a result of the business in hand, to a primitive state of mind which opened the door to a sneaking regard for the miraculous."[11] Soldiers learned to manage death by accommodating it, making light of it, embracing it, and scoffing at it. The trivial—in the form of charms and superstitions—became the sacred.

The trench soldier's most common defence mechanism was the development of a fatalistic attitude. With so many men killed around them, soldiers were left with little choice but to fully accept the possibility of death or wounding at the front. Wilfred Kerr of the 11th Battery shared his thoughts on this widespread surrender to fate:

> There was a common saying: 'If your number's on the shell, it'll get you, if it isn't, you're all right; and you can't do anything to avoid it.' More and more this attitude impressed itself on one; and it afforded a certain amount of comfort, since it relieved one from the necessity of worrying whether this path or that path, this step or that step, this job or that job might lead him into serious harm's way.[12]

Those who could not see themselves as already dead, or their fate as sealed, had a harder time dealing with the lethal randomness of the war. Private George Bell, who served four years at the front before he stopped a bullet in the last months of the war, described his own sense of fatalism: "I had adjusted myself to the abnormal conditions under which we were living, one in which we were likely to meet death at any moment."[13] In a desperate bid to grasp life, soldiers embrace death.

But death was not inevitable, regardless of the odds. And despite the deterministic attitudes that enabled men to carry out their duties, most trench soldiers hoped that a shell or bullet did not indeed seek them out. A popular tune among those in khaki, "The Bells of Hell Ring for You, but Not for Me," summed up their perspective nicely. As part of this bravado, many men made light of their fears, often by renaming weapons of war with slang, and even referring to the dead as having "gone west" or having been "napooed." Joking about the dead was a defence mechanism for the soldiers, and psychiatrists would have had the whole of the army on their couches if anyone had cared to investigate.

Trivializing and scoffing at death, normalizing the abnormal—all played their part in helping soldiers to cope.[14] Such measures acted as a defence against death. It was hard for the men not to embrace this ghoulishness when they inhabited open graveyards: corpses not only lay in No Man's Land but jutted out from the trench walls. Front-line soldiers could be callous, even cruel to the unknown dead. "The boys used the shin bones as racks for their gas masks and canteens, and one of them made a point of combing and arranging the blond hair of a head," wrote Gunner Ernest Black.[15] Engaging in such gallows humour was another means of psychological survival. Charles Roy Grose of the 102nd Battalion, a farmer from Rossland, British Columbia, told the story of one hand that jutted from a communication wall: "Men used to walk by and joke, 'Well, old timer, you are in a good place there.'"[16] Louis Keene described another grimly surreal image: "One man had the misfortune to be buried in such a way that the bald part of the head showed. It had been there a long time and was sun-dried. Tommy used him to strike his matches on. A corpse in a trench is quite a feature, and is looked for when the men come back again to the same trench."[17]

However, the constant presence of death was clearly not always a joking matter. The stench of rotting flesh assaulted the nostrils of men entering the front lines and could not easily be scoffed away. Private Frank Hasse of the 49th Battalion described the smell as "gut-emptying."[18] The reek of death came from No Man's Land, filled as it was with corpses reduced to a cheese-like consistency by the elements. But the

Two soldiers hold a human skull and perhaps ponder life and death on the Western Front. As trench warriors often fought and lived in open graveyards, it is not surprisingthat many embraced death as a coping mechanism.

smell of decay also wafted out from the trench walls, where the dead had been interred.

Soldiers stood on corpses, stabbed shovels and pick axes through the dissolving remains, even slept next to them. They necessarily grew callous to the dead, and sometimes even to their comrades who were killed. Lieutenant J.S. Williams remarked rather casually in a letter home: "My batman had his head blown off. It's extraordinary, really, what one can stand when one's put to the test. Now, before I came here I had never seen a dead person in my life before, and yet I do not seem to feel badly about it."[19] He was not alone. Private John McNab of the 38th Battalion, accustomed to the terrible fighting on the Somme, recounted his unit's experience of coming back from the line one day:

a big coal-box [large-calibre German shell] landed in the trench in front about thirty feet way. We stopped to let the dirt and shrapnel get down then we went on, and when we got round the turn in the trench it was all blown in, and right in the middle was a lad named McDonald. His head was shot off and his clothes torn nearly off, and he was buried to the waist. It was an awful sight, but we took a look at him and went on our ways. I was used to that by then so it did not bother me any.[20]

"Life was cheap," wrote Ralf Sheldon-Williams. "One soon grew thick-skinned on the subject [of death], both personally and vicariously, and felt a shock only when a man who had shared parcels and blankets with us for months went west hurriedly. That *did* bring it home to you, and set you wondering if Fritz had also pulled your number out of the grab-bag."[21]

THE RANDOMNESS OF DEATH reinforced the constant sense of risk at the front. John Cadenhead, who had enlisted at the young age of sixteen and served much of the war as a runner—dodging dangerously from shell hole to shell hole and down crumbling communication trenches as he moved from front to rear and back again to deliver messages—remarked: "Every time you went near the line you were gambling—it was a gamble whether you came out or not."[22] And as risk-takers facing the highest of stakes, men looked for patterns that led to winning and survival. Within the chaos and randomness of death, soldiers tried to find rituals, superstitions, or magical devices to beat the odds. "I am afraid that I am getting superstitious since I came over here," admitted Lieutenant Lawrence Rogers, only a few months before he was killed in battle.[23] Men tried to do the same thing every day in the trenches, patterning their behaviour rigorously to avoid any deviation that might lead to their luck changing. Such actions did not make rational sense, but there was little that was rational about life in the trenches. The longer they survived, the more soldiers clung to their rituals that seemed to be working, and few paid much attention when luck ran out. Wounded men thanked their rituals for preserving them from a worse fate, while the dead could offer no comment. Ways of acting or not acting, patterns that needed to be followed, and rules that had to be heeded were all essential in the minds of many men who lived in a world run by chance and chaos.

Some of the superstitions were in fact cautionary tales that kept men alive. The warning about "three on a match" remained an important one in the mind of many men. The refusal of a light to a third man was almost a rule on the Western Front, but it was born from long experience. The flare of the match could draw a sniper's attention, and, should the glow persist, he might decide to fire a shot through the trench parapet, which could be weakened from the weather. Even if it may have been overly cautious to assume that a sniper could target the glow of a match in a few seconds, the soldiers believed it. D.E. Macintyre described another superstition: "There used to be a saying that the same spot is never hit twice by a shell."[24] While this was of course not true, the idea was perhaps calming in the middle of a barrage, and it was in fact good advice to dive into a still-smoking shell crater, as at least the hole provided some cover.

But many superstitions had nothing to do with actual physical survival and were useful only as psychological coping mechanisms. Padre George Wells, known as the "Fighting Bishop" for his service in three wars—the South African War, the Great War, and the Second World War—described how one popular belief increased the difficulty of identifying the dead. After some time involved in this dismal work, he noted,

> A large number of soldiers carried no identification. This was against regulations; each man was issued with a disc which he was supposed to wear around his neck, but for some reason many of them didn't want to wear them. Perhaps they derived some comfort in believing they would never need to be identified but would survive to identify themselves. To be sure, I never wore mine."[25]

The discs were worn exclusively so that the slain could be identified; many men refused to apply such thoughts to themselves, or believed that wearing the disc invited death. The sheer number of unknown dead from the war may provide some grim evidence of how widespread this belief was, although the lack of formal identification tags until late in 1916 and the dismembering effects of shellfire were no doubt a greater factor in the difficulty of identifying the dead.

Medical officer Captain J.C. Dunn of the Royal Welch Fusiliers reflected the opinions of many combat soldiers when he scoffed at the superstition that pervaded the trenches: "There was no limit to the fanciful tales that ran riot, gaining currency and prompt discredit.... Superstition preyed upon many; it was among the youngest that I remarked it." Dunn saw much of the horror of war and could rightly distinguish some of the silly superstitions, but it was not just the young who believed in them; for good measure, Dunn's brilliant memoirs are rife with rumours, superstitions, and other soldiers' beliefs.[26]

Even as unlucky numbers, such as thirteen, were avoided, and signs and portents were studied, some soldiers were aware enough of their own irrationality to allow themselves to hold it up to ridicule on occasion. They might one minute be following their personal patterns of actions and whispering their silent prayers, and in the next moment take the piss out of what they were doing. One of their jokes cheekily summed up their gallows humour and superstitions: "It is considered very unlucky to be killed on a Friday."[27]

WHILE SUPERSTITIONS swirled from man to man, shared as communal stories of warning and means to govern actions, every man had his own private form of protection. Amulets and relics, magic coins and bullets, sacred bibles and photographs of loved ones—all of these, and more, became talismans used to ward off the fear of the unknown.[28] Most of the items had an intimate meaning to the owner: a piece of shrapnel might be kept as a reminder of a tangible brush with death—or to ward off its return.

Soldiers could be given talismans by worrying loved ones at home. Daughters and sons often sent along toys and drawings, and photos were highly prized objects, charged with meaning: "I want [a photograph of you] to carry for my own edification to act as a talisman to ward off the enemy bullets," wrote Corporal Harry Hillyer to his wife. "I have sufficient faith in your goodness and prayers that I believe if I carry your photo with me I shall not meet with any serious injuries."[29] Sadly, in this case, the longed-for photo did not ultimately ward off death, but Hillyer likely faced it more easily with the photo in his pocket. Georges Vanier wrote to his friend Frances, a nun: "I was very, very glad to receive the relic of St. Sebastian [the patron saint of soldiers] given to you by your mistress at Convent and I will always carry it with me. This relic, coupled with your prayers and those of my dear relatives and friends will protect me."[30]

Many men carried bibles, often strategically placed over the heart, in part because a convenient pocket on their khaki jacket was located there, but also because of the stories—some true—that bullets had been stopped by the Good Book. Chas Henderson of the 19th Battalion carried a Flemish bible in his lower left pocket, which stopped a bullet during the first hour of the Battle of Vimy Ridge. "The little book at least slowed the bullet down in its progress through my 'innards.'"[31] Henderson survived the war, as did Lieutenant Gregory Clark, who also had faith in the power of his bible: "As a superstition, I carried a new testament in my left breast pocket of my tunic—in which were preserved the 4 leaf clovers I found—and I never read any of that except Chap. 21 of Revelations."[32] Perhaps he found comfort in the lines, "And God shall wipe away all tears from their eyes; and there shall be no more death, neither sorrow, nor crying, neither shall there be any more pain: for the former things are passed away."

Soldiers' rituals, superstitions, and talismans offered protection to the vulnerable. Every man had a different belief system, although each was influenced by the myths and stories shared by the group. However, one soldier's belief or talisman could be another one's object of derision. The famous British war correspondent Philip Gibbs met a colonel in the North Staffordshires who honestly believed it was his will power that deflected flying metal away from him on the battlefield. "I have a mystical power. Nothing will ever hit me as long as I keep that power which comes from faith. It is a question of absolute belief in the domination of mind over matter." Gibbs noted, "He spoke quietly and soberly in a matter-of-fact way. I decided that he was mad." Indeed he may have been, but within the asylum that was the Western Front he was likely not too out of place.[33]

SOLDIERS' BELIEFS and actions also shed light on their fears. These men lived in the scarred wasteland of the war's front lines, a haunted place if ever there was one, and it should surprise few that No Man's Land spawned its own stories of dread and terror. Here, the dead inhabited the same physical and metaphysical space as the living. Their presence was more than felt: the living in fact seemed to be intruding into the world of the dead. The bewildering nature of such a place, where death seemed to stalk every man, led many soldiers to perceive the enemy's death-dealing weapons—or even No Man's Land itself—as monsters that lurked in the shadows to take their lives. Harry Coombs wrote to his brother about a mate in his section: "He is among the missing, another victim of No Man's Land."[34] Most of Coombs's friends had been killed or maimed, and only one original section mate remained; the rest had seemingly been swallowed by the darkness—consumed by the living entity that was No Man's Land.

George Magee, a gunner in the 43rd Battery who would be killed in the last months of the war, described the foreboding menace that seemed to lurk among the dead in No Man's Land:

> In those shallow trenches others had perished in the defence, as they thought of their Fatherland. By that scooped out hole yonder, where empty cartridges still strew the ground, a husky German machine gunner had lain beside his gun, repeatedly bayoneted and his head crushed in. At the bottom of those dugouts by the sunken road lay what had been men before Mill's bombs bounded down the steps. Over the field to the left of the wood were the ghastly remains of Frenchmen mowed down in rows in earlier fighting for Hangard, but why dwell on the scene? In and around that demolished village the dead of three nations rest. There is something eerie still in the air, even the hardened soldier feels it. It is a cemetery.[35]

Similarly, Major D.J. Corrigall of the 20th Battalion recounted the uneasy, even haunting, quality of the battlefield around Lens in the summer of 1917: "When there was a moon, the weird shadows kept us continually 'seeing things.' During these queer nights angle iron posts could be seen forming fours, patrolling, advancing, et cetera. Imagination ruled the nights."[36]

Many men believed that in the broken wilds that separated the two warring sides lay an army of deserters, reduced to surviving like ghouls, or so the stories went. British infantryman and poet Osbert Sitwell wrote of this international band of outlaw deserters:

> They would issue forth, it was said, from their secret lairs after each of the interminable check-mate battles, to rob the dying of their few possessions— treasures such as boots or iron-rations—and leave them dead. Were these bearded figures, a shambling in rags and patched uniforms … a myth created

by suffering among the wounded, as a result of pain, privation and exposure, or did they exist? It is difficult to tell. At any rate, the story was widely believed among the troops, who maintained that the General Staff could find no way of dealing with these bandits until the war was over, and that in the end they had to be gassed.[37]

This was little more than a "monster story" for sentries and those men who patrolled the blasted No Man's Land.[38] Another soldier described the deserter army that lived "like ghouls among the mouldering dead, and who came out at nights to plunder and kill."[39] The rumours and tales of horror continued to be fed by the soldiers who waited on the liminal boundaries of the battlefield, staring into the darkness. Many of those who entered into this unholdable land did not return, being snuffed out in ambushes, killed by stray fire, or, perhaps, captured and murdered (some claimed eaten) by the deserters. Putting a face on the unknown—even if it was a fantastic or grotesque one—helped soldiers deal with the uncertainty of what was "out there," and perhaps make sense of their senseless environment.

"IF YOU START DIGGING, you turn up what's left of something human," wrote a shaken Coningsby Dawson. "If there were any grounds for superstition, surely the places in which I have been should be ghost-haunted."[40] Many battlefields have stories of haunting attached to them. These places of mass trauma still have a presence, a sense of unease, grief, even of sepulchre. On the edge of the Western Front, the soldiers stood, ate, slept, and shit in a mass-murder site. And there was no escape, only temporary respite. The extraordinary violence and savagery of the Western Front was a solid presence.

Many soldiers experienced supernatural premonitions of death or of escaping near-death occurrences. William Green of the 4th Battalion wrote, "A lot of men had premonitions during the war of never coming home and a lot them, sorry to say, came true."[41] Harold Baldwin testified that his friend Morgan had "a second sight, a gift of foreseeing things," which he used to accurately predict when Baldwin and Morgan would be wounded in battle.[42] Sergeant Chester E. Routley told of being in the line with a normally rock-solid mate who "came to me and said that he was scared as he could be. He said that he wouldn't let the boys know it for anything, but he just had to tell someone." Routley reacted strongly when his friend, a fellow sergeant, informed him that he had foreseen his own death in a premonition:

> It made me feel sick, for I had heard of men saying that same thing before and they always got it. I tried to cheer him up a bit. I told him that he was alright and going to be alright, but I had known him for a long time and had never heard him talk like that before. He had done some pretty risky things too, such as putting out barbed wire in no man's land and patrolling our company frontage. To my knowledge, he had never been scared before. I tried to cheer him up, but I guess that my best was very poor.[43]

The sergeant was killed the next day, by taking a piece of shrapnel through his heart. The soldiers' tales described many similar cases, with contemporary studies by spiritualists and ghost-hunters claiming that such premonitions (or at least stories of them), were common at the front.[44]

"I have just come through another German hunt. Quite a few of my old pals are either wounded or otherwise. And I feel as if my turn to follow some of them is pretty near."[45] So wrote Frederick Barnes to his girl, Katie; he was killed at the age of twenty-two less than three weeks later. Barnes statement was perhaps based on a premonition, but more likely on an acknowledgment that he had served long past his due date in the cruel world of the Western Front. What, though, are we to make of the hard, even cynical, Will Bird, who offered caustic observations on his mates and officers throughout the war, and who would return to Canada afterwards to become a much-loved journalist and historian in Nova Scotia?

While on the Vimy battlefield, Will Bird of the 42nd had a unique premonition. After working through the muck and slime in No Man's Land, he finally made it to a dugout in a reserve trench and bunked down with some "decent chaps" from the 73rd. Deep in slumber, he awoke as his groundsheet was pulled away and a warm hand pulled him to a sitting position. Groggy and unhappy about being awakened, Will was surprised to see his brother, Steve, staring at him. Half asleep and fully exhausted, he could not believe it, largely because his brother had been listed as "missing, believed killed," almost two years earlier. When he blurted out a surprised word, his brother put his warm hand over his mouth, told him to grab his gear and follow him. He did, amazed that somehow his brother was alive, and somehow had found him on the Western Front. Will followed Steve down the communication trench, wiping sleep from his eyes, but unable to catch his brother, who was a few steps in front of him, and moving with pace. Stumbling along in the dark, he called to his brother to slow down, and then he rounded a corner and found himself alone. A devastated Will could not believe he had lost his brother again. Collapsing in despair, he rationalized that in his exhausted state he had imagined his brother had been in his billet. Distraught from the stirred-up memories of his brother's death, he fell asleep in a funk hole.

Bird was found the next day by surprised mates, who roughly shook him awake. "'What made you come here?' Tommy was asking. 'What happened?'" He recounted his story to shocked faces: his mates could not believe it, and then they told him that his bivvy mates, the men he bunked down with, were now little more than pieces, as a high explosive shell had landed on their dugout. Bird's surviving comrades had assumed he was part of the spongy, red mess left behind, and had even pulled a leg out that they thought was his. His story made its way around the ranks, and his officer and sergeant were suspicious, wanting to know why he had left the dugout. He told them the truth, the sergeant staring incredulously while the officer, a true believer, only nodded and said reverentially: "You have had a wonderful experience."[46] Bird and the officer were sure that the apparition of his brother had saved his life. One wonders if such believers were the majority or the minority of soldiers at the front, and how many were like the hard-bitten sergeant, who thought Bird's story was nonsense but could offer no more rational answer to explain his survival.

Premonitions and precognitions had long been part and parcel of the psychic's trade, but attention to these phenomena was further enhanced during the trauma of the war years, with soldiers' accounts similar to Bird's littering the pages of contemporary journals devoted to the field.[47] Impending events, psychics and like-minded believers suggested, cast shadows, which were imprinted on the ectoplasmic substance that was read or interpreted by a medium. Other psychics, who had heightened senses of perception, could feel the future as it touched them through conduits from the spirit world. While no séances, Ouija boards, or ectoplasmic projections were recorded at the front, many soldiers felt the shadow of the future cast upon them, and they made their final farewells accordingly.

Some soldiers were visited by premonitory warnings in the form of voices, images, and ethereal forms, all of which were recorded, but we can never know what uncanny experiences were never put to paper. In stories similar to that of Bird and his warm-handed brother, soldiers were saved by unseen powers or loved ones. Canadian serviceman Wallace Reid wrote to his mother of suffering under the strain of waiting to attack behind a crushing shellfire bombardment in the trenches; when he went over the top, he saw friends and comrades killed all around him by enemy fire, and at one point a shell landed nearby, rendering him senseless and throwing a corpse on him that bled all over his face, drenching him in blood. When he cast aside the body, he realized that everyone around him was dead: "whole bodies, pieces of bodies, single bodies, piles of bodies, all stark and still." And then, within this ghastly landscape, he felt a presence: "For a few seconds some magic hand held up all the hellish forces that were playing over that tortured land. I waited, scarcely breathing, for something—waited, it seemed minutes that could only have been seconds. Then it came—invisible, intangible, but nevertheless, very real. Something came to that place of desolation, stopped a moment and passed on again, and I was the only living witness." Reid never again felt the invisible presence that he attributed with his salvation on that day. But another soldier is said to have written home to his mother: "One night while carrying bombs, I had occasion to take cover when about twenty yards off I saw you looking towards me as plain as life. Leaving my bombs I crawled nearly to the place where your vision appeared, when a German shell dropped on them, and—well—I had to return for some more. But had it not been for you, I certainly would have been reported 'missing.' … You'll turn up again, won't you, mother, next time a shell is coming?"[48] The pathetic nature of the account might suggest it was written for a worrying mother, perhaps by an unhinged son. But the story seems more credible for the similarity of its events to those recounted by Bird—a much-respected veteran of the war who believed in his brush with the supernatural so fully that he entitled his memoirs *Ghosts Have Warm Hands*.

Hereward Harrington, a contemporary occultist who compiled an account of soldiers' "scientific" tales of the paranormal and the supernatural, recorded the story of a Canadian officer who was unnamed but assured to be of "fine family and un-questionable veracity." The story went that after an exhausting tour in the front lines, in which many men had been killed and all pushed to the limits of endurance, the survivors were being led from the trenches by their lieutenant. Seeing one of his men lagging behind the rest, and worrying about his welfare after the terrible tour, the officer dropped back and asked Private Rex, who was very pale, if he felt ill. He offered some food to the private, who thanked him softly and took the nourishment with "icy cold" hands. Just then, the lieutenant was diverted by something up ahead, and when he looked back the private was gone. He halted the unit and they looked for the private, the officer wondering if he had been felled by a bullet or had per-haps deserted. When a fellow officer ran over to help the puzzled lieutenant, the lat-ter explained the situation and the other man, with a look of concern, replied that there must have been some mistake as Private Rex had been killed three days earlier and the officer had himself been present at the burial. The disturbed lieutenant was stunned to remember this fact; according to Harrington, "because of the stress of subsequent fighting and of the death of so many others, he had momentarily forgot-ten." This would appear to have been a case of shell shock or battle stress, but the lieutenant in question testified to having touched Private Rex, and claimed, perhaps to justify his vision, that "it was quite a common occurrence for men in the war zone to see the ghosts of their comrades who had been killed."[49] A psychologist would easily chalk such a sighting up to the exhaustion of battle, the stress of an over-worked man who was close to collapse and perhaps internalizing the grief of having lost soldiers whom he was to care for in a paternal manner. Perhaps. But certainly the officer in the story believed in the veracity of what had happened, as did count-less others.

In his much-respected memoir, *Good-bye to All That*, Robert Graves criticized the formulaic themes that ran through many soldiers' memoirs, one of which was the obligatory ghost story: "There must, in every book of this sort, be at least one ghost story with a possible explanation, and one without any explanation, except that it was a ghost."[50] Yet none of the above Canadian soldiers' accounts ring false or sug-gest that the soldiers were trying to deceive the reading public. Perhaps Graves was simply writing cynically a decade removed from his experience in the war, or it may be that, in fact, many of the Canadian soldiers' ghost stories were simply the sort "without any explanation."

FROM THE DERANGED and damaged to the visionaries and true believers—and the vast number of soldiers who fell in between and were simply struggling to cope with a fate they could not control—men looked for patterns and trusted in their magic talismans and superstitions to guide their actions. Garnet Dobbs wrote of his chances of survival in the summer of 1918, with half a year of brutal fighting still in front of him: "If we carry on to the end in the same manner that we have so far, we have a thousand to one chance of getting home again."[51] The odds were in fact better than that, but not by much for front-line infantrymen. Dobbs was one of the lucky ones, surviving fifteen months at the front before returning to civilian life after the war, and eventually running a successful plumbing business in Belleville, Ontario. More than 60,000 of his companions were not so lucky. Despite their best rituals, talismans, and superstitions, death had eventually called their numbers.

CHAPTER 15

THE BREAKING POINT

Collapse and Punishment

Men are brave because of many motives. When they are standing shoulder to shoulder facing an enemy, few of them flinch, no matter how dark the outlook is at the moment. Their pride in themselves, their loyalty to their native land, their love of their comrades, and their hatred for the enemy combine to prevent them from allowing fear to conquer them. Fear, *per se*, is another matter. Practically all men experience fear under fire at times, but they grit their teeth and push on. The quality that makes them do this is what we call courage. Any man who could look into a hole in the ground into which you could drop a small house, and, knowing this hole was made by a large calibre shell, yet feel no fear on going through a barrage of such shells, is not a brave man, he is an imbecile.[1]

So wrote Lieutenant Ralph Lewis, who saw the many ways that soldiers at the front found to endure, to push past the fear that gnawed away at them. Men relied on comrades, faith in their leaders, small rewards, and newly formed belief systems to keep going in the face of the storm. But no one—no matter how fatalistic, nonchalant, or hard-minded—could completely disregard fear. It could be pushed aside but never smothered—and it often reared its unwelcome spectre in the psyche when least expected.

Alexander McClintock believed that it was not only sustained combat and unceasing pressure that wore on the men but also the quiet periods, when there was too much time to reflect or brood on what had happened to them and their mates: "The hardest part of soldiering is mental; and the times when men are not fighting, but just sitting 'round are the hardest times to bear—the times that break men down if they're not careful.'[2] The mental attrition of the war wore away at the soldiers, grinding them down, day after day, month after month.

Lance Sergeant William Curtis described this torment in a letter to his mother: "Ten days under heavy shell fire all the time, day and night. Our casualties were heavy, mostly wounded. It is nerve shattering to be under shellfire. No matter how strong a man's nerves are they are affected. I have seen many a poor fellow break down under the strain. I'm sticking it fairly well myself, but I'm not as steady as I was a few months ago."[3] Curtis's candid letter to his mother captured the stress of life at the front, where men became more and more unstable. "It was just a case of sit and take it," wrote Gunner Herbert Irwin of the 41st Battery. "I've seen big strong men cry like babies after things quieted down."[4] There was no escape and no rest from the battering—both physical and mental. Standing shoulder to shoulder with comrades helped, but as Fred Bagnall noted, "There is a limit to physical endurance linked with the endurance of the mind." Most men were hounded even in their dreams. Bagnall himself noted that, while sleeping, he often "rolled in sweat and fought more Germans than were in the Ypres Salient."[5]

While the high command acknowledged that the strain of war had to be combated, there were few who initially paid much attention to this mental erosion. Lord Moran, Sir Winston Churchill's Second World War personal doctor and a regimental medical officer in the trenches of the Great War, wrote that most officers "did not bother about men's minds; we did what we could for their bodies."[6] In this war of industrial might, it was hard enough to deal with the physical wounds to the body, but it was also the minds of men that began to break down. The physical strain could be seen as trembling hands tried to pull mugs of cold tea up to cracked, twitching lips. Bloodshot, hollow eyes looked out from cadaver-like faces afflicted with tics. The youth of many of the soldiers helped them to cope and to recover faster than older men, but combat veteran Louis Keene was also right to warn, "Young men grow old quickly here."[7]

The unceasing stress increasingly ate into their reservoir of endurance. One of the first danger signs was progressively reckless behaviour. Exhausted and drained, soldiers often chose to jump out of the trenches at night, walking back to the rear overland rather than through the shattered, muddy, and labyrinthine communication trenches. The route was shorter, but it obviously made men good targets for sniper fire when flares went up, as well as leaving them vulnerable to stray shrapnel bursts. This type of unwise behaviour was a sign of impending problems. Lieutenant William Gray noted that all of the men grew fatalistic when they were "five seconds away from death for twenty-four hours a day." More troubling, however, they tended to "grow rather careless."[8]

AS MENTAL EXHAUSTION set in, the reckless behaviour among some soldiers transformed from not caring about being harmed to actually embracing being wounded. "I began to wish that a bullet would wound me sufficiently to give me that coveted thing called 'Blighty,'" wrote George Bell, during his third year of service at the front.[9] A "Blighty wound" was a legitimate escape from the front, as a wound, if not fatal, would take a man back through the medical system to recover in a clean hospital bed in England. The conditions at the front were so debilitating that, over time, men chose maiming and possible disfigurement over the seemingly inevitable prospect of insanity or death. Hume Wrong, later to become an influential Canadian diplomat, wrote after the slaughter on the Somme: "My great desire is to get out honourably, and I don't mind what the end may be. I've seen too much death to be afraid of it anymore."[10]

Men who received "clean" wounds—injuries in which bullets or shrapnel passed through flesh and avoided bone, and therefore complications; or which, no matter how painful, did not look like they might kill a man—were often viewed as "lucky beggars."[11] "I suppose a man is justified in saying he's got off lightly when what he expected was death," reflected one trench warrior.[12] With a cigarette clenched between gritted teeth, a wounded man waved goodbye to his mates as he was transported to a hospital in the rear. For good measure, he might even thank the enemy who did him in. In a letter that J.H. Thompson wrote home—one that surely must have been bewildering for his kin—he recounted how, after having his arm wound dressed, "I then blessed Fritz for letting me out of it so easily—I had been cursing him right along up to this point—and I was more than thankful to get out of it alive with my limbs secure."[13] The usually gruff Agar Adamson—commanding officer of the PPCLI for the later part of the war, after his superiors were killed or injured— remarked after the sustained fighting on the Somme: "The strongest fellows are beginning to show the strain, but won't chuck it until they are quite done or I insist upon them going down for a few days. A great many court wounds, as an honourable way of getting out of the line."[14]

But receiving one of these honourable wounds wasn't easy. Ensuring that a shrapnel wound would not become infected or that a bullet through the leg did not cut a femoral artery was impossible. It was simpler for men fed up with the front to malinger. Soldiers could push themselves hard when they believed in the cause or were following trusted leaders, but when they felt they were unfairly treated they often faked ill health to show their displeasure. Medical Officer Captain Harold Hart of the 25th Battalion noted frankly in the official war diary that after the hard fighting at St. Eloi in April 1916, heavy artillery fire and a gas attack, the sick wastage rate (the number of soldiers who were, or who professed to be, ill) shot up. Of the fifty-three men and officers who stood before him on the last day of April for his medical inspection, no doubt many were suffering from exhaustion, but being aware of a number of obvious malingerers, Hart noted sharply to his superiors, "I would suggest that the health of the men might be better if the issue of rations was not short so often!"[15] The medical officer (MO) for the 85th Battalion observed a similar trend after the terrible fighting at Vimy: "There were 127 on sick parade this morning. I attribute this large amount of sickness to the fact that our men were not given sufficient rest to recuperate after the strenuous week on Vimy. If this policy is to be pursued it will prove disastrous economically, as it is bound to put a large number of men out of action for an indefinite period."[16] Without proper rest and a sense that their sacrifice in battle was being acknowledged with small rewards such as rum, adequate food, leave, and time in the rear areas, soldiers embraced their personal agency, deciding on the limits of their service themselves.

One of the MO's jobs was to patrol the men, acting as a detective and disciplinarian. Sick soldiers lined up in a medical parade before the MO and his senior orderly. It was usually a distasteful job for the doctor—a man who had sworn an oath to take care of those who needed his help—to now act as a disciplinarian, but success in the war depended on it. The high command ordered that soldiers could not be allowed to escape from their duties at the front through feigned illness. And indeed, malingerers and "lead-swingers" (a prewar nautical term for an easy job aboard a ship, adopted by soldiers to refer to those shirking their duties) were mixed among the truly sick. Lew Perry of the 52nd Battalion, who was gassed during the war and had respiratory problems for the rest of his life, described the medical parade:

> There was a whole bunch of us—various complaints—some real but most of them "lead swingers," trying to dodge a working party. Crozier was clever with those fellows. He would listen to nine men at once, telling pathetically of all the kinds of ailments you can find in the almanac or in the patient medicine— and some that no one ever heard of before. He would take six temperatures at once. He didn't really take them—but he didn't need to—he went through the motions. If he diagnosed your case as "acute lead swinging" or as a slight cold with exaggeration complications, the Doc would very sympathetically hand you a couple of no. 9 pills. Now a no. 9 pill is an effective form of bowel activity stimulant. Of course the lead swingers didn't take the 9's. They threw them away when they got outside the MO's tent. It is a blessing that those pills were not seeds—else there would be immense forests of no. 9 trees all over France today.[17]

The infamous pill No. 9 laxative vexed most of the soldiers, who were not shy about disparaging it in their letters, poems, cartoons, and prose. Other doctors issued palliative saltpetre or nutmeg. Frank Maheux of the 21st Battalion wrote to his wife sputtering with rage that even the legitimately wounded suffered under the callous regime. Maheux was injured by two shell fragments at Mount Sorrel, but even worse, his ears were ringing continuously and he was in constant pain from throbbing headaches. He went to his medical officer, but received only castor oil: "No matter if it was sore eyes he always give Caster Oil[;] we call him Caster Oil King."[18] Private Archie Selwood, who went to France with the 72nd Battalion at age thirty-five, commented similarly on the stringent medical examinations: "Unless there was blood, we got little sympathy."[19] Even the truly wounded found it difficult to bypass the gatekeepers to receive a rest, even a temporary one, while serving in the trenches of the Western Front.

"NERVES ALL GONE," was D.E. Macintyre's sad commentary about a fellow officer who had succumbed to the unending stress of battle.[20] The pressure was too much. With no honourable escape from the front, men began to retreat into themselves. Battered bodies and shaken minds were an increasingly fragile defence against an outside world of unending destruction. Will Bird provided a particularly chilling account of the types of experiences and images that assaulted men's minds and senses on the field. In the middle of a push during the bloody Passchendaele battle, Bird saw many of his closest friends killed around him. He, too, had nearly been snuffed out by a shell that had exploded near him. He awoke to find himself in a swamp of mud, having been blown from the spot where he was standing and knocked unconscious; but luckily he landed on his back, thereby avoiding drowning. Upon returning to consciousness, he wiped away the swamp slime and the blood pouring from his nose, but his head felt like a hammer had been beating on it—no doubt the effect of a concussion. When Bird and the survivors tried to dig in, the enemy shelling reduced time and space to a blur as they suffered the sonic boom of the shells and the utter terror of seeing men killed and dismembered. Bird described one man standing "rigidly, feet braced apart. He had been killed by concussion, and his body was split as if sliced by a great knife." Such bleak sights shocked even hardened trench warriors.

Only minutes later, when Bird and his battalion mates were working furiously to dig a hole in the mud for safety, one man "straightened to say something to us, and the next instant a shell cut the top of his head away, leaving but the jaw and neck." Some time later in the bombardment, an even heavier shelling opened up: "We crouched, grey faces under muddy helmets, our brains numbed by incessant explosions." But the hammering did not end there. Bird remembered a shaken British soldier sliding into his shell crater half filled with fetid water as the shells rained down:

> Twice I asked him questions but he was too dazed to answer. The shelling was heavy and never let up. Soon the lad snuggled tight against me. I moved over and he followed. Each shell that lighted near made him cringe. He kept saying

something in a high-pitched voice. I caught him by the shoulder and shook him. "What on earth are you saying?" I asked. He shook more violently. "I'm a shepherd boy from Hawes," he gasped. "That's the way we count sheep. I can't stop."

Other soldiers around Bird were twitching and convulsing, and Bird would likely have found himself doing the same had he held up a mirror. Dirt and slime showered down; then came a haversack packed with a toothbrush, towel, and socks, which Bird could not avoid studying with shock. It was followed by a man who was blown into the crater, most of his equipment lost, although he somehow looked undamaged. Still, when Bird tried to right him in the mud, the man "shook as with ague, making animal noises." Another man emerged from the geysers of shells and mud. "Fear had relaxed the muscles on his face and it had become like dough. His mouth dribbled. I could not look at him." The explosions continued until they could no longer be distinguished from each other. They stopped at some point, but it took several minutes to notice, so numbed were the men. Bird survived the ordeal, but he was badly shaken from the violence—both physically and mentally.[21]

Such experiences were enough to destroy a man's sanity. The breakdown, called shell shock, was a seemingly new and bewildering wound for doctors to diagnose, let alone cure.[22] Shell shock was initially viewed as a physical wound: with tens of thousands of shells exploding over the battlefield and sending out enormous shock waves, it was felt that these reverberations and atmospheric changes damaged the brain. It was soon found, however, that men who were nowhere near shellfire were breaking down. Prolonged exposure to stress was the culprit, and without rest or respite from the strain of war, most soldiers inevitably developed some form of this nervous disorder.

There was no single symptom experienced by the shell-shocked: for most men the effects began gradually and gained progressively in intensity. Tremors were common—most visible through shaking hands. Twitches caused by overtiredness and stress developed in the face but then progressed through the body. Lines were etched deep into the skin. Exhausted men found they could not sleep, as they were forever playing the events of the war over in their minds. For many, the dead continued to haunt the living, with past companions and mates tracking them through their night- and daytime hours. "Our casualties are mounting up and are more than twenty now," wrote Basil Morris. "Sgt. McDonald has gone nutty over it and it is fierce to watch a big husky man like that jump whenever a door slams. He used to be so cheerful and now he looks scared all the time. He likely will be sent to the base for shell shock."[23]

Like clothes increasingly worn threadbare until they finally ripped along unknown seams, soldiers were steadily worn down to the point where the slow descent into breakdown was accelerated by a traumatic event. The death of a close friend, a shocking artillery bombardment, an underground mine explosion: all could drive men from the precarious razor's edge upon which they perched. When men cracked, it was a terrible sight to observe, and utterly unnerving to the rest of the soldiers who were barely holding on to their own sanity. Some would stammer and shriek, their palsied mouths drooling; others convulsed in silence while their haunted eyes stared ahead unseeing. Daytime nightmares, delusions, and even the paralysis of limbs could turn men who once were warriors into twitching hospital cases.

These sick soldiers were taken from the line to be treated. Although there was no consensus on the reasons for, or treatment of, this seemingly new affliction, by the mid-point in the war shell shock was generally regarded as a psychological disorder rather than a physical wound. Most of the doctors were gentle in their methods, subscribing to prewar treatments of rest and recuperation with quiet, rest, and baths.[24] But not all were so compassionate, and brutal electric shock therapy was certainly applied in order to return soldiers to the front as quickly as possible. One wonders how many doctors shared the perspective of Andrew Macphail of the Canadian Army Medical Corps (CAMC): "Shellshock is a manifestation of child-ishness and femininity. Against such there is no remedy."[25] This was an ungenerous statement, to say the least, and medically inaccurate, for there were indeed remedies. Rest and recuperation got fighting soldiers back into the line, but the hospitals were under pressure to send patients back to the front, and so extreme measures were sometimes a final resort if rest and relaxation were not producing useful results. Sergeant Arthur Hickson recounted the story of Old Tom from his battalion—a friendly, balding man in his late thirties who was well liked by his companions.

During one tour in the line, a shell landed near him, killing his two mates and leaving him shell shocked. "After a series of electric shock treatments at the base hospital he was returned to us though still very shaky," wrote Hickson. "Lighting a cigarette for instance was very difficult for him. He told me that the patient would do or say anything to stop the treatment. One had to guess what the doctors wanted to hear."[26] Hospital records indicated that between sixty-three and seventy-one percent of shell-shocked patients were returned to their units for service, but one wonders how many of the soldiers came back in a condition similar to Old Tom's.[27]

The strain of shell shock was unavoidable in this new, industrial war, and despite the best ministrations of officers, NCOs, and medical officers—many of whom put their No. 9 pills away when they encountered truly damaged men—there was no escape from the destruction. According to official records, at least 9,000 Canadians were diagnosed with shell shock, but one contemporary wartime CAMC doctor later claimed that there were at least 15,000 diagnosed cases, and this did not include all the men who were killed even before they made it out of the line to be diagnosed.[28]

"During a spell in the 'Glory Hole,' when Fritz was particularly active with his trench mortars," wrote Private Donald Fraser, "one of our fellows, Butson, lost his nerve and went semi-insane. After the fireworks quieted down a bit, Butson was found crawling around the trench on his hands and knees quite demented. He was taken out. Returning to the Company a few months later, when word was announced that the Company was leaving Scottish Wood for the line, Butson became unnerved again and threatened to shoot himself. He said he could not face the music."[29] Sympathetic officers stepped in, and the unfortunate Butson, who had clearly not recovered from his shell shock, was sent to the rear, lost to the unit for the rest of the war.

Many men were not so lucky. Mentally damaged soldiers who threatened to shoot themselves did not always receive a "bomb-proof" job in the rear. Good officers and NCOs tried to manage their men, accounting for the wear and tear on them mentally, but a unit that was already short of bodies or had a hard-nosed commander might not make these allowances. This refusal to alleviate men's suffering could in part be attributed to pure bloody-mindedness, but it could also be put down to the threat of an unknown tipping point at which the army might disintegrate under the strain. Everyone was under terrible stress: how long did a man have to serve at the front before earning some relief? Certainly there was a desire by officers to have long-service men eventually rotated to the rear to keep them alive, but this also denuded a unit of its most experienced soldiers. As well, if they let every man out from front-line duty who had experienced too much stress, there would soon be no army left to fight. There were simply not enough soldiers. Between a rock and a hard place, the combat soldiers were forced to hold on as best they could.

With little relief from the front available, some men took matters into their own hands. They not only sought Blighty wounds but created their own. Known as self-inflicted wounds (SIWs) in army parlance, the soldiers sometimes called them "left-hand wounds," as they often were caused deliberately to a soldier's less dominant hand. One can only imagine the strain felt by soldiers compelled to wilfully drive their seventeen-inch steel bayonet through their hand or fire a bullet into their foot. The former type of injury was harder for the wounded man to explain—although there was a remarkable number of legitimate cases of men falling accidentally on bayonets. But the latter was harder to get away with, as gunpowder residue often revealed that a man had fired into his own flesh.

Often officers on the scene did not need scientific or detective skills to determine that a soldier had injured himself. Many of the cases were similar to that of Private Joseph Renaud, a twenty-one-year-old from Montreal who served with the 87th Battalion. He was found with a bullet wound through his left foot in the early hours of July 31, 1918. When an officer asked him what had happened, he said he had been shot by an airplane. Renaud had wisely left his rifle in his dugout, which had a pull-through in it and therefore could not fire, but he had neglected to ditch his friend's recently discharged rifle before the officers arrived on the scene—perhaps being too overcome by pain.[30] A quick interrogation of some of Renaud's dugout mates had revealed that he and a friend had been playing around with bullets earlier that day, removing gun powder from them, presumably to lessen the bullet's velocity when it was fired into his foot. Despite his blatant wounding of himself, however, Renaud was not charged or hauled before a court martial.

Desperate men could attempt to rub infected soil into their wounds, deliberately court a venereal disease, or breathe poison gas. The authorities especially feared the rising number of gas casualties in the last two years of the war. They knew the escalating rate was due to the increased dissemination of gas on the battlefield, but there was the nagging concern that perhaps soldiers were also deliberately subjecting themselves to these chemicals to escape service.[31] But how much gas was needed to damage lungs only temporarily was impossible to know, even though some men at the breaking point were willing to try anything. After the gruelling Passchendaele battle in the last months of 1917, George Bell of the 1st Battalion noted,

> Malingering was becoming too common, not only among those who were naturally shirkers, but among those who had been good soldiers. They had seen so much death, bloodshed and suffering that they were sick of it all…. Some cracked open a cartridge, extracted the cordite and chewed it to produce a pallor, quickened heart action and frothing at the mouth. Some bound a bandage over a copper coin placed over a well scratched flea bite, causing local infection.

Bell testified that some men went to brothels in the "hope of getting a disease that would send them to a hospital. Bell's verdict: "Cowards? Not at all. Some of these men had proven their bravery time after time."[32]

There were 729 identified SIW cases among members of the CEF, although more men must surely have been wounded this way but gone undetected, lumped in with those suffering from general venereal disease, gas, bayonet or bullet wounds. These wounded soldiers were sent to isolated hospitals, and after their recovery they received varying sentences, the most severe of these appearing to be two years' imprisonment with hard labour.[33] For men pushed past the limits of their endurance, the SIW was a way out of the line, and most neither thought nor cared about whatever form of punishment they might face.

While an SIW involved, at some level, a desire to survive—even if it was by suffering a painful wound—some soldiers were too despondent to seek a temporary escape and could only find peace through a permanent solution. Having lost all hope, men were driven to take their own lives. John Edward Luxford, whose brother Harry had been killed only a few weeks before, wrote a suicide note to his already devastated parents. "Dear Mother and Dad, I cannot stand it no longer, Goodbye and Godbless you all.... Don't worry I will soon be with Harry. Goodbye."[34] Herbert Burrell wrote sadly in his diary about another suicide:

> He had been previously wounded and then sent back to the front with a hand that was almost useless. He was also wounded in the legs. A visit to the doctor resulted in his getting 2 weeks rest at Boulogne. He was then sent back to the line yet again, still unfit for duty. He was then sent back to the line yet again, still unfit for duty. Once more he saw the doctor and got no satisfaction, and after this killed himself.[35]

And Medical Officer Harold McGill of the 31st Battalion told the story of one distressed soldier who had stolen a stock of morphine and consumed it in a suicide bid. The overdosed soldier was saved by McGill's performing "artificial respiration" on him after his heart had stopped.[36] These suicides appear to have been rare—if the number recorded in the official records are any indication—although no doubt many men committed suicide in battle through intentionally reckless or berserk behaviour. And, of course, some men who were invalided out of the line, either with physical or mental wounds, never recovered, taking their lives after escaping the front but not the torment in their minds. Major George McFarland of the 4th CMR told of 116th Battalion's commanding officer, Lieutenant Colonel Sam Sharpe, who, after returning to Canada, "killed himself by jumping from the upstairs window of a hospital in Montreal."[37] The story served as a poignant reminder that the war would never end for some, even for those seemingly lucky ones who escaped its clutches on the Western Front.

AS SOME MEN struggled for their very lives in internal psychological battles, others did what their bodies told them to do in times of fear: they ran. "Any NCO or man who absents himself without leave from the trenches, from a parade to proceeding to the trenches, or from a working party which is to work in an area exposed to fire, will be tried for Desertion," warned the 7th Battalion commander, Victor Odlum. "The penalty for Desertion is death."[38] The same threat was wielded across the Canadian Corps and the entire BEF, the exception being the Australians, who refused to allow their men to be shot. Soldiers had been warned of these severe penalties from the start of the war, but few took it seriously or even gave it much thought in the early days.

Since forces on the Western Front could disintegrate if enough men refused to fight and instead fled, the army was left with seemingly little choice but to respond with the most draconian aspect of military law: the threat and carrying out of the death penalty. The fear of rot spreading among the troops led to a powerful imposition of the full weight of military justice to curb men's normal inclination to flee. The penalty had to be severe for soldiers who were already sentenced to a death row of sorts in the firing line.

The most severe penalty was given to soldiers who deserted their units permanently. Lesser penalties were applied to men who were absent without leave—the label applied to soldiers who left their units but returned a few hours or days later. It took a brave or desperate man to challenge the system, as penalties were imposed seemingly at random. Punishments differed from unit to unit, from occasion to occasion, and from man to man. Much depended on the perceived strength or slackness of discipline in the soldier's unit. If the battalion commander or its brigadier considered a unit in good shape—perhaps with a strong combat record, low trench foot wastage, and regular punishments—transgressions could be overlooked, or treated leniently. If there was a sense that the men were grumbling more than usual, if SIWs were on the rise, if the sick parades were full, then woe to the soldier who pushed the limits.

Major Agar Adamson of the PPCLI noted that a young rascal in his battalion, Donald Gray, was finally run to ground after being absent for twenty-four days. Adamson believed he had probably been drunk the entire time, and the usually gruff major was opposed to a court martial, believing he ought simply to "be kicked around a three acre field. We are trying to get Loomis to cancel the Court Martial for the sake of the good name of the Regiment but I doubt if he can."[39] Many units did not want to air their dirty linen by going through official channels, preferring to take care of their own problems through the "justice" delivered by the fists of hard NCOs.[40] Indeed, some battalions had a poor reputation because of their number of courts martial, although most units were indistinguishable from any other. Only the

22nd Battalion stood out for having especially grievous discipline problems. Some have suggested that this reputation was born of bias against the only French-Canadian battalion in the Canadian Corps, but this appears not to be the case, as the unit's morale was plagued by crippling casualties, undisciplined drafts of reinforcing soldiers, and officers who at times could not exert a firm control of their men.[41] It was the battalion's own French-Canadian commanding officer, Lieutenant Colonel Thomas Tremblay, who recommended and carried out death sentences to restore order during a few critical periods in the 22nd Battalion's history—usually after it had been savaged in battle.

Although military law was applied unevenly, its potential ruthlessness is beyond question. Certainly soldiers were punished for everything from failing to salute to the more serious offence of refusing to follow orders, a range that afforded officers wide leeway to charge a man. Herbert Burrell of the 1st CMR wrote of "two young lads" who were given forty-two days of field punishment for being absent without leave:

> I was told that these lads had never been granted any leave—so they took it. If this is so it puts a very different complexion on the offense and the sentence is altogether too severe. The men are getting very dissatisfied with the system of leave granting.... There is a great need for reform in the method of Army court martial. It is seldom a fair proceeding for the men.[42]

Harsh punishments might be inflicted on a charged soldier to deter others in the unit who were toying with committing crimes. This uneven application of justice was either deliberately incompetent or necessarily vague, but without any sense of what their actual punishment might be, some soldiers simply took their chances and hoped for the best. Military justice, and the corresponding punishments, were perceived as a dangerous lottery, and nowhere was this more evident than in the handing out of death sentences.

The most serious offenders in the military were subject to court martial. Regimental and district courts martial dealt with minor crimes, while general and field general courts martial were reserved for serious offences that could potentially result in a death sentence. A tribunal of officers sat in judgment of the prisoner, who was brought before them, cap in hand. Most of the officers had little or no law train-ing, and many went by the book. Using justice to enforce discipline sometimes resulted in harsh punishments that were suggested by the letter of the law.[43] Witnesses were called to bolster the case and the prisoner was allowed a short state-ment, although many men "up on a charge" could find few convincing justifications for running from the front or striking an officer. The prisoner was given a "friend"— an officer to act as his defence lawyer—but most soldiers would have agreed that the court martial system was stacked against them. Attesting to the lopsided nature of the process, eighty-nine percent of the accused brought before courts martial in the BEF were found guilty, although some of the charges that might have resulted in a finding of "not guilty" had likely been dismissed without going to the court martial, or were light enough to be treated more informally within the unit.[44]

The most common crime soldiers were charged with was drunkenness, and the punishments for this and other minor transgressions were generally trivial. No treat-ment of alcoholism was considered or provided. Instead, pay was docked, leave was withheld, rank was often reduced down to the level of private, and offenders might be given extra duties or fatigues. Punishments varied according to which officers were sitting on the court martial. More serious cases would receive field punishment numbers 1 or 2. Number 2 was the less serious of the pair, and involved two hours a day of heavy exercise in full kit and close confinement, while number 1, as described by H.R. Butt, was much more severe. Butt, a machine-gunner who would be killed by a bullet on April 9, 1917, described seeing two men from the 47th Battalion, "doing 1st Field Punishment on a little hill in front of our huts. There were a few trees and the men were tied to the trees at a distance from each other without any coats on in the snow where it was freezing. They were tied so that they couldn't move about to keep warm. I don't know what they had done to get it, but it's a very inhuman treatment I think."[45] Butt was not alone in being shocked by the infliction of such a humiliating punishment on Canadians in a volunteer army. The ordeal did not cause terrible physical strain, although muscles were left sore; it was the flies and lice that tormented the helpless men. The soldiers called field punishment number 1 "crucifixion," and their harsh reactions against it sug-gest that it was in fact bad for morale. Nonetheless, it seemed to work, at least to some degree, as a deterrent. Arthur Jarvis, the assistant provost marshal for the 2nd Division—the senior officer responsible for policing the soldiers in that formation—remarked that the men hated field punishment number 1, but that "even the most hardened characters rarely come back for a second dose of this treatment."[46]

Despite its name, not all field punishment was carried out in the field. Each of the Canadian divisions had a field punishment station, which was in effect a prison. Soldiers given more than fourteen days of field punishment number 1 could be sent here. These camps were brutal places where the military police and guards regularly beat the prisoners. To break the prisoners, their hair was shorn, they were denied tobacco, rum, and care packages, and they were worked ruthlessly in carrying out mundane yet physically punishing tasks such as piling rocks or digging ditches, filling them, and digging new ones.[47] The severe punishments in the prisons were

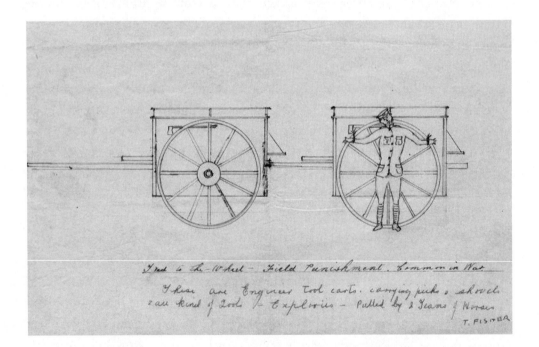

A sketch by Private Thomas Fisher of a comrade undergoing field punishment number 1. The prisoner was tied to a cart's wheel and left there for two hours a day for the duration of the punishment, which generally ranged from a week to a month. The punishment was humiliating and much hated by Canadians.

unmitigated, whereas a prisoner who stayed in his unit was unlikely to receive the harshest of punishments from his NCOs and officers, if only because the prisoner would soon revert to being a soldier under their command and grievances could carry a long time on the Western Front. No doubt the wardens and military police wanted to make the prison a far more inhumane place than the trenches, to ensure the compliance of men in the line and the desire of prisoners to get back to their unit, even if it was at the front.

It was not uncommon for soldiers to receive punishments of one or two years of hard labour in a prison camp. After serving several months, however, prisoners could have their sentence commuted under the 1915 Suspension of Sentences Act. This act allowed convicted men to escape the prison, avoided overcrowding of these depressing sites, restored soldiers' reputations, and brought fighting men back into the line.

Though field punishment number 1 and jail time in a military prison were harsh ordeals, some men faced worse punishments. "The crime of absence without leave was very prevalent in my Battalion until 2 men were shot a short time ago," wrote Lieutenant Colonel Tremblay of the 22nd Battalion. "The prevalence of this crime was due principally to the extraordinary leniency of the previous Courts Martial, especially at the end of last year and during the first two or three months of this year. Conditions in the Battalion are much better now with respect to absences without leave, since the two men were shot."[48] In total, 216 Canadians were sentenced to death by firing squad during the war, and 25 of the sentences were carried out. Of these, 22 were meted out for desertion, 2 for murder, and 1 for cowardice. But these 25 deaths out of the more than 60,000 total Canadian deaths weigh heavily on the popular memory of the war.

The two men executed for murder might have been killed in Canada for their crime, as capital punishment was still practised there, but the execution of soldiers at the front remains one of the grimmest legacies of the war. Those who condemn the practice often suggest that it was shell-shocked men who were put before the rifles. This was clearly not the case for the majority of Canadian soldiers sentenced to death, as they were generally repeat offenders with long charge sheets, and at least two of them had been reprieved from earlier death sentences. While they were not the eighteen-year-old victims that inhabit popular memory, they were indeed young, at an average age of twenty-four.[49] Regardless of their age, though, something had broken in them, and their number had come up. Moreover, all of the executed men were from the rank and file, and the few officers who were charged were acquitted, although cashiered from service, leaving them with a stain on their character but alive.

The sentence of death was not carried out lightly. When it was ordered by the court martial, it went up the chain of command and had to be approved by each succeeding general in the hierarchy. Finally, the decision went all the way to the commander-in-chief, Sir Douglas Haig. The field marshal rarely added any notes to the file in question, but on a single case—that of a private who quit his post on the eve of the Somme offensive and towards whom the court martial recommended mercy—he wrote: "How can we ever win if this plea is allowed?"[50] While the Australians refused to allow their soldiers to be executed, the Canadians had no such qualms. Of the twenty-five executed Canadians, at least a handful suffered injustice—even within the accepted parameters of justice at the time—their deaths clearly being meant to strike fear in the hearts of their comrades-in-arms. For example, Private Eugene Perry of the 22nd Battalion seems to have been one such case. A labourer from Boutouche, New Brunswick, who had enlisted at age nineteen, he was initially part of the ill-fated 41st Battalion, a unit troubled by gravely bad discipline that was broken up and its reinforcements (including Perry) sent to the 22nd Battalion.[51] Perry had served with apparent good service, fighting and surviving the Somme battles in which the 22nd Battalion had lost over 600 men, but he had worn thin by early 1917. On April 2 of that year, a week before the Vimy battle, Perry deserted from the front. He was caught the next day, confessing that he could not physically return to the trenches, that he was simply too nervous to stand the shelling and anticipation of battle. With his record of good service, he should have been let off, but instead he was tried and received the death penalty, which was carried out. Perry died not for his crime but for his comrades: the high command felt that the 22nd Battalion was a little "windy," and that the men needed their will stiffened. A firing squad carried out the court's verdict, with soldiers from the condemned man's unit performing the horrible task.

Kenneth Foster, who enlisted in Vernon, British Columbia, and served as a machine-gunner in the 2nd Battalion, was involved in a firing squad. Writing about it after the war, he still had a hard time coming to grips with what he had been ordered to do in the name of discipline. The condemned man had been "court martialed on two previous occasions and was let off on some pretext or other." This was where Foster entered the story:

> The third time he met his doom and the execution was carried out in this manner. The prisoner, a man of about thirty-five years of age, was placed in a chair, tied and blindfolded, with a piece of paper over his heart. The rifles, previously loaded with half live rounds and half blanks, were placed on the ground about thirty feet away. The firing party then marched in, for it took place in an old farm yard. No verbal command was given, the party acting on the blast of the Officer's whistle. We were first reminded that failure to carry out instructions would mean the same fate. In the event of no one hitting the mark, the Officer in charge would carry out the ghastly deed. Not being murderously inclined, it can be readily understood when I say that it was some time before I could get the disagreeable subject off my mind. Such is war. The ways of mankind are strange. At war, the penalty for not killing is death, in peace, the penalty for killing is death.[52]

After an execution was completed, the unlucky officer in charge was forced to examine the body and finish off the man with a pistol shot to the head should he have somehow survived. Often a battalion was marched past the corpse of the condemned to hammer home the point, and the record of the execution was read out to all units in the BEF. Many men felt grave discomfort about executing fellow soldiers who could not stand the strain of war. At the very least, these were men who had volunteered to serve but could not endure army life or the trials of combat. If we condemn the practice, however, the question becomes, what was the alternative? Though men were motivated to fight by much more than the threat of the revolver, it was certainly a factor. Should soldiers have been allowed to leave the front if they no longer wanted to fight? This would have been a recipe for losing the war.

Certainly these and other queries have been posed over the last century, but the most important question is whether the threat of the firing squad deterred soldiers' unruly behaviour. Ernest Black concluded emphatically that it did not when he wrote of one poor, wretched soldier who had deserted three times before he was executed. "It was a nasty, beastly business and generally speaking quite useless. The rest of us did not need the example, and the poor fellows who were shot for the most part could not help what they did. I doubt if any man ever did his duty from fear of being shot."[53] D.E. Pearson and his comrades were enraged when one of their own was shot: "Some thought the Colonel was responsible and threatened to shoot him the next time we were in action."[54] In this case, not only did the use of capital punishment fail to act as a deterrent—it in fact encouraged even more dangerous behaviour.

More venom might have been expected from soldiers who had been effectively abandoned by their mates who deserted the front. But men at the sharp end experienced and understood the severity of strain in the trenches. F.W. Bagnall of the 14th Battalion recounted the shock that rippled through his battalion when his officers read out that two British soldiers were to be shot at dawn:

> We felt extremely uncomfortable, and one is strange who would not. This was so different from being killed in battle. It will not be necessary to remark that few of us were asleep at dawn, nor did the boys have an idle curiosity. There was a setting of wills and stiffening of morale. We were in a terrible school for which we had volunteered and there are rules necessary to discipline. Hard, but the whole business of war is hard.[55]

Was the death penalty in fact too hard a fate for damaged men or even bad soldiers who had volunteered for a war experience that they neither understood nor could endure? This complex problem yields no easy answers, but certainly a trench warrior should have the final word. George Bell, who witnessed the execution of a fellow Canadian, was profoundly unsettled by the experience: refusing to watch, he closed his eyes—though he did not denounce it outright. When another soldier was condemned to death, only to have his sentence commuted at the last moment, the tough-as-nails Bell posed a question in his memoir that bears repeating: "The man had already fought through the battles of the year. Nerves shot. Why murder the remnant of him?"[56]

CHAPTER 16

A CANADIAN CORPS COMMANDER

Sir Arthur Currie

Field Marshal Sir Douglas Haig had been planning his offensive in the Flanders region since 1915, as a breakthrough on that front would drive the Germans back, forcing them to retreat and lose their U-boat ports that were the source of much anxiety to the Royal Navy and the entire Allied war effort. In the summer of 1917, Haig also believed that he needed to attack the Germans and purchase time for his French allies to gain control of the desperate situation in their armies, where tens of thousands had mutinied, refusing to allow themselves to be killed off in fruitless and callous operations. While these mutinies were largely under control by the summer, Haig, who mistrusted the French and found their Gallic temperament at odds with his stern soldierly and religious beliefs, was quite unsure about the quality of the French *poilus*.

Haig had wanted to start the Flanders offensive earlier in the summer, but he had been forced to prolong the Arras campaign in support of the French, which delayed his operation in the north. He was undeterred. And so, after months of stockpiling millions of shells and bringing together two of his five British armies, Haig launched his Passchendaele offensive on July 31, 1917. While the first phase of the attack made some initial progress, it almost immediately degenerated into a quagmire of mud and misery, as rain drenched the shell-cratered battlefield. The Flanders forces needed assistance.

In the hope of drawing German reserves away from the battlefield, the Canadian Corps, as part of the British First Army, was ordered to capture Lens. Thirteen kilometres northeast of Arras, the objective could be seen from Vimy Ridge. An ugly city at the centre of the coal-mining area of France, Lens was pitted with enormous mines, slagheaps, and tailings. These were ideal defensive positions, and the town and the outlying structures—now mostly reduced to ruins that provided good cover—had been heavily fortified by the Germans. The bones of thousands of British troops were littered throughout the forming-up area, as Lens had been reached during the Battle of Loos on September 25, 1915, but not captured.

By the middle of July, the 1st and 2nd Canadian Divisions were opposite Lens. The summer of 1917 had so far been warm, and although the fighting battalions had raided aggressively, this had remained a quiet front, especially in comparison to what the BEF was facing further to the north in the Flanders region of Ypres. While the infantry battled the lice and flies, and shared their trenches and dugouts with rats that left their feces everywhere, they took some excitement from watching the air armadas that fought high above Lens. British contact patrols flying up and down the line were interrupted only when enemy fighters dove on the slower planes, shooting many of them down. The action provided entertainment for the earthbound troops, who often viewed the aerial dogfights above their dirty homes in the ground as a sporting event of sorts.

Disrupting this period of relative calm, in early July the First Army headquarters ordered new Canadian Corps commander Sir Arthur Currie to launch a frontal assault against the southern portion of Lens to draw pressure away from the Passchendaele front. First Army commander General Henry Horne, an experienced gunner who had been instrumental in introducing the creeping barrage to the BEF, had already, in May of 1917, called upon his staff to prepare a detailed plan to attack Lens. That operation would have involved a six-battalion assault supported by a paltry eleven tanks, which was surely too small a force to overrun the fortified city that was heavily defended by dug-in German infantrymen trained for street fighting.[1] Horne had a reputation as a fine commander who listened to his subordinates, and his rise from colonel to general in the course of the war left him with a better understanding of the troops under his command than was shown by some of the elites with whom he shared the rank of general. But the First Army's plan was flawed from its conception, and one wonders what the general imagined the tanks would be doing in the rubble of Lens. Fortunately, he would not find out. The tanks were allocated by Haig's headquarters to another front, and Horne shelved the wholly inadequate plan to capture the city. But he still had orders to draw enemy reserves away from the Flanders front, and so he instructed Currie to prepare an assault plan to capture Lens. Currie well understood the need to divert reserves from Haig's offensive to the north, but he would attack the fortress on his own terms.

THE FORTY-ONE-YEAR-OLD CURRIE had taken over the corps in June 1917, after Byng had been promoted to command the Third Army. British GHQ recognized Byng as having performed brilliantly in a tough, and initially thankless, command, and noted that he was especially adept at transforming the wild Canadians into a disciplined fighting force. That he was admired, even loved, by the Canadians, attested to his charisma as a commander. "He is to a very great extent responsible for the good name of the Canadians in France," wrote Lieutenant Maurice Pope. "We have, I believe, a good and efficient body of troops who will do big things soon and much of the credit should go to him."[2] The hard-to-please Brigadier General W.A. Griesbach was no less effusive in his praise:

> Byng had keen insight and an active mind—constantly speculating and enquiring, a wonderful sense of humour, which was always just beneath the surface. He understood us. He was … supple in unimportant things and rigid in vital matters. He took us as he found us, with all our faults and imperfections and our good qualities as well, and by skilfully ignoring and correcting the former, and playing upon the latter, created for us our own standards, giving free play to our national characteristics and peculiarities. The Canadian Corps under Byng became the most powerful and efficient fighting machine on the Western Front.[3]

While Bungo Byng was promoted to a prestigious British army command—where, it must be said, his performance was mediocre at best—he always retained a soft spot for the Canadians. Tellingly, when he was raised to the peerage after the war, he took his title as Baron Byng of Vimy. As a British commander, Byng's contribution to the Canadian Corps is sometimes overlooked as it sits uncomfortably with the colony-transformed-to-nation paradigm that emerged from the war. Overseas, the Canadians stepped onto the world stage and out from under Britain's shadow, but they were nurtured by many Imperials—a fact which the popular Canadian memory would rather ignore. Byng was the single most important person in shaping the Canadian Corps during the war, and the respect and admiration he received from the men of the corps continued into the postwar years, and especially during his appointment as Governor General of Canada from 1921 to 1926. Bungo left his Byng Boys with tears in his eyes, but he had long groomed his protegé to take the reins. Yet having Currie appointed corps commander was a near-run thing, as several powerful intriguers were looking to install their own champion as corps commander: Sir Richard Turner, the current chief of the general staff in England.

Sir Arthur Currie, commander of the Canadian Corps (on the left), stands with Sir Douglas Haig, commander-in-chief of the BEF. Currie and Haig were not close friends, but Haig respected his Canadian corps commander and often allocated additional resources to meet Currie's requests for guns and ammunition.

Currie had proven over two years of command that he understood how the war had to be fought on the Western Front. The former militia gunnery officer enjoyed a meteoric rise in command during the war, but it was well earned. He devoted nearly every moment to finding better ways to train and support his troops, and his division and later corps headquarters were a welcoming place where officers were encouraged to question orders or offer innovative solutions during the planning phase. The supportive atmosphere of Currie's headquarters was noted by visitors, including the American commander, General Jack "Blackjack" Pershing.[4] Currie carried himself casually among his trusted staff, laughing and swearing freely. However, though Currie was comfortable among his officers, he rarely communicated this easy style to his men in the field, which would have gone over well with the rank and file. Instead, he was usually stiff and formal among them, unable to find the right words as an inspirational general and unable to intimidate by staring in severe silence like the equally challenged orator, Sir Douglas Haig. Nonetheless, Currie was far more open in his headquarters and he ran it like the CEO of a company, taking the best from his subordinates, talking through issues, and then choosing a path forward. His staff was always amazed at how he went to the heart of the matter, clearing through a mass of details and complexities. When he had made up his mind, he could be stubborn, but he delegated freely and had faith in his staff and his divisional commands to devise plans.

This managerial style suited Currie well for command at the Western Front. Trench warfare was "simply a problem of engineering," wrote General Monash, the last commander of the Australian Corps, who, like Currie, was a prewar militia officer and an outsider to the British professionals.[5] Battles had to be fought through a planned, methodical approach, and the efficient management of men and munitions helped to underpin victory. Currie listened to his subordinates, relied on his experienced British general staff officers, worked hard, was morally brave, and, although it was not always apparent to his men, always tried to ration their lives in the attritional battles of the Western Front. As one subordinate officer noted, Currie sought to spend shells rather than the lives of his men to achieve his objectives.[6] But he, like all the generals, had learned warfighting the hard way. Currie made his mistakes, and few found him to be a military genius. He admitted as much to one subordinate, T.G. Roberts, brother of the famous Canadian poet, Sir Charles G.D. Roberts. On the subject of planning operations, Currie confessed: "I'm not clever enough to guess in this game. I have to set everything down and figure it out. It's harder work than being brilliant—but safer."[7] Currie relied on hard work and detailed planning to win battles on the Western Front.

Byng had been grooming Currie as his successor since the Somme battles. Currie had also been recognized by Haig, who had been more than a little interested in the youngest major general in the BEF. Consistently distinguishing himself as a commander and trainer since the start of the war, Currie was, in Haig's eyes, the only Canadian-born choice for the top position of command. Major General Louis Lipsett of the 3rd Division was acknowledged by many as having corps commander potential, but most Canadian troops and politicians had now fully embraced the emerging national spirit of their corps and were demanding a Canadian to lead their force in the field.[8] Turner had claims as the senior Canadian officer, but he had been outmanoeuvred when he was sent to England as the CEF's chief of the general staff. Although intriguers such as Lord Beaverbrook tried to use their influence to impose Turner as commander, they had lost much of their sway with the British after the firing of Sam Hughes. Moreover, Turner had proven himself a far more adept administrator than operational commander, and he could ill be spared from his important position as the senior soldier responsible for manpower, training, and all military matters relating to the CEF that did not fall under the purview of the fighting forces in Europe, especially that of the Canadian Corps.

The bickering over the corps command went on for several days in June, especially when it was found that the Canadian cabinet in Ottawa was angry about not having been consulted over who would command the Canadian national force. When Currie worriedly visited Sir Douglas Haig for advice on what to do, the field marshal, who always displayed canny political survival skills, advised Currie to stop dickering with the opposing camp in England or politicians in Canada and take over command of the corps, assuming that possession would be nine-tenths of the law. He was right. Despite Turner's claims, Currie was soon confirmed by the Canadian cabinet, which was not about to overrule Haig and the British high command.[9] Currie would be the Canadian Corps commander for the rest of the corps' existence.

If Turner would not command the corps, then Beaverbrook and others thought they should receive some concession in exchange for their loss of potential influence over military matters. Aware that Sir Sam Hughes could still cause problems, Borden, ever the politician, felt that the command of Currie's former 1st Division should be given to Garnet Hughes. Overseas minister Sir George Perley, although no friend of Sir Sam's either, agreed, hoping that such a conciliatory move would mollify the senior Hughes. It appeared that a deal had been made that appealed to everyone—except that no one had discussed this political concession with Currie, and the new corps commander refused to cave in to the pressure. He would not accept an inferior general within his command for the sake of political expediency. After Perley pressed the matter, Currie threatened to resign unless the fiery and experienced fifty-three-year-old Scottish Canadian Archibald C. Macdonell, of the 7th Brigade, was given the division. The politicians blinked.

"Fighting Mac" or "Batty Mac," as he was known to the troops, was an inspired leader, whose fearlessness, flamboyant language, and charisma made him loved by his men. In between the swearing and cheering on of his men, he liked to speak Gaelic to his Highlanders, and was probably not too worried that most of them had no idea what he was saying.[10] He stood ramrod straight and had military experience dating back to the South African War. At the start of the Great War, he had commanded Lord Strathcona's Horse and had been twice wounded in as many years—once by a sniper's bullet, after which he stunned his men by yelling a string of colourful expletives at the sniper and had to be forcefully restrained from trying to go over the top to pay that bloody Hun back for his insolence! While Batty Mac was a good choice for commander of the 1st, the denial of the division to Garnet Hughes was a crushing blow to the Hughes family. The younger Hughes had helped Currie get his brigade in 1914, and Currie had even written to him as recently as May 8, 1917, seemingly indicating that he would like to see Garnet as a divisional commander in France.[11] Despite his debt to Garnet, however, Currie turned his back on him, instead rightly choosing the more experienced and successful Macdonell.[12] Hughes did not take it well. After a meeting at a London hotel while Currie was on leave, a three-hour screaming match ensued between the two men, with Garnet eventually storming out and promising, "I will get you before I am finished."[13] The incident marked the end of their friendship. And by denying Garnet the coveted command, Currie also earned the lasting enmity of his father. "From the time of my refusal," wrote Currie, Sam Hughes "never ceased to blackguard me and to minimize my influence and authority with my own men. The things to which he and his associates resorted would bring a blush of shame to the face of every decent citizen of this country."[14]

But these same decent citizens might also have blushed at the prewar actions of their war hero. Currie had invested heavily in Victoria real estate before the recession of 1913. When the booming market collapsed, his finances were tied up in what was now severely overpriced property. To stave off bankruptcy, he stole $10,000 from the 50th Highlanders' regimental funds to pay off his debts. Although the theft weighed on his mind throughout the war, Currie did not hasten to pay back the money—despite his substantial rate of pay as a major general and then a lieutenant general. His actions were bizarre and reckless, and he chose to ignore rather than rectify the problem. Currie's pilfering past eventually came to the attention of Sir Robert Borden and his cabinet ministers in the fall of 1917, during the corps commander's early days at his post, and they were disturbed to find that their brilliant general was only a court case away from being a felon. Although a crisis was averted when two of Currie's subordinates lent him money, the incident must have left some of the ministers wondering about the character of the man who commanded their land forces in the field.[15] However, it did not outwardly change their view of Currie as a military commander, and the politicians refused to force Garnet Hughes on their decorated general. Hughes retained the lesser prize of the 5th Division, which most thought would eventually make its way to France. It did not, and Currie broke it up for desperately needed reinforcements in early 1918: this was definitely the right decision, but one that further angered Hughes and his powerful father. They would later pay Currie back with an insidious campaign to undermine him in England and back in Canada. But in preventing Garnet Hughes from commanding the prestigious 1st Division, Currie had won an important first round and ensured that he would continue Byng's legacy of blocking politicians from diluting the effectiveness of the Canadian Corps.

AS A ROOKIE CORPS COMMANDER, Currie might have been expected to be nervous in orchestrating his first major battle and to acquiesce to the British high command's calls for a frontal attack on Lens. He did nothing of the sort. After surveying the front, Currie felt it would be a costly attack—a "bloody fool operation," remarked Gunner Andrew McNaughton—more likely to destroy the Canadian attackers than the dug-in defenders.[16] He went forward to his superior, General Henry Horne, on July 10 and declared that if they "were going to fight at all, let us fight for something worth having."[17] Horne, who had a reputation for caring for his men, sensibly agreed and presented Currie's recast plan to Haig. Instead of a frontal assault into the low-lying parts of the city, Currie consulted his divisional commanders and planned for an assault on Hill 70, a desolate, blasted chalky hill, mined and bristling with machine-gun strongpoints, to the north of Lens. The British had attacked it as part of their failed Loos offensive in September 1915, but the Germans had driven them off it. As Hill 70 overlooked and outflanked the city of Lens to the south, Currie knew the Germans would not relinquish it without a fight. General Haig told Currie as much, but authorized the operation, as his goal was not for the attack to capture Lens but to draw German reserves away from the Flanders front.[18]

Currie's proposed operation against Hill 70 was more practical than an attack on Lens as it would avoid costly urban fighting, in which the Canadians had almost no experience. In such an operation, the attackers would be at a disadvantage as they picked their way through the brick-strewn ruins, moving from ambush to ambush and harassed by fire coming from the heights of the hill. However, the defenders' advantage would be reversed if the Canadians could capture Hill 70 to the north. The Germans would be forced to counterattack—moving from their strongholds to cross the fireswept ground—or to suffer punishing fire within the city as Canadian gunners laid down bombardments from above. By biting off a limited objective on Hill 70, Currie planned to hold the high point and then bleed the German counterattack forces white by preparing a killing zone of concentrated artillery and machine-gun fire. It was, in effect, a plan much like that of the Germans at Verdun in early 1916.[19] The Canadians would capture a key enemy position but then use the German tactics of lightning counterattack against them, chewing up the enemy forces in a metal firestorm.

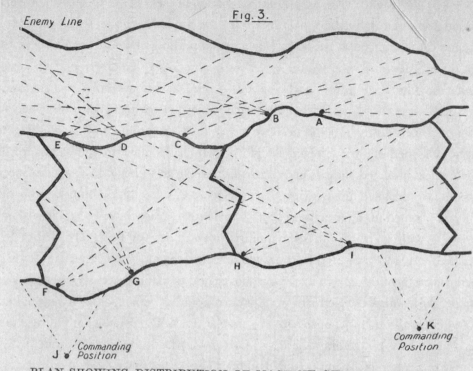

PLAN SHOWING DISTRIBUTION OF MACHINE GUNS IN TRENCHES.
A, B, C, D, E, F, G, H, I, AND J ARE MACHINE GUN POSITIONS.

Currie's plan to hold Hill 70 involved setting up a kill zone of artillery, machine-gun, and rifle fire. This diagram from a 1917 training manual illustrates the crossfire from multiple machine guns sweeping over fixed fire zones. After the Canadians captured Hill 70, 192 heavy Vickers machine guns and thousands of additional rifles and Lewis machine guns, all backed by artillery fire, would tear apart the counterattacking German forces.

Horne left the planning in Currie's hands, and when the corps commander asked for a delay beyond the tentative attack date of July 31, Horne replied: "My boy this is your own battle; attack when you are ready and I will hold you responsible."[20] While Currie was preparing his operation, the Canadian assault battalions practised behind the lines. "Nothing is left to chance," declared Currie, and as Vimy had shown, success rested on junior officers and NCOs knowing the terrain and their role in the battle.[21] Practice grounds, map readings, and lectures were used in the classroom of war before the infantry were unleashed onto the battlefield. This training occurred throughout July, and then into early August as the operation's date was pushed back due to heavy rain. The 25th Battalion had an astonishing twenty days to rehearse their part in the attack.[22] This extended practice was good for confidence, but not always for morale. The 1st Brigade, for instance, was bizarrely ordered to train in open ground that was under partial observation from the distant enemy lines, and sporadically under fire, because much of the area in the Canadian rear was covered in ripening crops.[23] Most of the enemy shells missed their mark, but more than a few soldiers must have wondered at the decision that placed greater importance on wheat crops than on their lives.

Following a sequence of heavy raids in the Avion sector in May and June 1917, a new series of minor operations was carried out to hone battlecraft skills, and as part of a deliberate policy to draw German attention away from Hill 70. The largest assault was the 116th Battalion's night operation on July 23, directed against the Sallaumines-Méricourt Line to the southwest of Lens. Currie hoped the attention of the German high command would be drawn here after the raid, and would therefore move some of its reserve forces away from Hill 70 to strengthen this southern sector. While Horne and Haig wished to see Currie launch an operation that would retain ground instead of just inflicting damage through a raid, the Canadian general resisted the pressure from his superiors and stuck to his policy of fixing the enemy to this front by taking action rather than retaining useless trenches that would only leave his forces more vulnerable to enemy fire on two sides.[24] Haig and Horne eventually agreed and dropped their orders to bite and hold rather than smash and retreat.

The Germans kept an active defence on this front and frequently shelled the area. In fact, as the 116th prepared for the raid, they did so while forming up within clouds of gas that the Germans had projected over the front. But the battalion's three companies were ready for the stealth operation. The 116th closed with the enemy behind a massive barrage after 1 A.M., and then crashed into the German trenches. Sentries were shot and stabbed; grenades were tossed into dugouts as terrified defenders milled about in confusion, trapped in the dark; trenches were captured in fierce hand-to-hand battles. After thirty-five minutes of frenzied fighting, the Canadians retreated to their lines, but not before blowing in a number of deep enemy dugouts with large satchel charges. It was a desperate retreat, however, as German counterattacking forces harassed the Canadian rearguard. An emergency barrage was called down to help the Canadians extricate themselves from the enemy trenches, but it landed behind the Germans, who were determined and quick to avenge the assault. They closed the gap and heavy fighting ensued in No Man's Land among the craters and corpses, with the Canadians making it back to their lines only after a running gunfight. It was impossible to estimate the number of killed, though the Canadians' fifty-three scared prisoners, perhaps too willing to please their captors, testified to whole sections of Germans being wiped out. The raid had been a success, but the retreat had been harrowing: the 116th lost seventy-four men, including seventeen declared missing, who had either been killed or taken prisoner.[25] This minor operation had been costly, but the Germans responded by strengthening this front as Currie had hoped.

On August 1, the infantry moved forward towards positions near Hill 70. The hill itself was unimpressive, amounting to little more than a gentle ridge. But with the city to the south in the low ground, the hill offered a point of observation into the enemy trench system and the maze of suburbs that ringed Lens. The Germans were aware that something was happening: too many troops were in the area, too many ammunition stockpiles, too many guns. German intelligence had already determined that the troops opposite them were the Canadians, who had long been identified as an elite shock force that "the British Higher Command always employ for the most difficult and costly fighting."[26] This knowledge made the defenders warier still. They continued with their searching artillery and chemical barrages in the hope of wreaking havoc among the Canadians. Captain Harold McGill of the 31st Battalion noted ruefully in his memoirs that "shelling was almost continuous…. Our daily activities went on in an atmosphere of shell smoke, poison gas and brick dust."[27]

As the Canadians moved closer to the front, the trenches and dugouts constructed by their engineers were essential to saving lives. But there were not enough to provide cover for all the men, and many Canadian assault units were housed in the cellars and basements of local houses in villages behind the lines. The Germans shelled day and night, but torrents of rain affected the accuracy of the gunners, which lessened the Canadian losses. The rain would prove disastrous for the British on the Passchendaele battlefield to the north, but Currie, with more limited objectives, was able to delay the zero hour, pushing back the operation until he was satisfied that all the necessary arrangements had been made. "Swiftness in war," wrote British general Sir Ian Hamilton, "comes from slow preparations."[28]

Crash bombardments over the next two weeks killed and maimed hundreds of enemy soldiers within artillery range. Canadian Corps siege guns fired at targets of opportunity, and always to prevent the Germans from repairing their destroyed trenches and barbed wire.[29] However, the corps still suffered from a shortage of field guns, and the preparatory barrage necessary to soften up enemy strongpoints and clear wire took more time than planned since many of the Canadian Corps gun formations—including five heavy-artillery-group headquarters, two heavy batteries, ten siege batteries, and five brigades of field artillery—had been moved north to support the Passchendaele offensive.[30] The Canadians were left with older, more decrepit guns, most of which had fired thousands of rounds past their life expectancy, so that barrels were worn down and melted, decreasing the accuracy of fire. The bad weather also hindered Canadian gunners' attempts to target their objectives.

Major General E.W.B. Morrison, commander of the Canadian Royal Artillery, turned to trench mortars to clear many of the barbed wire obstacles so that his guns could more effectively target enemy trenches and lines of communications.[31] The Canadian "destructive fire," noted one intercepted enemy report, "[has] turned the foremost German positions into a shell hole like that in Flanders."[32] The front was honeycombed with shellfire, and the broken battlefield was flooded beyond recognition. Although the Canadians' old and worn out guns presented a danger to the gunners (as shells could blow up in the barrel) or to the infantry (as short shells could drop on them), scientific gunnery skills and the assistance of aircraft from the Royal Flying Corps had enabled the artillery to neutralize 40 out of an estimated 102 enemy batteries by the time the infantry went over the top.[33] In both the destructive bombardment and counter-battery work, the Canadians used an enormous number of shells to complete their missions, and Currie refused to rush the plan even though he was pressured by the British to hasten his assault. He even had the audacity to ask for a few more precious heavy howitzers from the British, which Haig supplied, going so far as to overrule his own artillery officer, who objected to the disruption of his own barrage plans in the Flanders region. An anxious but supportive Haig could almost be heard sighing to his diary when he wrote, "The Canadians always open their mouths very wide!"[34]

THE ENEMY'S POSITION on Hill 70 was divided into three distinct lines. Scraggly woods marked the lower part of the hill, but the top had been blasted clean. The chalk outline of the enemy trenches could easily be observed by RFC planes supporting the Canadian gunners. The enemy's fortifications were some 2.5 kilometres deep, and spread over the hill and outlying parts of Lens's suburban villages, which were incorporated into the lines. To protect against the bombardment, the enemy had thinned out its forces to create fewer targets for the Canadian gunners, thereby forcing a greater expenditure of ammunition. The first line was defended lightly, but the second line, known as the Catapult-Hurdle Line, was held in far more strength. The third line was even tougher, as it was situated on the reverse slope of the hill and therefore harder to target with plunging fire. The entire position was held by German troops from the 11th Reserve and 7th Division, both of which were assessed by Canadian intelligence officers as good troops, although the 11th Reserve was thought to have some weak regiments.[35]

As the Canadian battalions moved into position on the night of August 14, the Germans continued to saturate the area with high explosives, shrapnel, and hated chemical agents that forced many units to advance with respirators attached, stumbling and wheezing their way to the front. Front-line German formations had been warned about an attack, as their intelligence officers had observed the changing density of the saturation bombardment and the intense activity behind the Canadian lines, and some units were told to expect the assault on August 15, the actual day of battle.[36] Gunner Basil E. Courtney of the 3rd Garrison Artillery recounted in his diary the day before the battle: "Fritz was giving us hell ... strafed us for three hours steady this A.M. Parkinson here only six days [before he was] killed outside our gun dug-out. Went out with stretchers but was dead when he arrived [at the clearing station]."[37] Another gunner, J.C.K. Mackay of the 20th Battery, who observed German interdiction fire sweeping the known road system and setting several ammunition wagons on fire, noted that August 14 was a "disastrous night for the battery."[38] Hundreds of Canadians were killed and wounded before the battle had even started.

Currie's plan called for a limited three-phase attack into the German lines along a 3,600-metre front: in the first phase, the Canadians would take the top of the hill; in the second, they would overcome a series of trenches to the east and on the downward slope of the hill; and in the third phase, pushing to 1,300 metres from the start line, the Canadian infantry would capture the remaining positions that ran in an arc around the lower edge of the eastern slope. So they could be sure to hold the position once they captured it, the infantry were laden with equipment and supplies. Sandbags, shovels, wire cutters, and water were added to the usual extra ammunition and bombs. Their burdened state was not unlike that of the British infantry on the Somme, who carried more than sixty pounds on their back. However, whereas in the Somme battle units were to achieve victory in one big leap, at Lens the front-line infantry would take their positions, dig in, and have follow-on units pass through them to stab deeper into the German trenches.

Behind a 400-metre-deep creeping barrage laid down by 204 18-pounders, forward waves would be supported by second and third waves, which were to advance in a loose, skirmish order that was more spread out, thereby allowing the reinforcing troops to flow around strongpoints if they were held up by enemy fire. The barrage could not destroy all of the enemy positions along the ridge, but it would hopefully paralyze defenders long enough for the spearhead units to overrun them. After the first objective was captured, a barrage of machine guns and artillery was to pound the front during a forty-minute pause for the lead infantry units, as they waited for the next wave to push through. The pause at Vimy had been longer and had allowed the Germans to recover in places, so it would be a hurried assault at Hill 70—long enough for the second-wave troops to move forward, but, hopefully, not long enough for the enemy to recover. For the plan to work, however, these second and

THE BATTLE OF HILL 70: AUGUST 15 TO 25, 1917

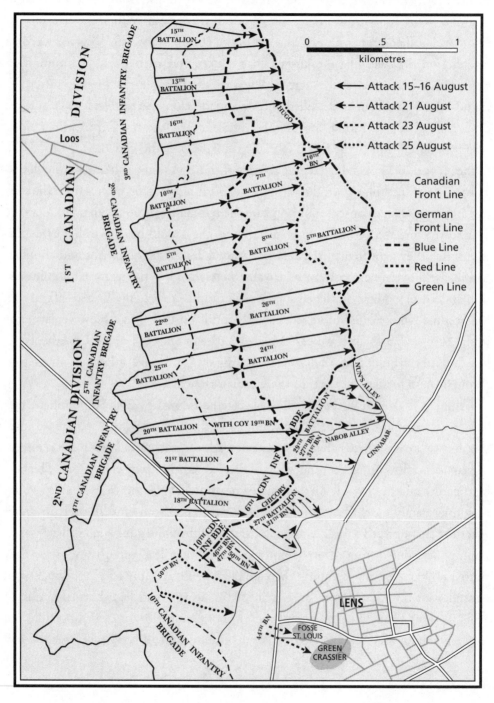

third waves would wait—bunched and vulnerable—in the communication trenches and second-line defences closer to the front. Behind these units, moppers-up would follow, spending extra time on mine-shaft entrances and redoubts where the Germans would likely go to ground as the first wave of men crashed over their lines. Orders stipulated that "every shell-hole and every apparent German corpse should be investigated."[39] If the attack were a success, a final group would be sent forward, with barbed wire and sandbags, to immediately consolidate the positions.

Currie's plan was to overrun the limited objectives on Hill 70 and then hold the hill against counterattack. The latter part of the plan would be accomplished through the establishment of a kill zone. More than 200 artillery pieces, 192 heavy machine guns, and several thousand riflemen and rifle grenadiers would be brought to bear on the ground in front of the newly captured positions. The astonishingly large force of machine guns would anchor the defensive line, around which the infantry would form their own battle groups. Even if the guns functioned at only one-quarter their optimal rate of fire—for reasons related to placement, stoppages, availability of ammunition, and the guns' destruction by enemy fire—they could lay down some 20,000 bullets per minute. If Currie's men bit off the hill, the Germans would have to pass through a holocaust of fire to wrestle it back from the jaws of the Canadian pit bulls.

CHAPTER 17

OVER THE TOP

August 15, 1917

"Dawn is coming; and my heart is filled suddenly with bitterness when I realize that the day may be my last.... I am aware of an intense desire to live," wrote Arthur Lapointe of the 22nd Battalion in his diary before the battle for Hill 70.[1] Pre-battle rituals were hurried under the fall of shells—from the spiritual to the practical to the superstitious, including whispering litanies, foregoing food that might keep a stomach wound from going septic, and giving away money, as it was considered bad luck by some to go over the top with unspent funds.[2] Whatever soldiers felt they needed to do to better their chances in this war of long odds was generally considered appropriate by mates who had their own rituals they used to master their fear. Last-minute adjustments were made, and orders were given to load ten rounds in rifle magazines and fix bayonets. Then silence. Luminescent in the pre-dawn light, wristwatches ticked off the minutes as zero hour drew near.

The barrage lit off at 4:25 A.M. More than 5,000 Canadians in 10 battalions crashed forward behind a barrage rained down by more than 200 artillery pieces. There was one 18-pounder for every 18 metres of the front. Gunners fired a frenzy of shells into the scarlet-streaked eastern horizon. "How anyone could live through the bursting of thousands of shells on these few miles of targets was a mystery," remarked Gunner Gurney Little of the 7th Siege Battery, a twenty-one-year-old bank clerk from Toronto.[3] Ahead of the infantry's protective creeping barrage, heavy guns dropped a second, jumping bombardment, while ahead of this, in a third wall

Despite the Canadians' intricate preparation and the heavy artillery and machine-gun barrage that would clear the way into the enemy lines, the minutes before the attack were agonizing for the infantry who waited on death row before surging forward into No Man's Land.

of steel and fire, the largest siege guns focused on strongpoints, communication trenches, and suspected battery positions. The creeping barrage landed on the enemy front line to inflict six minutes of hell. Then, at the designated time, it moved off 90 metres forward, and the infantry surged ahead to clear the smoking ruins. Thereafter, the barrage lifted at 90-metre bounds every four minutes, with attacking waves following it.

The Canadian Battle of Hill 70 was supported by more than 200 artillery pieces, all of which were directed on the limited front of Hill 70 and Lens. One Canadian gunner remarked: "How anyone could live through the bursting of thousands of shells on these few miles of targets was a mystery."

The regimental history for the German 165th Reserve Regiment observed that the speed of the Canadian attack took them by surprise, even though they were apprised of the exact day of the operation.[4] The rapid advance was assisted by Royal Engineers, who sent drums of blazing oil and poison gas from mortar-like Livens projectors into the enemy lines, which burst in pools of hissing flame and chemicals. The city of Lens was bombarded, and although the oil and gas caused little damage, the resulting smoke set up an effective screen for the Canadian infantry along parts of the front. An inferno of artillery fire further confused the enemy about the actual time of the attack, as communication was severed from front to rear, and laterally among now isolated units. To the south, the 4th Division's 12th Brigade was to offer a feint against Lens in the hope that the Germans would suspect that it was the main axis of the attack and focus their forces on that sector of the front. Brigadier J.H. MacBrien's soldiers discharged their Lee-Enfields in the direction of the Germans, supported by artillery and mortars, and sent battle patrols into the outskirts of Lens. They accomplished their goal of drawing heavy artillery fire to their position, thus freeing up the assault battalions advancing against Hill 70. It was a tough job for the men of the 12th Brigade, but they had prepared by digging deep dugouts, and lost fewer than two dozen men.

"SHELLS PASS IN SALVOS over our head and through the deep roaring of the guns I can hear the staccato rat-a-tat of machine-guns," described Arthur Lapointe. "I scramble over the parapet.... Our company is forming up and the moments of delay seem endless. A few hundred yards in front of us, red, yellow, and green rockets rise from the German lines, as the enemy tells his artillery, supports, and reserves that we are attacking."[5] Against the primary objective of Hill 70 to the north of Lens, ten Canadian battalions charged behind the barrage, passing over shell-torn landscape. They were under strict orders not to stop for the wounded, as that would slow the advance. The lead infantry units had to close the gap in the killing zone before the barrage got away from them. Dismembered, shattered German corpses were scrambled over in the rush, but not all defenders were killed. Sergeant J.E. Laplante of the 21st Battalion described the fierce fighting: "We advanced towards each other, neither side flinching when the collision came, fierce hand to hand fighting occurred, no quarter was asked, none was given."[6]

To the north, Brigadier George Tuxford's 3rd Brigade attacked with the 15th Battalion at the far north and the 13th and 16th Battalions further south. On the far left, the Highlanders of the 15th Battalion moved forward in three waves, each a company strong, with two mopping-up platoons following at their heels, along with two platoons of wirers to consolidate the position in the final phase. The lead units were also supported by ten Vickers machine-gun teams and another ten Stokes mortar bomb teams. Each company had to capture approximately 200 metres of frontage, to a depth of between 900 and 1,300 metres.[7] This amounted to roughly 272,700 square metres of ground to be taken by only about 150 men. And although the barrage tore up great chunks of earth, the terrain still afforded many places where enemy troops could hide, especially in narrow, slit trenches in front of or behind the main defensive line.

To protect the 15th Battalion's flank, engineers propelled forward ninety drums of blazing oil that exploded over the front, creating a temporary firestorm and then a billowing cloud of black smoke. On this front, the 46th British Division, which was supporting the Canadian Corps to the north, also laid down heavy fire with their artillery and machine guns in the hope of drawing the Germans' attention to their front, away from to the Canadians to the south. With the flank largely secure and the 46th Division sacrificing themselves for the good of the Canadians, the 15th pushed ahead, bayonets first. Most of the enemy positions were overrun, but a few strong-points on the right held up the attack until a left wheel of advancing infantrymen took them from behind. As the dawn broke around 5 A.M., the 15th had made good progress, with prisoners moving back to headquarters providing the first indication of the success. The first line was captured, but then the fighting started in earnest.

These Canadian signallers are repairing telephone wire along a communication trench. Shellfire frequently cut the wire, thereby isolating the soldiers at the front. The communication challenge was never overcome during the war, but new inventions such as the wireless set helped commanders better control the battle once soldiers were in contact with the enemy and lost in the chaos of close-quarters combat.

In the rear, the battalion headquarters waited impotently for runners to bring them information, anxious for answers to their many questions. Was the attack a success? The high number of prisoners indicated that some positions had been overrun, but at what cost? And where would the Germans counterattack? Signallers began to run their wires from the front to the rear, but, as in all battles, artillery fire either disrupted the lines or disintegrated the signallers. New continuous-wave wireless sets were lighter and had a greater range. Those few that were available were used later in the day to coordinate SOS artillery fire in support of breaking up counterattacks.

At 5:40 A.M., the second waves of the 15th Battalion attacked over the cratered battlefield, with bagpipers playing them into battle. Picking their way through shredded barbed wire that tugged at their legs, and scrambling from crater-lip to crater-lip when German gunners opened up on them, the 15th closed the distance. As in most battles, the company commanders' control broke down as shouted commands were lost in the cacophony of shrieks and crashes. But the trained infantry moved forward in smaller battle groups, advancing, firing, and then going to ground while others crept ahead. "It seemed to me," wrote an NCO in the 16th Battalion, "that we must have advanced for miles, so little does one understand time and space on those occasions, or what is happening on the flanks."[8] Countless small battles and engagements took place—from brutal firefights to easy strolls to the objectives. There was no uniform experience in the battle for Hill 70.

Those at the sharp end that day performed stunning acts of bravery. Private E.G. Raymond of the 15th Battalion rushed one machine-gun nest that was playing havoc with his section. As bullets sprayed all around his bare legs, the Highlander tossed his grenade into the pit, but was killed by the last burst of a machine gun before the crew was wiped out.[9] His section and company mates pushed deeper into the enemy lines, scanning and then stalking the next machine gun, the next dugout, the next German defender. No one will ever know how many acts like this—of soldiers sacrificing their lives so that others might live—went unrecorded.

The 13th and 16th Battalions had equal success to the south of the 15th, and were on their objectives at a little past 6 A.M., at which point they exchanged rifles for shovels. Lance Corporal Alvin Kines, who served with the 16th and had survived the Vimy battles though most of his friends had been killed or wounded, remembered taking over the defence of several sections as his sergeant "lost his nerve and hid in a German dugout along with some others."[10] Kines noted sympathetically that the sergeant in question was a "very fine Sgt. all other times," but had simply cracked during the battle. Kines did not, however, and was awarded the Military Medal for his work in holding the front. The counterattack was coming, and the now exhausted Canadians moved with the speed known only to those who stand condemned. Firing steps were ripped out and rebuilt on the back part of the trench, which, through the Canadian victory, had now become the front. Machine-gunners situated their guns with clear fields of fire. Sandbags were stuffed and barbed wire unrolled outside the new parapet and even in the trenches, especially to block enemy counterattacks rushing up through communication trenches. Liaison men braved the increasing weight of enemy fire to report back to headquarters, while others raced to contact units on the flank and ensure there were no gaps in the line between battalions that could be exploited by the enemy. Throughout the battle, the 3rd Brigade kept up nearly continuous contact with the British 46th Division to the north, which had inched forward after the initial German bombardment landed on their front lines. The Canadians and British worked closely to coordinate their defence against probing German attacks that looked for weak seams in the Allied lines, but the battle raged on to the south.

IN THE CENTRE of the battle, the 5th and 10th Battalions, from Brigadier Frederick Loomis's 2nd Brigade, stormed the first objective. The Fighting Tenth had had trouble reaching their jumping-off trenches the night before because of a heavy gas barrage that saturated the front, but they were ready by 4 A.M. Once they went over the top, "It seemed to us as if every machine-gun in Creation opened up all at once," recalled Private Norman Eastman.[11] Bullets and shell fragments whirled over the battlefield, as both the Canadian barrage and German counter-barrage chewed up the front. Enemy SOS flares lit the sky in reds and blues and the Canadians had to push into the enemy lines to find cover before the counter-barrage thickened and caught them in the open. Leapfrogging their way forward, platoons and companies passed through each other, clearing strongpoints and establishing a defence-in-depth. Stubborn German machine-gunners put up a strong defence, but they were wiped out by bullet, bomb, and bayonet. Sixty members of the 10th Battalion would be awarded the Military Medal for their role in the battle, including Privates Masumi Mitsui and Tokutaro Iwamoto, just a couple of the 222 Japanese Canadians who served with the CEF.[12] By 6:12 A.M., the 10th had captured their objectives, and the 7th Battalion passed through them to continue the assault.

The 5th Battalion experienced equally hard fighting to the south, as it was held up by several heavy German machine-gun crews. The battalion's objectives were on the reverse side of the hill and therefore harder to hit with plunging artillery fire. "There was much close-quarter fighting," reported one senior officer.[13] The second-wave battalion, the 8th, moved through the shattered lines of the 5th, whose two forward companies had started the battle with over 100 men each and were now reduced to 6 in one and 9 in the other. The 8th Battalion's Little Black Devils made good progress behind their barrage, but were raked with enfilade fire. Around 300 defenders dug-in at a spot identified on the Canadian maps as the Chalk Quarry were shooting into the exposed advance. With men cut to pieces and going to ground, the battalion lacked enough "push" to reach its final objectives. Though two Canadian machine-gun outposts were established to suppress the Quarry fire, both were wiped out by heavy howitzer shells that dropped short from Canadian guns.

But war's pendulum of fortune swings both ways. The few surviving officers of the Little Black Devils force decided by midday that a further attack by the battalion's remaining eighty men would be suicide. They therefore scratched out slit trenches in the chalk to meet the expected German counterattack with Lewis-gun and rifle fire. But the runner who was headed to the rear to alert the artillery to call off the barrage never made it to the gunners. The creeping barrage that was to carry the 8th Battalion forward fortuitously came down on the enemy trenches just as the Germans were carrying out their own counterattack. The shells, according to Canadian infantrymen, caused "tremendous execution." Nonetheless, brutal battles still took place among isolated outposts of men, who fought with little mercy, rifles firing until the ammunition ran out, bayonets stabbing red. According to the official report, "The fighting which took place from the crest of Hill 70 forward was the fiercest and most bitter which the Battalions of this Brigade have ever experienced or seen."[14] The 8th Battalion suffered 400 casualties out of an estimated 720 men committed to battle; seventy percent resulted from small-arms fire, indicating that the Canadian counter-battery work had largely silenced the enemy artillery guns but that many German infantrymen and machine-gunners had survived the creeping barrage.[15] While the determined survivors of the 8th Battalion held out against the German counterattack, the two reserve companies of the 5th Battalion leapfrogged over the 8th Battalion and fought their way to victory. To the north, as well, the remnants of the 10th Battalion, along with what was left of the 7th, had captured their final objectives by the late afternoon, including the Chalk Quarry, which was taken from the flank. Captain William Thompson, who led his B Company in the final assault over 80 metres of open ground, remarked, "We went through them like a dose of salts."[16] By the end of the day, the 2nd Brigade was on all its final objectives and was digging in to hold them.

TO THE SOUTH OF HILL 70, the 4th and 5th Brigades were to attack through the outskirts of Lens. The southern and southeastern slopes of Hill 70 ran into the northern suburbs of Lens, consisting of a group of brick miners' houses, now mostly in ruins after months of shelling. The setting would make for difficult city-fighting, even if pre-battle training had focused the infantry on how to move effectively down cobblestone streets, identify street signs, and clear the enemy from houses with grenade tossing followed by bayonet rushing.

The 5th Brigade led with the 22nd and 25th Battalions, which almost always attacked together. Lieutenant Colonel Thomas Tremblay of the 22nd gave a pre-battle speech: "Tonight you will fight as you fought at Courcelette and Vimy and the people back home will be proud of us."[17] The chaplain recited his benediction in a soft rain as the battalion stood bareheaded, and the assault troops moved up the line to prepare for the barrage. Right behind them were the follow-on battalions, the 24th and 26th, who were to advance with the lead units to avoid being caught by the expected enemy counter-barrage. This was a good decision since the counter-barrage started at zero hour plus three minutes and increased in intensity during the morning.

The two lead battalions followed their creeping barrage, laid down by more than 150 guns and howitzers, into the enemy lines. The hill felt like it was moving beneath the infantry's feet, and orders shouted by officers and NCOs were drowned out by the ear-shattering explosions. The creeping barrage had crushed most of the barbed-wire obstacles, and the infantry punched their way through the remaining forward German defences on the outskirts of Lens at the bottom of Hill 70. The enemy front lines were held lightly: the 22nd Battalion captured 150 prisoners and the 24th took 100 more, all from the 165th Regiment. One report classified the prisoners as "very young and of very poor physique."[18] But they were useful in carrying wounded Canadians back to their trenches. The first German line of resistance, known to the Canadians as the Blue Line, was overrun easily at 4:50 A.M., and the secondary battalions pushed forward.

The 24th Battalion, or the Victoria Rifles as they preferred to be called, passed through the Nova Scotians of the 25th Battalion at 5:20 A.M. and pushed to Cité St. Émile, on the outskirts of Lens. William Morgan of the 24th testified in his diary that they had trained so effectively for the operation that, "We even know the names of the streets we are to march up and the actual houses we are to mop up."[19] Knowing the terrain helped, but the fighting was difficult and costly as the Germans clung to the rubble of houses and dug in to cellars. Lead officers were shot down, but junior men rose to the occasion. Enduring casualties, dust, and explosions, attacking platoons clawed their way forward over the rubble and along pitted roads. Several spearheading platoons got lost, drifting into the 4th Brigade's territory to the south. The battalion's two lead companies were reduced to twenty and thirty infantrymen by enemy fire, the grinding attrition of house-to-house fighting, and the belief of some soldiers that going to ground was a more prudent course than advancing in the face of sweeping enemy fire. A desultory counterattack was beaten back by concentrated fire at 8 A.M., but it was a costly morning that left the 24th Battalion reduced to 5 officers and 132 men.

A stronger counterattack was defeated by the Victoria Rifles at 7:45 P.M. through well-coordinated crossfire kill zones and prompt action by the artillery in response to SOS rockets.[20] This type of grid firing was particularly lethal for breaking up enemy concentrations and isolating their forward forces, who were then beaten piecemeal by the infantry. Rifle fire from the infantry was acknowledged as providing essential killing power in this battle. While the Canadians had received some criticism for relying too much on the grenade and Lewis gunners at Vimy, here every rifle was needed to hold off the enemy onslaught. The 24th were to be relieved on August 16, but the enemy artillery fire was so heavy that no unit could be brought forward through the storm of steel. Even the attempts of smaller parties to carry water ahead were often little more than suicide operations, which left forward units, and their wounded, to suffer in the front positions without relief. They were eventually relieved on the night of August 17–18, but like most of the battalions in the assault, they limped to the rear after the devastating fighting; they went into the line 593 strong and emerged with a strength of only 278.[21]

To the south, the 4th Brigade sent the 20th, 21st, and 18th Battalions forward, along with the 19th, who would pass through the lead battalions to exploit success. These experienced combat units had been guided into No Man's Land before the battle to ensure that they could quickly get forward of the enemy's expected counter–barrage so that the shellfire would fall behind them. Despite forming up under gas clouds, the 4th Brigade had the easiest time of the Canadian brigades, and most of the battalions were on their objectives between 5 and 6 A.M., having covered a distance of 550 metres. At 5:50 A.M., the first walking wounded reported to headquarters that there had been "little opposition" from enemy troops or machine-gun fire.[22] At 7:35 A.M., however, it was reported that a German officer had been captured, and during his interrogation, he revealed that there would be a counter-attack within the hour. Suffering mounting casualties from artillery and small-arms fire, the Canadians all along the front dug in and prepared for the wave of assaults.

The 19th Battalion, in reserve, was rushed forward by mid-afternoon after it was reported that the 21st Battalion had been cut up badly and driven from their objective, an area marked as Chicory Trench on the maps. Private Deward Barnes recounted advancing through an enemy counter-barrage and losing men all around him. When his company reached the front line, they charged the German position, capturing it from the scared defenders who surrendered or retreated. Outposts were set up to slow a counterattack, although the men in the front lines knew that their role was really a sacrificial one: they were to punish the enemy with fire—and likely give their lives—so that their comrades could blunt the wave of weakened attackers when it crashed over the main line of defence. "Heavy casualties and the trenches were all torn to pieces by shells," wrote Private Barnes. "I picked out the best place I could see but a 21st fellow was right behind it with half his body shot away. It was the best spot, so I dug a hole in front of him and threw dirt over him. Maybe he was never found. War is hell. I did not get his disc, hadn't time."[23] Barnes and his companions spent the day and night desperately fortifying their weak and overextended positions. They did not sustain a counterattack against their trenches during August 15, but almost everyone else did along the new Canadian Corps front.

CHAPTER 18

BLEEDING THE GERMANS WHITE

August 15–18, 1917

The German regimental historian for the 2nd Reserve Guard Regiment, a formation moved from reserve "to hold Lens under all circumstances," noted:

> Our opponent was a Canadian division. An officer of the General Staff had specifically added that this Canadian division was composed of first-rate men, of our quality, and in the published description of [this division] it was noted with six exclamation marks: "They take no prisoners!" Accordingly, everyone knew that they could not be allowed to fall into captivity.[1]

Few Germans contemplated surrender as they were ordered to snatch back Hill 70 from the elite Canadian Corps.

The first of more than a dozen counterattacks against the Canadians began at around 8:15 A.M on August 15. The German doctrine called for lightning counterattacks to throw back the invaders before they had a chance to consolidate, but the Canadians had based their entire operation on anticipating and defeating these rapid attacks. Brave and disciplined, the Germans advanced in daylight and under full observation. Currie's plan to push his more than 250 machine-gun teams ahead—both the heavy Vickers and the lighter Lewis guns—was the death knell of these forces, as the Germans were cut down in droves. The infantrymen with their Lee-Enfields were also particularly deadly as they fired from the protection of slit

trenches and shell craters. Forward observers added to the efficiency of the holocaust, using telephones or wireless sets to direct gunners, who then saturated the
front with shrapnel.[2] Spotter aircraft from No. 16 Squadron, Royal Flying Corps
circled the battlefield looking for targets, and an incredible 240 calls for artillery fire
came from the aircraft alone, with more coming from the infantry in the trenches.[3]
Unlike at Vimy, where the artillery was forced to move forward during the battle in
the hope of breaking onto the Douai plain, here the shallow battlefield allowed the
artillery to remain back in their protective gun pits and rain down a deadly hail of
shrapnel. With the enemy infantry vulnerable in their shallow jumping-off trenches
or out in the open, the Canadian gunners could send shell after shell to explode
widely over the German forming-up points and lines of communication, saturating
the enemy front with shrapnel or explosives. The Canadian gunners also targeted the
shattered city of Lens. There would be no respite. "Your gas shells descended on us
by the ton," recounted one German prisoner, "and life in the underground defences
of Lens is simply Hell."[4]

If Lens was hell, the open battlefield across which the Germans attacked was
something almost indescribable. A carpet of bodies covered No Man's Land, with
blood, entrails, and body parts thrown into the air as shell after shell slammed into
the narrow killing ground. After the first counterattack was shattered, eight more
attacks fell on the Canadian lines during the day.[5] More bodies were added to the
charnel house that passed for a battlefield. A German in the 1st Battalion of
the 65th Infantry Regiment described one of the confused counterattacks against
the 2nd Canadian Brigade's front on August 15, during which their force had to
advance over open ground with little artillery support:

> After they crossed the [St. Auguste–Lens Road], the British [i.e., Canadians]
> called for barrage fire. The already substantial English artillery fire strength-
> ened in combination with the English machine-gun and infantry fire—which
> was now beginning to rage—into a veritable hurricane that welcomed the
> brave men who rushed forward. Our artillery preparation was imperceptible.
> It was only after the English barrage fell on our lone advancing battalion that
> our artillery responded. Although the enemy had not been weakened and we
> had suffered severe casualties, we still managed to take and hold the former

third battle line located 300–400 metres past the second railroad cut.... Everyone cursed [this] hastily ordered attack without sufficient artillery preparation."[6]

But still the Germans continued their attacks. Surrender was not an option, even in the face of such odds; but German determination was no match for Canadian steel.

Fighting was just as furious on August 16. The eight battalions opposite the two Canadian divisions were joined by seven more counterattacking battalions from the 4th Guard and 185th Division.[7] In places, the Germans advanced in columns, five abreast. Little mercy was wrung from the Canadians, who laid down withering fire. Black, smoke-wreathed bursts of shrapnel exploded over the surging Germans, while

This gruesome image depicts a Canadian standing over the buried body of a German soldier, who was likely killed by shellfire. The Germans launched at least twenty-one counterattacks against the Canadian positions from August 15 to 18, 1917, and suffered horrendous casualties in their failed attempt to recapture the heights of Hill 70.

high explosives sent up geysers of solid earth and bodies. Attacks wavered, then broke. New ones were launched over the still-warm bodies of men cut down in previous operations. Despite their disadvantage, determined German forces pushed through the firestorm and charged into the Canadian lines several times, where they encountered fierce hand-to-hand fighting. "The enemy has offered a most determined resistance throughout and the bayonet has been freely used," attested one captured German report.[8] The Germans were thrown back. The line held.

Fresh Canadian battalions had been cycled into the trenches to replace those shot up on August 15, but now the fighting had degenerated into an artillery duel, with the ground-pounders caught under the fall of shells. Kenneth Foster, a 2nd Battalion Lewis machine-gunner from Vernon, British Columbia, who enlisted at age eighteen, recounted the enemy bombardments on the night of August 16, after the Canadians had captured the last of their objectives in a series of limited, sharp engagements throughout the day:

> Fritz opened up with everything he had. Immediately the word was passed along to "stand to" and send up the S.O.S. which was a red light. Then our own artillery opened up with everything they had and between the two, there was hell let loose in several different languages. Never before or since had I been in a worse bombardment. Pretty soon the boys began to drop all round me, some killed, some wounded. My Lewis Gun was behaving splendidly. Any moment though, I expected to see it blown up and me with it, but fate said no.[9]

Foster survived the battle, although his platoon was reduced to seven men by dawn.

On August 17, the Canadians again met the Germans in a day of desultory battle that was often carried out within chemical clouds. Sweating profusely behind their bug-eyed respirators, men squinted through the fogged-up lenses looking for German targets in the swirling poison gas that blanketed the front. It was terrifying and exhausting work, and nerves were worn thin; many felt relief when the alert sentries sounded the alarm for an impending attack—by shouting or banging on old shell casings—as the cacophony broke the terrible stress of waiting for the inevitable. "Our gunners, machine-gunners and infantry never had such targets," wrote Currie in his private diary.[10] The 1st Motor Machine Gun Brigade, fighting in a dismounted role, and as only one of many Canadian units taking part in the battle using heavy Vickers machine guns, fired an average of 120,000 rounds per day.[11]

While the Canadians held their ground against artillery fire and probing enemy attacks, they also created an all-around defence to protect against rearward assaults. Isolated pockets of German troops had survived the Canadian storm crashing over them. Many surrendered, having been trapped behind Canadian lines. Others were ground away in vicious little battles involving mopping-up units that often chucked bombs first and asked questions later. But not all such survivors had been found, and in several instances German units raided behind Canadian lines at night, ambushing vulnerable men and then returning to their hideouts. The 15th Battalion's commanding officer, C.E. Bent, was almost killed when a party of Germans emerged from a hidden dugout. Bent held off the group of Germans with his revolver before his men rallied around him. The lurking presence of the enemy behind lines also caused dangerous—and potentially fatal—misunderstandings. Lieutenant Colonel G.E. McCuaig of the 13th Battalion was nearly shot by his own men when he was interrogating a group of German prisoners who passed by his location. A mopping-up patrol fired on them, presumably unsure if they were prisoners or combatants, and McCuaig was nearly hit, with his runner unfortunately killed by friendly fire.[12] Confusion reigned over the battlefield, and while the front line was held fairly solidly with outposts and newly dug trenches, there were porous gaps. Soldiers were continually getting lost at night—walking to the front, passing through their own lines, and finding themselves trying to relieve German sentries. Such was the chaos of battle and its aftermath.

On August 17, the Germans' suicidal mass-wave attacks were replaced by smaller groups of attackers worming their way forward, hoping to avoid being caught in the open. Many were shot down, but others made it into the Canadian trenches and had to be ejected in hand-to-hand combat. And always the shells fell with earth- and body-shattering explosions. Lieutenant J.C. Smythe wrote of how the men were hit all around him: "Our casualties were very heavy, and one could not help but wonder when his turn would come."[13] Smythe would be struck in the shoulder with shrapnel, and, while laying wounded, collect wounds to the chest, right thigh, knee, and right calf from the enemy's bombardment before he evacuated to the rear.

Miniature battles raged day and night along the Canadian front. A few failed attempts were made to push into the enemy lines, but mostly the Canadians dug in, defending against persistent German attacks. Often the isolated Canadian garrison outposts were outnumbered. On August 18, Sergeant Frederick Hobson and Private A.G. Fuller of the 20th Battalion were instrumental in holding the front against a German attack by elements of the 55th Reserve Infantry Regiment. Behind a concentrated barrage, the enemy moved forward, killing or stunning many Canadians and burying an essential Lewis-gun position. The forty-three-year-old Sergeant Hobson raced forward, dug the gun out of the debris, and put it into action, firing at the advancing enemy troops. He cut them down before the gun eventually jammed—likely clogged with dirt. Although bleeding profusely from a wound, Hobson handed the gun over to Fuller to clear it as he rushed a group of Germans. Firing, bayoneting, and even clubbing the enemy, Hobson—drenched now in his own blood and that of others—held off an entire section. He bought precious time for Fuller to get the Lewis gun into action, but his heroic efforts cost Hobson his life. When the enemy retreated, fifteen dead Germans were found around Hobson. He was awarded the Victoria Cross and Private Fuller received the Military Medal. Small, deadly engagements like these raged all along the front.

THE BODIES LAY THICK over the battlefield. The hot sun bloated the corpses, forcing out odoriferous gasses day and night that jerked soldiers to attention. Mounds of bodies were reduced to mounds of body parts as dead flesh was dismembered and churned up by the cascading shells. "The sights I observed beggar description," wrote Captain John Preston. "My goodness, if only some of those famous orators, who shout fight to the finish, could only see this sight, they would pause, and would wonder whether they were in hell, instead of living in this supposedly enlightened twentieth century."[14]

Among the dead, the wounded lay helpless and in shock. Those who could crawl moved to the rear; those too weak to go that far made for shell holes, often later falling victim to the poison gas that shrouded the battlefield. Private Fred Robichaud took a bullet through his leg and lay bleeding in a shell crater: "I undid my puttee and wrapped the leg to cut the flow. If I hadn't done so, I would not have lasted four hours. Furthermore, I had to keep my head above the rapidly raising water level. At the same time, I wanted to keep it down to save having it blown off."[15] Robichaud, like so many Canadians, waited in alternating numbness and agony for a shell or bullet to end his suffering or a stretcher-bearer to find him. But stretcher-bearers were in short supply since many were killed as they traversed the open ground: shells and bullets made no distinction between combatants and non-combatants. Nor did they differentiate between the able-bodied and the wounded, but Robichaud was one of the lucky ones, and was carried out of the line by a few men braving the fire.

Hundreds of other wounded men dragged themselves back to the forward trenches. In between counterattacks, the Canadians tended to their mates' suffering, trying to staunch their oozing wounds. The injured lay slumped where they would not be trampled, slowing turning from white to grey as blood pooled under them, slipping into unconsciousness and eventually death. Many died unnoticed by their companions, who were fighting for their lives.

Some battalions had medical officers in the front lines, but more often they were positioned to the rear since this was a more suitable collection point. Hundreds, then thousands, of Canadians and Germans passed through the medical system. Understaffed medical officers and stretcher-bearers performed emergency surgery or the more difficult role of triage: deciding who, in the crush of casualties, could be saved, and who would be left to die. The massive suffering and gore was a horrible sight, wrote Signaller Sandy Bain, who had carried wounded from the front to the rear: "Men, who a few minutes before were brave, cheery and full of life, [were] now being carried in shattered and broken, groaning or making horrid gurgling noises if wounded in the lungs or throat."[16]

THE GERMAN ARTILLERY had recovered from the Canadians' initial counter-battery blasts and began to sweep their own former lines, which they had wisely plotted on their artillery boards. As well, the rear areas of the new Canadian trenches were targeted to slow the forward movement of essential war supplies: ammunition and Mills bombs were running low all along the Canadian front, and they formed the difference between life and death in the trenches. Reinforcements were being brought up from the rear, too, and it was easier and safer for the Germans to kill them coming overland than to send their own infantry to perform the task in the trenches. Victor Wheeler, a signaller with the 50th Battalion, wrote of the grim tension:

> There was no let up in shelling by either side, and our casualties continued to mount as we crouched in our trenches.... The strain on everyone's nerves in this scorching furnace of Lens became more apparent each day, and a few chaps sought escape through the S.I.W. route. I, who had also known such temptation, could not condemn them.[17]

The soldiers of the corps displayed iron courage on the battlefield, steeling them for the inevitable. But there was too much whirling metal and fire for some. "I haven't slept for three days and jump at every noise," recounted a brutalized Arthur Lapointe.[18] More than half of his company was knocked out in the fierce fighting before they were relieved on August 17.

It was as bad on the German side of No Man's Land. The Canadian artillery kept up their fire, which was essential in breaking the German will. During a twenty-four-hour period from August 17 to 18, for instance, the 1st Brigade, Canadian Field Artillery, which wielded 24 guns, fired 11,366 shells.[19] One German recorded in his diary, "At times we suffer heavily from the numerous burst of fire and methodical drumfire of the Canadians.... The amount of ammunition they fire away is indescribable."[20] So many shells were being used by Canadian gunners that a First Army staff officer came to corps headquarters to complain: "General Morrison, do you know the Army Commander is appalled at the amount of ammunition you have used today?" An exhausted Morrison replied dismissively, "So are the Germans."[21]

Assisted by observation aircraft, which provided aerial photographs, the gunners had the essential role of engaging targets of opportunity and responding to the infantry's SOS rockets that fired up from the Canadian trenches. Intelligence reports noted that the use of gas, shrapnel, and high explosives had neutralized thirty enemy batteries on August 17 and 18.[22] But the Germans responded in kind. With the artillery shattering their infantry attacks, the enemy knew it had to either stop or smother the Canadian guns. And so on the night of August 17, the Germans turned to mustard gas. Unlike phosgene or tear gases, the effects of which could be fended off by wearing a respirator (even if the cumbersome contraption reduced combat efficiency), mustard gas was a persistent agent. It did not disappear as quickly as gas that attacked the lungs, such as chlorine and phosgene, but instead polluted the battlefield for days or even weeks as it lay dormant and deadly. One contemporary soldier labelled it the "King of the War Gases."[23]

Gas shells spewed the mustard gas over the Canadian front. Unlike chlorine, which had an almost immediate effect on terrified soldiers, this new gas was difficult to detect right away. Soldiers initially noted a light smell of mustard, followed by the first symptom—a tendency to sneeze. Thousands fell victim because, from experience, they associated gas attacks with violent choking, raw throats, and suffocation; the slight tickling of the nose and throat caused by this new agent was seemingly among the least of a soldier's worries at the front. In addition, mustard gas was a slow-acting agent that killed the nerve cells so that the victim would only start to feel the effects hours after being poisoned. Eyes were inflamed and swollen, skin blistered, and men vomited uncontrollably. Upon being taken to the clearing stations, the gas cases became hoarse, coughed harshly, and went blind.[24] The victims began to die on the second and third days after the attack. "There was nothing more horrible than to see men dying from gas. Nothing could be done to relieve their suffering. The body, as well as the throat and lungs, were burned and blistered by the poison," wrote Canon Frederick Scott, who saw men die in almost every conceivable way during the war.[25]

Between 15,000 and 20,000 mustard gas shells were fired on the Canadian artillery positions during the early hours of August 18.[26] The 1st and 2nd Artillery Brigades were the hardest hit, but the sweating and straining Canadian gunners—aware of the need to keep firing so as to protect the vulnerable infantry—removed their fogged-up respirators, refusing to be slowed or hampered in laying their sights and setting their fuses. Working beyond the limits of endurance, and aware that gas shell fumes swirled around them, the Canadian gunners did not let up, and further German counterattacks were beaten back. But by morning, the 183 heroic gunners lay in agony, suffering from blindness and burns to their bodies.[27] Almost nothing

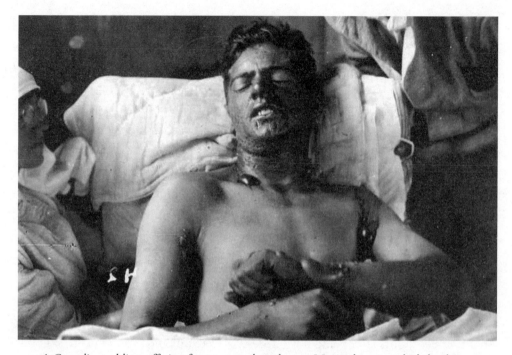

A Canadian soldier suffering from mustard gas burns. Mustard gas attacked the skin, leaving blisters and boils as well as blinding the victim. At Hill 70, the Germans unleashed this gas against the Canadian lines in the hope of preventing the gunners from laying down their devastating bombardments against the counterattacking German troops. It failed to stop the hurricane of fire, but the Canadians paid a heavy price for operating in the corrupted, chemically saturated environment.

was left of the two brigades, and Gunner K.B. Jackson of the 1st Divisional Artillery noted, two days later, "We had only five sergeants and cooks, and lord knows what, manning the guns."[28] This sacrifice was recognized by the infanteers, who viewed the gunners as heroes: "The assaulting infantry maintain that the artillery preparation has never been more complete, that the support has never been better, and that the liaison has never been so nearly perfect," wrote Sir Arthur Currie on behalf of his ground-pounders.[29]

The Germans attacked for the fourth day in a row on August 18, and made some headway against two forward companies of the 2nd Battalion—who had come into the line as reinforcements in the northern part of the line during the previous night. Despite their protection behind killing arcs of artillery and machine gun fire, the

Canadian attackers-turned-defenders were exhausted, thirsty, and hungry. Food supply had broken down, and most men were subsisting on their iron rations and whatever water could be scooped from muddy puddles or from the water bottles of the dead. Flamethrowers led the enemy troops into the Canadian trenches, but fierce hand-to-hand fighting drove them out again.[30] Major Okill Learmonth, a handsome twenty-three-year-old from Quebec City who was already a veteran company commander and wearer of the Military Cross, directed the resolute defence, encouraging the men during the barrage, directing the defence, and fighting in the front lines. During the battle, he caught enemy grenades in mid-flight and threw them back before they exploded. He could not get them all, and soon his body was torn through with metal. But Learmonth continued to battle the enemy even though he was bleeding to death from the wounds; and when he could no longer stand, he directed the defence of the area from the bottom of the trench. His men finally carried their hero to the rear, but he refused to go to the dressing station before he made a full report at headquarters. He did, but later died from blood loss, never knowing that he had been awarded the Victoria Cross.

THE GERMAN FORCES had been crushed by the end of August 18, their troops shredded by artillery, machine-gun, mortar, and rifle fire.[31] No fewer than twenty-one counterattacks had been fought off, and one Canadian intelligence report observed that a captured German battalion commander made the "unusual admission that he considered our troops superior to his own."[32] Whether this was true or not, certainly the German soldiers responded to the lopsided nature of the battle with a stubbornness that impressed even the phlegmatic Canadians, who had battled many of the enemy troops in hand-to-hand combat during the desperate engagements in the shattered trenches. While Currie's plan had undoubtedly been responsible for the mass killing of German troops, it would not have succeeded without the tenacity of his troops, who fought tooth and nail, with bombs and bullets, to hold the position against an equally tenacious enemy. There were no easy victories on the Western Front, but at Hill 70 and Lens, the Canadians had forced the enemy to pay a steep price: an estimated 20,000 casualties in comparison to the 5,600 suffered by Currie's corps.[33]

CHAPTER 19

"SWALLOWED UP IN THE SWIRLING MURK OF THE BATTLE"

Hill 70 and Lens, August 18–25, 1917

"The entire area was strewn with the dead of friend and foe alike so that the smell of the corpses, made worse by the increased heat, was almost unbearable," wrote a German soldier in the 2nd Guard Reserve Regiment, after surveying the carnage of No Man's Land.[1] Sergeant John Davis, serving with the Canadian Machine Gun Corps, also remarked on the gag-inducing stench of the rotting dead, but he was more worried about his hacking cough and wheezing lungs, as the pulverized battlefield on and around Hill 70 was polluted with the "distinct smell of gas."[2] With the infantry consolidating their positions, both the German and Canadian forces were deluged in chemicals and high explosives, but Currie's corps now held the hill firmly. Yet even as howitzers pounded the shattered enemy trenches and dugouts in Lens, the Germans refused to pull back from the city. Currie was frustrated. His corps had bled the enemy white over the last four days, but he had little to show his superiors, as the ultimate prize still remained out of his reach. With pressure from his senior commanders to finish the job, the corps commander ordered a push into Lens to see if the city would be relinquished.

Currie consulted Harry Burstall and David Watson, of the 2nd and 4th Divisions, about the feasibility of the operation. His divisional commanders felt that the objective could be achieved, but they committed a reduced force to the attack, planning for a probing assault with a much smaller scope than the enormous battle that raged on Hill 70 from August 15 to 18. The multiple objectives would fall across a wide front of 2,700 metres, and taking them fell to the 6th and 10th Brigades of the 2nd and 4th Divisions. A two-brigade attack could muster significant striking power, but they would be engaged in difficult urban combat in which the Germans had all the advantages, lying dug-in to their rubble fortress with full observation over their prepared kill grounds. Canadian intelligence had tracked at least six enemy battalions in the ruins, and another six were in close support. Despite the Germans' near parity in numbers and the advantage they enjoyed by holding the key terrain, a Canadian heavy bombardment of artillery fire might even the odds, and would certainly make the enemy infantry pay for their obstinate defence.

The assault would go in at 4:35 A.M. on August 21, but few of the front-line soldiers were sure about what they would encounter in the rubble, as intelligence was weak on enemy strength—and especially their location. Unlike in previous set-piece battles, the assaulting infantry had almost no time to reconnoitre the front and next to no time to train. German positions were likely strong, but it was felt that perhaps the morale of the enemy had been shattered after the four days of battle from August 15 to 18. This was an optimistic guess at best, however, as the obscuring ruins of the city rendered aerial photography and other traditional intelligence-gathering methods such as raiding and patrolling next to useless.

In fact, an elite German formation, the 1st Guards Reserve Division, had been moved into the line to blunt the expected Canadian assault. Basing their strong defence on an active offensive, one of the Guards' battalions launched a pre-emptive strike against the Canadian lines just as the 6th Brigade's 27th and 29th Battalions were preparing to attack. Ten minutes before the Canadian assault was to kick off at 4:35 A.M., the Germans came overland in a bayonet charge behind a heavy artillery and mortar barrage. Within this maelstrom, the German *frontsoldaten* thrust into the Canadian lines, engaging the 29th Battalion in desperate close-quarter fighting, and driving them from their trenches for a few hours.

Whole sections of Canadians were wiped out, while others, surrounded, held their ground until reinforcements relieved them. With most of the officers at the front soon killed or wounded, NCOs stepped up to fill the gaping holes in command. Company Sergeant Major Robert Hanna led the survivors of one assault party into a German strongpoint that was set up in the Canadian trenches. Three previous attacks on this position had failed, but Hanna and his men cleared it, destroyed the machine gun, and repelled repeated counterattacks. For his thrusting leadership, not to mention his act of knocking out the machine gun and several of its defenders, Hanna received the Victoria Cross. But despite such localized victories, this was a chaotic engagement. Dense fog and smoke smothered the battlefield, as "figures were swallowed up in the swirling murk of the battle."[3] Then, at 4:35 A.M., the Canadian gunners opened fire with their creeping barrage, sending shrapnel shells screaming into the enemy's ranks, many of whom were still in No Man's Land. The hammer of the artillery combined with the fierce Canadian defence held off enemy attacks.

The 27th and 31st Battalions were able to move off behind their barrage, with the 29th, supported by the 25th and 28th Battalions, regaining their lost trenches later in the day, followed by parts of the enemy lines. The 25th Battalion's war diary observed that the German defenders were "probably the best which [the battalion] ever encountered."[4] While the 29th was fighting for its life, the 27th and 31st continued to advance across the 500 metres of open ground that lay before them. Out in No Man's Land, they ran bayonet-first into hundreds of Germans coming over the top from their own trenches—advancing to support their success on the 29th Battalion's front and to punch through the rest of the Canadian line. What ensued was brutal hand-to-hand combat. Private Donald Fraser of the 31st Battalion described the chaos: "Both sides met one another in No Man's Land and a battle royal took place. After bombing and bayonet work, we slowly forced the enemy back, meeting another line later on."[5]

Having overcome this obstacle, the Canadians moved on to crash into the outskirts of the city, where German defenders counterattacked, rising up from cellars, shooting from second-floor windows, and racing forward from blind alleys. Men found cover where they could, but it was hard to coordinate a coherent defence in the rubble, which was dominated by houses and buildings. Sections, even platoons, were cut off from each other, as they had to go around and through the devastated city. Many Canadian combat units were destroyed, as they were overwhelmed piece-meal by superior German forces. The officers on site realized they could not defend what they had bitten off, and by the end of the day most of the Canadians had retreated to their start line. An official report noted, "The day's fighting had been of a more severe nature than any previously taken part in by [the 2nd] Division, and although the objectives were not gained and held, this was compensated for by the very high number of casualties inflicted on the enemy."[6] It was hard to tell which side had won the engagement, so thick were the bodies lying in the trenches, No Man's Land, and the outskirts of Lens.

TO THE RIGHT of the 6th Brigade, the 46th, 47th, and 50th Battalions of the 4th Division's 10th Brigade reached enemy lines without running into any German forces in No Man's Land, but they also suffered heavily under artillery fire while forming up and while crossing the killing zone in front of Lens. Advancing through the city in the dark left soldiers confused, a condition made all the worse as officers were increasingly knocked out by enemy fire. The 46th Battalion suffered a cruel fate when one of their two lead companies, B, lost every single officer when a stray shell landed in a shell hole where the officers were holding an emergency conference. Yet new leaders took their place. "We were engaged in nothing less than a battle-to-the-death with an enemy who was equally determined that we should not pass," recounted Victor Wheeler of the 50th Battalion. "Many individual acts of bravery among our heroic men were exploits of self-sacrifice—sacrifice that might, some-how, enable their buddies to go forward and gain the Battalion's objectives."[7]

Flares were fired by both sides, bathing the ruined city in an eerie glow. Coloured flares were used by the Canadians to signal to rear gunners and headquarters where to rain down fire, but the Germans had learned from previous battles that this was a key means of communicating from front to rear. They deliberately fired flares of similar colours to the Canadians', which resulted in some Allied guns dropping shells into the Canadian lines.[8] In fact, during the confused fighting, the artillery on both sides seemed to pound the city indiscriminately. The infantry could only dig in further to the rubble. Cellars became dugouts; a house was a strongpoint that cen-tred a ragged defensive line. The fighting was nerve-shattering as Canadian battle patrols went out in search of enemy outposts. Short, chaotic engagements erupted alongside frustrating actions in which snipers fired and retreated, and all the while the Canadians lost men to booby traps—usually grenades attached to doors that would detonate when opened. Corporal Filip Konowal of the 47th Battalion, a Ukrainian and former bayonet-fighting instructor in the Russian army, rose to the occasion. During one fierce engagement, he single-handedly cleared a number of German machine-gun positions and personally dispatched at least thirteen Germans. His inspired leadership and ferocity on the battlefield brought him a Victoria Cross from the high command. Despite such valiant efforts on the part of Canadian infantrymen, the Germans were not willing to give up the city, and they rained down shell and mortar fire on the Canadian front. The slain lay where they fell, slowly covered in dust and plaster, their blood soaking into the rubble. Victor Wheeler recounted how he "saw his chances of getting out alive disappear by the hour. We no longer wondered whose Number would be called; we speculated whose would not."[9]

August 21 had been a bad day for the Canadians, as the Germans had thrown the full weight of counterattacking forces against them. British war correspondent Philip Gibbs remarked, "This siege of Lens is the most frightful episode of the warfare on the Western Front.... It was all close, hard, grim, bloody fighting." The Canadians battled "from house to house, and in the cellars and tunnels and over trenches dug across the streets."[10] Currie's corps had chewed up the Germans from August 15 to 18, but their attack on August 21 had left them, in the words of an officer in the 165th German Reserve Infantry Regiment, "biting into granite."[11] The Canadians retreated with broken teeth, having lost 1,154 men on that single day.[12]

THE GERMANS were clearly holding onto Lens, and at this point Currie should have called off the battle. The Canadians had won the high ground and could bombard Lens at their leisure rather than engaging in costly urban warfare for which they had no training, and for which they had no time to prepare and plan in their usually thorough way. Currie had been right to test the strength of the enemy's defences on August 21, but now he had hard evidence that the Germans were not going to fold.

Unfortunately, however, the corps commander allowed Major General Watson to launch one more attack with his 4th Division. Watson reported to Currie that Brigadier Edward Hilliam's 10th Brigade could drive the enemy back in another assault. To the south of Lens was an imposing slag heap (or *crassier*, to the French) known as Green Crassier—a reference to the grass that was poking through the rock and rubble. The capture of this manmade mountain that towered over the city would allow the Canadians to encircle Lens from three sides, virtually guaranteeing that the Germans would have to pull out. The Germans were aware of this danger, and had not lost any opportunity to fortify the massive mound of mine refuse. Forward reconnaissance units noted that the Germans had turned the slag heap into a fortress, which was separated from the Canadian start lines by a narrow valley and protected by a canal behind it in the southern sector of Lens. The Canadians would have to assault it frontally.

After nearly a week of battle, the Canadian Corps was tired, and although wasted units had been rotated out of the line, the commanders and staff officers in the rear had received almost no time to rest. The attack on Green Crassier can only have been the product of tired minds, for wishful thinking does not win battles. No serious feint was made up the line to draw off the enemy's attention, and only a single battalion, the under-strength 44th, was ordered forward. While it is surprising that Currie did not wait a few more days to see if his battering artillery bombardment could convince the Germans to retreat, it is almost unbelievable that, if he and his subordinates were serious about taking the Crassier, such a half-hearted effort was made. Ordering forward four weakened companies for what was at least a brigade-level objective betrays not only the inexperience of Currie, who might have overruled the operation, but also the poor performance of Watson, who should have forced his brigadier to modify the operation. Far more damning is that the commanding officer of the 44th Battalion, the experienced Lieutenant Colonel R.D. Davies, objected to the attack, and presented his argument to Brigadier Hilliam. Having reconnoitred the ground, Davies had observed that the thrust into enemy lines would send the 44th Battalion forward to capture the Crassier on a cramped front only 200 metres wide, but that the axis of the advance was overlooked by other high German strongpoints, including the Fosse St. Louis, another slag heap closer to the

Canadian front. This would make a successful capture of the Crassier impossible to sustain unless St. Louis fell, and any loss of St. Louis during the battle would result in the forces on the Green Crassier being cut off from the resupply of reinforcements, ammunition, and water.[13] Despite a severe protest, Davies was overruled by Hilliam, who promised airily that St. Louis would be secured. By whom and how was not explained; even when Hilliam realized at the last moment that the 44th needed more support and ordered the 50th Battalion forward, the battalion could not get organized in time for the assault. Hilliam seemed nonplussed by the failure of the 50th to reach the front, however, and did nothing to try to call off the operation.[14] Such inattention to the details of reality was the stuff of the Somme, and could only end in disaster.

The attack went in at 3 A.M. on August 23, behind a creeping barrage that tore up the German defences, shaking the ground so intensely that it felt like an earthquake, remembered Allen Hart.[15] The men of the 44th—mostly drawn from southwestern Manitoba—followed the curtain of steel across the fire zone. They faced elements from two German battalions on both the Fosse and the Crassier, meaning that the small attacking Canadian force was vastly outnumbered. Through fierce fighting, two platoons cleared out at least a company of Germans on the Fosse St. Louis, while the main Canadian force, composed of a company and a half of infantry, converged on the Crassier. The remaining company and a half was split up so that its six platoons could ferret out the enemy that swarmed from the rubble of the shattered buildings and houses that ringed this sector of the front. Many Germans had gone to ground when the first waves of Canadians overran their positions, but now they kept emerging behind the Canadian advance, requiring a continual doubling back to clear trenches and positions that had already been won.

The six platoons captured the Crassier in hard fighting, but then found themselves atop the slag heap with the sun rising. They had battled fiercely to stick their neck on the chopping block. Low on ammunition and cut off from reinforcements, who could not push beyond the Fosse because of enfilade and crossfire, they were the object of savage enemy attacks all day long. Forward units swept the German attackers with Lewis-gun fire, but the ammunition was used up quickly, leaving the gunners to conserve their ammunition by firing off shorter and shorter bursts that betrayed their increasingly desperate situation. Canadian artillery gunners, severed from their forward observers, fired blindly for much of the battle. When the bombardment landed accurately on the enemy lines, the Germans would take shelter in their deep dugouts and call their own artillery down on the front. The Canadian artillery and machine-gunners had no means to set up any sort of a kill ground as they had in the Hill 70 battle a week earlier.

The situation was desperate. The 44th had only shallow trenches and lacked the deep dugouts and tunnels that protected the enemy troops forming up for their assaults. Canadian runners were sent to the rear followed by sombre gazes from those left behind, but whether staying or leaving, the men realized that their fates would likely be the same. None of the runners made it through the enemy barrage or sniper fire. By late afternoon, with water gone, bombs spent, ammunition low, the wounded in agony, the final Canadian defenders, skin black from dust and coal except for where sweat had pushed rivulets down their faces, were being pressed in from all sides. Resistance was systematically crushed as outpost after outpost was obliterated in a hail of grenades and mortar fire. The Germans were in no mood for mercy. Wounded soldiers were fired on as they tried to crawl for cover. By the end of August 24, the Crassier had been lost to German counterattacks, and even the dwindling Canadian garrison on the Fosse St. Louis had been driven back to their lines. The 44th Battalion took 258 casualties during the operation, with entire platoons annihilated to a man.[16] It was a harsh end to what had been one of the most successful operations of the war, proving that even elite formations like the Canadian Corps could stumble badly at times. Doing battles by half measures resulted in full defeats.

CURRIE ENDED the operation on August 25, following the 50th Battalion's capture of a number of enemy trenches. Hill 70 had been a significant Canadian victory even though the Germans had refused to retreat from Lens. If the operation had failed to achieve the tactical success of taking Lens, it had resulted in a rare strategic victory of attrition. The Germans had been forced to redirect two reserve divisions that were headed to support forces at Passchendaele, in order to use them at Hill 70. "The fighting at Lens cost us, once again, the expenditure of considerable numbers of troops who had to be replaced," wrote German General Hermann von Kuhl. "The whole previously worked out plan for relieving the fought-out troops in Flanders had been wrecked."[17] This was exactly the support that Haig's beleaguered Flanders forces needed.

By the end of the Lens offensive, Currie estimated that some 25,000 Germans had been killed or wounded in the storm of shell and bullets. That figure was probably too high, although it was hard to judge with the battlefield strewn with field-grey corpses. Intelligence officers identified seven German divisions that had been mauled and sixty-nine German battalions met in battle.[18] Except for the blowing of almost two dozen mines beneath the German lines on June 7, 1917, to kick off the Battle of Messines—which was really a one-off for the entire war as it had taken the British over a year to lay the explosives—the Germans had not previously suffered such a lopsided defeat as at Hill 70. General E.W.B. Morrison—whose artillery had performed brilliantly during the Battle of Hill 70 despite their inability to support the overextended Canadians who had put their head onto the Lens chopping block in attempting to capture the Green Crassier—wrote to his friend Garnet Hughes in England: "It is the greatest Boche-killing week that anyone on the Canadian Corps has ever taken part in."[19] Such chest-thumping was not out of place in a battle that Sir Douglas Haig described as "one of the finest minor operations of the war."[20] Haig also mentioned breezily:

> The experience and training of the past year had done wonders for the Canadians. Their morale is now very high, and though they have been opposed by the flower of the German Army (Guards etc.) they feel that they can beat the Germans every time! They have now made up their minds to take more prisoners in future. It will be less trouble, because now they have to dig so many graves for the slain Germans! This is hard work!![21]

The commander-in-chief's faith in the Canadians was well placed, and he would increasingly call upon them to deliver victory. But as Currie also noted in his diary, the Battle of Hill 70 "was altogether the hardest battle in which the Corps has participated," and most of his men would have agreed.[22]

Attrition is usually viewed as a bankrupt strategy employed by generals who have failed at manoeuvre warfare. But the Allies had nowhere to manoeuvre on the Western Front, as there were no flanks. And sideshow operations such as those at the Gallipoli and Salonika fronts wasted men and materiel equally. Nor did the Allies have the option of sitting back and waiting for Germany to strangle as a result of their naval blockade. They had to attack on land and force the enemy out of occupied Belgium and France. And so attrition was the only strategy the multi-million-man armies could pursue, as unpalatable as it was. Yet the quality of attrition could be both physical (in the sense of killing or maiming the enemy) and psychological (in the sense of breaking his morale). Up to mid-1917, most of the Allied attempts at attrition had been failures that had resulted in their own forces taking higher casualties. At Hill 70, however, the Canadian Corps had revealed how to carry out a minor operation that successfully ground away the enemy's morale, killed his troops in greater numbers, and assisted with the overall British strategy of attacking along multiple fronts.

Despite their overwhelming victory at Hill 70, 9,198 Canadians would be listed as killed, wounded, and missing from August 15 to 25 (8,677 at Hill 70 and another 521 at other locations along the Western Front) with another 2,000 Canadians added to the casualty lists in the first two weeks of the month of preparation for the battle.[23] "I shall soon have few of my Canadian friends left," wrote Herbert Burrell. "It's dreadful to think of the valuable lives lost in this insane combat."[24]

The campaign for Hill 70 was the second-largest Canadian military undertaking up to that point in the war—taking a back seat only to Vimy. The first phase of the battle had been almost as perfect an operation as had ever been carried out on the Western Front, but the second phase's two probing attacks on Lens were clumsy, hurried affairs that betrayed Currie's inexperience. From August 21 to 25, the Canadians suffered close to 4,000 casualties—almost half the total for the battle. If the successful strategy and tactics used at Hill 70 had their intellectual origins in the careful planning of Vimy Ridge, the disastrous approach of the Lens engagement seemed closer to the unimaginative attacks of the Somme. While Currie had likely saved his corps from a defeat by modifying the initial operation, he was guilty of rashly allowing the same frontal attack against Lens on August 21 and 23—although much more of the blame must fall to division and brigade commanders Watson and

Hilliam, the latter of whom should have been fired. Army commander Henry Horne, when meeting with the battered survivors of the 10th Brigade a few weeks after the battle, stated firmly and without hesitation—no doubt to Hilliam's great embarrassment—that the attack on Green Crassier was an "ill-advised plan which should never have been undertaken."[25] Most of the survivors were probably surprised at hearing such candour spoken by an army commander, but they likely remained unmollified, especially since Hilliam remained in command. That Currie refused to remove Hilliam can only mean that he kept faith in his brigadier, something that did not reflect well on the Canadian Corps commander, although Hilliam lost his command a few months later, after the Passchendaele campaign.

On the Lens battlefield, Canadians had once more shown themselves to be the storm troopers who could best the Germans, even if the ruins of Lens remained in enemy hands until the last months of the war. "Canadians, whom the British Higher Command always employs for the most difficult and costly fighting, advanced with obstinate bravery," observed one captured German report.[26] The corps had proven its mettle again, and Currie had distinguished himself as its commander in his first major engagement, even if he had diluted his gains by allowing the ill-advised assaults against Lens. With Haig's armies mired in the mud in Flanders, he would soon call upon Currie and his Canadian Corps to deliver victory once again.

CHAPTER 20

CALLED TO BATTLE

Passchendaele, October 1917

The word "Passchendaele" conjures vivid images of the Great War's fruitless slaughter and epitomizes the nadir of warfighting. This was the place where seemingly homicidal, chateau-dwelling generals sitting kilometres behind the lines clucked their thin gums in delight as they planned to murder off their troops in one hopeless assault after another. The horrific pervasiveness of quicksand-like mud and unburied corpses brought to mind Dante's images of hell. This blighted battlefield has maintained a firm grip on the popular memory of the war. For most of the British troops it was an unwavering horror show of defeat and destruction, but for the Canadians it provided another victory—which seemed pyrrhic at first, but played a key role in restoring the British army's morale, and probably saved the Sir Douglas Haig's job as commander-in-chief.

THE CANADIANS deserved a rest after their victory at Hill 70. During the harsh fighting for the barren wasteland of slag heaps and the surrounding ruins of Lens, the Canadians had chewed up the German defenders and inflicted a significant defeat on the enemy. Yet it had also cost almost 10,000 of the corps' 100,000 men, and most of those casualties fell again to the infantry. The Canadians were exhausted, but First Army commander Sir Henry Horne was planning to keep the pressure on the Germans, and was soon to order Currie to launch a new attack against Lens from the Canadians' anchor on Hill 70.

But Haig's offensive to the north was not going well. He had wanted to attack in the Flanders region of Belgium since 1915 for several reasons. Behind the German lines in this region ran railways that were essential for moving men and supplies. As well, the German U-boat pens were located on the coast, and the submarines were raiding Allied shipping—the essential lifeline from North America—with devastating effectiveness. The Royal Navy supported Haig's Flanders plan in the hope that his land armies would drive the German U-boats from their raiding pens.[1] Further, on the Allied side of No Man's Land, the British relied heavily on the nearby Channel ports that were guarded by the Belgian and British armies. The area around Ypres was a key logistical one that had been a central cockpit of the war—fought over continuously since the first days in August 1914—and in fact had been a battleground for centuries.

In 1917, neither side could afford to give up much ground. This was important to Haig, who also believed that he could continue to wear down the German forces through a campaign of attrition. By attacking where the enemy had to defend and could not retreat without giving up the U-boat pens, he aimed to grind them out of existence, at least enough to weaken them to allow his troops to break through to the green fields far in the rear. As well, with Russia and Italy in desperate straits as their armies crumbled, with their societies close behind, a British offensive might draw off some pressure from those fronts. Haig refused to entertain the French idea of waiting for the Americans, as he had little faith in the American "doughboy" as a saviour and, no doubt, did not want to go down in history as having been rescued by the Yanks. With the navy supporting Haig's offensive, British prime minister Lloyd George could do little but fume, as he feared his detested general would again throw away tens of thousands of lives in a Somme-like futile stagger to defeat, or at best a draw.

The deteriorating relationship between Haig and Lloyd George had reached its lowest point earlier that same year. The British prime minister, who was always at his best when he was battling someone—first the upper classes when he was a supporter of labour, and later the inertia of the British war effort—felt that his field marshal was an incompetent, monosyllabic martinet who could offer no solution to the stalemate except to plunge ahead and commit more men to the slaughter.

FLANDERS: 1917

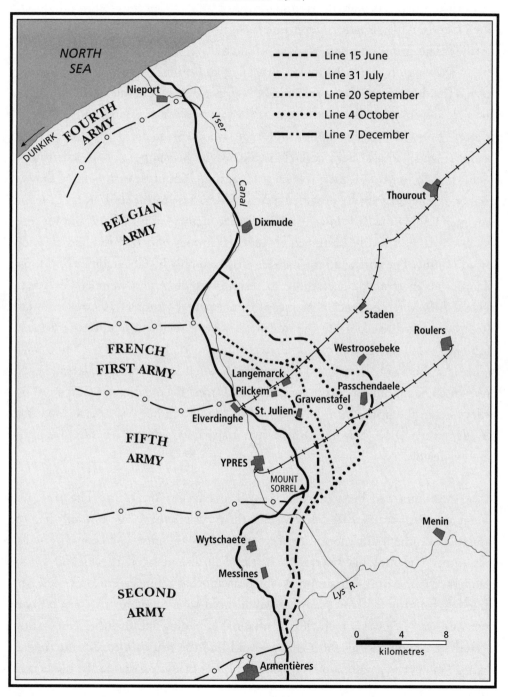

NORTH SEA

Nieport

DUNKIRK

FOURTH ARMY

----- Line 15 June
—·—·— Line 31 July
········· Line 20 September
•••••• Line 4 October
—··—··— Line 7 December

Yser

Canal

BELGIAN ARMY

Dixmude

Thourout

Staden

Roulers

FRENCH FIRST ARMY

Westroosebeke

Langemarck

Pilckem

Passchendaele

St. Julien

Gravenstafel

Elverdinghe

FIFTH ARMY

YPRES

MOUNT SORREL ▲

Menin

Wytschaete

Messines

SECOND ARMY

Lys R.

0   4   8
kilometres

Armentières

"Seniority and Society were the dominant factors in Army promotion," commented Lloyd George with disdain. "Deportment counted a good deal. Brains came a bad fourth."[2] The prime minister wanted an alternative—anything, he despaired—to simply chewing on the barbed wire. But Haig and other Western Front adherents sneered that his support for other "sideshow" campaigns, including the Dardenelles, Salonica, and Italy, had done little to hurt the German war machine, and in fact had diverted essential Allied supplies and men from the main battle front. Lloyd George's hand had also been severely weakened by his support of the charismatic fraud, French general Robert Nivelle. Charming, sophisticated, and a flawless speaker of English, Nivelle provided a marked contrast to the dull, dour, grunting Scotsman leading the BEF. Nivelle had promised victory in April 1917, but his reckless offensive had nearly destroyed the French armies and had resulted in widespread mutiny. The army, and the nation, was saved only by General Henri-Philippe Pétain, who intervened successfully to restore discipline and morale. For several months, however, the French were incapable of battle. Fortunately, German military intelligence failed to report on the mutinies—one of the great intelligence debacles of the war—and the Allies escaped relatively unscathed. Against this backdrop, Haig argued that he had to attack and draw German attention to the Flanders region in order to allow his ally to regain control of its forces. Even if Lloyd George did not believe Haig, the prime minister had backed the wrong horse when he supported Nivelle in early 1917. Now the British field marshal would have his offensive in the Flanders region.

BUT HAIG, too, had been dragged deep into Nivelle's quagmire. The BEF had fought a series of costly battles that formed the Arras offensive, and not only had the casualties been high but enormous stores of materiel and guns had been diverted to that front. The prolonged series of battles had also delayed the kickoff to the Flanders offensive until late summer, which meant that a long campaign would continue late into the fall, and planning would need to account for the possibility of poor weather. Haig was nonetheless adamant about going ahead with the operation.

Herbert Gough and his Fifth Army would lead the British forces in the drive to victory. Gough had a reputation for being a thruster in comparison to the methodical

Sir Henry Rawlinson of the Fourth Army and Sir Herbert "Daddy" Plumer of the Second Army. Sadly, both of these latter generals would have been far superior choices. Plumer's forces had held the ground in Flanders for months, his fighting troops and staff officers having walked almost every inch of it. On a battlefield where the Germans enjoyed the advantage of terrain—from their position on the high ground, with trenches situated along ridges to offer protection to reserve troops in "dead ground" and hollows that were hard to strike with artillery fire—Plumer's forces knew what would work and what wouldn't. Gough's men did not, and his staff were known for being especially careless—some said reckless—in their planning of operations. Gough and his senior staff officers looked too far ahead to the great breakout battle, without paying enough attention to the break-in that would take the infantry across the killing ground of No Man's Land and through the first series of trenches. Haig wanted a breakthrough, so he ambitiously called for large-scale attacks that would crash into the enemy lines and punch through the other side. Plumer and Rawlinson had argued that victory would be achieved only through a slow, methodical series of set-piece battles, while Gough "outbid" the other two generals, promising Haig that he could deliver the goods.

Haig, not surprisingly, had been drawn to Gough's assurances, even though the breakthough plan was, according to his most sympathetic biographer, "probably the most wildly optimistic to which he ever put his signature."[3] But Haig was no idiot, and he too realized the importance of the slow, methodical break-in, even as he was looking beyond it to the breakthrough. The plan therefore remained a strange hybrid: a slow, set-piece battle followed by a gallop to glory. Haig's tepid guidance to Gough to proceed carefully in a methodical manner seemed at variance with where his heart was directing his subordinate general.[4] The balding if boyish-looking Gough, who exuded cheerful confidence, failed to recognize this contradiction and looked to please his commander with a dashing operation. Gough sought the breakthrough, which resulted in a series of plans—including a thinning out of artillery fire and a holding back of critical assets to prepare for mobility—that contrasted markedly with the bite and hold operations which were the only type of limited attack that had resulted in any kind of success on the Western Front to date.

After a fifteen-day pre-battle bombardment in which the British fired an astonishing 4.3 million shells against the German positions, Gough's forces surged forward on July 31, 1917, in the Third Battle of Ypres—or Passchendaele, as it would be forever known.[5] After some initial success, the driving infantry formations soon ran up against a formidable enemy. Heavy rain fell during the first evening of the assault, and it rarely stopped for the next four months. Soon, the Germans found that their greatest battlefield assets were Generals Mud and Rain, which reduced the battlefield to a quagmire of glutinous sludge and water-filled shell holes. The million-shell bombardments that now preceded all major offensives also shattered the terrain. The effects of this iron assault were particularly bad in the Flanders region since the water table was very high. With a pulverized irrigation system, the heaviest rain in years had nowhere to drain, and the water therefore lay pooled on the broken landscape. With each offensive, the British artillery mulched the ground that their infantry then had to advance over; but when they tried to attack without artillery barrages, they were massacred. There was no alternative but to inch forward. Within a few weeks, it should have been clear to all that a breakthrough was not in the cards. But still the British Expeditionary Force fought on in unspeakable conditions.

A Canadian soldier stands in the wasteland of Passchendaele, where millions of shells and weeks of unending rain had reduced the battlefield to a bog of water-filled craters and unburied corpses.

PASSCHENDAELE was a "hideous dream," recounted one Canadian trench soldier. "Pitch-black, the rain came down in torrents. The clinging mud was waist-high everywhere, and when one fell, or stepped, off the bath-mat [i.e., duckboards] it was literally a life-and-death struggle to get back."[6] The only way forward through the sea of mud was to lay down tracks on which to walk; narrow wooden roads criss-crossed the battlefield, swaying drunkenly as they floated in the mire or were propped up on a few islands of solid ground—or on the thousands of decomposing corpses that rested in the quagmire. To fall off of these perches meant to sink into the morass. With heavy kits, it was not uncommon for soldiers to slip off the wooden boards and drown. The duckboards or duckwalks, as the soldiers often called them, also attracted the attention of German gunners and snipers. Geysers of mud exploded as shells dropped into the morass day and night.

In this charnel house, the British and Dominion forces attempted to wade through the mud and overrun the German defences, which now consisted of a complex system of concrete pillboxes, rows of barbed wire, and countless machine-gun nests built to a depth of several kilometres. The Germans had learned from the meat-grinder battles of Verdun and the Somme in the previous year: no longer would they hold the front with a series of continuous trenches, as these had been too easily targeted by Allied gunners. This newly dispersed force centred around mutually supporting strongpoints that could better survive the monstrous artillery barrages that preceded each battle. Haig scoffed at the new German system, deriding this porous shell-crater defence as "simply the refuge of the destitute," but it achieved the purpose of saving German lives and leaving the British infantry exposed for longer periods—advancing through more mud and enemy fire—before reaching the main battle zone.[7] "The further we penetrate his line," lamented one British Second Army document from August 1917, "the weaker and more disorganized we are liable to become."[8]

A month of fruitless battles pushed Gough's army to the breaking point in late August, and then the primary thrust was taken over by Plumer's Second Army. Plumer's bite and hold tactics scored some limited victories against the Germans, as his gunners not only laid down monstrous bombardments but also planned for the enemy counterattacking forces that were then chewed up in prearranged artillery fire. Battlefield conditions were beyond dreadful and, by October—after almost three months of fighting—the BEF had advanced less than 10 kilometres at the expense of almost 200,000 casualties. The German forces could not escape the slaughter either, and General Ludendorff noted, "Our wastage had been so high as to cause grave misgivings, and exceeded all expectation."⁹ The crippling casualties on the British side, coming as they did after the failure of the Arras and the Somme campaigns, left Haig's career on the line. A victory was needed to save the field marshal and, perhaps, the entire BEF—for, after fighting through the "Slough of Despond," the level of troop morale was at an unprecedented low.¹⁰ But fifty-one of the sixty British divisions on the Western Front, including the Australians who had suffered a crippling 38,000 casualties, had been cycled through Flanders. There was almost no one left, yet too much blood had been spilt to simply pull out from the muddy wasteland. While the breakthrough was no longer possible, the British now sought to capture the town of Passchendaele, which had once sat on the ridge but had been erased from the face of the earth by shellfire. The breakthrough plan had been reduced to the goal of capturing a now non-existent town surrounded by acres of shattered farmers' fields. And so, by the first half of October, when another series of Australian and New Zealand offensives were failing to dislodge the enemy, Haig called upon his other shock corps, the Canadians.

HAIG VISITED Currie's headquarters in early October. He had a long talk with the Canadian Corps commander about the need to send his troops to Flanders. It was not common for Haig to dicker with his generals, but although Currie was positioned within the hierarchical chain of command in the BEF, he also had a duty to the Canadian government. He did respect Haig, who he had always felt was a fine commander and a gentleman far superior to the political curs running the war effort in England, but he served two difficult masters and was not above playing one off against the other to get what he wanted. In this case, he did not want to send his corps to Flanders, and was hoping instead to have a chance to finish off Lens with another attack there or to go north with Byng's Third Army and take part in an innovative tank battle pitted against Cambrai. Passchendendaele offered nothing but a slaughter in a quagmire. Currie pleaded with Haig: "Let the Germans have it—keep it—rot in it! Rot in the mud! There's a mistake somewhere. It must be a mistake! It isn't worth a drop of blood."[11] While Currie's understanding of the situation was bang-on, he did not have the power to turn down Haig. But he still tried to convince the field marshal that the objective was not worth the lives it would cost. Currie later testified that his insubordination in this instance would likely have resulted in his firing had he been a British general.[12] Haig eventually impressed upon Currie that he must take the commander-in-chief's word that the situation at Passchendaele was an emergency, and that victory was needed. Even with the leeway afforded to the Canadian Corps commander, Currie could not, in the end, argue with Haig's word. After the war, the field marshal told Currie that he had needed to keep the offensive alive in Flanders because the French had not yet recovered from their mutinies and would likely fold in the face of sustained German pressure.[13] He may have been right, but the French generals believed their army was largely under control by the time Haig turned to the Canadians. Nonetheless, Haig wanted to give his ally's forces time to fully recover, for although he disliked the French, he knew that Britain could not fight Germany without them. Equally important, however, Haig needed a victory to salvage his reputation, and that of his forces. The latter goal was indeed an emergency worthy of further sacrifice, as sustaining the army's collective morale was essential in a war that demanded so much from the soldier. Haig's army needed to capture Passchendaele Ridge in order to avoid the necessity of pulling back his forces when the campaigning season came to an end in November or December—which would result in the disastrous situation of giving up all the terrain that his soldiers had bled and died for in the last few months of terrible fighting.[14]

Although Currie agreed to go north, he demanded additional artillery pieces, guaranteed authority to plan the battle on his own timeline and, perhaps most surprising to Haig, not to serve in Gough's Fifth Army. The Canadians had fought in Gough's army on the Somme in 1916, and the feeling among the Canadian high command was that his general staff was sloppy and wasteful with soldiers' lives. That this sentiment also ran through the BEF had been confirmed for Currie recently by several British divisional commanders with whom he spoke in confidence. Although Haig had already recorded privately his own misgivings about Gough's staff, he could scarcely believe Currie's demand. Neither could General Horne, who quite liked Currie but responded with shock: "My God, Currie, that is a terrible thing to say."[15] But all of the Canadian general's demands were met, and the battered Canadian Corps was off to Flanders to fight in Plumer's Second Army. Although Currie respected Plumer for his careful planning and his understanding that terrain sometimes dictated what could be accomplished and at what speed, the corps commander remained wary of the conditions on the Passchendaele battlefield. Before Currie left for Flanders, he predicted ominously that the operation would cost 16,000 men. Sadly, Currie's grim assessment was nearly accurate.

"I DON'T SUPPOSE there is any place on earth in quite such a mess as the surface of the earth surrounding Ypres. For over six miles in depth the land is nothing but a sea of shell-craters, the majority of which are full of water," wrote Sergeant J.A. Brice of the PPCLI.[16] Added to this slough of greasy water were unburied, bloated corpses that gave the battlefield an odour that could be detected kilometres to the rear. But even before the first Canadians encountered the rotting stench, Ypres and the Flanders region had a bad reputation among the old veterans in the corps. The Canadians had fought here since the start of the war and left behind thousands of comrades. They had seen bad places before, the Somme undoubtedly topping the list, but nothing could prepare the Canadians for the absolute desolation of the battlefield.

"Considerable shelling in our neighbourhood all day," wrote machine-gunner J.S. Davis. "Many landing uncomfortably close to entrance of our pill box."[17] The shell eruptions sent mud in giant showers of brown liquid, and roused the decaying smells of rotting flesh and gas. Even battle-hardened veterans were speechless as they stared at the putrid desolation, wondering how anyone could survive, let alone fight, in this wasteland. In his diary, signaller John Poucher described the exhausted Australian soldiers who passed them on their way from the front: "Their eyes are enough. One can't be fooled by such eyes."[18] Past their weary comrades-in-arms, the Canadians were marching straight into battle, with eyes wide open and aware of what was in store for them.

Only detailed preparation and planning might deliver victory on this terrible battlefield, but the Canadians had less than two weeks before they were to attack.

Currie sent out senior staff officers to survey the ground, which was situated on almost the same front lines that the Canadians had occupied before the 1915 Second Ypres battle. The battlefield did not look good. Villages such as St. Julien and Wieltje had been pounded out of existence. Roads were nearly impassable. The artillery and machine-gun positions indicated on tattered, stained maps often simply did not exist, leaving Currie's staff to guess at where they had been swallowed by the mud. Those weapons that could be found were in poor condition. Because it was almost impossible to move the Australian guns already situated on the islands of solid ground amidst a sea of mud, and equally difficult to bring in their own, the Canadians took over the guns of their dominion comrades. These were worn out and in some cases had barrels melted from overuse; guns in such condition always sent shells either long or short, but always on a skewed trajectory. Of the roughly 550 heavy and light British artillery pieces that should have been in place on this front, only about half could be located or were in working order.[19] Anxious to confirm the bad reports of his officers, Currie lumbered to the front, hunkering down in the mud to study the terrain.

It was as bad as he had been told. Perhaps worse. Passchendaele Ridge dominated the Allied front with spurs and heights that channelled attacking soldiers into killing grounds and provided the enemy with sweeping fields of fire. The frontage was small, at only about 3,000 metres. This meant that the Canadians could concentrate their forces, but also that the Germans could do the same. In fact, the Germans were firing from an arc of guns that wrapped around the Canadian front nearly 200 degrees. "Fritz has his guns all nicely registered," wrote Donald MacPherson of the 9th Battery, a University of Toronto graduate, winner of the Military Medal at Vimy, and one of three brothers serving on the Western Front. "Day and night he searches up and down [our front] with his shells."[20] As Canadian shells were also falling short into their own lines from the worn-out guns, the front-line infantry were literally being fired at from every direction.

Beyond the field of unburied corpses and shell craters extending to the left and right as far as the eye could see, the Canadians were confronted by the gentle slope of Passchendaele Ridge. Atop it lay the ruined village that gave the ridge its name. A fit man could probably have run up the ridge in ten minutes; through the glutinous mud, barbed wire, and enemy fire, it would take the Canadian Corps nearly three weeks and every step cost a few lives. And they would succeed only by scrambling over the open graves of those who had tried and died before. The eviscerated dead and desiccated horse corpses jutting from shell craters or pushed off the few dry roads provided clear evidence of the terrible battles that had been fought over this godforsaken land.

The ridge was divided in two by the Ravebeek, a shallow river that had overflowed and was now an impassable lake. There was no way through it, although the floating and submerged corpses of hundreds of men attested that many had tried. The western side of the ridge was dominated by Bellevue Spur, a German strongpoint that was also surrounded by marshy land that channelled soldiers into killing grounds. On top of the ridge, and to the east where Passchendaele village lay, the

This aerial photograph captures the effects of Allied shellfire, which has erased the village of Passchendaele. The thousands of shell craters filled with water in the photograph also illustrate the shattered nature of the battlefield over which the infantry had to assault.

ground was equally flooded and nearly impassable. All of this Currie surveyed, with the aid of aerial photos, and tried to formulate some plan of action to assist his troops in at least gaining a foothold on the ridge. Massive artillery firepower might allow for limited bite and hold operations so that the infantrymen could pull themselves from the mud at the base of the ridge. But there did not appear much to bite for the infantry surveying the ridge from their slush-filled rifle pits.

Currie needed more guns to adequately prepare for the battle. Returning from his tour of the front, the red-faced general barged into GHQ demanding replacements for the guns that had sunk beneath the mud. Kilometres from the front, the British staff chided Currie and asked how he could know for sure if the guns were there or not. Currie exploded, cursing and pointing to his mud-stained uniform; he had been there to inspect the bloody guns, he bellowed, and there were far fewer of them than the British claimed in their handover reports! The surprised and chastised British acquiesced. Currie got his guns, including heavy and light artillery, on top of his own corps artillery, which had recently been augmented by the 5th Division's guns from England. That made for 587 artillery pieces: 270 18-pounders, 90 4.5-inch howitzers, 48 60-pounders, 106 6-inch howitzers, 32 8-inch howitzers, 26 9.2-inch howitzers, 10 naval guns between 6 and 9.2 inches, and 5 super-heavy howitzers from 12 to 15 inches, although only sixty percent of the guns could initially be dragged close enough to the front for their fire to reach enemy lines. Lieutenant Colonel Andrew McNaughton estimated that the entire expenditure of artillery in the four years of the South African War was some 273,000 rounds, which weighed roughly 2,800 tonnes; at Passchendaele, the Canadians would fire this amount in two days.[21]

Some British troops were a little resentful of the Canadians. It appeared that they had been called in to play clean-up when the battle had already been raging for months. One sharp-faced staff officer, Captain Bernard Montgomery, who would rise to field marshal in the next world war and command a different generation of Canadian troops in battle, wrote ungenerously: "The Canadians are a queer crowd; they seem to think they are the best troops in France and that we get them to do our most difficult jobs."[22] Montgomery noted rightly that the Canadians had a great deal of confidence in their abilities and were not afraid to tell anyone of their superior skills, although the captain clearly had his doubts. After Vimy and Hill 70, the

Canadians felt they could crack almost any nut. "We thought of ourselves as a special combat group," recounted infantryman Arthur Hickson.[23] Such self-assurance was needed in the mud of Flanders, but the Canadians would also require élan, determination, and a hell of a lot of artillery firepower to break the German front.

HALF SUBMERGED IN THE MUD, the Germans' spread-out pillboxes presented very low profiles and were hard to locate even by low-flying aircraft. Each was a miniature fortress with the capacity for an all-around defence—and they were nearly impregnable. Postbattle reports noted that the heaviest shells (15-inch) could destroy these concrete shelters, but almost nothing else cracked the surface: "Our field artillery shells would bounce off them like tennis balls off the sidewalk."[24] The tactic of saturating the area with smaller-calibre shells, used in the hope that the concussion would drive the inhabitants mad—which it sometimes did, or simply killed them from the force of the explosion—was found to be ultimately unsuccessful, as it chewed up the ground around the strongpoint, making it even harder for the infantry to advance towards it.[25]

Facing the Canadians was the 11th Bavarian Division, which had three regiments, of three battalions each, and all echeloned deeply. With the British and Dominion forces having eaten into the German buffer zone to the west of Passchendaele Ridge, the Germans were forced to crowd their forces into a narrow front, and almost all of it within range of the Canadian guns. The three battalions in each of the German regiments were arranged in-depth, with the first echeloned on the closest line of resistance—which the Germans called the Protective Line of the Forward Zone. It was expected that this position would be overrun but that machine guns and riflemen would exact a toll on the enemy. The second area of fortifications, known as the Line of Resistance of the Forward Zone, was located some 500 metres behind the Protective Line. This was the area to which the front-line screen of defenders would retire to join the second battalion when they were close to being swept aside by the attacking infantry. Where possible, the Line of Resistance was situated on the reverse slopes of hills and ridges to offer some protection from Canadian fire. A single German company—comprising about 120 men and 5 machine guns—held about 230 metres of frontage; the defenders were spread out in a series of isolated strongpoints, which remained a serious challenge for the Canadians to locate amidst the filth.[26] The forces on the Protective Line would have fifteen minutes to retreat across the fire zone before the German artillery would bring down devastating fire on the Protective Line, where the primary, secondary, or tertiary waves of Canadian attackers would be passing. The Line of Resistance—in fact a thick zone several hundred metres deep and structured as a checkerboard defence in which strongpoints were laid out to support one another and sweep advances in their sector and others—formed the buffer in front of the Main Resistance Line, located a further 500 metres to the rear. This last position was more heavily defended and needed to be held at all costs.[27] By October, counterattacking forces had been moved closer to the front than they had been located during the initial phases of the Battle of Passchendaele in August and September. This tactical revision had been a response to Plumer's adoption of more limited bite and hold operations, which included using prepared artillery fire to smash the expected counterattacks; the shellfire had taken its toll on the German forces that travelled exposed overland behind their own lines. The Germans' elastic defence no longer had the same power in the snap back—with the counterattacking forces now accounted for by artillery fire—and so their various lines of resistance were based around heavy MG-08 teams, of which there were to be twenty-four to twenty-eight in any given regimental sector.[28] As on the Somme, the German high command ordered that "Every man had to fight where he was stationed. Only over his dead body could the enemy advance."[29] By holding the front in strength, the Germans suffered heavily, with one infantryman lamenting, "It makes me cry to see our dear soldiers disappear. This butchery is madness."[30] Few Allied infanteers would have disagreed.

THE CANADIANS would achieve no single breakthrough battle against these formidable defences. At the division and corps level, it was understood that the only method of capturing the heavily fortified and flooded Passchendaele Ridge was to take it one chomp at a time. Currie and his staff planned to overrun the ridge in four set-piece battles, on October 26 and 30 and November 6 and 10. In the first phase, the forces would pull themselves from the mud, and then, in the second and third phases, they would claw their way forward up the ridge to capture the village.

THE BATTLE OF PASSCHENDAELE RIDGE: OCTOBER 26 TO NOVEMBER 10, 1917

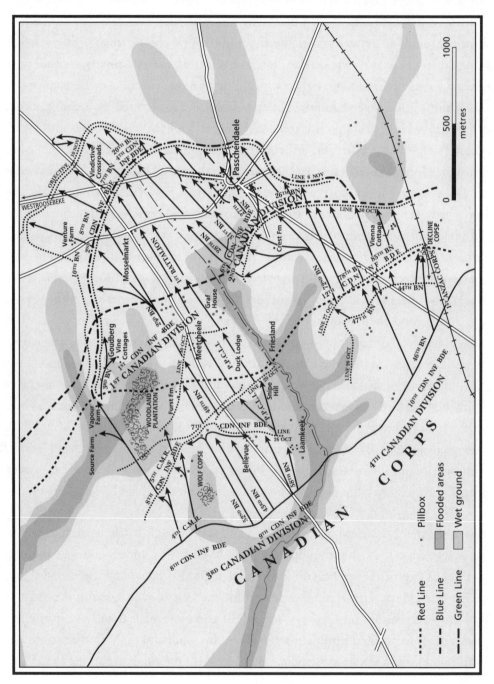

The fourth and final phase would involve the capture of what was left of the ridge to the north of the village. Through the use of limited operations, the Canadians hoped to successfully capture ground and also avoid driving too deep and getting caught in the main German battle zone where the enemy's counterattacking forces were positioned. To overextend would be to risk losing all that had been overrun.

While the Canadians had had over six weeks to plan for the Hill 70 battle, now they had only fourteen days to prepare the battlefield for the forthcoming offensive.[31] In the quagmire, roads had to be built across the swamp, both forward from the rear and laterally. Engineers and labour battalions expanded the logistical system to accommodate the movement and needs of tens of thousands of soldiers. The Germans well understood the importance of this preparatory work, and from atop the ridge they directed accurate fire along known roads and dry spots to engage all "living targets" and, according to established doctrine, harass "the enemy's service of supplies."[32]

Currie believed that the Canadians could succeed on the swampy Passchendaele battlefield only if they laid new roads and dug additional gun pits to prepare for the coming battle. It was a slow and costly process, as the Germans rained down shellfire day and night, but the logistical support—especially the laying of wooden paths or "duckboards," as illustrated in this image—would at least give the infantry a fighting chance.

The Canadian labour groups paid for this necessary work with more than 1,500 casualties. Currie lamented the losses, but the logistical work had to be pushed through "at all costs."[33] The infantry would not stand a chance in the muck without the support of the guns, and his batteries needed shells. It was not uncommon to see groups of men 50 to 100 strong straining at pulling the guns over the boggy roads in a manner reminiscent of siege warfare of old, in which sappers hauled forward their siege guns or catapults for a long, drawn-out campaign. The gunners needed solid ground on which to situate their batteries, and intelligence reports noted bluntly that without proper logistical support and battery positions, "it was impossible to support further operations."[34] As it stood, the guns were grouped on what little firm ground there was in the salient, and were easy targets for enemy counter-battery fire.[35] Hundreds of new gun pits had to be built to protect Canadian artillery from enemy fire. There was a lot of sweat and swearing in preparation for the battle before a single bullet was fired. The service corps lived up to its informal motto: "The impossible we do immediately; the miraculous takes a little longer."[36]

The marshes of Passchendaele consumed men, ammunition, and guns at a shocking rate. In the absence of firm ground, the artillery guns became buried in the mud by the force of the recoil during firing.

Night after night, units worked in muck, laying duckboard to provide firm footing. These planks soon became greasy with ooze, but they were often the only pathway connecting the front to the rear, and were travelled by hundreds of men as they braved enemy shellfire. "There was no escape," wrote Private John Becker. "No cover of any kind."[37] Since much of the movement along the wooden paths took place in the dark, it was common for men to step forward and disappear into the mud after a shell had shattered the pathway and left a yawning gap. Heavily laden soldiers might never surface from a deep sinkhole, while others found footing on submerged corpses or other buried debris and were able to wade to the next slimy duckboard. The dead populated the landscape, clutching the duckboards with rigor-mortified fingers or bobbing as bloated corpses on the surface of slime-filled shell craters.

AS THE CANADIANS hammered out their plans, the attacking infantry slithered into what passed as front trenches. It was hard to hide several thousand soldiers in the desolate wasteland: there were no tunnels as at Vimy and no deep cellars for sections to huddle in as at Hill 70. The Germans responded to the vulnerability of the Canadian positions, blasting the infantry at the front and the gunners in the rear. Because of the low water table, most of the Allied line had been built up using sandbags, and these were constantly being scattered about the battlefield by gunfire, as were the soldiers hiding behind them. The Canadians were aware that attacking with surprise would be impossible. Captured enemy prisoners later revealed that the German high command had warned their troops of another offensive on October 26, the exact day of the Canadian attack.[38] German intelligence had been tracking Currie's troops very closely since they considered the Canadians to be an elite force.[39]

While the infantry went to ground in the holes they were able to scoop out of the soft earth, the Canadian gunners proved harder to hide, especially from searching aircraft and balloons. Wilfred Kerr, a lieutenant in the artillery, observed that the enemy pounded their gun pits with searching high explosive and shrapnel fire: "We would have moved the guns; but in that awful sea of mud it was impossible either to move the guns or bring in new ones. We stayed and endured and paid the price."[40] Gun batteries crowded islands of dry land within the wasteland of muck. The gunners dug down, built up gun pits with sandbags, and tried to camouflage positions with tarp or canvas, but often their muzzle-barrel blasts gave away their locations, which were soon shelled with high explosives, shrapnel, and poison gas. Everyone was exhausted, and most units suffered 100 percent casualty rates, which included many of the experienced officers and NCOs.[41] One after another, the guns and their crews (six of which were in the battery at any one time) were blown apart, replaced, and knocked out again. Gunner Ernest Black endured the strain and survived the German destruction of twenty-three guns in his battery, revealing an almost 400 percent casualty rate. "I spent thirty-one months in France and Belgium and I would do all of the rest of it again rather than those six weeks at Passchendaele," wrote the beleaguered gunner.[42] Almost everyone at Passchendaele would have agreed with Black, and the battle for the bog had not even begun.

CHAPTER 21

"I DON'T KNOW HOW THE HUMAN FRAME STOOD UP"

October 26, 1917

As dawn appeared on the horizon through a fine mist on October 26, the Canadian guns unleashed hundreds of shells at exactly 5:40 A.M. The barrage forced the defenders into their dugouts or pillboxes, and targeted the hidden batteries that had been identified via aerial observers or sound-ranging techniques. However, the mud swallowed many of the shells, so the Canadian gunners adapted by firing more air bursts, with seventy-five percent of all shrapnel shells fused to explode at higher heights than the typical 5.5 metres. This alteration made the shells less effective but ensured that fewer exploded harmlessly in the mud. The 700-metre-deep creeping barrage, composed of several walls of artillery fire coming from field guns and howitzers, remained stationary for eight minutes on the enemy front lines, and then lifted at the rate of 50 metres every four minutes.[1]

The pre-battle gunfire and creeping barrage cleared most of the barbed-wire obstacles, although the ground was churned up further—if that were possible. When the barrage went off in a blinding light, the infantry hugged the moving wall of fire and steel into the enemy lines. Private Arthur Turner remembered the high explosive and shrapnel shells exploding above as the soldiers pushed forward: "The concussion was terrific; it made me feel as if my chest was being ripped open."[2]

On the left sector of the front, to the west of the flooded Ravebeek valley that divided the battlefield, Major General Louis Lipsett ordered his 3rd Division's

4th CMR, 43rd and 58th Battalions, and supporting companies from the 52nd Battalion to advance up the ridge some 1,100 metres. Although their objective was limited, it was heavily fortified and protected by imposing geographical features. The primary objective was Bellevue Spur, which was a knoll that ran down from Passchendaele Ridge and overlooked the Canadian lines. The ground was entirely flooded on the eastern side of the spur, and considered impassable. On the western side, the Germans had heavily fortified the low ground around an area called Wolfe Copse. At least fourteen pillboxes dotted this narrow divisional front. They were placed in the customary checkerboard formation across the battlefield, some situated on forward slopes while others were hidden in rear positions, all protecting machine-gunners and riflemen.

To the right of the 3rd Division, but separated by the marshy ground that had been transformed into an impassable lake, Major General David Watson's 4th Division had room for only one battalion to attack 550 metres through the muddy porridge. The 46th Battalion was ordered to take Decline Copse, a section of broken ground protected by mature trees and logs that offered protection to the defenders. At least ten German pillboxes were situated on this front. Mud was expected to slow soldiers to a mere crawl, leaving them exposed for longer in No Man's Land. It was a recipe for disaster.

THE 4TH CMR went over the top in a light rain, attacking with two companies forward, on the far left of the front. The infantry started the attack in a poor mood, having spent the night in the sludge that passed for the front line and, because carrying parties had gotten lost, being forced to attack without water in their bottles or rum in their bellies. When they "hit the bags"—which in this battle was truly just a metaphor since the forming-up trenches contained almost no sandbags—they found the ground choked with mud the consistency of soft cheese, and almost nothing on the horizon, as all the trees had been blown away. To the right was the strongpoint of Wolfe Copse, and behind that were at least four pillboxes, but it was hard for the Mounted Rifles to see much in the gloom.

The 4th CMR were supported by an awe-inspiring artillery force: 180 18-pounders, 125 siege guns, and additional mortar and machine-gun fire.[3]

This mass of Canadian gunfire tore up the enemy lines, with the creeping barrage marching forward slowly at only 50 metres every four minutes to account for the infantry's difficulty in crossing the mangled terrain. Even at this crawl, however, the barrage was soon outpacing the foot soldiers, who also had to deal with enemy retaliation from artillery, machine guns, and rifles.[4] The Mounted Rifles' objective, to the northwest of Wolf Copse, was a little wood of elm trees and a few ruined houses. As they moved towards it, the deep and numerous water-filled shell holes required that the soldiers advance in small sections, as there was no way to keep assault formations intact.

The infiltrating CMR units were augmented by Vickers machine guns from the 9th Canadian Machine Gun Company, which provided essential firepower against targets of opportunity. Despite this reinforcement and a heavy supporting barrage of bullets and shells, the attackers ran up against strong enemy resistance. All around them the water was quivering as the shells screamed overhead. The enemy's counter-barrage in return was throwing up geysers of mud, and the occasional bloody rags of what had once been men. The CMR struggled forward, but rusty barbed wire, hidden beneath the scummy water, clawed at their legs, holding up the attack. German snipers, situated in isolated pillboxes or in Wolf Copse, began to pick off the officers and lead infantrymen. Reserve Lieutenant Pätz of the 9th Company, 164th Infantry Regiment, testified that the Canadians: "offered amazing targets."[5] But still the Mounted Rifles came on, moving from one water-filled crater to the next, bombing or bayoneting the enemy to death when they got within range to make a final charge.

Despite the heavy Canadian barrage, the guns in fact provided little help, as they were now being fired erratically. The gunners had difficulty staying on target as lift after lift moved further away from their sights, and they faced the enormous challenge of coordinating the large number of staggered guns so that all lifted at the same moment and came down on the next objective with precision. On the far left, the barrage was falling short, and one company of the 4th CMR was torn apart by Canadian shells. Across the divisional boundary to the north, the British 63rd Division—which was advancing in unison with the 3rd Division but was not controlled by Currie's headquarters—had been checked short of its objectives by unrestrained enemy fire, and so the German defenders on that front, especially in a position called Source Trench, turned their guns on the CMR. Men were hit and, though they suffered seemingly non-fatal wounds, were knocked out and then drowned in the mud.

The losses accumulated as the forward units of the CMR were pinned down. Success came from an unlikely soldier, the boyish and shy nineteen-year-old Private Tommy Holmes. With bullets flying and men being killed as they peered above the shell craters for a way through the mud, Holmes charged headlong into the German machine-gun nests, weaving in and out of craters, crawling through the muck as the bullets tore up the ground around him. The few survivors of the 4th CMR in the front lines could not believe what they were seeing. As Holmes closed on the enemy, desperate and panicky enemy machine-gunners and riflemen trained all their guns on him. A barrage of bullets flew around him, but still he avoided what seemed certain death. When he was within 30 metres of the German lines, he threw a grenade and knocked out a pillbox. A few more well-thrown grenades silenced other defenders, but then he was out of bombs. Instead of digging in and saying his prayers, the private returned to the CMR's forward positions to get more grenades. Mouths agape, soldiers pooled their grenades and handed them over. Holmes made the insane return trip through a hail of bullets as German units on the flanks fired at him, but he seemed to be protected by some unseen force. With seemingly no fear, he got in close and wiped out a second machine-gun crew, which allowed his platoon to keep driving deep. Holmes was awarded the Victoria Cross and later remarked, "I thought everybody did that sort of thing." Many Canadians did, but Holmes's action was extraordinary; in the words of one soldier, "As an example of sheer unadulterated bravery it could hardly be surpassed."[6]

CMR leaders pushed forward through the muck, their men falling around them. Though the battalion was attempting to advance in a triangle formation, with one platoon up and two on the flanks, the formation had lost all coherency in the mud and under enemy fire. Men went to ground and stayed there. Others stumbled forward, losing their mates, attaching themselves to new sections, following new leaders who waved them onward. Lieutenant Tom Rutherford, a platoon commander from Owen Sound and soon the last standing officer of A Company, found himself almost alone at one point, the few men still with him shot down by enemy fire.

"Every Officer, NCO, and man was on his own," wrote Rutherford. "There was no way to control such a battle under such conditions."[7] After tripping and falling headfirst into a pool of fetid water, he discarded his soaked and now sodden equipment. He slipped through the enemy defences, which were porous because of the Germans' inability to man a continuous trench in the mud. Slithering forward, Rutherford entered what remained of a German position, but was attacked by a defender. As they grappled, the German lost his rifle, but he tried to choke Rutherford to death. A revolver shot to the belly ended the struggle in the lieutenant's favour. Rutherford had the strange experience of being alone in the enemy trench and looking back over the battlefield to see his fellow

Nineteen-year-old Private Tommy Holmes was awarded the Victoria Cross for his gallant action on October 26, 1917, when he charged frontally and knocked out a series of enemy machine guns—all on his own. Holmes's action was, in the words of one of his comrades-in-arms, "sheer unadulterated bravery."

Mounted Rifles struggling to advance. The Germans were brazenly standing on the ground above the rough trench lines, discharging their rifles at the Canadians. Shaking like a leaf from the cold and adrenaline, Rutherford slowly began to snipe Germans, who had no idea that their line was breached and that they were vulnerable from within their own trenches. Rutherford was alone, but by taking ammunition from the dead, he continued to widen the gap in the enemy line, and soon the CMR began to pour through it, after which they quickly cleared the enemy positions. Rutherford would continue to serve with the 4th CMR until August 25, 1918, when he was invalided home with gas poisoning.

On October 26, the 4th CMR sustained 321 casualties, with most of the survivors reporting uncanny escapes from the nearly suicidal charge. The operation would have been more costly if not for heroic infantrymen like Rutherford and Holmes. Attesting to the severe difficulties presented by the blighted battlefield, the 4th CMR, who had eventually been supported by three companies of the 1st CMR, successfully captured their objectives but were forced to pull back their left flank 300 metres to avoid enfilade fire coming from the British sector.

The two battalions on the right of the 3rd Division's front, the 43rd and 58th Battalions, supported by two companies of the 52nd Battalion, initially had better luck than the men of the 4th CMR, as the Canadian artillery had been very effective in cutting the German wire, despite many of the shells falling short into the ranks of the lead units. The battalions had been ordered to attack relentlessly, and even if "part of the line be held up by machine guns … units on the flank must push on through the gap and endeavour to envelop the obstacle."[8] The 43rd Battalion, a Highlander unit raised in Winnipeg, was advancing on the front and made good progress, but as the infantry instinctively let their guard down a bit, they climbed a small hill and passed through the rotting corpses of previous attackers in what was obviously a kill ground. Within minutes, the Highlanders ran into heavy rifle and machine-gun fire from pillboxes and German infantrymen who had set up a deadly crossfire.

Almost all of the Canadian infantry were pushed back, with dozens left behind to add to the field of corpses, but a platoon of the 43rd held on to a portion of the Bellevue Spur, where it withstood a series of counterattacks. Lieutenant Robert Shankland organized the desperate last stand, keeping the Germans at bay with just his machine gun; later, he went to the rear, found reinforcements and brought them up in an impromptu counterattack. This assaulting force, led by Captain Christopher O'Kelly, caught the Germans in a flanking attack, crashing through a number of pillboxes and machine-gun positions, and taking more than 300 prisoners. O'Kelly and Shankland were each awarded the Victoria Cross for their inspired leadership. A fellow infantryman attested that Shankland "saved all the rest of us."[9] Reinforced by reserve forces drawn from the 52nd Battalion—men who had initially enlisted in towns around Lake Superior—sections of the 43rd began to fight their way forward, attacking pillboxes from the flanks, firing through the slits or passing grenades through openings like postmen inserting letters. Rifle grenades were effective in providing extra firepower, and by the end of the day the Bellevue fortress had fallen to the Canadians.

The 58th had gone over the top and struggled through the same slimy and glutinous ground as the 43rd. In places, the soldiers waded forward up to the waist, trying to keep their Lee-Enfields from dipping into the mud. With shells dropped all around them, soldiers had to fight the urge to dive headlong into the false security of the slime. But the only way to real safety was to push forward and capture the enemy strongpoints.

Spread out to avoid machine-gun fire, the 58th closed on their objectives, located some 400 metres from their start line. The distance felt more like 4 kilometres in the glue. Enemy riflemen and machine-gunners slowed the advance further and had to be knocked out by Canadian rifle-grenade and Lewis-gun fire, which pinned down the enemy while riflemen and grenadiers crept forward close enough to snipe or lob grenades. A number of Maxim posts were captured this way around Dad Trench, a position about halfway to the battalion's objective. Yet the lead units were thinning out as a result of casualties, and a reserve formation of 100 men, cobbled together from previously wounded soldiers who had just returned to the battalion, was thrown into the line. All sixteen officers who went forward with the 58th that day were shot down, and men of lower ranks took over the leadership, including Company Sergeant Major Andrew Anderson, who received the DCM for his gallantry in battle. More than sixty percent of the unit's attack force would be killed or wounded by the end of the day; capturing half of a farmer's field had cost the battalion more than 300 men. The 58th held their objectives, even against counterattacks: too many men had been lost for the survivors to allow themselves to be pushed out.[10]

On the 4th Division's front, the Canadians had an equally hard fight. Like the other units, the 46th Battalion lost men to both German and Canadian artillery fire before the battle. The enemy held the high ground in strength, with strongpoints at places such as Decline Copse and Crest Farm, and with reinforcements in Passchendaele village. Several field guns were known to be near the front lines, where they had wreaked havoc on previous Australian attacks, but they could not be conclusively located by Canadian intelligence.[11] Private Percy Hellings of the 46th recounted the minutes following zero hour:

> We didn't go far. Our own guns were in this sloppy muck and they couldn't keep the range and they dropped short…. We were right in the middle of it— getting shelled from both sides…. They were coming down like rain and I don't think I went twenty feet and there was dozens like me. When I was hit, the sergeant alongside me got his shoulder shot off with a piece of shrapnel.[12]

Once again, victory came down to the individual bravery of men doing the incredible and the impossible, inching their way forward through the storm of steel. In a few short hours, two-thirds of the attacking force was knocked out. The survivors took Decline Copse, but the two lead companies, C and D, had been reduced from 8 officers and 255 men to a shockingly meagre 1 officer and 65 men.[13] The 46th had captured Decline Copse, but holding it against counterattack with such a small force was another challenge entirely.

Reinforcements from the 50th Battalion were rushed up to support the 46th, but they first had to cross the fireswept battleground. Signaller Victor Wheeler described the advance: "The enemy fire grew steadily in intensity. Veterans and recent reinforcements alike fell with every yard of mud gained. The nearer we advanced … the more tremendous the firepower we faced."[14] Sometime after 1:30 P.M., the 50th Battalion arrived in time to fight alongside the 46th to repulse two enemy counterattacks.[15] But the German barrage played havoc with the Canadian position. Private Arthur Turner of the 50th recounted one part of the fight:

> There are only about four of us left then in our platoon. All the rest had been wounded. And I says, "Keep your eye on the front, and the first Heinies you see, let them have it." And just then three Heinies appeared about fifty yards away…. I ripped off the breech cover and there was my mechanism all caked in mud. I scraped away the mud. There was one shell already in the breech and I aimed point blank at them three fellows and all three heads disappeared and then I tried to re-load but I couldn't.[16]

Turner and his small group decided to retreat to a better position, but could not get out of the slimy hole that they had fortified. With the Germans advancing on them, they tried three times to scramble out of the ooze before they finally found their footing. Regrouping several hundred metres back, they were then led forward in another assault by an officer. The see-saw fighting continued for about ten hours before the 50th were finally overrun. But the 46th, which had also been pushed out of Decline Copse, turned around and attacked over the same ground, behind an accurate machine-gun barrage. They almost retook it, capturing the upper slopes, but were unable to drive the enemy from the entire position. The shattered units dug in around their own fresh dead along with the maggoty corpses of Australian Diggers who had fallen there several weeks earlier.

A German infantryman from the 2nd Battalion, Bavarian Reserve Infantry Regiment, was involved in the counterattack against the Canadians on this front. He offers a vivid account of the fighting:

> The enemy had overrun and captured the outpost company, so quickly that it had no time to react.… they simply had to be driven off.… Our companies lined up along the railway embankment. All our batteries concentrated a short period of drum fire on the enemy. Then we stormed forward. Of course it was nothing of the kind. Wading up to our knees in the bog, we made our way forward from crater to crater and on up the hill. Enemy machine gun fire mowed down many, but the courageous troops pressed on.… Suddenly flares went up! The enemy had fled; the position was ours once more.… We were relieved at 2:00 A.M. and were very happy about it. It had become an eerie experience, rather as though we could hear the beat of the wings of death, which had already reaped a dreadful harvest earlier that day."[17]

Brigadier Edward Hilliam, commander of the 10th Brigade, ordered a counterattack that night, declaring that the copse had to be taken "at all costs." The brigade's 44th and 47th Battalions carried out the operation, but in the mud and darkness, they got lost and failed to capture the now ruined copse, instead occupying a series of positions before the remains of the wood. Much like at St. Eloi a year and a half earlier, the men at the front, fighting for their lives, thought that one muddy hole looked like another, especially when the enemy was firing at them. However, a second counterattack was launched the next night, in which the 44th Battalion and an Australian force cleared Decline Copse after a fierce bayonet fight. It was held that night, but half of it was lost the next night in an enemy counter-attack, before it was finally recaptured and consolidated for good.

In the fighting on October 26, the use of reserves to support attacks teetering on the brink of failure had won the day in several cases. Contact patrols from the RFC helped to establish where advance infantry were dug in, and forward artillery observers tried to keep in touch with the gunners. Communication between front and rear remained problematic throughout the battle, as telephone wire was cut, sig-nal lamps were destroyed from the blast of shells, and pigeons became so disorien-tated from the shelling that they refused to leave their baskets.[18] The infantry at the sharp end were therefore left to fight it out on their own. This was understood by the rear commanders: for much of the battle, brigade headquarters devolved all deci-sions to the battalion commanders, advising them to "use your own judgement and do the best you can."[19]

The Canadians fell a little short of their final objectives on October 26 and in the days that followed, but they had moved on to higher and drier ground. The British and Australian attacks on either side of the Canadian assault had limited success. On the Canadian front, Bellevue Spur was captured and would enable further attacks up the ridge. The long process of consolidating this position began after the battle in the foul stench of gluey muck and dismembered corpses. Those pillboxes not destroyed during the battle were used as command headquarters or forward medical units. But not all soldiers were comfortable in the drier pillboxes. W.A. Crouse, who had enlisted at age sixteen and was only eighteen during the battle, was looking for a dry spot when he came across a section of dead Canadians in a pillbox. They were sitting upright like statues and none of them showed visible wounds. They had died from the concussion of a shell that landed on the pillbox, which had not broken through but had sent such a killing reverberation through the cement that all the men inside had died of ruptured internal organs. After that, Crouse chose mud over concrete. He lived into the 1960s.

"EVERYTHING TURNED into porridge, a ghastly dreadful porridge, thigh-deep, in which if you got hit on the shoulder blade with a bullet that merely knocked you unconscious for two minutes, you drowned," remarked Gregory Clark of the 4th CMR.[20] Those wounded men who avoided drowning in the mud still faced the conventional dangers of passing into shock or bleeding to death. Quick care was the solution, but how were they to get to the surgeons in the rear? The mud was so thick that it could take six hours to get a wounded man to a medical unit. "One thing about Passchendaele I'll never forget was the endurance, the fortitude and the courage of the stretcher-bearers," remarked one infantryman who described the burdened men's struggles through the mud. "I don't know how the human frame stood up."[21] Prisoners were employed to help, but even so the transporters ran a race against time. Relays were established to reduce the strain posed by inert, water-soaked men, but as Private Deward Barnes of the 19th Battalion recounted, the experience was always horrible: "Carrying the wounded out, most.... had parts of their faces shot away, some nearly all of their face."[22] The sound of men's feet being

Within the desolation of Passchendaele, it could take eight hours for men at the front to make their way backward to the first line of medical officers—far too long a wait for severely wounded soldiers, who would bleed out or slip into shock and then death.

pulled repeatedly from the suctioning mud could be heard all across the battlefront, and the mud-bespattered ordeal of stretcher-bearers emerging from the ghostly vapour became an iconic image of the battle.

The moaning or crying of wounded Canadians who had crawled onto dry ground wafted over the front, especially at night. Trench soldiers were warned not to go to their aid, for they would likely not find them and they could stumble into an ambush. Men who lost buddies to the wasteland usually ignored these orders, however, and spent the nights crawling through the muck in search of the maimed. Some were rescued, but others were too far gone. Machine-gunner Ray LeBrun remembered his horror upon coming across a severely wounded infantryman in the mud: "I nearly vomited. His insides were spilling out of his stomach and he was holding himself and trying to push this awful stuff back in. When he saw me he said, 'Finish it for me mate. Put a bullet in me. Go on. I want you to. Finish it!' He had no gun himself. When I did nothing, he started to swear. He cursed and swore at me and kept on shouting even after I turned and ran."[23]

THE FIGHTING on October 26 and the three-day defence to hold the front cost the 3rd and 4th Divisions 1,276 and 942 casualties, respectively. The two infantry divisions' losses formed 2,213 of the total 2,791 sustained by the Canadian Corps in this phase of the battle, with the remaining casualties falling to those involved in the lines of communication or to men attached to the corps.[24] In comparison to the results of previous British attacks, this was not an unusually high blood sacrifice for a two-division attack, but its effects were spread, for the most part, among only seven battalions, each with an average strength of just 600. The beleaguered Canadians had captured thirty-three machine guns and blown at least a dozen more to pieces in the battle for control of a front that General Lipsett described as the "strongest position I have ever seen."[25] The casualties to the fighting units were proof of that claim. And the Canadians would face another battle against equally formidable positions in less than a week.

CHAPTER 22

CRAWLING OUT
OF THE MUD

October 30, 1917

Private A.J. Foster of the 38th Battalion spent most of his time during the Battle of Passchendaele carrying wounded men back to the Canadian lines. It was exhausting work, and at one point he collapsed in a shallow trench. When he awoke, he forced himself to swallow some cold bully beef, trying to erase the memory of men he had seen simply vanish in a burst of smoke and mud when shells had landed on them. Then the shelling started again. Within seconds, a shell landed above his trench parapet, and the concussion of the blast left him stunned. "I sat there on my knees with a piece of meat between my teeth for possibly fifteen minutes while eight more shells cracked the trench all around," sending dirt and filth raining down on him. A little dog, also rendered insensible by the concussions, was running in panic along the parapet. Hearing it yelp in between the sounds of explosions, Foster looked up just in time to see it blown through the air and land on top of him. Trembling man and dog clung to each other for a while, but after a few minutes Foster came to and sent the dog on his way with the gristle that had been clenched between his teeth. Before the day ended, the private was buried again and gassed. He testified that his nerves "were shattered."[1]

THE CANADIANS could throw more battalions at the German forces in the second phase of the Passchendaele operation, as the attacks on October 26 had won them a solid foothold on the ridge. The objective for October 30 was only some 600 metres beyond the Canadian lines, but assault formations would need to pass through a grid of fortified houses, farms, and concrete pillboxes, all of which overlooked the Canadian front from higher ground. This position was held by the 465th Infantry Regiment, which was determined to retain the front.

The second phase of Currie's attack was also part of a larger British offensive, the seventh since the Passchendaele campaign had started on July 31. The Canadian Corps would be supported by two British divisions to the north and I Anzac Corps (an Australian/New Zealand force) to the south. Despite the support of the other formations, the Canadians would spearhead the force, and the capture of the ridge was still the primary objective. So when General Gough pressured Currie to move his attack back one day to October 29—to accommodate the British and Anzac forces that were already in the line, suffering casualties from enemy shellfire and facing another night of waist-deep mud—Currie refused. He believed that he owed Gough very little and advised the British general that he would not send his troops into battle without every possible means of support he could muster. The Canadian corps commander was serving his men, but his refusal to change his attack no doubt cost the lives of other Allied troops.

Engineering units turned their expertise to the drainage problem on the battlefield. A complex series of troughs and lateral runoff systems was dug along the front to help relieve the infantry of their struggle with the suctioning mud. In some spots, trenches could actually be dug into the soggy earth. But all of this labour was carried out under shell- and sniper fire, and the poison gas that was becoming a constant factor on the front. This spadework, along with the movement of the Canadian lines up the ridge as a result of the first phase of the operation, allowed the gunners to build new gun pits from the refuse of the battlefield: wooden planks, corrugated tin, even bully beef cans. These innovations helped to stabilize the guns, but the stop-gap measures were not ideal, as many gun pits were exposed to enemy fire. After three days and nights of miserable hulking through mud and preparing jumping-off positions while dealing with stray firefights along the front, Canadian assault forces readied themselves for the second phase of the attack on October 30. Infantryman G.R. Stevens wrote that many soldiers felt "they were alone in a dead world," and that only the "treasured fellowship" of their comrades kept most soldiers going.[2] The troops wrapped themselves in their ground capes, smoked cigarettes, and guzzled rum to stay warm. Waterlogged boots were taken off so that feet could be examined by officers who feared reprisals from above in the event of a trench foot epidemic, but even deep waders and a steady supply of dry socks could not keep the men's feet dry. In between shifts of sentry duty and applications of whale oil to tired, damp feet, mates checked with one another to make sure that grim promises would be fulfilled: a letter would be sent home telling of a brave and painless death should their comrade not emerge from battle.

FOUR HUNDRED AND TWENTY GUNS opened fire at 5:50 A.M., and the Canadians attacked under a blood-red dawn sky. Although it had not rained for three days, the ground over which the Canadians advanced remained a quagmire, and the smoke and exploding shells reduced visibility to less than 20 metres along most parts of the front. Into the gloom the infantry pushed.

Three battalions of the 3rd Division—the PPCLI, 49th Battalion, and 5th CMR—assaulted on the left. Several additional battalions would be thrown in later to consolidate the line, reinforce success, or provide a backdrop against defeat. One of these units was the 42nd Battalion, whose Major C.B. Topp was correct to note that the role of a reserve battalion "was not always a desirable one for the incentive of the attack was lacking, but the unceasing labour and the punishment of the retaliatory barrage had to be endured."[3] William Breckenridge, a Highlander from the same battalion, wrote: "I don't believe a single man went into the battle with the expectations of returning with his limbs. Each and every man felt it was a sure death trap."[4] The three spearhead battalions in this sector would face strongpoints at Meetcheele, as well as Furst, Source, and Vapour farms, and Duck Lodge on the far right.

Across the Ravebeek valley, on the right sector, the 4th Division could attack on a wider front as a result of the capture of Decline Copse a few days earlier. Brigadier J.H. MacBrien committed three battalions of his 12th Brigade to the operation—the 85th (from Nova Scotia), the 78th (Winnipeg Grenadiers), and the 72nd (Seaforth Highlanders)—their objectives being Crest Farm and less identifiable fortified shell craters. Positioned on the far right, the 85th faced a daunting task.

Pre-battle reconnaissance had revealed the Germans holding this front in strength and equipped with machine guns on dry land. They also appeared to have advance posts jutting into No Man's Land, which would likely survive any barrage that was directed on the German trenches. At the last moment, the fireplan was revised to bring the bombardment further back to grind out these forward German defences, and the Canadians were forced out of their trenches at 4 A.M. to avoid short-dropping shells. After the bombardment, however, it was not clear if any of the enemy defences had actually been destroyed.

When the creeping barrage opened up, the fire was light and scattered (possibly because the Canadian guns were sinking in the mud)—and did little to suppress enemy fire, its eight-minute duration on the first position only alerting the enemy to the coming attack. Chomping at the bit to follow the barrage, as soon as the 85th went over the top they were greeted by what one man described as a "continuous sheet of machine-gun bullets."[5] Within four minutes, the German shellfire had also begun to fall among the Canadians. Nine officers were knocked out in the first minutes of battle; on the Somme, a year earlier, this likely would have resulted in the attack being stopped cold. But the ensuing training had freed the lower ranks to act independently and assume positions of leadership. The Canadians now regrouped in shell craters, fired rifle grenades, and brought forward Lewis guns to lay down a suppressing fire. The rifle grenadiers proved invaluable, and the Canadian infantrymen's rifle fire was reported to be effective. The resulting iron storm allowed the infantry to wriggle their way forward, finding the folds in the land where a depth of eighteen inches made the difference between life and death.

The 85th's surviving senior officer at the front, Major P.W. Anderson, had been entrusted with control over the battalion's only reserve company, because it was felt that communications from front to rear would likely be severed during the battle, leaving the battalion headquarters unable to respond quickly to emergencies. With the Canadians pushing forward but paying for every inch of ground, Anderson ordered the reserve D Company into the fray. This addition of troops turned the tide. The surge of fresh Canadians drove some of the Germans to flee in panic while others shifted their fire to engage the reinforcements. Though the hail of bullets slowed the reserve company's attack, it gave the forward, surviving stragglers time to punch into the enemy lines. By 6:38 A.M., the 85th were on their objective. Lewis-gun magazines, small-arms ammunition, and grenades were rushed forward by tumpliners. They lost men all along the way, as well as the ammunition and supplies those unfortunates were carrying, but some of them got through the enemy's inter-dictory barrage.

Few of the gallant 85th were left standing, but the survivors kept up a fierce fire on the Germans, especially with the heavy Vickers that were rushed up in the second wave to help with consolidation. Several German counterattacks were beaten back by the "Breed of Manly Men"—as the motto emblazoned in Gaelic on the 85th Battalion's cap badge, "Siol na Fear Fearail," described them. They were indeed a tough breed: Private Walter Wyman, a thirty-one-year-old plumber from Westville, Nova Scotia, took over his section after his superior was knocked out. Under heavy shellfire, he reorganized the troops, calmed the men, maintained contact with units on the flank, and even dressed the wounds of two men. Other brave soldiers rose to the challenge all along the 85th's front, even as the lead units were pounded by artillery fire and poison gas. The position would not be relinquished. Taking it had cost the battalion 23 officers killed and wounded, and 371 casualties to the other ranks, from an initial force of just 26 officers and 662 men.[6] One of the dead was Major Anderson.

To the left of the 85th, positioned in the centre of the 4th Division's front, the 78th Battalion waited in makeshift trenches before going over the top. Eighteen-year-old Archie Brown's company was crammed into a shallow ditch, where there was not enough room for the officer to move along the trench to pass out the rum. Trusting the men, he simply sent along the jug of battle rum, and each man took a gulp and passed it along. They passed it back to him a quarter full. Brown remembered looking down the trench and seeing a chubby-faced youngster with whom he had served in an underage battalion before they both turned nineteen and were sent to France. Their eyes locked and they smiled reassuringly at each other. Then the boy's body exploded as a dud shell passed through him. It would be a bad day.

The lead platoons went over the top and encountered withering small-arms fire. All company commanders were knocked out in minutes, and soon the four waves of men, set 50 metres apart, went to ground. Brown was among them, but he had been forced down when a bullet hit him in the helmet, leaving him dazed and bloodied.[7] He woke up in a shell crater, his body twisted around, blood temporarily blinding him. Brown wiped his eyes, untangled himself, and kept going when he heard an order to rise and attack. That order might have come from Major John McEwan, the battalion's second-in-command, who saw the attack falling apart and rushed forward. He rallied the troops from their temporary cover and led them on a full-out bayonet charge across 800 metres—the equivalent of half a dozen football fields. They overran the German positions, withstood three counterattacks, and held the captured ground.

Attacking on the left was the 72nd Battalion; their objective was Crest Farm, a strongpoint defended by twelve machine guns on-site and another dozen spread out over the flooded front. The Highlanders of the 72nd had additional support from Canadian light mortar and machine-gun units, but the forward infantry companies still held little hope of taking the powerfully entrenched position, which was protected by a small lake.[8] Any assault seemed like suicide. Only a few hours before the attack, Lieutenant Colonel J.A. Clark made the gutsy decision to withdraw the battalion's D company and funnel the other three companies through a gap only 50 metres wide in the hope of surprising and overpowering the enemy defences. This stacking of the front could have resulted in a disaster, with one machine gun annihilating his battalion in this narrow formation—let alone the two dozen guns available to the Germans. But the experienced Clark, who had a reputation as a disciplinarian but also as a man who cared for his troops, realized that only a gamble would stave off slaughter.

Clark's forward infantry were situated on the reverse slope of a hill, waiting for zero hour and aware that the unorthodox manoeuvre would either save or shatter the battalion. Yet unlike the two battalions on their right, the 72nd were supported by a near-perfect artillery barrage. Supporting Vickers machine guns also fired hundreds of thousands of bullets, saturating the enemy front for miles. One Canadian after-battle report noted, "the casualties caused to the enemy by the [machine-gun] barrage are probably over-estimated but moral effect is undoubtedly considerable."[9] Perhaps the Canadians were in fact underestimating the effectiveness of the machine-gun barrage, as several prisoners testified that front-line units were "entirely cut off" by the hail of fire.[10] When the barrage lit up, the three companies fanned out and followed their shrieking shells right into the German trenches.

The 72nd's infantry were hugging their barrage closely, with the lead troops only a terrifying and lethal 20 metres behind the moving wall of fire. The mud swallowed much of the shrapnel and high explosives, but the soldiers' situation was still very dangerous. Some Highlanders even went forward through their own barrage, taking their chances with friendly fire rather than with German machine-gunners. Experienced infantry officers had drummed it into their men's heads that the more quickly they crossed the killing ground the briefer their exposure would be to the enemy's counter-barrage, which fell quickly on the expected axis of advance. Captured documents later revealed that the German outpost positions were given fifteen minutes from when the first Canadian shells were fired to fall back to their main resistance line before their barrage came down in full force. Although the Canadians were not aware of precisely how long they had before the full force of the German artillery fire came down, they knew they had only minutes to close the gap.

This they attempted through harsh fighting against enemy strongpoints. The Highlanders moved fast—faster than the Germans thought possible in the mud and under fire. Several prisoners later remarked that the attack was a surprise as they had been led to believe that the "swamp would protect them."[11] The Canadians broke through with a combination of fire and movement. On the far left, A Company killed at least fifty Germans and captured another twenty-five, including two machine-gunners, whose weapons were promptly turned on the enemy. In the centre, B Company pushed on to Crest Farm, bombing and shooting their way forward. Lance Corporal S. Irwin, in charge of a Lewis gun, crawled ahead in a desperate race to get the drop on three German machine-gun crews who were holding their fire as they waited for the Canadians to advance into a low gully that served as a killing ground. Irwin sprinted for the flank, got there with only seconds to spare, and opened fire, killing and scattering the gunners.[12] All along the front, platoons swung forward and advanced on the enemy—some wiped out in short, sharp affairs, others clawing their way to victory.

The 72nd were on their position by 9:30 A.M., and an entire counterattacking German company was ripped to shreds by the Highlanders, who let loose some

35,000 rounds during the day.[13] The Germans, unwilling to send more men into this killing ground, withdrew their forces but responded by blasting the front with an artillery barrage for eighteen hours. The German gunners were assisted by spotter planes that circled above the Canadian's newly won trenches, and these aerial observers were largely unharried by the Allied air forces, who were strangely absent from the skies on October 30. The German airmen even provided some harassing fire as they swooped on the Canadian lines, shooting up the trenches. Orders were issued for the soldiers not to look up, as their white faces might draw attention to the trenches.[14] Some obeyed while others fired a few useless shots at the planes.

Even the Canadian counter-battery work was desultory at best, with the sound-ranging sections producing few useful targets as the analysts were positioned too far from the front and the weather played havoc with their scientific readings.[15] Little could be done to silence the German guns; even worse, because most of the forward artillery observers had been shot down, many of the Canadian shells fell short. The 72nd were bombed from ahead and behind as they frantically dug into the mud to find protection. Over the day's fighting, 50 of the 72nd's men were killed, 220 were wounded, and 6 went missing. The battalion accounted for an estimated 200 Germans and took 130 prisoners, most of whom were used to carry back the wounded.

Douglas Haig called the 72nd Battalion's attack "a feat of arms which would go down in the annals of British history as one of the great achievements of a single unit."[16] This may sound excessive, but Haig was not one to lavish praise frivolously on the "colonials." The three battalions of the 12th Brigade lost about 1,000 men, with the two on the right—the 78th and 85th—losing more than the 72nd Battalion, even though they had a shorter distance to travel. The key was the artillery barrage on the 72nd's front, and the battalion's aggressive tactics.

ON THE OTHER SIDE of the Ravebeek, the 3rd Division was less successful. General Lipsett used three battalions in the assault: from right to left, the PPCLI, the 49th Battalion, and the 5th CMR. With the entire front gently running down towards the Canadians from the high point atop the spur, where the Germans held the ruins of a few houses around Meetcheele, its full length could be swept with enemy small-arms fire. There was no denying the hard truth that lay before all soldiers: with the bog sucking men and materiel into its dark grasp, the attacking formations would essentially be sitting ducks for the German defenders.

James McBride of the PPCLI remembered the anxiety that the soldiers suffered before going over the top:

> Many strange thoughts come into a man's mind. The next few hours might be his last in this world and he thinks of Home and ones he loves. It is an awful feeling. We did not know how hard the fight was going to be and you would ask yourself the question, has our artillery done its work, has it smashed his wire, has it broken his trenches, has it destroyed his machine gun emplacement, has it broken down his strong points, has it broken the spirit of the men.[17]

On the PPCLI front, the infantry was faced with one of those awful cases where the artillery had not done its job. As the lead formations rose from their slit trenches and muddy holes, they were mowed down by machine guns left unhindered by the barrage. Yet still the Canadians pushed forward, even after all their company commanders were knocked out. The 49th Battalion on their left had not been able to keep up, so the PPCLI drove deeper on their own, capturing at least five pillboxes.

As infantry officer Robert Graves noted, referring to the Great War in general, "A man's average expectancy of trench service before getting killed or wounded was twice as long as an officer's."[18] Aware of the seemingly suicidal orders that often came from headquarters, officers led from the front, refusing to force their men to go where they would not. While officers learned to remove their distinctive Sam Browne belts before battle, snipers could still tell which men were leading and which were following. One such officer at Passchendaele with the PPCLI was Captain Talbot Papineau, the great-grandson of Louis-Joseph Papineau, leader of the *patriote* rebels of 1837. He had served in the front line for over a year earlier in the war, but had been removed from the infantry battalion because of his father's political connections and the recognition by many that he would be groomed for politics on his return from the war. Papineau rejoined the PPCLI at the front for this battle, unwilling to abandon his men to their fates while he lived a slightly better life in the rear.

Fully bilingual and at ease in both anglophone and francophone cultures, Papineau was a witty, dashing, and intelligent young man. "Papineau endeared himself to me in everything he did," wrote Sergeant P.H. Ferguson of the PPCLI. "He worked as hard as any of us, and in every word and action he showed himself a great gentleman."[19] The captain's star was clearly soaring, and many predicted a rich postwar political career, especially after he had publicly called on his cousin, Henri Bourassa, to support the war and the boys overseas. But it was not to be; Papineau was cut in two by a shell during the offensive on October 30. The PPCLI lost eighty percent of their officers and sixty percent of the rank and file who attacked; it was another bloody day for the regiment. Commanding officer Agar Adamson wrote to his wife:

> The ridge we took is a commanding one and I do not expect the Army (although they ordered us to do so) thought we would be able to hold it, even if able to take it. The higher authorities are themselves out in expressing to us their appreciation of our efforts, but I cannot help wondering if the position gained was worth the awful sacrifice of life.[20]

To the left of the PPCLI, the 49th Battalion suffered as well. Their opening barrage was irregular and ineffective because of the awful conditions, so that in several places along the line, the shells fell short and landed in the midst of the Edmontonians who formed the bulk of the "Fighting Forty-Niners." An accurate German counter-barrage caught the Canadians, too, and the right-front company was almost wiped out before they even left their trenches. While the 49th Battalion took their first objective at Furst Farm, they could go no further as snipers killed them with wild abandon. The battalion went in with 21 officers and 567 other ranks and it lost a staggering 443 men in total.[21] October 30, 1917, was one of the worst days of the war for the 49th Battalion.

The 5th CMR on the left occupied the most difficult position. In front of them lay the swamp of Woodland Plantation, which was strongly defended by a number of machine-gun teams. The strongpoints of Vine Cottages and Vapour Farm dominated the terrain. A little outside of their divisional boundary—in the British sector to the CMR's left—was Source Farm, a machine-gun post that had to fall if the battalion were to make any progress. Two companies were ordered to advance on

Woodland Plantation, but they made little headway against the unsuppressed fire. Despite a curtain of Canadian shells tearing through the mud, the creeping barrage soon began to move away from the infantry as they could not keep up in the dreadful conditions. Men fell left and right, some finding protection in a shell crater, others drowning as they lay unconsciousness in the mud. The attackers went to ground and stayed there in the face of the unceasing enemy fire.

On the far left, two companies of the 5th CMR were led forward by Major George Pearkes to capture Vine Cottages and Vapour Farm, and to establish a position to protect against the enemy at Source Farm if the 63rd British Division could not capture the strongpoint. Pearkes was already an inspirational leader at the age of twenty-nine, having risen from the rank of private, survived several wounds, and received the Military Cross for bravery. He had a reputation for being a hard man to kill. Early in the battle, he was knocked out by a shrapnel wound through the thigh. But he struggled to his feet and led his men through hundreds of metres of mud to their objectives. In the final push, Pearkes took forty men and attacked Vapour Farm, which was little more than a "rotten haysack" bristling with machine guns. They captured the position at the point of a bayonet (and it was the furthest objective captured by the Canadians that day). Holding it, however, would be more difficult. Ammunition was running low, the wounded were piling up, and both flanks were in the air. But the small, ever-dwindling battle group was inspired by their blood-stained leader, with one soldier later remarking, "I would have followed him through Hell if I had to."[22] And they did.

Around 10 A.M., two companies of the 2nd CMR were rushed up as reinforcements, but they became trapped in a deadly German crossfire of bullets and shells and were cut up terribly. The Germans counterattacked against Vapour Farm but had their own problems going through the mud. Pearkes organized a series of resolute defences based on slit trenches manned by only a few riflemen, who would be supported by a Lewis machine-gunner 20 or 30 metres to the rear. Enemy attacks were thrown back twice. Desperately low on ammunition, the infantry crawled through the slime, rifling through the bodies of the fallen to retrieve precious small-arms ammunition, grenades, and Lewis-gun pans. When the amalgamated CMR battle group was relieved, only thirty-seven men and officers of the 5th CMR and eighty-five men and officers of the 2nd CMR stumbled out of the line.[23] Pearkes was awarded the Victoria Cross; he would go on to be a Second World War general and lieutenant governor of British Columbia. Pearkes's significant wartime and postwar accomplishments put into stark relief the loss of men such as Talbot Papineau and the thousands of other promising Canadians killed in the wasteland. What would they have accomplished and contributed to Canada after the war?

THE SECOND PHASE of the battle allowed the Canadians to further drag themselves out of the mud through the use of deliberate bite and hold tactics. The condition of the battlefield was among the worst in the history of warfare, but still the infantry had found ways to reach their objectives. The supporting shellfire had been sporadic, but the gunners were firing in truly debilitating conditions and had been bombarded continuously with counter-battery fire. Although there were countless examples of short shelling and ragged barrages, General Lipsett thought that the gunners "did well under the circumstances."[24] But it was a terrible battle and the Canadian Corps suffered 884 killed and 1,429 wounded, including 130 gassed.[25] In turn, the German regiment holding this front was "finished as a fighting force."[26]

There were likely more casualties that remained unreported, and therefore uncounted, among the hard men at the front. Medical Officer Joseph Hayes noted, "Nearly everybody had been more or less gassed" during the heavy fighting. It took several days for straggling survivors to make their way out of the quagmire and for the lightly wounded to return from hospitals. Heartfelt reunions took place between men who thought their mates had been swallowed by the mud. But as Hayes noted, "Many of the smiles were exchanged through glistening tears. It was a terrible feeling to miss so many familiar faces, friends true and tried for their noble qualities of real manhood. A great affection existed among all ranks because of the magnificent loyalty and devotion to each other such as can never develop in the ordinary pursuits of life."[27] Such elevated diction might have seemed out of place at Passchendaele, but it was the mutual support of comrades as they faced nearly insurmountable odds that had allowed the Canadians not only to endure but also to grind out victory on an unspeakable battlefield where men might be shot and then buried a heartbeat later in the swill of mud and waste.

CHAPTER 23

"THE DEVIL HIMSELF COULDN'T HAVE STOPPED US"

November 6–10, 1917

"Here and there, arms and legs of dead men stick out from the mud, and awful faces appear, blackened by days and weeks under the beating sun," wrote Private A.J. Lapointe of the 22nd Battalion. "I try to turn from these dreadful sights, but wherever I look dead bodies emerge, shapelessly, from the shroud of mud."[1] The Passchendaele battlefield remained a nightmarish mess of rotting corpses, lung-searing gas, and glutinous mud, over which hovered the ever-present spectre of death.

The second phase of Currie's offensive came to a halt on October 30. Hundreds of wounded had pulled themselves into shell holes, where they passed the hours, and then the days, trying not to drown in the mud. Numbness spread to the extremities as men slipped into shock. Others were tortured with agonizing stomach or abdominal wounds, and lay screaming themselves into unconsciousness. Some of the dead were later found having gnawed their fingers off in their pain-induced madness.

Along parts of the front, informal truces were established to allow both sides to collect the bodies of their dead.[2] These temporary ceasefires never lasted more than a few hours, but they had an unreal quality: men who had been killing each other for days now moved about together above the trenches, searching and poking through the debris to find the slain and the near-dead. While temporary truces applied to the wounded, one Canadian officer noted that in trying to bring in the casualties, a number of apparently unwounded Germans tried to surrender. German officers quickly ordered their own troops to fire on the surrendering Germans, and at least one Canadian was hit in the crossfire.[3] Though the small mercy of clearing the dead was afforded by each side to the other, neither the Germans nor the Canadians were ready to give up the battle.

The Germans saturated the front with poison gas in the hope of catching unconscious or exhausted men without their respirators at the ready. Gunners masked the sound of poison gas shells within the cacophony of high explosive barrages. And even if soldiers were alerted to the gas, the force of the high explosions could, as Victor Wheeler of the 50th Battalion attested, blow "respirators ... completely off [their] faces."[4] At other times, the mustard gas lay dormant in the mud, only vapourizing when the sun rose the next morning. Soldiers were gassed without even realizing it, and hundreds were sent to the rear with blindness and terrible blisters that were almost always infected. In this chemically saturated environment, poison gas silently took many of the helpless wounded as they lay immobile and defenceless, indistinguishable from the corpses around them.

Gas was but one more horror in a hideously eviscerated landscape. Day and night, the shells searched the battlefield as soldiers huddled for safety. "It was only by providence that we lived through the bombardment," remembered Private Herbert Cooke of the 75th Battalion. "I think I was never so faithful in prayer to God as I was those last two nights. It made one consider that someone higher than all is caring for you."[5] But hundreds were hit every night by the artillery fire, their bloated bodies added to the flooded landscape.

AFTER THE TWO COSTLY PHASES of the previous week, new forces were needed to push the advance further into enemy lines. The 1st and 2nd Divisions were moved to the front, and all reliefs were completed on November 5. Attack plans were hurried, and the infantry had not had time to carry out extensive battlefield preparations like those at Hill 70 or Vimy. However, in the month before the battle, the

Canadian machine-gunners holding the soggy Passchendaele front. Note the lack of trenches and sandbags. The only advantage the mud offered was that most of the enemy's high explosive shells buried themselves deep in the slough before exploding, thereby saving many lives.

chief object of training was to enforce in "platoon and other commanders … [the importance of] exercising their initiative in dealing with the unforeseen situation, and in the assault and mopping up of isolated strong points."[6] The decentralization of command emphasized in training during the winter of 1916–1917 had become fully ingrained in the Canadian Corps. Victory, they knew, could only be won at the sharp end.

"I was in for three days and we only took in one day's rations. Of course they send us in some rations but the rations party would get blow[n] up and we had no water for three days," wrote Private Henry Savoie, who operated a machine gun during the battle. "But we had took in lots of rum that was the only thing that keep us up."[7] Plastered with mud, soaked to the skin, the infantry lived on rum and cigarettes and whatever rations they could steal from the dead bodies around them. It was very difficult to get hot food from the company cooks in the rear to the soldiers in the front lines, but brave groups of men transported stew or water in large containers or emptied gasoline jars to the front lines. All soldiers remembered drinking water that reeked of gasoline and chlorine. One of the many ironies at Passchendaele was that soldiers—voices raw from countless minor gassings—were constantly thirsty despite being surrounded by water. None of the abundant fluid was drinkable, having been polluted by poison gas and rotting bodies. And so men were killed as they brought forward food and drink to the desperate front-line soldiers. Yet no life was worth losing for a cup of hot soup, even if receiving a jar of rum might have a few old hands thinking long and hard about the need for sacrifice. Despite the risks taken to get supplies to the front, even if a runner did succeed, some of the ravenous, gaunt men found that they could barely stomach food with the stench and sight of rotting bodies assaulting their senses.

Along the front there was a frenzy of activity as jumping-off trenches were prepared and stealth patrols investigated enemy defences—while all remained acutely aware of the looming spectre of an order to attack. This third Canadian set-piece battle would encompass the ruined village of Passchendaele; if the November 6 attack was successful, four days later, a final assault would push out the advance and seize the crest behind the village. The first operation would involve six attacking battalions from the 1st and 6th Brigades, as well as several units on the flank to broaden the attack and draw away enemy fire and reserve formations. While the Canadians were now higher on the ridge than at the beginning of the offensive, the front was still a quagmire and scouting officers spent the night before the battle attempting to locate dry paths through No Man's Land and the enemy's barbed wire. The Germans had their own patrols locating the driest ground, and they situated their machine-gunners to guard the passes.

One of the bizarre features of the battlefield was the porous nature of the front lines between the opposing forces. There were no front-line trenches and so soldiers moved through the muck, slithering from shell hole to shell hole. Officers established forward listening posts and battle posts consisting of groups of heavily armed men who could be rushed forward or backward to fight at a moment's notice, but enemy patrols and raiders moved throughout the lines. It was not uncommon, as well, that rear units bringing up food or ammunition might pass through their own lines mistakenly and blunder into enemy strongpoints, to be shot up or captured.[8]

In one such case, as noted in a German prisoner report, a Canadian private got lost in the dark and was captured by the enemy. The Germans brought the despondent soldier to a dry pillbox, gave him a warm drink, and got him to talk. He revealed that the Canadians would attack on the morning of November 6.[9]

"MY IDEA OF HELL, mother, can't be any worse than Flanders," wrote Bombardier Bert Walker, who had just received his medical papers stating that he would be relieved from front-line duty due to deafness brought on by the unending firing of the guns.[10] Walker was poisoned by mustard gas before the battery could find a replacement, and so he was carried out of the line, temporarily blind and permanently deaf. There were others to replace him. The 1st Division front was supported by 144 18-pounders and 42 4.5-inch howitzers, although on the day of battle only 134 of the former and 33 of the latter remained after enemy pre-battle counter-battery fire had done its work. Despite the heavy losses to the gunners, there was still one 18-pounder for every 8 metres of front and one 4.5-inch howitzer for every 32 metres of front. This high concentration of guns created a dense barrage, and forty Vickers machine guns were allocated to thicken it further; another twelve machine guns would play a mobile role, being moved forward to bring firepower to bear on key parts of the front.[11]

Horses and mules continued to feed the guns with ammunition brought up from the rear. On the 1st Division's front, the machine-gunners fired 730,000 rounds over a two-week period and the artillery unleashed 184,000 shells over an eight-day period. In the Passchendaele battle alone, animals made more than 35,000 trips from the dumps to the gun pits.[12] To sever this essential lifeline at Passchendaele, the Germans deluged the area with shrapnel and poison gas in the hope of killing or debilitating the beasts of burden. Yet through the storm of steel they came, with legs and hoofs scarred and burned from mustard gas, and past the bloated corpses of other animals. The animals' average life expectancy could be measured in weeks. Private J.R. Johnston, who had enlisted when he turned eighteen, remembered the piteous whine of trembling, shell-shocked horses. In his words, they "suffered beyond all description."[13]

On the 1st Division's front, General Macdonell's 1st, 2nd, and 3rd Battalions were ready in the jumping-off trenches by 4 A.M. They would have to cross about 1,100 metres to reach their objectives. As the assault units prepared for battle, the enemy artillery searched their lines. The shuddering of artillery fire in the dark rocked the Canadians' weak trenches, many of which began to collapse. Realizing that even an advance of 50 metres would save lives, senior officers in the 1st, 2nd, and 3rd Battalions pushed forward into No Man's Land, leading their jumping-off forces into the mud to occupy shell craters and any fold in the ground they could find. The battalions sustained a few casualties as the German bombardment lit up behind them, but most of the enemy shells were missing their positions. Senior NCOs moved from crater to crater, dispensing rum and whispers of good luck in the hour before battle.

The Canadians attacked under cover of darkness at 6 A.M. behind a heavy bombardment and creeping barrage, the latter of which consisted of three waves of shellfire, each 230 metres deep, and moving at different speeds—faster on the 1st Battalion's front on the right than on the 2nd and 3rd's to their left because of the nature of the terrain. Even though the Germans had been warned of an attack on November 6, the Canadians' creeping barrage was extremely fierce and one enemy prisoner testified, "The Canadians came over practically in their own barrage and attacked so suddenly that they had [no] opportunity to use their machineguns."[14] Smoke from the gunfire helped to temporarily blind enemy strongpoints and bought precious time for the spearheading forces. Canadian assault troops overran pillboxes and continued their advance underneath the fall of green rockets that German forward defenders had fired to signify an attack. The 2nd Battalion's commander, Lieutenant Colonel L.T. McLaughlin, had told his subordinates to "use their initiative and adapt their formations to the nature of the ground and the character of the opposition that developed."[15]

On the far right of the division's front, the 1st Battalion encountered machinegun fire coming from Graf House, but as this was an anticipated strongpoint, two Stokes mortars had been brought forward with the infantry. Under supporting fire from Lewis guns and grenades, the mortars fired sixteen rapid rounds that stunned the defenders, and a platoon, according to the official report, "easily dealt with the enemy, who were busily engaged in preserving their lives."[16] Objectives began to fall and the forward companies dug in, allowing follow-on units to pass through them and drive into the enemy lines. Camouflaged shell holes and machine-gun nests that had not been located by intelligence contained enemy troops who caused dozens of casualties, but they were overrun as the infantry advanced with fire and movement tactics, dealing with each problem as they encountered it. Even though the set-piece battle was predicated on a rigid artillery plan, the infantry were now routinely manoeuvring within the barrage. Innovation and adaptability were the key to victory, with the Canadians surging around the enemy defenders and attacking them from all directions. Even when ammunition ran low, the Canadians did not hesitate: grabbing the captured machine guns, they turned them around and fired into the enemy lines.

To the 1st Battalion's left, the 2nd Battalion also had to navigate the swampy battlefield, and were forced to compress their forward battle lines into a narrow 80-metre frontage. Having left their weak trenches to slip into No Man's Land, the infantry moved to within 50 metres of the enemy's forward defensive crust. But two companies of 300 or so men could not advance without noise, and the Germans opened up with bursts of machine-gun fire in nervous anticipation, aware that something was happening in the darkness.

As soon as zero hour hit, the 2nd Battalion's lead units shot forward, moving into attack formation: two waves of four skirmish lines each. The first two lines were assault troops, the third was mopping-up forces, and the last was in reserve. Intelligence had located a cluster of six pillboxes spread out in a 100-metre square on the battlefield, which was the Canadians' first objective. The advance was a complicated one and evidenced intricate training; Lewis machine guns and grenades played an important role in clearing positions, but infantry riflemen also engaged their targets from a distance of several hundred metres. The soldiers fired, moved, went to ground, and fired again, to ensure that other sections and platoons could continue the advance. Then they were off again, as other sections laid down suppressing fire on the enemy lines to keep the defenders behind cover instead of shooting down the advancing infantry. Position after position was destroyed or overrun as the Canadians employed these "fire and movement" tactics. While the German defenders seemed demoralized and willing to surrender, they took their toll on the Canadian forward waves: 41 were killed, 211 wounded, and another 28 missing.[17]

At 7:40 A.M., the 1st and 2nd Battalions were on their final objectives. Lewis-gun teams were pushed forward into mutually supporting shell holes, creating a forward crust that would break up enemy counterattacks. On the far left of the 1st Division's front, the 3rd Battalion had experienced a tougher fight with defenders at Vine Cottages, who stubbornly held out to the bitter end, offering "formidable resistance."[18] The entire garrison, including five machine-gun teams, was killed, wounded, or captured.[19]

THE 2ND DIVISION attacked with the 28th, 31st, and 27th Battalions of H.D.B. Ketchen's 6th Brigade on the right side of the Canadian front. The 28th Battalion, on the far left, had flexible orders that depended on the 1st Brigade across the divisional boundary. If their comrades succeeded in passing through the flooded areas, the 28th could go like hell's bells; but if they became bogged down, one company of the 28th would have to set up a defensive flank and pour fire into the enemy lines while the main group assaulted forward. The 1st Brigade hit their objectives, and so the 28th were free to punch forward, although they encountered waist-high mud in places. They advanced into a dense haze and mist that helped to mask their assault.

Fighting within the creeping barrage, the Canadians' three battalions were seemingly supported by "every gun on the Western Front," observed an officer of the 28th Battalion. A German officer on the receiving end wrote, "The explosions of the shells came so thick and fast that it was no longer possible to distinguish between them."[20] Pushing forward within this shower of metal, the Canadians methodically snuffed out the enemy positions.[21] The primary weapons were the rifle, grenade, and Lewis gun, but official reports contained a surprising number of references to fierce bayonet use, such as that of Lieutenant J.A. Cameron of the 31st Battalion, who charged an enemy group and ran through two defenders with his bayonet, causing the survivors to panic and surrender.[22] Another official report noted that the lead waves "freely used the bayonet.… No prisoners were taken," and most of the dead were later found to have "bore the mark of the bayonet."[23] No doubt many of the Canadians' rifles were clogged with mud, but it is also clear that an advance made behind a seventeen-inch steel blade was both reassuring for the attacker and terrifying for those about to be skewered.

As they moved forward, the infantry passed dozens of shredded corpses of Germans who had been caught in the barrage as they had no effective dugouts in the mud in which to seek protection. Nineteen-year-old Sergeant A.O. Hickson remembered stoically accepting what lay ahead: "Most of us would shy away from the thought of being one of the shattered figures we saw too often. A combat man would be a nervous wreck if his imagination was given free reign."[24] Perhaps it was all summed up in the lines of a popular soldiers' song: "The bells of hell ring ting-a-ling, a-ling, a-ling; for you but not for me." The bells rang for too many Canadians on this day.

COUNTLESS ACTS of self-sacrifice by the Canadians at the sharp end allowed the three battalions of the 6th Brigade to pass through Passchendaele and capture both the town and the upper part of the ridge. The defeated Germans made them pay for their success with artillery fire, but the dug-in victors would not be dislodged. The Canadians situated a defence-in-depth and received much-needed time to prepare their positions when the British formation on the flank launched a "dummy assault" and drew fire onto themselves.[25] The forward slopes of the hills were manned by isolated combat groups, each consisting of a few men in a crater with a groundsheet pulled over top. These positions had wide fields of fire, but they were also vulnerable to snipers and artillery fire. The lives of many in the forward units were traded for security against full-scale counterattacks. Behind them, the Canadians set up isolated but mutually protecting defensive nests, as continuous trenches were not sustainable in the muck. Prisoners told the mud-splattered soldiers that the German troops had orders to hold the ridge, "or, if lost, recapture [it] at all costs."[26]

The Canadians dug in, cleaning the mud off their Lewis guns and Lee-Enfields and laying out their grenades within easy reach. Then they waited. During the rest of the day, the German 11th Division refrained from a full counterattack but laid down heavy machine-gun fire all along the front. Hostile aircraft circled in the air and the Canadians turned their Lewis guns on them—this ineffectual act being more to relieve frustration than to comply with orders demanding that a steady stream of fire be maintained to try to scare them off. These airplanes strafed the forward trenches, but most of the infantry kept out of sight in their craters, hunkering down under muddy groundsheets and munching on cold rations as the planes circled overhead like angry hornets.[27]

At around 6 P.M., forward observers could see the enemy forming up for a counterattack. SOS rockets fired from specially adapted rifle grenades alerted Canadian gunners, who found their mark and scattered these forces. Throughout the rest of the day, the Canadian artillery laid down a protective barrage and carried out a neutralization program on the enemy's batteries.[28] Communication from the front lines to the rear was carried out by power buzzers, which transmitted only ten words per minute. The task of expediting communication again fell to the runners, who were handed dispatches and sent in pairs to the rear: "We never expected to see any of them again, for they dashed fearlessly into the German barrage that was falling in rear of the front lines," wrote signaller William Breckenridge.[29]

Prisoners were also ordered back through the barrage, dodging shells and scrambling from shell hole to shell hole. More than 1,000 prisoners were captured by the Canadian Corps during the third phase of the operation, and many of them were involved in carrying out wounded Canadians. One prisoner from the 38th Fusilier Regiment of the 11th Division informed his captors that German officers had told their men that the Canadians "have instructions to take no prisoners and show the utmost cruelty to any Germans that fall into their hands."[30] The man was no doubt grateful to find that the officers had been lying, and that he was not to be summarily executed.

By the end of November 6, the Canadian Corps had captured and consolidated Passchendaele village, and were not likely to be dislodged by enemy counterattack. Flights by aircraft from the 21st Squadron, RFC, helped to apprise the divisional headquarters of further attacks being readied by the enemy, and aerial photographs taken at low altitude—some from as close as 100 metres—confirmed ground intelligence reports. Despite poor weather and aggressive German fire, slow-moving RFC observation planes radioed in more than seventy separate calls for artillery to fire at targets of opportunity.[31] Over the next five days, the Canadian gunners would fire tens of thousands of shells in an attempt to both hold the rubble and expand the Canadian front to make it more secure. In fact, records show that by battle's end, over a period of less than a month, the Canadian gunners fired an astonishing 1,453,056 shells in support of the operations.[32] This was indeed a storm of steel.

Within this maelstrom, Currie moved on to the fourth phase of the offensive, ordering one final assault to expand the line to the north of the village. Behind a thunderous barrage and advancing against dispirited troops, four battalions from the 1st and 2nd Divisions threw the Germans off the remaining part of the ridge on November 10. The German infantry fought poorly, with more than 1,150 making their way to prisoner of war cages by the end of the day.[33] One proud Canadian remarked, "We went through the bloody village and over the hill like all hell alight; the devil himself couldn't have stopped us."[34]

But if the devil could not have stopped the Canadians, the Germans certainly gave them hell. While the ground defenders meekly surrendered what was left of the ridge, their artillery made the Canadians pay for their final advance, bombarding them all day long. Canadian guns could do little to suppress the enemy fire as they were still down the ridge and locked fast in the mud. The Germans also flooded the skies with their greatest concentration of fighter squadrons in weeks, which not only fired on the advancing Canadians but also denied the Canadian gunners the invaluable guidance they normally received from their RAF observatory aircraft.

The experienced commanding officer of the 8th Battalion reported that the enemy bombardment on November 10 was "the heaviest I have ever known and coming from every direction except straight upwards."[35] The Canadians sustained more than 1,000 casualties in this limited attack, the scope of the assault making little difference to those annihilated under enemy shellfire. But Haig had his victory, and the offensive was called to an end.

SERGEANT L.M. GOULD of the 102nd Battalion recounted the Canadians' experience at Passchendaele: "We had just done the little that we had been set to do, but had suffered casualties out of all proportion to our task, and that it is which makes the memory of Passchendaele a nightmare."[36] Passchendaele broke many men; those who fought there would never be the same. "It was really hell on earth," recounted

A British tank mired in the muck at Passchendaele. This forlorn image sums up the terrible reputation of the battle that one Canadian called "hell on earth."

one Canadian gunner, while infantryman Tommy Adams of the 85th Battalion saw the battlefield as "a complete nightmare of mud, slush and everything else. It was frightful, and if I'd been in for a week I'm sure I'd have gone mad."[37] Despite the horror of combat suffered by those thrust into the charnel house, the Canadian Corps had once again reaffirmed its reputation as shock troops. But it had been done with the assistance of the rest of the BEF. British, Australian, and New Zealand units, through previous offensives, had put the Canadians within striking distance, and during the four phases of the battle, Currie's Corps had been supported on their flanks by other national formations. The Canadian logistical and artillery units had been augmented by the British, too. Notwithstanding this support, it had been the Canadian infantry who delivered victory at the sharp end. The success achieved via careful planning, artillery and infantry cooperation, and flexible tactics revealed the effectiveness of the Canadian attack doctrine. Currie had not only resuscitated a dying campaign, but had likely saved Haig's career.

"ONLY THOSE that saw it will ever know just what it cost to take Passchendaele Ridge, in [terms of] sheer grit and bull-doggedness," wrote infantryman Garnet Dobbs.[38] The four Canadian set-piece battles here were intricately planned by Currie and brilliantly executed by his men on the front lines. Currie gave full credit for the victory to those at the sharp end. Looking back on the battle, the corps commander remarked proudly, "The fighting spirit of the men, tempered by discipline, developed by training, and enhanced by the confidence in themselves and their officers created a year of unbroken success."[39] For the soldiers on the field, however, the campaign amounted to little more than mud and blood. "Men go to their deaths cursing the imagined stupidity of a staff who are working day and night to help them," wrote D.E. Macintyre, whose comments on the St. Eloi battle a year and a half earlier applied equally to the Passchendaele mud campaign.[40] None of the men knew of Currie's protestations to Haig, or of his stubborn refusal to attack before enough guns could be marshalled to protect the infantry who would go over the top. Instead, the soldiers saw only the misery around them, and another 16,404 casualties for the corps—almost the exact number that Currie had forecast in the hope of changing Haig's mind. Of this total, 12,403 were sustained between October 26 and November 11, and the remaining number before and after the battle. The ratio of killed to wounded—one to two instead of the usual one to three—was higher at Passchendaele because the wounded often drowned after being rendered unconscious.[41]

Many of the Canadian Tommies, men who "would never be the same again," blamed the general who planned the operation and "sent us to appalling sacrifice."[42] In the eyes of many of the rank and file, that callous general was Sir Arthur Currie, rather than the one who gave the order from further to the rear, Sir Douglas Haig. But the commander-in-chief did not escape condemnation. When Winston Churchill referred to Passchendaele as a "forlorn expenditure of valour and life without equal in futility," his voice was but one in a chorus that accused Haig of squandering approximately 275,000 British and Dominion soldiers in the wasteland of Flanders over the 109-day campaign.[43] The battle stands in the popular memory of the Great War as a monument to the seemingly intractable stupidity and callousness of the generals—especially Haig. While recent historians have placed more blame on the politicians—men such as Lloyd George, who could, and perhaps should, have forced Haig to call off the battle."[44] None of the armies escaped from Passchendaele unscathed.

Was the Passchendaele campaign worth the sacrifice? For the soldiers at the front, there was no escape from the misery. While the battles at Passchendaele were not as fierce as those on the Somme, the conditions were unspeakable. And at the cost of approximately 275,000 British casualties, in comparison to some 220,000 German losses, the attackers again suffered more than the defenders.[45] But it was the Germans who could least afford these losses. "Unimaginable things had been suffered and performed by the troops and unimaginable were the demands made upon the nerves of the commanders," wrote German general Hermann von Kuhl. "Neither the Somme nor the battles of Arras had reached the ferocity of the struggle in Flanders."[46] Through blockades and battles on many fronts, Germany was being bled white. Starvation rations at home were leaving a nation weakened and increasingly unable to provide the necessary millions of munitions and weapons of war. Despite the bloodletting, however, few could foresee an end to the war any time soon, as the battered and spent nations had suffered too much to lay down their arms: only victory could assuage the grief caused by the terrible casualty lists. And so all nations, with their million-man armies, steeled themselves to fight to the bitter end.

CHAPTER 24

"EDUCATED LARGELY BY OUR OWN MISTAKES"

November 1917–March 1918

"The year 1917 has been a glorious year for the Canadian Corps," wrote Sir Arthur Currie to William Hearst, premier of Ontario. "We have taken every objective from the enemy we started for and have not had a single reverse. Vimy, Arleux, Fresnoy, Avion, Hill 70 and Passchendaele all signify hard fought battles and notable victories. I know that no other Corps has had the same unbroken series of successes. All this testifies to the discipline, training, leadership and fine fighting qualities of the Canadians." Currie only regretted the high casualties sustained by his "gallant comrades."[1] The record of the Canadian Corps surely revealed its soldiers to be the shock troops of the BEF, but those at the sharp end had far different concerns in the aftermath of the battle for the bog.

The more than 16,000 casualties suffered at Passchendaele had dulled the corps' blade, with morale among front-line troops having taken a significant blow during that terrible month of fighting. Private E.W. Russell of the 5th Battalion witnessed a veteran soldier, who was returning from a tour in the front lines, snap under the pressure. When the survivors limped to the rear, the veteran "made a hole in the ground, drew out the safety pin from a Mills bomb, put it in the hole, his foot over it, and thereby lost a leg."[2] He had calculated the odds and was willing to trade a leg for freedom from hellholes like Passchendaele. Russell was understandably shaken.

In the aftermath of battle, the regular grumbling and grousing of soldiers began to take on a sharper edge. William Antliff, a former commerce student at McGill University and a member of No. 9 Canadian Field Ambulance, remarked in one revealing letter that, no matter what the politicians or generals were telling the public back home, "In the opinion of a great many [fighting men], we can never hope to break thru in the West." He believed that talks should be started to find a peaceful solution, and declared, "Put to a vote of the Tommies, I guarantee it would be passed by a majority of 9 to 1. Of course it is all very well to say let the war go on when one is sitting in a comfortable chair before the fire ... but it is a different thing when one is a poor infantry man who has to go into a living hell which is his lot every time he goes over the top!"[3] Never had morale been lower in the elite Canadian Corps, or in the larger BEF; British war journalist Philip Gibbs, who observed the British force in the months following Passchendaele, remarked: "For the first time the British Army lost its spirit of optimism, and there was a sense of deadly depression among many officers and men with whom I came in touch. They saw no ending of the war, and nothing except continuous slaughter."[4]

The Canadians had been pushed to the limits of endurance, and many felt the front-line soldiers had been abandoned by their commanders, who rested safely in the rear. Rumours circulated about Currie's eagerness to throw his troops against the enemy to improve his own reputation among the other Allied commanders. Canadian soldiers were increasingly accusing Currie of being a butcher. However, while Currie's reputation suffered among his men, that of his corps soared. With its successes at Hill 70 and Passchendaele, the Canadian Corps solidified its reputation within the BEF as a fighting formation that could be called upon to deliver victory. "We look back on the year 1917 with a great deal of pride," wrote Currie, "feeling quite sure that in that period the Canadian Corps more than did its share in helping to win the war."[5] Indeed it did, but the 40,000 casualties sustained since April had put a terrible strain on the corps. Not enough men remained in the training camps to make up for the debilitating losses, and enlistment in Canada had slowed to a mere trickle since the new year.

In January 1918, the CEF consisted of 6,147 officers and 133,768 NCOs and men in France, for a total of 139,915. The losses to date had been horrendous, and a tally of numbers in medical records on January 31, 1918, revealed that nearly

150,000 Canadians had been killed, wounded, or taken prisoner since the start of the war.[6] The breakdown was as follows:

Killed in Action	25,367
Died of Wounds	8,492
Died of Disease	1,787
Wounded	103,669
Prisoners of War	2,753
Presumed Dead	3,694
Missing	1,247
Total	**147,009**

Prime Minister Borden had visited Canadian soldiers after their victory at Vimy, and had not shied away from the wounded in hospitals. Talking to the amputees and men who had been wounded two or three times and were set to return to the front, he had come away shaken. If new recruits could not be found, these wounded heroes would be forced to keep fighting until they were maimed, killed, or driven insane. He resolved to spread the burden among all Canadians, and on August 29, 1917, his government invoked the Military Service Act, which would bring about conscription of young men for service. Unable to form a coalition government with Sir Wilfrid Laurier's Liberals, who realized that support of conscription would effectively annihilate their power base in Quebec, Borden set his will to fight the bitterest election campaign in Canadian history.

Borden formed a new Unionist party of Conservatives and Liberals, which supported conscription and weakened Laurier's Liberals by siphoning off many of his English candidates. With vitriolic accusations ringing across the country in newspapers and election campaigns—on the one hand about the traitors of Quebec not pulling their weight and on the other about the "Prussians of Ontario" forcing war on all—the nation was on the verge of tearing itself apart. While the war effort had unified many parts of English Canada in a crusade to the bitter end, in which any price would be paid and any burden shouldered, it was also bringing out the worst passions of intolerance and divisiveness. No compromises would be made: too much blood had been spilt.

The election revealed fault lines along linguistic, cultural, and regional divides. English were set against French, but the bases for division were not only cultural and linguistic. Labour unions suggested that if conscription were to force men to fight, a conscription of wealth should also be required—meaning that the wealthy should divulge their riches to the government in the name of the war effort. The well-connected scurried to their members of Parliament, calling in favours and warning about the downfall of democracy, capitalism, and a Western way of life. Outside the cities, farmers were doing their best to feed the nation and the Allied armies. They rightly pointed out that they could not do so without the assistance of their children, especially their sons. Anxious for the farmers' vote, the government promised to exempt their sons from conscripted service. Many farmers voted for the Union government, only to find a few months later that the government would break its promise and begin snatching their sons for service to fight overseas.[7]

Pulling out all the stops, the government offered enfranchisement to women who had a relative serving overseas. Some women had been fighting for the vote for years, and it would have come at some point, but it was certainly hastened by the war effort. Although it was sold as a reward for women who had done their bit in supporting the country, many accused the government of simply creating new votes for itself, since it was almost assured that the vast majority would support the soldiers overseas and the Union government's primary platform of conscription. In a far more controversial measure, the government rescinded the enfranchisement rights of immigrants who had arrived in the last fifteen years from "enemy countries" (those now at war with Canada). Most immigrants voted Liberal, and this disenfranchisement was a shocking display of political skulduggery—and perhaps the most far-reaching anti-democratic act in twentieth-century political history. Most soldiers were unconcerned, but Henry Baldwin, a steadfast Liberal who was later a political secretary to Prime Minister W.L.M. King, wrote while serving in uniform overseas, "The Canadian elections were in my opinion the most corrupt event in our history. To have enfranchised all those women—relations of soldiers, and denied the vote to Aliens and the womenfolk of Anties [those who were anti-war] was unforgivable. I cannot see where even a Union government built on this rotten foundation can succeed."[8]

The soldiers put up candidates for members of Parliament, and a number of officers were eventually elected. Canadians overseas were lectured to as part of the campaign process, and the Liberals objected that they could often not find anyone to
speak on their behalf. Thousands of underage soldiers were allowed to vote, their
record of service trumping their illegal voting age. "Politics to us front line soldiers
was rather academic," wrote Private Victor Wheeler. "However, if a National Election
was unavoidable in war time, we men wanted to see sent to Ottawa the Party we
believed would be most likely to prosecute Canada's part in the war with maximum
vigour and effectiveness."[9] Soldiers voted overwhelmingly for the Union government—to a level of ninety percent—and they were even allowed to assign their votes
to key ridings, which helped to sway some tight races towards Union victories.

As part of the campaign, Currie was asked by the Unionists to support conscription. The Canadian general had tried to stay clear of political issues as corps commander, but he was certainly in favour of having more men at the front. Without
them, his beloved corps would inevitably be forced to disband divisions. Currie
noted in a letter to J.J. Creelman, one of his former artillery officers, now back in
Canada:

> The men who are here now are committed until peace is declared. If no oth-
> ers are sent to help them they can look forward to nothing else but to be killed
> or permanently maimed. Many of our men have already been wounded three
> or four times. Yet the exigencies of the service deemed that they be again sent
> to the firing line.[10]

When some of Currie's statements in defence of conscription were printed in conservative newspapers, Liberal campaigners attacked the corps commander, trying to
discredit him as a callous incompetent who had wasted the lives of his men in brutal tactics and battles. Of course he needed more men after spending their lives so
freely, they thundered. Currie was outraged by these false accusations, and urged the
government to deny them officially.[11] He found it incredible that while his corps was
recognized as an elite formation, and he personally had received gallantry awards
and international recognition for his leadership, his own "countrymen should do
their best to knife [him] in the back."[12] For Currie, it was clear that he had enemies

both in front of him and behind. After this experience, the general harboured a life-long distrust of politicians and a refusal to engage them at their "dirty game," as he saw it. It was an honourable, if naive, stance for an important public figure to take, and would later leave him susceptible to further unscrupulous public attacks.

Despite the Union election victory—which was convincing across the country except in the province of Quebec, where the vote was overwhelmingly against conscription—several months would pass before any of these new men were trained and ready for combat. Some 24,000 conscripts would eventually serve at the front, and be instrumental in shoring up the ragged Canadian infantry battalions by the last months of the war. Tens of thousands more would have been essential replacements had the war gone into 1919, as almost all generals and politicians predicted at the time of the vote.

IN EARLY 1918, the British War Office, anxious for more men to strengthen the depleted BEF, began to pressure the Canadian overseas ministry to establish an army of two corps. The BEF comprised sixty-one infantry divisions in eighteen corps, which moved within five armies.[13] While British divisions formed the core of the BEF, the force also included five Australian divisions as well as one New Zealand, two American, two weak Portuguese, and four Canadian. The ten dominion divisions of Anzacs and Canadians were considered shock troops, although there were at least another dozen hard-hitting British divisions, including the 9th, 29th, 50th, 51st, and Guards Divisions.

Despite the effectiveness of these formations, the British had been forced to cut the strength of each of their divisions from twelve to nine battalions to free up troops for new divisions, and—in a move almost as detrimental to divisional *esprit de corps*—to juggle battalions and brigades, transferring them from their divisional "homes" to new units. To find new infantrymen, an astonishing total of 141 BEF battalions were broken up—comprising almost three times the total fighting strength of the Canadian Corps' infantry battalions.[14] These changes were absolutely devastating for morale, as long-service units were dismantled and orphaned men, many of whom became demoralized and disgruntled, were sprinkled throughout the ravaged British fighting units. The move clearly indicated to every soldier that

Britain was desperately short of men, no matter what the propagandists might say about the fighting British bulldog spirit and an enemy on its last legs.

To address the imbalance among BEF divisions, the British War Office pressured the Canadian Corps to make similar changes. It was to follow suit by reducing its infantry divisions from twelve battalions to nine, and then shuffle the surplus battalions of its four divisions at the front, which, when combined with Garnet Hughes's 5th Division in England, would eventually form two corps, each consisting of three weak divisions. Many Canadian politicians and soldiers wished to follow the War Office's suggestion, as it would create a multi-corps Canadian army. The command would surely have gone to Currie, thus making him the only dominion-born army commander in the BEF. Rising to this position would have been an enormous honour for Currie. In fact, it was even rumoured that Lloyd George had toyed with the idea of removing Haig and making Currie commander of the entire BEF, with the Australian general Sir John Monash as his chief of staff. But Currie did not believe it would be wise for him to replace Haig, as the British general still engendered respect among the troops, and it was unlikely that the British professional officer class would have served readily under a colonial; however, that Lloyd George even entertained the thought was an indication of the Canadian Corps commander's elevated status in the minds of British generals and politicians.[15]

Yet even as he was feted by the British during intense discussions in England in February, Currie was not blinded by the accolades. Surprising friends and foes, he fought against the reduction in battalions in the four main Canadian divisions, making the difficult case that diluting the Canadian Corps' strength and its cadre of experienced officers would only weaken its formidable striking power.[16] Showing his political acumen by meeting with soldiers and politicians, Currie got his way and even broke up the 5th Division in February, which he used to reinforce his forces throughout 1918. The surplus of men enabled Currie to add 100 infantrymen to each battalion; these infantrymen, along with the conscripts coming from Canada, would be essential during the grinding battles in the final year of the war.

His refusal to dilute the Canadian divisions left Currie with almost 12,000 infantrymen per division, in comparison to a British division's 8,000. This total referred to units at full strength, which was never the case, but even when a unit went into battle at a strength of sixty percent—which was increasingly common in the last year of the war—the higher number of soldiers in the corps gave the Canadians more men at the sharp end. The over-strength Canadian divisions, which now numbered almost 22,000 men each, in comparison to about 15,000 for a British division, would prove essential in the climactic battles of the Hundred Days offensive in the war's final months, as attacks required that units pass through one another to prevent the momentum from being lost. Canadian brigadiers could, and did, throw their extra battalion into the line to support success or prevent failure, something the British could not achieve with their smaller forces.

While Currie's decision against creating a Canadian army was unpopular among officers aching for a promotion, it was undoubtedly the right one. Many of these "unwanted" officers—those waiting in England for a command, including much of the senior staff of the 5th Division—had powerful connections. Currie paid the price for his stand, and remarked that the "air in London ... was filled with rumour and suspicion."[17] Another commentator noted at the time that because of Currie's uncompromising position in favour of quality rather than quantity—the latter of which would have led only to unnecessary deaths—"slander had never been so reckless, unreason never so wild, suspicion never so cruel."[18] All of this venom was directed at Currie. It took moral courage for the corps commander to refuse the laurels offered and withstand the pressure executed, but he held to his convictions. Currie's refusal to weaken his Canadian Corps, and to ensure the combat efficiency of his fighting force, may have been the single most difficult and important decision of his career.

Napoleon had written that, in battle, God was on the side of the big battalions. He was probably correct, although there have been countless smaller armies in history that have defeated larger, more disorganized ones. But modern warfare required bodies. Even when forces were winning, they were always losing men. The combat power of fighting forces hinged, in Currie's mind, on three important factors: sufficient manpower, increased firepower, and a refined attack doctrine. Fortunately, by early 1918, Currie had solved his manpower problem, but he also needed to implement structural changes in the corps to further increase combat power and flexibility.

The need for more firepower in the Canadian Corps had been evident since the beginning of the war, and improvements had consistently been made in this area. By 1916, the weight of artillery had reached the point where attackers could make some headway by suppressing enemy strongpoints and clearing barbed-wire obstacles. The next year had seen a refinement of artillery tactics, especially in conjunction with the infantry's use of weapons. During the first two and a half years of the war, the machine gun had been a devastating defensive weapon, but in 1917, it was incorporated into the attack doctrine to give the infantry control over their own firepower assets. Heavy machine guns were used to thicken up creeping barrages or saturate the logistical lines with curtains of lead; light Lewis machine guns had proven invaluable in enabling the infantry to suppress enemy fire in battles at Vimy, Hill 70, and Passchendaele. The artillery barrage was essential to victory, but Currie also recognized the importance of the machine gun and he demanded more of these crucial weapons.

To better utilize the firepower of his machine guns, Currie amalgamated his independent machine-gun companies into larger, more powerful machine-gun battalions in early 1918. These four battalions—one per division—were three times as large as their British counterparts, with the Canadian unit now consisting of 1,039 men and sixty-four machine guns. During the multiple German offensives of March and April 1918, in which the Canadian Corps at one point held one-fifth of the entire British line, Currie added another thirty-two guns no longer needed by the defunct 5th Division in England, which raised the strength of these battalions to ninety-six heavy machine guns.[19] Each of the four divisional machine-gun battalions could now offer devastating firepower when coordinated against limited objectives. These machine guns, organized into sixteen six-gun batteries, were essential in the consolidation phase of the battle, but could also offer devastating fire against targets of opportunity.

At the same time, more light machine guns were issued to the fighting units at the sharp end. By May, the Canadian Corps had equipped all infantry platoons with two Lewis-gun teams, and all men underwent a short course of training in how to operate the guns. As a result of further restructuring, the platoon dropped in strength to about forty and consisted of a lieutenant, two sergeants, two corporals, two lance corporals, and thirty-three privates. A platoon now consisted of two half-platoons of roughly twenty men, each of which had a Lewis-gun team and a balanced complement of riflemen and rifle grenadiers.[20] The grenadiers reverted to riflemen since rifle-grenade fire had greater range, and all infantrymen now carried grenades into battle. While these new formations, comprising about forty men, were smaller than the fifty-strong platoons of previous years, the enhanced firepower made up for the loss of manpower. The two half-platoons would work together on the battlefield, supporting each other with overlapping fields of fire. The increased firepower meant that the Canadian infantrymen, operating in smaller subunits but ultimately better supported within the larger battalions, had significantly more striking power than they had wielded earlier in the war.

In addition to amplifying the Canadians' machine-gun power, Currie had also augmented their artillery. In September of the previous year, the corps commander

INFANTRY BATTALION, 1918

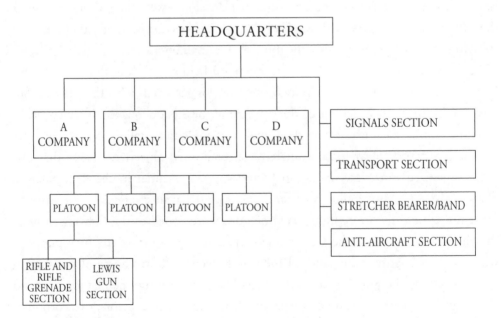

had poached the artillery and mortars of the 5th Division, still training in England at the time. This gain had increased Currie's arsenal at the front to 350 field and heavy guns, manned by 20,000 gunners.[21] These extra guns—in effect, the four Canadian infantry divisions were supported by five divisions' worth of artillery— allowed corps headquarters to control greater firepower assets and apply them where intelligence indicated. The Canadian Corps' ratio of 6.3 guns per 1,000 infantry- men in 1916 had doubled to 12 guns by 1918.[22]

Other structural changes to the artillery included the addition of two trench mor- tar batteries, one light and one heavy, to each division. The heavy 6-inch mortars were of limited use on the open battlefield since they were difficult to move forward and keep supplied (even with the addition of a mobile platform), but the infantry understood the importance of the light 3-inch, which could be more easily trans- ported to bring plunging fire down on a strongpoint. The additional mortar fire- power was appreciated in battle, even if it was not relied upon, and it became another useful weapon for counter-battery work and clearing barbed wire.[23]

To support the sharp end, Currie increased the size of his engineering battalions, a change that came into full effect at the end of May 1918. The resulting 3,000- strong brigade per division (in comparison to the British brigade of 700 men) gave each divisional commander greater flexibility in employing his engineers to support the all-important logistical system by building roads, pontoons, and railways that allowed the infantry to move forward rapidly during the preparation phase, during the course of battle, and as they were exploiting success.[24] The enlarged engineering brigades, which had swallowed the pioneer (work) battalions and most of the tun- nelling companies, were now to carry out much of the work that previously had fallen to the infantry. Relieved of having to dig kilometres of trenches or fill tens of thousands of sandbags, the infantry could devote more time to training for upcoming battles.

To feed Mars, the Canadian Corps added two mechanical transport companies to the order of battle, which provided about 100 more trucks than were available to a British corps.[25] New workshop units further greased the sinews of war. With trucks running almost twenty-four hours a day and over shell-pocked roads in the dark, mechanical work was constantly needed. All of these changes to the corps were increasing its combat effectiveness and making strides towards Currie's goal of transforming the Canadians Corps into "as self-contained an institution as possible."[26]

Concurrent with these structural changes within the corps, Currie had another hard look at how his forces were functioning in battle. As in the winter of 1916–1917, the Canadians again returned to the classroom to study the previous year's fighting. "As far back as Vimy, the [General] Staff had earned encomiums by the excellence of its organisation, but we had learned many things in a hard school since Vimy," wrote Sergeant Ralf Sheldon-Williams. "We had been educated largely by our own mistakes."[27] Questionnaires circulated among battalions, brigades, and divisions to identify the lessons of battle learned at Passchendaele. The machine gun and artillery were consistently acknowledged as the weapons that had paved the way to victory. In contrast, the tank was almost ignored, likely because the Canadians had had so little experience working with it, and when they had done so, as at Vimy, the tanks had failed to overcome the broken ground. There was also no champion of the tank at Currie's headquarters, and battlefield examples from outside the family—the primary one being the Third Army's tank breakthrough at Cambrai in November–December 1917, which had been strongly rebuked by German counter-attacking forces—lessened the apparent exploitation value of tanks. Betraying a conservatism not normally associated with the Dominion troops, the Canadians would stick with the weapons that had got them this far.

THE ENTIRE CORPS STRUCTURE continued to exert a strong influence on the combat effectiveness of units in battle. The Canadians, like the Australians, had a permanent corps structure. British corps, in contrast, did not have permanent divisions; instead, the divisions were posted to a corps headquarters for a time and then moved elsewhere, like cards shuffled in a deck. "I am constantly being told by divisions moving from corps to corps and from army to army that they are being taught different doctrines as they move from one command to another," wrote Guy Dawnay, the deputy chief of staff at British army GHQ. Lieutenant General Ivor Maxse, one of the finest Imperial generals of the war and an acknowledged expert trainer of his men, revealed the incoherence of the British policy when he noted that, in a period of less than a year, thirty divisions had passed through his corps.[28]

In contrast, the Canadian Corps' permanent structure allowed the four divisions and their staffs to get to know one another. They also worked together with the corps headquarters, a relationship that became less strange and foreign as time went on. Currie believed that while the Canadian Corps was "technically an Army Corps of the British Army, [it] differed from other Army Corps in that it was an integral tactical unit, moving and fighting as a whole, retaining the same Canadian troops though British Divisions and troops were often attached to it."[29] The "splendid organization" of Currie's Corps, in the words of one officer, fostered "a good under-standing ... between the various formations making up the Canadian Corps."[30] Brigadier General Ox Webber, a professional British soldier who was the last of Currie's brilliant GSO1 staff officers, remarked, "The Canadian Corps was an organization. It had life; there was a family feeling present. British Corps was a machine to supply the necessary formations ... the British Corps had no life."[31]

Lessons could be imparted more easily within this cohesive organization, as demonstrated by the Currie and McNaughton reforms after the Somme. Other advantages inherent in the corps' separate, self-contained structure ranged from a greater control over the flow of reinforcements to an ability to establish independ-ent training schools. The organization was not without its rivalries, of course, nor its dysfunctional relations, but the structure provided a context for learning, dissem-ination, and progress. The Canadians' permanent corps structure was far superior to the empty British corps shell.

The corps' structure also allowed for the creation of a stronger sense of Canadian identity—a sensibility reinforced by the rise of more Canadians to higher positions, from NCOs to subalterns to senior officers, and of course by Currie's assuming com-mand of the corps. British accents began to be replaced by the many dialects from across Canada. E.L.M. Burns, a junior officer during the war, believed that the Canadians had their "sentiments of nationality greatly intensified in the war, [and increasingly wanted] to fight all together in a homogeneous Canadian higher forma-tion."[32] The Canadians almost always fought side by side, and when they hit together they punched far above their weight. Would Vimy or Passchendaele have been as well remembered as Canadian victories if half of the units had been British? In truth, a good number of supporting units were in fact not Canadian, but the Canadian Corps was a recognizable central structure that incorporated other

Imperial units into its fold, rather than the other way around, which allowed for greater recognition of Canadian wartime deeds by Imperial and Canadian newsmakers, propagandists, soldiers, politicians, and citizens back in Canada.

Perhaps almost as important as the corps' individuated structure was the view many Canadian soldiers held of themselves as an elite force. The corps' publicity machine, orchestrated by Lord Beaverbrook and his Canadian War Records Office, disseminated stories of heroism and endurance, a task made all the easier by the string of Canadian operational victories since Vimy.[33] As part of the development of a unique identity within the BEF, Canadians and others sometimes attributed the corps' successes to national characteristics held by or forged in the Dominion troops, who had carved out a civilization from a rugged land of snow and ice. "There seems to be a great difference between a Canuck and a British Tommy, we seem to be more free and easy among ourselves in a distinctly Canadian way," opined Corporal John Becker. "The Tommy does not seem to understand our bluff friendliness, they are much more reserved.... Mind you, they are downright good fellows but they need a couple of years in Canada to put some backbone in them."[34] Currie, too, was not above promoting this Canadian uniqueness, declaring:

> Our men are full of resource and when a difficulty or situation confronts which has not been provided for, they are not the kind to stand around and do nothing simply because they have "no instructions." It is always well in such circumstances to do something, and the natural common sense, which is such a pronounced Canadian characteristic, usually tells one the best thing to do nine times out of ten. Then our chaps are peculiarly quick to learn, and they are not casual.... Our fellows are also full of grit, determination, and initiative. Where there is a will, there is a way, and with us difficulties are made only to be overcome. I can give so many instances to show where the initiative of the Canadians has helped greatly.[35]

Many Canadians played up this frontier spirit and uniqueness. Toronto-born Private Ronald MacKinnon told his father that "we tell the 'Tommies' stories about wolves and bears and climbing up trees to sleep at night, so they must think we are a rough lot."[36]

The Canadian troops believed that they were a distinct force from the British. Accounts of Canadian swagger and nonconformity were rife in soldiers' letters and published accounts; Arthur Chute, for example, an artillery officer from Lunenburg, Nova Scotia, noted that he and his comrades refused "to be hammered into automatons" through drill.[37] And Corporal Hugh Monaghan remarked that in the Canadian Corps, "discipline was necessary and always enforced, but there was an easy camaraderie between officers and men that the old line British troops never understood or wished to copy."[38]

The Canadian soldier, according to Lieutenant Herbert McBride, "was better educated [than his British counterparts] … has lived a freer and more varied life and, as a result, possesses that initiative and individual ingenuity."[39] The flip side of the Canadians' fiercely nationalistic pride in their armed force was the need some felt to denigrate the British. It was not uncommon for Canadians to refer uncharitably to the British as "Woodbine divisions" or "Woodbine units," after the undesirable and cheapest cigarettes that often went up in flames while being smoked.[40] This maligning of the British was no doubt due in part to the Canadians' self-satisfaction about their series of victories in 1917, which contrasted starkly with the British operational failures, but the behaviour also evidenced an emerging sense of distinctiveness, founded to some extent on a corresponding process of disparagement.

"The Corps became a sacred word…. Men felt a strong devotion to Canada and the Corps," wrote Gunner Wilfred Kerr.[41] Currie put no less stock in the Canadian Corps and the men who formed its lifeblood: "Confidence in each other is an outstanding feature, and without confidence you cannot win many battles. Then the morale is very high. This is owing chiefly to the record of victories won. Our Corps has been uniformly very successful. The men have tasted victory, and nothing but victory will satisfy them."[42] Such a devotion to the corps, and the sense that Canadians were a part of something special, would be tested in the cauldron of battle that would mark 1918, the most devastating and final year of the war.

CHAPTER 25

BACKS TO THE WALL

The German Peace Offensive,
March–May 1918

1917 had been a disastrous year for the Allies. Although the Canadians had won significant victories at Vimy, Hill 70, and Passchendaele, the French armies had mutinied and, even after they recovered, morale was fragile at best; the Italians were hemorrhaging men at a crippling rate, had been soundly defeated at the Battle of Caporetto in late October, and were resorting to mass executions to keep soldiers in the line; the British Army had endured a series of costly defeats, with the Arras and Passchendaele campaigns resulting in terrible casualties; and while much hope rested on the United States to tip the balance, its forces had not yet arrived at the front in great numbers. Far worse, however, the Russian army and nation were in full revolt, with Communist forces vying for control against weakened government supporters, and having all but pulled out of the war against Germany. Although the ponderous Russian armies had been incompetently led, their loss to the Allied cause was nothing short of devastating.

With Germany soon to knock Russia out of the war, the German high command of generals Erich Ludendorff and Paul von Hindenburg turned their attention to the west, concentrating their forces against the British and French, who had moved to the strategic defensive in early 1918 in preparation for a German onslaught. The Germans planned an offensive aimed at knocking the Allies out of the war before the United States' forces were fully committed to battle. The draconian Treaty of

Brest-Litovsk imposed by the Germans on the Russians had been shocking in its savage terms, which included Russia's surrender of its territories in Finland, the Ukraine, the Baltic States, and the Crimean peninsula—about 1.5 million square kilometres containing some 62 million people, not to mention vast war supplies of oil, grain, and heavy guns.[1] These harsh terms of peace required that the Germans garrison more troops on the Eastern Front to protect against the possibility of a Russian revolt, but they were able to free up thirty-three divisions that were transferred to the Western Front in support of the coming offensive. The settlement from Brest-Litovsk, and the severe treaty imposed earlier on Romania—which had entered the war on the side of the Allies in August 1916 and had promptly been crushed by the Germans—revealed that the losers in this titanic war would pay a heavy price beyond the hundreds of thousands of men already sent to the abattoir. Germany aimed to be the victors, and its armies on the Western Front swelled to hold 4 million men in almost 200 divisions.[2] A decisive battle was coming, directed at the British forces whom the Germans believed had exhausted themselves during the Passchendaele offensives in the previous year.[3]

OVER THE WINTER OF 1917–1918, the Canadians had carried out their orders to hold the front around their prize of Vimy Ridge and the surrounding area. While no set-piece battles took place during this period, the trenches were alive with crash bombardments and harassing chemical attacks. Both sides raided furiously, vying for dominance of No Man's Land. Even at Christmas, when the Canadian troops behind the lines were treated to special dinners of turkey, vegetables, and wine, there was no respite. Major George Franklin of the 4th CMR described in his diary an incident near Lens, where the opposing lines faced each other across a narrow No Man's Land. Both the Canadians and Germans could be heard singing Christmas carols. "Just about dawn one of our snipers saw a Hun making his way overland from one trench to the other, evidently thinking the light was not yet good enough for rifle-fire. Our fellow 'drilled' him clean, and was heard to remark as he ejected the empty shell, 'Merry Christmas Fritz, you ———!'"[4]

From atop the ridge, Currie's men transformed Vimy and the surrounding region into a fortress. The French generals and politicians stressed that no ground could be given here, as the area contained the northern collieries of France, whose yield was crucial to the Allied war effort. The Canadians knew they had been entrusted with a key part of the line, but few needed to be reminded of the imperative to hold fast unto death. None of the Canadians wanted to have to recapture Vimy Ridge.

"Nearly everyone has more or less bronchitis," penned Major G.S. Strathy in his diary in early 1918.[5] Hacking and coughing in the cold, the Canadian Tommies dug some 400 kilometres of trenches and laid more than 450 kilometres of barbed wire that criss-crossed along the 12,000-metre front.[6] Telephone cables were buried and laddered (laid in multiple strands to better avoid shellfire); water mains were sunk deep, running from front to rear. Sturdy dugouts supported by steel scrounged from the surrounding mining towns were constructed to house the troops during the artillery bombardments that raked over the front like angry storms. Situated all over the ridge, machine-gun strongpoints would provide sweeping fields of fire and

Canadians in a communication trench near the front. Note the width of the trench and the funk hole carved into the wall on the left that houses a grinning Canadian. Trenches like these criss-crossed the Vimy sector held by the Canadians in early 1918, creating a formidable defence against the expected German offensives.

harass low-flying observation planes. Snipers' posts were built not to be seen. Successive defensive lines created a cushion for any attack, and were compartmentalized so that the loss of ground in one sector did not compromise the overall defence. Supporting the battle front, the artillery in the rear—protected against enemy shelling by their placement in sturdy gun pits with brick ceilings—had all parts of the front mapped out on a grid system so that shellfire could be called down with devastating accuracy. This defence-in-depth worked with the favourable topographical features as the Canadian defenders stared down from the heights of Vimy Ridge. Lieutenant Colonel D.E. Macintyre observed correctly that the Canadian front was "the best fortified sector on the Western Front."[7] Defended by the elite Canadian troops, Vimy was low on the Germans' list of targets.

Over the winter, not all soldiers were needed in the firing line, so fewer troops were held closer to the front. John Baird of the 5th Pioneer Battalion wrote on January 9 that his unit "went for a bath, first one for about three months."[8] Long-service battalion commanding officers and brigadiers were relieved for up to a month so they could go back to England—an essential respite for men who had fought for several years in some cases. The long-awaited furlough for First Contingent men was approved as well, and several hundred married originals were sent back to Canada to see their families. Also provided leave were those soldiers who had loved ones back home suffering severely, such as children who had been left alone after their mother's death.[9] Most of those who went back to Canada never returned to the front. Commanding officers took the opportunity to give long-service officers and NCOs a rest by sending them off to one of the divisions', corps', or army's many specialist training schools, where the soldier-pupils took courses in leadership, Lewis-gun operation, raiding, gas warfare, and a host of other necessary skills and specializations. "It was indeed pleasant to be out of the line in the dead of winter," wrote A.L. Barry, who would rise from batman to brigadier in the course of his military career.[10] Another Canadian, William Breckenridge, was not too sure about the value of being sent on one questionably relevant training course, but he sounded like the long-service veteran that he was when he acknowledged, "A live man is better than a dead one and taking a pigeon course was better than exposing your body to the merciless weapons of war."[11]

As those soldiers who remained at the front shivered in the February and March cold, wrapping and rewrapping themselves in blankets, coats, and anything else to protect against the wind that whipped along the Douai plain, bombardments took place almost every day. The enemy deluged the front with poison gas, and the Canadians responded in kind. This chemical environment created "a waking nightmare to haunt the memory forever," swore Victor Wheeler.[12] Phosgene, chlorine, and various irritants that caused sneezing or vomiting were among the witches' brew that smothered the front. Mustard gas was especially insidious as it remained active for days and weeks in the snow and frozen mud. Soldiers could easily get infected mud on their clothing during a crawl through No Man's Land or while on routine trench fatigues. When they burrowed into the dugouts to escape the cold, the heat of the central fire and of other men then began to vapourize the mustard gas. Its deadly fumes attacked those soldiers near the carrier, like some deadly plague. Men could wake up blinded and with grotesque blisters on their back, armpits, and groin. And even if they got through the night unscathed, the morning could bring new horrors: "When the sun rose, the gas, which had lain dormant in the shell holes and among the brick-piles, began to vaporize, and our men, going about without respirators, began to collapse in scores," wrote Major George McFarland. "[One company] had ten men killed, and seventy seriously gassed."[13] The toxic environment eroded morale and created a breeding ground for fear, with one official report noting a pervasive "tendency for men who have smelt the gas to believe that they have been poisoned."[14] Uncertainty about whether or not a respirator was attached quickly enough to prevent a chemically induced death wore away at the exhausted and weakened soldiers, whose minds played terrible tricks on them as they waited in terror to see if gas symptoms would be revealed. Sadly the men often faced far more than just this psychological strain. The Canadian Corps suffered 519 gas casualties in the first nine weeks of the year, meaning that more than one out of every seven casualties was caused by chemical weapons.[15] Thirty-seven-year-old Corporal Albert West responded angrily in his diary to one devastating gas attack on his battalion that left sixteen dead and eighty wounded: "This is not warfare, it's sheer brutality and murder."[16]

AS THE CANADIANS dug in for the coming battle, the British forces were suffering through the aftermath of their forced reorganization and reduction of fighting units. A further draw on their numbers was Prime Minister Lloyd George's insistence on withholding troops from the Western Front, as he believed that Haig would only use them up in another irresponsible and wasteful offensive venture. The prime minister had raged at his own impotence during the Passchendaele campaign, declaring, "I am the butcher's boy who leads the animals to the slaughter."[17] But refusing Haig troops was not the answer, as it weakened the entire BEF and would result in unnecessary deaths as skeleton-thin units fought battles with insufficient soldiers.

Although the British were short tens of thousands of men, at least Haig's intelligence corps had successfully pinpointed the timing of the forthcoming German offensive, which was revealed through countless intelligence reports that tracked the movement of enemy divisions and the stockpiling of ammunition. Not only did the British have a firm appreciation of German intentions; they in fact welcomed an attack. If they could shatter this final assault, then the war might be won in 1919 or 1920 with the aid of fresh American troops. Yet the BEF also knew that it could not rely solely on the fledgling U.S. forces to support them in the coming battle, as the brash doughboys—or "Sammies," as the Allied soldiers called them when they felt mean-spirited—were not yet ready to take on the battle-hardened German forces. The British and French would have to beat back the coming German offensive on their own.

Despite forecasting the German offensive, and courting it, the British were ill-prepared. The Canadians had worked to strengthen their positions like men possessed, but many British divisions had taken a lackadaisical approach to finishing their defences-in-depth upon which the German infantry were to be slaughtered. Even worse, the concept of the flexible defence was poorly understood by British troops and their officers, who had difficulty jettisoning the concept of refusing to give ground.[18] All forces had long relied on deep trench systems, but the flexible defence required lightly held buffer zones that would slow and wear down attacking forces, allowing aggressive counterattacking forces to drive the exhausted enemy back. British orders to hold to the last man were perhaps inspiring, but were entirely counter-productive, and in fact worked against the very principle of the defence-in-depth. The confusion about how to hold the front was most evident in the Fifth Army's sector, where forces there were thinned out, vulnerable, and not fully trained in the elastic defence and the rapid counterattack. The Fifth Army was not to blame for all of these deficiencies, as it had only twelve weak divisions spread over a large front. The army's brash commander, Sir Hubert Gough, who was usually teetering towards arrogance, was particularly timid around Haig, as he owed his meteoric rise to the field marshal, but the situation was so desperate that he had no choice but to object to the shortage of men. Haig's GHQ promptly told him that there were no more men, and that even if the Germans broke through, their advance could be better contained on the Fifth Army's front, as stronger forces on the flank would eventually pinch in and decapitate any enemy force. No one told the Fifth Army's men that they were the bait for the Germans, and one wonders what the Tommies at the front would have thought of Haig's remarks to his wife just before the battle: "Everyone is in good spirits and only anxious that the Enemy should attack."[19]

BY THE BEGINNING of March, the Germans had firmed up their plan to launch their multi-army offensive on the 21st of that month against the British Third and Fifth Armies behind a hurricane bombardment of 3.2 million rounds of high explosives, shrapnel, and chemical shells.[20] This peace offensive—intended to shatter the Allies and end the war—would rely on a new strike force to spearhead the attack. Dozens of German divisions had been stripped of their elite troops, which had been grouped to form new aggressive attack formations. These storm troops had trained intensely for open warfare, in which assault forces flowed around areas of resistance and kept driving into the rear areas to sow confusion. On the eve of the offensive, one of the elite soldiers, Rudolph Binding, wrote excitedly that: "The preparations are quite inconceivable in detail."[21] This would be the Germans' final roll of the dice.

Behind a cloaking mist, and hugging the artillery and machine-gun barrage, the Germans made enormous gains on March 21, with their troops moving forward aggressively. These special storm troops advanced in small groups of twenty to sixty, relentlessly pushing deeper into the British lines, refusing to be held up by strongpoints, and instead washing over and around them like a tidal wave.[22] Employing tactics honed on the Eastern Front and armed with a high concentration of light

MG-08/15 machine guns, these units were instructed to "act on their own initiative."[23] British soldiers in forward positions that were not destroyed or deluged in gas soon found themselves far behind the thrusting German forces who had moved swiftly past them. Captured German documents indicated that the swarming infantry were not to "give the enemy any time to re-organize."[24] British battalion, brigade, and then divisional headquarters were cut off from their front lines and unable to react to the rapidly changing battlefield. This was no set-piece battle that inched forward a few kilometres and then waited for the artillery guns to catch up to the infantry, but a plunge ahead and past areas of resistance, leaving the artillery far behind. British casualties on the first day of battle were 38,512, but a disturbing 21,000 of the total had surrendered.[25]

By the third day of the offensive, the Germans had driven back the Fifth Army some 20 kilometres behind the Somme, and were closing in on the vital city of Amiens, a key logistical junction. There was panic in the British high command: the Germans had scored an impressive victory. But amidst the chaos of the collapsing Allied front, brave groups of British defenders made the Germans pay for their thrusting tactics. While these tactics would foreshadow the blitzkrieg of the next world war, here they were carried out without supporting armour. Despite the confusion in the British lines, machine-gunners and riflemen still cut down the elite German light infantry with ease as they advanced in the open.

The British, after their initial shock, fought back hard. Trading control of blasted farmers' fields for space and time, British forces drew the Germans into an over-extended position during the next few days, as the storm troops plunged deeper and deeper into the British lines but became increasingly vulnerable as the jolt of their surprise wore off and they were left without the support of their artillery. Much desperate fighting ensued over the next weeks, especially during the second German offensive that attempted to drive through Flanders to the Channel ports, in what became known as the Battle of the Lys. Here, the British could give little ground, and when the Germans attacked on April 9, the British Tommy was forced into another fighting retreat. But this withdrawal was not like the seemingly panicked rout of March 21, even though the normally inarticulate Sir Douglas Haig felt compelled to rouse his men for a last stand on April 11, with "their backs to the wall and believing in the righteousness of their cause." The fighting battalions did not need such appeals, however, as the British force had not suffered a serious blow to morale or its combat effectiveness. Although the British gave up all they had captured during the Passchendaele battles of the previous year, the German offensive slowly ground to a halt at the end of April, without having endangered the all-important logistical system of Allied train lines nor split the French and British forces.

As they overran British lines, the malnourished German troops who had subsisted on low-grade black bread and meatless sausages—all the while aware that their families were suffering even more at home—were shocked to discover the British dugouts and stores to be full of food. The Allies, they found, were not as close to defeat as the German propaganda insisted. In fact, it was reported that the gorging German troops, who fell upon the food stores, disrupted several offensives as they fed themselves rather than crashing deeper into the British lines. The looting of some two million bottles of whiskey sent many a German soldier into a deep dugout for days.[26] More damaging to their forces, though, was the increasingly stiffening British defence that made subsequent German attacks—still employing light infantry tactics, yet now with all strategic and tactical surprise lost—costly and ineffective. In order to slow the lightning enemy attacks, the British blanketed the front in poison gas to further slow the logistical support of the lead German troops.[27]

"The giving over of ground is not so much to be feared or regretted, and believe me he has paid a long price for it," wrote one Canadian about the apparent large enemy gains. "His victories are all of the Pyrrhic sort and if we had cared to throw our men away we could [have] had all sorts of such 'victories.'"[28] Having suffered some 800,000 casualties by the end of the summer, which included the death or wounding of many of its crack troops, Germany was left in a far weaker position than before the offensive, as now it was overextended and holding a longer part of the Western Front. The German offensives ended with a whimper.

THE CANADIAN CORPS was not, for the most part, engaged in the hard fighting, although its lines were bombarded heavily. The Germans well heeded the reputation of the Canadian troops and noted their deep entrenchment on and around Vimy. But Currie was ready for a fight, and one set of orders to the troops concluded harshly: "You will hold your position ... to the last man."[29] Spartan sacrifices were not needed, however. On the first day of the assault, the Canadians pre-empted the German offensive with a massive gas attack that projected hundreds of large mortar-like chemical shells in unison to saturate the enemy front. Corporal John Becker remembered, "It was an inspiring sight and an inspiring sound and I gasped at the suddenness of it, notwithstanding the fact that I thought I was fully prepared for it."[30] With the enemy troops floundering in gas, the respirator-clad Canadians peered down from the stronghold, awaiting any assault. Although thousands of terrified rats scurried away from the chemical clouds, moving through the Canadian line as a twitching, screeching mass of fur and legs, the German forces never crashed against the Vimy breakwater.

As the British were pressed back all along the front, Canadian infantry, cavalry, and motor machine-gun teams fought in support of the beleaguered Fifth Army. Brigadier Raymond Brutinel's Motor Machine Gun Brigade attracted the most attention. The twenty cars, protected by armour plating and equipped with two Vickers machine guns, combined manoeuvrability, defensive strength, and firepower. The vehicles had been ready for battle in 1914, but the British had never found an adequate role for them during trench warfare. Their reliance on good roads meant that they were held back for the exploitation phase of the battle. But trench warfare never offered a chance to "hit the gap," as the cavalry were fond of saying, and so most of Brutinel's forces had fought in 1916 and 1917 in a dismounted role, usually thickening up the creeping barrage with hundreds of thousands of bullets or supporting the infantry holding the line.

Since the British trench lines had been broken on March 21, the armoured cars now found a role as they raced across the front, providing much-needed firepower and shoring up desperate situations. After driving 150 kilometres north from the Vimy front during the last week in March, the armoured cars covered British withdrawals and punished German spearhead units with raking fire. "The situation was very confused and very fluid," remembered Second Lieutenant Frank Worthington, who would be awarded the Military Medal and Military Cross and survive the war to become a leading proponent of armoured warfare in the Canadian Army.

We would take the four or eight guns of a battery and open fire as the enemy would be advancing and bring them to a halt. Then the enemy would be ready to shell us out and the thing to do was to move your guns back to a rear position—maybe a thousand yards, maybe five hundred—and as the enemy started to move forward again, then you'd give it to them again. Day after day it was the same sort of thing.[31]

The armoured cars made a significant contribution to the British defence in this battle. During desperate fighting on March 27, for instance, an aerial observer noted that just two armoured cars were holding up 600 German infantry along the roads west of Cerisy.[32]

But the cars, though armoured, were far from bulletproof, and their 5mm side armour did not always stop high-velocity bullets fired from close range. As well, the vehicles' open top left the gunners and drivers susceptible to shrapnel bursts and plunging mortar fire. Snipers were increasingly employed to knock out the Canadian gunners.[33] In their desperate attempt to shore up the British lines, many motor machine gunners paid for their rear-guard actions with their lives: 37 were killed, 11 were reported missing, and 116 were wounded, combining to a casualty rate of over forty percent of the force's men.[34] But despite these heavy losses, the "Motors" served as a powerful backstop for the retreating British units.

The Canadian Cavalry Brigade also found an important role in this new open form of warfare. The war had thus far been unkind to the cavalry, as the awesome firepower of dug-in defenders had rendered it largely impotent on the Western Front. Although the cavalry were chomping at the bit to exploit a gap in the enemy line, local successes never translated into a large-scale breakthrough. The enemy's barbed wire, trenches in depth, and machine guns had shut down the cavalry charge, but now the fighting retreat opened up the battlefield again, and the cavalry were able to exploit their strengths: rapid mobility, the shock of the massed horse charge, and the power to pursue and harass the enemy through their fluid lines. Unlike the dismounted Canadian Mounted Rifles of the 8th Brigade, the Royal Canadian Dragoons (RCD), Fort Garry Horse, and Lord Strathcona's Horse fought astride their horses, employing lances and swords as often as their cut-down, lighter Lee-Enfields. German units found during the dark days of March that facing several hundred men and horses riding en masse, with swords drawn, covering 350 metres per minute, was a terrifying experience.

On the morning of March 30, the Canadian Cavalry Brigade was ordered to support British infantry units near Moreuil Wood. The lead squadron of the RCD ran into enemy fire at about 9:30 A.M. and was forced to dismount. Taking casualties, the Dragoons charged on foot with speed and fury, routing an estimated 300 enemy troops in the wood.[35] The most famous charge involved C Squadron of Lord Strathcona's Horse, commanded by Lieutenant Gordon Muriel Flowerdew, a thirty-three-year-old British Columbia fruit farmer. Flowerdew led his galloping force around the northeastern part of the wood to cut off the enemy from reinforcements. Seeing the enemy caught in the open 300 metres away, Flowerdew half-turned in his saddle and urged his men onwards: "It's a charge, boys, it's a charge!"

It was indeed a glorious charge, reminiscent of the Light Brigade's mounted thrust at Balaclava in 1854. Swords drawn and leaning low over the necks of their horses, the squadron rode down the enemy. Flowerdew and his men were decimated by concentrated fire: twenty-four of the seventy-five who went in were killed, and fifteen more later died of their wounds; most of the remainder were wounded.[36] Acting Squadron Leader Thomas Mackay was found to have fifty-nine bullet and shrapnel wounds in one leg; his other leg had more, but it was so badly pulped that individual wounds could not be counted.[37] Although the Germans had savaged the Strathconas, the sight of this charging force was too much for them, and when the surviving cavalry wheeled for another pass, most of the surviving enemy fled the battlefield. They left behind dozens of slain companions run through with swords. Flowerdew was hit four times but continued to lead his men before he died of his wounds. His gallant action was the stuff of heroes and he was recognized as such with a Victoria Cross. Despite their losses, the Canadian Cavalry Brigade had stabilized the front and had, with their lives, purchased precious time for the retreating British forces to establish a new defensive line to the rear.

As the armoured cars and cavalry attacked, counterattacked, and held the front, the Canadian Corps remained largely untested. Though probing assaults and heavy bombardments hit their lines, the Canadians were never threatened. But up and down the line, the Canadians knew the British were being thrashed, and many whispers and rumours circulated about the magnitude of the catastrophe. Grousing was the infantryman's way, and more than a few wags suggested that the Germans were simply trying to isolate the Canadian Corps by attacking to either side of them, in order to strike a separate peace with the Canucks.

But it was hard to joke away the dire situation of the Fifth Army. In the days following the near breakthrough, Haig pulled three of the four divisions from Currie's corps to support the beleaguered British to the north. Balking at seeing his Canadian Corps broken up piecemeal, Currie complained to the field marshal, informing him that his small army could not be treated like other British formations. Currie's grievance was the last thing that Haig needed to hear or discuss at this critical point in the battle. But as commander of the Canadian army formation, Currie had a duty to his political masters to keep the corps a coherent fighting unit. It was never an easy role for the Canadian Corps commanders: Alderson had been sacrificed on the cross formed between the British high command and the Canadian politicians; Byng largely ignored the Canadian politicians since he did not care about the consequences; and, at risk of being crucified himself, Currie benefited from the experience of his predecessors but still often found himself staring down his two opposing leaders, who came at him with nails in hand. Still, he was becoming more adept at making such high-level manoeuvres, and he learned how to play the Canadian politicians and the British high command off against each other when it was required for the good of the corps.

Confronted by Currie and his political supporters in London, a fuming Haig soon returned all but one division, but grumbled darkly in his personal diary that he and General Henry Horne felt that "Currie is suffering from a swollen head.… He wishes to fight only as a 'Canadian Corps' and got his Canadian representative in London to write and urge me to arrange it. As a result, the Canadians are together holding a wide front near Arras, but they have not yet been in the battle!"[38] Haig's anger made its way to the Earl of Derby, his political superior, who may have agreed with the field marshal but politely reminded him, "We must look upon them in the light in which they wish to be looked upon rather than the light in which we would wish to do so."[39] Since the Canadians had begun to see themselves as "junior but sovereign allies," Haig would need to treat them as such.[40]

Currie and the corps continued to hold an enormous part of the British line; by the end of March, two Canadian divisions were manning 15 kilometres of front; less than two weeks later, the Canadians were holding an astonishing one-fifth of the total BEF frontage.[41] Even though many of Currie's troops were not in the direct path of an enemy assault, their role was crucial in freeing up the British to concentrate their forces on holding the Germans at bay. All the while, Currie defended his dangerously thin lines with fierce artillery barrages and aggressive infantry patrolling.

To bolster the desperate situation and help to quell some of the darker rumours about the British forces' collapse in the face of the German onslaught, Currie issued a statement at the end of March, congratulating his men on their fortitude and imploring them to fight to the bitter end. While the communiqué was enormously popular back in Canada where it was widely published, it was much too windily heroic in tone for the battle-hardened Canadian soldiers to take seriously:

> I place my trust in the Canadian Corps.... Under the orders of your devoted officers in the coming battle, you will advance or fall where you stand facing the enemy. To those who will fall I say, "Your names will be revered forever and ever by your grateful country and God will take you unto Himself."

Soldiers scoffed at Currie's words. Too many friends had already been embraced by God at that point in the war for the survivors to be placated by grandiose speeches. One of Currie's friends revealed after the war that the message "was not the stuff to feed the troops. Appeals to the higher ideals only made them ill."[42] R.G. Barclay of the PPCLI noted that, after Currie's speech, the boys in the trenches chirped facetiously to each other, "Did you stand where you fell?"[43]

Tired of their monotonous food, some of the soldiers snickered that the corpulent Currie did not appear to have missed too many meals, and the shy and stiff general was disdainfully referred to as "Guts-and-Gaiters."[44] H.W. Johnston recounted after the war that despite Currie's operational success, "Oddly enough we didn't love him.... I don't think we realized exactly how good a man we'd got."[45] Currie was never a chateau general, even if his awkwardness was misconceived by some as arrogance. He never enjoyed a luxurious life in the rear. Soldiers did not see the hours Currie worked late into the night at headquarters, bent over maps, eyes darkened with fatigue, demanding more guns or supplies, sending out officers to collect information from the front, and standing up to both British and Canadian superiors to ensure that his soldiers had a fighting chance in battle. To his men, unfortunately, he was only an absent superior who called on them to fight and sacrifice, while he did neither. While Currie remained unloved by some of his men, his corps was recognized as an elite combat formation. Moreover, the Canadians had survived the greatest threat of the war with their forces intact and would remain a key weapon in Haig's arsenal when the Allies counterattacked.

CHAPTER 26

"OUR NERVES GREW STEADIER; OUR TEMPERS IMPROVED"

Training and Rest, Summer 1918

The Canadian Corps had escaped the worst of the grinding German battles of early 1918. It had done so partly because the Canadians had fortified strongly and deeply around Vimy Ridge, and because their first-class reputation drove the Germans to look elsewhere for supposedly easier pickings. While the BEF suffered close to 300,000 casualties during March and April, the Canadian Corps, despite having fought in a series of intense minor engagements, remained a strong and efficient formation on which Haig relied.[1] Sir Arthur Currie wrote to his prime minister shortly after the war about this grim period in the history of the BEF: "Sir Douglas Haig himself told me that in the dark days of last spring, the one comforting thought that he had was that he still had the Canadian Corps intact, and that he should never regard himself as beaten until that Corps was put into battle."[2]

From the early days of the German offensive, the corps was not intact, with the 2nd Division having been moved to serve with British VI Corps. Here, the Canadians of this division made it their business to patrol and raid frequently, retaining an aggressive policy of dominating No Man's Land. During the three months in which the Canadians held the line in VI Corps' sector, they carried out twenty-seven raids.[3] Robert Inglis, who served as a Canadian heavy-siege gunner in support of the 2nd Division, remembered that Major General Henry Burstall's men soon acquired a reputation as "master raiders."[4] Trench warrior C.J. Albon of the 25th Battalion saw some of this action first-hand, noting the debilitating effect of raiding on German morale: "It's one thing seeing a man lying there dead but it's another thing when a man just disappears, and night after night men disappear and you don't know where they go."[5] Under the constant threat of either phantom stalkers or smash-and-grab raiders, few Germans slept well when opposite the Canadians.

Throughout the summer, the Canadians of the 2nd Division were acknowledged for their aggressive tactics, but some of this division's men grumbled that they were still in the thick of holding the front while the rest of the Canadian Corps had been in reserve since the first week in May. Burstall's division had suffered heavy losses in the three months of holding the line: 120 officers and 2,647 other ranks. By comparison, casualties in the rest of the Canadian Corps during the same period totalled to 185 officers and 2,556 other ranks.[6] The 2nd Division had been busy and aggressive: Burstall claimed that his men beat the Germans into a "state of docility." The 2nd Division infantry also pioneered deep-raiding techniques: the raiders did not stop at the first or second enemy lines but pushed further, often 1,000 metres into German-held territory. This created additional confusion and allowed raiders to kill more of the enemy as they lay trapped in their dugouts, unprepared for such extensive assaults. Lieutenant General Aylmer Haldane, the commander of the VI Corps, noted in a letter about the Canadians that the "Germans have been given no peace" on their front.[7]

However, the bitterness of the Canadians' heavy losses was felt throughout the 2nd Division, and a pervasive rumour circulated through the ranks of the division that they were being punished by the corps commander for supposed crimes they had committed. Wild accusations of the 2nd Division troops having looted Arras were patently false, but still the rumour created bad feelings among the men towards the rest of the corps—and especially towards Currie. Responding to the intensity of the slander, Currie remarked, "The lie was spread so systematically that I believe it was done maliciously"; he felt sure that the accusations were part of the ongoing campaign by Beaverbrook, Hughes, and other supporters of Turner to undermine his authority.[8] No evidence of such a plot exists, even if Currie soothed his frayed feelings by blaming the rumours on this shadowy group, but the 2nd Division's men were angry about their long service in the line away from the rest of the corps, and so were susceptible to the suggestion.

By June, the multiple German offensives had been defeated on the BEF front. The Allies had held the line, but it had required a gut-wrenching effort. In the British forces, tens of thousands of unhealed wounded men and underage eighteen-year-olds had been rushed to the front. "We seemed to have stopped Fritz's mad rush so far," wrote Canadian Lieutenant Bill Hutchinson, who was recovering from inhalation of gas. "To my mind and to many others, it's his last grand stab for victory and to use the language of the Army I think he's 'out of luck'. Here's hoping. He can't last forever at the rate he's getting casualties. It must be pure slaughter when he comes over in close formation."[9] The fighting had indeed been reckless and costly. By the end of their offensives, the Germans had suffered almost 800,000 casualties, and the combined Allied losses were almost as high.[10] The Fifth Army had suffered the brunt of the attack, and had indeed fought well after the initial reversal, but General Gough was fired as a convenient scapegoat. Gough held the unique record of never having won a major battle, although ironically it was his depleted forces that had held off the Germans during the darkest hours of the offensive. But someone had to take the fall, and Gough was more expendable than Haig. The German high command also slashed and burned its way through its own generals, but Germany was in an increasingly desperate situation as the British blockade strangled the nation's food and munitions supply, and as hundreds of thousands of American troops poured into Britain and across the Channel. At the front, soldiers struck in the ranks, refusing their orders.[11] Germany's last gamble had left it weak and exposed to a strategic counterattack.

DURING THE DARK DAYS of the German offensive, the French and British armies had almost been split by the German wedge, which would have disastrously exposed their strategic flanks and rear areas, and the French had been understandably wary about rushing emergency divisions north to help their allies when they expected to face their own attack, which eventually came the next month. The normally staid

Haig nearly had a breakdown on March 25, when he implored his superiors to "make peace on any terms we could."[12] The British regrouped after their apparent rout, but it was clear that the Allies needed to better coordinate their armies, which were superior in numbers to the Germans but plagued by an excess of commanders, politicians, and national agendas. The man to bind the Allies together would be French general Ferdinand Foch. The British agreed to appoint Foch as General-in-Chief of the Allied Armies, in part because he had ordered French troops north at the end of March to backstop the British. While Foch was far from brilliant, he was a pit bull who refused to concede defeat. He was fond of making Churchillian speeches: "I shall fight in front of Amiens. I shall fight in Amiens. I shall fight behind Amiens. I shall fight all the time."[13] General Henri Pétain would command the French armies, while Haig would remain as commander of the BEF. The Americans, Italians, and Belgians were also under Foch's command, although answering as well to their own national commanders. Like Dwight Eisenhower's role in the next world war, Foch's in this one was unenviable, as he was called on to herd his cat-like generals with their enormous egos. But his role was essential to maximize the Allies' striking power against the enemy and coordinate the offensive of the principal armies, which numbered 1.8 million in the BEF, 1.7 million in the French forces, and now over 2 million Americans, although most of the doughboys were still in England.[14] Against them were 3,576,000 Germans, but many of their best troops had been ground away in their previous offensives.[15] Now they would return to the defensive and wait for the Allied onslaught.

MOST CANADIANS had rarely met Haig, and would most certainly have failed to pick Foch out from a crowd, even with his chest-full of medals. Foch did make one formal inspection of the Canadians and was deeply impressed, writing that Currie's Corps was "an army second to none, deriving its immense strength from the solid organizations of each of its component parts, welded together in battle conditions."[16] Even if Foch knew little directly of the Canadians, their reputation had made its way to his headquarters, and he would draw upon them in the final year of battle to spearhead several offensives. In the meantime, this first-rate fighting formation was pulled from the line and put into strategic reserve, meaning that there would no longer be the cycle of units through the front lines. This was the third time during the war that Canadians had been provided the chance for an extensive rest and "refit": the first having been after the Somme, the second after Passchendaele.

While in reserve and far from the fall of shells, the Canadians rebuilt their battalions and units up to full strength. Currie had a ready-made reserve in the broken-up 5th Division, and these well-trained soldiers joined established fighting units. As well, a steady trickle of Military Service Act (conscripted) men were coming overseas and training in England, and would soon be replacements for the several thousand casualties the corps had suffered during the last four months. While the 24,000 MSA men may not have been worth the cost of nearly tearing the country apart during the conscription crisis, no one expected the war to end in 1918, and the generals planned to use the MSA men in the 1919 and 1920 fighting campaigns. While some of the veterans who had volunteered for service treated the conscripts roughly—taunting them or generally giving them a cold shoulder—these MSA soldiers soon adapted to regimental life. Captain Claude Williams thought that the "draftee's path is not to be strewn with roses," but Private E.W. Russell was surprised at their combat effectiveness during the final fighting, noting in his memoirs: "Such of those that I met were definitely good material and they had come at a time when their mettle would be proved."[17]

Before the Canadians engaged in the brutal battles of the final Hundred Days campaign in 1918, they had time to train and recover. The Canadian Corps rose to a strength of 103,530, all ranks, in June 1918. Another 35,491 were part of the Canadian Expeditionary Force in the European theatre of war, including men in the cavalry brigade, railway troops, forestry units, and lines of communication, who did not serve with the Canadian Corps. The total strength of the CEF in Europe reached a high-water mark of just under 150,000 men in July.[18]

The seemingly endless cycle of training began again, and the major goal in the summer was to transition from trench fighting to semi-open and open warfare. But after three years of siege mentality, it was not easy to change soldiers' view that a 1,000-metre gain was the limit of a day's advance. While the artillery and infantry were to work in unison, open warfare would soon result in the infantry outdistancing its protective artillery screen. The strengthened infantry platoons were to "stick the enemy" with concentrated fire by pinning them down with Lewis guns or rifles, and then infiltrate along the paths of least resistance to encircle the position before destroying it. Lieutenant Colonel Hugh Urquhart of the 43rd Battalion described the challenges posed by this new type of fighting:

> These were tactics which called for an exceptional degree of daring and resource in the infantry. Front line men had not only to close with the enemy in circumstances of comparative isolation—that is, without the moral support of the old close order formation—but they had to think and co-operate skilfully with the other troops engaged alongside of them; there could be no more blind charging. "Cannon fodder" had to give place to a high type of disciplined manhood, if attacks, under the new methods, were to carry the day in the face of a determined enemy.[19]

Although the Canadian infantry had long abandoned the "cannon fodder" approach of advancing in long lines of men, Urquhart was right about the need for the infantry to fight their own battle at the sharp end.

Weak points in the enemy's defensive positions were to be penetrated. Plunging through the enemy line, even if it meant bypassing strongpoints, would create confusion in the German command-and-control structure, and lead to mass surrenders as positions were cut off and surrounded. Mopping-up units would later destroy these "bitter-enders" if they continued to hold out. All the while, onrushing platoons and companies passing through one another were to dig in and prepare for possible counterattacks. Each bound forward to create a new defensive line was to be protected by firepower, allowing the infantry platoons—working in conjunction with increasingly mobile field guns and machine guns, aided by combat engineers—to knock out enemy defences and then better withstand the expected counterattacks.[20] Smoke was to be used more frequently to cover troops as they advanced vulnerably across open ground, and heavy machine guns would lay down interdiction fire behind the enemy lines to suppress counterattacks.

Despite these refined tactics and evolutions, the ever-present bugbear remained of how to support troops that were exploiting success. Any deep advance usually meant that the all-important logistical support was left behind, as was the protection of heavy artillery. The conundrum of the Western Front revealed that the further the infantry advanced, the less artillery cover they received—and the deeper they put their head into the enemy's noose. The tempo of future battles was also expected to change, with less time available for senior staff to work out elaborate set-piece battles resulting in a need to rely more on junior officers in the field. Yet this combined-arms warfare, which joined the infantry, artillery, machine guns, engineers, logisticians, and signallers together into a tightly mailed fist, remained the key to victory, and so the various components had to train together for the coming battles.

The Canadians studied tactical and doctrinal documents, both Allied and German, that were circulated throughout the British armies. Currie felt that his staff officers and soldiers, benefitting from the unique corps structure in which lessons could be shared and absorbed quickly, were "peculiarly quick to learn, and they are not casual. This is a job which must be done, and the more we learn about killing Germans the sooner peace will be declared and the sooner we can get back to Canada, therefore, we study our job thoroughly, and in the execution of our plans nothing is left to chance."[21] In accord with the British, Currie believed that any open warfare would occur after the shock of a set-piece battle sent the enemy reeling. As the Germans withdrew from the battlefield, the Canadians were to pursue, scouts in the lead, attacking in successive bounds of platoons passing through platoons. It was not much different from what the 1914 armies had planned for—with the exception of the essential combined-arms battle, which would hopefully suppress enemy fire.

Much of this warfighting was expected to take place on the chemical battlefield. Both sides were increasingly using gas shells to disrupt and attrite enemy morale. In an attempt to prepare for the confusion of battle, men wore respirators as they carried out their training exercises. While soldiers "perspired profusely inside the nasty rubber things," the respirator was essential for surviving on the Western Front.[22] The interaction of infantry and tanks was also practised, with platoons and sections advancing in front of the metal behemoths, and tanks generally moving forward in the second wave in order to avoid German anti-tank guns. To perform their role of destroying enemy strongpoints or wire, the tanks would be called up or directed by flag-waving signallers (a job only slightly less lethal than that of the flamethrowing troops, who also had to reveal themselves on the battlefield). But the Canadians did not train as hard or as frequently with tanks as they might have, perhaps because of their ongoing mistrust of the machines' usefulness on the battlefield. Since Vimy, Canadians had loaded many of their eggs into the artillery barrage basket. The combination of the creeper, destructive fire on strongpoints, and all important counter-battery work, would pave the way to victory. But the high command still needed boots on the ground, and success or defeat would rest on the shoulders of the infantry.

Lack of reliable communication methods continued to present a problem in the coordination of any attack. The artillery's solution was to put a forward observer in the field to track the fall of shells and help to correct errors, and to support the observer with a small team of signallers who communicated to artillery headquarters by all means possible. Telephone wires were the most effective means, but as forward observers moved with the troops, the wires had to be strung above ground (instead of buried in a laddered manner six feet underground as was customary), and so they were often cut by enemy fire. Backup systems of wireless radio, flags, mirrors, pigeons, and runners were all employed. The infantry had an even harder time, as they had to coordinate not only from front to rear but also laterally. The small armies of signallers tried to keep the communications working through methods similar to the artillery observers', but the infantry at the front had far fewer resources, and so they often relied on runners, who were the most effective means of locating units on the flank and grouping together disparate platoons. The lack of reliable communications remained an essential motivating factor in the push to further decentralize the command and control of infantry units at the sharp end.

Despite the corps' intense training for the breakthrough battle, few in the general staff were optimistic enough to believe the Germans would break entirely as a result of one attack. The key to open warfare was to transition effectively from attack to pursuit to defence, likely all in the same day, and then to be able to resume battle again. The tempo of operations would be even more rapid than in the battles of the previous year. Casualties were expected in high numbers, so while the infantry had become specialists in particular weapon systems, they were also trained in other roles to enable them to take over as cogs in the machine. All the while, soldiers were urged to thrust deeply into the enemy lines, notwithstanding the loss of officers, key fire support, or enemy strongpoints.[23] Always the infantry were to keep moving, keep attacking. Deep penetration would confuse the enemy and send him reeling.

Indeed it would, but the loose talk of exploitation and hounding advances was processed warily by trench warfare veterans who remembered such hopes before the Somme in 1916, and understood well that—even taking into account the doctrinal evolution over the last two years—no matter what tactics were employed or how much firepower was brought to bear, in the open it always came down to flesh and blood against steel and fire. In June and July, the realistic training sessions employing open tactics met with only limited success, prompting a brigade major in the 1st Division to declare, "The tenets of trench warfare hung around their necks like a millstone."[24] Urging men forward to assault machine-gun positions in depth might lead to success, but regardless of new weapons, tactics, and doctrines, it would also surely result in a heavy butcher's bill. After months of training, and a growing confidence in their tactics, the Canadians had an inescapable sense, wrote Sergeant L.M. Gould, that they would soon be engaged in "the bloodiest fight" of the war.[25]

IN ADDITION to the rigorous training, however, the Canadian Corps were also afforded an extended refit period. "Our nerves grew steadier; our tempers improved," remarked one long-service veteran.[26] Life behind the lines was spent playing sports, visiting *estaminets*, and preparing for the coming offensive. With the corps out of the line, Dominion Day 1918 was celebrated by some 50,000 troops in a medley of competitions and sporting events that the prime minister and corps commander attended. Several squadrons of RAF patrolled the skies to ensure that the Canadian high command was not decapitated with one well-placed aerial bomb. Celebrated ace Billy Bishop stunt-flew over the crowd, and men from the 1st CMR marched past the dignitaries led by a mounted band of pipers and drummers. With snaking lines of soldiers queuing up for beer, it was a day of spectacle and national celebration; morale was high and the troops well rested.

"We, the Canadians, are apparently being held for the last innings, which should indeed be a battle royal," wrote Captain Maurice Pope to his father as he rested comfortably in the rear.[27] Some officers despaired at the inactivity or the relentless wiping out of haystacks in farmers' fields during mock battles. Lieutenant Henry Baldwin, a Liberal Party supporter whose service in France began only that summer, wrote home: "Every day we march, or maneuver or watch sports—the greatest of these is sports. Caesar fiddles—England plays football."[28] This swipe would perhaps not have gone over well with long-service veterans, most of whom were content to recuperate after years of battle and brutality. Baldwin had just arrived at the front, had avoided the killing battles of the last three years, and would just as quickly return to the rear after being hit by falling shrapnel from Canadian anti-aircraft fire before the battle of Amiens.

Though the respite was desperately needed by the beleaguered men of the corps, it could not last forever. Rumours about Allied counterattacks circulated up and down the line. On July 4, an Australian-led operation, which used a few American companies, resulted in a brilliant small operation at Hamel. The Germans folded easily in the face of the assault, which involved infantry, artillery, and tanks in a combined-arms limited smash. The British high command was suitably impressed and wondered if perhaps the earlier offensives had rotted the core of the German army. Having escaped most of the fighting in the previous months with little damage, the Canadian shock troops had no doubt that they would soon be thrown into the line to test the German will to continue prosecuting the war.

CHAPTER 27

THE EMPIRE STRIKES BACK

The Battle of Amiens

After suffering a series of German hammer blows since March, the Allies, by late summer, were anxious to counterattack the exhausted enemy forces that appeared demoralized and weakened from their failed exertions to win the war. General Erich Ludendorff, chief of staff of the German army, had gambled that he could break the Western Front in one final titanic battle before the full weight of American armies drove him from the field. But although the series of battles had been tactically successful, nothing had changed strategically. No major cities were gained, nor were the Channel ports taken. The Allies had been pushed back, but, like a spring coil, they were now ready to blast forward. And the Germans, who had lost 800,000 casualties in the spring and summer fighting, were a battered force, with the ongoing naval blockade strangling all parts of the war machine and morale low among many front-line units.

General Ferdinand Foch ordered a counterattack, and Haig, agreeing, commanded General Rawlinson of the Fourth Army to deliver it. The minor operation at Hamel on July 4 by Australian troops using tanks and new infantry tactics had proven that enemy positions could be overrun. Perhaps the many patrol and intelligence reports coming in from front-line units that observed listless defences were accurate? Even more revealing, in the weeks that followed, the Australians steadily chewed away at the enemy line, ruling No Man's Land and slowly but efficiently capturing and consolidating outposts and forward positions. This policy of "peaceful penetration" chipped away at the German buffer zone, eating into their lines all along the front.

Far more important was the enormous counterattack by the French-led force at the Second Battle of Marne. The Germans had attacked on July 15 near Reims, the fifth of their major offensives since March. Behind a heavy bombardment, they crossed over the Marne after pushing through American and French forces, making a strong advance of several kilometres but unable to go much further in the coming days. Three days later, an enormous counterattacking force of fifty-seven French, British, and American divisions—almost the size of the entire BEF—crashed into the Germans.[1] Spearheaded by 225 tanks—most of them the new Renault light tank—the counterattack drove 10 kilometres into the enemy lines, throwing the Germans back behind the Marne. Within two weeks, the Germans had lost 793 guns and 168,000 men.[2] Morale was shaken in both the German army and its high command, and a sixth offensive was cancelled. It was a shocking reversal, which revealed that Pétain's strategy of waiting, making reforms, and rebuilding had restored morale fully in the French army and that the Americans were finally ready to contribute to battle. Now it was the British army's turn. Haig planned a counterattack using elite troops and armour. Would it also punch a hole through the German line?

DURING THEIR SPRING and summer offensives, the Germans had nearly captured Amiens, an important railway junction between Paris and Boulogne. To ensure the safety of this logistical hub, it was essential that the Germans be pushed back, as they could bombard the city. Currie was called to a commanders' conference on July 20 to meet with Rawlinson, his staff, and the Australians. Rawlinson wanted a limited attack—an advance of only about 12 kilometres to the old Amiens defences (which had been overrun in March)—but Haig pressured him to be more ambitious, pushing for an advance of some 45 kilometres. In his vision, the smaller bite and hold tactics would be replaced by one big swallow. Haig's legendary method of communicating inarticulately in grunts and half-sentences—along with his forceful presence, which conflicted with his general refusal to interfere in the planning of his subordinates—resulted in confusing orders and counter-orders among Haig,

Rawlinson, and their supportive staff. In the end, the battle would be planned as Rawlinson wanted it: with a limited objective. Nonetheless, the operation would require a powerful spearhead force to hack a hole in the enemy lines. Rawlinson also demanded, and received, the dominion shock troops from Australia and Canada.

"The Canadian Corps, magnificently equipped and highly trained in storm tactics, may be expected to appear shortly in offensive operations," warned one captured German document in the summer of 1918.[3] The Canadians had earned their reputation as an elite force. The reverses of 1915 and 1916 had long since been obscured by the corps' string of operational victories since Vimy. Fresnoy, Hill 70, and especially Passchendaele had proven that the Canadians could capture the most fortified enemy positions. Moreover, since three of the four Canadian divisions had avoided most of the fighting during the German spring and summer offensives, they were considered fresh, and had been training for open warfare. The shock troops were ready for battle.

THE AMIENS OPERATION was planned as a surprise attack, although it was impossible to hide the movement of more than 300,000 Allied troops. If the enemy caught wind that both the Australians and Canadians were coming into the line together, they would know for certain that something was afoot. An elaborate deception plan was needed.

Several Canadian infantry, medical, and signals units were moved north. The infantry were ordered to carry out small raiding actions, purposefully losing some of their equipment in enemy lines. Signals groups passed messages back and forth in the north with deliberately sloppy telephone secrecy, which allowed the Germans to pinpoint their location. All of this was to distract from the main Canadian Corps force that was forming up for battle near Amiens. No one in the corps was told anything, but, as usual, the rumour mill had picked up on the coming offensive. Lieutenant Brooke Gossage of the Royal Canadian Artillery noted in his diary for August 2, "This is a most secretive move and nobody has any idea what we are here for." But he guessed: "Big Scrape coming off."[4] Every Canadian soldier also had a message put in his paybook instructing, "KEEP YOUR MOUTH SHUT." So secretive

Canadian gunners firing a heavy howitzer. The 646 Allied gun teams supporting the Amiens operation often had little cover from which to fire, but they nonetheless laid down a punishing bombardment and creeping barrage against the enemy lines.

was the operation that even the divisional commanders were informed only on July 29 about an attack that would be carried out in a little over a week's time. While secrecy was important, it was also overplayed as the divisional and brigade general staffs had almost no time to plan this massive operation.

Amateurs talk tactics; professionals know logistics. The experienced Canadian divisions had pulled off many intricate jobs in the previous years, and the veteran core of staff officers at every level worked well with one another across divisions and up and down the command hierarchy. Yet the days before the battle provided this well-oiled system with an enormous challenge. Light railways, motorized trucks, and horses were essential in transporting the more than 10 million rounds of small-arms ammunition, 291,000 artillery rounds, and all manner of other war supplies from the railheads.[5]

Arrangements also had to be made to move the Canadian Corps, which, at 100,000 strong, was equivalent in size to the population of one of Canada's largest cities at the time. The staff officers at corps headquarters and down the chain of command struggled to pull together plans, movement orders, medical arrangements, materiel, food, and water, identifying problems and improvising solutions on the spot. Despite the officers' expertise, the preparations were hurried and strained, and the traffic jams were enormous. A 26th Battalion officer noted that his men were forced to march along a secondary road, which could barely accommodate two lanes of traffic and was now crowded by five lines of moving soldiers. It took seven frustrating hours for the men to march 7 kilometres.[6] Other problems arose too, including the impossibility of moving sufficient medical field units to the front in time for the battle; and the failure to accommodate the nearly 20,000 horses that needed a steady supply of water resulted in long queues of animals travelling in the open that could have given away the surprise attack. However, the Allies had command of the air, pitting 2,000 aircraft against 365 German ones, which ensured that the enemy did not spot the horses, or at least did not have time to draw the right conclusions with a Nieuport or Sopwith Camel on his tail.

But the Canadians lived in fear of their preparations being discovered. Lieutenant Colonel G.C. Chambers of the 2nd CMR noted in his diary, "Nothing short of a disaster could have befallen us had the Bosche suspected anything and shelled the vicinity."[7] But they did not, except for sending a few stray shells. All of these practical details—the essential sinews of war that provided support for the fighting arms—were hammered out by the corps and divisional staff officers, who started early in the morning and worked late into the night, day after day. This work ethic started at the top, and Currie could be found studying maps at 2 A.M. and then up for more work only four hours later.[8] At the front, the infantry dug temporary slit trenches, pulled their groundsheets over top and waited for the inevitable orders to attack.

ALLIED INTELLIGENCE had revealed that the German defences were weak, and the defenders not of high quality. During the battles in the first half of the year, many of the Germans' best soldiers had been stripped from the regular divisions, and thousands of them had been killed or wounded in the fighting. Furthermore, the Amiens region was considered a quiet sector by the Germans, who had not seen much fighting since the summer. The garrison forces here were recuperating, both from the earlier battles of the year and from the deadly influenza epidemic that had

The Battle of Amiens: August 8 to 14, 1918

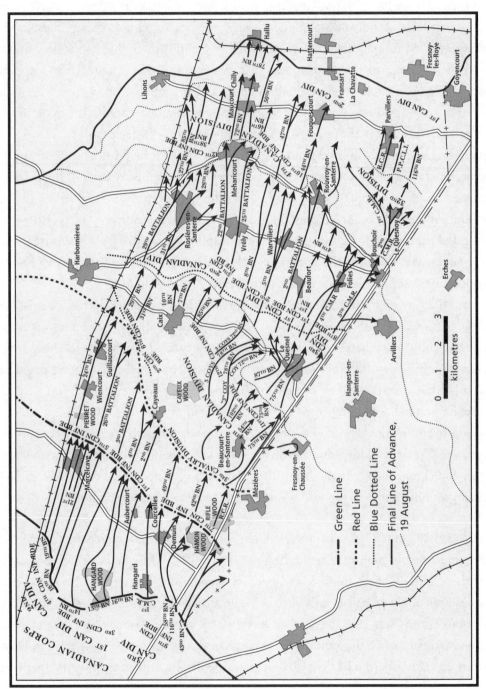

raced through the ranks. Although ten depleted German divisions manned the front, with four stronger ones in reserve, they were spread thin.[9] As a result of indifference and exhaustion, front-line troops and the high command had prepared few fortifications, and the defenders had missed the telltale signs of the impending Allied offensive.[10] Even if they had been alerted, they would have had a hard time beating back the formations opposite them. The Allies outnumbered them all along the front and were supported by overwhelming firepower from the artillery, the largest tank force ever assembled to that point in history, and almost complete command of the air. However, the German infantrymen at the front were far from incompetent, and they continued to base their defensive lines on machine-gun positions that were spread over the battlefield, were difficult to spot, and were so effective that just a handful in a sector could destroy an attacking force.

The Allied attackers would again find gunnery essential both for suppressing enemy battery fire and for "shooting the infantry" onto the enemy positions behind the creeping barrage. The secrecy of the operation made ranging the 646 guns for the complicated creeping barrage difficult, but the Canadians had calibrated their guns in May and June during the rest period, with many gunners boasting that they knew the range from their guns to the targets to the exact metre.[11] In this battle, the gunners would be firing from map references and factoring in atmospheric conditions. They were faced with a difficult task, but proceeding this way would ensure that the element of surprise was not surrendered by telltale ranging shots. Fourteen brigades of artillery would fire together to create the creeping barrage, and, depending on the sector, there would be a gun for every 5 or 10 metres of frontage.[12]

As in previous battles since Vimy, the Canadian Corps relied on devastating counter-battery work to suppress enemy artillery fire. Lieutenant Colonel Andrew McNaughton used intelligence gathered from aerial and forward spotters, battle patrols, and prisoners to build up an appreciation of the enemy's battery strength. McNaughton's protégé, Harry Crerar, who would replace him as commander of the CCBO, and as army commander in the next war, applauded McNaughton's "elasticity of methods and procedure" in finding solutions to targeting and destroying the enemy.[13] With only a week to prepare for the assault, McNaughton's headquarters used sound-ranging and flash-spotting technology to spot enemy guns and gradually knock them out before the battle. In the days before zero hour and during the early stages of the attack, shrapnel, smoke, high explosives, and poison gas were used against all known targets, and eighty percent of the German guns were destroyed or neutralized at the start of the battle. Currie and Morrison had faith in their gunners. It would not be misplaced.

Zero hour was fixed for 4:20 A.M. on August 8, just over an hour before sunrise. The time was chosen to give the infantry a chance to advance within the relative safety of darkness and break the outer crust of the Amiens defences before driving deeper into the heart of the German lines. Tanks were to assist in mopping up and to support the infantry push, and 168 of the BEF's new Mark V tanks were available to the Canadian Corps. The lumbering tanks still had problems, even though they had improved in speed and reliability since their introduction on the Somme two years earlier. At a weight of 29 tonnes and a length of 8 metres, the armoured vehicles were hard for enemy gunners to miss, and while they were bullet-resistant, they were not bulletproof. Tank crews were issued with chain-mail masks that would have been easily recognized by a medieval warrior, to protect against the "splash" of metal that flew around the interior of the tank as pieces of the interior walls were dislodged and turned into projectiles when bullets and larger ordnance hit the tank's hull. Perhaps worst of all, the metal beasts were poorly ventilated. Despite these problems, the tanks were a significant threat and still a terror to the enemy troops, who had almost none of their own to support them.

REFERRING TO THE CANADIANS, General Rawlinson confided to his diary: "They are my chief anxiety as they have the most difficult job."[14] The Canadian front was crossed by the 200-metre-wide Luce River and was flooded and swampy in many parts. As well, the axis of attack was from northwest to southeast, which would require the infantry to carry out some complicated manoeuvres to ensure they did not gravitate to the south by following the natural geographical patterns of the battlefield. This situation was made yet more difficult for the Canadians by the deception plan, which kept them out of the front lines during the week before the battle, seriously hampering the ability of battalion and brigade officers to reconnoitre the battlefield.

The Canadian Corps had an 8.5-kilometre-wide front and had to advance about 14 kilometres to reach their final objectives. All four Canadian divisions would be involved in the battle on August 8, as well as the Canadian Cavalry Brigade. The plan divided the battlefield into Green, Red, and Blue lines. The Green Line was the forward or outpost zone that needed to be overrun quickly; it was not held in strength and had little wire and few dugouts. The Red Line was more strongly defended and contained many of the reserve units and dozens of artillery positions. The furthest objective, the Blue Line, ran through the rearward zone of enemy strongpoints and counterattack positions. Beyond this lay the Allies' outer Amiens defences, which dated back to the Battle of the Somme in 1916 and had been lost during the German push of early 1918. This final rear area was criss-crossed with old trenches, supporting lines, and rusting barbed wire. Attacking battalions would move ahead with fresh formations passing through them to keep up the forward momentum of the attack. This would be an operation based on speed, with the goal of gouging a hole through the first-line German defences and plunging deeper before the enemy could react.

For the Canadians, the operation was informally known as *Llandovery Castle,* in homage to the hospital ship of that name that was sunk at the end of June by a German U-boat. Eighty-eight of the ninety-four Canadians on board died, including fourteen nurses. Even worse, the U-boat had machine-gunned and rammed a number of lifeboats. This was viewed as the height of barbarity, and as the Canadians moved into the line on the night of August 7, many felt that revenge was in order. Brigadier George Tuxford, a former homesteader from Moose Jaw, Saskatchewan, gave orders that the "battle cry on the 8th of August should be *Llandovery Castle,* and that cry should be the last to ring in the ears of the Hun as the bayonet was driven home."[15]

The assaulting divisions moved into their jumping-off positions just south of Villers-Bretonneux. Tens of thousands of troops lay in the wet grass or in shallow slit trenches. "If the Germans had ever got wise as to how the troops were massed down there, it would have been a terrible slaughter, because we were packed in the lines so tight," recounted R.H. Camp of the 18th Battalion.[16] A poison gas bombardment remained one of the high command's greatest fears, as the chemical clouds would throw the operation into chaos. One stray German shell did find a fuel dump, causing a massive explosion and burning up a number of tanks. But although the surrounding area was bathed in fiery light, the Germans did not follow up by sending over additional shells. The infantry, who had been ordered to shed most of their equipment and go in "battle order"—equipped with only emergency rations and water, 250 rounds of ammunition, an entrenching tool, two grenades, two sandbags, a respirator, and their weapon—shivered as dawn's dew collected on the grass where they lay prepared to jump off, waiting for the barrage. The staff officers and commanders in the rear could only hope that all had been done to ensure success. The Canadians, as Sir Arthur Currie noted with pride, "were the spearhead of the attack."[17] If they were stopped, the offensive would likely fail with them.

CHAPTER 28

THE EIGHTH OF
THE EIGHTH

The Battle of Amiens, August 8, 1918

"A great white light went up and our guns started firing rounds," recounted
D.J. Pearce of the PPCLI. "The whole German Trench rose up in the air with everything in it."[1] At 4:20 A.M. on August 8, 1918, 2,000 artillery pieces ranged along the
entire Allied front fired almost as one in a devastating bombardment. In the
Canadian sector, 646 guns were firing in support of the corps' assault. The starry sky
was rent by a "furnace of orange lightning and the noise came in a continual roll,"
remembered gunner Wilfred Kerr.[2] Shrapnel, smoke, high explosives, and poison gas
were used against all known targets. According to one official report, "Not only was
the artillery retaliation very weak throughout the advance, but also on reaching the
lines of enemy guns the effect of our counter-battery work was conclusively evident."[3]

The creeping barrage moved forward at 200 metres per minute, quickly tearing
up the enemy's lightly held forward defences. Its speed was six times that of the
Vimy barrage, reflecting the high command's hope for a rapid advance. The infantry
and tanks moved with the curtain of fire, storming over and through smoking
craters, shredded barbed wire, and German corpses. The assault advanced so quickly
that most of the German first-line defenders were caught unprepared. Along most
of their front, new troops had been cycled into the line only the night before—a
disastrous move by the German high command as the new soldiers had almost no
time to reconnoitre their positions. As the attackers moved forward, a dense fog

reduced visibility to only a few metres, and before the sun burned it off, units got lost all over the battlefield, straying into other sectors. Few incidents of Canadian friendly fire were reported, but there must surely have been some, especially with nervous soldiers mucking through the fog and running into other units unexpectedly. But the thick haze worked both ways, preventing the blinded defenders from seeing and targeting the advancing Canadian troops.

On the left, Major General Burstall's 2nd Division employed the 18th, 21st, and 19th Battalions of the 4th Brigade in the initial assault, their main objective being the fortified village of Marcelcave. The divisional front was about 2,000 metres wide, and the morale of the assault force was described as being "extraordinarily high."[4] The Canadians were itching for a fight. However, for more than an hour before the attack, their forward positions of linked shell holes had been heavily bombarded by searching German artillery fire, indicating that the enemy was obviously aware that something was occurring opposite them. Private Deward Barnes of the 19th Battalion noted in his diary: "His batteries opened up and he made an awful mess of us. A large number of us were wounded or killed."[5]

Despite the effects of the enemy bombardment, at zero hour, the 19th Battalion, supported by two sections of tanks and four Stokes mortar teams, launched themselves forward, with three of their four companies making deep inroads. The first 2,000 metres of German front were lightly held and quickly overrun, but stray machine-gun fire increasingly swept the Canadian advance. The tanks were to clear the machine-gun nests, but they got lost in the fog, and so, unable to wait, the company commanders organized small battle groups to flank the MG-08 positions.[6] Short, sharp battles ensued, which succeeded in clearing the way for the drive forward. In other cases, the fog effectively covered Canadian sections and platoons as they infiltrated past machine-gun nests; secondary waves then cleared the positions or the first wave of attackers doubled back to destroy them from the rear when they opened fire and revealed themselves. The strange, ghostly battlefield must have been terrifying as shadows of soldiers and units filtered through the murk, and all the while the combined cacophony generated by the metal clanging of tanks, the horrendously loud high explosive bursts, the distinctive crack of rifle fire, and the shrieks of the wounded added to the nightmarish quality of the scene.

Allied tanks passing through a field during the Battle of Amiens. While the tanks initially proved effective in surprising the enemy and in grinding out strongpoints, many were knocked out during the succeeding days of battle, leaving the infantry to fight their way forward often without armoured support.

The men of 4th Brigade worked their way forward towards the Green Line objective, but first they had to push through the village of Marcelcave. It was a long advance of over 3.5 kilometres, and indiscriminate long-range machine-gun fire caught many Canadians in the open, including the commanding officer of the 21st Battalion, Lieutenant Colonel Elmer Jones, who had fought with the battalion since its first days and was killed here by a bullet to the lung. With the 19th and 21st Battalions in the lead, heavy howitzers began to rain down devastating fire on the German defenders dug-in and around the village. As the infantry rested in sunken roads and craters catching their breath or smoking, a punishing forty-five-minute bombardment reduced much of the village to rubble. At the prearranged time of 6:23 A.M., the barrage moved off and the Canadians attacked from three directions through the dust, smoke, and fire. The Germans were not quick to surrender, but they were eventually overrun, room by room, house by house, street by street. The 4th Brigade pushed another kilometre beyond the ruins. The advance had been successful but costly, with the 18th and 19th Battalions losing about 150 men each, and the 21st about half that many.[7]

THE 5TH BRIGADE passed through the 4th Brigade's Green Line positions at around 8:20 A.M., with the 24th and 26th Battalions advancing 4.5 kilometres against Pieuret Wood, Wiencourt, and Guillaucourt. Only one tank remained in this sector (the rest having been lost in the mist), but the Canadians had the support of three captured 77mm German field guns, which they turned on the enemy and fired at point-blank range. The normally effective sweeping artillery barrage was ragged on this front, and had a difficult time keeping a uniform wall of fire, so that shells were landing ahead of and behind the barrage line, leaving some German positions unscathed while shells fell into the Canadian lines. There was harsh fighting for Pieuret Wood, but eventually the Germans were overrun, with the Canadians capturing a number of anti-tank guns, four 4.2-inch mortars, two 5.9-inch howitzers, a handful of machine guns, and 150 prisoners.[8] The position fell by 8:50 A.M., and the 24th Battalion, with Lieutenant Colonel W.H. Clark-Kennedy in the lead, drove his companies towards Wiencourt.

The 26th also had to fight its way forward, but the New Brunswickers did so behind their skirling pipe band. Advancing over open ground to the right of the 24th and to the south of Wiencourt and Guillaucourt, they began to take casualties from hidden machine-gun nests to their rear, which were behind the now advanced Canadian lines. Before these posts near Marcelcave were wiped out, the men of the 26th "suffered considerably from enfilade machine-gun fire," wrote Captain C.A. Moore, who was leading A Company.[9] With the enemy in front, on the flanks, and behind, it often fell to the rank and file to destroy the pockets of resistance without the assistance of tanks or artillery. Private L.D. Chase of the "Fighting Twenty-Sixth" and a few other men rushed one machine-gun strongpoint after their officer had been shot dead. In the ensuing battle, Chase and his companions killed and captured four times their number, and Chase was awarded the Military Medal for his bravery.[10] The tanks were also useful on this front (much more so than on the 24th's), zigzagging their way across the battlefield to avoid presenting easy targets and eventually grinding out a series of machine guns and a German battery that was firing from only 400 metres away. Several times the advance was held up by machine-gun fire, and the infantry succeeded in moving forward only by crouching behind the metal monsters, which provided effective cover. The 26th regrouped and, with elements of the 24th Battalion, pushed on in the face of stubborn small-arms fire. Capturing the village of Guillaucourt by 10 A.M., they moved on to the Red Line objectives a further 1,500 metres to the east.

After-battle reports noted that most of the Canadian casualties were caused by machine-gun fire, attesting to the effectiveness of the Canadian counter-battery work. The day cost the 24th Battalion 31 killed and 152 wounded; the 26th lost an unknown number in the fighting, but seemingly even more than the 24th, as most of the battalion's infantry companies suffered casualties in excess of half of their strength.[11] The only saving grace was that the ratio of dead to wounded appeared to be roughly one to five—the number of deaths thus being far lower than in previous engagements. The reduction was likely due to the Germans' heavy reliance on their small arms—rifles and machine guns—rather than their artillery, which created more lethal wounds as the uneven shrapnel and shards of shell casings tumbled and tore through the body at irregular angles.

ABOVE THE FRONT, the RAF aircraft bombed and machine-gunned enemy positions. To the south of the 24th and 26th Battalions, the 49th felt secure in their advance with a low-flying aircraft circling the battlefield over them, ready for targets and communicating with ground forces by dipping and wagging its wings. The 49th came across a machine gun holding a dug-in position, and the infantry projected several rifle grenades in its direction to alert the fighter plane. The aircraft spotted the target and dove, firing its machine guns, raking the position.[12] When it dove a second time, the German machine-gunners ran for cover, hands in the air and shouting out their surrender.

But deployment of tactical airpower was dangerous work. Raymond Collishaw, a native of Nanaimo, British Columbia, and one of the highest ranking aces of the war, described the cost of this battle for the airmen:

The fighter Squadrons suffered heavily and the whole Roye road was strewn with hundreds of aircraft and derelict tanks. Each time the fighter pilots were launched to assault the infantry, they could see the aeroplane graveyard beneath them, and one was conscious, while passing through a hail of fire, that at any moment the frail shell, in which the pilot felt poised precariously, might join its kind below.[13]

Slower observation planes circled the front at low levels, running contact patrols that reported on the extent and speed of the infantry advance, and correcting the fall of artillery fire. Basic wireless sets, which could transmit but not receive, provided real-time intelligence. The infantry, in turn, used flares and reflective markers to communicate with the eyes in the skies. The Allies also tried to compound the confusion in the enemy rear areas by bombing a number of key road and rail bridges, to slow the ability of the Germans to reinforce their crumbling front. Day-bombers flew over 200 sorties, with the support of fighter planes, but they were unable to damage the rail structures with their light payloads of only eight 11-kilogram bombs. Still, the German air force was pushed to fight and defend these logistical areas, and their planes were systematically shot down in an aerial war of attrition. The RAF even engaged in the complicated act of supplying forward troops with air drops of ammunition and supplies. With the addition of this aerial support, Amiens was truly an all-arms battle: artillery, mortars, armoured cars, tanks, and airplanes supported the infantry fighting their way forward through the German defensive lines.[14]

TO THE SOUTH, in the centre of the Canadian front, General Macdonell's 1st Division attacked with the 3rd Brigade forward, with the other two brigades poised to cycle through it later in the day. The terrain was heavily wooded, and the attack along parts of the front would be funnelled into a valley, flanked on the sides with ravines that offered the enemy additional cover and natural defensive positions. The primary objectives on this front were Hangard Wood and Demuin, the latter situated across the Luce River, about 5,500 metres away. This sector was well suited for the defence, since it was level and therefore ideal for sweeping defensive fire. Only overripe rye covered the battlefield that had to be traversed by the 14th, 13th, and 16th Battalions, and while it provided some cover from searching eyes it offered only a false sense of protection against whirling metal.

The 13th, in the centre, had swarmed forward at zero hour into the heavy fog that had reduced vision to a mere 10 metres. Their support tanks were soon hopelessly lost, and the situation would get worse: within a few minutes, at least thirty of the Highlanders were wounded or killed by friendly artillery shells. But still the ghostly figures pushed on through the mist to Hangard Wood.

The Germans had established a number of machine-gun positions throughout the wood, on its edge and in its interior. The 13th advanced, passing through hundreds of rotting bodies—the remains of fierce fighting here earlier in the spring. Amidst these macabre sights, the Canadians employed their flexible infantry tactics to pin down enemy positions and then attack them from the flanks, wiping them out one by one. But these encounters were costly, and men were lost while drawing fire or engaging in firefights with the enemy in order to allow their comrades to move up. One of them was Private John Croak, a miner from Glace Bay, Nova Scotia, who, according to one mate, "feared nothing. He always carried a revolver on his hip and I don't think he would have been afraid to use it on anyone who crossed him. It was a saying in our company that if you went on a patrol or out on a working party with Johnny Croak you'd come back."[15] With his unit under fire, Croak charged single-handedly, tossing a grenade and killing the gunners in an MG-08 post. Though severely wounded in the right arm, he organized his battalion mates for an assault on another German position. They took it, but Croak was killed in the process. The gallant action was recognized with a Victoria Cross, which was awarded posthumously to his family.

Corporal Herman Good lived to see his Victoria Cross, awarded for his gallant action of taking out several machine-gun posts that were holding up the advance. A lumberjack from New Brunswick, Good continued his drive with his remaining surviving companions following him until they encountered a battery of 5.9-inch guns. Realizing that his section of men would provide a big target, Good ordered most to dig in, choosing to lead three privates in a wild bayonet charge against the more than forty gunners who were furiously pounding the Canadian lines. The three men shot and stabbed more than a dozen enemy before the rest surrendered their position and guns to the bloodstained Canadians. Courage and luck carried Corporal Good through the rest of the battle, and the war.

Despite such individual acts of heroism, the 13th Battalion ran into determined opposition at Croates Trench, where sixty defenders and several machine-gunners held up the advance for forty-five minutes. It was a fierce firefight, and the Highlanders suffered because they were out of rifle grenades. Two tanks were signalled for and brought forward but both were knocked out by German artillery fire.

The German anti-tank doctrine called for the evacuation of outposts in case of armoured attacks, and for flanking units to direct their small-arms fire against the supporting infantry to prevent them from exploiting the breakthrough.[16] In this case, however, the enemy artillery directed all fire on the lumbering beasts, completely destroying them. These two tanks were the last of seven assigned to the battalion, raising the casualty rate to 100 percent. High velocity 77mm shells had torn through the metal hull, ricocheting inside, shredding the inhabitants. Few ever forgot the smell of roasted flesh wafting over the battlefield, and Frederick Noyes of the 5th Canadian Field Ambulance attested that "tank crews died horrible deaths inside their steel pyres."[17] After much sniping back and forth, a Stokes mortar team was brought forward, which pulverized the German trench. Despite the deep advances, this was no walkover.

The 14th Battalion, to the left of the 13th, crashed through a series of German outposts. Their infantry and tank coordination was strong, and one concealed German position containing six MG-08s was knocked out by an attack formation of tank and infantry working together. The Royal Montreal Regiment pushed deep but also ran into fierce machine-gun resistance at Croates Trench. After they deluged the trench with rifle fire and grenades, a white flag was raised by the Germans. The Canadians rose tentatively from their cover but were fired on, several being killed. It was unclear whether the Germans' act was treachery or just the result of confusion as one part of the German defence sought to surrender while another continued fighting. The answer was irrelevant to the Canadians after their brethren were killed in cold blood. Frontal and enfilade advances began to close the ring on the Germans. When the enemy later raised white flags, an official report by Lieutenant Colonel Dick Worrall—a prewar soldier-adventurer who had served in the American army before 1914 and would be awarded two Military Crosses and two Distinguished Service Orders before the end of the war—testified, "No notice was taken of this, and when the garrison stepped out with raised hands—they were annihilated almost to a man."[18] It was blood for blood on the Western Front.

On the division's far right, the mist was combined with a smokescreen, ensuring that the 16th Battalion's senior officers had a difficult time exerting control over their diffused fighting units. It was a corporal's battle. The Canadian Scottish groped their way forward, and then, passing through the mist and smoke, made strong advances, meeting little opposition for the first 2,000 metres. But again it was machine-gun nests that made the push costly. When concentrated fire opened up against them, the lead units went to ground. One group of men were inching their way forward towards the enemy lines under a hail of bullets when a bagpiper made his way up to the front. An officer told him to pipe "The Drunken Piper," and the men charged to the strains of the tune. The roused Highlanders overran the machine guns and a heavy trench mortar, flooding into the enemy's elaborate trenches. Throughout the rest of the morning, the infantry continued to surge forward, and though they were supported by seven tanks, as Lieutenant Colonel Cy Peck observed, the success of the attack came down to "these veterans, heroes of many battles, who advanced with their old-time steadiness, discipline, and dauntless courage." The men of the 16th drove the Germans before them, capturing, by the end of the day, more than 900 prisoners.[19]

The 3rd Brigade had advanced so quickly that the 3rd and 5th Battalions, which had been held in reserve to provide an extra push to the Green and Red Lines, were not needed, and spent most of their time dealing with areas of enemy resistance that had been bypassed. By about 8:15 A.M., the lead units of the 3rd Brigade were on the Green Line, and Brigadier General Griesbach's 1st Brigade pushed through them on their way to attack the Red Line, some 3,500 metres beyond. The 2nd, 4th, and 3rd Battalions drove forward, shifting from line tactics to smaller, forward-rushing sections when they encountered pockets of resistance. Here, with their fire and movement tactics—which involved scouts and snipers pushing forward and Lewis machine-gunners developing "superiority of fire," as one official document observed—the infiltrating infantry neutralized most of the opposition.[20]

The tanks struck fear in the hearts of the enemy, but most of them could not keep up with the infantry; nor could the artillery, as the advance had moved outside its range. At this stage, the infantry were fighting their battle with little support from the gunners, who were in the process of moving their weapons forward. Even the infantry's own heavy Vickers machine-gun teams lagged behind. Lieutenant James Pedley of the "Mad Fourth" recounted that his platoon went forward in diamond formation, with the "four sections spread out, advancing by rushes," pinning down the enemy positions with fire and attacking them one after another.[21] The three battalions engaged in some hard fighting, but the low number of casualties to the brigade—68 killed, 353 wounded, and 15 missing—was an indication of the swiftness of the advance.[22]

All of Griesbach's men were on the Red Line by 12:30 P.M., and had established their fortified outposts, many of which were across the Luce since the Canadians had, through their rapid advance, captured bridges that the German defenders did not have time to blow up.[23] In other spots, Canadian engineers built cork footbridges to allow the infantry to cross the marshy waters. The front had narrowed considerably here, so that Brigadier General Loomis's 2nd Brigade was forced to squeeze through a 1.5-kilometre-wide gap, which was dangerous since the Germans now had a better appreciation of the disaster that confronted them, and had already moved reinforcements forward and saturated the front in shellfire. Moreover, the 7th and 10th Battalions would have to overrun the German-fortified small village of Caix before reaching the Blue Line.

Despite a logistical jam caused by long cavalry columns that advanced very cautiously, and a shortage of bridges to cross the Luce, both battalions pushed forward, infiltrating through and around areas of resistance. By 2:30 P.M., they were on their final objectives, and hundreds of Germans had been captured or were fleeing. The 10th Battalion alone accounted for eighty machine guns. The enemy was disorganized and in full retreat, but by around 5 P.M. enemy trucks could be seen rushing troops to the front, backstopping the wavering defence.[24] The glimpse of the breakthrough disappeared.

ON THE RIGHT of the Canadian front, the 3rd Division had the most difficult task of the three divisions. It had to secure the Amiens-Roye road and cross over the Luce River, all in full view of the German trenches. But fortunately for the attackers, the fog was also heaviest on this front due to the presence of the marsh, and the Canadians would go forward into, and be screened by, a dense mist as thick as smoke.

General Lipsett and his staff conceived of a daring operation. To the south of the Luce, the 9th Brigade attacked with three battalions up. The 43rd Cameron Highlanders from Winnipeg, on the far right, followed the creeping barrage and a special smokescreen into dead ground in front of the Germans—an area out of direct observation and relatively safe from enemy fire. They occupied this position by overrunning machine guns and a battery of 5.9-inch guns that were torn apart when eight Lewis guns laid down a heavy crossfire on the static defenders. The battalion then held the dead ground, which focused the Germans' attention, as they were rightly worried about a strong force digging in under their noses.

With the 43rd Battalion's thrust drawing enemy fire, the 58th and 116th Battalions delivered a left hook, moving along the river bank towards Demuin. The 116th, the least experienced Canadian battalion, was lucky to be commanded by Lieutenant Colonel George Pearkes, who had been awarded the Victoria Cross at Passchendaele for his bravery and leadership under fire. The "Umpty Umps," as the 116th called themselves, advanced steadily on a wide front of 1,000 metres. Control was difficult to maintain since the company commanders had been given almost no time to reconnoitre the front. They crossed the open fields in a spread-out formation, aware that the woods in front of them likely contained enemy troops all drawing a bead on them. The lead company, A, was the bait, and it marched into a crossfire killing zone in front of Hamon Wood. Within minutes, every officer was killed or wounded, and the survivors frantically found cover. There was almost no possibility of pushing forward without artillery support. But Pearkes, who had already shown legendary bravery on the battlefield, amalgamated a number of shattered platoons and companies into a composite unit and, bringing all Lewis guns forward, led his men to enfilade the German trenches. Driving their defences in from the flanks, Pearkes's force killed dozens and took some 400 prisoners. E.P.S. Allen, the battalion's adjutant, noted, "The dash of our men was most marked, showing a marvellous difference from the old staid method of following the barrage shoulder to shoulder."[25] Trophies including an 8-inch howitzer and two other field guns were marked with the battalion's number and reversed against the enemy by specially trained gunners. The shattered trees of Hamon Wood had fallen to the 116th, but at the cost of 32 killed and 158 wounded or missing.[26]

The 58th advanced to the north of Hamon Wood against Demuin by working closely with its tanks. Despite marshy ground and belts of uncut barbed wire, three companies hit the fortified town, spread fanwise, and crashed over dozens of machine-gun positions. Fierce fighting raged for several hours. Major Henry Rose, a thirty-six-year-old company commander, recounted his experience of leading a platoon to outflank the position where his men were pinned down by enemy fire:

> I led my motley platoon across the Hun zone of fire, with only two casualties, I think, and got fairly close in to the flank of the strongpoint without being discovered. I was not quite certain where the Hun was, so I went on ahead of my men to reconnoitre. I worked along a sunken road about 150 yards to a bit of a bank running at right angles. The patter of machine guns seemed closer, but I thought I was yet some distance from them, so I stuck my head over this bank, and found the whole thing on the other side. I drew down very quickly of course, but not before a Hun bomber had spotted me, and then over came the cylindrical stick bombs. I dropped into a shell-hole and did some hard thinking. I only had my revolver and there were some three Hun guns and about 30 of the enemy.[27]

Reacting almost instinctively, Rose jumped over the top and charged the Germans, emptying his revolver into them. And then everything went black. Rose woke up in a hospital with multiple wounds from bullets and shrapnel. His men had rushed to support him and all of the Germans had been killed or captured. The 58th continued their advance. By the end of the day, Demuin was in Canadian hands and the 58th had bagged at least 400 prisoners and 40 machine guns, at the cost of 150 casualties.[28]

ON THE NORTHERN SIDE of the Luce the 8th Brigade attacked with a single battalion, as it was squeezed between the river and Hangard Wood. The 1st Canadian Mounted Rifles' rapid advance, assisted by the fog, carried them into the small village of Hangard, and then Courcelles. The infantry had outpaced the tanks, and so, with their refined tactics, the enemy's "machine-gun nests were surrounded and put out of action before they could inflict many casualties."[29] This was open, manoeuvre warfare, and a spirit of aggression and sacrifice reigned among the Canadian troops. The 2nd CMR passed through them and pushed to the brigade's final objectives on the Green Line.

Because of the difficult frontage that was cut by the Luce River, the 3rd Division received two additional artillery brigades, for a total of six. Brutinel's Canadian Independent Force (CIF)—formerly the Motor Machine Gun Brigade (having recently been renamed)—was also provided to protect the division's right flank, since the French to the south were not attacking until forty-five minutes after the Canadians went in. The core of the CIF was composed of twenty armoured cars, each armed with twin Vickers machine guns, but also supported by motorcyclists and mobile mortar teams. Acting as a hard shoulder for the operation, the metal-clad machine-gunners used their mobility to race off down the shell-pocked Amiens-Roye road to attack and take Mézières.[30] With significant firepower from their Vickers, as well as from newly mounted Newton 6-inch mortars that fired 52-pound bombs up to 1,200 metres, Brutinel's force knocked out a number of enemy positions, including three villages where Germans were holding up the French advance to the south. Here, the machine-gunners outflanked the enemy, shooting them up from the side and rear. Seventeen Croix de Guerre gallantry medals were awarded to the motors by the appreciative French forces.[31] Despite the glamour associated with this armoured warfare that combined speed and machine guns, the cars were limited in what they could accomplish against dug-in forces in wooded areas, as they had almost no off-road capability. Due to the cars' high visibility and vulnerability, the armoured formation was forced to retreat several times in the face of heavy artillery fire, but they had achieved Lipsett's goal of engaging the enemy on this front and ensuring that the main attack to the north would not be assaulted from the flanks.[32]

THE BATTALIONS of Brigadier H.M. Dyer's 7th Brigade moved forward in the secondary waves at about 6 A.M., and the divisional engineers played a key role in building pontooned cork footbridges over the Luce River and across surrounding marshy ground.[33] As these secondary force units queued up before the bridges that would take them over the Luce to catch up with the 8th and 9th Brigades in contact with the enemy, more than a few of the infantrymen could not help but glance worriedly at the water over which they crossed, which was "fouled with human and animal corpses."[34] At 8:20 A.M., the 49th Battalion attacked on the left, the 42nd in the centre, and the Royal Canadian Regiment (RCR) on the right along the Roye road, leapfrogging through their sister brigades. Behind a barrage that was so loud that shouting officers and sergeants could not be heard, the RCR made quick progress moving along the side of the road, and were on their Red Line objectives in less than two hours. But the French advance to the south pushed a number of retreating German troops across the divisional boundary into Canadian territory. The lead RCR units could have been wiped out, stuck as they were between hammer and anvil, but RCR Lieutenant J.W. Miller and his support platoon rushed up and engaged the German forces in several fierce firefights. All enemy soldiers were cut off, killed, and scattered, and the RCR advance continued.[35]

In portions of the 49th Battalion's sector, the ground was so pitted with shell holes that the crater lips almost touched one another. Advancing through the deluge of fire and steel, the 49th Battalion carefully avoided stepping on the dismembered bodies of horses and men. George Maxwell of the 49th described a group of dead machine-gunners, likely killed by the concussion of a high explosive shell, since they had no visible wounds: "Some were in a crouching posture, as if tending their guns. They looked as if they were still alive; some resembled wax figures. One that especially caught my attention was in the act of lighting his pipe, his hands still cupped around where the match had been ... and there he knelt, stone dead."[36] Further advances were made, and prisoners were disarmed and sent to the rear. Maxwell offered some insight into the dangers of close combat, and remembered one of his companions, who "in the welter of bloodshed and emotion upheaval" killed a prisoner. Later, the man confessed: "Jesus! Will I ever forget it? I stuck the poor bastard with his hands up!" Maxwell also anguished over the act, but felt that the "unhappy soldier was pressing forward, overwrought like most of us, through shell-shocked enemy soldiers who had survived the murderous barrage. One can do nothing about the nervous strain engendered, especially in those on the 'receiving end.'"[37]

In the centre, the 42nd was harassed by gas shells that forced the infantry to don their respirators, leaving them bathed in sweat and gagging on the chemicals. However, Padre G.D. Kilpatrick noted, "The platoons went forward in rushes.... it was clear that those hot and dusty days spent in training had not been wasted."[38] But small-unit tactics could not save the Highlanders from the counter-barrage that was landing on their lines and the direct artillery fire that was being coordinated by a low-flying German spotter plane above them. The Highlanders, led by Captain J.D. MacLeod, who took over B Company after its commanding officer had been knocked out, overran two enemy batteries of 4.1- and 8-inch howitzers, manoeuvring his sections close enough to fire at point-blank range. Both batteries were captured. With four tanks, the Highlanders overran Hill 102, a German strongpoint, and the metal monsters were, according to the 42nd's commanding officer, Lieutenant Colonel R.L.H. Ewing, "largely responsible for the success of the whole operation."[39] He was overstating the case, as there had been much terrible, chaotic, close-quartered fighting, in which soldiers lived on the razor's edge between life and death—a nightmare fraught with confusion and savagery, split-second decisions and heart-rending choices.

As the 7th Brigade dug in, the grim-faced soldiers were struck by an incredible image: from behind them came a massed cavalry attack. Here, finally, the cavalry was "hitting the gap," which the infantry had hacked open. The Canadian Cavalry Brigade, led by Lord Strathcona's Horse and the Royal Canadian Dragoons, rode towards Fresnoy-en-Chaussée, and then on to Les Quesnel. They were supported by small groups of Whippet tanks, but these were too slow to keep pace with the hell-for-leather cavalry. More than 125 prisoners were taken at Fresnoy, but the cavalry was an arm to attack and exploit rather than hold and defend. After the cavalry rode off, the Germans reoccupied the position. Overall, the cavalry met mixed success: they were breaking into the enemy positions, but, just like the infantry, they found that even a few machine-gunners could shatter a charge. Since these mounted soldiers lacked the specialized weapons and tactics of the infantry, the bodies of horses and their riders were increasingly dotting the landscape. The Canadian Cavalry Brigade suffered 245 casualties from August 8 to 11, and proved once again that sabres could not defeat machine guns.[40] "Their charges at many times ... were exceedingly gallant, but futile," was the assessment of Brigadier Robert Rennie of the 4th Brigade.[41]

Another attempt at combining fire and movement was the use of the new Mark V* tanks—known as the Mark Five Star and measuring longer than the Mark V by about 1.5 metres—which would act as armoured personnel carriers. The innovative plan called for the tanks to transport a section of twenty soldiers each, supported by three machine-gun detachments that would attempt to keep up on foot. The tanks were to drive to the Blue Line, past Le Quesnel; but very quickly the debilitating heat and gasoline fumes sickened almost everyone inside the suffocating machines. One officer noted, "The bullets striking the tank made a noise like riveters working in a shipyard," and left those on the interior bleeding from nasty scrapes and cuts.[42] Major George McFarland of the 4th CMR recounted his experience in a tank: "The awful heat, the ear-splitting roar of the engines, and the fumes of the oil and petrol made the place a veritable inferno."[43] The armoured advance ground to a halt as wheezing, exhausted men rolled from the tanks. As well, a single German battery, in a fortified, hidden position, destroyed ten tanks as they rumbled forward. Although eleven tanks (relieved of their cargo of infantrymen) reached their objectives, they were attacked in strength and forced to retreat.[44] The Germans, too, had learned from the previous two years of fighting—having trained to knock out the feared tanks. The Mark V* operation had been a complete failure. With the cavalry shot down and the tanks knocked out, it once again fell to the infantry to smash their way forward. Third phase formations on the 2nd and 1st Divisions' fronts pushed on to their final objectives, although there was harder fighting to the south.

DAVID WATSON'S 4th Division passed through the 3rd to continue the drive on that front. Odlum's 11th Brigade attacked on the right, along the Amiens-Roye road, and MacBrien's 12th Brigade advanced on a similar axis to their left. Odlum pushed forward with a thick assault force: the 54th and 102nd Battalions, followed closely by the 75th and 87th, which would have to crack through Le Quesnel.

The 54th moved forward from the start line at 5:30 A.M., advancing several kilometres before they even reached the front-line troops. As they marched to close with the enemy, they passed the walking wounded and prisoners of war moving in the opposite direction. While pushing into the mouth of hell, Captain John Preston recounted the surreal scene of watching a group of infantrymen throw their steel helmets at an apple tree in the hope of bringing down some fruit.[45] The opening phase of the operation had been an obvious success: would it be as easy for follow-on forces, or would the enemy's resistance stiffen?

Shells started to fall around the 54th as they approached the front, increasing in density with each step towards the firing line. During the march, one shell landed on B Company, wounding fourteen men; a second came roaring through the air "wiping out a Lewis gun" and twelve men.[46] Such casualties could not be avoided in open warfare. Upon reaching their jumping-off positions, the infantry waited for the barrage, scheduled for around 1:30 P.M. The noon-day sun had burned away the fog, increasing visibility, but also revealing the truth of reconnaissance reports by scouts that the "entire frontage was swept with machine-gun fire" from the woods behind Beaucourt. Three tanks went forward, but almost immediately two were knocked out and set on fire, and the third was disabled. The sight and smell of roasting flesh and oil spread over the front.

Lieutenant Colonel A.B. Carey, the 54th's commanding officer, thought the battalion might charge quickly through the smoke and catch the Germans off guard. A cavalry section was in the vicinity, which would have added shock value, but it refused to advance. A disgusted Carey would not be dissuaded. He gathered two reserve platoons and charged frontally. There was almost no barrage, and only a few survivors gained the trees—most with bullet holes through their clothes, water bottles shot away, lives spared by the barest of inches. They dug in and tried to return fire against a "hail of lead" coming from German guns. The 54th responded with Lewis-gun fire. "The bands of their guns fairly smoked," wrote Lieutenant T.S. McLanders, commanding officer of B Company, "as drum after drum, almost as fast as the No. 2s could hand them up, were used up, pouring accurate and death-dealing fire." But as these two ragged platoons drew fire onto themselves, they allowed three advancing companies to clear the woods from the flanks, surging around strongpoints and into the German rear areas. In the face of this Canadian pressure, the Germans fled from their positions or surrendered.[47]

The 75th passed through the 54th, whose men were digging trenches or enlarging still-smoking shell holes under fire. But the 75th had lost a steady stream of men in the advance to the front. Private John Becker remembered flopping to the ground as a shell whirled over his head, landing some 200 metres behind him and sending three or four men into the air. "I was genuinely ashamed of myself for flattening out as I was familiar enough with shelling to know by the sound if it would not be close.

I realized then that my nerves were going and that I wouldn't be much good in action if I kept at it many weeks longer."[48] But the nerves of many experienced combat soldiers were on edge as they stared at their objective: the village of Le Quesnel. The Torontonians who formed the 75th would be facing their objective with no tanks, little artillery (since much of it was left behind the rapid infantry advance), no cavalry, French forces that were unable to keep up on the flanks, and motor cars that had been beaten back twice as they tried to advance and offer supporting fire. Three companies went forward in the attack over open ground and were cut to pieces. The commanding officer called off further suicidal charges.[49] The Canadians would wait for darkness before attacking again. Le Quesnel was the only planned objective that did not fall on August 8.

THE FIRST DAY OF BATTLE had been a terrible blow for the Germans, as the British armies had achieved their greatest single-day victory of the war, thrusting 13 kilometres. Weak Germans forces had bent, but they had not broken. There would be much hard fighting for the Canadians and other spearhead formations as they tried to turn the enormous gains of the 8th into a breakthrough on the 9th, and possibly end the war.

CHAPTER 29

"I THINK THIS IS THE BEGINNING OF THE END"

August 9–14, 1918

"August 8th was the black day of the German Army in the history of the war," lamented General Erich Ludendorff.[1] The German general, who virtually ran the nation's war effort in the west, was shocked by the Allied advance. Along the Amiens front, three entire divisions had been shattered, and an astounding total of 5,033 of his troops had been captured. The Allies' unqualified success was a bad sign that rot had set into the core of the German army.[2]

As the spearhead of this force, the Canadians had advanced 13 kilometres, the Australians 11, the French 8, and the British a disappointing 5. Currie's refusal at the start of the year to reduce his infantry brigades by a fourth of their strength had paid dividends on the first day of the battle, especially in comparison to the British force on the flank, which often did not have enough men to cycle through the lead units to keep the drive from grinding to a halt. Captain C.E. Montague, who observed the battle as part of British GHQ Intelligence, despaired at the British divisions' "colourless, stunted, half-toothless lads from hot, humid Lancashire mills," whom he contrasted with the "Dominion battalions of men startlingly taller, stronger, handsomer, prouder, firmer in nerve, better schooled, bolder … men who had learned already to look at our men with the half-curious, half-pitying look of a higher, happier caste at a lower."[3] Despite this unflattering portrait of the British troops, and a glorification of the dominion soldiers that seems heavily influenced by the myths of the colonial frontiersmen—either the Digger or Kiwi from the Australian or New Zealand bush or the Canuck who had carved civilization out of the northern wastes—it is worth remembering that the French and British were added to the attack at Amiens to broaden the Allies' base and not allow the Germans to concentrate their artillery fire on the central thrust made by the dominion formations. That said, the Australians and Canadians had distinguished themselves, and perhaps deserved the acclaim offered by Charles Carrington, a British combat veteran, who wrote that the dominion forces were "the best fighting troops in any army."[4]

DESPITE THE EXPECTATION of a coming breakthrough, the fighting on August 8 had been intense and costly, with the Canadians having lost 1,036 killed and 2,803 wounded. Moreover, the Canadian infantry were now spread over the battlefield and out of range of many of their own artillery guns. Exhausted and spent, most of the infantry were content to finger their newly acquired German souvenirs and smoke captured cigars in between furtive catnaps. Excited about their gains, the Canadians were more susceptible than normal to the regular flow of rumours, most of which were elaborated upon by ample quantities of wishful thinking. A report went down the line that not only had the Canadians and Australians broken through, but so had the British at Passchendaele, the French on the Chemin des Dames, and the Americans somewhere else. There was excited chatter that the war could soon be over. When the men learned that the other operations had not produced such stellar results—or, in many cases, had not even been carried out—"Even the let-down … did not spoil that day of excitement," wrote Sergeant Ernest Black, but more than a few veterans were embarrassed that they had been taken in by a trench rumour.[5]

Small-arms and artillery ammunition, field kitchens, and reinforcements jostled for space on worn roads with the wounded, prisoners, and relieved units marching to the rear. Although several mobile batteries of the 18-pounders had been rushed forward under enemy fire, the heavier guns and their ammunition lay mired several kilometres back to the west. The Germans targeted the rear areas with interdiction fire, aware that the best way to slow the infantry's advance was by denying them the supplies and support they needed to continue the push.[6] But the Canadians had a robust service and engineering arm, and while the brave horse-and-mule drivers led their equine friends forward, the engineers were rapidly building new roads. William Stewart, whose big 8-inch gun had been designated to advance early in the battle, remembered the incredible sight of Canadian engineers building a narrow-gauge railroad, from the rear to the front: "Three or four men in front, shovels and picks, filling in the shell holes and levelling the terrain with others carrying up lengths of rail clamping each piece of rail to the last. These sections were about twenty feet long."[7] By the end of the day, light rail cars were bringing ammunition forward—a process that went on all night long. Horse teams pulled their guns forward and gun pits were dug to fill the requirements of the new fireplans that were being prepared through the night for the coming day of battle.

With the Germans fully prepared to defend their lines on August 9, the Allies had no choice but to launch a frontal assault. While the enemy had been shaken on August 8, they were not shattered. Elements of three German divisions, with two more following, were rushed to the front and dug in opposite the Canadians—who had succeeded in the previous day's battle, according to a few German reports, because they had been drunk.[8] Though rum had no doubt helped fire the infantry up for their harsh task, this was no raging army of alcohol-soaked warriors. On the morning of August 9, however, more than a few Canadian units lamented the fact that the pre-battle rum could not be brought forward in time for the kickoff of the second day of battle. Even worse, it was clear that the German positions were now far stronger, as they were defending the old Somme battlefields of 1916, which were criss-crossed with derelict trenches and rusty barbed wire overgrown with grass. Fresh German forces provided a steel backbone to the defenders. These improvements in the Germans' defensive position aside, however, it was the disarray in the Allied headquarters that most limited the attack's momentum.

The Fourth Army headquarters was mired in confusion, largely because of the astounding success at the front. Orders were issued, then cancelled, and then issued again. This vacillating caused problems all down the chain of command as the orders and counter-orders rippled through the ranks, resulting in units setting off for the front or rear and then being forced to return to their original position. Other units were lost on the enormous battlefield, making it impossible to coordinate attack times with them. And even the cardinal sin of command was committed: moving a

division, the 3rd, into reserve some 10 kilometres behind the lines and, later, ordering it back into the forward positions for battle. It was disheartening and tiring for
the infantry to prepare themselves psychologically to be pulled from the line only to
find that they needed to march back into the mouth of the guns. As Charles Bean,
the Australian official historian, noted bluntly, the operations on August 9 would
"probably furnish a classic example of how not to follow up a great attack."[9]

But there was no doubt that the Allies would exploit their success of August 8. All
four Canadian divisions would be involved in the assault to determine whether the
German system might again collapse. But the first step was to secure key objectives
on the 4th Division's front, especially the village of Le Quesnel. At 4:30 A.M., the
75th Battalion, supported by elements of the Canadian Independent Force, stormed
the important village. The few guns that had been brought forward were ineffective,
except to alert the enemy to the attack. One gunner on an 18-pounder crew remembered that the "volume of sound was poor compared with that on the eighth; we
wondered where the heavies were and feared that our light shells would not do much
for the infantry."[10] Shells also fell short in the dark, and many of the Torontonians
who formed much of the 75th were torn to bits by their own armaments. Far worse,
the Germans knew exactly where the attack would fall; as one officer remarked,
Canadians pushed forward "in the face of a murderous machine-gun fire."[11] Yet a
combination of dogged frontal assault and quick-moving flanking attacks pierced the
German lines. Within an hour, two companies had overrun the fortified village, capturing over 100 prisoners, several machine guns, three forward medical units, and a
large supply of cigarettes and cigars, which were passed out to the appreciative survivors. Further consolidation by the 87th Battalion ensured a strong jumping-off
position for the 3rd Division units, which would attack later in the day.

Throughout the morning, Currie tried to marshall his forces for the follow-on
assaults, but several times the artillery units could not get into the line quickly, and
one postponement followed another. These difficulties were worrisome, as the set-
piece battle was reliant on the guns, especially since the Germans could no longer
be taken by surprise. Making matters worse, many of the Canadian troops had
fought the day before, were now exhausted, and had endured hours of shellfire
during the night. As the victorious infantrymen crouched with the worms in their

slit trenches, bloodshot eyes staring out into the enemy lines, only the most naive of newcomers would not have realized that the second day of fighting would be far more difficult than the near breakthrough on August 8.

ON THE FAR LEFT, Burstall ordered the 2nd Division's 5th and 6th Brigades to attack at 10 A.M. But the 1st Division, on the right, notified Burstall that its forces would not be ready until 11 A.M., and then, only forty-five minutes before zero hour, Macdonell was forced to postpone the attack until after noon. This left the 2nd Division with the unenviable prospect of attacking alone, thereby allowing the Germans to focus their guns on them from several parts of the battlefield. Burstall's staff scrambled and was able to delay the 5th Brigade's attack until noon, but on the left front, the 6th Brigade had to attack at 11 A.M. in conjunction with the Australians.

The 6th Brigade's commander, A.H. Bell, ordered the 29th and 31st Battalions to capture the village of Rosières and a light railway running behind it. Officers of the spearheading forces had spent the night studying the battlefield and sending out patrols, which had captured and killed a number of isolated German sniper teams. But an exploratory cavalry force that unwisely strayed into the area took heavy casualties from numerous machine-gun pits, and it was clear that this would be an assault against an alert enemy who was well fortified.

Bell's infantry had to cross more than 1,000 metres of open ground in daylight. Making this task more daunting, when the barrage opened up, it was weak and ragged: experienced soldiers could see right through it, and few believed it would even keep the Germans in their dugouts. But they had to move, and they did. The 29th and 31st fought their way forward, knocking out position after position. Firing from the hip, Lewis gunners deluged the enemy front in bullets and were decisive in suppressing enemy fire.[12] Still, the 29th Battalion alone ran into at least 40 Maxim machine guns, and the brigade captured over 200 guns by the end of the day. Three Whippet tanks, which rolled southward from the Australian front, helped to clear some of the stubborn positions. But still the rate of fire was extraordinary, and even long-service veterans looked with awe upon the storm of steel rained down by enemy defenders. "It looked like certain death and the effect it seemed to have on me was to cause my mouth to go dry just as though I had a mouth full of cotton wool," wrote Lieutenant Colonel W.S. Latta. "The only other sensation I can remember was hoping that it would not be a stomach hit and that I would get it swift and sudden."[13]

The Germans seemed to have fortified every part of the village, and three machine guns were firing down from the town's church steeple. The only solution was a rapid advance, and surviving officers ordered the men forward. Latta was hit in both legs during the assault. As he lay in a shell hole, the bullets flying above, shrapnel falling around him, he was forced to wave his steel helmet desperately to alert a Whippet tank that was grinding over the ground in his direction. At the last moment, it veered away. Led by Captain R.S. Moore, B Company of "Tobin's Tigers" (as the 29th Battalion were known) broke through the northern part of Rosières, and after fierce street-fighting—including the killing of enemy troops who had attempted to trick the Canadians by posing as prisoners—the village was cleared by early afternoon. Though Moore survived, more than sixty-five percent of his company was knocked out.[14] The 31st, which was initially held up on the right, cleared the rest of the village, but lost most of their officers and suffered 253 killed and wounded in the operation and subsequent German counterattacks.[15] Even without artillery, the Canadians could capture the strongest of positions, but the task required grim fighting of the most resolute kind.

To the south, the 5th Brigade attacked an hour later, at noon, and profited from the 6th Brigade's capture of Rosières. But the 22nd and 25th Battalions were also disorganized as a result of the difficulties of kicking off the second day of battle, and companies attacked at various times between 11:45 and 12:30, depending on when they hit their start lines.[16] Luckily, though, the French Canadians of the 22nd and Nova Scotians of the 25th had fought together successfully in the past and their officers communicated well with each other. The battle groups pushed forward, aided by tanks, crashing through Vrély and to Meharicourt beyond.

The enemy's defence had stiffened, and the Canadians experienced tough fighting since the Germans were able to concentrate their fire on the attackers' piecemeal thrusts. The 25th Battalion's A Company reported that with enemy machine guns and field guns "firing at point blank," the attack was halted until enough Lewis gunners could be brought up and grouped together to lay down a wall of fire and allow enveloping troops to circle the positions from the flanks.[17] On other parts of the front, according to official reports, "small parties of scouts followed by Lewis gunners worked up ditches, sunken roads, and other dead ground until the enemy's Machine Guns were put out of action or forced to retire by enfilade fire from a flank."[18] This was open warfare at its best, but it was also costly. The commanding officer of the 5th Brigade, J.M. Ross, was injured by a shell during the advance, along with his brigade major and senior intelligence officer. Yet showing its experience and interoperability, the 5th was able to draw on senior officers: Lieutenant Colonel Thomas Tremblay of the 22nd Battalion took over the brigade while Major Georges Vanier assumed command of the battalion. There was no predicting where the losses would fall, but the previous three years of fighting had proven the necessity for officers and NCOs to be prepared to fill the roles of their superiors. Leaders in the ranks were found in the coming days, as the 22nd lost more than 150 men, while the casualties for the Nova Scotians were even heavier, with the lead companies of A and B alone losing 148 over the two days.[19]

Yet once again it was the determination and bravery of the infantry that clawed victory from the enemy. Lieutenant Jean Brillant, a twenty-eight-year-old from Assametquashan, Quebec, and already a winner of the Military Cross, led two platoons in a bayonet charge that captured 150 men and 15 machine guns. He was wounded, but killed five Germans. Despite heavy blood loss, Brillant organized what was left of the ad hoc unit to dig in, while he took a small force and charged again over open ground against a field artillery piece that was harassing the Canadians' position with shrapnel fire. They captured the guns, but Brillant was again wounded and died the next day. A posthumous Victoria Cross was awarded for his bravery and leadership.

In the course of five hours of battle, the 5th Brigade pushed deep into the enemy lines and secured several important villages, allowing follow-on forces a strong jumping-off place for the next phase of the battle. Over August 8 and 9, the four battalions of the 5th Brigade had advanced 12,000 metres, but at the cost of 48 officers and 950 other ranks killed and wounded.[20]

Macdonell's 1st and 2nd Brigades attacked to the south, with four battalions in the first phase, and despite being poorly supported by the artillery and having almost no tanks, they mirrored the success of the 2nd Division to the north. The fierce resistance of dozens of machine-gunners prolonged the battle throughout the day, but all were gradually knocked out. Sergeant R.L. Zengel of the 5th Battalion and Corporal F.C. Coppins and Lance Corporal Alexander Brereton, both of the 8th Battalion, were awarded Victoria Crosses for their work in single-handedly knocking out enemy machine-gun nests. In Coppins' case, the corporal was leading his platoon when it was caught in the open in a machine-gun ambush. Thousands of bullets whizzed around the soldiers, with the tall grass affording little cover. In an act of desperate heroism, Coppins grabbed four men and they charged the machine guns; the four were killed, and Coppins was wounded, but he got close enough to knock one out and allow his platoon to find some dead ground. From there, they slowly manoeuvred around to destroy the remaining gun crews. His duty done, and suffering from a wound, Coppins could have been sent to the rear, but he kept leading his men to their final objectives.[21] Similar incredible acts of bravery were carried out all along the front, making the difference between defeat and victory.

On the far right of the Canadian front, the 4th and 5th CMRs of the 3rd Division passed through Le Quesnel, which had been captured earlier in the day by the 75th Battalion. With the support of tanks, the two battalions pushed southeast, through the small town of Folies. But the 5th CMR ran into trouble along the French army boundary, and were forced to cross it to destroy a series of machine-gun positions that were shooting into the Canadian sector. Lieutenant Thomas Philips of the 4th CMR wrote after the battle to his sweetheart: "The machine gun and shell fire was pretty heavy at times and we had several nasty spots over which to pass. Out of the platoon, 1 was killed and 14 wounded. I was near to some who were wounded but thank God I didn't get a scratch. A bullet hit my coat sleeve but a miss is as good as a mile."[22] Later in the day, friendly fire from Allied planes raked the positions held by the CMR and even a few tanks fired at them mistakenly. The second day of the battle had been characterized by ongoing confusion.

THE CASUALTIES were far lighter in the southern Canadian sector than in the north, with the 1st and 3rd Canadian Divisions taking just under a quarter of those suffered by the 2nd Division. Yet still Captain Thomas Hazel Whitmore, the medical officer of the 5th Battalion, was up to his elbows in blood as he performed emergency battlefield surgery on the wounded who pulled themselves towards his front-line dugout hospital. Captain Whitmore saved the life of Private H. Badeu, who, a week later, was still too injured to write, but expressed his appreciation through an unknown writer, possibly a nurse: "I shall never forget you. I should very much like a photo of you to keep as a souvenir to say to my people that it was you who saved my life, may God always have you safe."[23] Sadly, his dear doctor, Whitmore, had been mortally wounded only a few hours after he had saved Badeu.

Inefficient clearing of the wounded was in fact one of the ongoing problems of the battle. With casualty clearing stations too far to the rear, Canadians were dying of shock and loss of blood before getting to medical attention. The primary dressing station on the Canadian front received 2,622 wounded in the first twenty-four hours, then 1,334, 2,544, 1,615, and 702 over each of the next four days.[24] Broken men lay everywhere. Even when they managed to arrive at the stations, the wounded lay for as long as twenty-four hours without treatment. At one point, there were as many as forty light rail cars filled with bleeding men, and no one to drive them to the surgical wards. There were simply not enough doctors and orderlies to keep up with the onslaught of wounded.[25] The hurried and secret nature of the Canadian operation had resulted in inadequate medical preparations, and the problem was compounded by the incredible success of the front-line troops, which had placed them far forward of their medical facilities, thereby making the process of clearing the battlefield and the progress of the wounded to the rear much more time-consuming than in normal static warfare.

THE ADVANCE SLOWED and then ground to a stop, as fighting raged along the front. Far fewer German prisoners were making their way to the prisoner cages on August 9, which one official report interpreted as an "unmistakable sign of determined resistance" from the enemy.[26] Trench warrior Thomas Dinesen noted that the "Germans had recovered from the first blow ... and were ... fighting furiously for every yard of ground."[27] With surprise lost, artillery fire sporadic, enemy batteries out of counter-battery range, and casualties heavy, the fighting felt more like the

Somme battles than the previous day's tantalizing brush with a breakthrough. At the sharp end, a lack of ammunition and supplies among several of the spearhead units was discouraging the infantry from pushing forward, and Lieutenant James Pedley noted that by the morning of August 9, only hours before he was shot through the legs, "There was hardly a round left in my platoon."[28] Under these conditions, the infantry were not generally inclined to risk their lives by pushing forward, and while the high command tried to urge them on, many of the front-line troops made their own choices, digging in to shallow hollows and shell craters rather than sacrificing all in ill-prepared frontal assaults against an alert and tenacious enemy.

AUGUST 9 ENDED with the Canadians having advanced another astonishing 6 kilometres—deeper than any of the other national forces involved in the battle. They dug in amidst the destruction, waiting for enemy counterattacks, steadily losing men to artillery fire. "The shell holes were our only shelter, and each of these was occupied by dead soldiers whose eyes were crawling with maggots, their faces turned practically black, and their bodies swollen to twice normal size," recounted J.E. Duggan with horror. "The smell of decaying flesh was overpowering and all of this enabled us to give free reign to imagination. Am I going to become one of these?"[29] Such thoughts wore away at the infantry as they sat among the putrid dead, the clouds of black flies buzzing through the air interrupted only by the fall of enemy shells.

The Canadians' success had again worked against them. The logistical system spasmed and the men in the front lines, while not abandoned, certainly did not have the same overwhelming artillery support as on August 8. As the gunners dragged their heavy cannons forward and the service corps tried to get shells to them, water was also slow in making its way to the front to soldiers waiting with parched mouths. Private James Johnston recounted that he and a small group of men were thirsty and came upon what had once been a small stream. "The water was very stagnant and there were several dead Germans lying around in it, but we still drank the water."[30] Despite such challenges, however, the infantry fought their way forward and around areas of resistance. But the real difference in the advance on August 9 had been the strength of the German defence. Surprise was no longer a factor and the Germans responded with a vigour born of desperation. The previous day's Canadian success had been a harsh rebuke, but Ludendorff had rushed thousands of troops to the front, including independent machine-gun units. These new defenders were disorganized and unfamiliar with the terrain, but they made the Canadians pay for their own increasingly ragged assault. The 6-kilometre-deep advance had cost 2,574 Canadian killed and wounded on August 9, but the fighting would only get worse.[31] The Australians were no better off, having sustained nearly double their August 8 casualties on this second day of the battle. It was clear that the hope of a breakthrough was quickly dissolving: "To continue fighting," remarked Brigadier J.A. Clarke of the 7th Brigade to General Currie, "will break the spirit of our men."[32]

With the greatest victory of the war unfolding before them, Haig and Rawlinson's reluctance to close down the battle is not surprising. Yet August 9 had revealed confusion in the Allied command, which contributed to the deaths of the infantry thrown into battle unsupported. The Germans continued to rush in reinforcements, many of whom were thrown piecemeal into the battle and chewed up by the Allies, but many more dug in along the old Somme lines. With the Allied artillery short of shells and having lost more than half of their tanks, a breakthrough was no longer possible, and to continue pushing forward without sufficient supplies and reinforcements would only result in crippling casualties.[33] But there would be two more days of battle, and several additional days after that of sporadic fighting as the lines continued to stiffen.

ON THE CANADIAN FRONT, Currie, discerning that further attacks would only waste his men, divided his sector among two divisions, bringing the 1st, 2nd, and 3rd into reserve. The British 32nd Division, temporarily attached to the Canadian Corps, joined with the 4th Canadian to carry out a series of attacks throughout August 10, gaining 2 kilometres through further hard slogging under a scorching sun. "We are dead tired," wrote Captain John Preston of the 85th Battalion. "Fritz has rushed up fresh guns.... I think we are held up, until we can get up sufficient of our heavies to blow him out of this position."[34] Desultory fighting on the fourth day of the battle chewed up another kilometre of territory, but the Germans were no longer surrendering, and the Allies were paying for every metre of territory. "For God's sake stop. Don't push us in any farther. We'll get smashed. Take us out,"

The Germans suffered a shocking defeat during the Battle of Amiens. The Canadian Corps,
as a spearhead force in the battle, met and defeated elements of fourteen German divisions and
captured 9,311 prisoners. This photograph portrays some of the young Canadian and German
soldiers who were called upon to fight for their nations during the last year of the war.

pleaded a desperate Canadian engineer, Maurice Pope, in his diary, likely voicing the worries of many of his comrades-in-arms. "We'll fight better somewhere else."[35]

Even if Currie, in his position at the rear, could not hear the complaints of his men, he could see the writing on the wall. On August 13, the Canadian general, supported by Australian corps commander John Monash, appealed to his superiors that the battle should be called off before his corps was "pounded to pieces."[36] Haig and Rawlinson listened to their generals and, after facing Allied supreme commander Foch's anger about letting up pressure on the enemy, they ended the fighting. Haig had learned from his past experiences of prolonging a battle to the point of diminishing returns, and he must be given credit for closing down the Amiens offensive against his superior's wishes. But he also believed in keeping pressure on the enemy, and so Haig's GHQ began to plan for another blow against the German lines to the north.

FOR THE ALLIES, August 8 was the single most successful day of the war. The secrecy of the operation had caught the Germans unprepared, affording the Canadians an initial advantage. However, the challenges of open warfare—in which troops continued to drive deep into enemy lines with artillery and logistical supplies left behind and with casualties to tanks and infantry not replaced—could not be overcome. Not only did the combined arms of infantry, tanks, and artillery break down as communication failed in sustained combat, but the Allies ran into increasing levels of resistance from an enemy who had withstood the initial shock and was now fighting obstinately. In this type of warfare, where trenches were few and far between, both attackers and defenders had countless opportunities to attack from the flanks or provide enfilading crossfire that tore up troops on the advance. Success was found in the mutual support of attacking battalions, brigades, divisions, and even corps. When they advanced together, they reinforced one another, allowing for flanking units to attack strongpoints laterally or from the rear. When they failed to coordinate their assaults, they created opportunities for the enemy to concentrate fire and destroy piecemeal attacking troops as they crossed the killing ground.

Amiens has often been characterized as a tank battle, but it was not. Although the tanks assisted the infantry, too many times they were late for battle, fought uncoordinated skirmishes, or broke down over the terrain. Throughout the fighting, the advancing infantry passed the smouldering hunks of derelict metal, shattered by direct hits from artillery that, according to one Canadian Highlander, left the "inside of them like charnel houses."[37] Although the Germans found it convenient to attribute their losses at Amiens to their opponent's tanks, time and time again the Canadian front-line units had been forced to attack without the assistance of armour.[38] The threat of the tanks was important, however, in that it forced the Germans to bring more of their artillery guns closer to the front to assume an anti-tank role, which made the guns more vulnerable to deep thrusts of the infantry.[39] But the tank and infantry arms had been afforded little time to coordinate their training, and while the behemoths undoubtedly saved lives by assisting in the clearing of machine guns or just drawing fire, they were not essential, and Amiens was anything but a victory based on the tanks.

Amiens was in fact an all-arms battle, which was taken deep into the enemy lines with shellfire and made three-dimensional with aircraft. The infantry were supported, as always, by the artillery, but also by tanks, mortar teams, machine-gun units, and even airpower. The artillery fired a punishing 409,838 shells during the battle, but the enemy's positions were often dispersed, and so many of these shells simply dug up the battlefield.[40] Enough shells found their targets, though, with enemy gunners in particular being harassed and killed through brutally accurate counter-battery shellfire. With their supporting artillery overwhelmed, the German infantry were forced to defend their front with rifles, grenades, mortars, machine guns, and field artillery firing over open sights. The Allied wounds attested to this shift, as official medical records for the Fourth Army indicated "very few cases of shrapnel wounds among British [and Dominion] troops, about 70% being rifle and machine gun bullets and about 27% shell wounds."[41]

IN THE AFTERMATH of the battle at Amiens, Frederick Barnes wrote to his girl, Katie: "I have just come through another German hunt. Quite a few of my old pals are either wounded or otherwise. And I feel as if my turn to follow some of them is pretty near."[42] He was killed at age twenty-two less than three weeks later. Amiens was no walkover, and the fierce nature of the battle cannot be overlooked. An analysis of the hundreds of individual battles fought by battalions, companies, and individuals allows for a better appreciation of the difficult fighting. The Germans were routed for many reasons—partly because they were hampered by weak morale and dispirited troops, but also because they were soundly beaten. Flexible and refined Canadians tactics allowed for fire and movement: Lewis gunners pinned down the enemy, rifle grenadiers used their weapons like mobile mortars, and riflemen systematically flanked and destroyed. But there were no bloodless victories. The sheer weight of fire on the battlefield meant that the Allied troops still took heavy casualties, although the statistics speak for themselves: The Canadians met and defeated elements of fourteen German divisions, capturing 9,311 prisoners, 201 guns, 152 trench mortars, and 755 machine guns.[43] Three whole divisions were destroyed, and would disband by the end of the month. While the defeat had stunned Ludendorff, who had neither anticipated a British offensive nor imagined an enemy advance of more than two dozen kilometres, the almost 30,000 prisoners lost to the Allied forces could be seen as nothing other than an indication that rot had set into the army. The Kaiser viewed Amiens in equally bleak terms: "We have reached the limits of our capacity. The war must be terminated."[44]

The Battle of Amiens, from August 8 to 14, 1918, consisted of fighting of the most testing nature. Ten Victoria Crosses and 3,000 other decorations were awarded to the corps' soldiers.[45] At the same time, the corps of a little over 102,000 strong suffered 11,822 casualties, and most of these losses fell on the infantry.[46] Despite this decimation in battle, conscripted men, returned wounded soldiers, and remnants from the broken-up 5th Division combined to provide Currie with 12,000 reinforcements shortly after the battle, bringing his corps up to strength again. The Australians, in contrast, were desperately short of men and could not make good their losses. They would fight one more brilliant battle at Mont St. Quentin on August 31, but their bolt was nearly shot. In contrast, the Canadians were able to keep fighting, even if their combat efficiency was also dulled, since veterans were replaced with inexperienced recruits. Still, Currie's corps, unlike the Australian and British formations, would at least be up to full strength for the coming battles. "I think this is the beginning of the end," wrote Private George Anderson of the 2nd Battalion to his mother. "The Kaiser and his mob will be driven to the farthest end of Hell.[47] Driven back they would be, but not before much hard-pounding warfare.

CHAPTER 30

HARD POUNDING

Breaking the Arras Trench System

The hammer blow at Amiens had shaken the Germans. But it had not shattered them. Despite the Allies' deep advances over the first three days of the battle, the enemy defences had stiffened and Allied casualties had mounted. The supposedly callous Haig called off the operation to save his soldiers' lives, much to General Ferdinand Foch's annoyance since the supreme commander felt the British could have pushed it further, which might have chewed up more German troops. But all armies were weary now and had to be treated carefully: throwing men into battle with no hope of success could destroy their fragile morale, at the individual and unit level. This Haig refused to do, but he compromised and offered a new campaign to batter the reeling enemy armies that were wracked with exhaustion, hunger, flu, and crippling casualties.

Foch urged all the Allied armies forward: *"Tout le monde à la bataille."* There was nothing special about the Allied strategy, which consisted of hard-pounding, driving assaults against the German forces, all along the line. Hit them hard, hit them everywhere; destabilize their positions, force them backward, use up their reserves of men and materiel. While a breakthrough was not likely, the Allies continued to press the Germans in a strategic policy of attrition, hoping that they would crack under the strain.

French, British, Belgian, and American armies attacked the Germans along the entire Western Front. On August 21, the French and British Third Armies renewed

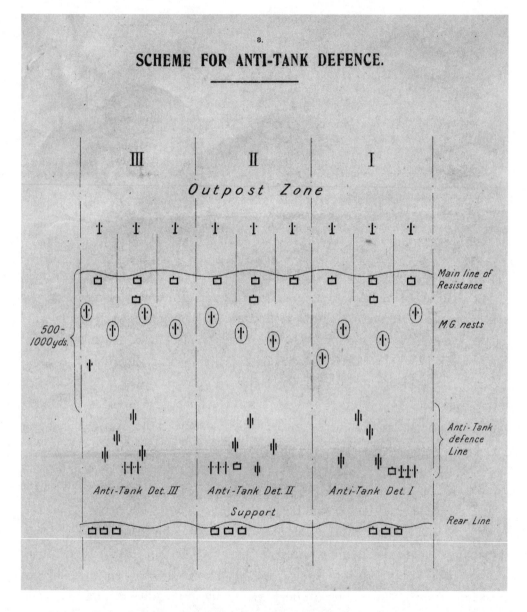

German sketch of an anti-tank defence. Note the various lines of resistance as well as the staggered machine-gun and artillery anti-tank defences. While the German artillery proved effective at blunting the effectiveness of the tanks, this threat forced the defenders to bring their field guns forward into the battle zone, which made them more susceptible to the Canadian infantry that were surging forward.

the offensive. Byng's army advanced cautiously and produced disappointing results. Haig was not pleased. "Risks which a month ago would have been criminal to incur ought now to be incurred as a duty," Haig declared angrily in a general order sent throughout the BEF. "It is no longer necessary to advance in lines and in step. On the contrary, each division should be given a distant objective which must be reached independently of its neighbours even if one flank is thereby exposed."[1] Haig was calling for stormtrooper tactics to be implemented at the operational level, although his troops exhibited far more caution as they only had to turn their minds back a few months to remember how they had ground out the Germans, who had employed similar tactics.

The Allied forces continued to apply vise-like pressure on their enemy all along the Western Front. On August 24, the Fourth Army made good progress, again shaking the German high command, which watched helplessly as reports indicated its troops were surrendering by the thousands. The Canadian Corps, as part of Sir Henry Horne's First Army, would be part of a spearhead force tasked with crashing one of the most heavily fortified German positions, the Hindenburg Line, to the east of Arras, where the Canadians had distinguished themselves at Vimy, Fresnoy, Hill 70, and during the enemy offensives of early 1918. Haig and Foch saw this battle as a decisive blow as it would smash the Germans where they were strongest.[2]

The German strategy was to hold the Hindenburg Line, inflicting maximum losses on the Allies and surviving until the winter, after which they would try to find a way to withstand the overwhelming Allied numbers—with the recent addition of the Americans—or to seek a negotiated peace before the campaigns of 1919. The Allied naval blockade was biting deep, causing terrible suffering and starvation throughout Germany, but the Imperial German Army seemed capable of holding off the enemy. Most of the Allied generals and politicians believed the Germans would do just that, and were planning for at least one, likely two, more years of fighting. But any victory would depend on breaking the Hindenburg Line. It was where the German armies would make their last stand.

THE HINDENBURG LINE was not a single line but a series of strong defensive trenches, 30 kilometres deep on the Canadian front—twice the depth of anywhere else along the Allied front. These trenches centred around the strong 1916 Somme defences and the former British lines that had been lost to the Germans during the 1918 offensives. Cratered and broken, the battlefield was littered with rusting barbed wire often obscured by untended crops. Concrete pillboxes and tunnels offered the Germans protection against all but the heaviest of artillery bombardments. A kilometre and a half behind the forward line centred on Monchy-le-Preux was the Fresnes-Rouvroy Line, and the strongest of them all, the Drocourt-Quéant Line, was another 2 kilometres to the east and situated along a series of topographical strengths in the form of hills and river-cut valleys. Behind the Drocourt-Quéant Line was the yet unfinished Canal du Nord, which incorporated marshes and deep trench systems into its defences, and then Cambrai, a key logistical and railway hub. The defensive lines were composed of fortified villages, dozens of additional trench lines, hundreds of interlocking machine-gun positions, and unseen artillery guns in reverse slope positions to the rear. The trench system was set up so it could absorb a series of infantry assaults: if one line fell, the attackers would be jutting their head into a salient where it would be cut off.

The normal period of rest and refit had been denied the Canadians after Amiens. Reinforcements had been rushed to replace the almost 12,000 casualties, but the Canadian Corps had lost many of its battle-hardened veterans. Soldiers resented the corps' being called on again. "I can't understand it ... it looks to me as though the Canadians are the only troops in France," remarked a disgruntled William Breckenridge of the 42nd Battalion.[3] There were of course other troops, but at the end of August neither the French nor the Americans were ready to commit to a long offensive. The former were worn out and overly cautious, the latter brash but too inexperienced. It fell to the BEF and its dominion troops to lead the offensive.

The Canadians marched north to the familiar Arras battlefield. First Army Commander Sir Henry Horne selected the Canadians for a key assault, and left most of the planning and execution of the operation to Currie. Horne and Currie respected one another, even if the British general occasionally thought the Canadian was too big for his already oversized britches. But Horne recognized talent, praising Currie's "many great qualities as a leader, commander and organizer," and he let the well-oiled Canadian Corps staff prepare the difficult campaign."[4] Horne's appreciation was

The Battle of Arras: August 26 to September 5, 1918

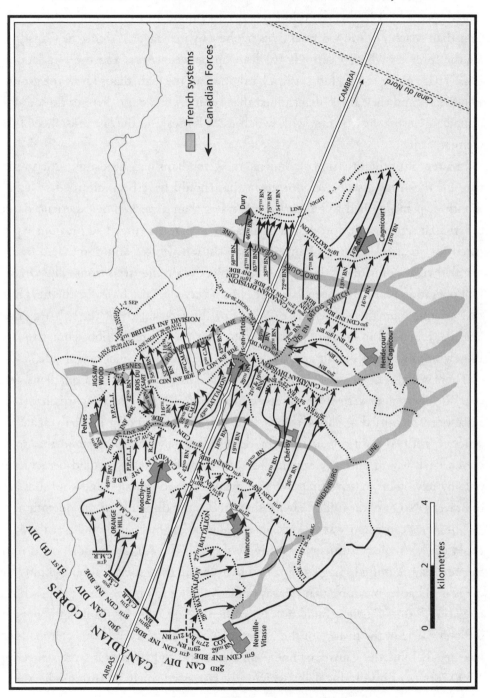

shared by Marshal Foch, who told Brigadier Raymond Brutinel, commander of the Canadian Machine Gun Corps and his nephew by marriage: "I think the Canadians are the force on which I can rely to clean up between Arras and the Hindenburg Line. That's going to be a long task, a hard one, but the Canadians know the ground so perfectly and they are so determined that I think I can trust them to do so." The Canadian Corps was "the ram with which we will break up the last resistance of the German army."[5]

In a repeat of the situation at Amiens, the Canadians had almost no time to prepare for the Arras assault. An operation that should have been afforded at least a month of planning had to be carried off in less than a week. The experienced and expert staff set to work, fortunately assisted by a plan that they had previously prepared for an attack against Orange Hill, a position west of and dominated by the fortified village of Monchy-le-Preux, a key objective on the Arras front. The Orange Hill operation had never been executed, but it served as the basis for the new hurried assault. Nonetheless, Maurice Pope, now brigade major of the 4th Engineer Brigade, remarked in one letter: "Vimy took months of preparation. Four days ago I knew nothing of this affair and this job is at the least the equal magnitude."[6]

There was also no hope of surprising the Germans, who knew the Canadians were opposite them and were always prepared for an attack, as Currie's corps had long since been identified as shock troops. The assault would go in frontally against a series of fortified positions manned by desperate forces who understood that to be driven back would hasten Germany's defeat. Canadian success would be achieved only by relying on massive firepower, innovative infantry tactics, and countless acts of bravery. No one was under any illusions about the difficulty of the operation.

The Arras campaign was to kick off on August 25, but Currie did not think he could get his artillery sufficiently ready by then, so the attack was postponed until the next day. A miffed Haig complained that Currie was "sticky" about sending his corps into battle, meaning that he was perhaps taking too much time to launch the operation.[7] But Currie would not be rushed—especially in planning the most difficult battle in the history of the Canadian Corps—not even by his commander-in-chief. Behind the Canadian lines, engineers and light railways were delivering 1,800 tonnes of munitions daily, which, if it consisted solely of 18-pounder shells, would have amounted to roughly 80,000 shells.[8] Every hour allowed more time to equip the Canadians with the means of destruction. Currie had again proven that he would not sacrifice his men simply to meet the timetables set by high command.

Currie had great faith in his corps, but an anxious Haig, despite pressing for the attack, was worried about it and even took the uncommon measure of visiting Currie's corps headquarters. The corps commander reassured him that the Canadians would succeed. Currie ordered the 2nd and 3rd Divisions forward, with two British divisions on the flanks to draw off attackers and to exploit success if the Canadians crashed the enemy's lines. Each of the Canadian division's three brigades would be sent into the line over the next three days to keep fresh units at the front.

On August 26, the 2nd Division would attack south of the Arras-Cambrai road, which split the battlefield, with the primary objectives encompassing Chapel Hill, Guemappe, Wancourt, and the southern part of Monchy-le-Preux. The 3rd Division was to take the heights of Orange Hill and Monchy to the north of the road. These offensives would be supported by 762 guns manned by Canadian, British, and other Allied gun teams.[9] Currie and his gunners acknowledged the importance of knocking out enemy batteries before they had a chance to kill the Canadian infantry advancing vulnerably in the open by allotting two-thirds of the heavy batteries to engage in counter-battery work.[10] The best way to save one's own infantry was to paralyze or kill the enemy's gunners.

The gunners were assisted by Royal Air Force (RAF) spotter planes, which were essential in tracking the fall of shells and reporting information back to headquarters in real time through wireless radio. But the job of the observers was difficult and dangerous, as they flew low and at predictable heights. They remained the primary targets for enemy fighter planes that knew well the importance of shooting down these "eyes in the sky." There were also cases of friendly artillery shells obliterating the planes that circled the battlefield at heights of less than a kilometre. T.W.L. MacDermot of the 7th Siege Battery remembered seeing one of his gun batteries' heavy howitzer shells hit an RAF plane that was spotting for them. The aircraft, composed of wood and wire, was blasted out of existence. The next day an RAF plane dropped four light bombs treacherously near the battery.[11] Accidents happened in war, but the flyers no doubt wanted to impress on the Canadian gunners that they should be kept to a minimum.

While the Canadians had almost no support from the tanks, which were in short supply and would have had trouble crossing the numerous trenches and ditches that scarred the battlefield, the land armies would be protected by a strong aerial armada. I Brigade RAF, consisting of thirteen squadrons of reconnaissance planes, fighters, and bombers, provided valuable intelligence and firepower in shooting up targets of opportunity.[12] Furthermore, for the first time in the war, the counter-battery officer, Lieutenant Colonel Andrew McNaughton, had a light bomber squadron placed under his command to engage targets beyond the range of his guns with 25-pound fragmentation bombs.[13] The all-arms battle was increasingly extending into the important third dimension of warfare, as the land armies could better control air assets. The Canadians would need everything they had on the ground and in the air to defeat the tenacious enemy.

WITH NO CHANCE to surprise the Germans, Currie opted for a risky night operation. He did not like ordering his men forward at night, as experience told him that the darkness caused more confusion to the attackers than the defenders, but he needed to do something to tip the balance. The attack would go in at 3 A.M. on August 26 under a bright moonlit sky.

General Lipsett's 3rd Division stared at the heights of Orange Hill and Monchy-le-Preux. Both were well fortified and on high ground so that their defenders could sweep the Canadian forces as they advanced in the open. The initial plan had called for a frontal assault on Orange Hill behind a barrage, but after surveying the ground, Lipsett revised the approach. Instead of sending his forces against the enemy's strength, he would go around it. Three battalions attacked: the 5th CMR had the unenviable role of leading a frontal feint to draw German fire and attention, while the 4th and 2nd CMRs were to attack along the Scarpe River to the north, breaking through the weak defences there before cleaning up the enemy from the flank and rear.

The combat veterans prepared for battle. William Breckenridge of the 42nd Battalion described the pre-battle rituals he and others engaged in as they waited:

Long before the zero hour some of the men begin to worry; they look on the gloomy aspects and perhaps think of the loved ones at home. Then there are the hypocrites, who suddenly become filled with religious notions; but most of the men only think of getting to the final objective in safety. At least that is all I think about. I never think about getting hit. If the shells are coming over fast I get my wind up; but I just carry on with most of the men and take my chances. Any prayers that I offer are very short; but the favourite is "Damn that Fritz," and I say it quite often.[14]

It did not require years of battlefield experience to know that this would be a brutal battle. Adding to the misery, heavy rain drenched the exposed troops anxiously hunkered down in their forward trenches. Soldiers could barely see 5 metres into the darkness. But that changed at 3 A.M. when the black sky was ripped with brightness as the creeping barrage thundered into the earth, chewing up No Man's Land, and then worked its way towards the enemy trenches.

The 5th CMR moved forward, aware of their sacrificial role. Almost immediately, the operation went from bad to worse, as the Mounted Rifles soon found that their own artillery was laying a sporadic barrage and, in parts, firing short into their ranks. The battalion advanced 1,000 metres across the open terrain, all the while taking casualties from the enemy's machine-gun and trench-mortar fire, but finding enough folds in the land and shell craters to keep the casualties to only a few dozen. Private William Ogilvie remarked of these machine-gunners, whom he held in grudging admiration: "Left to man their machine-gun post until death, these brave Huns caused untold casualties amongst our advancing infantry.... such a nest could hold up the advance for hours."[15] The gunners sold their lives dearly and had to be knocked out one by one.

The Canadians battered their way forward, firing and advancing over the broken ground. There were hand-to-hand battles as soldiers shot and stabbed each other in close quarters, but also inspired acts like that of Lieutenant C.S. Rutherford, who forced the surrender of German troops through gruff and bluff when he came across a position while reconnoitring by himself. Upon surprising the Germans, he demanded roughly that they surrender to him and his "troops." The smoke and dust of the barrage made visibility almost non-existent, but the German officer was hesitant to surrender his force of almost fifty troops to one man. He stalled for time, but Rutherford would have none of it, threatening the group of fifty with his six-shot revolver until they surrendered. Marching them to the rear, he was just in time to meet his forward units rushing up to clear the position. Rutherford was awarded the Victoria Cross, which he would later wear with the Military Cross and Military Medal that he had won earlier in the war.[16]

To the north of the 5th CMR, the 2nd and 4th CMR advanced through and around Orange Hill, encountering little resistance, as many German forces were focused on the 5th CMR, who were shooting up the front. The Mounted Rifles were soon covered head to toe with mud from crawling and wriggling forward during their alternate charges of fire and movement. "As we moved up the flank of the hill we could see the flashes from the German machine guns firing to their front down the slope until stopped by the bombs or bayonets of our men taking them in the flank," wrote Lieutenant Colonel G.C. Johnston of the 2nd CMR. "One sacrifice 7.7 field gun was also taken in this way, the gunners dying at their guns, which was afterward swung round and used against its previous masters."[17] The 4th, furthest to the north, set up a defensive position to prevent a flanking counterattack, and the 1st CMR passed through the 2nd at 5:25 A.M. Together with the 5th CMRs, they captured Monchy over the next two hours. The two battalions held it for the day, but the Germans punished them with heavy mortar and howitzer fire.

To keep up the momentum, the 7th Brigade passed through the Mounted Rifles units of the 8th Brigade, pushing into the enemy lines with all four battalions. The 42nd and RCR began their assault to the east of Monchy. The enemy here was the 262nd Bavarian Regiment, the same formation that the 42nd Battalion had faced at Vimy Ridge. While the Canadian barrage had pulverized many of the German positions, the 42nd's Highlanders took casualties from the arcs of enemy fire. But they kept driving forward. On the left flank, Lieutenant W.G. Scott's B Company destroyed or captured twelve enemy machine guns in one position alone. "For six and a half hours the Companies were heavily engaged at close quarters pressing home the attack with bomb and bayonet," claimed the battalion's report.[18] The RCR had an equally stiff fight, but they too wrested more than 1,000 metres of wired-in trenches away from the enemy, east and south of Monchy.

To the north, the PPCLI and the 49th Battalion followed the barrage as it crashed through the enemy positions. On the right, the PPCLI's thrust towards Jigsaw Wood was carried out by about 600 men. The battalion was supported by two tanks, but both were knocked out early in the advance. However, the tenacious tankers dismounted their Vickers machine guns and assisted the infantry, moving forward with them on foot. Lead units passed through the enemy counter-barrage, attacking and clearing a series of trenches. "There was hand-to-hand fighting in the wood," recounted T.T. Shields of the PPCLI. "Grenade, bombing, and small-arms fire."[19] Later in the day, and throughout the night, the Germans launched at least five counterattacks, all of which were beaten back. Small pockets of defenders and attackers engaged in a fury of chaotic fighting, and survivors remembered a burned-out tank that lay blocking the front on the left flank, which the Germans used as cover to advance on the PPCLI lines. At one point, two parties fought over the tank, both sides sniping and tossing grenades around the smouldering hulk of metal.[20] Fewer than 10 metres separated the warring sides. The enemy was finally forced to retreat, but it was a night of hard-fought actions.

On the PPCLI's left flank, the 49th Battalion from Edmonton had started the day billeted in woods behind the lines, where, to the delight of the soldiers, wild blackberries were growing. Lips smeared black, the 49th advanced into the heavy fire. As always, the fortunes of war were not split evenly. Although the battalion's casualties were fairly light, one platoon of B Company sustained seventy-percent losses by mid-afternoon—the work of a few artillery shells or an obstinate machine-gunner, perhaps. There were not enough survivors among the officer corps to pull together a coherent postbattle operational report to indicate what had in fact happened to B Company. At the whim of fate, best friends and mates, men who relied on each other for emotional and physical support, were annihilated as a fighting unit while other platoons lost only a man or two to stray fire.[21]

ACROSS THE ARRAS-CAMBRAI ROAD to the south, the 2nd Division fought an equally hard battle. Major General Burstall was confronted with a series of German positions to the east of Neuville-Vitasse, a prewar health resort that had been reduced to rubble. His gunnery background told him that, with his forces facing thick rolls of barbed wire and pillboxes, he did not have enough artillery to clear the whole front. He therefore ordered the 27th and 28th Battalions to attack from a north to south direction, allowing him to concentrate his artillery fire on a smaller front and, at the same time, outflank the enemy positions to the east of Neuville-Vitasse, and near the village of Wancourt. When the two battalions attacked, many of the German machine-gun positions further to the south saw no action at all, while the northern ones were overwhelmed and crushed.[22] Outflanked, most enemy positions surrendered after a short fight, and Wancourt fell to the Canadians.

On the left of the divisional front, the 4th Brigade attacked along the Arras-Cambrai road. The 18th Battalion assaulted the village of Guemappe, overrunning it after some difficult fighting, and the 19th, 20th, and 21st pushed through it, advancing side by side in the late afternoon behind a renewed creeping barrage. The opposition was light, but men were still hit by stray shrapnel or small-arms fire. The Canadians encountered gas during the push, losing men and time as gagging and hacking soldiers fumbled with their respirators, and then blindly groped their way forward over the cratered ground.[23] But the chemical clouds did not smother the penetrating forces as the Germans had hoped. The Canadians were trained to fight in a gas-saturated environment, and sectional rushes and a handful of tanks helped the infanteers of the 4th Brigade deal with isolated enemy positions that had survived the barrage. However, the resolute infantry of the 363rd German Infantry Regiment fought hard here, and most had to be shot, bombed, or bayoneted to death, as they had, as stated by their own intelligence officers, "morale beyond expectations."[24]

On the 20th Battalion's front, a series of tenacious heavy Maxim machine-gun crews threw up a wall of metal. The battalion received little support from their own barrage, which was sporadic and, in places, fell short into the attacker's lines. This was the nature of the creeping barrage, which moved over hundreds of metres: depending on which batteries were manning a sector of the front, the fire could be strong or weak, and could be interrupted or disrupted by enemy fire, poison gas, or problems with ammunition. Regardless of the cause, the 20th Battalion was in trouble. Caught within the barrage, the men were blinded by the shells exploding around them; the commanding officer sent two runners back to call off the guns and get armoured assistance to grind out the defenders. A tank eventually rumbled forward and put an end to the enemy's close-range firing, but it was then knocked out by a direct hit from an enemy artillery shell fired over open sights.

Lieutenant R.C. Germain, in his first battle as an officer with the 20th Battalion, wrote to his mother after the fighting while "spitting up slime" in the hospital as he recovered from gas poisoning:

> We were held up by machine gun fire from a ridge in front. We had got into the Boche transport lines. What do you think they did? They tied their horses, placed machine guns under the horses' bellies and fired point blank into us. I don't know how I escaped because I was lying right out in the front. Well after losing half of my company there, we rushed them and they had the nerve to throw up their hands and cry, "Kamerad." All the "Kamerad" they got was a foot of cold steel thro them from my remaining men while I blew their brains out with my revolver without any hesitation. You may think this rather rough but if you had seen my boys go down you would have done the same and my only regret is that too many prisoners are taken.[25]

There were no easy battles in the 4th Brigade's advance to the Drocourt-Quéant Line: during the three days of fighting, the four battalions in the brigade suffered 155 killed in action and 1,049 wounded.[26]

With the division's northern flank secure, and sensing a chance to exploit success, Burstall ordered the 27th and 28th Battalions to push towards Cherisy. They had the support of a strong artillery barrage, but the direct route was blocked with row after row of barbed wire. Experienced front-line officers shifted their advance to the southeast to avoid the razor barrier, but forward movement was slow, and numerous casualties were caused by enfilading German machine-gunners firing from the British sector to the south. A company of the 28th was forced to cross the corps boundary and take out the position. The attackers traversed the dry bed of the Cojeul River at 4:40 P.M., but were cut up badly as they tried to drive through more uncut barbed wire. Realizing the futility of pushing further into enemy lines, both battalions dug in on the hill, with Cherisy almost 1.5 kilometres away and the only route of advance a gentle plain that would make for a natural killing ground should the Canadians be caught there in the open.

*An example of the depth of barbed-wire defences protecting the German trenches
along the Arras front. Note the knocked-out Allied tank on the far left of the horizon.*

ALL ALONG THEIR FRONT, the Canadians had bitten off a significant chunk of
German real estate. Several thousand Germans had been killed, and more than
2,000 captured, but the defenders had survived the day to fight on.[27] Shell and mortar fire fell continuously, sending all for cover except for the bluebottle flies that
infested the battlefield, smothering the freshly slain. Exhausted Canadians fortified
their new trenches during the pitch-black night, while new soldiers moved into the
jumping-off lines, slipping and sliding through the muck of a heavy rainstorm. And
then they waited for the second day of crashing warfare against a prepared enemy
who was engaged in a desperate last stand.

CHAPTER 31

"HAMMER AND TONGS FIGHTING"

Set-Piece Battles
August 27–September 1, 1918

"Our casualties were very heavy and some of the best have gone," wrote a saddened Canadian infantryman, J.P. Van de Water. But he also recognized the importance of breaking the Germans where they were strongest, and that meant attacking in the Arras sector. Although disheartened, Van de Water noted proudly, "We fought him to the finish and beat him at every turn."[1] The fighting on August 26 had brought the Canadians success, even as they had frontally attacked one of the most fortified positions on the Western Front. The corps had punched forward, but was still far from the Drocourt-Quéant Line.

AFTER A DAY of withering battles, the Canadians would continue their push on August 27, with the aim of breaking through the Fresnes-Rouvroy Line, which was still more than 3 kilometres to the east of their newly consolidated positions. Fresh brigades were cycled through the line for both the 2nd and 3rd Divisions. The primary objectives of Burstall's 2nd Division were the villages of Cherisy and Vis-en-Artois, and Lipsett's 3rd Division would attack the Bois du Vert and Bois du Sart, with the village of Boiry to the rear, before both forces tried to pierce the Fresnes-Rouvroy Line. As on the second day of Amiens, the Germans knew the Canadians were coming, and the friction of battle was again working against the attackers, who, in coordinating multiple forces, always suffered greater confusion than the defenders who were fighting over the terrain that they knew intimately.

But these obstacles would not stop the offensive. North of the Cambrai road, the 3rd Division's 9th Brigade attacked with the 52nd and 43rd Battalions forward at 4:55 A.M. Attesting to the prevailing confusion, the 52nd Battalion commander had received his orders from the brigadier at 11 P.M., and by the time these were communicated to the company commanders, they had almost no time to prepare for the battle. Attacking companies were rushed forward and arrived in their trenches just as the creeping barrage began to walk through the enemy lines. Tank support was late, as the armoured commander received an erroneous message that the attack was to be delayed by five hours. But he was experienced enough to have his force rolling forward when he heard the barrage begin, even though his tanks took nearly two hours to reach the front.[2] The Germans had reinforced their wobbly positions after the previous day's losses by rushing the 35th German Infantry Division to the area. Three regiments defended the front with several thousand men and more than a hundred machine guns.

But the Germans were in dire straits, having had little time to adapt to their new front, especially given the confusion raging in their own lines as a result of the Canadian rupture the day before. Many front-line units were cut off from the rear by shellfire, and morale was low even as the positions bristled with defenders. Exploiting this weakness, the Canadians cut right through the fresh German defenders. The barrage was brutally effective, but strongpoints that had avoided destruction remained intact all over the front. When the Canadians ran into fire, they went to ground but kept pushing forward. The 43rd Battalion, the Cameron Highlanders of Canada, innovatively attacked along the old communication trenches that lay abandoned across the battlefield, racing forward below the ground to close with the enemy. But despite the element of surprise that their route afforded, they still engaged in many fierce clashes.[3] Corporal Albert West, a teacher in civilian life, recounted in his diary immediately after the battle that, as a result of heavy casualties among the junior officers and senior NCOs of the 43rd, "every man was a leader."[4] The northern part of Vis-en-Artois fell to the Highlanders, who would push on the next day with the 4th and 5th CMRs to clear additional positions. The

Bois du Vert and Bois du Sart were also overrun by the 52nd and 58th Battalions.

The 116th passed through them towards Boiry, which lay perched on top of a hill overlooking the two woods. The trenches around Boiry were captured, lost, and recaptured three times. Isolated Canadian sections and even a few individuals held out in pockets of resistance as posts around them were overrun; men made prisoners were freed again when counterattacking forces swallowed parts of the enemy front. The Canadians held the line, and would capture Boiry the next day.

The 2nd Division had been unable to coordinate its action with the 3rd, and it was not until 10 A.M. that its battalions finally attacked. This later kickoff finally relieved pressure on the 3rd Division's front, especially where the 9th Brigade was battling, as it had taken the full brunt of German defensive artillery fire all morning. The 2nd Division pushed towards Cagnicourt, with the 4th and 5th Brigades advancing along the front and making good progress against heavy and persistent resistance, especially around the village of Cherisy and then through to the Sensée River that ran behind it. The 18th, 19th, 22nd, 24th, and 26th Battalions drove into the enemy lines, from north to south, despite their disadvantage of crossing the battlefield in broad daylight.

The 4th Brigade's 18th and 19th Battalions pushed south of Vis-en-Artois and on to the Fresnoy-Rouvroy Line. The first 1,000 metres was easy, as the Canadians snuffed out the remnants of the German resistance that had not been mashed by the barrage. Nine officers and 257 ordinary rank prisoners were captured by the 19th and sent to rear cages, most carrying wounded Canadians as they went. Enemy field hospitals were found to have only flimsy paper bandages—the shortage of German medical supplies being one of many tangible effects of the ongoing British naval blockade—and the stretcher-bearers of the 5th Field Ambulance observed that the "wounded Germans seemed quite pleased at finding themselves in our hands."[5] As the enemy troops streamed to the rear, the 18th and 19th drove onwards. But the barrage sputtered after 1,000 metres, and the German machine-gunners were able to emerge from their dugouts and trenches. The official report of the 19th Battalion noted that the "line of the barrage was very irregular, and some guns were about 30 seconds after others in lifting, which caused many casualties. These operations were very costly to the Battalion."[6] The 18th and 19th were forced to dig in along a series of shell craters, using dead bodies to form the parapet. They were well short of the Sensée River and the Fresnes-Rouvroy Line beyond it.

To the south, the 5th Brigade had equally hard fighting. Lieutenant A.L. Barry, a scout officer for the 26th Battalion, remarked as he looked out over the battlefield, "I never saw such a naturally good defensive position … the ground sloped down to the German front line which had been taken, then upward to a rise held by heavy machine guns." Beyond this, witnessed Barry, "enemy light artillery was firing at us over open sights about three-quarters of a mile away—a real Balaclava."[7] The 22nd, 24th, and 26th Battalions converged on Cherisy at 10 A.M.

The 22nd, on the far left, jumped out of their trenches as the barrage crashed down. The enemy resisted fiercely, having grown bold in its desperation, and pockets of defenders—riflemen and machine-gunners—refused to surrender. Advancing troops passed some of their corpses and noted that the gunners were chained to their guns.[8] There would be no retreat. The Van Doos, as the French-Canadian 22nd Battalion were informally known, drove through the outskirts of Cherisy and crossed the Sensée River but it cost them 22 dead, 207 wounded, and 11 missing, including Major Arthur Dubuc, the commander of the battalion, who received a bullet in the eye.[9] With dozens of German machine-gunners firing thousands of bullets a minute, such attacks were nearly hopeless, for, as Canadian machine-gun officer Armine Norris noted, "The bravest men can't stop bullets without going down."[10] As a long-service veteran, Norris had seen many a good man go down; he too would fall victim, being killed during the Cambrai campaign at the end of September.

The 24th, under the inspiring leadership of Lieutenant Colonel W.H. Clark-Kennedy, a First Contingent survivor who was deeply respected by his men for his utter fearlessness in battle, advanced closely behind their barrage that was lifting 90 metres every four minutes. Cherisy fell at noon to the vomiting and sneezing Canadians, who were reacting to the Blue Cross irritant gas shells (named after the blue cross marked on the casing) that the Germans fired in the hope of slowing them. The tactic worked to some degree, as the Canadians donned respirators or choked back vomit—but they still pushed forward. The Victoria Rifles of Canada, as the 24th Battalion continued to call themselves, drove to the Sensée River bed, where they captured a series of enemy field guns; but a crossfire of machine-gun

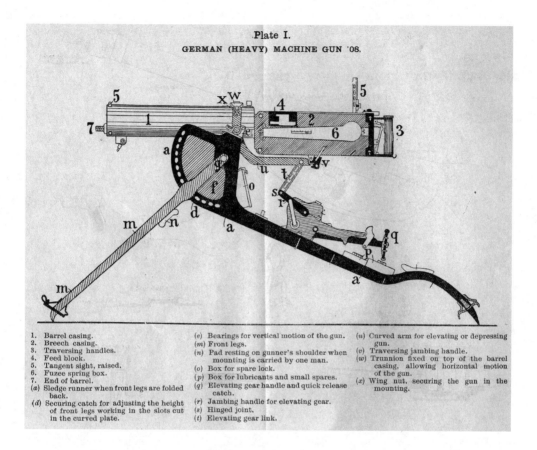

Plate I.
GERMAN (HEAVY) MACHINE GUN '08.

1. Barrel casing.
2. Breech casing.
3. Traversing handles.
4. Feed block.
5. Tangent sight, raised.
6. Fuzee spring box.
7. End of barrel.
(a) Sledge runner when front legs are folded back.
(d) Securing catch for adjusting the height of front legs working in the slots cut in the curved plate.
(e) Bearings for vertical motion of the gun.
(m) Front legs.
(n) Pad resting on gunner's shoulder when mounting is carried by one man.
(o) Box for spare lock.
(p) Box for lubricants and small spares.
(q) Elevating gear handle and quick release catch.
(r) Jambing handle for elevating gear.
(s) Hinged joint.
(t) Elevating gear link.
(u) Curved arm for elevating or depressing gun.
(v) Traversing jambing handle.
(w) Trunnion fixed on top of the barrel casing, allowing horizontal motion of the gun.
(x) Wing nut, securing the gun in the mounting.

Diagram of the German MG-08 heavy machine gun. This water-cooled machine gun, capable of firing several hundred bullets a minute, was kept in action by a team of five. During the Hundred Days, the German artillery was consistently overwhelmed by Canadian counter-battery fire, so the defenders at the front relied increasingly on machine guns to hold their positions.

bullets forced them to dig in along Occident Trench, about 500 metres east of the river, in the late afternoon. Ten officers, all with combat experience, and many having won commissions from the ranks, were killed and wounded, along with 242 non-commissioned men.[11] One stretcher-bearer at an advanced dressing station noted that "pretty well every man that come down here is done in by machine-guns."[12]

On the far right, the "Fighting Twenty-Sixth," from New Brunswick, had jumped off from their forward lines secured the previous day, but they were met, almost immediately, "with terrible Machine Gun fire."[13] The German counter-barrage was firing erratically, but enough shells were landing among the troops to do serious damage, with small groups of men vapourized by high explosive shells while others were shredded by shrapnel and shell splinters. But the Canadians remained ferocious and relentless as they closed the killing ground between the two forces. The battalion commander, thirty-eight-year-old Lieutenant Colonel A.E.G. McKenzie, winner of the DSO and Bar, inspired his men by calmly walking back and forth across the front, the bullets flying around him, as he rallied the troops to move forward. He survived the battle but was killed the next day while once again at the head of his troops.

The New Brunswickers fired and advanced, but were eventually forced to dig in after crossing the Sensée because British troops on the far right had, according to Lieutenant W.A. McDougall, "lost direction," leaving the flank open for German enfilade fire.[14] This in fact was part of the German tactical doctrine: to situate machine guns to fire obliquely to the front, sweeping other sectors.[15] The attackers had a difficult time knocking the guns out since they were on another battalion's front, and to cross over risked friendly-fire fratricidal battles in the smoke and confusion. In addition to these flanking guns, however, there were also dug-in positions on the hills in front of the Canadians that could not be dislodged without additional fire support. The 26th had nowhere to go, so they hunkered down and fortified the captured enemy trenches. Equal punishment was meted out to the enemy: the historian for the German 132nd Infantry Regiment, whose troops held this front, lamented that during the early hours of August 27, "There was much quiet heroism in a desperate resistance to the bitter end."[16]

The failure of British troops failing to keep up on the flanks angered more than a few Canadians. Often the British seemed overly cautious, and at all times they suffered from having fewer men and fewer machine guns than the Canadians. Brooke Claxton, a gunner whose wartime experience turned him into a Canadian nationalist, keenly felt the difference between Canadian and British troops: "We get into a hole & our feeling is 'come on boys, this ———— thing is a hole. We've got to get into action as soon as possible so let's get it out and get to bed' & everyone jumps & pulls & heaves and uses the brain. The Imperial says 'fuck the fucking thing. I'm going to fucking well stay in the bloody hole.'"[17] While Claxton's observation provides a colourful illustration of how many combat soldiers employed the ubiquitous "fuck" as a noun, adjective, and verb, his characterization of the Canadians' comrades-in-arms was broad and unfair. Many British divisions fought furiously along the front, but certainly the Canadians, from lowest private to corps commander, felt that the British did not have the same thrust as the dominion storm troops. Of course, this is the type of feeling typically exhibited by elite troops.

ON THE NIGHT of August 27, the 2nd Division's staff again faced logistical problems: the limited roads were clogged with troops, guns, horses, munitions, and the wounded, a traffic jam that degraded the operational tempo of the Canadian Corps as they tried to transition from set-piece battle to open warfare on the third day of battle. With the lines of communication a mess of men and machines, Major General Burstall was unable to relieve the 5th Brigade, which had fought in savage battles during the day and whose four battalions were reduced to the strength of nearly a single battalion. To the east of the Sensée River lay row after row of barbed wire and the fortress-town of Cagnicourt. Although they were, in the parlance of the time, "played out," the men of the 5th Brigade received their orders to press the attack along a narrow front the next day even though they lacked sufficient soldiers and functional tanks, had no hope of surprise, and were unlikely to have the support of a good barrage with which to drive the enemy back. This would be, as Lieutenant Armine Norris described it, "hammer and tongs fighting."[18] Since most of the senior officers of the 22nd Battalion had been knocked out the day before, Lieutenant Colonel W.H. Clark-Kennedy coordinated the operation for the 22nd and 24th. But both regiments were so weak that the cooks, batmen, and other usual non-combatants were ordered forward to fight. Major Georges Vanier, later Governor General of Canada, was the senior ranking Van Doos, and so he went in search of Clark-Kennedy to formulate some sort of plan. Exhausted and having been awake for nearly forty-eight hours, he stumbled in search of the 24th Battalion's headquarters in the dark. Vanier found Clark-Kennedy in a shell hole and they discussed the nature of the attack. The prospect looked grim, and although Clark-Kennedy tried to assure Vanier, both knew their situation was hopeless. Nonetheless, the officers shook hands and tried to organize an assault force. Soldiers know that there are sacrifices to be made in war, but nobody likes to be the sacrifice.

At 12:30 P.M., the barrage opened up and the disciplined Canadians surged from their shell-crater defences in broad daylight. They did not get far. Accurate enemy machine-gun fire played along the front, and officers and men went down by the dozens every minute. Barbed wire had remained uncut by the weak barrage, leaving the lead soldiers to search in panic for what narrow openings had been cut in the wire. Vanier, whose leg was shattered by a shell after he was shot in the stomach, had his life saved by a stretcher-bearer who was killed while shielding his body. Clark-Kennedy also had his leg shattered, but he continued to direct the battle, encouraging his men to go forward through both the writhing and still bodies. He remained an inspiration for his men, and would be awarded the Victoria Cross for his leadership. But inspiration could not suppress enemy guns. The infantry from all three battalions were torn apart as they struggled forward, their bodies left hanging on the barbed wire or splayed over the killing ground. Over the three days of battle, the 22nd Battalion lost every one of its officers and suffered 501 casualties overall; the 24th was down to three officers and 150 men; and the 26th suffered 57 killed and 199 wounded.[19] Surely too much had been asked of the depleted Canadian forces, and the decision to both leave them in the line and not postpone the attack must rest heavily on Burstall and Currie, either one of whom could have, and should have, called off the operation. The Canadians had indeed been pushed too hard.

TO THE NORTH, the 3rd Division fought again on August 28, and while they had more luck than the 2nd Division to the south, their supporting artillery fire was sporadic at best. Along the front, uncut barbed wire held up several of the advances, but Jigsaw Wood fell to the Highlanders of the 42nd Battalion and the PPCLI. The most impressive battle, however, was on the 9th Brigade's sector, where Brigadier Dan Ormond concentrated four battalions to attack along a 1,000-metre corridor. While the Germans appeared weakest here, it was an extremely dangerous operation, as mounting an attack with so many soldiers packed together could have resulted in a bloodbath. But this assault exemplified the decentralized command that was prevalent in the Hundred Days, which called for brigadiers and even battalion commanders, close to the front and studying the terrain, to react to the ever-fluid nature of the battle.[20] Despite having only a few hours to prepare for the attack, battalion officers rushed their exhausted troops forward to catch the barrage. At 11 A.M., the four battalions punched through the German defences, driving deep. Even though some of the battalions were down to just a quarter or third of their full strength—the 73rd, for example, had only 220 men—they pushed out the salient into the enemy lines.[21] Unafraid of leaving their flanks open to attack, and relying on the shock of the mailed fist delivered by the riflemen, rifle grenadiers, and machine-gunners of four battalions, the 9th Brigade broke through the Fresnes-Rouvroy Line, making them the only Canadians to do so on August 28.

Fighting through a maze of trenches, uncut barbed wire, and hundreds of machine-gun nests, the Canadians had clawed their way forward 8 kilometres all along the front through three days of brutal fighting. Several German divisions had been shattered, some 3,300 prisoners captured, and countless more killed. But Currie realized that his two fighting divisions had suffered crippling casualties, having lost 254 officers and 5,547 other ranks.[22] Indeed, the Canadians had pounded the Germans, but they had paid for it on the most intense battlefield in the history of the corps. And still they faced the imposing Drocourt-Quéant Line.

THE FIGHTING since August 26 had been of the worst kind. The Canadians had excelled at plunging ahead behind the battle-winning artillery barrage and, when that failed, at employing fire and movement infantry tactics. Currie was a champion of the bite and hold method of limited attacks, but he refused to be rushed into the next phase. The British First Army ordered the kickoff for September 1, but Currie demurred, delaying an additional day. The Drocourt-Quéant Line was "the back-bone of [enemy resistance]," he wrote in his diary, and "we have decided … not to attack it until we are ready, then go all out."[23] Horne understood and acknowledged this, but hoped that Currie's men would spend the next few days penetrating soft parts of the enemy line from which to launch the main attack.

The Germans, too, would be going all out to defend this important position. They had three divisions holding the front, and five in reserve positions. Even accounting for the Germans' low strength, taking the objective seemed an impossible task for only two Canadian divisions (although backed by the corps' full artillery) against eight enemy divisions.[24] As the Canadians prepared for the attack, German artillery saturated the front day and night, and laid down interdiction fire against the logistical lines. Harvey Spencer, a twenty-year-old former student from Picton, Ontario, noted in his diary the terrible German bombardments: "Concussion very heavy. Three men killed and several wounded. One of them was blown across the street with one foot off, one arm and part of his jaw missing, and his legs a mass of broken bone and flesh."[25]

While most of the infantry and gunners sought cover in trenches or dugouts, Canadian drivers were forced to direct their mules or trucks carrying essential ammunition and food along the muddy, shattered road, weaving around craters and dismembered animal carcasses, and all the while praying that shells would go long or short. Private Clifford Johnston, a devout Christian who had curtailed his studies in engineering at Queen's University to enlist in the final year of the war, was part of the continuous Canadian Army Service Corps convoys to the front:

> There is a big rush on so we had to go out hauling ammunition from railheads to the dumps. We went in convoy and it was pitch black.... As we arrived on the scene Fritzie was throwing over high explosives all about ... then he put up big flares which illuminated the place like day. We had to wait in line 3 hrs. in this before we got unloaded for there was such congestion... The worst part of the trip though was driving over the roads full of shell holes in the black dark.[26]

Night after night, Johnston and his companions along the logistical lines fed the sharp-end units. When their trucks returned to the rear—and many did not—they were often shredded with shrapnel and shell splinters. After these marathon voyages, some of which ran for twenty-four hours straight, through shellfire and in the dark, the drivers were "numb, cramped, [with] headaches, and eyes running."[27] Light railways, tramways, trucks, mules, and men all humped ammunition, food, and weaponry forward. Without this logistical lifeline, the combined-arms battle would have ground to a halt.

The key to success was a multi-layered artillery fireplan to clear the three successive belts of barbed wire, each 50 metres deep and about 100 metres apart, which protected the Fresnes-Rouvroy Line. The line had been breached north of the Arras-Cambrai road but was still a formidable position to the south, and the gunners pounded it day and night to tear a gap for the infantry.[28] Aerial photographs indicated a mass of strongpoints composed of reinforced dugouts, supporting trenches, and dead ground where the Germans were likely holding counterattacking troops in dugouts. Gunner Wilfred Kerr recounted that the "prospect of an offensive against an enemy warned and prepared by five days of battle, was far from inviting."[29] All expected resistance to be strong.

THE FRESNES-ROUVROY LINE had to be captured south of the Arras-Cambrai road, along with several other deep trenches, including the Vis-en-Artois Switch, a heavily fortified trench that ran off the main Fresnes-Rouvroy Line. On the night of August 28–29, the wasted 2nd Division was relieved by Macdonell's 1st, while the 4th British Division replaced the 3rd Canadian, pending the arrival of the 4th Canadian from the Amiens front.

Macdonell's 1st Division was ordered to clear the Vis-en-Artois Switch on August 30. The objective comprised two main trench lines—Union and Unicorn—that branched southward from Vis-en-Artois, both sited on the gently rising forward slope, and overlooked by Upton Wood. At the 4:40 A.M. zero hour, a complex and innovative barrage was unleashed that first boxed in the German trenches and then moved from south to north across the front, rather than taking the more traditional west-to-east direction that would march towards the German lines. Brigadier William Griesbach, the South African War veteran and former "boy mayor" of Edmonton, pushed his 1st and 2nd Battalions to attack with the barrage, while the 3rd Battalion held the enemy's attention with a frontal assault. Following the barrage of bullets and shells, the Canadians wheeled north from their positions, surprising the Germans, many of whom later reported that they thought the Canadians were attacking them from all directions. Furthermore, the German counter-barrage landed in front of the German trenches, where they thought the Canadians were going to attack—unfortunately catching the sacrificial 3rd Battalion, but missing the spearhead 1st and 2nd Battalions, who were driving from the south.

Still, there were no easy victories. The Germans had been ordered to hold the front against all attacks. Private George Bell, who had served since Second Ypres, observed the frenzy of fighting:

> Within two minutes after the attack I could see that we were in for tough going.... We had no tanks to aid us and we had to go it alone. We had run into trouble as men were falling to the right and left, and it began to look as if the attack was going to break down. We continued to send up rocket signals to our artillery asking for more support, and those of our platoon who were not hit reached a slight slope of ground which afforded some protection and a chance to collect ourselves.[30]

Bell's section commander found an overgrown communication trench, which they moved down, bombing several enemy positions. The weakened defenders, whose companies numbered only about fifty men each, were swept aside, but enemy machine-gunners caused significant casualties as they raked the Canadian advance from their position in the village of Hendecourt, which had been captured but later lost by British units on the flanks. Nonetheless, by 7 A.M., the 1st Brigade was on all of its objectives. But because of the unconventional attack that was launched from south to north rather than from west to east, many of the exhausted attackers of the 1st and 2nd Battalions were dug in facing the wrong direction.

The transport of food and water to the front and the consolidation of the trenches by the 1st Brigade infanteers, were completed under the fall of shells. Private George Bell was hit in the leg by a small shell splinter and, during a lull, he went to a stretcher-bearer in the rear to have it bound. Returning to help his mates in the firing-line, he found only a charred, twisted mess of flesh, mud, and sandbags. A shell had landed almost where he had been sitting. One man had been killed by the concussion of the shell blast; a second was drenched in blood but alive; another was eviscerated. It was the third time in the war that Bell had avoided death by mere inches; he would also be injured and gassed a few weeks later at the Canal du Nord, but he survived the war.

"Artillery and machine gun fire from the enemy's position made it virtually impossible to evacuate the wounded during the day," lamented one officer. A little before noon, the Germans attacked in strength, and got into the Canadian lines after some of the defenders fled in the face of the assault.[31] But Lieutenant Colonel L.T. McLaughlin of the 2nd Battalion—the fifth commanding officer over the course of the battalion's three and a half years at the front—ordered a counterattack that pushed the enemy out "in spite of stubborn resistance."[32] He was shot in the thigh, becoming one of an estimated 175 wounded, but continued to direct operations from a shell crater.[33] At this point, though, all the reserves of the three forward battalions had been thrown into the line, along with two companies from Griesbach's last reserve battalion, the "Mad Fourth." With the Canadian defences spread thin, a second German counterattack at 3:50 P.M. formed a significant threat. All lines of communication were cut by the German bombardment, leaving the front-line garrisons isolated and facing the enemy alone. But an alert sentry spotted the Germans advancing, using their "'dribbling' method of attack"—which consisted of crossing the battlefield in loose formation—and a runner braved the shellfire to get to the artillery in the rear, which soon unleashed a devastating bombardment. The German attack was shattered by shellfire and the survivors shot down by the Canadian infantrymen at the front.[34]

Later in the day, as the sun was going down, Griesbach threw his last two companies into the battle to take tenuous parts of the front. The Germans were surprised by the attack, as the Canadians had seemed content with what they had already captured. Lieutenant George McLean of the 4th Battalion led his platoon through the rats' maze of German support trenches, where they ran into opposition:

> Fritz was just on the other side of a barricade we made in the same trench, we had plenty of bombing back and forth—all day and in the evening he counterattacked us bombing down the trench and coming across from in front. He drove us a short distance down but we got going again and we had him on the run back down the trench.[35]

In this see-saw warfare, the Canadians attacked, retreated, were overrun, and overran in return. Dozens of individual battles swirled throughout the day, but the Canadians held the front.

As part of the fighting, McLean made the dangerous decision in a lull to get above the trench to survey the battlefield and hopefully see from where the next enemy counterattack would come. Almost immediately he was shot in the chest, with a bullet piercing his lungs. He fell back, spitting pink froth. A few of his subordinates cast experienced gazes over him and gently placed him in a dugout to die. Alone in the dark, wheezing and coughing up blood, he readied himself for a "nice long sleep." But, as McLean later noted in a letter to his sister, "after a quarter of an hour, seeing I was alright," a number of his men carried him to the rear through a high explosive bombardment and down shattered communication trenches.[36] They took him halfway, then raced back to defend the front. McLean staggered on through shattered trenches and eventually walked overland when he became too disorientated to find his way back. He met a fellow officer who had a gaping head wound from a bullet or piece of shrapnel, yet was somehow still alive. The two of them staggered back, bullets and shells falling around them. McLean survived, but the other officer died of his wound.

Many of the slain were left in the trenches until they could be carried out during a lull in the fighting or by proper burial units. The walking wounded dragged themselves to the rear, biting back the pain of a shredded arm or shattered leg. Despite the Canadian divisions being larger than British ones, they were afforded no additional stretcher-bearers or motor ambulances to assist in the clearing of the wounded.[37] Often, then, it fell to the terribly wounded to make it to the rear on their own, usually driven by survival instinct alone.

The 1st Brigade had cracked the Fresnes-Rouvroy Line, even if the enemy held many of the commanding heights from which they directed machine-gun and artillery fire into the brigade's position. Over three days of battle and consolidation, the brigade lost 106 killed, 499 wounded, and 47 missing, but they captured over a 1,000 prisoners and 99 machine guns.[38] Intelligence reports noted that the "enemy resistance during these days was fairly severe, large numbers of Machine Gun nests being encountered and destroyed."[39]

A SERIES OF OTHER ATTACKS was carried out over the next two days to secure stronger jumping-off points. On August 31, the 2nd Brigade captured key remaining portions of the Fresnes-Rouvroy Line, including a series of trenches called the Ocean Work that had bedevilled the Canadians for days. Lieutenant Colonel

E.W. MacDonald of the 10th Battalion attested to the savage engagements against enemy troops who "fought bitterly until the end in almost every instance, and in many cases were killed rather than captured."[40] In these days of harsh fighting before the big push of September 2, the 1st Division lost some 50 officers and 1,200 other ranks.[41]

The 4th British Division, to the north, had also chewed their way through a series of tenacious limited engagements, but had lost a prohibitive number of men from their already weakened ranks in securing the ground for an attack on the Drocourt-Quéant Line. Their commanding officer told Currie that he did not think his division could fight another battle, and not one that had any hope of piercing the Drocourt-Quéant Line. Currie was forced to move his reserve, David Watson's 4th Canadian Division, to support the 1st Division already in the line. This addition created a crowded front and more targets for the enemy gunners. At the same time, if the infantry could get off the mark quickly, driving through the enemy positions with speed, they would be able to push deeper, harder, and longer with the stronger force. It was a gamble that Currie was willing to take.

And so was Haig, who had received a thinly veiled threat from the War Cabinet that he would likely be sacked if the offensive failed or if it resulted in heavy casualties. Neither Haig nor Currie was under any illusions about the risks involved in the plan. Currie's one-day delay of the attack gave his gunners more time to clear barbed wire and crush the formidable enemy defences, but regardless of the weight of firepower, the Drocourt-Quéant Line would not fall easily. The heavily fortified objective consisted of a front and support line, both protected by dense rolls of barbed wire, concrete pillboxes, and hundreds of machine guns. A young Howard Graham, who would later rise to the rank of lieutenant general in the Second World War, was surveying the enemy defences as he compiled an intelligence report; there appeared to be "fields of ripened buckwheat as far as one could see" in front of the enemy trenches. Only later did he realize it was "roll upon roll of rusted barbed wire."[42] To hold the essential line, eight fresh German divisions were situated in depth: forward slopes allowed them to set up killing grounds, while the reverse side on hills hid reinforcing troops from much of the plunging Canadian artillery fire.[43] Villages such as Cagnicourt and Dury were incorporated into their positions, becoming miniature fortresses.

CURRIE ORDERED the main axis of attack, along the Arras-Cambrai road, for September 2. The 1st and 4th Canadian Divisions were to hit it hard and push through the Drocourt-Quéant Line, pressing all the way to the Canal du Nord before turning north and south to roll up the enemy lines. This was a grand operational objective and a dangerous one, as it would leave the flanks open and exposed to counterattack. The four-phase attack was supported by 72 Mark V tanks, but again it would be the infantry and artillery who paved the way to success. More than 740 guns and howitzers would lay down crushing fire—the most artillery support for any Canadian attack during the Hundred Days battles. Over the eight-day battle, the Canadian gunners would fire an astonishing 847,990 rounds.[44] The softening of the objective via bombardment should have taken weeks: the Canadian gunners were called on to do the job in mere days.

Minor skirmishes continued through the night before the battle on September 2. The Germans knew an attack would fall on their line, and they sent spoiler forces against the Canadians to disrupt plans and destroy jumping-off trenches. The Canadians fought back just as hard, and even in the hours before the offensive was to begin at 4:50 A.M., battles were raging back and forth in the Canadian outpost zone. Front-line soldiers and rear-echeloned generals realized that the enemy would defend his powerful Drocourt-Quéant Line to the bitter end.

CHAPTER 32

"IT WAS MURDER TO MOVE AND SUICIDE TO STAY PUT"

Breaking the Drocourt-Quéant Line,
September 2, 1918

"The Drocourt-Quéant Line is to be held at all costs," a German prisoner warned his Canadian captors.[1] Having punched through several kilometres of cratered positions, concrete machine-gun nests, interlocking trench systems on forward and reverse slopes, rusty barbed wire, and several German divisions, the Canadians now faced the fiercely held Drocourt-Quéant Line. The attack on this objective would become the hardest single battle of the war for the Canadian Corps.

In contrast to major set-piece operations such as those at Vimy or Passchendaele, the tempo of the fighting during the previous week had allowed the Canadians almost no time to prepare for the battle. Despite the formidable objective to be assaulted, Haig could not meet Currie's request for extra guns or tanks, as they were being used on other key army fronts. But Haig cautioned Horne and Currie not to attack the German defences "if they [had] any doubts about taking it," although he acknowledged that there was enormous pressure from the French to push on, as the British forces could not drive deeper into enemy lines unless this front fell to the Canadians. Few could have been confident in the plan, and even Major General David Watson of the 4th Division, who had a reputation for being rash, wrote in his diary: "It is a very ambitious programme and I doubt if it can be carried through to the extent they have laid down."[2] No matter what feints were made up and down the line, the Canadians had almost no chance of surprising the enemy, and they had already been involved in almost a week of continuous high-intensity combat. Further, aerial intelligence was spotty at best, as the German fighters harassed observer planes. The Canadians would be going in blind.

The "Boche will fight us very hard," noted Currie in his diary several days before the battle.[3] The desperate corps commander was looking for anything to tip the balance in the Canadians' favour. While the main assault would be carried out by the 1st and 4th Divisions behind the usual creeping barrage, Currie also wanted to unleash Brutinel's armoured machine-gun brigade, the Canadian Independent Force. With the Canadians attacking astride the Arras-Cambrai road, they would have to storm through the Dury sector, a series of ridge lines where the Germans were dug in both on and behind. The advancing Canadians would be exposed to sweeping fire from the Germans atop the ridge and from outpost lines on the forward slope, and would then have to defend against fierce counterattacks coming from the enemy forces on the reverse side of the ridges. Enemy artillery batteries also had these areas covered, waiting and ready to lay down shrapnel and high explosive shellfire. The prospect was grim, and Currie did not think he had enough time to plan for the preparatory bombardment to shatter the enemy defences. Instead, he hoped for the methodical set-piece infantry and artillery battle to break through the Drocourt-Quéant Line and reach its first objective, the Red Line, which ran south from Dury in front of Cagnicourt, about 1,000 metres from the Canadian start position. Upon reaching this point, Currie would order forward Brutinel's armoured forces through the German lines, using speed instead of massive firepower. For this phase of the operation, the artillery barrage had to be held back along a 900-metre-wide lane across the Arras-Cambrai road in order to avoid cratering the front and killing the advancing Canadian forces with friendly fire.[4] But as had become clear during the gas raid before Vimy Ridge, combat formations—even innovative ones like the armoured cars—needed artillery support, and without it commanders were risking the lives of their men. Brutinel's cars, which often seemed to be a weapon in search of a purpose, were to lead the axis of the exploitation, with the goal of charging through the enemy lines and capturing bridges across the Canal du Nord, several kilometres to the east. It was an ambitious plan, and one that bore the stigma of being rushed by tired commanders searching for a solution to the difficult fighting that they knew was in store for the troops at the sharp end.

"At dawn the whole valley and the hills around burst into a living hell of flame and of hunks of shells," wrote R.A. MacKay, a gunner in the 43rd Battery and a future diplomat.[5] The 13th, 16th, and 7th Battalions of the 1st Division, ranged across the southern sector of the corps' front, leapt from their forward trenches behind the creeping barrage at 4:50 A.M. The enemy was ready for the operation and their counter-barrage came down within a minute, catching the attackers in the open.[6] But tanks assisted on various fronts, and when the infantry was held up by concentrated machine-gun fire, the increasingly robust machines were welcome distractions that drew enemy fire.

The 16th Battalion ran up against a line of German machine-gun nests midway through their advance. After the lead troops were ripped apart, the follow-on forces

A rare photograph of Canadians advancing under fire. Note the single-file advance as they move forward in open warfare. When the infantry encountered the enemy, they would spread out and engage the position with rifle, Lewis-gun, and grenade fire and then manoeuvre around it to attack from the sides or rear.

were driven to the ground. Under a hail of fire, the rankers dug deep; junior lieutenants looked around for a way through, and more than one was shot in the face. The situation was desperate, and growing more deadly as Germans began to vector on the now grounded Highlanders. From the rear, Lieutenant Colonel Cy Peck strode forward, even as the air around him was rent with bullets and shrapnel. Peck, who was described by none other than Currie as the "soul of the battalion," and was known throughout the corps as "Cy," "performed wonders in reorganizing and encouraging his men, exposing himself most fearlessly," noted one observer.[7]

The Highlanders were being massacred as they dug for whatever cover they could find in the rough ground, but a tank several hundred metres away was guided to their location by Lance Corporal W.H. Metcalf—an American with the 16th Battalion who had already been awarded the Military Medal—even as the bullets slashed past him. For their seemingly suicidal actions on behalf of their comrades, Metcalf and Peck were awarded the Victoria Cross. Yet even after Metcalf directed the tank under fire, it did not advance far since the enemy swung their guns around in a desperate bid to slow the metal monster. But with the weight of fire slackening, the Highlanders—sensing that the time to act was now or never—surged forward behind smoke grenades and captured the position, shooting the enemy at close quarters. They pushed on through the smoke, which gave them temporary cover, but nothing could stop the hail of bullets against them. An infantryman from the 16th Battalion noted: "I got a machine-gun bullet in the shoulder, and it entirely dispelled any preconceived notions I had as to the burning pains or sting of a bullet; it was more like the village blacksmith swinging on one with a thirty-pound hammer. It whirled me round and round."[8]

Along with the Highlanders, the 13th and 7th pushed forward 1,000 metres through the Drocourt-Quéant Line after more than two hours of fighting, with several ad hoc battle groups—usually the remains of a few platoons—slinking around strongpoints to snake into the enemy positions where they could shoot up increasingly vulnerable rear units. The infantry on this front had also been supported by two artillery batteries that had advanced with the ground-pounders. Horses strained to pull these guns over the broken ground, and several times during the battle the guns intervened successfully, firing against targets of opportunity and knocking out a few of the German anti-tank guns.[9]

When the 13th and 7th finally captured their objectives, the reserve 14th Battalion pushed through them to capture Cagnicourt. At 8 A.M., the Montrealers of the 14th climbed uneasily from their positions of relative safety in their makeshift trenches as the barrage crashed down. The men advanced in "blobs," according to the multi-decorated Lieutenant George McKean, who wore the Victoria Cross, Military Cross, and Military Medal. "Spread out in this fashion, they lessened the risks of sustaining heavy casualties, a single shell rarely claiming more than half a dozen victims."[10] The creeping barrage was effective, and the rank and file followed their NCOs and officers through No Man's Land. Long-service veterans tried to hold back new men who tended to get excited and tried to charge too quickly, often being lost to their own barrage. Lift by lift, the infantry slowly advanced behind their wall of fire, 90 metres every three minutes, and then decreasing to 90 metres every five minutes.

The Royal Montreal Regiment (RMR), as the 14th liked to be called, broke the outer defences of Cagnicourt and, pushing through the crater-scarred cobbled streets, took hundreds of prisoners, most of whom were found cowering in cellars and dugouts. A much-respected and decorated officer, Lieutenant A.L. McLean, led a small party to capture a stubborn machine-gun post. They outflanked it and forced its surrender. As the remaining two German machine-gunners offered their surrender, one treacherously shot down McLean.[11] His men, enraged, killed the gunners without mercy, and later gave the same treatment to other groups of innocent enemy troops attempting to surrender. Such were the hard rules of the Western Front, as the act of surrender held dangers for both sides. At the same time, the sheer number of prisoners captured by the 3rd Brigade—2,800—confirms that there was no unfettered retaliatory bloodbath.[12]

Having cleared Cagnicourt, the 14th then pushed on, overrunning positions to the east of the village. The Canadian shock troops followed Currie's order to "remember Stonewall Jackson's motto and 'Press Forward.'"[13] Despite the lack of protection on their flanks, the spearhead formations of the 14th Battalion exploited their successful attack after a short break to reorganize, allow officers to confer, and pass around water bottles to relieve parched throats and perhaps splash water on a sweat-stained face. Away they went again, advancing behind groups of Germans streaming across the valley, many of whom were shot down by a single 18-pounder gun firing shrapnel shells. Tanks had been useful in parts of the battle, but most had been knocked out at this point. Of the 3rd Brigade's nine tanks, three were stopped by direct fire, two were ditched because of mechanical failure, three were immobilized after the crews were gassed, and a final tank assisted the British division on the flank.

In support of the RMR, the 13th Battalion moved forward to establish a hard flank to the north, but throughout the day, more than thirty enemy aircraft raked the Canadian lines with machine-gun fire.[14] Far worse was the artillery bombardment that shattered the newly captured positions. Runners, with their "utter disregard for danger," kept open the lines of communication, which had been so severely cut that for much of the day Brigadier Tuxford admitted that he was out of touch with divisional headquarters and the brigades on either side of him, and had only a tenuous link to his intelligence officer, who was near the front lines reporting back to him.[15] It was only the brave runners' exposure of themselves to enemy artillery fire that allowed the Canadian gunners to send down destructive bombardment to stave off the worst enemy assaults.[16]

The 3rd Battalion, who, along with the 4th Battalion, advanced behind the 3rd Brigade battalions to clean up missed strongpoints, noted that in their push forward, their riflemen engaged targets from a distance of 50 to 400 metres, and a postbattle count of the infantrymen's ammunition revealed that most fired between 50 and 90 rounds.[17] The barrage had shocked the Germans, but the job of clearing out enemy positions always fell to the infantry, even though at times those at the sharp end had bunched together or drifted into other zones of the advance, often in an attempt to escape enemy fire or strongpoints. The fighting wasn't always pretty, but it ultimately succeeded. The Germans had been driven out of the main part of the Drocourt-Quéant Line—to the south of the Arras-Cambrai road—although the 3rd Brigade had lost 55 officers and 1,064 other ranks in the process.[18] The 1st and 2nd Brigades had also suffered heavily, but they had fewer infantry units in direct contact with the enemy, and most casualties came from enemy shellfire that pounded the front all day, as well as from the smothering effects of poison gas.

TO THE NORTH of the road, the 4th Division attacked into the heart of the line. Major General David Watson had stacked his front with all four battalions of the

10th Brigade on the left to crash through Dury and the 12th Brigade's 72nd, 38th, and 85th Battalions on the right to capture a position known as Mont Dury—a long, low rise astride the Arras-Cambrai road—after which the 11th Brigade would send through its battalions in support of Brutinel's armoured force to drive to the Canal du Nord. This was an all or nothing charge, as there were not many reserves left behind these forces.

The 47th and 50th Battalions spearheaded the 10th Brigade's assault, with the 46th and 44th driving through them to Dury. Nine tanks would assist the infantry, and these were ordered to lead the push by advancing even before the barrage was finished. But they were slow in getting to the front, and the infantry attacked without them, moving forward behind the heavy barrage that shattered the enemy's trench lines. Smoke concentrations helped to mask suspected enemy positions, allowing time for the infantry to advance and knock them out. But as the creeping barrage moved off, thick pockets of barbed wire remained uncut, forcing sections to clip wire with hand-cutters while the bullets cut many of them down in the open. The job took iron patience and men willing to sacrifice their lives to give their mates a chance to survive. When the tanks finally arrived, however, they did wonderful work, driving back and forth over the wire to allow the infantry to break through. The two lead battalions were on their objectives by 7:10 A.M., and the 46th and 44th Battalions passed through them.

The Saskatchewaners of the 46th pushed through Dury, which fell remarkably easily, despite being on a slight hill surrounded by good fields of fire. Germans had no stomach for battle in the northern part of the village, and soon the Canadians were outnumbered by their prisoners. The disarmed Germans were sent to the rear in small groups. However, on the right flank, C Company ran into concentrated machine-gun fire from the southwest corner. A tank was brought forward, and two sections advanced along sunken roads, the bullets kicking up dirt around them. Outflanking the position of 150 Germans, two sections consisting of no more than 25 men charged with bayonets. The German will to fight was broken, and the gunners quickly surrendered. At 7:45 A.M., the village fell to the Canadians, although holding it would be another thing.

At noon, a heavy German counter-barrage of high explosives, shrapnel, and

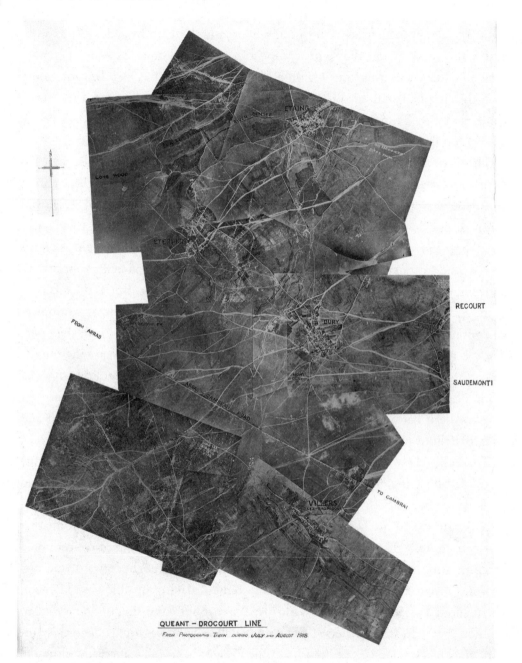

Several aerial photographs arranged in a montage to create a map of the Drocourt-Quéant Line.
Dury is in the centre of the map, just to the east of the Drocourt-Quéant Line, and was assaulted
by the 10th Canadian Infantry Brigade on September 2, 1918.

poison gas rained down on the Canadians holding the area to the east. The 46th were spread out over the battlefield with no definite series of trenches, instead lying two or three men to a slit trench no more than a metre or two wide and half as deep. But they arranged their defence in a series of mutually supporting positions that unleashed interlocking fields of fire. When the Germans attacked in strength in the early afternoon, these Canadian outposts were driven in by the hurricane of bullets and the village was threatened, but battalion headquarters ordered it held at all costs. Vickers machine-gun teams and light trench mortars laid down withering fire, and the 46th were supported by their sister battalion, the 44th, on the left, but German probing attacks were on the verge of punching through the thinly held front when the Canadians rallied. In a position of growing weakness, the Canadians charged. Sergeant George Kenter described the scene: "In an instant we were all over, racing forward, yelling and screeching and cursing as wildly as men ever did. One element in our favour was surprise. The sight of us charging across the open ground, with fixed bayonets, and our weird, wild, almost insane cries disheartened Fritz."[19] Lewis-gun fire from the flanks supported the Canadians, some coming from positions whose capture had gone unnoticed by the enemy. The Germans faltered and then broke. Their turned backs were easy targets, and only a dozen or so were made prisoners, the rest lying splayed out across the open fields. Dury was held, but the day had cost the 46th 310 casualties while the 44th lost 278.[20] For the 44th Battalion, the deaths of long-serving leaders such as Lieutenant Reg Bateman, a professor of English from the University of Saskatchewan, and Lieutenant Hugh Rising, the third of four brothers to be killed in action, weighed heavily on the surviving junior officers and the new men who looked to experienced leaders for guidance.

The lead troops of the 50th, on the far left of the divisional front, advanced behind one of the "heaviest and most effective barrages ever experienced by our troops." They overran the enemy outpost machine guns and pushed 500 metres into the first trench. After clearing it, they waited for the barrage to move off the German main trench system. When it lifted, the battalion moved forward, led by officers such as Lieutenant A.J. Slade, the commander of D Company. Slade was all over the front, rallying men and organizing assaulting forces. Twice, he frontally charged machine-gun nests: the first time with a small group of men, the second time with only his batman. Slade survived the battle and his company captured at least 400 prisoners and several dozen machine guns. In the end, a shocking total of ninety machine guns were captured in this battalion sector alone.[21]

By 10 A.M., three of the company commanders in the 50th Battalion had been knocked out, and an hour later, all communication from front to rear had been lost.[22] All but swallowed up in the chaos of battle, the lead units of the 50th Battalion found themselves facing three enemy machine guns. Several rushes against the position were tried, and brave Canadians were cut down ruthlessly. With communications severed, there was little hope of reinforcements or artillery support. As H.B. Coldwell, a signaller in the 50th Battalion, observed: "It was murder to move and suicide to stay put."[23] Volunteers were asked to run a message back to the artillery, to help them pinpoint and destroy the position. Two men stepped forward but were cut down within metres of leaving the trenches; two more men stepped up, and in a lull, made a break for it. Both were cut to bloody ribbons as they sprinted for the rear. Two more runners stepped up, knowing the odds. The wait was agony for the men and officer, who watched with "lumps in their throats."[24] One runner was killed, but the second made it through the crossfire, even as bullets tore through his clothing. He was successful in reaching brigade headquarters, and within minutes 18-pounder shells crashed down on the German position, annihilating it. The 50th eventually took their objectives, but over the bodies of their brave comrades. Such willing sacrifice could not be taught through training; it could not be inculcated via discipline or fear. The soldiers' selfless acts can only be understood in terms of the bond of camaraderie between brothers-in-arms.

TO THE 10TH BRIGADE'S RIGHT, J.H. MacBrien's 12th Brigade ran into fierce enemy small-arms fire as they tried to push through four lines of distinct trenches that were heavily wired and resolutely defended. The Germans had packed their main and second lines of resistance, which were more than a kilometre deep, thus concentrating their defenders further forward than in previous battles. The Canadians would have the hardest fighting here as the defenders' front was dominated by medium- and long-range fire that the Canadian guns could not suppress. Against such formidable defences, Brutinel's Independent Force would make its dash to victory—if MacBrien's force could first punch through the four series of trenches.

The Canadian artillery supported the infantry of the 85th, 38th, and 72nd Battalions, who were to go ahead in a spearhead role—each on a frontage of 500 metres—to capture key objectives south of the village of Dury. The smoke barrage that the gunners fired on the flanks to mask the leapfrogging units failed to blind the Germans, but the high explosive and shrapnel barrage was heavy and accurate, with artillery batteries pushing forward to keep up with the infantry. MacBrien noted that the "vigorous and self-sacrificing support" of the 3rd Brigade, Canadian Field Artillery, was particularly important to the infantry, as the gunners engaged enemy machine guns and artillery at "point-blank range."[25] But even with the artillery and twenty-four tanks of No. 9 Tank Battalion supporting the thrust, it would be a brutal frontal assault for the infantry, who would have to claw their way into the Drocourt-Quéant Line.

On the far right, the 72nd Battalion, Seaforth Highlanders, found themselves raked with enfilading fire from uncleared enemy positions across the divisional boundary. The 7th Battalion's infiltration tactics on that front had allowed them to break into the Drocourt-Quéant Line, but it had left too many strongpoints intact, and it was fire from these positions that was harassing the 4th Division on the flank. Caught in a crossfire, the kilted soldiers of the 72nd Battalion went to ground, but then pushed forward doggedly. Through the efforts of combined-arms infantry units—Lewis gunners laying down a screen of bullets and infantrymen firing their No. 36 rifle grenades—the 72nd pierced the enemy defensive system. The casualties were heavy, but pockets of men continued to crash forward. Sergeant K.A. Campbell and two privates advanced some 400 metres into the enemy line through a gap, and then set about clearing enemy positions from behind. Several strongpoints fell to them, and when their grenades and ammunition ran low, they picked up enemy supplies. The three men took no fewer than fifty prisoners and cleared a path for exploitation.[26] The Seaforth Highlanders, along with their sister battalions, the 38th from Ottawa and the 85th from Nova Scotia, captured almost 3 kilometres of enemy trenches.

The 85th's kilties' experience of battle was representative of the other battalions'. They knocked out an astounding thirty enemy machine guns on their limited front, although they had terrible fighting from the start of the battle, losing fifty percent of the total casualties within the first 300 metres of the start line.[27] The Highlanders had advanced into the face of tens of thousands of bullets, and had done so through countless acts of bravery. One of these was carried out by Private Solomon Pitts, who with a small group charged just one of the enemy machine-gun nests that was holding up the advance. He alone reached the enemy, shooting several defenders and capturing the gun, somehow surviving the hail of fire that ripped around him. Pitts was absolutely fearless and unstoppable, as were many of the Nova Scotians on that day.

As the lead units were reinforced by follow-on forces, primarily the 78th Battalion, Canadians had little room to manoeuvre on the eastern slopes of Mont Dury, which the Germans swept with heavy machine-gun and artillery fire.[28] The congestion of the front intensified the carnage, as the Canadian spearhead forces were dug in but now had reinforcements pressing up against them from behind. Heavy Vickers machine-gun teams kept some of the enemy fire suppressed, but as Lieutenant Colonel C.M. Edwards of the 38th Battalion remarked in an official report, once his men hit their objectives, they could go no further as they faced "a veritable stronghold of T.M.s [trench mortars] and M.G.s [machine guns] backed by a heavy garrison fully armed."[29] There was no way to work forward, even using fire and movement tactics, and according to the 72nd Battalion's official report, many of the soldiers "bunch[ed] together" under fire, refusing to advance without their leaders, who had been killed or wounded.[30]

As per Currie's plan, the armoured cars raced forward to hit the Red Line (which ran through Dury) at 8 A.M., in the hope of punching deep into the enemy's rear zone and capturing intact bridges that spanned the Canal du Nord. A pre-battle order noted that "a certain amount of resistance will be encountered," but the resistance was to be dealt with by "vigour[ous] machine-gun fire." Machine guns and determination were all the Canadians would have, however, as the artillery barrage on this front had been called off along a 900-metre corridor in the hope of surprising the enemy and allowing the armoured cars to race along the Arras-Cambrai road that split the battlefield.[31] Even though the infantry had secured their objectives on the Red Line, they had no effective way to suppress the enemy fire that was tearing them apart. The armoured cars would be riding straight into the enemy guns, like a glorious yet futile mechanized Charge of the Light Brigade.

Even if the operation had been perfectly timed (and it was not, as the cars were late in hitting their start line, and were then delayed by wire and felled trees along the road), they stood little chance against the heavy enemy fire without a supporting bombardment. Two failed attempts were made to punch through, showing the vulnerability of the armoured cars, which had no off-road capability. Moreover, erroneous reports received at the rear via the fractured communication system suggested that one of the armoured cars had broken through and reached the Canal du Nord, and the artillery was curtailed further for fear that friendly fire would kill the Canadians. It was six hours before the artillery started firing again, and without the creeping barrage it was impossible for the infantry to advance, or even suppress enemy fire, in the face of what one survivor described as "the most severe Machine Gun opposition which this Brigade has ever encountered."[32]

ALONG THE CANADIAN FRONT, the battered infantry had broken the Drocourt-Quéant Line and consolidated their new gains against the expected enemy response. All the while, they were bombarded mercilessly by enemy shellfire and raked by machine guns that caused terrible casualties. With the Canadian guns not firing because of the confusion over the advance of the armoured cars, the infantry had no chance to exploit their break-in and dash to the Canal du Nord. Instead, they hunkered down in clouds of poison gas, gas masks affixed, hugging shallow trenches, and waiting for the German counterattack. It never came. The German forces were beaten, even though they were dug in along countless strongpoints to the east of Dury and Cagnicourt, and outnumbered the shattered Canadian units. Thousands of German infantrymen streamed eastward across the Canal du Nord on the night of September 2–3, leave the battered Canadians in command of much of the western side of the canal.

Despite having broken the formidable Drocourt-Quéant Line, the Canadians had been unable to "bounce" the Canal du Nord as the wildly optimistic plan from GHQ had called for. The Canadians were dogged by the same problem as all of the

Allied forces: as they pushed deeper into the enemy lines, the artillery and logistical train struggled to keep up. This failure had often left the infantry fighting against dug-in defenders without proper artillery support. That they succeeded was astonishing; that they suffered heavily was not surprising, especially given that individual battalions, ranging from 300 to 600 strong, were knocking out 30 to 40 machine guns on their front. On the Somme, a few machine guns had wiped out battalions at least this strong, and here the Canadians faced guns in ten or twenty times the density.

When the bone-tired Seaforths of the 72nd Battalion were relieved after losing a staggering total of 448 officers and men, they trudged out of the line, half-dead from exhaustion. But when they heard that their fallen mates were going to be picked up and placed in temporary mass graves by divisional burial parties, they showed their mettle and *esprit de corps*, and marched back into the line.[33] Exhausted sweat- and blood-stained infantrymen collected the remains of their comrades and interred more than sixty of them, side by side, thus ensuring that their comrades were buried with dignity by the men who had stood beside them in battle. Private George Bell volunteered to help clear the battlefield as part of a separate burial party. The strength of his platoon had been reduced from forty to fewer than ten in two days of fighting, and he helped to carry the bodies to a mass grave. Bell and the burial team received a stiff tot of rum to help deal with their grim work, and after arranging the bodies in the grave, they began to search them, taking identification tags and emptying pockets to identify the slain. An anguished Bell remarked, "Too often we pull out a picture. There he stands and she stands beside him. How smart he looks in his new uniform and how proud and happy she looks. Here's a family group. There he is, the others must be his father and mother and kid sisters.... Damn this dirty, lousy, stinking bloody war."[34] In the wake of another stunning victory for the corps, the survivors of the two Canadian divisions surveyed their smashed battalions: during just two of days of fighting, they had suffered the crippling loss of 297 officers and 5,325 other ranks killed and wounded.[35]

"HARD POUNDING, THIS, gentlemen; try who can pound the longest."[36] Such were the words of Lord Wellington at Waterloo in 1815, which were also easily applied to the fighting during the Arras campaign. The Canadian advance, in the face of concentrations of enemy troops and machine-gunners almost unparalleled in the war, was the finest set-piece battle fought by the corps, and certainly one of the greatest achievements of any part of the British Army during the four years of the war.[37] Attesting to the tenaciousness of the Canadian infantrymen, seven Victoria Crosses were awarded for uncommon valour exhibited on September 2, most given to soldiers who had single-handedly charged machine-gun nests. Countless other acts of unacknowledged bravery had allowed the Canadians to succeed against nearly unimaginable odds.

Currie also believed the Canadian operation at Arras was one of the hardest-fought battles of the war. He wrote of Arras in comparison to the stunning victory at Amiens:

> There we went up against an enemy who was unprepared for the offensive; here he was prepared for the defensive. There his trenches were not particularly good ones; he had no concrete emplacements; he had little wire; his guns all were all well forward in order to help him in the advance he proposed to make.... Here we went up against his old system, than which he has never had anything stronger anywhere. His guns were echeloned in great depth, and so we were constantly under artillery fire, whereas down south, when we overran his guns in the first day, there was little artillery fire until he had time to bring up additional guns.[38]

The Canadian crashing of the Drocourt-Quéant hinge sent reverberations all along the line, allowing forces to the south to push forward and, in combination with the Australian penetration at Peronne, forced the Germans to relinquish all the remaining territory they had captured in March and April.

Currie's corps, almost 150,000 strong with the addition of the British division in this battle, had steamrolled through 10 kilometres of the strongest trench system on the Western Front. Elements from at least seven German divisions had been met and defeated on the Canadian front; 10,492 prisoners had been captured, as well as 123 artillery guns, 99 trench mortars, and an astonishing 927 machine guns, in what one British newspaper called "the greatest fighting exploit in the annals of the Canadian nation, [which] stands unsurpassed in the entire war."[39]

A senior German officer ascribed the defeat to insufficient artillery support; inflexible control from above, which was impossible to exert over the large battle-field; and the order for forces "to resist everywhere [until] every part is individually defeated."[40] The Somme-like approach of rigidly holding every metre of the front had not helped the Germans, and many times the Canadians, though attacking out-numbered, had found ways to capture or destroy a dozen or two machine guns per battalion front. But these guns had taken a terrible toll: the six days of battle had cost the Canadian Corps 11,423 casualties, and almost another 3,000 men fell in the week following the battle during a supposedly quiet period that in fact witnessed heavy bombardments and cross-canal raiding.[41] The corps had suffered more than 23,000 casualties during less than a month of battle, and most of those fell on the infantry. As long-service veteran R.J. Manion observed, "The odds are against you, and if you keep at it long enough you are almost mathematically certain to lose out in the end."[42]

While the Hundred Days were the pinnacle of the Canadian approach to warfighting, an analysis of the battles at the sharp end shows clearly that the opera-tions during the Arras campaign had sometimes been hurriedly and haphazardly planned. Certainly the attack on September 2, against one of the most difficult posi-tions on the Western Front, had relied on brute force rather than careful planning. After nearly a week of continuous fighting, the infantry and gunners had been worn down, despite the rotation of front-line troops. The shift from the set-piece infantry and artillery engagement to an experiment in punching through the lines with the armoured cars was a failure, but the two Canadian divisions had also attacked piece-meal and often in an uncoordinated manner. Watson's headquarters at 4th Division was particularly angry about the 1st Division's failure to keep up on the right, and their use of sunken roads to move forward.[43] This no doubt saved lives, but it allowed the Germans to converge much of their fire on the 4th Division's front. But the infantry in the 1st Division's spearhead units can hardly be faulted for their innovative use of the terrain, irrespective of the consequences down the line.

The set-piece battle approach is often all too easily defined according to the old dictum: "the artillery destroys, the infantry occupy." The sophisticated artillery system of the Canadians—and of the BEF as a whole—had reached a new level of professionalism by the time of the Arras battle, and the German defenders had been consistently dominated by shellfire. But the eyewitness accounts and official battle reports reveal the stark reality of the infantry's brutal engagements, in which close-quarter gun battles and hand-to-hand fighting were common and provided the only way forward through the enemy's fortress trenches. The Canadian attack doctrine was based on an intricate all-arms system combining infantry, artillery, machine guns, tanks, and airpower, but it frequently broke down in the face of massed enemy machine-gun formations and counterattacking troops, and then it fell to the infantry to carry the day. And the Canadian storm troopers did.

Sir Julian Byng cabled Currie after the battle, telling him that the Canadian Corps' "smashing of the Quéant-Drocourt Line was the turning point in the campaign."[44] Indeed it might have been, since the corps' success proved to the Germans that even their most fearsomely protected defences could be smashed. While the Canadian survivors could look back on the series of trenches they had pierced with pride, they also probably hoped that some other BEF units would be ordered to finish the job. But that was not likely. The corps' experienced combat veterans realized that the elite, if battered, Canadian shock troops would again be called upon to deliver victory in the final campaigns of the war. Most cared not a whit for their corps' reputation and instead would have traded it for a rotation to reserve. The Canadian Corps may have played an essential role in shattering the German line, along with the defenders' hopes of prolonging the war, but as one Canadian infantryman observed ruefully: "We have won our victory, but where have we landed? In the heart of No Man's Land, stretching to our strained imagination in all its horror."[45] Were the 10 kilometres of machine-gun posts, concrete bunkers, shattered trenches, and blasted landscape worth the butcher's bill of 10,000 men? Currie was proud of his corps' accomplishments, but not unaware of the costs: "Many old and trusted friends have gone, and we are bound to feel the loss of our Officers and N.C.O.'s very, very much…. It is truly impossible for me to find words to adequately express the truly wonderful fighting qualities our men have displayed. I cannot say any more; a lump comes in one's throat whenever you think about it."[46]

CHAPTER 33

"BE BOLD—ALWAYS BOLD"

Preparing for the Battle of the Canal du Nord,
September 1918

The Canadian Corps had achieved two significant victories at Amiens and Arras, but it had been nearly shattered during the ordeal. The two battles had accrued almost 25,000 casualties, more than eighty percent of which had been gouged from the infantry.[1] Experienced officers and NCOs were killed and wounded, and long-serving privates knocked out. The self-repairing ability of the infantry battalions was put to the test as battle-hardened men rose from the ranks to fill the holes above them. Most units' experience was similar to the 44th Battalion's, which lost 278 men in the Arras fighting and was forced to promote twenty-six of its best NCOs to the rank of officer, but then lost them for several months as they attended officer training schools.[2] As a result of the high number of casualties, along with the promotion of men to fill the ranks—which in turn created gaps lower down the hierarchy, at the NCO level—combat effectiveness was steadily dropping, even though, after receiving new recruits, most of the Canadian infantry battalions were back to a full fighting strength of 900 to 1,000 men—almost double that of most British infantry units.[3] The survivors contemplated their fate, passing critical eyes over the seemingly ill-trained newcomers, some of whom were conscripts. They might well have believed that they had earned a rest.

After they were driven from the Arras trench system, including the powerful Drocourt-Quéant Line, the Germans retreated to the other side of the Canal du

Nord. The setback was serious, but it also allowed the Germans to shorten their line and concentrate units in an echeloned defence. The canal was part of the Hindenburg Line, and the last trench system of German defence. Cambrai, a major logistical hub and railway nexus, was located on the Canadian front, and the Germans would defend it with a ruthlessness born of desperation, for to lose it would imperil the supply of war materiel and reinforcements to the entire sector. While German defensive doctrine from the summer fighting noted, "We shall have to make up our minds to a greater extent than in the past to abandon outpost lines and forward systems … and to give up the idea of retaking them," there was no such flexibility on this front.[4] As the canal was the linchpin to the whole Hindenburg Line, it had to be held. Ludendorff observed that this was the last line of defence— the "very furthest we can go."[5]

Foch and Haig suspected that the German army had rotted at the core, and that one more drive might bring them down. Even though it would mean another blood-letting, Haig called on Currie's battered corps to spearhead a final attack. Anxious to end the war in 1918, Currie complied, although his own men grumbled that he was too willing to sacrifice their lives for the greater good of the BEF.

The corps had almost a full month to plan for the next phase of the attack: the crossing of the Canal du Nord and the capture of Cambrai. It was a formidable position that would require enormous preparation and coordination to overtake. Separated by the canal, the opponents dug in and fortified their fronts. Observation balloons, tethered to the ground and protected by anti-aircraft batteries, floated high behind the lines, acting as "eyes in the skies." They were winched down quickly when fighters swooped on them, but the observers had a dangerous job and were issued with parachutes to jump out of their baskets should the incendiary bullets reduce their hydrogen-filled balloon into a flaming death trap. Reconnaissance flights also circled the battlefield, taking hundreds of photographs of the road systems and trenches. These, in turn, guided the gunners on both sides, who targeted the enemy's fortifications and logistical infrastructure. German Gotha bombers also flew tactical runs, dropping their payloads on Canadian rear areas. George Maxwell of the 49th Battalion described one direct hit near his trench: "A number of us were sent to clean up the gory mess. Severed arms and legs and other bodily organs were gathered up in sacks, identification tags were collected, and the dead were separated from the living. Those not seriously wounded, who had a chance to live, were given priority in medical attention. It seemed heartless, but it was a military necessity."[6] The two enemy bombers were shot down, but that afforded little consolation to those under the fall of their bombs.

With the enemy guns searching their lines, the Canadian Tommies remained out of sight during the day, hiding in their trenches, often with their muddy ground-sheets thrown over them. At night, they expanded the trench system, unrolled barbed wire, fortified dugouts, sent out intelligence-gathering patrols, and prepared to defend against enemy raids. Not many raids were attempted, however, since the canal acted as an effective barrier for both sides, although more than a few listening posts that reached deep into No Man's Land were wiped out by aggressive combat patrols. Currie also thinned out his front to allow his troops to rest, although the outpost and main line were still held in strength.

The battlefield continued to be raked with high explosives and shrapnel. The Germans also employed their chemical shells in localized, heavy concentrations, mixing their gases to form a witches' brew and often firing the combination within high explosive bombardments or at night so that the quietly exploding chemical shells were effectively hidden.[7] Will Bird of the 42nd Battalion recounted that his mates' "grousing was stopped by the arrival of gas shells. This lasted for an hour and by that time our box respirators had become a misery. We took them off and twenty minutes later came the gas again. Another session with the masks. Another brief respite, and more gas. It went on all night."[8] Notwithstanding their own counter-barrages directed against the enemy across the canal, the Canadian Corps suffered 553 gas casualties in the second week of September alone.[9] This Canadian soldiers had been taught to protect themselves while fighting in the gas environment, but there was no escape from the pervasive mustard gas that polluted their trenches. For those men who were not immediately affected, the mustard gas remained active in the mud to be breathed later. Nor was there relief or escape for any other soldier along the Western Front—whether Allied or Central Power—and by the last year of the war, gas was used before, during, and after every battle, in the only continuous chemical battlefield in the history of warfare.

Within this shell- and chemical-plagued environment, the battered Canadians continued to prepare for the Canal du Nord crossing, and the new recruits learned to survive in the trenches. Several thousand of the recent arrivals were conscripts, and most of them had been rushed through basic training, missing key aspects of instruction. Tensions were anticipated, but most of the veterans warmed up to the new men. All hands would be needed to refashion the fighting efficiency of the corps. Reflecting these constant changes at the bottom of the Canadian Corps pyramid were similar ones at the top. Major General Louis Lipsett—the prewar British officer who had served since the First Contingent, rising from a battalion to divisional commander—had a falling out with his old pupil (and now commander) Sir Arthur Currie. Some of Lipsett's powerful British political and military friends had ill-advisedly visited him and his division on the field, without first informing Currie. The Canadian Corps commander was one of the finest generals of the war, but he had his flaws, and he was particularly thin-skinned with regard to Lipsett. Some of Currie's men, and even Sir Julian Byng, had advised Currie to dump Lipsett as 3rd Division commander because of rumours that circulated suggesting the British general should have received command of the corps instead of Currie. But Currie told one of his staff officers that notwithstanding their differences, "Lipsett was too good a soldier to ever let him down in a military way."[10] Indeed he was, but Currie reacted to this perceived slight in early September in an unseemly manner, even going so far as to complain to the British high command. An outraged Lipsett called in some favours and left the division. Currie later claimed that Lipsett wanted to stay, but it was clear that the two men had reached their limits after four years of war.[11] Sadly, Lipsett was killed later that month while reconnoitring near the front lines. Frederick Loomis, a former Canadian militia officer and First Contingent veteran, was given the division. Now, in the final months of the war, all four divisions were commanded by Canadians.

SUSTAINED OPERATIONS were afoot all along the Allied front. General Foch ordered that the British, French, and American armies be thrown against the Germans to use up their reserves by battering them all along the line. With a series of hammer blows, the formidable German lines would first bend, then break. The

Canadian part of the massive assault would be to cross the canal and capture Bourlon Wood, a fortified strongpoint in front of Cambrai. Removing this obstacle would enable the British Third Army to advance to the south. But few parts of the German line were as strong as the sector across from the Canadian Corps.

The Germans had flooded the region to recreate a Passchendaele-like bog. Within this marsh, the Canadians had little room to manoeuvre, except for a narrow, dry corridor only 2,600 metres wide. Luckily, the canal was dry. Currie planned to send his divisions across it and then to fan out on the other side. They had to keep plunging forward as the enemy's front was based on a defence-in-depth, with Bourlon Wood and Cambrai acting as fortresses in their wake, all protected by a series of deep trenches. Because of the gentle forward slope on the other side of the canal, the Canadians needed to push deep into the German lines or they would be massacred in the open, especially by fire from Bourlon Wood. Eight divisions were entrenched across from the Canadians, three in the line and five in reserve.[12] The Canadians would have to hit hard and fast. "Do not do away with necessary precautions," advised General Archie Macdonell, "but be bold—always bold."[13] A force attacking through the slow, plodding approach of a set-piece battle would likely be annihilated.

But with the enemy defences established in depth over several kilometres, and spread out over the front to diffuse the effect of artillery fire, Currie also acknowledged that any success in the battle would require that his artillery move across the canal quickly to assist the infantry in the deep thrust to the east. Engineers would be called on to coordinate the building of roads and the throwing of bridges across the canal—all of which had to be done under fire. This challenge would indeed push the operational art of the Canadian Corps to new limits, calling for all the lessons of the previous three years to be coordinated in a combined-arms method of warfighting.

The first phase of the attack involved crossing the Canal du Nord and pushing out across the open ground behind it. The canal was uneven in width, ranging from 40 to 60 metres wide. It was not an imposing obstacle, but it was surrounded by marshy ground and enemy strongpoints. A strongly fortified enemy trench system, the Marquion Line, ran almost the entire length of the front behind the canal. Situated on the reverse slope of a gentle hill, it not only offered protection for the core of the defenders dug in on the other side, but also provided a devastating field of fire for the machine-gunners and riflemen who were situated on the frontal slope. The latter were more vulnerable to Allied shellfire, but they could shoot at will at the infantry closing the distance. The Canadians' other immediate objective, Bourlon Wood, which overlooked the canal and was bristling with machine-gun emplacements and artillery batteries, had to fall before the British could advance to the south. The nature of many of these defences could only be guessed at because ancient oak trees covered the ground and shrouded aerial observation. Intelligence and previous harsh fighting in the area during the Cambrai offensive of November 1917 had revealed a series of interlocking and fortified positions. Further on, the second phase of the attack would involve the breaking of the Marcoing defence system that ran along the Canal de l'Escaut and the high ground north of the city, which dominated Cambrai. The entire area was also known to be protected by row upon row of barbed wire, much of it obscured by overgrown fields. Infantryman Harold Cline remembered looking out at the density of the wire and despairing at "how it could be broken."[14] The Canadians would have to crack the canal, punch through the Marquion Line, capture a series of fortified towns, trenches, and woods, and then move on to deal with the Marcoing Line and, finally, Cambrai.

The Germans were complacent behind their superior defensive and geographical position: they did not expect an attack in that area, as it went against all conventional military thought. While Currie's audacious and aggressive plan therefore had the advantage of striking the enemy where he least expected it, the operation must also be recognized for the danger it involved. The problem for the corps remained the necessity of squeezing through the narrow opening and breaking out on the other side before the Germans could blunt the attack. If the lead storm troops were stopped short or wiped out, all chance of throwing the rest of the formidable forces into the line would be lost.

Currie acknowledged this obstacle, but he knew his corps and his men: this was not a blind stumble and gamble. But even Currie's commander, General Henry Horne, considered the plan too dangerous. He worriedly visited Currie in an attempt to convince him to try something less complicated, even though he was always supportive of the Canadians. But Currie refused to budge. Even when Horne appealed to Haig and roused the field marshal to visit Currie on September 21 at Canadian Corps' headquarters, Currie would not significantly alter his plans. The high command nonetheless remained worried about the daring nature of the plan. A final private visit by Currie's old mentor, Sir Julian Byng, must have left the Canadian commander a little shaken, especially when Byng asked: "Old man, do you think you can do it?"[15] Currie responded in the affirmative, and Byng left confident that his old Canadian Corps could pull it off. Currie had faith in his men, and Haig and Horne backed their dominion general.

The generals' plans would rise or fall based on the performance of the hard-driving soldiers at the sharp end. And it was clear that they were nearly worn out. Too many experienced soldiers were now missing from the ranks. Would the new men rise to the occasion? Maurice Pope described the precarious nature of morale among the fighting forces as they prepared for battle.

> I feared before the attack that our men might not have sufficiently rested after their two strenuous struggles. In battle one is subjected to two distinct fatigues, one to the muscular system, the other to the nervous system. A few days rest repairs the former, the repair of the latter is problematical. One's surroundings, the weather, and a hundred and one other things, contribute towards it and in my humble judgment, one cannot be too certain.... Once the Corps had proved itself, I never bothered much about the plan of the attack when I was weighing the chances of success, but that always I tried to gauge the feelings of the men who were to do the job. Granted our fellows were in the right mood for a scrap, then all the devils in hell could not stay them. On the other hand, should the men feel that they are being asked to do more than their share, the most carefully planned attack is bound to go "phut" and the wires are bound to state that "the situation is obscure," i.e., they have not got there.[16]

As Pope observed wisely, combat motivation remained the essential ingredient in determining victory: if the men felt they were being callously sacrificed or ill-treated, battlefield victory was almost impossible. No one was sure how the Canadians would respond to being thrown into one final titanic battle against seemingly impossible odds and a desperate enemy whose back was against the wall.

CHAPTER 34

SHOCK AND AWE

Crashing the Canal du Nord,
September 27–28, 1918

The attack was set for 5:20 A.M. on September 27. The operation was to be a sledge-hammer assault, although bouncing the canal would initially require a crowbar to wedge open the door. Tanks would assist with the wire, but each division had only eight, and no one was relying on them for much since most had already seen fierce action, as evidenced by their scarred hulls. If the advance forces were stopped in the narrow gap or constrained from fanning out to the full 9,700 metres on the other side (eventually pushing to 15,000 metres), they would be slaughtered. The Germans would be able to concentrate their fire on a constricted portion of the front and kill Canadians by the thousands as they scrounged for cover, trapped by fire in front and the mass of their comrades to the rear.

In the days before the battle, the infantry of the 1st and 4th Divisions moved into their jumping-off positions. The confined front allowed only four battalions to attack at once, although several more would leap through them in quick succession. Corps commander Currie wrote worriedly, "The assembly of the attacking troops in an extremely congested area known by the enemy to be the only one available was very dangerous.... A concentrated bombardment of this area prior to zero, particularly if gas was employed, was a dread possibility which could seriously affect the whole of the operation and possibly cause its total failure."[1] The 4th Division, on the right, would have to neutralize Bourlon Wood, while the 1st Division, on its left, would capture the high ground to the north of the wood, which was riven with trenches and strongpoints, although less densely so than the fortress around Bourlon Wood.

The Canadian infantry's assault would be supported by a complicated creeping barrage that also included a backward-moving barrage. The artillery fire would jump away from the Canadians in the conventional manner, but would also roll back towards the Canadian lines, giving the enemy the impression that their own guns were raking through their positions since the shells were coming from the opposite direction. The density of the attack was striking, at one 18-pounder gun for every 14 metres of frontage. The creeping barrage consisted of shrapnel and high explosives, with ten percent of the total shells containing smoke to further obscure the front.[2] As well, the counter-battery section played a key role in targeting enemy guns, of which 113 had been located. While not all were destroyed, enough were harassed to interrupt enemy fire. Additional Canadian guns were brought forward, camouflaged, and silenced in the pre-battle barrage so as not to give away their positions. The full weight of the Canadian Corps' Royal Artillery—comprising 785 guns manned by 37,879 gunners, drivers, and planning staff—was thrown behind the infantry's asssault.[3] It would indeed be a shock and awe operation.

A STEADY DRIZZLE rained down on the night of September 26–27, stirring up old memories and pungent smells. Lewis gunners sacrificed their rain capes to protect their guns; greatcoats were pulled tight around the neck as soldiers scooped out runny mud from their slit holes. The heavily clouded sky made movement extremely hazardous as scouts traversed the cratered ground in the inky darkness, reconnoitring the terrain over which the infantry force would pass. In the nights before the attack, the Germans launched some probing raids to secure a prisoner, but these were beaten back along the front. The Canadians tried to remain as passive and quiet as possible as they prepared, but all of their activity, which could not be masked, alerted the Germans that the operation was impending. With two Canadian divisions in the line and two more supporting them from behind, it

THE BATTLE OF CANAL DU NORD: SEPTEMBER 27 TO OCTOBER 11, 1918

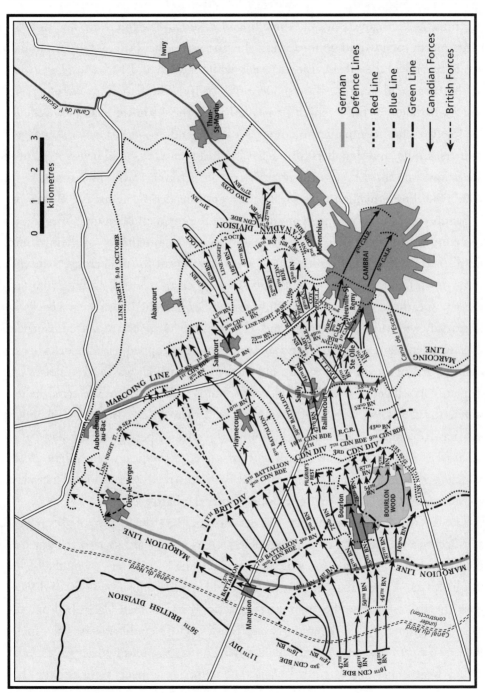

appeared on maps as though the whole 100,000-man Canadian Corps was ready to tear into the Germans. But only three brigades were in the forefront, and only four battalions in total would go forward in the first wave: the 44th and 46th Battalions would spearhead the 4th Division's attack, while the 4th and 14th Battalions would be the first to advance on the 1st Division's sector. The battalions were depleted: while a battalion at full strength had 1,000 men, the 44th, for example, went into the line with four companies totalling 24 officers and 509 other ranks. Another 96 runners, scouts, and signallers from battalion headquarters would be involved in the operation, but these men were not part of the striking force. The attack by the 100,000-strong Canadian Corps was in fact spearheaded by about 2,100 men.

Scouts crept into No Man's Land in front of the canal and laid tape lines to mark company boundaries. Then the platoon and section commanders led their men forward to scratch out their positions in the earth and wait for the barrage that would come down in a few hours' time. Chain-smoking cigarettes and guzzling rum-laced tea, the spearhead forces of the assault companies had shed their heavy packs and were ready with rifles, Lewis guns, and Mills bombs. Many had also been issued ladders, wooden planks, and rope, and some units were equipped with life belts to assist them in getting down into and up out of the canal, which was 3 to 4 metres deep in places. Intelligence patrols and aircraft photos indicated that the canal held no water, and that its western side was only 1 or 2 metres deep, but none knew what the massive Canadian barrage would do to the terrain: perhaps entire parts of the canal wall would collapse and become impassable, or the heavy rain might create a stagnant pool that could slow the attack or even drown advance troops. Uncertainty gnawed away at bellies in the long hours before the battle.

The key to the corps' victory was its barrage, but the depth of the planned advance meant that most of the final objectives were out of range of the guns. For the infantry to have any chance of success, the Canadian batteries would also have to quickly cross the canal. Such a move would require enormous skill and would push the artillery to use the open warfare tactics the Canadian Corps had practised over the summer. While the infantry and Mark V tanks could traverse the canal on their own steam, the artillery guns would need horses to pull them across, especially if they were to get over the canal walls. The combat engineers were essential here, and they would follow the first wave closely. As the infantry surged across the canal, the engineers would begin to build bridges to allow the guns to follow and support the increasingly overextended infantry. Without the guns on the eastern side of the canal, the infantry would be forced to launch frontal attacks against fortified enemy positions with little protection against the enemy's counter-barrage fire. These various obstacles that would need to be overcome rested heavily on the minds of the generals and those at the sharp end, but all they could do was wait and hope that their preparations would not be upset by the enemy.

THE BARRAGE lit off at 5:20 A.M. and was magnificent in its ferocity. German positions and barbed wire were thrown into the air by a continuous blast of fire and steel. Within the cacophony, experienced soldiers could pick out the different sounds of shrapnel bursts and high explosive shells, and the larger explosions caused by the heavy siege guns. Canadian Vickers heavy machine-gunners thickened the barrage with tens of thousands of bullets, and then drove forward with the infantry to add much-needed firepower. Lieutenant Hans Krieghoff of the 2nd Battalion, German 188th Imperial Regiment, recounted the panic of men caught in this maelstrom:

> Each connection with the companies is immediately severed, our runners don't return. Due to the powder fumes and smoke, visibility is zero … the enemy artillery fire blocks our rear and the British release their armored vehicles and tanks upon us, their victims. Infantry columns staggered in-depth followed. They are coming! They are coming! We defend ourselves with a rage that positively escalates into a frenzy."[4]

Above the battlefield, Lieutenant Warren Hendershott of the Royal Flying Corps looked down on the battlefield, capturing the experience in a letter to his parents in Canada:

> I have never in all my life and never again do I ever expect to see anything to equal this morning's war. We crossed the lines just as the sun was coming up out of the east and it certainly added to the wonderful scene that was going on below. The whole front was one mass of smoke, dust and flames. How anything

or anyone could live through it, I do not know. I do know though, that all the time I was buzzing around through the air I was thanking my stars that I was not on the ground.[5]

Rising from their forward trenches into the seemingly solid cloud of explosions, debris, and smoke, the infantry of the four lead battalions started forward at a measured pace. Yet the pent-up anxiety of waiting for hours to begin the assault, combined with the adrenaline rush of battle, compelled soldiers forward too quickly. Officers and NCOs tried to hold back some of the battle-crazed men from the creeping wall of shrapnel that tore up the ground ahead of them. But since the front was not straight, the sectors were at varying distances from the canal and in the 44th Battalion's zone of advance the troops had to wait longer than those on the far left, whose barrage was moving forward at a different pace to account for the terrain. Over-anxious infantrymen from the 44th charged into their own shrapnel barrage and were shredded by their own gunfire. With voices lost in the banshee wail of explosions, officers and NCOs were reduced to waving their arms and forcibly holding excited men back from the barrage. Racing back and forth, all four company commanders were soon hit by artillery fire or the steady raking of the ground by German machine-gunners who had not yet been knocked out.

On the 1st Division's front, the 4th and 14th Battalions followed the barrage over No Man's Land, through some isolated German outposts, and into the canal. The "Mad Fourth" made a quick advance, and soon the 1st Brigade headquarters lost all touch with the forward units. But at 6:05 A.M., the first prisoner arrived at the rear: he spoke broken English well enough for intelligence officers to understand that the "'English' were over the Canal and all his comrades were killed."[6] The supporting 1st, 2nd, and 3rd Battalions passed through the 4th, which had hit their objectives quickly, although they still lost 142 men by the end of the day.

On the 14th Battalion's front, to the north, a hidden German machine-gun nest had moved forward and set up in the Canadians' assembly area. The gun could have crippled the attack, but it was overrun by the swiftly advancing Royal Montrealers at the start of the battle, before it had the chance to fire even one shot. Attacking through rain and gas clouds, the 14th crossed two water-filled ditches and torn wire, stumbling nearly blind in their respirators. Often the enemy bullet fire was lost in the cacophony of shelling and explosions, and obscured from view by the soldiers' cumbersome respirators, resulting in several men being killed before it became clear that the whirling metal was tearing holes through their ranks. The survivors then had to determine where the fire was coming from along the front. Were these stray shots from machine guns firing on fixed points in sweeping arcs, or was the unit being targeted by specific enemy snipers? Tenacious groups of infantry knocked out several machine-gun nests to the west of the canal, fighting their way forward and using the folds in the ground for cover until they were close enough to kill with a rifle shot or shrapnel grenade. While the German defences on the western side of the canal had no chance of survival, as they were isolated and vastly outnumbered, reports noted that the Germans were relying on this type of suicidal tripwire defence to slow up the Canadian assaults and cause terrible casualties. The machine-gunners were abandoned and ordered to "fight it out or hold out until a counterattack restored the situation," but the experienced German machine-gun teams must have known that their fate was sealed.[7] While many German positions fought to the bitter end, others were abandoned, their defenders quick to surrender or flee to the rear. The German offensives of early 1918 had taken their toll on the morale of the German army. One captured report noted that many Germans no longer had faith in their high command's order to hold all ground no matter the cost. The cost was literally their lives, and some Germans voted with their feet.[8]

When the barrage lifted over the canal at 5:45 A.M., twenty-five minutes into the operation, the Montrealers drove forward through the garrison troops that were dug in to the canal, often in dugouts, caves, and funk holes along the western side of the wall. The historian of the 188th Infantry Regiment noted ruefully that "at the end of the day only a little band of men was left."[9] Leaving detachments of guards to cover the prisoners, the Canadians pushed past them, crossing the 40 metres of dry bed and scrambling up the far wall. Throwing up ladders or scrambling up the 1.5-metre-high slope on the backs and shoulders of others, the forward men made it over the top. Then they stepped into the great unknown.

The opposite side of the canal looked like something straight out of hell: the barrage had torn up the ground, leaving behind smouldering shell holes and dismembered body parts. The rows and rows of barbed wire had been crushed or thrown about the battlefield to form twisted metal mountains of wire. The barrage was still moving out from the Canadian advance, but German defenders, including the machine-gunners who had survived the bombardment, were emerging from their protective areas and beginning to pour fire into the advancing troops. Bullets raked the Canadians, but casualties were minimized by experienced troops who advanced in single file and knew when to go to ground in shell holes, sunken roads, or whatever other shelter they could find. The battle group leaders pushed the thrusting units forward, realizing that any delay could result in their losing the barrage, and would at least allow the enemy troops to emerge from their holes. Sections advanced in short rushes, laying down fire to provide cover for other units as they moved ahead. German positions were wiped out by grenade or Lewis-gun fire, while riflemen sniped at enemy heads as they popped up to survey the chaotic situation.

On the far left of the narrow opening, the Royal Montrealers waited in smoking shell holes to widen the front on the eastern side of the canal as a special barrage wreaked havoc on the defenders of the small village of Sains-lez-Marquion. Code-named the "monkey puzzle barrage," it was a reverse barrage that started beyond the town and then moved backwards, raking the ground in reverse to the usual creeping barrage. Within minutes, houses were on fire and ammunition was exploding. But the resilient Germans held on, with a few gunners firing from upper storeys of buildings. At the same time, the 14th advanced on the buildings behind the fire of a regular creeping barrage, with Lieutenant C.E. Tuttle, commander of A Company, leading the assault from atop a tank. The Canadians laid down a screen of Lewis-gun fire while rifle grenadiers fired their grenades and riflemen closed with the enemy. A number of wobbly grenades were accurately projected through windows, shredding the German defenders within. Some 350 prisoners surrendered, but a number of machine-gunners fought to their last bullet.[10] The first objective position, known as the Red Line, was captured by 10 A.M., and secondary units pushed through to the next objective, the Green Line, which ran behind the Marquion Line to the Bourlon Wood fortress.

ON THE 4TH DIVISION'S FRONT, the 50th Battalion passed through the 46th and raced towards the Marquion Line, the German trenches in front of the village of

Bourlon and Bourlon Wood. On their right was the 44th Battalion, which, unlike the 46th—which was ordered to dig in and hold the east bank of the canal in case of counterattack—had no unit to pass through it and therefore pushed on, capturing prisoners from the elite 4th and 11th Ulanen and Dragoner cavalry regiments, who were fighting in a dismounted role, as well as Bavarian and Prussian infantry units and an independent machine-gun company.

The 50th moved quickly, destroying a few enemy machine-gun posts through envelopment, but took casualties from long-distance fire. The only small consolation was that many of these bullets had lost much of their deadly velocity in flight, and the normal three to one ratio of wounded to dead shifted to six to one. Nonetheless, the battalion faced a firestorm. D Company, one of the two lead companies, lost every officer, and a tough company sergeant major, W.L. Watkins, rose to the occasion, leading the men forward. Despite taking a bullet through the hand, he continued to direct the 50th to their objectives.[11] Victor Wheeler, who had watched many of his friends fall victim to enemy fire, noted grimly, "Men fought and fell, rushed machine-gun nests, and annihilated the gunners who were not given the opportunity to surrender."[12]

Behind this advancing system of infantry, the combat engineers scrambled into the canal and crossed to the other side to build the vital bridges across. Major General William Lindsay, Currie's chief engineer, ordered his men to work under fire to construct these logistical arteries that would allow artillery to pass over to the east of the canal. With one bridge completed, the first guns crossed the canal at 8:40 A.M., but almost all of these were quickly disabled when the Germans trained their machine guns on the horses, killing them and grounding the guns. The dead horses were unlimbered and pushed off the bridge, and the rest of the guns were man-handled across by available men. Enemy fire slackened as the Canadian infantry pushed eastwards and German machine-gunners were overrun. An hour later, the guns of the 3rd and 4th Divisions began to cross the canal in strength, with horses and drivers straining to clear the easily targeted canal. Four more prefabricated bridges were in place within four hours, with three larger bridges available for bigger guns by 6 P.M. The heavier guns started to roll forward in the early afternoon. The combat engineers of the Canadian Corps, who had at times put down their tools and raced forward with rifles to knock out areas of resistance, had done their job—often under intense fire—to ensure that the infantry would not be isolated on the eastern bank of the canal.[13]

THE FOLLOW-ON FORCES WERE PUSHING through the spearhead units that were digging in furiously under fire. To the north, the 1st Division's 15th, 13th, 1st, 2nd, and 3rd Battalions were all fanning out, driving deep to create space for the rushing torrent of the two divisions pushing from behind. At one point, the troops were fighting in four directions simultaneously: north, northeast, east, and west. They were also receiving much-needed help from British units to the north, which were pressuring the enemy.

On the 1st Division's front, the barrage was strong and the infantry surged ahead, moving in a diamond formation to pin down and then envelop strongpoints. The German counter-barrage increased in intensity in the initial hours of the battle, but the Canadian counter-batteries destroyed many of the guns as they revealed themselves. In fact, Canadian artillery reports crowed that eighty percent of the enemy's identified guns had been destroyed within the first few hours of the battle, although the heavy German counter-barrage throughout the day would seemingly bring this claim into question.[14] The 1st Battalion, for instance, was held up later in the battle by shrapnel bursts near a railway embankment on the northwest outskirts of Bourlon, forcing them to establish a screening flank that allowed the 2nd Battalion to push through.

Each of the 2nd Battalion infantrymen were, like most soldiers in the corps, laden with 220 rounds of small-arms ammunition, 2 water bottles, and 2 sandbags, as well as 1 shovel per 4 men and 23 wire-cutters per company. Notwithstanding their eighty pounds of equipment, the men were expected to move quickly. The enemy counterattacks would require lead formations to dig in and have ample supplies if they hoped to hold their newly won ground. This was the challenge of open warfare, in which boldness could catch the enemy unaware and therefore result in the overrunning of his position, but at the same time could leave attacking forces vulnerable to decapitation if they pushed too deep without flank support. But Major General Archibald Macdonell of the "Old Red Patch"—as the formation was proudly known in reference to its divisional shoulder patch—was not too worried, and, quoting Wellington's notion that "People with too nice notions about religion had better keep out of the army," declared, "we felt the same to be true of people with too nice notions about flanks." He further noted that assault formations would need to prepare "all-around defences," as attacks could come from every direction in this open warfare environment.[15] For the attacking battalions to survive within the ever-changing sea of battle, they had to be self-contained fighting units, with their own firepower, command structures, and supplies.

The waves of 2nd Battalion men continued to advance to the north of Bourlon, their numbers thinning as enemy shelling and machine guns "increased in intensity."[16] Having recovered from the shock of the initial attack, the Germans were making a determined stand. Around noon, a series of MG-08 teams had pinned down the lead elements of the 2nd Battalion, many firing from the strongpoint of Pilgrim's Rest (some 500 metres to the east and situated near the Blue Line). Fragile wireless sets were knocked out early, and officers were unable to call down supporting artillery fire. Backup rockets and flares remained unseen amidst the smoke and dust that filled the air, although they cast a weird orange glow over that part of the front. It fell to brave runners, who dodged from shell hole to shell hole, to deliver a message about their predicament back to brigade headquarters. In response, additional runners were sent forward to the 72nd Battalion on the right, which curled back and knocked out the positions from the rear. The depleted companies of the 2nd, which had lost more than half of their lead force, pushed on to their objectives on the Blue Line. The 47th and 50th would then pass through them and into the fortified village of Rallencourt.

To the north of Bourlon and Rallencourt, the 2nd Brigade leapfrogged over the deep advances of the 1st. They had the furthest objectives of any brigade for the day. The 2nd Brigade had advanced from their start lines at zero plus four hours, and while the German counter-barrage was heavy, as the enemy guns laid down interdiction fire, it was "ill-directed," falling all over the battlefield. Nonetheless, for soldiers with no bird's-eye view of the battle, confusion reigned. The lead battalion, the 7th, got mixed up with the 3rd Brigade's 13th Battalion, on the left, which was battling fiercely for its objectives at Marquion. The delay resulting from the process of sorting out the mixed-up units left the lead companies watching in anguish as their barrage moved off without them, abandoning them to face the fire naked. Aware that the enemy would soon begin to emerge from his dugouts, two lead companies of the 7th pushed desperately through the 13th behind accurate sniper and Lewis-gun fire that cleared the way, men sacrificing their lives by drawing fire onto themselves so that others could advance. Captain H.C.R. Clarke led his company forward in the assault for two hours, "through a maze of wire in an almost untenable position," an official report noted, "until he himself was mortally wounded."[17] Four tanks tried to assist the 7th, but they drew heavy fire from enemy field guns and were forced to retire, spewing smoke from gaping holes in their metal hulls. There was nothing left for the battalion to do but push ahead, as the battle had "developed into a straight fight with Lewis guns and rifle fire against large numbers of the enemy ... who was putting up a stubborn fight with machine-guns and rifles and also firing over open sights from two field guns dug in along the ridge."[18] The determined men of the 7th finally captured their objectives on the Blue Line at around 2 P.M.

The other three battalions of the brigade, the 8th, 5th, and 10th Battalions, marched through them, following a new barrage at "zero plus 9.40," or 3 P.M. Clouds of dust and debris from the barrage blanketed the front, making it difficult for the lead units to locate not only their objectives but, more importantly, the enemy that was firing upon them. Brave scouting officers exposed themselves as they raced forward looking for telltale muzzle flashes and the origins of tracer bullets; often they made themselves targets to draw enemy fire, the direction of which was communicated back to company commanders by the men themselves if they were lucky, or by companions who saw the enemy who had riddled the brave bait. Again it fell to the junior officers or NCOs to gather together men who had thrown themselves into craters or depressions in the land. Clods of dirt were banged off helmets; shrapnel sizzled into the ground; men passed hurried orders after snatching quick glances above the crater's lip. With forces spread across the battlefield, soldiers waited for a few more men to arrive in their shallow craters and then pushed forward again. The dispersal of infantry in hundreds of shell holes could result in a battalion's battle degenerating into dozens of disparate engagements. Along the front, one section might be battling for its life while another group of men caught their collective breaths in a crater. In such a diffuse battlefield, not all men went forward, as some were unable to find the courage to leave the relative safety of their craters. But most did, a fact that attested to the discipline and camaraderie among the infantry, who refused to allow their mates—their family members—to take all the chances.

The 2nd Brigade worked its way forward, steadily driving through the enemy positions, many of which were situated as slit trenches. By mid-afternoon, the 5th Battalion had captured Haynecourt and a series of trenches to the north, before digging in facing Epinoy, which would be overrun later in the day by the 11th British Division. As the "Fighting Tenth" passed through them, pushing out in a two-company advance, indirect machine-gun fire deposited burning lead all around them. Their right flank, facing the south, was in the air, and the enemy enfiladed the men as they overran enemy outposts through the nearly flat, treeless terrain. With almost no cover and innumerable rows of uncut barbed wire in front of them, the battalion relied on designated wire-cutters to creep forward, cutting paths through the wire by hand, protected by the fire laid down by their sections. The 10th reached their objectives, but these were in the middle of a field some 200 to 300 metres from the Marcoing Line. The lead units dug in here were dangerously exposed after a day of fierce fighting. Under the cover of darkness, the infantry enlarged their slit trenches, but the company commanders ordered roving battle patrols all night to act as a forward defence. The 8th Battalion, which was mixed up with the 10th, set up a hard flank to protect against incursions from further to the south, but they too were in danger of catching it in the neck from enemy counterattacks.

DESPITE THE 1ST DIVISION'S strong advances to the north, the battle hinged on the capture of Bourlon Wood, at the south end of the Canadian front, in the 4th Division's sector. The heights of the wood towered over the battlefield, and this strongpoint had been the German army's springboard from which its counterattacking force drove Byng's Third Army back during the December 1917 fighting in the Battle of Cambrai. Maps showed that the wood rose just above the 100 contour mark (at 110 metres), while the canal was at about the 40 contour.[19] Bourlon Wood was expected to be the most difficult objective on the entire front. In fact, the Canal du Nord set-piece battle was sometimes referred to as the "B.W." operation in official documents.

The 85th Highlanders from Nova Scotia were tasked with capturing the village of Bourlon, to the north of the wood. After an hour and a half of anxious smoking and the gulping down of fortifying rum as they waited for their staggered start, the Highlanders crossed the canal at about 6 A.M., stumbling through debris, shattered bodies, and clouds of gas that the enemy had loosed to slow the assault. Advancing platoon by platoon, in single file to minimize the damage wrought by sweeping machine-gun fire, they pushed into the battle zone. The blasted battlefield was a far cry from what was shown on the aerial photographs and maps that the officers held in their hands. Frequent rests were needed to gather the men together and determine objectives, which was almost always done while shells and bullets crashed or whizzed overhead. Enemy troops in stray positions that had escaped the notice of several Canadian formations as they passed over them re-emerged to raise havoc on supporting waves of troops and units, including the 85th. They were systematically wiped out, but most took a toll on the advancing Highlanders.

Having cleared these isolated positions, the Nova Scotians pierced the Marquion trench system as they hugged their barrage into the village of Bourlon. One platoon seized the moment and passed through their own barrage to capture the enemy trench system where all the defenders had sought safety in their dugouts, and then hurriedly went to ground in the same German dugouts as their own barrage passed over the trench like a storm. The commanding officer, Lieutenant Colonel J.L. Ralston, a future minister of national defence, supported the drive, sending his third and fourth companies, along with three tanks, through the gap in the enemy lines to exploit success. "A gentleman, scholar, brilliant, courageous beyond words," was how one soldier in the 85th Battalion described Ralston.[20] His face would stop some shrapnel later in the day—his third of four wounds during the war—and he remained an inspiration to his men.

The forward companies of the 85th were now reduced to about fifty men, and commanded by lieutenants. As the Highlanders swarmed through the village, they saw the Germans fleeing to the rear, where they were picked off by Canadian snipers who scrambled for high ground, usually atop the rubble of what had once been a house. One enemy supply wagon was captured, containing hot soup, which was eagerly downed by sweaty-faced soldiers. But there was no time to rest, as the battle was far from over. Several counterattacks from the northeast were turned back by concentrated Lewis and Vickers machine-gun fire, and the enemy bombarded the village with explosives and gas all day. Lewis gunners played an essential role in holding the front; one gunner, Lance Corporal Auguste Lauren, fired pan after pan as his crew was slowly cut down around him during the next forty-eight hours. Despite being an obvious target for the enemy, he somehow survived, although his gun, by the end of the fighting, was riddled with machine-gun bullets and shrapnel.[21] In front of him, the crimson bodies of Germans lay in the fields of wheat. Behind, tumpliners rushed forward ammunition and water, and then helped to carry out the wounded. The 85th would fight for another week, patrolling actively, hunting snipers, and destroying enemy outposts that crept forward. By battle's end, the Highlanders had lost more than sixty percent of their fighting strength, but had captured and held every one of their objectives. They lived up to their informal motto: "To do their bit and a bit more."[22]

To the left of the 85th, once the village fell, the 38th carried the advance forward, and was then leapfrogged by the 78th and 72nd. The spearhead units ran into increasingly heavy opposition past the Marquion Line, and concentrated fire from a sunken road on the outskirts of Bourlon held up the 38th, until Captain W.R. Ross pulled together a small battle group and captured eight field guns. Further on, the 72nd ran into several machine guns and a 77mm field gun, which raked the forward units with direct fire. Private A.J. Foster recounted that the enemy fire was knocking his mates "down like nine-pins." Everyone went to ground. Worse still, the Canadian gunners were almost out of range, and many shells were dropping short. Foster remembered the nightmare of watching a phosphorous shell explode near two men. Their hair and heads began to catch fire like roman candles, their bodies slowly enveloped in flame. Nothing could be done, as the napalm-like phosphorous came off on the hands of men trying to help them. The screaming of the two damned men could be heard above the wail of the shells.[23]

Driving forward behind a smoke and high explosive barrage, the 78th pushed ahead to the left of the 72nd, although the two forces soon became intermingled while working together to clear obstinate positions. Lewis guns supported by 3-inch mortars—along with the 6-inch Newton mortar, which fired a heavy bomb that tumbled over and over in flight before it landed with a devastating detonation— helped to soften up the strongpoints around Pilgrim's Rest, a small hill with a commanding view of the front. As well, the few roving-commission 18-pounders attached to each of the battalions were used in a direct fire role.

Again, though, it often fell to individuals to find ways to win on the battlefield. Most of the 78th Battalion's commanding officers had been knocked out by noon, and Lieutenant Samuel Honey took over B Company. He rallied the troops several times, travelling back and forth across the sector as bullets and shrapnel whizzed around him. As the sun set, the 72nd and 78th charged one final time at 8 P.M. to crash the Marcoing Line, located about half way between the Canal du Nord and Cambrai. A bayonet charge by the 72nd over open ground against Pilgrim's Rest forced the surrender of more than 200 Germans. The Germans almost immediately counterattacked, but their assault was broken up when signallers got a message back to Canadian headquarters and a savage bombardment tore into the massed enemy groups.[24] On the 78th's front, Honey led several additional attacks with his depleted company that was down to forty men by infiltrating forward to clear machine-gun nests that were harassing the consolidating forces. At one point, Honey rushed a machine-gun nest and single-handedly captured a series of guns and ten prisoners. This quiet, self-effacing former teacher, after rallying his depleted battle group to repulse four counterattacks, continued to patrol the front throughout the night, and captured another German outpost. Honey's commanding officer wrote to his family, "Nowhere have I seen such gallant work as this boy of yours displayed…. He was the first to reach the final objective during the first day and throughout the days that followed he was an example of grit and determination that was the talk of the whole command. The men idolized him."[25] For his bravery and inspiring leadership in battle, he was awarded the Victoria Cross, but he did not live to see it. On September 29, he led his wasted forces against a strong enemy position and was shot in both legs. Despite being mortally wounded, Honey stayed at the front, organizing the attack and defence, until he died from shock and loss of blood.

It was junior officers like Honey who often turned defeat into victory. Hugh Urquhart, who rose from a subaltern to a lieutenant colonel during the war, noted that, by the Hundred Days, many of the lieutenants who commanded the battle from the front had risen from the ranks. Battle-tested, experienced NCOs had been promoted, and they "possessed a treasure of experience and ability."[26] In the 16th Battalion, for example, of the forty-seven lieutenants who served in the Hundred Days battles, thirty of them had been promoted from the lower ranks. As a body of men, such experienced officers were essential in turning the tide of battle.

ALTHOUGH BOURLON VILLAGE had fallen, the German defenders remained hidden in the dark reaches of Bourlon Wood, spraying the front with bullets and shrapnel bursts. Because of the wood's strength, Currie had ordered that phosgene shells be fired into the area to disrupt the enemy defences. The heights of Bourlon Wood were shrouded in a death haze, but the explosion of shells in the mist lent it a quality of unreal beauty. The gas, smoke, and dust also helped to provide cover for the 87th, 54th, and 102nd Battalions that were tasked with clearing the position.

The British division to the south had been stopped short of Bourlon Wood, which presented problems for the Canadians. The initial plan of a double-envelopment was no longer possible, and the Canadians' southern flank was left open. But the wood had to fall, and so the three lead Canadians battalions would attack. Three tanks were to support the infantry, but the tank commander refused to advance into the woods. He may have had good reason to do so, as this was not good tank terrain, but his refusal left Brigadier Victor Odlum fuming, and he later wrote: "I had no further time to waste on him."[27] The 102nd and 54th cleared the way through the northern part of Bourlon Wood with fierce fighting. Throughout the push, the 102nd needed to avoid the southern part of the forest, as they were raked by "direct artillery fire over open sights." A quick-thinking officer of the 2nd Machine Gun Battalion took seven Vickers machine guns under his command and situated them to cover the exposed flank. The gunners, with the support of two companies of the 75th, destroyed a strong German counterattack in the late afternoon. In other parts of the forest, the Canadians advanced, creeping from tree to tree, bush to crater, routing enemy artillery positions and machine-gun nests.[28] High explosive shells shattered trees, adding lethal wooden stakes to the lengthy list of means by which men could be killed on the battlefield. The 102nd and 75th Battalions lost so many casualties that they were amalgamated around noon. But robust Canadian fighting units, equipped with similar doctrine and weapons, proved adept at forming these ad hoc fighting formations. Enemy strongholds fell one by one, or surrendered when they encountered Canadians in front, around, and behind them. Several counterattacks were beaten back throughout the day, and by dusk the fortress of Bourlon Wood had fallen to the Canadians and would not be recaptured.

AT THE END OF THE DAY, the Germans had lost the canal, the linchpin position of Bourlon Wood, and the Marquion Line. The Canadians had advanced nearly 8 kilometres. It was a shocking success, on par with the initial breakthrough at Amiens and against a far more difficult position. On the other side of the battle lines, the German high command was desperate to hold Cambrai, which was now within Canadian shellfire range. Seven German divisions were rushed to the front on September 28 and 29. The Canadians' aggressive advance, with battalion passing through battalion, had German intelligence mistakenly believing that they were facing twelve Canadian divisions! There were in fact only three (and one British to the north), and now the Canadians, despite their oversized divisions, were outnumbered. The German high command also sent a number of elite machine-gun companies to stiffen the backbone of the defenders. Well-trained and with strong morale, these gunners often fought to the death and would be incredibly difficult to overwhelm in the coming days. Although these new German forces would make the fighting far more difficult, the Canadians played their part in the larger Allied offensive by drawing limited enemy reserves to their front.

THE NIGHT OF SEPTEMBER 27–28 was spent digging and preparing new jumping-off trenches within the haunting red glow cast over the battlefield by the burning villages of Rallencourt and St. Remi. The Canadians had made good progress, but they also knew that the enemy was responding to their advance by massing counter-attacking forces and by fortifying their own positions. German units holding the Canal de l'Escaut, including the 26th Wurttemberg Reserve Division, had been personally visited by Field Marshal von Hindenburg, who urged them to hold the line to their collective deaths. No retreat, no surrender.

The Canadians pushed out their lines on September 28 in a renewed attempt to exploit the success of the previous day. But now the Canadians were spread out over three times the space, on almost a 10,000-metre front, and the density of the barrage therefore suffered. All along the front, the Canadians were to attack just after dawn, but the assaults were uncoordinated as a result of general confusion in the lines and a breakdown in communication. As with other set-piece battles, the success on the first day had resulted in the infantry advancing to the outer edge of the gunner's range. Horse teams and tractors dragged the field guns and heavy howitzers forward, but it was a night of confusion as ammunition trains tried to prepare and supply gun crews for the next phase of the offensive, while under enemy fire.

Canadians hold a ditch during the Canal du Nord battle. The Hundred Days campaign was a mixture of open and trench warfare. On the road are Canadian infantrymen riding on armoured cars and trucks, presumably moving towards the battlefield.

To fill the widened front, Currie had pushed the 3rd Division between the 1st and 4th. It would attack along the heavily defended Bapaume-Cambrai road. To the south, Watson's 4th Division had been reduced to a one-brigade front, with the remaining units so badly cut up as to be all but operationally ineffective. To the north, Macdonell's 1st Division had the widest sector and benefited from the support of the 4th British Division. On paper, the Canadian operation looked like a four-division assault, but in reality most of the divisions employed only a few battalions in a spearhead role. All those involved, whether at the front or rear, expected hard fighting.

The 3rd Division, now under the command of Major General Frederick Loomis, had elbowed its way to the front during the previous night, pushing northeast from Bourlon Wood. Officers had almost no time to reconnoitre the ground, and many of the division's battalions entered the line only to run into German counterattacks. This was chaotic fighting in which the defenders relied on the resilience of platoons, sections, and even groups of individuals to hold key portions of the front, with almost no direction from the high command. The enemy forces crashed upon the Canadians, but in running up against the strong fields of fire and SOS artillery bombardments, they made little impact, leaving hundreds of dead and wounded on the battlefield. Just as there was confusion in the Canadian lines, the German counterattacks were hastily planned and often uncoordinated. The tempo of the Canadians' assault played havoc with the enemy's ability to react in a timely way and with concentrated forces. But there was no questioning the Germans' drive, and the Canadians were frequently down to their last reserves as overextended units were pressed in from three sides, with enemy infantry attacking wildly over open ground and often without artillery cover. Brigadiers and divisional commanders felt constant pressure to commit new troops to the front, but they had to maintain a fine balance: to stabilize the line now would mean depleting the forces available for the follow-on battles in the morning. The Canadians would have to hold with what they had. And they did.

The attack by the 3rd Division on the morning of September 28 involved both the 7th and 9th Brigades. The 9th, under the temporary command of Lieutenant Colonel Donald Sutherland, a future minister of national defence, unleashed a series of headlong assaults against the enemy positions. They closed to within a kilometre of Cambrai, but the main attack was mounted further to the north by the 7th Brigade. The Royal Canadian Regiment, leading the 7th Brigade's drive, got away quickly behind the 6 A.M. barrage, but took casualties from flanking machine-gun fire. Three supporting tanks were knocked out by anti-tank guns along the Marcoing Line, and while the commanding officer later suggested that smaller but faster Whippet tanks might have closed the gap more quickly, it is not clear how they would have had any more success in the face of unsuppressed enemy fire. As on the previous day, the Canadians were often facing enemy field guns that were employed in a direct fire role. These were positioned far closer to the front than normally situated guns, in part to stop the Allied tanks but also to hide them from the now punishing counter-battery fire of the Canadian guns.

In the face of bristling enemy guns along the German-held Marcoing Line, the Canadian infantry infiltrated forward, looking for seams in the enemy positions. Lieutenant Milton Gregg of the RCR was a former teacher from Mountain Dale, New Brunswick, who had risen from the rank of private and had been awarded the Military Cross twice for battlefield bravery. During the fighting on the morning of September 28, Gregg crawled forward alone, through a hail of fire, and found a small gap through which he led his men into the enemy lines. Two reserve platoons widened the breach by bombing up and down the trenches, and the Canadians were pouring through the enemy trenches by 9 A.M. They held it through several counter-attacks, with Gregg coordinating the defence even though he was twice wounded. He personally killed or wounded eleven enemy troops, took twenty-five prisoners, and captured twelve machine guns. The RCR tried to push out with further assaults, but were stopped by concentrated machine-gun fire from the village of St. Olle. By the end of the day, some 54 machine guns and 130 prisoners had been captured, and an estimated 700 casualties inflicted on the enemy.[29] Lieutenant Gregg was awarded the Victoria Cross, survived the war, and had a distinguished postwar career as a soldier, diplomat, and president of the University of New Brunswick, as well as holding several ministerial posts in Liberal governments.

The PPCLI and the 49th Battalion passed through the RCR to restore momentum, but despite individual heroics made little progress. The zero hour was not until

7 P.M., and by then the sky was nearly pitch-black. Worse still, two tanks that were to support the advance never arrived. Nonetheless, the 49th Battalion jumped off as arranged, but ran into concentrated machine-gun fire from several directions and uncut barbed wire that was hidden in overgrowth. The Germans had spent most of the day fortifying their positions, and they knew that once the RCR had breached the Marcoing Line another attack would follow. Stiff enemy resistance, ongoing casualties, and shortages of grenades plagued the attackers. Both battalions went to ground in front of St. Olle, where the entire brigade front was raked with artillery and machine-gun fire, and smothered with poison gas throughout the night. "I can never believe how I got through it," wrote Octave Pineau of the RCR, who was a little behind the lead 7th Brigade forces. "My friends were killed standing along side of me."[30]

TO THE NORTH of these 3rd Division attacks, the 4th Division's 10th Brigade was tasked with capturing Rallencourt and Sailly, both situated along the Arras-Cambrai road. The Germans had stacked their defences here in a formidable system of inter-locking machine-gun and artillery fire, and the Canadians going up against this strength were far weaker now, having lost hundreds of their most experienced men in the previous day of battle. Zero hour was at 6 A.M., but the lack of time to pre-pare had left the attack disorganized, with the two lead battalions, the 50th and 47th, forced to assemble their lines in the open—a veritable death sentence—as the sun rose. The two follow-up battalions, the 44th and 46th, were only 100 metres behind them, and all would push together to capture the two fortified villages. Even before the battle began, the four battalions began to take casualties from searching fire rained down by defenders who must have stared in bewilderment as more than a thousand men lay fully exposed in the long grass.

Yet the Canadian barrage was effective, chewing up the ground in front of the lines. For the second-echelon 44th and 46th Battalions, both with depleted compa-nies, capturing and holding their objectives would be even more difficult than for the lead battalions. On the 46th's front, the Saskatchewaner ran up against four machine guns sweeping the front. The position fell after fierce fighting in which lit-tle quarter was asked or given. Once this strongpoint was captured, sunken roads provided cover for the advancing infantry, who also pushed through hedges and barns in a desperate bid to find cover. Rallencourt and Sailly fell to the two battalions by late morning; holding them was no easier than capturing them had been, but at least the Canadians could dig in deep and wait for the enemy gunners to spend their fury.

The Canadians established flanking strongpoints with their weak forces, but they faced tense moments: counterattacks started at 10 A.M., and three were crushed before lunch. Vickers machine guns from the 2nd Machine Gun Battalion, assisted by the Lewis guns of the 44th, were especially effective in setting up a kill zone. On the right side of the brigade's sector, Captain H.D. Thomas of the 44th rode back and forth through the bombed-out villages on a bicycle to coordinate the defence, until he was wounded later in the day from a low-flying plane that was strafing the Canadian lines. Another round of counterattacks was destroyed starting at 3 P.M., but these were desperate affairs for the defenders, and several SOS calls by Canadian infantrymen went unsupported by the Canadian artillery. Ammunition was running low, and still the Germans came on, sometimes played forward by drummer boys. Parts of the line crumpled under the weight of assault, but reserve units marched forward to hold the front and the Germans were driven out again. By 7 P.M., the 3rd Division, on the right, had finally secured its objectives, which reduced the pressure on the Manitobans in the 44th. By the time the 44th were relieved the next day, they had lost 76 killed and 152 wounded.[31]

The 46th on the left had an equally difficult time. The barrage sputtered and the beaten ground in front of the Marcoing Line was alive with spewing bullets. "Machine-guns are the chief weapon of defence used by the Boche," wrote Lieutenant R.D. Borrette. "[When] we advance we have to take cover behind a blade of grass if necessary."[32] In the open, and with little cover, the 46th were cut down. Regardless of the bravery of individuals, the Canadians had no chance of pushing through where the Germans were in full strength, unsurprised, and sweeping the battlefield. One tank lumbered along parallel to the enemy front, unable or unwilling to get closer despite desperate attempts by two Canadians soldiers to direct it by banging on the armoured hull. The tank moved off in another direction, away from the front, and the two brave Canadians were riddled with bullets in the open. The four companies of the 46th were cut to ribbons and soon amalgamated to form two under-strength companies. But at 7 P.M. Brigadier Ross Hayter ordered another attack, which was supported with a heavy barrage. Somehow survivors dug deep and breached the Marcoing, capturing and killing hundreds of Germans. "In our particular company we had one officer, one sergeant, myself, and I think eleven men," remembered one survivor.[33] The 46th had lived up to its name as the Suicide Battalion.

ON THE FAR NORTHERN FRONT, the 10th Battalion spearheaded the 1st Division's attack on September 28 at 9 A.M., about three hours after the two divisions to the south advanced. Here, between Sancourt and Epinoy, as along most of the front, the ground was flat and gently rolling, so the defenders could sweep it with impunity. The 10th were not informed of their attack until dawn, not long before they were to strike at the enemy. When the officers looked at their orders, they noted with shock that the creeping barrage was to come down on their very coordinates. The 10th scrambled from their trenches in the pale dawn light and retreated several hundred metres to the rear. A bitter battalion report noted that they "suffered at least 50 unnecessary casualties" as the Germans harassed them in their vulnerable state. Sadly, the 10th should probably have stayed where it was, since when the barrage came down it was so feeble as to be "practically useless," and only served to alert the Germans to the forthcoming attack.[34]

According to one official report, as soon as the forward companies left their trenches, "Enemy machine guns, unmolested, fired at point blank range. A perfect hell of bullets swept them.… A finer thing was never attempted. For two hours they fought the enemy artillery, and his machine guns, and his wire, and his snipers, clustered at every point of advantage."[35] The bravery of the men was unquestionable: Captain Jack Mitchell of the 10th Battalion led his men forward into the Armageddon of fire, where a bullet smashed his hand, and he went back to the dressing station. He later returned to the front, his hand bandaged into a bloody club, and rallied his men again from their shallow cover in the farmers' fields that were now open graveyards. Moving from crater to crater, Mitchell coordinated a second attack. Another bullet struck him, this time tearing into his foot. He was bandaged up, and continued to hobble back and forth with the aid of a batman. As bullets whirled around him, Mitchell went up and down the uncut enemy wire looking for an opening, "cheering his men, helping his men, tireless, undismayed, fighting a hopeless fight with a courage that went beyond all praise."[36] In a final attempt to cross the wire obstacles, he was hit again, this time fatally. When darkness permitted, Mitchell's men carried him out, refusing to leave him on the battlefield where the 10th had been stopped short of its objectives during an engagement that one officer characterized as an "attack worse than useless."[37]

SEPTEMBER 28 was a bad day for the Canadians. The multi-pronged attacks were uncoordinated and costly, and artillery support was sporadic at best. Far more damaging was a determined enemy who was desperate to hold back the Canadian advance. The Germans were not only willing to fight for almost every metre, but they proved reckless in their counterattacks, moving in bunched formations over open ground. Although the Canadians made the Germans pay for their massed attacks, forward units found themselves outnumbered and often overwhelmed. Isolated forward outposts of infantrymen were severely pressed, but, in a testament to the high Canadian morale, these sacrificial posts that were not wiped out in the fighting often held on until counterattacks from their own reserves freed them from their trapped position behind the German lines. During both the day and night, the forward Canadian lines were held by fewer and fewer men, the dead lying around them, the wounded mercifully sent to the rear. Clifford Johnston, an ambulance driver, recorded in his diary the "many gruesome sights" that greeted him as he scoured the battlefield looking for the wounded:

> Dead men lay here and there, ours as well as Germans. Those with heads torn off, sides shot away and bullet holes through many heads—many soaked in blood and lying in it…. The expression on the dead men's faces was also one to make a person shudder. Some had a smile, some appeared to have died instantly, while many had the most agonized looks, as if they had suffered untold pain.[38]

As at Amiens, the second day of battle revealed diminishing returns. Could Currie have done anything different? He had secured the all-important Bourlon

Wood, and now Cambrai was within his grasp. The corps had to push further to reach the prize, and, of course, its commander was under orders to do so. On the positive side, the Canadian operational goal of drawing enemy reserves to the front was working according to plan, and in fact beyond all expectations. Just as the Canadians had supported Haig's Passchendaele offensive by drawing German troops to their attack on Hill 70 in the previous year, so too were they chewing up essential reserves at the Hindenburg Line. The attack had to be pressed, but, as always, it fell to the poor bloody infantry to do the fighting and dying. Those who survived into the night must have wondered if there would be anything left of the Canadian Corps come morning. Certainly another pitched battle seemed out of the question against an enemy force that now held almost all the advantages: terrain, firepower, and tenacity born of desperation. But the operation would go forward. A beleaguered force of too few Canadians was now called on to do too much against nearly impossible odds. After losing almost eighty percent of his company in the futile fighting, and facing the prospect of further losses, Lieutenant Joseph Sproston of the 10th Battalion complained to his commanding officer: "This isn't war, it's murder. It's just pure bloody murder."[39]

CHAPTER 35

"EVERY TIME I LOOK AROUND FOR A FAMILIAR FACE, I FIND THEY HAVE GONE"

September 29–October 9, 1918

"The Canadians have suffered terrible losses during the last 3 days," wrote Gunner Bertram Cox. "Some companies have fought to the last man, but we have taken all our objectives."[1] The fighting on September 28 had been brutal, plunge-ahead warfare. While the Germans were left disorganized and scattered as a result of the unyielding pressure, the Canadians were hampered in organizing and getting troops to the battlefield to coincide with artillery barrages. Too often units on both sides were thrown into the battle piecemeal, in desperate attempts to either stem the advance or meet objectives set kilometres behind the lines at headquarters. September 29 would prove no better.

THE 4TH DIVISION'S 12th Brigade had sidestepped the 3rd Division's forces and was now in the centre of the corps. It kicked off the day with an attack by the 38th and 72nd Battalions, which both went into the line for the second time in three days. The 38th Battalion, from Ottawa, mustered 24 officers and 445 men, but the 72nd Battalion had fewer than 400 men in the front lines.[2] As the two battalions attacked through the 50th and 46th at 8 A.M., a powerful artillery barrage tore a hole through the Marcoing Line, crashing on the enemy front line for twenty minutes and then lifting 90 metres every four minutes. The 12th Brigade punched through, capturing Sancourt, but the two battalions were reduced to such a paltry force that prisoners outnumbered the surviving attacking Canadians by a ratio of four to one.[3] During one enemy counterattack, which was destroyed by concentrated Canadian fire, the defenders also had to deal with a few German officers who were already prisoners and attempted to encourage a revolt among their men. The inciters were silenced with Lee-Enfield bullets.[4]

The fiercest battles centred around St. Olle. During the previous day, the 58th had moved to within a kilometre of the village, allowing the 116th to launch a morning assault. The barrage at zero hour was effective, but the Germans had established a crossfire of machine guns from St. Olle and a hidden position further to the south. The lead companies of the 116th, A and B, were "practically annihilated," with A reduced to five men and B down to thirty-three by the end of the day. What was left of the two remaining companies, led by a single lieutenant, raced through the maelstrom and captured the main enemy trench, killing dozens and taking more than 100 prisoners and fifteen machine guns.[5] After nearly three days and nights of continuous fighting and almost no sleep, the 9th Brigade was relieved late in the day by the 8th Brigade.

To the 8th's left, the 7th Brigade, consisting of the RCR, the PPCLI, and the 49th and 42nd Battalions, was thrown into a narrow front along the Douai-Cambrai road. Under a cloudless sky, the mass of infantry waited in the tall, wet grass. When the barrage opened up at 8 A.M., they watched with growing apprehension; the fire was thin and ineffective. Officers took control as the companies advanced in long, thin lines towards the towers of Cambrai that stood out boldly against a horizon of blue sky. The men of the 7th Brigade cautiously grabbed 1,000 metres, facing almost no enemy fire. Combat veterans knew something was wrong. Had the Germans perhaps retreated during the night? The attackers found out soon enough when lead units ran into uncut low-lying wire, at least five rows deep. The infantry was slowed here as they were forced to step over each strand and cut through denser portions. And it was here that the enemy opened his fire, having withheld it as the Canadians moved within range. Lines of men were cut down as bullets snapped and

Defending to the last bullet, this slain German defender was armed with the MG-08/15 light machine gun and firing from a slit trench to the east of the Canal du Nord.

ricocheted off the wire while others found flesh. Most of the officers were killed within a few minutes; the 42nd Battalion's Highlanders, for instance, lost all four company commanders and all four seconds-in-command.[6] "It was certain death to breathe deeply," wrote William Breckenridge of the 42nd, remembering his experience of playing dead along with his section mates as they lay in shallow craters, pinned down by raking enemy fire. "The moaning and groaning of the wounded put fear into those who were more fortunate; but still we could not move to help them. As the wounded rolled over to ease the pain of their wounds, the Germans would riddle them with bullets."[7]

But even within the firestorm, the Canadians found ways to advance, moving from a smoking shell crater to a ditch, from the ditch to a depression in the ground, and so on, pushing ahead one or two men at a time, metre by metre. Fire-unit teams, comprising a Lewis gunner and a few riflemen, banded together to move forward on the battlefield. Private W.G. Roberts of the PPCLI recounted that a bullet hit him smack in the middle of the head: "As luck would have it, however, it hit the rim of my steel helmet and traveled up and over the top. It knocked me silly for a few minutes and I called out, 'I'm hit!'" As Roberts knelt stunned, feeling his head for blood, an officer passed him and barked, "'Put on your helmet, you damn fool,'" which he did, and continued to advance.[8] Senior corporals and even privates gathered survivors together and led them forward into the inferno, destroying position after position—but behind them lay the red wreckage of their battalions. Despite deep Canadian inroads, and almost a kilometre of captured ground, Tilloy remained in German hands. It was a key objective, however, and would have to be assaulted again on September 30.

The 1st and 2nd CMRs, to the south of the 7th Brigade, made only a slight advance against concentrated fire. The artillery barrage had almost entirely overshot the enemy strongpoints, leaving the battalions exposed, and as they tried to move forward in the face of uncut barbed wire and sweeping machine-gun fire, the CMR took heavy casualties. With soldiers cut down around him, Captain James MacGregor of the 2nd CMR, who had risen from the rank of private and already wore the DCM and Military Cross, led the men forward, dangerously exposing himself to bullet and shell, waiving his revolver in one hand and shillelagh in the other. Fire from a machine-gun nest in a house across the Douai Road—outside of the battalion's sector—was tearing holes in the advancing sections, so MacGregor ordered it destroyed. Several of the 2nd CMR survivors refused to move from the relative safety of their shell holes. With the makings of a mutiny on his hands, MacGregor grabbed a rifle from a soldier and, leading by example, charged the machine-gun nest, followed by his batman, who was shot down within a few seconds. Somehow MacGregor reached the house almost unscathed, with only a bullet hole through his tunic and a slight wound in his knee. In the fierce fighting that followed, the captain killed four Germans with bullet and bayonet and captured another eight. The push continued and MacGregor was later awarded the Victoria Cross for his bravery and leadership in this part of the battle. Throughout the rest of the day, MacGregor rallied the troops, many of whose officers had been killed or wounded and lay spread out all over the battlefield. Just as brave as MacGregor was Lance Sergeant Henry George Sivertz of the 2nd CMR, who single-handedly wiped out a machine-gun nest that was holding up an advance, and was awarded a second Bar to his Military Medal. Sadly, the twenty-five-year-old Sivertz was killed later in the day by a sniper. The two CMR battalions captured their positions, but suffered almost 500 casualties in the process.

Along the front, the Canadians had attacked and counterattacked in bitter battles. In the three days of fighting, the Germans had reinforced their original four divisions ranged against the Canadians with six more, also adding thirteen marksman machine-gun companies. In contrast, only three divisions and a brigade had been ordered to the British portion of the front, which was twice as large.[9] The cycling of Canadian infantrymen through battered units had kept up the corps' momentum, but the Canadians' lack of concentrated artillery fire and the enemy's desire to hold the front by pouring in reinforcements reduced the battle to hard-pounding, attritional warfare. Daunting acts of bravery and tactical innovation continued, but too often the infantry were called on to attack without time to prepare or even to reconnoitre the ground. There would be no rest in the face of this bristling defence. Currie believed that the enemy was on the edge of cracking, or were at least desperate enough to keep shovelling precious resources into the open maw of his forces, but he also admitted, "The Germans have fought us here very, very hard."[10]

ON SEPTEMBER 30, the 3rd and 4th Divisions continued to press the attack against the outskirts of Cambrai. After waiting in misery through a rainy night, the 11th Brigade led the push to capture the canal crossings at Eswars. The see-saw battles here were the "hardest battles in which the brigade ever engaged," confided Brigadier Victor Odlum to his diary.[11] The brigade was to attack into a gentle valley, where the Germans held the heights on both sides. The operation, wrote Odlum, "was based on false assumptions, namely that the enemy was beaten and would withdraw." The attack could only succeed if the artillery smokescreen blanketed the flanks, but the screen was weak—"a total failure," according to Odlum; it did nothing to suppress the attack, and the brigade's entire front was exposed to German guns firing from Abancourt.[12] When the strike force left their trenches at 6 A.M., a full ten minutes after a few of the Canadian guns had mistakenly opened up to give away the time of the attack, the 75th, 54th, and 87th were torn to shreds, eventually being forced to pull back from most of the gains achieved during the day since the front was untenable.

The 75th lost so many officers and NCOs that it could not be put into the line the next day, and one veteran of the 87th Battalion, John Preston, recounted his shock as he marched to the rear with the remnants of his battalion: "The last five days and nights we have been in battle ... the shattered remnants of our battalion, to the number of 60, groped our way out of death and hell.... I bore a charmed life through it all, of close calls, I ceased to count them. I am still numb ... every time I look around for a familiar face, I find they have gone."[13] Suffering from buzzing ears and numb at the loss of his best friends, Preston spoke for most of the infantry who had been through the meat grinder of battle.

The harsh fighting of the previous day in front of Tilloy had allowed the 7th Brigade to push within a few hundred metres of the village. All night there was activity as battle patrols moved through No Man's Land to prepare for the assault, dodging the sputtering German machine-gun fire under the ghostly glow of flares. The attack went in at 6 A.M., but the barrage was weak, partly because German aircraft were swooping down and harassing the gunners with machine-gun fire. Nonetheless, after ninety minutes of fighting, Tilloy fell to the PPCLI. The Germans counterattacked throughout the day, throwing in piecemeal forces, all of which were consumed in the sweeping fields of fire laid down by what was left of the four Canadian battalions.

The attack on September 30 had gained the Canadians about 1.5 kilometres of territory, but prisoners from dozens of German battalions clearly indicated that the enemy was throwing everything into holding the line. Four days of continuous fighting had left the Canadians exhausted and spent, although they had captured more than 7,000 prisoners and 205 guns, and had drawn six more German divisions to the Canadian front to reinforce the four mauled ones barely hanging on.[14] Cambrai had not fallen, but the attackers now surrounded it on two sides, and the strongpoint would become untenable for the defenders when the Canadians brought up their artillery. The Canadians had ground out the enemy, and in carrying out their operation they had also provided a strong flank for the British army attacks to the south.

THE 1ST DIVISION had not been involved in any pitched battles on September 29 or 30, although its units had been engaged in constant exchanges of fire. The men of the Old Red Patch had outdistanced the two divisions to the south in the first days of the advance, but now the division's renewed set-piece attack on October ran into problems, as the German lines had stiffened considerably. The 1st Brigade's 1st and 4th Battalions, supported by six batteries of machine guns (thirty-six guns in total), were to mount a frontal assault on the Marcoing Line, which had been breached to the south but remained firm on their front. One report noted that the terrain leading up to their objective, Abancourt, was "as flat as the palm of the hand."[15] This was not quite true, but it must have appeared so to the Canadian infantrymen staring at the fortress from their trenches. In fact, the ground rose slightly to the north and northwest, providing the enemy with a commanding field of fire. The attack was the type of operation that brought a large lump to the throat. But because Abancourt dominated the entire battlefield to the town's south, including Bantigny and Blecourt, located in the 3rd Brigade's sector, it had to fall.

At zero hour, 6 A.M., the 4th (on the left) and 1st (on the right) surged forward. The men of the 4th made good progress within their strong barrage, and had little problem with enemy troops, who fought poorly. The Germans had been force-marched 20 kilometres to the front in the middle of the night, leaving some of them so tired that the barrage did not even waken them.[16] The "Mad Fourth" continued their measured advance until they were within 200 metres of the village, near a railway line, where they encountered heavy fire. The Canadian barrage dropped down in straight lines here, but part of the enemy front was not covered by the shellfire, as it was slightly outside the full fury of the shells. Dense machine-gun fire tore into the Canadians. Men were bowled over by the velocity as bones were shattered and flesh pulped. "Any man who exposed himself," noted one official report, "immediately became a casualty."[17] Even the wounded were targets, with survivors watching helplessly as the bullets dug into the earth around them, hitting the already injured again and again. One man could barely contain himself as a fallen chum was hit in the head six times, the final bullet decapitating his lifeless body. In the absence of artillery support, even the multiple heavy machine guns supporting the battalion were not sufficient to suppress the enemy fire, and the 4th had no choice but to dig in for the day amidst the carnage.

To the south, the 1st Battalion, which had a narrower front, made a deep advance of 700 metres. Thereafter, their barrage became ragged, with several guns firing short into the Canadian advancing sections. Many 1st Battalion soliders faded back from the barrage for their own safety, but the rest of the barrage, as weak as it was, carried on through the objective so that again, like so many times in the last two years, the attackers lost their artillery support. On the British front to the north, the British had attacked with only three companies from the 32nd Brigade, 11th Division, and their attempt had predictably failed. The commanding officer of the 1st Brigade, W.A. Griesbach, did not blame the Imperial troops, who had fought with determination, but he wondered why such a weak force had been employed in such a difficult operation. As a result of the British failure, dozens of enemy gunners remained unmolested and opened fire, raking the Canadian 4th and 1st Battalions to the south. The front was a cacophony of noise and spitting bullets, and the Canadians moving into the firefight even witnessed the rare sight of enemy field artillery, largely unhindered by the Canadian barrage, being pulled across the battlefield to fire directly into the attackers' positions. Enemy aircraft commanded the skies, too, acting as aerial observers and as an active part of the German defence by shooting up the Canadian forward units. During several hours of bitter fighting, in which the right-hand platoons crept forward to flank the enemy positions, the 1st Battalion was able to make some limited progress. But all the while, the enemy machine guns, firing from the British and 4th Battalion's fronts, raked their lines, making any advance, even a reconnaissance, costly.

At risk because of its open left (northern) flank, the 1st Brigade was supported by a successful right-flank attack by the 3rd Brigade to the south, which had captured Blecourt by 10 A.M. The 1st Battalion launched a second attack on Abancourt in the mid-afternoon, but that attempt also failed when it was shot down by hidden machine-gunners on the 3rd Brigade's front who had remained undetected until the men of the 1st Battalion left their shallow ditches. Realizing that any frontal assault was bound to fail, the commanding officer of the 1st Battalion sent out several battle patrols to find a way around the enemy strongpoints, but not one man returned alive. Adding salt to the unit's considerable wounds, Canadian artillery periodically fired short into the Canadian lines, injuring at least twelve men. It was a frustrating and bloody day, and the Canadians blamed the British for not keeping up and taking the objective on their own front.[18] It was true that they had not, but the Canadian artillery had also done little to support the two shattered battalions, each of which had strangely lost exactly 179 men. In fact, it was a near-miracle that the Canadians did not suffer greater casualties in the face of such heavy German firepower. To the south, the 3rd Brigade's 13th, 14th, and 16th Battalions captured their objectives and were forced to set up a hard flank facing north, as Abancourt would not fall until the British finally captured it several days later, passing over the bodies of the 1st Brigade as they did so. By the end of the battle, the 1st Division, which had a pre-battle strength of 13,791, but only a "fighting strength" of 12,270 when the administrative and headquarters staff were excluded, suffered 3,963 casualties, of which 558 were killed and another 530 listed as "missing."[19]

ON THE CAMBRAI FRONT to the south, one final set-piece engagement would be made by the 3rd and 4th Divisions. The elite 9th Brigade, which had proven itself during some of the hardest fighting to the west of Cambrai, was now shifted slightly

The Canadians in the Hundred Days suffered shocking levels of casualties, forcing the fighting units to engage in battle after battle at less than full strength, with inexperienced new recruits, and with the worn-out soldiers who had fought through the previous brutal engagements at Arras and Amiens. It was always one more push—and each time with fewer and fewer men.

to the north of the city to attack around it in a wheeling formation to avoid the enemy's strongpoints that were facing west. Passing through the 7th Brigade, the 43rd and 52nd Battalions attacked at 5:10 A.M. on October 1, following their barrage around the city and clearing out a series of German trenches.

The 9th Brigade had pushed the Canadian line almost entirely around the northern portion of Cambrai. But it was clear that the German defences were not going to buckle, and on October 1, prisoners from six infantry brigades from four different divisions were among the captured, indicating that new units had been thrown into the defenders' line.[20] The tempo of the battle had increased again, with attacks launched only hours after the orders were given. Since there was little time to prepare, lieutenants and captains, who were now leading companies, often had "only a vague idea" of operations and objectives, and when they were knocked out, the survivors had no idea where they were going.[21] This lack of organization, added to the fact that the Germans were throwing everything they had into the line, made for confusing, if brutal, battles. The Canadian attacks were met by counterattacks, with both sides employing tripwire defensive outposts based on strong machine-gun formations backed up by hard-hitting reserve troops who were thrown into the line when it began to waver. By the end of the day, the Canadians had stopped the German attacks cold. But their lines were still supported by a massive concentration of machine guns and artillery, and nothing would shake them loose except for a full set-piece battle. During three days of grinding warfare, the 9th Brigade lost 56 officers and 1,467 men, the losses spread almost evenly among the four battalions.[22] This casualty rate was a terrible burden for the brigade, and all the more shocking when compared with that of the 7th Canadian Siege Battery, a heavy howitzer unit initially raised in Montreal. Gunner T.W.L. MacDermot noted that October 2 was memorable for the battery because it was the day on which they suffered their first fatality of the war.[23] Without downplaying the crucial role of the gunners—and certainly other field batteries closer to the front were far more badly cut up—these divergent numbers can surely be taken as an indication that the brutal consequences of battle on the Western Front were not spread evenly among the fighting units.

DURING THE FIGHTING on October 1, the 1st and 4th Divisions, with some support from the 3rd, had engaged and defeated two entire German divisions, large portions of two more divisions, and elements of four other divisions.[24] General Currie wrote in a letter to Prime Minister Borden that the breaking of the canal and its eastern defences was "some of the bitterest fighting we have ever experienced.... It was attack and counterattack every day."[25] But despite the corps' success, Currie and Horne realized that further attacks would not be possible with the corps' battered troops, and the fighting in the first week in October was of a minor scale. Night patrols went out to harass enemy positions, but the battle had been ground out. Alternating between offensive operations and an active defence based on sited artillery gunfire and a heavy concentration of machine-gun teams, the Canadians kept the Germans back on their heels, and when the enemy attacked, his forces were destroyed, as in, for example, the one-battalion-strong counterattack against the 2nd Division's front, northeast of Tilloy at 6:15 P.M. on October 2.

Behind the lines, the ammunition columns, light rails, and pack trains caught up with the sharp end, and new stockpiles were formed and gun pits dug for the next—and hopefully last—phase of the offensive. Burial parties carried out their grim work. There would eventually be twenty cemeteries located along the 1st Division's front alone, to accommodate the 568 known dead and the more than 238 still missing in action, whose bodies or body parts were more slowly discovered.[26] The 3rd Division, having born the brunt of heavier fighting, was even worse off; their losses totalled 994 killed and missing and 3,017 wounded. Loomis's men captured twenty-one field guns, but also an astounding 351 heavy machine guns, a stark indication of the German reliance on their machine-gun teams to hold the front, as their artillery had been overpowered by the Canadian counter-battery guns.[27] Watson's 4th Divisional headquarters was not able to tabulate the final casualties for the division, but the figures were likely on par with those of the 3rd, at close to 4,000. However, the division's final report on the battle noted, "The enemy opposed this division with the heaviest concentration of troops that has yet been encountered."

In the five days of battle from September 27 to October 1, Watson's men met and defeated a staggering total of fifty-five enemy battalions.[28] Although some German units were weaker than their Canadian counterparts, the attackers-to-defenders ratio was 1 to 4.5 in terms of numbers of battalions pitted against one another. Such attacks depicted the desperation of both the Germans and the Canadians. While the Canadian Corps suffered some 10,000 casualties during the course of the battle, the real shock was that they did not suffer more.

BECAUSE OF CAMBRAI'S importance as a logistical centre, the French implored the Canadians not to destroy it with artillery fire. But although the Canadians had already smothered the German defences in front of the city with poison gas, Currie was not willing to throw his forces into battle without an adequate barrage. He would wait and see what the Germans planned to do with his corps on their doorstep. Several days of uneasy quiet ensued along the front, although shelling and gassing were still constant both day and night. But on the morning of October 6, Major A.L. Barry of the 26th Battalion knew he and his men were in trouble when their colonel brought out strawberry jam for breakfast: it was so rare that it was only issued before an operation.[29] A series of probing battles by the fresh 2nd Division on the night of October 7 was successful in gaining key terrain to the northeast of Cambrai, strengthening the Canadian hold on the city. But still the Germans held the bridges that criss-crossed the moats and canals near Cambrai, and capturing them intact was crucial to the final assault on the city. On October 8–9, combat engineers led by Captain C.N. Mitchell of the 4th Battalion, Canadian Engineers— a twenty-eight-year old construction engineer from Winnipeg—sought to disarm a series of charges that the enemy had attached to blow an important bridge. While his engineers dealt with the explosives, Mitchell held off a desperate party of Germans who charged him, anxious to set off the explosives. He killed three and captured twelve, and for his bravery and leadership, Mitchell became the only Canadian engineer ever to receive the Victoria Cross.

As the Canadians pushed forward to the north and northeast of Cambrai, the agonizing standoff to the west of the city continued. The high command could wait no longer: Cambrai had to fall. For the Canadians in their ragged battalions, an assault on Cambrai would involve devastating urban warfare among civilians, hostiles, and rubble, which would require that almost every position be dug out with artillery and hard fighting. The corps' only sustained experience in urban fighting had been against Lens in the second phase of the Hill 70 battle, and that had not gone well. "We knew that [Cambrai] would be desperately defended," wrote twenty-one-year-old John Lynch of the PPCLI.[30] And Corporal Albert West, who had seen his beloved 43rd Battalion almost annihilated in the attacks at Arras and around Cambrai, upon hearing that his surviving comrades were being readied for an assault on the city, wrote bitterly in his diary:

> In Heaven's name, surely we handful of men and so few officers (Lieut. MacIntosh is the only officer of B. left) are not to be put thro' the mill without more reinforcements. We need 400–500 men at once. If such a disorganized mob is sent "over" now I should call it a crime.… We hear General Currie has said he will have Cambrai tho' he lose 75% of his corps. If so he is a fool and a murderer. Cambrai can be taken but we do not need to be slaughtered to capture it.[31]

But as preparation for the Canadian assault was being made, the Germans pulled out of the city. They did so behind a screen of smoke, having first set parts of the city on fire. Flames leapt through the rubble and old buildings as the Canadians advanced gingerly. They chased a number of enemy units out of the city but stepped warily through the many booby-trapped streets.

Cambrai and its ashes had fallen to the Canadians. The Germans were again pushed back, and though it looked like a rout, the enemy still had fight left in him. Difficult assaults over the Canal de l'Escaut were made on October 9, and the Canadians followed the retreating enemy. But advance forces of armoured cars and cavalry seeking to close with the enemy were stopped cold around Iwuy on October 11, when German rearguard machine-gun units shot them to pieces. The fighting at Iwuy was also notable for its inclusion of a rare tank-on-tank battle, in which the German behemoth A7V ran up against the smaller Allied tanks. The A7Vs were 7 metres long and almost 3 metres high, presenting a strange, box-like target that was manned by a team of eighteen. Only twenty of the German tanks were used on the Western Front, but they made an impression far beyond their operational effectiveness. Corporal Deward Barnes of the 19th Battalion remembered the panic caused by these "great big square tanks," but eventually the metal monsters were knocked out by concentrated fire from field artillery pieces. Barnes's war ended at Iwuy, too, when after more than a year of combat his leg stopped a bullet.[32] Aware that no breakthrough would happen despite the German defeat, lead Canadian forces, still licking their wounds, followed the enemy carefully, no doubt remembering that they had been called on to spearhead too many operations in the last two months.

NEXT TO THE BREAKING of the Drocourt-Quéant Line, the taking of the Canal du Nord was the Canadian Corps' most difficult battle of the entire war. And because of its complexity—in contrast to the Arras fighting that had been characterized by brutal, plunge-ahead warfare—it provided the greatest challenge to Sir Arthur Currie as a commander. He and his men rose to the task and triumphed. This was particularly fortunate for Currie, for if the operation had failed it would have likely cost him his job. The corps' commander's detractors were always waiting in the wings, and would have portrayed the battle as little more than a clumsy frontal assault against a fortified position—in effect, a throwback to July 1, 1916. Currie was willing to take that gamble. The Canal du Nord operation was predicated on shock and awe, but it could only have been accomplished by experienced and confident troops.

Currie issued a special order on October 3, which was to be read to all of the men. In it, he applauded the corps' success in crashing the Canal du Nord, which had then provided a solid shoulder to the British Third and Fourth Armies to the south. Acknowledging the brutal fighting, he noted that while the two armies with more than half a dozen corps to the south had engaged thirty-six German divisions to date, the Canadian Corps, in the Canal du Nord battle alone, had met and defeated twelve divisions, supported by thirteen independent machine-gun companies. "As you formed the flank you suffered enfilade and frontal artillery fire all the way; and the hundreds of machine-guns captured testifies to the violence of the opposition," wrote Currie with pride.[33] Unlike some of the commander's previous communiqués, this one was not rife with hyperbolic calls for glory. Currie remarked on the difficulty and costliness of the operation, and praised the men who had been called on again to deliver victory. While most of the twelve German divisions met and defeated were depleted in strength or had been thrown into the line in desperation, the four attacking Canadian divisions' advance in the face of a dug-in enemy had nonetheless been a nearly unparalleled feat of arms. However, between August 22 and October 11, the Canadian Corps had suffered 30,806 killed, wounded, and missing. Attesting to the spearhead nature of the Canadian assault, when compared to the British XXII Corps on the right of the Canadians, and also to the rest of the First Army, Currie's corps suffered ten times as many casualties as the British.[34] General Henry Horne and his staff acknowledged that the Canadian Corps formed the "backbone" of the First Army.[35]

The Canadian Corps' attack doctrine had been honed to a fine art, but a series of sustained operations was still difficult to put together day after day. Communication remained a problem throughout the campaign (one that would in fact never be resolved during the war), leaving unit headquarters in the rear completely out of touch with soldiers at the front end during critical periods. In the days that followed the initial success, too often the battle degenerated into chaotic piecemeal assaults in which the infantry had little choice but to fight their way forward. They did so with bravery, self-sacrifice, and skill.

For the veterans of the infantry, it was heartbreaking to look around and see comrades, men who had survived Ypres, Somme, Vimy, Hill 70, Passchendaele—even Amiens and Arras—killed or maimed in the final stretch of the war. As they were forced to attack again and again, the troops began to listen to and spread rumours that their corps commander was sacrificing them to appease his British masters. Such false reports were unfair, as Currie always tried to ration his men's lives, and had stood up to the British in the name of his corps time and time again, but more than 42,000 casualties since Amiens seemed too many even for the battle-hardened Dominion troops. Unlike past similar instances, this simmering anger was not quelled after some rest and rum, as many Canadians continued to feel that they had been pushed too hard. While Currie and the British could point to the string of impressive Canadian accomplishments, it was also clear that even though the corps' fighting was informed by a refined doctrine, there were no easy victories on the Western Front. Every metre was paid for in blood.

The Canadian Corps' offensive at the Canal du Nord had been a part of the Allied multi-army offensive in late September. As shock troops with a dependable record, the Canadians had been assigned some of the most difficult fighting. They succeeded, as did most of the Allied forces, through grit, determination, and brute force. But to gauge the extent of the Canadians' success, it is perhaps worthwhile to compare them with the inexperienced Americans. In the Meuse-Argonne offensive, launched on September 26, an American army composed of nine over-strength divisions—even larger than the Canadian divisions—attacked five German under-strength divisions. The operation was largely unsuccessful because of a vigorous German defence and clumsy American tactics. In contrast, the Canadians, after fighting through the withering battles at Amiens and Arras, had defeated twelve enemy divisions, as well as elite machine-gun companies, during the Canal du Nord campaign. They had also captured 1,063 machine guns in the brutal fighting, raising the total to 2,745 since Amiens. The infantry's advance in the face of this blizzard of steel, and with the enemy fighting, as Currie described them, "like a cornered rat," revealed that the Canadians could deliver victory on the most difficult of battlefields.[36]

After the Allied hammer-blow offensives at the end of September, the Germans were unquestionably beaten. They would not be able to hold on until winter, and there would be no 1919 campaign, which most politicians and generals had planned for in the late summer of 1918. With the Germans in retreat, the Allies would chase them, nipping at their heels, all along the front. The Canadians, as ever, were in the vanguard.

CHAPTER 36

"WE STEELED OURSELVES NOT TO LET DOWN THE CORPS"

The Battle of Valenciennes, November 1–2, 1918

The Canadian Corps was battered and nearly broken after the three major Hundred Days battles beginning with the near breakthrough at Amiens on August 8. Currie and his staff officers noted proudly that the corps had advanced 37 kilometres since the opening of the Arras offensive, and most of it through the enemy's deep defences. Thirty-one German divisions had been met in battle, and many of them smashed decisively. Referring to the entire German force on the Western Front, Currie crowed, "We took care of 25% of that number; leaving it to the American Army, the French Army, the Belgian Army and the rest of the British Army to look after the balance."[1] It was an accomplishment well worth crowing about, even if the Canadian staff officers counted full divisions when sometimes they were in fact meeting only a regiment or an even smaller formation. Yet Currie also acknowledged the terrible sacrifice of his men against such a strong enemy force: "Many old and trusted friends have gone." Nonetheless, as he professed to the overseas minister, A.E. Kemp, "I do not consider that anyone can regard [the casualties] as excessive when the extent and severity of the operations are considered."[2]

Indeed, the operations had been the most impressive carried out by any combat formation on the Western Front—but despite Currie's protestations to the contrary, the numbers had unquestionably been excessive. From August 22 to October 11, the Canadians had suffered 30,806 killed and wounded, and another 11,822 casualties had been lost in the Amiens fighting from August 8 to 14. In all, during this period the Canadian Corps, some 100,000-men strong, lost more than 42,600 killed, wounded, and missing.[3] And the vast majority of these casualties would have fallen on the infantry at the sharp end, who were fewer than 50,000 men. The infantry had been thrown into battle after battle, and while they had often been ably supported by artillery, machine guns, armour, an effective logistical support system, and airpower, they had still been forced to risk their lives against one hardened position after another. Barbed wire hundreds of metres deep, concrete bunkers bristling with machine guns, and counterattacking forces had all been overcome. Currie, of course, had done his best to protect his men with every available gun at his command, and many more that he begged, borrowed, and stole from the British, but he also never considered pulling his men out of the line. He believed, like Haig, that the Germans had to be pressed, and that after their surprising collapse at Amiens, and then the systematic shattering of their defences at Arras and Cambrai, deep rot had set into their forces. He was right, but the Canadians also paid a heavy price for this continuous series of battles.

THE GERMAN POSITIONS had been broken all along the Western Front by the Allied forces, which were growing stronger with each month as the Americans arrived in force. New plans for 1919 included bomber raids on German cities; Plan 5000, which involved unleashing a massive tank armada attack to break a hole in, and then drive through, the enemy lines; and experiments with new, deadlier, and denser gas clouds that in test trials appeared to overpower German respirators. The Germans were degenerating into disarray. Morale had never been lower in the German army as a result of heavy casualties at the front, the devastating effects of the Spanish flu that had killed and weakened thousands, and the ongoing plight of loved ones starving at home—subsisting, in many regions, on 800 calories a day, the amount of nutritional energy needed to sustain a three-year-old. The Kaiser's forces were on the verge of a breakdown, and Germany's allies were in no better shape: Bulgaria sued for peace at the end of September, Austria-Hungary's forces were collapsing and retreating, and Turkey, on its last legs, would accept terms of surrender at the end of October.[4]

The German high command, still led by Ludendorff and von Hindenburg, had also accepted the harsh truth of their situation by the end of September, and so appealed to the Kaiser for an armistice. Some German generals and the politicians back home still held a vain hope that the American president, Woodrow Wilson, could negotiate a favourable peace settlement, and thereby avoid a vengeful victor's peace imposed on them by France, Belgium, and Britain. But too much blood had been spilt for any sort of compromise to be reached, and the Allied high command of politicians and generals soon made it clear that only unconditional surrender would be accepted. But diplomacy worked slowly. Ferdinand Foch and Sir Douglas Haig recognized that the Germans were on the verge of defeat, and they urged their tired forces to drive home the sword.

WITH THE GERMANS in full retreat, there were orders from Haig's headquarters to hound the enemy—"'Hustle the Hun!' was the watchword," although it likely resonated with few of the rank and file. Logistical problems slowed the British advance, and on the Canadian front, northeast of Cambrai, marshy land was made all the more impassable by the efforts of efficient German engineers who had blown almost every bridge during their retreat.[5] The Canadian engineers of the 3rd Division alone were forced to fill 135 craters along the roads from mid-October to the end of the war.[6] Given these logistical problems, the high command realized that, of necessity, the fighting in the next stage would be of a limited nature, with active battle patrols and artillery test barrages being the primary form of contact. The test barrages roamed over suspected German positions in an attempt to ascertain if they were holding the immediate front or were in retreat. Infantry and cavalry patrols advanced tentatively until they ran into fire. To purchase much-needed time as they retreated, the Germans placed sacrificial forces behind them to harass any Allied advance. These brave forces knew their fate, and often they were given little mercy as they held out to the last bullet.

The 1st, 2nd, and 4th Divisions pushed against the retreating enemy forces, and by October 17, the Germans abandoned strong positions along the Canal de la

Sensée. The Canadians followed them, making difficult marches through ankle-deep mud, but most were delighted to find themselves greeted as liberators by the French civilians they encountered along the way. From tiny villages to mid-sized towns of several thousand people, the French lined the roads cheering on the victors. The French tri-colour flew proudly, pulled from hidden storage where it had lain for four years. Wine bottles were opened and shared freely. Old men doffed their caps. Young women brazenly kissed the Canadians and hung from their necks.

Private George Anderson commented to a friend at home, "Instead of dugouts, we are living in houses, most of the time with civilians.... They don't seem to be able to do enough for you and should you offer them money they get peeved."[7] The civilians had initially had some reservations, however, as the Germans had portrayed the Canadians as wild colonials who would rape and murder their way through the French population. But these concerns were soon overcome as the Canadians were greeted into the French homes and told stories of the German occupation over cups

Canadian soldier trying to comfort a Belgian baby whose mother was killed by stray shellfire in the last days of the war. In the final month of the war, the warriors of the Canadian Corps became the liberators of tens of thousands of French and Belgian civilians, as they moved east in pursuit of the broken German armies.

of tea. The ill-treatment of the elderly and women, and the looting of livestock and destruction of houses left many Canadians cold with a desire to avenge these hapless victims.

The advancing divisions also found themselves in a relief role as they cared for malnourished and sick civilians. On the 3rd Division's front, the troops were responsible for over 31,000 civilians, to whom they issued daily iron rations consisting of bully beef, tea, and biscuits.[8] Many of the Canadian units voluntarily gave up their warm rations to feed the destitute and hungry.[9] Will Bird recounted that "at one place a pig was eating a dead horse by the roadside and was driven away with shrill cries as women attacked the carcass with knives and stripped every shred of meat for their own consumption. We gave most of our rations to the children."[10]

The Canadians continued pushing east throughout the third and fourth weeks of October. Enemy positions situated at bridges and water crossings slowed the advance, but these were dealt with by crushing artillery fire. Still, Canadians died by the score every day. Alva Kerman of Port Hope, Ontario, who had enlisted on January 3, 1918, arrived to the 20th Battalion during this supposedly quiet period as a reinforcement. His first tour near the front lines ended with his death by a stray bullet.[11] He was buried the next day, likely by men who never knew his name.

When called upon by their officers, the infantry attacked, but generally the enemy resistance was scattered by the gunners. Aggressive patrols kept close touch with the Germans, engaging in small-arms firefights, but there was little opportunity for a major set-piece battle against the retreating foe and the light screen of rearguard forces. Occasionally, jumpy and exhausted Canadians fought against one another as combat patrols roamed the front, but these fratricidal battles resulted in few casualties in comparison to the slaughter during the major engagements of the Hundred Days.[12] And just when it looked like a straight march to Berlin, the Germans stopped running at Valenciennes, a town of several thousand French civilians, strongly protected by the Canal de l'Escaut. And there, on superior ground, among civilians, they made a stand.

VALENCIENNES was the last major French city still in German hands, and its loss would entail another significant German retreat. After their experience at Cambrai, the enemy believed that the British and Canadians would not bombard French cities. The Canal de l'Escaut ran from north to south along the western part of Valenciennes and was a major obstacle. As at the Canal du Nord, the enemy had reduced the ground around the city to a soggy quagmire by opening up dikes and sluices, and had also wired the canal banks with explosives and situated machine guns in the outlying buildings. To the south of the city, Mont Houy was covered in woods and rose to a height of 150 metres, dominating the Canadians' avenues of advance. The hill was held in strength by determined German defenders ordered to make a last stand. In fact, elements of five divisions were situated on this front, and backstopped by additional defences in depth, secondary trenches, and the fortified city of Valenciennes itself.[13]

At an October 27 First Army meeting, Horne, his general staff, Currie, and a number of British commanders met to discuss how to capture Valenciennes while inflicting a minimum of damage to the city and its people. As at the Battle of Hill 70, it was decided that taking the high ground—in this case Mont Houy—was the key to the operation, as it overlooked the Germans' position within the city. The elite—although played-out—British 51st Highland Division was tasked with the initial part of the operation, and Watson's 4th Canadian Division would then link up on the left and assault the city in a two-pronged staggered attack: first from the south on October 31, and then from the west the next day.

At 5:15 A.M. on October 28, a single battalion from the 51st Division—the 4th Seaforth Highlanders—attacked Mont Houy behind a massive barrage from 176 artillery guns. It was an almost unheard of weight of shells to support one battalion, but irrespective of this firepower, capturing the strongly held enemy objectives would require a force larger than a single battalion. The British were even more depleted than the Canadians at this point in the war, but throwing a mere 500 men at the heights of Mont Houy was nonetheless inexcusable. The Highlanders did manage to capture the hill with the help of their barrage, and through some dogged fighting, but German counterattacks drove them from their gains. The British retained the low ground and the small village of Famars to the southeast of the hill, but they were far from the objectives where the Canadian 4th Division's 10th Brigade was to take over the line. Because of the instability of the position, the

THE BATTLE OF VALENCIENNES: NOVEMBER 1 TO 2, 1918

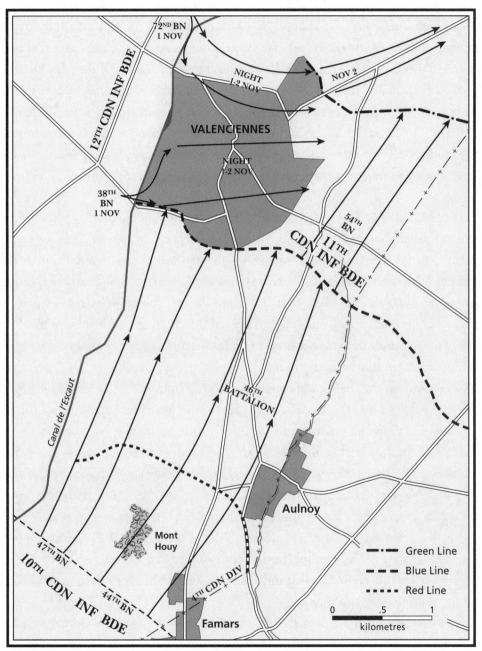

expected relief was delayed by a day, during which the British gallantly fought off several additional counterattacks to consolidate their gains. The Canadians were wary of repeating the error they had made at St. Eloi, almost thirty months earlier, where the then raw soldiers of the corps had taken over an unsecured British line and had been trounced partly as a result of this lack of consolidation. Now, with the 51st Division battered and unable to hold Mont Houy, it fell to the Canadians to capture the strongpoint and then Valenciennes beyond it to the north. But Currie had little time to prepare for the attack as the entire British front was planned to advance again on November 3. Valenciennes had to be captured by that date as it sat astride the main German line, in much the same way that Cambrai had a month earlier.

TWO LEAD CANADIAN UNITS, the 47th and 44th Battalions, took over the British lines on the night of October 29. Battle patrols were sent out to reconnoitre the enemy positions. Several enemy machine-gun nests were wiped out through this penetration, and a number of terrified, starving civilians that had been caught between the two armies were found and led to the rear. These active patrols cost the 44th one killed and two wounded, but crucial information about the extent of the enemy's front and wire was sent back to divisional and corps headquarters, where it was incorporated into artillery fireplans.[14]

Currie and his staff had worked almost non-stop over the last two days to prepare for the battle. Unlike the British, who had thrown just one battalion against the position, Currie employed the entire 10th Brigade, with two battalions up—the 47th and 44th, from left to right—and the 46th Battalion as a second-wave formation that would punch through Mont Houy and carry the attack up to the Canal de l'Escaut, on the other side of which was Valenciennes. The 50th Battalion would remain in reserve. But Currie also did not want to waste his men's lives. He first ordered his two senior artillery officers, Major General E.W.B. Morrison and Brigadier Andrew McNaughton, the new commander of the Canadian Corps Heavy Artillery, which also now handled much of the counter-battery work, to pound the enemy positions day and night.

This bombardment marked the culmination of the Canadian Corps' set-piece approach to battle. The 10th Brigade was supported by a hurricane of artillery fire from more than 250 field and siege guns—the largest force to support a single Canadian brigade in the entire war. The gunners would deliver 7 tonnes of explosives per minute on a front of less than 2.5 kilometres, totalling to 4,280 tonnes of explosives over the course of the battle—approximately 116 times the weight of shells fired during the empire-changing Battle of Waterloo in 1815.[15] McNaughton later testified that the First Army staff was horrified at the proposed expenditure of ammunition, and that the British staff officers attempted to overrule him. But Currie stepped into the breach, storming into army headquarters and demanding the necessary trucks to deliver the ammunition. His demands were met. McNaughton noted that his corps commander always wanted "to pay the price of victory in shells and not in the lives of men."[16]

The delay of two days before taking over from the British had allowed the gunners to advance both north and to the west of Mont Houy, so that they could now fire into the city from two sides. And the Canadian creeping barrage would move forward, backwards, and obliquely, creating an utterly terrifying experience for the German defenders, who would have three moving walls of fire raking over their positions.[17] Almost fifty of the Canadian guns were devoted to counter-battery work and to bringing down fire on enemy strongpoints, especially on known machine-gun nests situated in buildings along the canal. An artillery smokescreen and indirect machine-gun fire would also help to cordon off the battlefield. Currie tried his best to refrain from devastating the city, but he was not willing to sacrifice his men's lives to preserve it.

The night of October 31 saw a cold rain wash over the Canadians as they lay crouched in their shallow jumping-off trenches. Officers and NCOs took last looks at aerial photographs that had been issued to all sections, on which all known enemy positions were highlighted: dozens per grid reference, seemingly far too many for the limited attackers. All of the Canadians now knew that the war would soon be over, and it was the hard lot of the men of the 10th Brigade to be called in to fight the last set-piece battle. But they understood their role. Gunner W.B. Kerr echoed the thoughts of many ground-pounders: "We did not much relish the prospect, but we steeled ourselves not to let down the Corps. We would make the sacrifice, do our best and hasten the conclusion, and so we prepared again for combat."[18]

SEARCHING ENEMY artillery fire swept known roads, killing and wounding a number of service corps men and horses attempting to pass through shrapnel to deliver needed food and supplies to the front-line troops. Yet the German gunners were saddled with a surprising number of dud shells, a clear indication that the British naval blockade was tightening the noose around the Central Powers and their war-making capabilities. Periodic gas shelling from the enemy forced the Canadians to wear their respirators, which only added to the frustration of the assaulting troops. Many of the infantry harboured a palatable anger towards the Germans, who they believed did not have the sense to surrender when they had been beaten, and the ill-treatment of civilians added to the attackers' rage. Currie penned to a minister that he believed there would not be "as many prisoners taken as usual."[19]

At 5:15 A.M., the artillery bombardment opened up, shattering enemy strongpoints and artillery batteries with accurate fire. When the creeping barrage moved off, the two lead Canadian battalions—the 44th and 47th—advanced unsteadily, with the ground literally shaking under their feet from the pounding of hundreds of shells exploding every minute over and into the battlefield. The 44th on the right got away quickly, hugging the barrage. The battalion was so weak—down to a paltry 300 men—that it had amalgamated its four companies into two. The right one passed around Mont Houy to the east and near the smoking ruins of Aulnoy, a small village once crawling with Germans. So quick was the advance that a key bridge was captured with the demolition crew on it. The German engineers responsible for blowing it were shot dead before they could carry out their task.

On the left, the 44th's second company pushed through the charred tree trunks on Mount Houy. The Germans held a double line of shell holes that acted as their first line of defence. These were hard to spot as there were no telltale long trench lines, and harder to hit with artillery fire. Behind them lay a second line of crater defences, and finally a third support line that was held in more strength. Two of the three positions offered a dominating view of the ground from which the Canadians were forced to attack. But the Canadian barrage was punishing in its accuracy and weight of fire, and the advancing infantry stepped over many dead and dying Germans. The Canadians were so under-strength that one of the special mopping-up platoons consisted of a cobbled-together group of batmen, signallers, orderlies, and runners—men who rarely went into battle. Every man in the 44th Battalion was called on to fight: the luxury of reserve could no longer be afforded.

Within forty-five minutes, the 44th were on their objectives. The Germans had been demoralized and shocked by the power of the Canadian bombardment, and hundreds surrendered freely. Three field guns, twenty mortars, and an incredible eighty-three machine guns were captured by just this one battalion. This type of enemy defensive power on the Somme would have been enough to stop a division, let alone two companies. Here, the 44th found a way to drive forward, even if it cost the remaining force nineteen killed and seventy wounded.[20]

THE 44TH DUG IN on Mont Houy, establishing six Vickers machine guns as their central point of the defence against expected counterattacks. There were no attacks, however, as the momentum of the push by the 46th Battalion had disorganized the defenders, although the 44th were harassed by shell and gas fire, described as "heavy at first" but lessening steadily as a result of accurate Canadian counter-battery as the battle progressed.[21] With every available man used in the attack, the 46th Battalion—which passed through the 44th and pushed on to the canal to the north as low-flying aircraft raked their lines—was forced to further weaken their ranks as the junior officers believed that so many prisoners had been captured—between 600 and 800—that they had to be escorted to the rear. Their count of prisoners was in fact almost double the entire number of 44th Battalion men committed to battle.

The reduced 46th Battalion swept over the ridge, driving north to their canal objectives on the southern edge of Valenciennes. Under-strength at about 400 men, the 46th needed to push nearly 2,500 metres through residential areas heavily fortified by the Germans—a task that seemed quite impossible. But through four hours of desperate fighting, the small number of Canadians cleared positions held by two or three times as many defenders. Certainly the barrage helped to kill, maim, or at least demoralize the enemy, but the infantry were often left no choice but to advance in the face of heavy fire. Although the Lewis gun and rifle grenade were essential in suppressing enemy positions, dozens of enemy machine-gun teams defended the front, many of which fought to the last man. Incredibly, brave pockets of attackers, advancing in short sprints while other formations covered them, captured one position after another, including a German 77mm field gun that was firing over open sights.

Of the countless stories of bravery under fire, one must suffice as an example. With his section pinned down by the small-arms fire, as well as by plunging mortar and machine-gun fire, Private W.J. Wood leapt forward, firing his Lewis gun from the hip. His mates looked on with disbelief as enemy bullets tore up the ground around him, but he advanced machine-like into the fire, killing first the enemy machine-gunners, then the mortar team, and finally the artillery gun crew.[22] All along the front, the aggressive 46th were spread out, the gaps widening in their ranks, but still they pushed through the enemy positions. In house-to-house fighting, they swept forward past enemy positions while many Germans cowered in the cellars. "Those that offered any show of resistance were killed," and the rest, according to the battalion's commanding officer, were sent to the rear.[23] The 46th pressed on to their objectives, even as the German resistance strengthened closer to the canal and as the Canadians' barrage became more ragged, with some guns firing at their outer range.

But time and again, brave pockets of men, banding together behind a Lewis gunner or rushing forward as a rifle grenadier laid down a covering explosion, cleared the enemy strongpoints. Captain R.W. Gyles of A Company recounted the incredible story of Sergeant Hugh Cairns, a celebrated football player in Saskatoon before the war. In the advance towards the canal, the barrage had left a strong German force unscathed, and Gyles and thirteen other men, two of whom were Lewis gunners, advanced on the German position. Even though the strongpoint consisted of three field guns, a trench mortar, seven machine guns, and about 100 defenders, the Lewis gunners broke off to attack it from the flank. Led by Sergeant Cairns, one of the two Lewis machine-gunners who set up a crossfire, the Canadians laid a devastating stream of bullets into the enemy positions. Cairns had seen his brother, Albert, killed in battle at the Drocourt-Quéant Line only a month before, and he wanted blood. He got it: about fifty Germans were killed or wounded as the Canadians fired off pan after pan of .303 rounds. The survivors soon surrendered and the group moved forward again.

Further on, Cairns and a small party of four men came across a courtyard teeming with Germans. At the head of the Canadian vanguard, Cairns, who had been shot in the shoulder and was bleeding, sprayed the sixty or so Germans with his Lewis gun, firing from the hip. Half a dozen went down and the rest soon surrendered. But minutes later, the ranking German officer realized that the attacking group in fact consisted of only five Canadians, and he treacherously pulled his pistol free and shot Cairns in the body. Hughie, as he was known to his friends, was bowled over by the impact, but he twisted on the ground and sprayed several bursts of fire into the German, sending the officer reeling back in a mist of blood. Then all hell broke loose. The initially stunned Germans recovered and dropped to the ground to pick up their relinquished weapons. Raking their numbers back and forth, Cairns took down swaths of Germans while the other Canadians fought with a desperation born of men outnumbered by twelve to one. A bullet shattered Cairns's wrist in the mad minutes that followed, but he continued to operate his Lewis gun, cradling the weapon with his arm. More Germans were hit, bathing the courtyard in blood, but though Cairns was struck again, his companions were able to pull his shattered body back behind a broken wall. The Germans eventually surrendered, and Hugh Cairns was awarded the last Canadian Victoria Cross of the war for his double feat of bravery. He didn't live to see it, though, as he died the next day at a clearing station.[24]

Notwithstanding a punishing barrage and low enemy morale, the relentless tenacity of soldiers such as Cairns was the only explanation for the Canadians' defeat of dug-in forces two, three, and four times their numbers. But the attackers paid for their incredible success. Of the 405 men of the 46th Battalion who went over the top, 36 were killed and 90 more wounded.[25] One of those killed was Lance Corporal Harold Tallis, the fourth and final slain of six brothers who had enlisted during the war.[26]

On the left of the 10th Brigade's front, the 47th Battalion skirted Mont Houy, attacking through Le Poirier Station. They had been ready in their trenches since 3:30 A.M., and planned to advance with four companies. Again, the operation was to be an all-out assault, with no troops in reserve. Attesting to the battered condition of the battalion, all four companies were commanded by lieutenants. A fifth company of mopping-up troops was supplied by the 50th Battalion, under command of Lieutenant A.J. Slade. The 47th followed their barrage into the enemy lines. As on the right, the wall of fire was strong and tore up much in its path. In spite of the barrage, pockets of enemy formations held out, with an official report noting clinically, "In most cases enemy posts did not surrender until many had been killed by bayonet or shot down."[27] Vicious hand-to-hand fighting occurred in the fields and then in what was left of the houses around the rail station. Officers were hit and replaced by other officers, who were in turn replaced by sergeants and corporals, and finally long-service privates. Resistance remained strong along the entire front, and the 47th had to fight for nearly every foot of ground. At the halfway point, about ninety-five minutes into the operation, B and D companies cycled through the forward companies (A and C), waited fifteen minutes as the artillery played havoc on the enemy lines, and continued the advance towards the canal, which they reached at 10:20 A.M.

The dense artillery fire left the battlefield wreathed in a cloud of dust and explosions, and those enemy troops taking refuge in houses along the canal were soon lying bloodied and broken in the rubble. One captured German company commander noted that because of the density of the shellfire, and the fact that it came at him from three sides, "It was impossible to see or even know from which direction the attackers were coming."[28] The commander eventually surrendered what was left of his company.

The 46th and 47th spent the rest of the day trading fire with the enemy across the canal, calling down SOS bombardments, and providing the coordinates of targets of opportunity for indirect machine-gun, mortar, and artillery fire. German troops of the 6th Division were well dug in across the canal at Marley, where they fired into the Canadian flanks. Brigadier J.M. Ross of the 10th Brigade ordered his reserve battalion, the 50th, to present a hard flank to ensure there were no cross-canal attacks. The infantry were supported by twenty-four Vickers machine guns from the 4th Battalion, Canadian Machine Gun Corps. It looked as though the Canadians would hold the terrain south of the city.

AS THE 10TH BRIGADE pushed north to the canal, the 12th Brigade had launched a flanking attack from the west. A little before noon, the 38th and 72nd Battalions crossed the canal on rafts and on cork bridges laid out by the corps' engineers. It must have been terrifying for the lead platoons to expose themselves in the open on the water. But strong covering fire from rifle and Lewis guns, along with direct-firing field guns shooting over open sights at a mere 100 metres range, in addition to plunging mortar fire, forced most of the Germans to seek cover and stay there. Other enemy forces had been rushed to the south of the town to protect against the northern thrust by the 10th Brigade, thereby leaving this western flank position vulnerable. Although German machine-gunners and snipers harassed the lead elements of the canal crossers, the opposition could not have been very heavy given that the daylight operation resulted in 38th Battalion suffering only four killed and seven wounded.[29]

The 72nd had more trouble, with their cork bridge breaking in three places and the troops on rafts and boats engaged with heavy fire. At least one raft sank, but a vanguard section of Seaforth Highlanders scrambled ashore and drove in towards the occupied buildings. Other rafts and boats were pinned down by heavy rifle and machine-gun fire, but those Highlanders who made it ashore began to clear out the defenders, eventually reducing the amount of fire directed against their exposed comrades. An amphibious crossing under direct fire is one of the most difficult tactical manoeuvres in warfare, and the success of the Seaforths and 38th Battalion provides a glimpse of the sophistication of the Canadian attack doctrine towards the end of 1918.

Throughout the day, elements of the two battalions swarmed through the western part of Valenciennes, kicking down doors, tossing grenades into cellars, talking to the French civilians who freely passed on intelligence relating to the location of enemy troops. Although all four companies of both battalions were committed to the operation, the companies were severely under-strength, each having started the battle with only about ninety men and a few officers. Yet they pushed forward aggressively, and German units often found themselves surrounded and overrun without having fired a single shot. The weight of German numbers was of little use in the urban fighting since many of their positions were not mutually supporting, and were therefore easily attacked one by one while much of the German force simply waited, listening to the fighting and the steady engulfment of their comrades.

Further to the north, the 4th CMR of the 3rd Division completed the third side of the encirclement, crossing the canal and infiltrating through the northern part of

A rare photograph of a Canadian platoon, likely from the 38th Battalion, crashing through the outskirts of Valenciennes to close with the enemy.

the city under the cover of darkness on the night of November 1–2. On the morning of November 2, the 4th CMR were further supported by the 72nd and 38th Battalions, along with the 54th Battalion, who crossed the canal from the south; the battalions spread through the city from three directions. Resistance was light, but battalion reports contain throwaway lines such as "Three enemy machine-gun posts were wiped out at the above cross-roads."[30] What such incidents meant to the Canadians in terms of self-sacrifice will be known only to the men who fought and died at innumerable crossroads.

By the end of the day, Valenciennes had fallen and the Germans were in full retreat. The Canadians took some 1,379 prisoners from nineteen battalions representing five separate divisions, and from two marksman machine-gun detachments.[31] More than 800 dead were counted in cellars, strongpoints, and rubble. "We surely got ours back for almost a month of hard chasing and dirty fighting," wrote Lieutenant R.J. Holmes, a wearer of the Military Cross who had fought south of the canal with the 46th Battalion.[32] It was openly acknowledged among the Canadians that at least some of these corpses had been prisoners trying to surrender, but the wicked behaviour of the Germans in occupied French territory, the lessons learned from previous false surrenders, and the enemy's obstinate defence so close to the end of the war resulted in some German troops being killed while they reached for the sky. One battalion was even apologetic about the high number of prisoners taken on its front, noting, "It was impossible to avoid taking so many as they surrendered in batches of from 20 to 50, but some very useful killing was also achieved."[33] As always, there was safety in numbers. Cy Peck, the Victoria Cross winner who commanded the 16th Battalion, remarked after the war: "The Great War was one of ferocity, without chivalry and magnanimity, and sometimes without mercy." He noted further that, towards the end of the war, "Brass hats got very blood thirsty and we had thinly veiled hints from higher up to 'kill 'em.'" But if you kill prisoners, Peck pointed out, "there is a pretty good chance of getting killed yourself, and if people urge men to kill, they ought to be on hand to help the killing along. However, our troops used their own judgments. Men in the heat of battle are liable to be more vindictive than otherwise, but on the whole our troops were merciful, even tender-hearted."[34]

The Battle of Valenciennes raises a single question: how could the Canadians possibly have succeeded here? The enemy had every advantage. They were dug in; had flat, open fields of fire; and outnumbered their attackers by at least two or three to one. While German morale was close to collapse, and no one wanted to be the last soldier to die in an already lost war, the Germans also decided to make their final stand here, and elements of defenders fought resolutely. Ultimately, the Canadian success on this front was due to the power of the offensive, which had eclipsed that of the defence. Massive and coordinated artillery bombardments, when combined with determined infantry units that had the flexibility, training, and firepower to fight their way forward, proved that few defensive strongpoints could hold out against such an onslaught.

This last set-piece battle cost the Canadians 501 casualties, of whom 121 were killed or listed as missing. While the Valenciennes victory had been astounding, these casualties were bitter pills as the end of the war appeared to be at hand.[35] The weight of shellfire had clearly stunned the enemy, but, as in all previous battles, it fell to those at the sharp end to clear the enemy positions, one at a time, in countless stand-up battles that went largely unrecorded in the official records.

CHAPTER 37

"A BLOODY LONG
WAY TO MONS"

November 11, 1918

"We all felt that the end of the war was near and life became more precious than ever before," recounted William Ogilvie, a signaller with the artillery who had survived through two years of fighting. "No one wanted to lose it when the end of fighting was so near and the few scattered shells which the retreating Germans were able to fire were treated with the utmost respect."[1]

THE GERMAN ARMIES were drawing back again with the unhinging of Valenciennes and other strongpoints along the line. But there was no rest for the Canadians as Haig ordered a full advance against the seemingly broken German forces. And this was no rout, for rearguard forces made pursuit dangerous: enemy snipers and machine-gunners were eager to take a steady grind on the Hun hunters who advanced too quickly or without caution. As well, a steady rain falling on the soldiers' tin hats for a solid week had left men wet, exhausted, and chaffed from continual marching. The downpour also turned the few roads into a quagmire of water rivulets and mud. Such a bog couldn't stop the Canadian Tommy wrapped in his ground cape, water dripping from his nose, but it did slow the artillery. The 18-pounder gun teams coaxed their straining horses forward, but the bigger guns, which required tractors to drag them along, constantly needed to be dragged from the dissolving roads. The logistical system was strained to the limit, even though it had diversified among light rails, trucks, and pack animals.

For men who had spent years skulking beneath the ground to avoid the deadly firepower that scythed everything above, marching overland for kilometres produced a strange feeling of nakedness. While artillery fire continued to scar the landscape, this was not the lunar-surface No Man's Land the soldiers were used to; but it was still dangerous. The countryside was dotted with farms, hedges, and sunken roads, all of which were perfect spots for ambushes. Infantry scouting parties, motor machine-gun cars, and cavalry screened in front of the advancing forces, calling down artillery fire on suspected enemy positions. When the Germans were defeated or fell back, French civilians lined the roads, cheering on the Canadians. J.L. Melville of the 6th Field Company, Royal Engineers, noted cheekily that the slowness of the advance to Mons was not due to German artillery barrages, but rather to a "very effective barrage of coffee, cognac and kisses put up by the overjoyed inhabitants."[2] Marching through throngs of grateful civilians took time, as did the repair job necessitated by nervous civilians who continually cut the Canadian telephone wires, believing mistakenly that they were some form of mined booby traps left by the enemy.

AS THE WAR was ostensibly winding down, pockets of fierce fighting continued to rage, and Canadians were still being killed daily by the dozens. On the 4th Division's front on November 4, a German force made a stand around the village of Quarouble, which the 12th Brigade cleared in fierce combat. On the same day, three battalions of the 3rd Division's Canadian Mounted Rifles ran into two Germans battalions of the 115th Regiment spread in a strong defence around the mining town of Vicq. The 5th CMR, who mounted the main attack, attempted to drive the Germans back. They expected that the light screen of defenders would fold when they applied pressure, but the fighting here was ruthless as the Germans were dug in to slag pits, and machine guns, mortars, and snipers commanded the advance, as the surrounding ground was marshy, flat, and almost entirely devoid of any vegetation. Although the Germans had been retreating quickly, they chose places like Vicq, where the ground favoured the defenders, to hold on by teeth and nails. The 5th CMR captured many of the slag pits on the November 4, but were driven out by counterattacks later that day. The Canadians returned with a vengeance over the next two days behind a heavy artillery bombardment, again recapturing the slag pits, and then the villages of Vicq and the surrounding region. In the fighting here and until November 9, when the 5th CMR were pulled out of the line, the battalion lost 10 killed and 78 wounded. The Canadians were clearly furious about this ferocious last-ditch fighting, and many refused to extend mercy to the Germans after the bitterly contested battles; only eight prisoners made it to the cages from the 5th CMR's battle front.[3]

Single-battalion operations were carried out up and down the line on November 5 and 6, including the forced crossing of several rivers that required the engineers to work with the infantry under fire and throw down cork bridges and rafts to secure the bridgehead. Through numerous small engagements—involving the clearing of houses and farms, or the crossing of shallow river obstacles—the Canadians continued to drive through enemy positions, suffering casualties as they went. The 85th Battalion, for example, lost fourteen men killed and thirty wounded on November 6. One of the wounded was Captain Hugh Dickson of Truro, Nova Scotia, who was shot through the head from temple to temple, but somehow miraculously suffered no serious permanent damage other than seeing double in one eye. Freak survivals were as common as freak deaths on the Western Front.

Though the Canadians were exhausted, their infantry battalions were again up to full strength. The reinforcements from England kept the battalions at roughly 1,000 men—far stronger than the British or Australian units.[4] These impressive numbers did not mean that Currie was willing to sacrifice his men, as he well understood their fragile morale after the hard push of the previous three months. But he could have put his corps into another major set-piece battle, should the Germans have dug in. The Australians, by contrast, were down to the bone in strength, and effectively no longer able to fight. While Canada's conscription crisis had nearly torn the country apart in 1917, and had left deep scars, the recruits generated by the political battle would have been essential if the Canadian Corps had needed to keep fighting into 1919, as all expected at the time of the divisive federal election.

On the night of November 6–7, the 2nd Division replaced the 4th in the line, and Burstall's men, along with the 3rd Division to the north, continued to push towards Mons. This city was an important symbol for the entire BEF. While Mons dated back to Roman times and had been the prize of many armies over the centuries, the BEF troops viewed it foremost as the site of their first significant battle in 1914, and the spot from which the small Imperial professional army had been forced to retreat in the face of overwhelming German pressure. Its capture would have resonated throughout the BEF. The Germans had kept the city through the entire war, using it as a critical logistical hub for the movement of troops, and depending on its local mines to supply their army with much-needed coal. The prewar population of about 60,000 had been reduced when many had fled the city, aware that for the Allies to take the position, they would likely have to destroy it. But the city was in the Canadian sector, and Currie wanted it.

It was clear to all, including the German high command, that morale in the German army was at the breaking-point. Death, starvation, and now sickness from the Spanish flu had steadily eroded combat motivation. Bolshevik talk was rife among the soldiers, who openly questioned the war and why they, the soldiers, should continue fighting for a lost cause, seeing it as a "great swindle," as several captured enemy letters indicated after the fall of Cambrai.[5] Others whispered dangerously that the front-line troops had been let down by the civilians in the rear; the *frontsoldaten* had defended themselves against the multiple spears of the Allies, the rumours went, only to find themselves stabbed in the back by unworthy civilians, profiteers, and other nebulous undesirables. Such stories were untrue, as German civilians had supported the armies to the hilt, sacrificing much to keep the soldiers at the front fed, clothed, and armed. But the non-combatants provided the troops with a convenient excuse to account for their dissolving army. Since October, Germany had seen its allies surrender, one after another, and now it too was on the verge of defeat. The Allies' demands for unconditional surrender had been a stumbling block for Hindenburg, the Kaiser, and his advisors, but it was also true that the German forces were increasingly losing their coherency. Though they were still fielding armies of more than a million men, the will to fight was eroding in all but the most elite of units.

On November 7, the Canadians crossed into Belgium, continuing to push the Germans before them. An order from Canadian Corps' headquarters warned all units to be aware of the possibility of German officers surrendering, bearing flags of truce. Such prisoners were to be directed to GHQ.[6] On the southern part of the Canadian front, Burstall's 2nd Division was driving forward, with the 5th Brigade in the vanguard. This mobile force was supported by field artillery, motor machine-gun cars, cyclists, and two squadrons of the Canadian Light Horse. Engineers were stationed with this combined-arms force in order to provide bridging capabilities. Fighting against German bitter-enders was carried out from November 7 to 10, but the opposition was weak and sporadic. No one on either side wanted to be the last man killed in this very long and brutal war. Though few Canadian Tommies shirked their duty, most were showing extreme caution. But not all soldiers or units were in the know, as Lance Corporal Richard J. Alton of the 75th remarked to his former school teacher at Burlington High School: "There are some great rumours of peace going around just now, up here near the line however we practically know nothing of what is going on anywhere else."[7]

To the north, the 7th Brigade of the 3rd Division was that formation's spearhead unit, with the PPCLI and the 49th Battalion clearing village after village as they moved towards Mons. On November 9, the RCR and the 42nd Battalion took over the advance and were soon in the outlying suburbs of the city. The next day, they probed the enemy defences around Mons, but the Germans were holding tough, having established machine-gun nests and snipers at all of the bridges and canal-crossings leading into the city.

Rumours of the war's end had been running like wildfire through the Canadian ranks, but these were not new and had in fact been spread freely since the first months of the war. While Germany's war effort was disintegrating, to those Canadians at the sharp end the Germans did not appear to be folding. In fact, the enemy sent out at least five raiding parties from Mons on November 10, and throughout the day the Canadians were forced to revert to being defenders.[8] The fighting from November 7 to 10 cost 645 killed and wounded in just the 2nd and 3rd Canadian Divisions.[9]

Despite these losses, Currie wanted to continue on to capture Mons, a significant prize for the already heralded Canadian Corps. While the commander knew that the war would soon be over, he had received no confirmation of this by November 10.

Nor is there any indication that corps headquarters had heard of the Kaiser's abdication the day before, which surely signalled the end-game of the German Empire. Here at the front, the Germans were defending resolutely, and Currie believed that they would have to be firmly beaten in the field. To leave the German army with Mons at the Armistice might allow the nation to cling to the idea that it had negotiated a peace of sorts.

Currie ordered the capture of Mons through an encircling approach: the 2nd Division would attack from the south and southeast, while the 3rd Division would attack eastward. "It has never been the spirit of the Canadian Corps to relax in their efforts in killing Boshes," wrote Currie, looking back on this period a few months after the war. "From the very beginning, the Canadian Corps has killed the enemy on every possible occasion, and would no more have thought of easing up because an armistice might have been signed in three or four days than they would have thought of running from the enemy."[10] No senior officers questioned Currie's orders at the time, although a decade after the war the corps commander would be forced to defend his reputation in a nasty, slanderous libel case, in which he was accused by a small-town newspaper of callously ordering his troops to their death to achieve his own glory. The allegation was untrue, and it would in fact have been insubordinate of Currie to call off any attack, especially with the rest of the Allied forces pushing ahead, but these justifications would become blurred in the postwar years.

BACK ON NOVEMBER 10, the Canadians followed Currie's orders and pushed gingerly around the city. If the senior officers did not question Currie's plan, the rank and file were less pleased to be assigned the role of liberators. Reputations meant little to those who were required to possibly sacrifice their lives to confirm the Canadians' status as shock troops. Corporal Will Bird of the 42nd Battalion, a long-service veteran who had earned the respect of his mates through his survival skills, remembered that "every man argued bitterly" over the order to take Mons.[11] Some of the new junior officers were urging the infantry forward by extolling their bravery, but many of the older veterans understood that at this stage in the war caution was the better part of valour. A few were still bitter about a stray shell that had

THE FINAL ADVANCE: OCTOBER 12 TO NOVEMBER 11, 1918

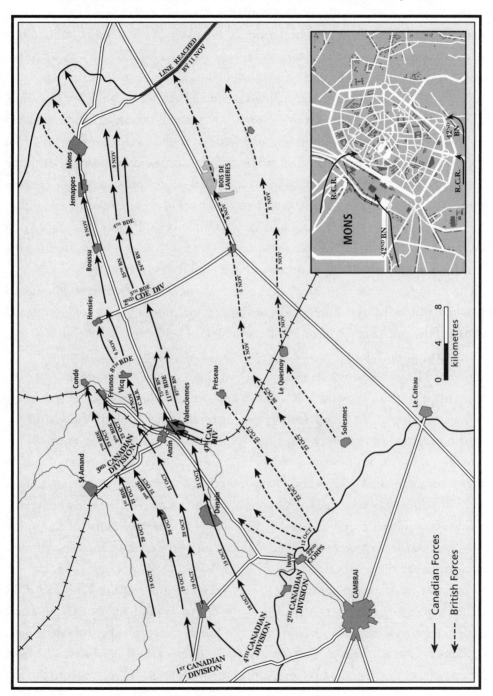

landed amidst a platoon three days earlier, killing six and wounding six more. Tragically, most of the men had been original members of the 42nd Battalion, having served some thirty-seven months in France. The long odds of the war, odds that these men had dodged time and time again, had finally caught up with them.

Now, with the war nearly over, the high command was sending the 3rd Division's 42nd and RCR into the breach one more time. Despite the anger swirling within the ranks, there were no mutinies; no one refused to obey a direct order. In a foul mood and with much swearing, Bird got his section to advance eastward towards the city. Once there, he and the other Highlanders looked for soft spots in the enemy's defence, but the Germans had several strongpoints that they refused to relinquish, and they were dug in along key woods, canals, and villages. Patrols fought it out on November 10, but with the Germans keeping up a heavy small-arms fire, the Canadians mounted no large-scale attacks that would be costly in lives.

The Canadians were also hamstrung since Currie—on orders from his superiors—had forbidden the unfettered shelling of the city, allowing only shrapnel instead of the usual high explosive bombardments. The Germans were initially cautious, firing off short bursts of machine-gun fire to keep from giving away their positions, but when no artillery retaliation arrived they became more brazen, engaging in sustained gun battles with the Canadians, who soon found they could not easily dislodge the dug-in defenders from their entrenched positions. If the Canadians could not blast their way forward, they would need to infiltrate the enemy lines. Throughout the night of November 10–11, combat patrols crept through the dark, looking for unguarded bridges and even slipping into the water-filled moats. One of the RCR patrols was shot up, as recounted by Lieutenant W. Martin King, leaving an officer and three men killed and several others wounded.[12] None of the routes were easy, but the Canadians determined that most of the enemy's machine-gunners were situated to the southeast of the city. They would look elsewhere to attack.

Finding a weak spot in the enemy lines, combat platoons of the 42nd and RCR crashed through the southern defences of the city at around 11 P.M., laying down Lewis machine-gun and rifle-grenade fire to suppress the stunned enemy defenders. Attackers infiltrated through the city streets. To the west and northwest of Mons, D Company of the 42nd and B Company of the RCR forced a crossing into the city at several bridges. By the early hours of November 11, elements of the two battalions were creeping through the streets, shooting up strongpoints and engaging in running gun battles with the enemy. Corporal Will Bird and his section, in the vanguard of the attack, lost at least three men, one of whom had both his eyes shot out while another was killed when shrapnel passed through his body. The latter had a brother who watched his kin die in front of him and for days afterwards muttered that he would assassinate Currie for murdering his brother. He didn't in fact try to shoot the general, but more than a few men felt anguish and anger over the final order to take Mons.

At 6:30 A.M. on November 11—about the time when the last of the German defenders in Mons were being killed or forced to surrender—Canadian Corps headquarters received word that the Armistice would be struck at 11 A.M., at which time all hostilities would cease. The signalmen in the corps sent the message to their companions in the divisions and brigades, after which runners raced across the battlefield with the good news. The Canadian Corps was spread out over several kilometres of frontage and to a depth of twenty or thirty kilometres, but most units, including the front-line ones, had received the message by 9 A.M.[13]

On the flanks, the Canadians pushed beyond Mons, still driving the Germans before them. In the city, the inhabitants had been awakened in the night by bursts of gunfire. Others slept through the fire, only to be roused by the mopping-up units of the Highlanders and RCR passing through the cobblestone streets, running their bayonets along the windows to stir the population. Morning revealed liberation. To drive the point home, the Highlanders even marched their pipe band through the city, stirring up the emotions of the soldiers and announcing their arrival to all the citizens of Mons.

The liberators were hounded, kissed, hugged, and backslapped. The Belgians, who had been better treated by their German occupiers than the French civilians, whose emaciated appearances had shocked the Canadians, broke out their hidden bottles of wine. "They were wild with delight," wrote Private Jerred Mansfield. "They embraced us, they kissed us, they cried over us, they whole-heartedly welcomed us. They hemmed us in and crowded around us.... We were their rescuers, their deliverers. They showered us with such poor gifts as they had, flowers, blessings, sweet biscuits, wine and this cheap bit of ribbon."[14] Embarrassed Canadians returned the gestures tentatively, then affectionately, passing out kisses and cigarettes, the only things they had in abundance. At least three large Canadian flags were hung from windows in the cities, as the citizens of Mons desperately tried to repli-cate the Red Ensign. Marching through Mons after the Armistice, the citizens greeted the Canadians with songs, including the popular "It's a Long Way to Tipperary." One exhausted Canadian was heard to mutter, "It's been a bloody long way to Mons."[15]

WHILE THE VICTORS at Mons were being greeted as liberators before the Armistice, pockets of German resistance were still holding out to the east of Mons. Snipers and MG-08s were met by Lewis-gun fire and the explosion of grenades. The fighting on November 11 resulted in a number of Canadian casualties. In the 3rd Division, whose 42nd Battalion and the RCR attacked Mons, fourteen were killed, seventy wounded, and two missing.[16] An unknown or undisclosed number of casu-alties was also suffered by the 2nd Division on this final day of fighting, the very last being the 28th Battalion's Private George Lawrence Price.

As the final hours ticked down, the 28th battalion was further ahead than any other unit, having just captured Havre, located about 7 kilometres east of Mons. The battalion's officers decided it had gone far enough, and Major A.F. Simpson ordered all the men to stay down and not expose themselves to more fire. Most men were silent, waiting for the guns to quieten for the last time. In a slit trench, only a few minutes before the Armistice, Private Price, a twenty-five-year-old farmhand who had been conscripted in 1917 from near Moose Jaw, Saskatchewan, looked around, perhaps dreaming of getting back to Canada. To his amazement, from a window of one of Havre's outlying buildings, a Belgian woman waved to him. She too must have tingled with anticipation at having her life return to normal after nearly four and a half years of German occupation. As his companions stayed low and out of sight, Price inexplicably jumped from his protective trench and ran to the girl, presumably to steal a kiss, perhaps to have a story to tell his grandchildren about what had happened at 11 A.M. on November 11, 1918. He never made it to those lips. A German sniper tracked him in the run and put a bullet through his chest. Price died almost instantly, at a few minutes to 11.[17]

The Canadians forged a tremendous reputation as shock troops in the Hundred Days campaign, but they paid a terrible price, sustaining more than 45,000 casualties from August 8 to November 11, 1918. By the end of the hard-pounding battles, many Canadian combat veterans, who had watched too many friends be buried in shallow graves, wondered if the results were worth the sacrifice.

During the ninety-six days of hard-pounding battle from August 8 to November 11, the Canadian Corps had suffered a devastating 45,835 casualties—almost an eighth of the total losses sustained by the entire BEF, which stood at 379,000.[18] This figure is all the more shocking given that the Canadians formed only about one-fifteenth of the entire BEF's strength. Haig had relied heavily on his Canadians in the final push for victory. Price was the last Canadian killed during the Hundred Days, and is believed to have been the last Commonwealth soldier killed before the Armistice. His death formed the tragic capstone for the millions of dead that came before him in the 1,561 days of slaughter and destruction during which the British Empire was at war.

CHAPTER 38

"I WANTED TO GET THE HELL HOME"

Demobilization, 1919

Private George Anderson of the 2nd Battalion wrote to his mother that November 11, 1918, was "the greatest day since I joined the Army." But with the war over, he wondered: "When do we start for the land of the Maple?" The private's enthusiasm dripped from the page, but he also ended with a sombre thought: "To tell the truth it seems hard to realize … that we are through with this awful slaughter."[1]

Many had imagined that the war would never end. Trench newspapers had lampooned white-bearded soldiers ensconced in their trenches in the year 1967. Front-line soldiers had spent months, even years, within the constant thundering of shell explosions, rising and falling in an ebb and flow of booms and earth-shattering explosions, but always there. And then it began to fade away like a storm moving off. After a few batteries tried to time the very last shot with an artillery shell at exactly 11 A.M., only eerie silence remained, later replaced by the ringing of church bells. The war had gone out not with a bang but with a whimper.

The survivors knew they had somehow beaten the odds. Everyone had buried friends or mates during the last hundred days of fighting. Lieutenant Donald Macpherson, who had been wounded at Amiens, marked the announcement with a deep sob for his fallen brother, Ross.[2] More than a few men mulled over the notion that perhaps the Allies should have kept fighting and driven the Hun back to Berlin. "I thought why if we have got them on the run do we have to stop right now?" remembered Bert Warren, an infantryman who had enlisted at seventeen and fought through three years of battle.[3] Captain William Hay, who had served with his two brothers and a sister as a nurse, and who would spend the rest of his life with shrapnel lodged in his head and the right to wear the Military Cross, wrote to his mother shortly after the Armistice: "A Devil of a war—thank God it is over, but I wouldn't mind going on for a bit more to crush the dirty and cowardly brute."[4] Perhaps this was simply tough talk, and no one really wanted more fighting and death, but many worried that Germany might rise up again. To fight another war of this magnitude was nearly unthinkable: soldiers, veterans, and civilians would soon refer to the Great War as "the war to end all wars."

ALTHOUGH THE LAST SHELLS had been fired, the generals of the victorious Allied armies realized that the war was still not over. The Armistice was simply a break in the fighting. The German Imperial Army had been soundly beaten in the field, having sustained 1.7 million casualties since March 21, but it was not yet destroyed, remaining at several million men strong.[5] No one was sure what kind of terms would be imposed on the enemy now that he had laid down his arms. If they were too draconian, would the Germans rise up and fight to the bitter end? The British were generally inclined to take a moderate approach, but the French, whose country and people had endured the worst effects of the war, wanted blood. The Germans should not have expected much leniency not only because they had prolonged the struggle but also because of the brutal terms that they had imposed on Russia in the Treaty of Brest-Litovsk. A high price had been exacted from the Communists, including the severing of Poland, Kars, and Lithuania, and their acceptance of Germany's occupation of Estonia and Latvia. The vengeful Allied politicians generally showed restraint in refusing to hang the Kaiser as many of their citizens demanded, but they eventually imposed dictatorial terms on their beaten enemy: Germany would pay billions in reparations; hand over most of its war materiel and weapons, including its navy; admit guilt for causing the war; and of course return to France the provinces of Alsace and Lorraine. Though the politicians struggled over these terms, it would be the soldiers in the field who would be called upon to enforce them.

An army of occupation would be needed in Germany to ensure that hostilities did not flare up again, but the Allied high command was asking important questions: Now that the war was over, what was the justification for keeping citizens in uniform? And how would the armies hold together now that emotionally and physically exhausted troops realized that the threat had seemingly passed? The soldiers of the Great War had served for years away from loved ones, barely holding on to their sanity in the firestorm of the front—often with only one fervent dream: of getting home again. No one relished the thought of asking these men to continue to serve for an indefinite period. "The Canadian Corps seem enthusiastic over the idea of being in the army of occupation, or rather the people at the head of it are, but I don't think the men will care about it for long," thought Canadian infantryman Stuart Thorne.[6] Sir Arthur Currie's Canadian Corps, recognized as one of the most disciplined and hard-hitting forces in the Allied order of battle, was asked if it would contribute two divisions to the occupation. Currie accepted this prestigious role on behalf of the corps, even as his men grumbled and groused at becoming a military gendarmerie that might have to deal with freedom fighters and terrorist attacks.

On November 17, the 1st and 2nd Canadian Divisions—the vanguard units that had been on French soil the longest—began the long, 400-kilometre march to the Rhine River, where they would occupy a series of bridgeheads. The German destruction of bridges and railheads, as well as logistical problems such as horses, mules, and motorized transport floundering on the muddy roads, caused delays. "No rations—no march," wrote Captain W.W. Murray, and several times the Canadian troops refused to advance until they received their food.[7] Their demands were reasonable for the most part, and staff officers scrambled to meet the desperate requests of regimental officers. An official report downplayed the problems by blaming a few bad seeds "with strong socialistic tendencies," and some senior officers looked for more power to transfer out to salvage units the "agitators" who "will soldier no more."[8] The Canadians addressed these difficulties quickly, but they were a sign that the rank and file were now more willing to kick against a system that was increasingly failing them.

During their advance on Germany, the Canadians had the satisfaction of passing village after village of liberated Fench and Belgians, as well as thousands of abandoned German guns, helmets, and destroyed equipment that had been left by the side of the road. The totality of the victory was evident. Civilians flocked to the streets, shouting, cheering, and waving; others stared sullenly from behind windows, having seen too many occupying forces pass through their villages and towns, bringing only death and destruction.

Blistered feet and dark rumblings from Canadian troops were not helped by the nasty turn in the weather towards the end of November, when cold sheets of rain drenched the marching men. Roads dissolved under the march of thousands of boots, and the logistical problems went from bad to worse. Grumbling could be heard from men's stomachs and then their mouths. Private F.R. Hasse of the 49th Battalion remarked on the increasingly angry denouncements: "What might have been a happy time is beginning to degenerate into a period of dissatisfaction and lowered morale."[9]

Tempers were wearing thin, and then the influenza epidemic struck. The first wave of the worldwide deadly flu had hit earlier in 1918, and while it had been utterly devastating to hunger-weakened civilians, its effects on the Allied armies had been minimal, although German fighting efficiency had suffered significantly when the flu had compounded the losses of the 1918 offensives and the steadily dwindling rations available to the men. The strain of the virus that struck at the end of the year was more virulent: this, the most terrible flu in human history, killed an estimated 50 million people globally over the next few months, including a shocking total of 50,000 in Canada. Within the CEF, an estimated 45,000 Canadians were afflicted with fevers, aches, and chills, and 776 died from the illness, although the number could have been higher, as another 3,049 were tabulated as having died under the generic category of "disease."[10]

Although it generally seemed similar to the trench flu that had affected most men at least once during the war, this far more lethal strain attacked the lungs, creating a pneumonia-like mucous buildup, which could not be expelled. It soon led to uncontrolled hemorrhaging and the coughing of blood, as blue-tinted, writhing patients slowly suffocated. Horrified soldiers were reminded of the suffering of gas victims. "The Spanish flu hit us hard and we lost a good many from it," wrote Lieutenant A.O. White of the 4th Canadian Siege Battery. "The Brigade MO, who was billeted with us got it and pleaded with us not to let him be moved to hospital! After four or five days, he got over it by taking large doses of quinine. I was detailed for burial duty as three of our men had died from the flu in hospital. It was very distressing. The hospital people told me ten men had died that morning and were buried quickly as infection spread rapidly. Last Post was sounded almost all day long."[11] The disease was a particularly bitter pill for men who had survived the machine-gun bullets and poison gas of the Western Front only to succumb to mucus-filled lungs and heart strain.

WHILE THE FLU was ravaging the ranks, the Canadians finally arrived at the Rhine in early December. The crossing into Germany was a significant event, with dignitaries, journalists, and photographers there to capture it for posterity. On December 13, the lead Canadian units marched over the bridge at Bonn in a steady downpour of rain. The dark and gloomy conditions did nothing to elevate the spirits of the men, many of whom cared not a whit for the symbolic event.

Currie was there to take the troops' salute. He was extremely proud of his men and the reputation they had won on the battlefields of Vimy, Hill 70, Passchendaele, and especially the campaigns of the Hundred Days. The corps commander had worked hard in preparing his corps for battle, and had sought few diversions. Through unending stress and lack of sleep, however, he had grown even pudgier, and now that the strain of the war was over he had savoured some of the rewards of a lieutenant general, including better food and staying in royal palaces. His men had received no such luxuries, and many were spitting mad. They blamed their corps commander for the losses suffered in the war and now for their delay in getting home.

While Currie had never enjoyed the same ease with the men as Byng, or the solemn bearing of Haig, he had always done his best for his Canucks. He had put his career on the line several times to ensure that more guns were available to support an attack, pushed back start times against his superiors' wishes, refused to let his forces serve under weak British generals, and even turned down an army command to preserve the fighting efficiency of his corps. "Currie was a very sound tactician," wrote Brigadier William Griesbach after the war. "He may have been in error upon occasion, but he made fewer mistakes than any one I know and that after all is as much as one can say."[12] But the corps commander's attention to detail, desire to learn, and moral courage was little known to his men, and dark rumours began to swirl and make their way through the angry ranks. One of the most virulent of these accused Currie of sacrificing the infantry and volunteering them for every battle, all in the name of elevating his reputation among the British. The nearly 46,000 casualties in the Hundred Days were proof, some argued, of Currie's uncaring nature. Bored and angry soldiers could look around and see how few of their mates were still with them and how many had been buried in shallow French graves.

The march past Currie at the Rhine on that dark December day was not a happy one. A sarcastic Garnet Dobbs of the 21st Battalion likely reflected the thoughts of many. Describing the viewing stand of dignitaries that the troops filed past, Dobbs sniped, "On this was our dear (?) Gen. Currie and his staff ... I'll bet that's the nearest he ever came to earning his day's pay."[13] This was an unfair statement, but the ranks' view of their commander was always different from that of the senior officers, many of whom admired Currie for his open style and moral bravery.

THE 2ND BATTALION entered the Rhineland with their band playing "O Canada," and the 14th Battalion were played forward to the tune of "The Maple Leaf Forever." Such Canadian music meant very little to the silent civilians watching the occupying force by the side of the road, but they were perhaps an indication that there was a new spirit of nationalism in this powerful land army that was the embodiment of the Canadian war effort.

Of the German army and its people, Lieutenant Colonel D.E. Macintyre observed, "It is a bitter dose for them to swallow, but it's the kind of medicine all Germany should be made to take. Most of them do not feel that their army was beaten." Macintyre, who had risen from a battalion scout officer to a senior staff position, and wore the DSO and Military Cross for bravery, believed that the Germans must be "thoroughly humiliated now."[14] The Canadians were ready for the worst. The British army had posted signs warning civilians that any acts of hostility or destruction of property would be punishable by death. Public gatherings were forbidden, except for church services, and civilians were forced to doff their hats as a sign of deference. The armies of occupation readied themselves for both a clandestine uprising and a major attack, with the Allied forces spread out in a massive defence-in-depth to fend off a Western Front–like assault by any rejuvenated portion of the German army.

But there was no enemy army waiting like wolves on the periphery. Even within the occupied zone, the Canadians found Germans who, while not welcoming the Canadians, certainly were not overtly hostile. While orders from the high command instructed that there should be "no intercourse" with the Germans, soldiers were soon mixing with the civilians during their off-duty hours.[15] Brigadier William Griesbach, who had been a fire-breather of a brigadier and was now looking to exert his will on the population, admitted in his diary that he found it very hard to act like the "heavy conqueror." The German people "are obsequious and anxious to make friends."[16]

Canadian guards were nonetheless posted at railways, dumps, and on the streets. German army barracks were taken over, but there were not enough to house the two divisions of men, even as they spread out through several German towns and cities. Canadian soldiers were therefore soon billeted among the civilian population. Joseph Buote wrote to his brother living in Rhode Island of his experiences as part of the occupation force in Bonn, where he stayed with a German family:

> … beds, real beds, can you imagine that.… Yesterday we all had a bath and all got new underwear, it seemed awful good to get cleaned up again after so long. The German people are very nice to us so far, all the men salute us when they meet us on the street, the fact is, they have to be whether they want to or not. But they are a good deal more polite than I expected they would be. I guess that they are afraid that we will do to them as they did to the Belgians.[17]

Another soldier—a Highlander from the 16th Battalion—noted in his diary that two shy little girls, ages four and eight, soon began to play with him, communicating through songs and nursery rhymes: "From lack of nourishing food the small child's skin is like sandpaper. Bought some chocolates for them which seemed a great luxury."[18] The rough and ready Private William Woods of the 1st Battalion, a long-serving veteran who had survived several years of sustained combat and had rejected every attempt by his superiors to elevate him in rank, recounted that he and two mates stayed with a German family who were very friendly towards their guests, even trying to teach them the language. But tension rose when their son came home in his army uniform and they all stayed under the same roof.[19]

Under such conditions, one would expect a rise in crimes committed by Canadian soldiers, who were fed up and perhaps harbouring anger towards the Germans, but there was very little evidence of this. The armies of occupation had been instructed to act with "courtesy and restraint." Second Army commander General Herbert Plumer, for example, somberly pointed out: "German troops have shown how infamously an army of occupation can behave."[20] The BEF would set a higher standard. And indeed, when a group of Canadians destroyed a statue of the Kaiser in Bonn's town square, they were punished by their own officers.[21] The ever-watchful Currie, who worried about discipline and the reputation of his troops, wrote of their "splendid" behaviour to the minister of militia and defence, S.C. Mewburn: "I am not going to try to make you believe that all our troops are Sunday-school lads. We have the foolish Officer, who so far forgets himself as to get drunk, but these are very, very few indeed. We have, too, the bad character, who meets the lone German in the dark and relieves him of his watch, but these cases are also negligible, and hardly worth mentioning."[22]

Although the Canadian troops were responsible for very little crime, the corps did house a criminal element. One of the more spectacular cases involved Canadian infantryman A.D. Norval, who, in Bonn on the night of December 28, 1918, held up a tram car, shot the conductor, robbed him of his money, held up two hotels, smashed their furniture, and finally stole their money boxes. He was ultimately caught and arrested by the Canadian authorities, and was given a lengthy prison sentence.[23] Such actions did little to help civil–military relations, but they were also distressing for the high command, who were always fearful that an angry, armed mob was waiting to break free from the disciplined army. The 3rd Division's Major General Frederick Loomis, worried that the ranks would be incited by agitators, ordered that "work was to be explained to the men," "trouble-makers to be watched," and all were to be kept busy. Discipline was essential, and "if officers did not correct men when men failed to salute, etc., they were laying a foundation for trouble."[24] Griesbach, too, ordered that discipline had to be enforced: "To depart in any way from this principle may result and probably will result in dissatisfaction and insubordination with possible rioting and mutiny."[25]

With many of the best officers having been killed or wounded during the Hundred Days, new officers, unsure of themselves—and their men of them—tried to impose parade-ground discipline on the battle-hardened warriors. Many of the rankers refused, engaging in minor strikes, work stoppages, failures to salute officers, and open threats when commanded to march with full packs. A member of the 49th Battalion remembered: "Myself, I had been in France for three years and the army for four.... I wanted to get the hell home."[26]

Ernest Black, an artilleryman with the 2nd Division, laid out the problem: "What does one do with an army out of work and waiting to be sent home. You cannot subject soldiers waiting for discharge to regular training. Even less can you let them sit idle with nothing to do but get into trouble.... The problem was to keep us occupied with light and interesting things."[27] Drill kept soldiers busy but it could only be pushed so far, especially now with the threat of the Germans increasingly fading. Sports remained a key leisure pastime, and all manner of games were played. Less traditional activities were pursued, too. The 2nd Battalion, for example, which was garrisoned around Cologne, went deer hunting in the Imperial Forest. After some close calls of Canadians shooting Canadians accidentally in the throes of their desire for fresh meat, the battalion's officers organized official hunting parties. The deer did not stand a chance; the 2nd Battalion's men had lip-smacking venison at Christmas.

Soldiers' theatre also gained in importance, and a school was established to train entertainers in the dissemination of songs, skits, and escapist jokes. As well, an innovative education program was carried out under the name The Khaki University of Canada, which allowed soldiers at all levels of education, from illiterates to university students, to learn new skills. At its closure in July 1919, this program had enrolled more than 1,000 Canadian soldiers in university courses in England and France, and over 50,000 had been instructed at more junior levels within the battalions and batteries.[28] All of these leisure activities—including the granting of more leave, which allowed soldiers to visit local towns—helped to ease the rising levels of frustration, but it was nonetheless a cold, unhappy winter for the Canadian troops, especially as it appeared that the Germans were not going to mount guerrilla attacks or resurrect their army to launch a full-scale offensive. The Canadian army of occupation seemed to have no reason to be in Germany—an observation increasingly not lost on the angry infantry.

THE HIGH COMMAND was as frustrated as the soldiers they led. While policy-makers had been preparing for the eventuality of getting hundreds of thousands of Canadians, and now over a million Americans, back to North America, the process would be long and trying as a result of shipping shortages, an increasing number of strikes in Britain, and a lack of suitable ports in Canada. The Department of Militia and Defence had always been aware of the difficulties in demobilizing tens of thousands of men, but by 1918 they had begun to devote serious attention to the obstacles. "Very quickly will the world realize how much easier it is to make war than to make peace," warned one report. The concern was how to get soldiers home, and quickly. Some men were unquestionably interested in seeing justice done—though usually to themselves—asking for a "first one in, first one sent home" policy. The government had different priorities, however, and wished first to reintegrate men with skills, known as "pivotal men," to guard against a recession and kick-start the economy after the war.[29] In contrast to both positions, Currie argued forcibly that his men should be sent back in their units and under their officers so that they would keep their discipline en route and receive the recognition they deserved back home. To send the men back in dribs and drabs based on a points system of service and age would be fair, but such an approach would denude battalions and batteries of some of their longest-serving leaders, as well as important bomb-proofers including cooks and clerks, just at the time when these men were most needed to hold together the steadily eroding morale of units.

The solution arrived at was a compromise: complete units from within the four divisions, and the rest of the Canadian Corps, would be sent back under their own officers and would account for approximately 100,000 men, while the rest of the CEF, from reserve units and conscripted men to the vast logistical apparatus that was established to support the corps in the field, would be organized into drafts and sent home piecemeal.[30] Amidst the grumbles, gripes, and hard words over how to demobilize Canada's overseas forces—which many had predicted would take some eighteen months—the first battalions were pulled out of Germany in early January 1919, with all of the 1st Division's forces departing by January 18. The 2nd Division soon followed. It looked to the men as though they were soon to return to their former lives. Hopes were raised and letters written informing loved ones that it was time to prepare for the homecoming. And then, like so many soldiers before and since, they found that theirs was a case of "hurry up and wait." England was the embarkation point for the troop ships since the demobilization camps were there and many of the soldiers in the CEF had family in England whom they wanted to see before they returned to the Dominion. The issues of how to transport the troops, where to keep them, and how to process their papers in a timely way were worked out like a military operation. There would be twenty-two dispersal areas in Canada, but the soldiers had to reach them first.

The general frustration felt by the bored and angry Canadian soldiers came to a head in a series of strikes and riots that punctuated the period from the Armistice to April 1919. These disturbances ranged in size and scope, and one of the more colourful ones involved the Young Soldiers' Battalion (YSB), comprising several hundred underaged Canadian soldiers. These adolescents had been trained in England throughout the war, until they hit the age of nineteen, at which point they were shipped to Europe. Many of these young men had seen combat in the trenches, and had been plucked against their will from their units because of their age. A few of these warrior adolescents had even tried to desert back to the front, wanting to avoid the stigma of holding a bomb-proof job and sitting out the war. Private C.A. Stranger, a long-service veteran who had enlisted at fifteen, had been pulled back from his unit in France to the YSB in early 1918. Unhappy about being away from the firing line, he deserted back to the front, where he was caught and sent back to England with a mild scolding.[31] In all, an estimated 20,000 adolescents between the ages of ten and eighteen served in the CEF, many with distinction, and an estimated 2,270 gave their lives for king and country.[32]

The YSB was in the process of being demobilized at the main camp at Kinmel Park in North Wales. The camp had a well-deserved dreadful reputation. Too many soldiers were crammed into the shanty town of corrugated iron huts and muddy roads. The food was bad, and few soldiers were paid regularly, leaving them unable to augment their revolting sustenance. Worse still, few forms of entertainment were provided, and the men had a great deal of time to grouse and complain as units repeatedly suffered delays of their scheduled embarkation on the ships home. Drill was half-hearted and disrupted as soldiers were less and less willing to engage in mindless activity, and officers and NCOs gained little by enforcing discipline as the men here were generally from conglomerate units.

Members of the YSB had been invited to a dance on the night of November 21. Cleaned up and eager to meet some women, a group of young soldiers arrived at the hall but were barred mistakenly from entry by British officer cadets. The young Canadians, many of them combat veterans, reacted badly. They left to fortify and arm themselves with alcohol, fence posts, and bricks, and then returned. The sound of shattering windowpanes alerted the British officers and women inside to the angry mob, and a company of British officer cadets rushed to the scene with bayonets fixed. But the boys of the YSB were not cowed. Some skirmishes ensued, with both sides suffering casualties—including bayonet wounds and brick lacerations to the head—and one poor British cadet was disarmed and non-fatally run through with his own bayonet. After some bruises and blood, the young Canadians were eventually persuaded by their officers to return to their barracks, but with 65 panes of broken glass and the remnants of some 400 dishes lining the floor.[33] The British high command reacted quickly, and most of the young Canadians were fast-tracked through the demobilization process and sailing home within a week.[34]

Other instances of Canadian soldiers' raucous behaviour occurred in and around the demobilization camps. At Witley camp, on a cold January 9, a party of Canucks stormed the police station at the nearby town of Godalming to free a decorated black Canadian soldier who had been unfairly arrested, at least in the eyes of the mob. The police were roughed up and their comrade freed. Two days earlier, more trouble had erupted within Kinmel Park camp in North Wales, when black soldiers were pitted against whites in what looked a lot like a race riot.[35] Razor blades and rocks were the weapons of choice, and half a dozen men were badly wounded. Tension was rising throughout the camp. A swill of bad feelings, lax discipline, and overcrowded space came to a boiling point here in early March.[36]

Kinmel Park camp had degenerated over the winter, as its already poor infrastructure was bursting at the seams with thousands of combat veterans, conscripts, and non-combatants, who had minimal supervision, often by officers who had not been to France and whom the experienced soldiers sneeringly called "chocolate majors" since they melted at the first sign of heat. With the influenza epidemic infecting half of England and forcing the closure of theatres and many social venues, troublemakers were stewing. Fuel shortages and bad food added to the general distemper of the times, and the soldiers' pay was also held up, with most of the men having long since spent their meagre earnings or lost them through gambling. Rumours that a group of conscripts was being demobilized instead of long-service men finally set the spark to the dry tinder. Bored and angry, some 17,000 men, many having waited restlessly in the camps for weeks, set off on an orgy of destruction on March 4. At 7:30 P.M., a group of soldiers crashed into a canteen. Consuming their fill of beer, they began to destroy the building, but not before passing out cigarettes and alcohol to a growing crowd of curious, gawking, and soon cheering soldiers. The drunken mob grew wilder and more destructive. Sympathetic or scared guards who had no desire to tangle with their comrades failed to suppress the activity, many later claiming that they could not find the thousands of looters in the dark.[37]

The temporary madness burned itself out by the next day, however, and smart officers quickly tried to round up ringleaders and get rid of the alcohol. Incentives to cooperation were also offered in the form of pay that would allow the soldiers to pursue other leisurely activities, but the camp was too big, and only a few units—which were divided within the camp by regions of Canada (Western Ontario and New Brunswick, for instance)—were actually paid. And soon much of the beer that the rioters had hidden away resurfaced again to be drunk quickly. On March 5, another mob of soldiers crashed through the camps, robbing canteens and stores, destroying and looting as they went. Some officers ordered groups of men to guard key areas, but others simply locked themselves in their barracks.

A few soldiers chose to even old scores, and several NCOs were battered. It would get worse: by late in the day, the mob of 1,000 men was armed with knives and clubs, and hand-to-hand fighting took place among roving bands. A few red banners had been raised in the name of Bolshevism, but the mob seemed little inter-ested in Communist sympathizers and more excited about bashing their way around the camp. Indeed, little leadership was evident, and an eyewitness, Grant Dean, recounted that the "unruly bunch" was simply bent on destruction. After the mob moved off, he watched a rioter with a pool cue systematically break every glass win-dow he could find. When Dean tried to talk to him, chastising him for what he was doing, the grim rioter pulled back his coat to reveal a few grenades, and told him to scram. Dean moved away speedily, realizing that a few panes of glass were not worth his life at the end of an already long war.[38] Sadly, not all involved on that day were so lucky. Bullets, bayonets, and fists killed five men, and another twenty-five were wounded seriously.

Witnesses picked out ringleaders, but many other men were scapegoated for the day's event as well. Some fifty-nine were court martialled for leading or inciting the riots, of whom twenty-eight were found guilty. The heaviest sentence handed down was ten years imprisonment (which was later reduced), and most men received lighter sentences. Private Victor Souliere of the 21st Battalion, who had served at the front for nineteen months and had been wounded, was one of the soldiers charged with inciting a riot, as he had urged his comrades to "get some ammunition" and use it against the authorities. He was sentenced to two years of hard labour but was "discharged with ignominy" on November 11, 1919, after his sentence was remit-ted. Many of the men charged for their role in the riots had recognizably foreign-sounding names such as Hiba, Miculka, Schmidt, and Wikle, and they received the harshest sentences, no doubt betraying the conviction of military authorities that Bolshevism had to be stamped out in the ranks, and that it was likely carried by "foreigners."[39]

But many soldiers escaped prosecution, as witnesses were demobilized and the men got on with the important business of getting home. The high command inves-tigated thoroughly, however, and was shocked to find evidence of some officers tak-ing bribes from men in return for an earlier ticket back to Canada. Moreover, there was a shocking lack of communication from officers to men about the reasons for the delays. Much could have been done differently to stave off the riots, the inves-tigation noted, but once the rioters started, only the unleashing of armed men might have restored the situation, but this surely would have resulted in greater death and destruction, and would have involved Canadians killing Canadians.

THE RIOTS were much reported on in British papers. Local civilians, already fed up with unruly and misbehaving soldiers, contributed to the stories. Rumours circulated, quickly becoming reported on as truth: Dozens of men had been murdered. Canteen girls had been ravaged by wild-eyed, frothing soldiers. A Victoria Cross–decorated soldier had been stomped to death by the herd-like crowd. Bolshevism was running rampant in the camps, and soon the soldiers might break out and take the country by force. None of these stories were true, but the Canadians were consistently depicted as thugs and criminals, wildmen who had fought well on the battlefield but who were no longer suited to civilized society. Frank Underhill, who would return to Canada and become one of the nation's most respected historians, remarked: "I fancy most Ripon inhabitants except the shop keepers will be rather glad [that the Canadians were leaving] for the Canadians haven't a good reputation. They are too wild for this peaceful market town. Every night there are scores of drunks rolling home from the pubs, singing and fighting."[40]

The Canadians reacted angrily to the accusations—Currie especially so. He wrote to the justifiably concerned minister of militia, S.C. Mewburn:

> The first accounts of the trouble … were shamefully and grossly exaggerated. We all feel very bitter at the attitude of the press. They gave an exhibition of yellow journalism of the rankest kind, and it seemed that they were willing to say anything if it could be to the detriment of the Canadians. I cannot understand the press of England at all…. Now that we are going home, they seem to take an unholy delight in referring in a much exaggerated way to any indiscretion on the part of Canadians.[41]

Currie blamed the riots on conscripts and men who had never been a part of the corps, and his view may have been accurate, although the mob had been large and many involved were clearly combat veterans of the trenches. Despite official protests from the Canadian government, newspapers' retractions of stories that one Canadian official described as "vindictive" were few, and the wild reputation of the Canadians lived on.[42]

With the Canadians branded as lawless toughies, the British War Office expedited the demobilization and more men and units were soon sailing for home. Before embarking, however, each man had to play his part in killing not only time but also a few more trees. Soldiers filled out 13 documents and answered 363 questions during the tedious process.[43] Amidst the lineups and seemingly endless waiting, many soldiers took the opportunity to be "dentally fit for peace."[44] Having half a dozen teeth pulled at a time was not an uncommon fate—and the procedure was often performed without anaesthetic. James Johnston, who had driven a mule through the firezone for two years, later remarked that the seven teeth he had removed at one sitting remained a pain he would never forget, even decades after the war.[45] Throughout the war, the plier-wielding dentists performed 2.55 million operations on Canadian troops—an astonishing average of five operations per man.[46]

Perhaps the most important administration form, at least from the soldiers' point of view, was the one carrying the results of their medical exam. Men suffering from venereal disease were held back until they were cured, as many in the senior ranks and at home feared the prospect of a plague of diseased soldiers descending on the helpless women of Canada. A medical exam would also determine if a man was eligible for a pension. However, many soldiers simply wanted out of the army and knew that admitting to a medical illness would delay their demobilization, as more tests would have to be performed. A persistent cough from relentless minor gas poisonings was shrugged off; an old bullet wound through the shoulder that never fully healed was downgraded to a nonchalant stiffness; recurring nightmares were kept from probing committee members who were forced by the sheer numbers to race through their patient files. Many of the men were labelled "fit" when they should not have been, and in the postwar years the information in these documents, which reflected the soldiers' desire to get out of the army more than their true medical status, was held against these veterans to deny them deserved pensions.

MOST OF THE CANADIAN CORPS was returned to Canada between February and May 1919, and almost all of the men were back on Canadian soil by late summer. The overseas ministry was dissolved in early 1920 after fighting its own battles with

Whitehall over the final tally to be paid to Britain for the full cost of its overseas contingent. The government blanched at the price tag: $252,567,942.03.[47] The amount was added to the enormous debt of over $2 billion accrued during the war.

The winter of discontent had blossomed into a spring of new futures, in which veterans would need to reconnect with loved ones and find their place in a society that had changed without them. But how many were like Will Bird, who felt that the brotherhood of the soldiers would never be understood by civilians? Those who had survived in the trenches and stared out into No Man's Land, he believed, "would remain a separate, definite people," forever haunted by the war.[48]

CHAPTER 39

"LIFE TO ME CAN NEVER BE THE SAME"

The Veterans' Return

"We all wanted to forget the war," wrote former stretcher-bearer Frederick Noyes. But he candidly lamented: "as if we ever could forget something which is imprinted so indelibly under our eyelids!"[1] Thomas Dinesen, a Victoria Cross recipient, remembered his anxiety about returning to Canada. During the heavy fighting in Flanders and France, he had embraced fatalism so strongly in the trenches that he "did not expect to come back," and wondered after the war how the dead were to again embrace life. "Now we return to civilization; once more the weary load of a future will fall upon our shoulders."[2] For men who had been away for years, some for almost half a decade, the future was dimly lit.

Upon returning to their homes by trains that took them through cheering villages and hamlets along the metal ribbon that connected the Dominion, the soon to be demobilized battalions, batteries, and units formed up for one last time before dignitaries. Speeches were given, soldiers stood proud, and then it was over. Demobilized men received their back pay, a bonus depending on their length of service, a maximum of $420 for single men, $600 for married men, $35 for a set of clothes, and the option to keep parts of their kit. Canada's most effective fighting formation ever fielded marched into history, its combat veterans swallowed by Canadian society.

FRANK MAHEUX, the tough NCO from the 21st Battalion who had survived the bloodbaths of St. Eloi, the Somme, and Passchendaele, returned to his wife and family. He hoped to learn how to farm, but that proved harder to do than his trench dreams had allowed. He eventually returned to the woods he knew so well as a pre-war lumberman, and his wife, as during the war, again endured long absences of her husband. Corporal Clarence McCann of the Royal Canadian Artillery had a fairly undistinguished postwar military career. Born in Windsor, Nova Scotia, he served throughout the war, returning home in apparent sound mind to his wife Ada. They would have fourteen children, but Ada died in childbirth with their fourteenth child in 1936. McCann remarried, having three more children with new wife, Gladys. Sergeant Chester Routley, a long-service veteran who emerged from the war fully deaf in one ear and nearly deaf in the second from a wound, felt lucky to be alive. But he was not sure what he was trained to do. "I had heard that once you had put in three years in the ranks, you were no good for anything else, so I made up my mind that the first job that I seen open, I would take and stick to it through thick and/or thin."[3] He became a farmer near Saskatoon. Many other men took the opportunity to work the land, too, aided by land grants from the government. These benefits were applied unevenly, however, and often the available land was barren.[4] Postwar inflation and a drop in inflated wartime wheat prices, combined with the poor quality of the land, meant that within a decade more than a half of all veterans had lost their farms. It has often been said that Canada has too little history and too much geography. In this case, most of the good "geography" had long been distributed, and many soldiers' dreams of a postwar farm soon became history.

The soldiers' transition to peacetime was difficult, but most men found ways to return to their lives. They reconnected with wives who had been forced to run the household without them; with children who had grown up with an idealized view of a soldier father that would now be tested by reality; with parents who had become aged by stress and strain. "Now I am back in my own country and, though memories sometimes overwhelm me and nightmares disturb my sleep, I am consoled by knowledge that I have been of use to Canada in a time of need and have paid my debt of gratitude to ancient France," wrote A.J. Lapointe, who had served with the Van Doos and had suffered the shock of returning to Canada to be greeted by a haggard father, who sadly informed him that most of his family had been wiped out in the flu epidemic.[5] Soldiers were well accustomed to death, but the blow of arriving home to the graves of loved ones felled by the flu broke many men who were already on the edge.

Warren Hendershott, whose brother had died in an aircraft training accident during the war and who had himself flown as a "knight of the sky," expressed to his parents his desire for something different: "Say, I don't know how I will go back to my old job after the war. I would go crazy standing behind a counter from morning till night. I think after a while at home the place for me will be out west. I may change my mind but after awhile at this life you become all nerves and are not contented sitting around. You want to be doing something exciting all the time."[6] It was not easy for a young man of twenty, who had commanded a dozen hard men in combat, to return to his job as a store clerk. Lieutenant Stanley Edgett was a little less guarded in a letter to his brother during the fighting: "This war game makes me wild & reckless and I expect there will be lots of shooting cases after all is over."[7] Such statements, joking or genuine, left some at home worrying that the civilian-soldiers had been corrupted into hardened killers and wondering how they might fit back into society. The men's participation in sports, education, and theatre was held up by the army as proof that they would make the transition easily, although the end-of-war riots raised concerns for many Canadians that the soldiers would need to be handled carefully. Edgett did not survive the war, and therefore never came home to see how most of his mates found ways to adapt rather than turning to violence.

But often violence seemed the only means by which veterans could assert themselves. From the first years of the war, wounded men were returning to Canada, and these former soldiers quickly formed into groups, the most powerful being the Great War Veterans Association (GWVA). Across the country, they pushed for government recognition and rewards, while often exerting moral authority in the streets. Many instances were reported of soldiers and veterans roughing up immigrant Canadians who had come from enemy combatant countries. Now, after the war, the GWVA and other veterans' groups set their sights on carving out a space for returned servicemen in a postwar Canada. A natural sense of resentment towards those who had stayed behind, and likely prospered, drove many veterans to demand not only recognition but compensation.

A debt-ridden government, dealing with a fragile economy, not only failed to find money for rewards in its coffers, but had no idea how to deal with the massive influx of unemployed veterans. Within days of the Armistice, the Imperial Munitions Board—the largest corporation to that point in Canadian history—cancelled all contracts, put its factories up for sale, and laid off 289,000 workers.[8] Those women who had filled the paid positions of the men at war were either pushed out or left voluntarily, but there were still not enough available jobs in the depressed market. For veterans who expected a "land fit for heroes," the reality generated growing dissatisfaction. What was a manager to do when faced with hiring either a man who had worked for five years in a job and done it well, or a serviceman, newly returned from the ranks, coarsened, perhaps suffering from a wound or less visible psychological scars? These ex-soldiers did not always receive their prewar jobs back, especially as the economy slipped into stagnation. Most Canadians believed they owed a debt to the veterans, but soon this debt began to weigh heavily, and all, including those who served king and country, were scrapping for their own piece of the steadily diminishing finances in the mean postwar world.

IF IT WAS HARD for able-bodied veterans, it was even worse for disabled men who came home wounded in body or spirit. The Canadian government, in the hyper-patriotic climate of the war, had publicly announced it would care for veterans— and to do anything other than treat wounded men humanely would have severely damaged the future strength of the voluntary war effort. But both the government and the fiscally minded citizenry were fearful of encouraging a repeat of the "pension evil" that had plagued the United States after the American Civil War, when tens of thousands of wounded veterans, backed by a powerful lobby force, increasingly consumed federal spending as the war had once consumed men in battle. In Canada, the government's desire to ensure that veterans did not become wards of the state was strong. This often meant that they were paid pensions they could barely survive on, which would, it was thought, provide an incentive for the recipients to find work. But the war had ground men out, and many would never again be able to hold gainful employment. An official medical report from 1921 observed, "Cases are constantly presenting themselves in which a nervous or mental disability is complained of or has become noticeable after the lapse of periods varying from a few months to several years since discharge from the army."[9] Sir Arthur Currie, who suffered from undiagnosed post-traumatic stress disorder, believed that

> [the] health of almost everyone who served throughout the war was, to some extent, adversely affected. Men may not have been wounded nor have suffered from any illness, but I do not believe that any man could go through the campaigns of the Great War without his power to resist disease being minimized. It might be difficult to say that an affection of the lungs, or heart or nerves is unquestionably attributable to war service, yet a man would have to be superhumanly wise to say it was not.[10]

Fifteen years after the war ended, 77,000 veterans were receiving pensions, and thousands more had died premature deaths or were living with daily pain.[11] Veterans fought hard to win this second war—against indifference, bureaucracy, and callousness—and the government generally responded with fairly progressive pensions for the time, especially in comparison to those received by veterans in European war-ravaged countries, although nothing could replace the Canadians' lost years or compensate for their dark nightmares.

Although the pensions were considered fairly generous by some, the process usually required a veteran, or his family, to plead his case before a jury of superiors. The boards assessed the damaged men before them, interrogating them, prodding them with new medical exams while studying old documents. These gatekeepers were looking for malingerers, much as the medical officers did during the war. Veterans who had claimed themselves of healthy status, usually to get out of the army and back to their lives as quickly as possible, now found these declarations of fitness held against them, despite evidence of gunshot or shrapnel wounds. A soldier coughing persistently through cancerous lungs was perhaps a genuine victim of chemical warfare; or was he instead suffering from tuberculosis, and therefore undeserving? Only wounds related to the war qualified men for compensation. How were the pension boards to decide? Sometimes they were generous, while at other times they turned deserving men away.

Full pension payments varied among the ranks, with privates receiving a maximum of $480 per year, plus monthly child allowances of $6 per child.[12] "That an officer with an arm off should get twice as much pension as a private with an arm off," raged blinded veteran Harris Turner, "is unfair, unjust, unsound, undemocratic, unreasonable, unBritish, unacceptable, outrageous, and rotten."[13] Those found pensionable did not automatically receive their full allotment, however, as grim tables assessed the portion of the pension available to them. The loss of both eyes, legs, or hands warranted a full pension, but the amputation of a single arm or leg was worth sixty percent of the pension (later reduced to forty percent). Minor ailments often did not qualify the sufferer for a yearly pension, but might bring a one-time stipend. Wounds to genitals generally elicited a sympathetic response, but only at rate of sixty percent. Shell shock and the equally unknown post-traumatic stress disorder were almost impossible for the boards to assess. The vast majority of disabled soldiers received pensions of less than twenty-five percent of the possible allotment for their rank, in a process that reduced wounds to percentages, pain to dollar figures.[14]

The surviving dependants of soldiers killed in the war also received compensation for their loss, but they too encountered the seemingly callous, if necessary, quantification of the unquantifiable—in this case, their grief. Since twenty percent of the Canadian Expeditionary Force were married, some 12,000 women would have been left war widows. Thousands of children were orphaned, countless lives disrupted, and families broken up. Overcome by grief, these families were forced to go before pension boards to receive their compensation for a father's or a husband's life. Robina Reid, a thirty-four-year-old mother, was one such widow. When her husband, Private William Reid, was killed on the Somme, she was left to care for seven children—aged one and a half months to thirteen years. Robina Reid was awarded the $384 per-annum allotment for a private's widow, plus $6 per child per month, provided that she did not remarry.[15] One wonders how a family of eight could possibly survive on that pittance, and in reality it is clear that they could not. It is not surprising that there was outrage among veterans when stories surfaced of lower-ranking men's widows and orphans nearly starving, especially while more senior officers received far more generous pensions.[16]

The Department of Soldiers' Civil Re-establishment, created to care for veterans, advised injured veterans unhelpfully that only those who "refus[ed] to try and achieve victory over [their] wounds were destined for hardship."[17] Veterans generally viewed the department as uncaring, overly bureaucratic, and pitted against them in an adversarial role. What of once-young men whose hair had turned white, who were wracked with strange afflictions, and who had taken up the bottle to escape their dreams? Will Bird, combat veteran and journalist in Nova Scotia, offered some scathing thoughts on behalf of his comrades. With more than 60,000 dead overseas, "now thousands more are in graves on this side, dead while they should yet be young, and the others struggle to live, plead hopelessly with soul-less powers who renege their promises made, who grind these broken veterans to starvation, shame and suicide."[18] Thousands of veterans were denied pensions, or never even applied for them, too proud to go before a board of "bomb-proofers," who would pass judgment on them and their service. Such men went through life hobbling on a bad leg or wheezing through gas-corrupted lungs.[19]

Those who did receive pensions had some of their burdens eased in life, although many veterans would have shared the sentiments of Stephen Beames, who, in his memoirs decades after the war, wrote: "[The] picture is getting dim now, but I can still see those dead men. For many years all I had to do was shut my eyes and let my memory loose."[20] Did all veterans—most of them, some of them?—suffer flashbacks, nightmares, and even daytime horrors? The mind remained a battlefield, as many veterans were never able to leave behind the Western Front. Some were so badly injured that they had to be shuffled off to the veterans' hospitals and renovated private homes that sprang up across the country to care for the legless, the armless, the blind, and insane. Harry Bissett of the 49th Battalion had served throughout the war, starting as a private in 1914 and eventually rising to a captain. But the war destroyed him both physically and mentally, and when he returned to Canada he entered a long-term hospital. He never left. For sixteen years he was bedridden, passing the time by drawing and making model ships.[21] Long-term illnesses from disease were common among many men, and resulted in more hospital cases than did wounds from the weapons of war. Amputees were fitted with prosthetics from limb factories that opened to meet a new demand. A small minority of the wounded had faces reconstructed in painful surgery, and the worst cases were consigned to wearing masks for the rest of their lives. In hospital, hacking, limping, sightless men were taught new skills and provided with relevant vocational training. Many took advantage of the chance to restart their lives, while others were gripped too tightly by despair and depression. These hospitals, sanatoriums, and private health organizations, numbering over 100 institutions at the high-water mark, cared for the veterans who were relegated to the periphery of society.[22] Even though the federal government's Department of Soldiers' Civil Re-establishment oversaw this early instance of state-run medical care—a progenitor of Canada's universal medical system—spending the rest of their lives in a long-term-care institution was a hard plight for young men who had once faced a bright future.

It is unknown how many former soldiers had their lives cut short after the war as a result of wartime injuries, disease, and long-term trauma to the body and mind. Private George Bell, who endured four years in the trenches, wrote that his sleep was filled with nightmares: of battles and shells; of waiting in the trenches to "go over the top;" and of dead companions and enemies, clutching at his mind, ever still. "Life to me can never be the same after those four years," he observed somberly.[23] Nor could it for any of the veterans. Although the number of pensioners grew year by year—from about 19,000 in 1921 to 78,040 in 1935—weakened in body and mind, they also began to die in the hundreds, and then the thousands. No one kept track of the deaths, although the regimental associations that formed in the 1920s began to note the steady loss of members. In the 1930s, men who were severely wounded and on pensions were dying at an average rate of between 990 and 1,100 per year. By 1937, the majority of the pensioners were over forty years old, but the youngest was thirty-four and the eldest ninety-one.[24]

VETERANS who were not badly enough injured to spend the rest of their days in a medical facility were often left to the care of loved ones. Or they fended for themselves, becoming less forgotten soldiers than invisible ones. "What of the thousands of unglorified men whose eyes were blinded, whose lower jaws were shot away, who are still paying [for the war]?" asked veteran and writer Theodore Roberts.[25] Crippled veterans begging on the street or selling small handmade goods were a common sight in most Canadian cities. "This war has made a horrible mess of everybody's plans," wrote Lieutenant William Gray, who had spent much of the war in a German prisoner-of-war camp. "I often sit and wonder what we should all have been today if things had gone otherwise."[26] But the war was now part of the veterans' history. Most steeled themselves and set to rebuilding the lives that had been taken from them. Two, three, four years had come and gone in training camps and trenches, but a lifetime lay ahead.

The lives of the returned soldiers followed no single narrative, but most would have agreed with the veteran who remarked: "The place we had left off wasn't there anymore." Indeed it wasn't, but nor were the men the same as those that had gone to serve overseas.[27] The war had changed everything. Many veterans flexed their new-found political powers by attacking temperance. This was bewildering to many of the good-hearted abstinence groups such as the Women's Christian Temperance Union and religious organizations that had banned demon rum and other forms of the devil's drink during the war, often in the name of the soldiers or to better prosecute the fight against Germany. But most of the men who had fought overseas did not take kindly to returning home to a dry country. Through the efforts of veterans, as well as civilians who felt that the same spirit of sacrifice was no longer required in the postwar years, temperance was slowly repealed across the country, province by province.

While the veterans had some influence in shaping the postwar Canada that they believed was owed to them for their wartime sacrifices, and a number of them went into politics at the national and provincial level, they never became a powerful, cohesive force in Canadian society. Although the veterans' organizations were amalgamated into the Canadian Legion of the British Empire Service League (now the Royal Canadian Legion) in 1925, much of the groups' political capital had already been spent in the early 1920s in trying to secure a $2,000 bonus for veterans. The debt-ridden government fought the veterans tooth and nail on this issue, and much of the political goodwill towards the veterans was expended in this eventually fruitless endeavour. As well, a strong sense of brotherhood prevailed among workers in the administration of the veterans' groups, and many officers—most of whom were very influential—were excluded from these groups. Currie, for example, wrote in

1925 that all the splintered veterans' organizations did was "keep up the old shouting that the country owes a living to every returned soldier. It is always a popular cry, but makes little impression on anyone except those who feel they would be benefited."[28] Currie may have been right, but it was certainly an ungenerous assessment of those who had sacrificed much, although within a few years of making this comment he was increasingly involved in the Legion and felt the organization was doing important work for the veterans. In the end, perhaps the power of the veterans dissipated simply because the former soldiers were dispersed across the country and most men and women simply wanted to get on with their lives. Those who had fought for their country were anxious to build it up again. They did so as they returned to old jobs on farms or in factories, or forged new ones, having grown, matured, and become surer of themselves and their place in Canadian society.

Some veterans, though, quite rightly wanted to change Canada for the better, or at least bring about more equity. During the war, Native soldiers had become the equals of their white comrades in the trenches and had enjoyed the right to vote in the 1917 federal election overseas. Mark Steinhauer of the Saddle Lake Agency in Alberta spoke for many of his fellow First Nations soldiers when he remarked: "What I want to find out is, is there a possible chance of us getting our franchise … in the reservation after the war is over? I do not think it would be fair not to get anything out of a country that we are fighting for."[29] However, the men returned to a land where they were still treated as wards of the state. Proud and fuelled by a new sense of entitlement, these veterans who had served their country fought back against the system. A long battle would ensue before Natives received equal rights in Canadian society, along with other visible minorities such as the Japanese, but the Great War veterans' voices were often among the most powerful and poignant of those raised against this injustice.

OSCAR ERICKSON went overseas in 1917 at the age of twenty-five. He had wanted to enlist earlier in the war, but he was the sole supporter of his mother. Day after day, however, Erickson felt the burden of the never-ending casualties reported from the front, as well as the growing realization that he was now virtually alone among his friends in Winnipeg not in uniform. His militia experience and relatively advanced age resulted in his receiving a commission as a lieutenant, but he reverted back to the rank of sergeant over in England when his battalion was broken up before they had even set foot on the battlefield. He arrived on the Western Front only a few days before the Germans unleashed their March 1918 offensive and survived it. Erickson's luck ran out at Amiens, however, when on the second day of battle, August 9, 1918, he was hit by a shell splinter that nearly amputated his left leg before burying itself in his right leg. He was carried to a dressing station by four German prisoners; when he got there, in agony, he asked for morphine, but it was denied to him because, as the medical officer told him, he was so weak that the drug would kill him. During a hasty operation, one leg was amputated; the second later developed gangrene and had to be amputated at the knee. At the Armistice, the former sportsman found himself "without any legs and a new kind of future to look forward to."[30] While not all veterans faced such a harsh future, all Canadians were forced to deal with the war's terrible legacy.

CHAPTER 40

THE BUTCHER'S BILL

All forms of death can be classified as heart failure. But the devil is in the details. The Great War casualty lists present some stark reminders of the difficulty of assessing casualty rates in war. Within the fighting armies on all fronts and in all theatres across the globe, an estimated 9.5 to 10 million soldiers were killed and another 15.4 to 20 million were wounded in this war.[1] The figure for the wounded is so inconclusive because not all armies tracked their number of wounded and many only episodically counted minor wounds. Moreover, in the final year of the war the Central Powers were in an ever-worsening state of administrative disarray, and many of their records were lost or never completed as the Allies systematically destroyed their forces on multiple fronts. But many statistics still remain to be picked through. Britain suffered 723,000 dead and 1,662,000 wounded. France had 16.8 percent of its total mobilized troops killed, while Germany lost 15.4 percent, which equated to 1,398,000 French soldiers' deaths versus 2,037,000 German deaths. Of the two powers, almost 900 Frenchmen were killed every day of the war, in comparison to more than 1,300 Germans.[2]

Although Canada's butcher bill cannot be compared to such a mind-numbing death count, the young Dominion suffered heavily during the war. The country of some 7.5 to 7.8 million citizens had contributed heavily to the war effort. Some 619,636 men and women were attested during the war and officially served in the Canadian army, but this does not include those who enlisted directly into the Royal Flying Corps or other Imperial services, of which there is no documented figure.[3] Of the roughly 620,000 attested Canadians, 424,589 served overseas as part of the Canadian Expeditionary Force. Another 8,826 Canadians sailed with the

Royal Canadian Navy (RCN) and the Royal Navy, some of whom would have served in European theatres of water but were outside the CEF. Of those in the RCN, an estimated 150 were killed in action or accidents, but no casualty figures exist for the 3,000 or so Canadians in service with the Royal Navy. There were some fatalities, however, and the first four Canadians to die on active service during the Great War were serving on the HMS *Good Hope*, a British armoured cruiser sunk on November 1, 1914. Another 13,160 Canadians served as aircrew in the British flying services, plus 9,652 ground crew. Many of these men had initially enlisted with the CEF and later transferred into the flying services, so most were likely already counted in the 619,636 figure.

The cost of the war was unbelievably high for the roughly 425,000 Canadians serving overseas as part of the CEF. Postwar analyses of the casualty figures calculated that 51,748 Canadian soldiers and nursing sisters were killed in action or died of their wounds. Another 7,796 died of disease or injury, which seems a high number but it included deaths resulting from accidents—everything from car crashes to falling down dugout stairs, and all the other ills that befall hundreds of thousands of men and women in dangerous places like the trenches, or in equally dangerous cities such as London and Paris, or in training camps where live ammunition and bayonets were used freely.[4] Within the British flying services, another 1,388 Canadians were killed.[5] Thus, a total of 60,932 Canadians met their death during the course of the war, as well as 1,305 Newfoundlanders, who were killed while serving with British forces.[6]

While the slain were much lamented, 172,950 members of the CEF were wounded (plus another 1,130 airmen). Of the CEF's total wounded, 138,166 suffered non-fatal battle casualties, the rest being injuries not associated with combat.[7] Some of the battlefield wounds were light in nature: a finger torn off, a clean bullet wound through a leg, a broken bone suffered while carrying supplies into the line. Other injuries were simply horrifying: eyes shot away, jaws ripped off, body parts amputated after being shattered beyond saving. Of the Canadians who survived the war, 3,802 had had at least one limb amputated; no figures exist for how many patients endured the agony of an amputation and succumbed to subsequent blood loss, shock, or infection.[8] The Canadian dead and wounded (excluding

Newfoundland) total of 235,012 casualties reveals that nearly 5.5 out of every 10 overseas Canadian servicemen were killed or maimed during the years 1914 to 1919, and the vast majority from 1915 to 1918.

These are astonishing casualty rates, but they are far worse when one considers that of the 425,000 men who travelled overseas in the land forces—plus an unknown number of airmen who might be double-counted—only 345,000 Canadians ever made it to France. Many of the remaining 80,000 were unfit, too young, or too old; other stray men—often officers who had been in command of a broken-up battalion—never found a spot in a new unit, their war thus being confined to England. Still others were involved in essential logistical or medical duties, or were recruits and conscripts who simply arrived too late in 1918 to be of service at the front. While the total Canadian dead and wounded of 235,012 includes men who were killed in training accidents, died of disease, or were injured accidentally in England, the vast majority lost their lives fighting on the European battlefields. While no exact number can be determined, if the figure of 345,000 is used to represent those Canadians who fought in Europe, then at least 6.5 out of every 10 soldiers, and likely closer to 7 out of every 10 soldiers, serving on the Western Front were killed or wounded.

Again, the facts cannot speak for themselves. The wounds did not fall evenly on the soldiers who formed the various arms of the CEF. It was the infantry—the spearhead of the forces—who most often had to face the enemy's barbed wire and machine guns on their own. Of the roughly 345,000 Canadians who went to France, 236,618 rank and file and 6,000 officers passed through the fifty Canadian battalions that served there and in Belgium.[9] The Kitchener divisions of the BEF each lost some 39,000 men on average. Most of these volunteer divisions arrived at the Western Front in early 1916, when three of the four Canadian divisions were already in the line. The four Canadian divisions all surpassed the average losses of the Kitchener divisions, with the 4th Division having 50,306 rank and file pass through it, the 3rd Division 55,634, the 2nd Division 59,186, and the 1st Division, in theatre the longest since February 1915, 71,492—and these figures do not include officers.[10] These numbers again reveal the "fighting" nature of the Canadian divisions, but fortunately none of them would reach the grim total of the 29th British Division, which led the BEF divisions with 94,000 men passing through the formation during the course of the war, indicating that every man in the division was replaced seven times over.[11]

Within the fighting divisions, the casualties were once again weighted towards those at the sharp end—the infantry and machine-gunners, rather than the artillery, engineers, or medical units. The front-line battalions were supported by the vast spear handle, but it was the infantry who were on the cutting edge. And they paid for it. Battalions were destroyed over and over again. Most hard-luck units lost 500 to 600 percent of their strength: starting with 1,000 men, by war's end more than 5,000 had passed through the ranks. The single most devastated Canadian Corps battalion was the 1st, through which 6,449 of the rank and file passed during the war, almost 700 more men than the longest-serving infantry battalion, the PPCLI.[12] Under such conditions, few of the old originals could possibly survive the war in the combat units. If they were not eventually posted to a "bomb-proof" job as a trainer or on the logistical lines, they had little chance of emerging unscathed. The 4th CMR offers a sobering example: as a 3rd Division infantry battalion, it arrived on the Western Front in early 1916, missing the Second Battle of Ypres, the Battle of Festubert, and the 1915 summer of trench warfare, but even so, only two officers and thirty-four men of the original thousand remained in the unit at the Armistice.[13] One postwar study attempting to determine pension rates noted that the Canadian infantry serving on the Western Front suffered a shocking eighty-two percent casualty rate.[14] There was no more lethal place to be in the war than with the infantry.

THE MACHINE GUN, with its arc of scything bullets cutting down advancing soldiers as they pushed their way around shell craters and barbed wire, remains an iconic image from the Great War. But shellfire was the great killer. It is often noted that close to sixty percent of all wounds were caused by high explosive shells or shrapnel and shell splinters.[15] According to the British official medical history, one sampling of wounds reveals that shells and mortar bombs caused 58.51 percent of British casualties, bullets 38.98 percent, bombs and grenades 2.19 percent, and bayonets .32 percent.[16] These statistics were taken from a sample of 212,659 wounded soldiers over an unknown time period, and have been cited extensively by historians for decades. However, even if these figures are accurate for British formations—which is by no means certain—they cannot be applied whole cloth to the Canadians. The number of shellfire wounds among Canadians decreased as the war went on, especially as enemy guns were destroyed or suppressed by counter-battery fire, or as German guns simply burned out through overuse and could not be replaced because of the naval blockade, resulting in the Germans' greater reliance on machine guns, mortars, and poison gas.

Moreover, the above statistics, though a useful starting point for analysis of casualty rates, reveal further inaccuracies and exclusions. Bayonet and hand-to-hand fighting wounds, for example, are grossly under-represented here. Countless combat reports provide evidence of the bayonet's value in battle, and it is important to remember that determining cause of death in the chaotic fighting of the trenches or in No Man's Land was nearly impossible. What of the nearly 10,000 cases of shell shock? The effects of poison gas, too, are wholly absent from the above casualty charts, whereas official records noted that the Canadian Corps suffered 11,572 non-fatal gas casualties during the war.[17] According to this figure, of the total number of deaths and wounds suffered by Canadians—233,611—approximately five percent resulted from gas.[18] However, gas killed only about three percent of its victims. Drawing on this percentage, if the ratio of poison gas casualties to non-fatal battlefield casualties—11,572 to 138,166—is examined, a much more startling finding emerges: over eight percent of all non-fatal casualties among Canadian soldiers resulted from gas.[19] And since the use of gas increased in intensity and frequency throughout the war, doubling each year, most of the gas casualties would have been sustained in the final two years of the war (except for the abnormal occurrence of Second Ypres in April 1915), further skewing the oft-cited British statistics listed above, and revealing the riskiness of blindly accepting statistics.

The changing nature of the warfighting during the four years of evolving battle—especially the Germans' increasing reliance on small-arms fire, mortars, and chemical weapons—resulted in a corresponding change in the types of wounds sustained by the Allies, and specifically the Canadians, as the war progressed. Sir Andrew Macphail, in his 1925 official medical history, tabulated the totals of various types of wounds suffered by Canadians in battle, basing his figures on the number of wounded men who arrived in hospitals.

Wounds in Action[20]

Type/Location of Wound	Officers	Other Ranks	Total
Head and neck	907	21,377	22,284
Chest	230	3,550	3,780
Abdomen	78	1,317	1,395
Pelvis	10	43	53
Upper extremities	1,895	49,615	51,510
Lower extremities	1,809	41,843	43,652
Wounded, remained at duty	904	6,698	7,602
Wounds, accidental	107	2,140	2,247
Wounds, self-inflicted	6	723	729
Effects of gas fumes	368	10,988	11,356
Total	6,314	138,294	144,608

When Macphail compiled these figures in the early 1920s, he was relying on incomplete statistics, but these numbers are nonetheless revealing. The low incidence of recorded abdominal and pelvic injuries reveal that wounds to these regions in the absence of penicillin and other antibiotics were usually lethal, either as a result of the initial trauma or the subsequent infection. Men found on the battlefield with stomach wounds were often left to die, as moving them caused the victims such terrible pain that stretcher-bearers (who were forced to engage in their own form of triage) often did not consider the transport worth the effort, especially given that carrying in a patient required several hours of backbreaking labour. While statistics suggest that almost nine of every ten men wounded survived if they reached a doctor, those who were left to die in the front-lines have not readily found a place among the body-bag accountants.[21]

If we acknowledge that the casualties were—in number, frequency, and location—more complex than historians have previously allowed for, the question remains as to why the figures were higher during the last two years of the war. By the end of 1916, the Canadian Corps had suffered an estimated 61,000 casualties, but in the final two years of the war, the Canadians suffered almost three times as many deaths and injuries. Much of this increase is due to the intensity of the fighting, and to the Allies' engagement in more intense set-piece battles. The major battles of 1917 and 1918—Vimy, the fighting at the end of the Arras campaign, Hill 70, Passchendaele, the 1918 German offensives, and especially the Hundred Days—were particularly costly for the Canadians. By 1917, as well, the corps was at its strongest, with four over-strength divisions. Bolstered by more men, the Canadian Corps could withstand more casualties and keep its operational effectiveness, which in turn meant that it could be kept in the line longer than British formations. Further, as a result of their larger divisions, the Canadians were ordered to hold broader sectors of the front—during the German 1918 offensives, for example, when the Canadians garrisoned one-fifth of the entire British line. With this large number of units in the front lines, and for more sustained periods, the attrition normally suffered by trench forces took a heavy toll.

WHILE THE RECORDED NUMBER of men killed and wounded during the war was terrible, the casualty list does not convey the full swath of destruction. Not represented in this already horrific tabulation is an unknown number of injured Canadians who returned to Canada and soon succumbed to their wounds. Do they too belong on the war's roster of dead? The story of Private John McKinnon is a sobering one. In the official military records, McKinnon was counted as one of Canada's 138,000 battlefield wounded. As a stretcher-bearer at Passchendaele, he had dressed more than forty men during the hour after his 85th Battalion had gone over the top. As he was caring for his comrades, a piece of shrapnel tore into his chest, penetrating his lungs. Coughing up blood, he refused to move to the rear, continuing to drag himself through the muck to locate and save the lives of his wounded mates. During McKinnon's convalescence in England, it was determined that he would never soldier again, and so he was evacuated back to his home town of New Waterford, Cape Breton, where he died of his wounds in August 1919.[22]

Without a doubt, McKinnon and other soldiers like him, who escaped the front with their lives only to succumb to battlefield wounds back on Canadian soil, should be counted as part of the war dead. But how can an accurate figure be arrived at to account for the many battle-related deaths that occurred in the years after the war? In compiling statistics, the Commonwealth War Graves Commission, which was charged with caring for the Commonwealth's war dead, considered August 31, 1921, to be the official end of the war. From August 4, 1914, to August 31, 1921, the commission listed 64,962 fallen Canadians and Newfoundlanders in its care. Of these, 3,792 died in the years 1919 to 1921. For the period 1920–1921, a year after the CEF was officially disbanded, 1,673 new dead were listed.[23]

Canada's Books of Remembrance—seven ornately designed memorials, every page of which is hand-illustrated and illuminated—are held in the Peace Tower, itself a memorial to the fallen, at the House of Commons in Ottawa. The books contain 66,755 names of Canadians who were killed during the Great War, and the number continues to grow as the Department of Veterans Affairs discovers new veterans who died of their war wounds before the department's established cut-off date of April 30, 1922. [24] While this appears an arbitrary date (and official records fail to

The Commonwealth War Graves Commission cares for 64,962 Canadians and Newfoundlanders from the Great War, who paid the ultimate sacrifice in their service of king and country.

reveal why it was selected), it does allow for the inclusion of several thousand Canadians who died of their wounds after the Armistice. But it is unclear as to how the government determined who of this latter group would be included in the books, as belonging among the war's dead. One might have expected that the list would account for only those wounded veterans who were confined to Canadian hospitals and never left them. However, a sampling of personnel files suggests that most of the dead included in the books did not spend time in hospital, although many had been wounded during the war. In fact, it appears that all veterans who had served overseas and who died during this period (from 1919 to April 30, 1922) were automatically included in the books, irrespective of whether they had suffered a wound while serving overseas—save for the occasional soldier inadvertently left out and the twenty-five executed soldiers who were deliberately denied recognition of their sacrifice, until they were added to the books in 2001. But it is hard to justify the inclusion of some of these men. For instance, Private A.P. Smith, a butcher from Edmonton who broke his leg badly in December 1916 when he fell off a trench mat, was discharged home after his recovery in England. He died at the age of forty-one on May 22, 1921, with nothing in his personnel file to suggest that his death was related to a war injury. A sampling of other veterans had suffered either gunshot or shrapnel wounds, although often to the extremities instead of the head or centre body mass, and many of the wartime slain had their deaths attributed to tuberculosis contracted while in uniform. Records providing a rationale for who was included in the Books of Remembrance have not been located, but the number of those listed must be viewed with some skepticism, or at least acknowledged as different from the battle-related deaths from 1914 to 1918. Notwithstanding the uncertainty and incompleteness inherent in statistics, it is surprising that historians are still struggling with the total death count of Canadians in the Great War. Now, however, the country has a better sense of its sacrifice, with the death figures ranging from 60,932 to perhaps as high as 67,000, and from 62,237 to around 68,656 if Newfoundlanders are included in the assessment.

With a population of less than 8 million at the time, Canada's losses in the Great War were proportionate to the 600,000 dead suffered during the terrible American Civil War of 1861 to 1865. And to view the numbers in the context of the twenty-first century, the current Canadian population of roughly 32 million citizens would have to suffer some 250,000 dead and some 550,000 wounded to rival the slaughter the nation experienced in the Great War. Such figures are simply mind-boggling and provide harsh insight into the war's level of human carnage. Whatever the total of Canadian war dead—and it changes depending on whether all enlisted Canadians are included or just the Canadian Expeditionary Force, and whether the cut-off date is considered the point at which the CEF was demobilized in 1919 or dates in 1921 or 1922 later imposed by administrative bodies—the Great War put a shocking number of young men in the ground. And it continued to kill Canadians long after the last bullet was fired.

CHAPTER 41

WHITHER THE GREAT WAR?

1919 to the Present

John Henry Babcock was born in July 1900, one of ten children from a farming family near Holleford, Ontario. Too young to serve in the war legally, Babcock lied about his age and went overseas at the age of fifteen and six months. He was subsequently caught by the military authorities and placed in the Young Soldiers Battalion in England, where he served for the duration of the war, never seeing action at the front. While his war service was undistinguished, Babcock will still go down in history, for he is the last man standing. John Babcock is the last living soul of the 620,000 Canadians who served in the Great War. The rest have marched into history, joining the comrades they left behind on the battlefields and those who later succumbed to their wartime wounds or the normal ravages of time.

The war thus teeters on the razor's edge and will soon pass over, moving from living memory to history. While it was the geography of the war that was so important to the soldiers of the time—the No Man's Land to be crossed and the enemy trenches to be captured before breaking through to the other side—it is the soldiers' history that has continued to exert a grip on the popular imagination. Over the last ninety years, the Canadian memory of the war has changed, being shaped and reshaped by each generation that has tried to make sense of the nation's appalling sacrifice on foreign battlefields. The Great War ended on November 11, 1918, but the reverberations of its terrible battles have resounded through the ensuing decades.

MORE THAN 61,000 Canadian dead, several thousand more succumbing to their wounds in the immediate postwar years, and others hobbled for life with missing limbs, scorched lungs, blindness, or abiding psychological trauma: this huge toll in a country of less than eight million might have left most Canadians in the early 1920s lamenting the war or cursing the government for allowing young men to serve in such a wasteful conflict. While the death pall indeed shrouded the country—as nearly every community had paid for the war with the blood of its young—instead of portraying the war as a meaningless slaughter, the vast majority of Canadians sought to make sense of their losses by elevating the war's ideological and moral importance. The soldiers who had fallen overseas, they proclaimed, had given their lives in a crusade for liberty and justice.[1]

Memorials erected in Canadian communities became sites of remembrance, as almost all of the bodies of the fallen had remained overseas, where the Commonwealth War Graves Commission was charged with caring for the Empire's million dead. Canada's tens of thousands of slain soldiers had been disinterred after the Armistice from their haphazardly dug battlefield graves and re-interred in new cemeteries in individual graves, all under uniform white crosses. The war's dead would remain a unique army of comrades for all eternity. After the war, thousands of Canadians paid their respects at these silent necropolises, both the enormous ones that housed tens of thousands and the smaller ones, now increasingly surrounded by farmers' fields as the land was slowly reclaimed from the ravages of war. But most families were forced to grieve without a body, or without an expensive overseas visit to a grave, thus unable to achieve the closure that was so important to those who had never had a chance to say a proper goodbye.[2] "Their name liveth for evermore," was inscribed on the Stone of Remembrance in each overseas cemetery containing 1,000 or more graves, but Canadians at home needed something more tangible.

Across the country, grieving citizens came together in the immediate postwar years to erect cenotaphs and memorials in their villages, towns, and cities to those men who had left and never returned. Hundreds of monuments were built in the 1920s, and while their size and scale varied, they were remarkably similar in their presentation and message. The symbol of Winged Victory and the Canadian uniformed soldier were often presented together. Very infrequently were the soldiers shown to be suffering, or represented in poses of grief or even exhaustion; instead, they were standing at attention, or with arms raised in victory, or marching forward, their duty done nobly in the Great War for Civilization. The just war needed memorials that marked it as such.

Local fundraising paid for the monuments of stone: though bodies were gone, the names etched in permanence lived on. The dead had given (not lost) their lives in the service of God, king, country, and justice, it was believed, and the cenotaphs almost always signified only the fallen—not all the soldiers who had served or even those who had been wounded.[3] Those patriotic Canadians who had done their bit for the war effort on the home front were often given their due through pins, publications, or other forms of recognition, but their efforts were not represented on the prominent local memorials. The cult of service was trumped by the cult of the dead. These sites of memory remained important gathering places on November 11 of each year, up to the present day, but there were other forms of remembrance as well. Soldiers' service and sacrifice were captured in commissioned stained-glass church windows; named streets, gardens, and buildings; commemorative books commissioned by businesses, schools, universities, regiments, and companies; and in sculptures, paintings, songs, and poetry.

Within the patriotic grieving of the first decade after the Armistice, little space was afforded for public questioning of the war. Dissenting voices were not wanted in a society intent on portraying the war's victory as a selfless sacrifice.[4] But thousands of parents, widows, and orphans still had to deal with their now broken families and individual personal grief, a reality that contrasted starkly with the idealism of collective community and national memorializing. There must have been little consolation for mothers and widows who received the Memorial Cross (often known as the Silver Cross) to commemorate a fallen son or husband. The Memorial Death Plaque, also referred to as the "dead man's penny" because of its similarity to a large, round coin, represented another attempt by the government to acknowledge sacrifice and service. It too named the dead and was embossed with the sentiment "He Died For Freedom and Honour." Families found other private ways to remember loved ones: treasuring and archiving letters from the front; displaying a slowly fading sepia portrait on the mantelpiece; and passing down to subsequent generations the personal possessions or artifacts of loved ones who never returned.

THE GOVERNMENT also felt the need to commemorate more formally, on a national level, Canada's shocking war sacrifice. While the Great War's butcher bill had nearly been equalled by the 50,000 deaths of Canadian flu victims in 1918 and 1919, the government offered little recognition of that natural disaster, but it made sure to establish a number of national memorials, both in Canada and overseas, to honour the war dead. Veterans took matters into their own hands as well, adopting the red poppy as their emblem in 1922, thus transforming into a symbol the flowers that had grown on the battlefields in Europe and had been immortalized in the lines of John McCrae's famous poem, "In Flanders Fields." The poppy was initially a commemorative device used in fundraising for soldiers' pensions, and later became a powerful icon of remembrance. But the most symbolic event associated with the war's remembrance was the ceremony in the name of Armistice Day, also known as Peace Day, on November 11, 1919, and every year since then, with the name changing to Remembrance Day in 1931. Two minutes of silence, the playing of "Last Post," the recitation of "In Flanders Fields," and the wearing of red poppies have all infused the meaning of these annual observations. While Remembrance Day has gone through cycles of importance to Canadians, ebbing and flowing with different generations, it remains a poignant symbol of the Great War and is still the most important collective state-sponsored ceremony carried out by Canadians, save for Canada Day on July 1—and some years eclipsing even that celebration.

Postwar governments responded to the desire of Canadians, and the pressure of veterans' organizations, to further mark the soldiers' sacrifice. In 1927, the Peace Tower was erected in the new Centre Block at the Parliament Buildings in Ottawa in recognition of both Canada's role in the war and the nation's hope for peace. The Memorial Chamber at the top of the tower houses a simple marble plaque that reads:

THEY ARE TOO NEAR
TO BE GREAT
BUT OUR CHILDREN

SHALL UNDERSTAND
WHERE AND HOW OUR
FATE WAS CHANGED
AND BY WHOSE HAND.

And within the chamber rests the handcrafted Books of Remembrance, which carry the names of those whose actions changed Canada. Further memorializing the fallen was the national cenotaph, unveiled in 1939 in downtown Ottawa—sadly and ironically only a few months before the outbreak of the Second World War. While some Canadians lamented various governments' decisions not to build a special Canadian War Museum in the 1920s to house the trophies, artifacts, and art related to the war, others took solace in the construction of overseas monuments on several Western Front battlefields—especially the "Brooding Soldier" at Ypres and the breathtaking memorial at Vimy Ridge.[5]

In 1922, 100 hectares of land around Vimy Ridge were ceded by France to the Canadian government in perpetuity.[6] Prior to this, discussions had taken place among government personnel and former CEF generals as to where the planned memorial for Canadian soldiers should be located—with one early and strange suggestion possibly selecting Mount Sorrel in the Ypres salient. Vimy was eventually chosen because of its imposing geography and the importance of the battle here to the collective memory of Canadians. Sir Arthur Currie had some reservations about the site, although he eventually agreed to it. He worried that

> [If] they place the large memorial at Vimy it will confirm for all time the impression which exists in the minds of the majority of the people of Canada that Vimy was the greatest battle fought by the Canadians in France. In my mind that is very far from being a fact. We fought other battles where the moral and material results were greater and more far reaching than Vimy's victory. There were other victories also that reflected to a greater degree the training and efficiency of the Corps. Vimy was a set piece for which we had trained and rehearsed for weeks. It did not call for the same degree of resource and initiative that were displayed in any of the three great battles of the last hundred days—Amiens, Arras, Cambrai.[7]

Canada's national memorial on Vimy Ridge was completed in 1936 and remains one of the most imposing and moving sites of remembrance on the Western Front. The names of 11,285 Canadians killed who have no known graves in France are inscribed on the ramparts around the memorial.

But Vimy was the site of Canada's first major victory of the war, one that solidified newly crafted tactics and the Canadians' reputation as elite troops, and thus was indeed a fitting place for the memorial. Sculptor Walter Allward's design was accepted by the government and he began work in 1925, labouring for the next eleven years. The stunning memorial was unveiled in 1936 to an audience of tens of thousands, including 6,000 Canadian veterans who had made the pilgrimage overseas. The twin soaring pillars of stone reach to the skies, representing France and Canada joined together in friendship, as well as forming, along with the sculpture's base, an unmistakable upper portion of a cross. On and around the memorial are twenty figures representing faith, justice, peace, honour, charity, truth, knowledge, and hope, as well as the allegorical mother, Canada, mourning her fallen sons. The names of 11,285 Canadian soldiers who died in France and had no known grave are inscribed on the ramparts of the memorial (with close to another 7,000 on the Menin Gate Memorial, in Ypres, erected in memory of Canadians with no known graves who fell on Belgian soil).

THE VIMY MEMORIAL WAS THE MOST IMPRESSIVE Canadian monument to the fallen built overseas, reminding Canadians and our Allies of the young country's sacrifice and success. It was erected a full five years after the British parliament passed the Statute of Westminster, the important act that finally extended full national rights to the British dominions, including Canada. From 1931 onwards, Canada would control its own foreign policy and, as a self-governing nation, would decide when it would go to war.

The Great War was Canada's war of independence. The Canadian forces' battlefield success pushed the nation towards full autonomy and international recognition. In 1919, Canada signed the Treaty of Versailles, which formally ended the war, and that signature, separate from Great Britain's, revealed that something had changed in the relationship between the two countries. Canada also joined the newly created League of Nations as a member state in its own right, although most of the prime ministers of the 1920s and 1930s did their best to avoid making any commitment that might again drag Canadians overseas from their isolated "fireproof house, far from the sources of conflagration," as one senator famously described it in the 1920s.[8] Even if Canada's politicians seemed reluctant to exert their own authority on behalf of the country, wartime prime minister Sir Robert Borden believed correctly that "The development of constitutional relations through which Canada and other Dominions have entered the portal of full nationhood ... was due to the valour, the endurance and the achievement of the Canadian Army in France and Belgium which inspired our people with an impelling sense of nationhood never before experienced."[9] Canada had come of age during the war, and it added a new dimension to its existing autonomy as it stepped beyond the national stage, first during the war with its contribution of the CEF, and ever afterwards as it partook in more frequent international diplomacy and involvement in world organizations.

Unlike the American war 150 years earlier, Canada's war of independence did not result in the nation's throwing off of the supposed shackles of British tyranny. The Dominion's relationship to Britain had changed during the countries' mutual death struggle of 1914 to 1918. Veteran and later historian G.R. Stevens recounted that during the war, "Canadians had become deeply conscious of a national identity and of their own superb performance in the field; they no longer felt it necessary to adopt without question usages, manners and behavior simply because they were British. They were a branch diverging from the parent stem and the relationship of Mother Country and offspring never would be quite the same again."[10] During the war, and ever afterwards, many Canadians saw themselves in a different light. It is too much to say that Canada was born on the slopes of Vimy Ridge in 1917, as surely Canada had been confederated for fifty years at that point, but what kind of country was it? Most Canadians had come from somewhere else: losers and castoffs, the displaced and unwanted, the prosecuted and those seeking a better life had all come to carve a new life out of the vast Dominion's geography. Until the early years of the twentieth century, those who lived in central Canada might never visit the east or west coast, and certainly the rural parts of the country spawned men and women less likely to travel beyond the closest towns or cities. The war changed that. Canadians from across the country were pulled from homes and hearths and sent overseas in the largest diaspora of Canadians up to that point in the Dominion's history. Close to seven percent of the country's total population left Canada during

SIGNS OF THE TIMES
John Bull alters the sign again.

This cartoon nicely captures the changing status of Canada in the eyes of the British (John Bull)—from colony to dominion to nation. Canada's wartime sacrifice, as embodied through the Canadian Corps, had fashioned a new identity and pushed the country towards full nationhood.

the war years, which included an astonishing twenty percent of the total male population between the ages of eighteen and forty-five. And when they arrived in the camps, and later in the fighting formations of the Canadian Corps or other units, they met men who hailed from across the country. English Anglo-Saxon Protestants served next to French-speaking Catholics; east-coast fishermen rubbed shoulders with big-city Toronto factory workers; Natives, blacks, and Japanese fought side by side with men who might never have seen them in Canada, let alone talked to them. This is not to suggest that the Canadian Corps was one big, happy family that experienced no friction or fights. But the country did come together in its corps, taking great pride in the significant victories on the Western Front, which created a new pantheon of national heroes. The corps' success in the war also created a new sense that Canadians had done something important together, that indeed something "Canadian" existed beyond the political federation of provinces and localities.

Although the Great War was Canada's war of independence, it both united and divided the country, which was forged in the fire of war, and nearly consumed by it. The extremity of the war effort brought out the best and worst in Canadians, and as it demanded increasingly greater sacrifice, tolerance and moderation were replaced by a crusading mentality. Those who questioned the seemingly unending sacrifice and the need for greater exertions were accused of being traitors. The war created new heroes, new myths, new legends, but it also nearly tore the country apart along linguistic, cultural, class, and regional lines. The horrifying loss of life, fiscal strain, and the trampling of minority rights were interwoven with the important steps to full nationhood. After the Great War, Canada became a far more difficult country to govern.

A.Y. Jackson enlisted as a private, was wounded, and finished the war as an official war artist before returning to Canada to make his reputation and achieve everlasting fame as a member of the Group of Seven, a collective of artists who depicted Canada's powerful geography and landscape. Years after the war, Jackson remarked: "My life divides from before and after the war, just like B.C. and A.D.... that's the dividing line in my life."[11] Indeed, the Great War would mark a line of division for all Canadians, as millions struggled with their conflicting senses of intense grief and enormous pride regarding what they had collectively done during those four and a half agonizing years. Canada and its people would never be the same.

DESPITE THE FRACTURING of the country and the excruciating losses it suffered, in the 1920s the Great War was seen as the good war. The Great War for Civilization had been a necessary conflict that many participants and supporters saw as a fight to ensure liberal values, to defend the rights of small nations, to protect the world from German militarism, and to support the British Empire in its time of need. No one had foreseen the tremendous sacrifice that would be required of all nations and citizens, but despite the huge losses, not many Canadians believed that the war should not have been fought or seen through to the bitter end. Even those vehemently against conscription in 1917 often framed their arguments to suggest that the war had to be won, just not at any cost, and certainly not at the price of free choice in a war that was supposedly about liberal ideas. Most Canadians believed that war was indeed awful, but that there were worse things than war. Enslavement, loss of empire, and allowing militarism to run wild were all cited by Canadians as justification for the fighting and dying during the war and afterwards.

In Canada, a surprising court case in 1928 marked a symbolic sea change in these attitudes. Then called the "trial of the century," Sir Arthur Currie, former Canadian Corps commander, went to court to fight for his reputation. The case centred around the question of how the Great War, and the high price paid by Canadians, should be remembered. Nearly a decade earlier, on March 3, 1919, the old war horse and former minister of militia and defence Sam Hughes had stood up in the House of Commons and launched a vitriolic attack against Currie. He thundered that Canada's victorious corps commander should be "tried summarily by court martial and punished so far as the law would allow."[12] Hughes had been denouncing Currie for several months in private as a "murderer, a coward, a drunkard, and almost everything else that is bad and vile," or so Currie had heard from friends in Canada, but he had chalked such comments up to Hughes's unstable mind and his bitter disappointment at having been eclipsed by Currie in leading Canada's war effort.[13] But in the House of Commons, Hughes had gone too far, putting into official record that Currie was an incompetent criminal, primarily because of his order for the corps to attack Mons on the last day of the war, but also generally because of the heavy Canadian casualties sustained during the Hundred Days campaign. The charges were outrageous, as was Currie's potential punishment of court martial resulting in death by firing squad. But despite Hughes's reputation as a discredited force within the Conservative/Unionist party, his tirade was a shock to members of Parliament. Few politicians knew the details of the fighting better than this former war minister, which left many with questions. Perhaps the casualties were too high? Victory had been won, but at what cost? Had there been callousness to loss of life in the Canadian high command?

Members in the House had difficulty responding to the condemnation of Currie without concrete evidence, an obstacle that never inhibited Hughes. In the uncomfortable silence following the attack, no members stood up immediately to defend the corps commander. Hughes's allegations hung like a pall, and more than ten days passed before newly elected member of Parliament Cy Peck, a former battalion commander, defended his former commander and shut down Hughes's rant. Although Hughes was soundly put in his place, the rumours lived on, dogging Currie in the postwar years, even after Hughes's death in 1921. By this time, an exhausted Currie had left the military and become principal of McGill University in Montreal, eventually reviving that then-moribund institution. Despite Currie's sacrifice for his country during the war, and his postwar success, he was never publicly thanked by the government or given a cash reward, as were other senior generals throughout the British Empire.

On June 13, 1927, a small-town newspaper, *The Evening Guide* of Port Hope, Ontario, re-accused Currie of sacrificing his soldiers at Mons on November 11, 1918.[14] The editorial repeated Hughes's attack of eight years before in the House of Commons. While parliamentary privilege had protected Hughes from any lawsuit, the same was not true for the newspaper. After years of trying to defeat the rumours, Currie was handed an easier target, and he sued the newspaper editor for defamation of character. The battle that unfolded in the courthouse of Cobourg was not, in the end, about punishing the staff of a small newspaper: it was fought to restore Currie's reputation and to run to ground the rumours that had plagued the former corps commander for years. As Currie wrote to one friend about the trial: "I thought the time had come when, once and for all, this spreading of lies should cease."[15] Ultimately, though, Currie's fight was about shaping the Canadian postwar memory of the conflict.

The trial was nothing short of a nationwide spectacle, with reporters rushing out after every session to file their stories with newspapers across the country. Canadians watched and waited as the general fought for his reputation. After bitter weeks of arguments and cross-examination, Currie won the case. Although the positive judgment, rather than the limited monetary compensation he received, did much to rehabilitate Currie's reputation, the trial broke his health. He recovered from a stroke suffered in 1928, but his health was much reduced in the last years of his life. When he died in 1933, his country finally seemed to recognize his important role in its development: his state funeral was a national event with an estimated 200,000 in attendance, including thousands of veterans. The newly founded Canadian Broadcasting Corporation transmitted the proceedings from coast to coast, and Sir Robert Borden commented that it was perhaps "more elaborate than ... any funeral in the past history of Canada."[16] The trial and time had restored Currie's reputation, but the memory of the war would soon go through a revolutionary change after Currie's trial and before his death.

FREDERICK NOYES, a stretcher-bearer during the war, still believed in the brotherhood of the trenches even a decade after the war, writing with conviction about the "Memory of comradeships dearer than any which peacetime could have brought; a Memory of experiences, trials and moral victories which are almost beyond belief; a Memory of sacrifice and self-abnegation of which we never dreamed ourselves capable before the war," and which had forever marked the men who made up the Canadian Expeditionary Force. But although Noyes avowed that he and most of his fellow veterans would not "trade our army days for anything," he noted too that they could not forget the heavy price paid.

> We were ... robbed of our boyhood, plundered of our youth, and flung deliberately into a hellish testing furnace before we were old enough, many of us, to know the ordinary ways and pitfalls of a peacetime world. Many of us came out of the war burned-out wrecks, possessed only of tragic disillusioned minds and broken bodies to carry us toward an old age from which we will, thank Heaven, be mercifully spared.[17]

Here, Noyes captured the contradiction inherent in war service, as well as the corresponding one that had begun to emerge in the memory of the war by the late 1920s. The war was now acknowledged as both glorious and tragic: it was the catalyst for shaping veterans, and subsequently, the nation, but it laid waste a generation and left lasting scars to survivors and society. It demonstrated not only the unimaginable courage and heroic sacrifice ordinary Canadians were capable of but also the rash, callous nature of rival imperialisms. After a decade, Currie had finally answered the rumours that had stalked him, but the notion of the "just war" had faded in the face of the reality of the increasingly disillusioned survivors. With their wounds refusing to heal, and the need to write the war out of their systems growing, many veterans put pen to paper.

The rise of the "disillusionment writers" of the postwar years is often associated with the worldwide success of Erich Remarque's *All Quiet on the Western Front*, published in 1929, which poignantly and powerful depicted the senselessness of war when viewed through the eyes of lice-infested trench soldiers who seemingly knew nothing of the larger war effort or why they were killing other men in similar circumstances. Much earlier than such dissenting prose accounts—indeed, dating back to the first years of the war—antiwar poetry had been written and published, but despite the fame of writers such as Siegfried Sassoon and Wilfrid Owen, this poetry did not resonate with most readers.[18] In fact, putting aside the special case of *All Quiet on the Western Front*, studies of postwar literature have found that the best-selling books were still romantic adventures: for every popular Wilfrid Owen poem there was a better-selling book or Hollywood film about a trench soldier and his dog engaging in a romping adventure.[19]

But this apparent lack of public interest did not stop dozens of Canadians—the "front generation" as they were sometimes known—from publishing their memoirs during and after the war. Of course, most veterans refused to share their war experience with anyone, even as families and friends were desperate to know more about what had happened to them overseas. One veteran advised his comrades: "Do not talk about the war, truthfully or otherwise, to people who weren't there. You will be misunderstood if you do.... Keep your war-talk for old soldiers."[20] This silence, deafening in most households, was broken periodically, but the better part of a decade passed before veterans began to write about the war, no doubt as an exorcism of sorts.[21] Most soldiers offered moving testimonials about the death, wastage, loss, and ruin that pervaded the trenches, but few questioned the need for the sacrifice. The war, they believed, had been a necessary evil, even if many of the front-line soldiers were portrayed as victims. The former fighting men offered a grim perspective on their experiences, but one that was, by its very nature, limited and intimate. No bland historical narrative of the importance of the balance of power could compete with a vivid account of a Canuck with his head blown off by a sniper, taking three hours to die.

By the 1930s, a strong body of such literature had been penned by Canadian front-line soldiers, veterans such as Will Bird, Peregrine Acland, Charles Yale Harrison, James Pedley, and William Kerr. The most aggressive antiwar novel, Charles Yale Harrison's *Generals Die in Bed*, railed against the war, but especially against cowardly generals who remained safe in their rear chateaux while ordering men to their deaths. Yet Harrison's book was vigorously attacked by veterans who thought it unrepresentative and the product of a "diseased mind."[22] As a contemporary veteran wrote in the early 1930s, Harrison's work and books of that ilk were the mere "whimperings of neurotic sensationalists."[23] But in Harrison's mind, and those of many veterans and civilians, someone had to be held accountable for all those deaths. It is worth noting that of the fifty-nine Canadian generals (those men at or above the rank of brigadier) serving in France and Belgium, seventeen were wounded and one was killed, but perceptions among those at the front rarely extended all the way back to headquarters.[24] These statistics are not as grim as those for front-line troops, but nor was a thirty percent casualty rate an indication that the generals never saw a shot fired in their direction. Nonetheless, the myth of the callous general persisted. While Currie was aghast at Harrison's novel but unwilling to publicly denounce it, his former divisional commander, Archibald Macdonell, had perhaps a better solution in hoping to "live long enough to have the opportunity of (in good trench language) shoving my fist into that s. of a b—— Harrison's tummy until his guts hang out of his mouth!!!"[25]

Despite their increasing disillusionment with the war, veterans found stability in one another and in their memories of the trenches. While some exorcised old demons through their writing, many more came together in Legion Halls to drink and sing and reminisce with old comrades. Regimental associations grew in strength, and veterans' tours revisited the Western Front. In 1934, in the midst of the Depression, 75,000 veterans from across the country converged on Toronto for a three-day reunion fuelled by camaraderie and nostalgia.[26] There is no doubt that the absence of the "Lost Generation" weighed heavily on the young country, but the war was certainly not universally lamented, and the constructed memory was very much fragmented, contested, and even used for new ends.

Peace groups had gained legitimacy in the 1920s as they called for universal disarmament in order to never repeat "The War to End all Wars," and while most Canadians were not involved in such organizations, these voices of peace seemed more relevant now than at any time in the preceding two decades, especially as they resonated in the unstable world that followed the seemingly unending war.[27] Resolve to end strife might have been strong, but the economy was not. The shattering effects of the Depression of the 1930s, which nearly destroyed the Western democracies, coincided with the rise of Adolf Hitler's Nazis in Germany, Mussolini's and Franco's Fascists in Italy and Spain, and intensified militarization in Japan. Rearmament, invasions of weak countries, and ongoing threats by these fascist and militarized nations increasingly revealed that no matter how the appeasing Britain and France, or the isolationist United States and Canada, tried to accommodate the new warlords, another war seemed to loom unavoidably in the future. The horror of No Man's Land beckoned with each account of Germany, Japan, or Italy flexing its new economic and military might. The maw of war appeared ready to make the new, younger generation into the next "Lost Generation."

WHEN WAR CAME in September 1939, Canada waited a respectable week before deciding to go to war on Britain's side. Ties of blood and belonging, and an understanding by many Canadians of the threat posed by Hitler's forces, meant that Canadians again joined the colours. But this time enlistment was accompanied by little cheering. Everyone knew what was in store: a long, grinding war against a powerful and resilient opponent. From 1939 to 1945, over 1.1 million Canadian men and women joined the services, fighting on land, on the oceans, and in the air. While some within the Allied high command felt that the Canadian Army did not live up to the performance of Currie's Canadian Corps in the Great War, the contribution of Canada's land forces, which included fighting in Italy and Normandy and their liberation of the Netherlands, was augmented by the navy's essential role in winning the Battle of the Atlantic, and the actions of thousands of Canadian airmen who bombed Germany into submission. As in the Great War, Canada punched above its weight, contributing mightily to victory and emerging in 1945 as an influential middle power.

As this second group of veterans returned to a more robust and progressive society and economy in 1945–1946—one that offered good jobs, affordable housing, and veterans' benefits—the Great War slipped from memory. The war against Hitler became the good war, and the Great War was soon crowded to the periphery, or dismissed as a war of rival empires in contrast to the clearly understood fight against Hitler's brutal and odious regime. The names of the Second World War's 42,000 dead were often added to the Great War cenotaphs, and the Legion Halls became more crowded with new generations of veterans. In public memory and popular culture, the Great War became the forgotten war over the next two decades, as the conflict was almost entirely absent from novels, films, documentaries, memoirs, and historical scholarship from 1939 to the end of the 1950s. Only in the 1960s, with the marking of the fiftieth anniversary of the war, did a new generation return to the Great War, but now the nature of its memory had evolved again. Viewed against the backdrop of the anti-authoritarian, anti-military, and intergenerational conflicts of the 1960s, the Great War seemed a perfect example of the stupidity and senseless of war—any war—not to mention a warning of how the callous and cruel old had sent the naive young to die in ditches that they dug with their own hands. The music-hall ditties had been replaced by psychedelic rock 'n' roll and folk-music protest songs, and the new, cynical youth sneered, "We won't be fooled again." The ongoing conflict in Vietnam during the 1960s, during which thousands of Canadians enlisted in the U.S. forces when Canada refused to partake in the war, belies the danger of absolutes, but most Canadians were against the Vietnam War, and proudly so. The legacy of the country's role as United Nations peacekeepers rather than warriors—along with Lester Pearson's 1956 Nobel Peace Prize—reinforced Canada's self-image as the "Peaceable Kingdom."[28]

And yet when the fiftieth anniversary of the Battle of Vimy Ridge coincided with the centenary of Canada's Confederation in 1967, it became clear that the Great War, as always, was hard to pigeonhole as simply a useless slaughter. In France, it had destroyed the country's will to fight, leading to the debacle of the shocking collapse in 1940, during the Second World War; in Germany, it had paved the way for Hitler's seizure of power; and in Britain, it marked the start of the decline in the Empire's worldwide influence. But in Canada, five decades later, new history books were published that spoke to the war's importance in paving Canada's way to full nationhood, now so widely and colourfully being celebrated in the country's centennial year. The popular perception of the war's role in the colony-to-nation arc was still strong, partially because it was true.

The Great War veterans started to pass away in noticeable numbers since the 1960s, and the ranks in all Allied countries were threadbare by the 1980s and 1990s. But beyond the men's immediate families, few seemed to pay much attention. The war was slipping more quickly into memory, moving almost entirely out of the hands of veterans, but new memory-makers filled the vacuum. Films such as *Gallipoli* (1981)—which had the obligatory ending of the mass slaughter of helpless Australian youth at the hands of callous British generals—built upon the grim tradition of *All Quiet on the Western Front* (1930), *Paths of Glory* (1957), and *King and Country* (1964). Television programs including Rowan Atkinson's *Blackadder Goes Forth* (1989) skewered the imbecilic generals. And novelists such as Pat Barker and Sebastian Faulks told moving tales of men and women caught in the bewildering and brutalizing grip of war.

In Canada, too, the Great War had its twin legacies. As in other nations, the horror and futility of the war were strongly present in cultural products of remembrance in the later decades of the twentieth century. Timothy Findley's widely acclaimed Canadian novel *The Wars* (1977), for example, offered a particularly moving portrayal of the senselessness of the war. But generations of Canadian schoolchildren continued to memorize John McCrae's "In Flanders Fields" (1915), which had transformed from a martial poem about picking up the torch from the fallen to continue fighting the enemy into a poem about the general need for remembrance of the war. And the vibrant memory-strand of the war as a coming-of-age event remained, too, captured best in Pierre Berton's bestseller *Vimy* (1987), with its hyper-patriotic, nation-build-ing narrative. Seven decades after the war, Canadians still could not agree on what the war had meant to the country. Whether referred to as the Great War, the First World War, or the War to End all Wars, it remained the enigmatic war.

Within this contested terrain of memory formation, historians had (rather curi-ously) long been absent. As the official archives had been closed for decades, few his-torians had delved into the war, and those who did generally produced dry-as-dust, little-read books. Canada's official historian, Colonel A.F. Duguid, a decorated wartime artillery officer and prewar engineer, was tasked with writing a multi-vol-ume history based on the official war records in his care. He started to organize the millions of pages of records and interview surviving officers in the early 1920s, but it was an enormous job, and Duguid was also the champion of the veterans of the Canadian Expeditionary Force, enthusiastically defending the reputation they had fought so hard to win during the war years. Duguid battled the British, Americans, and even Canadians to keep the memory of the war—and the elite reputation of the Canadian Corps—from being tarnished, pressing hard against other nations' official historians or supplying facts as ammunition to politicians when they needed to strike back at American writers who claimed that it had been their forces that had won the war. But although Duguid was lauded in his role as champion, his enor-mous research project suffered, and he produced only one of the expected eight vol-umes in the official history series after almost three decades of work.[29] While other countries told their own stories in official histories, the memory of the Canadian Corps was never fully codified in print. Even worse, Duguid hoarded the records, refusing to let most historians access them. And although the official war records were gradually opened to the public in the 1950s and 1960s, it really was not until the 1980s that a new generation of historians began to study the Great War.[30] The long-standing shibboleths of the war that had been so firmly entrenched in popular memory were prodded and analyzed against the archival records, which, while num-bering in the millions, were gradually sifted through and studied by historians. But while important work was completed in attempts to better understand the war and its multiple components, it was often difficult to break the stalemated memory of the Great War.

DESPITE THE WAR'S end result of pushing the Dominion to embrace full nation-hood, for many Canadians the end did not justify the means: the war was the epit-ome of industrialized, callous slaughter. Canada may have achieved its independence on the battlefields of Europe, but it had done so by stepping over the bodies of thou-sands of sacrificed youth. By the end of the twentieth century, the Great War was almost universally viewed as a war fought over nothing, and for the sake of nothing. The service and sacrifice of the soldiers had been glorious, but it had been wasted. Those who lived in the trenches, with the rats nibbling at their fingers and feet buried in a slough of mud and human remains, were first tricked into serving and then held against their will under threat of summary executions. The high com-mand, and especially the British generals, were incompetent, homicidal murderers, whose ossified minds could not process the lessons of warfare and instead chose, time and time again, to send the brave leonine troops in frontal assaults into barbed wire and massed machine guns, and, on top of that, forced the infantry to do it at a slow, methodical walking pace carrying crushing loads. Every battle apparently ended with the same result: soldiers cut down in bloody swaths while generals rested luxuriously in the rear sipping brandy and tut-tutting the weather, before returning to the task of studying their maps and finding new ways to kill their men in the hopes of garnering a "mentioned in despatches," a medal, or a knighthood from the King.[31]

One of the most enduring legacies of the war is the liturgy of hate and spite directed against the generals and high command. According to many present-day angry critics of the war, Sir Douglas Haig was the head donkey of this group, responsible for the slaughter of the brave lions. Soldiers often complained that they never saw the generals in the front lines. Indeed, most generals did not walk through the trenches; nor did they lead their forces from the front. But such was not the role of a general in the Great War. Even the lowest ranking general, a brigadier, com-manded 4,000 men; and a major general commanded a division, around 20,000 strong. Haig had almost two million men under his command. In this war of enormous numbers, there was no way for a general to be at the head of the army, rousing the men from a white charger. Direct vocal communication with so many men was impossible. This was a telephone war—albeit one in which the telephones rarely worked. But there was more to commanding a division than leading the infantry forward; artillery, engineers, machine guns, transport, and supply had to be coordinated, communications linked to flanking units, and reserves thrown into the line when necessary. Furthermore, generals had to be callous—willing to sacrifice some men to save others. In the case of Haig, few of his critics accounted for the constraints of coalition warfare, which often forced him to attack where he did not want to, as on the Somme, or for longer, as at Arras. Haig was surely no brilliant general, with the Somme and Passchendaele hanging like millstones around his neck, but one looks long and hard to find any "brilliant" generals in any of the armies involved in the war. Is it possible that every general was a donkey? Or is it more likely that the problems of modern warfare, such as command, control, and supply, and the inherent power of the defensive over the offensive, had led to the stalemate? Whatever the case, the collective endurance of the civilian-soldiers to withstand shocking punishment in the meat-grinder battles of the Western Front ensured that armies of hundreds of thousands would not easily crack, even in the face of such debilitating casualties.

One can be sympathetic to the problems of command without being apologetic, however. The British high command suffered from severe problems: it was too rigid and it did not encourage open criticism from lower levels in the hierarchy; neither did it disseminate the lessons of the war uniformly across the forces, thereby ensuring that some formations were ready for battle while others were hidebound and almost guaranteed to fail. David Lloyd George, no friend to Haig, wrote this of his headquarters: "The whole atmosphere of this secluded little community reeked of that sycophantic optimism which is the curse of autocratic power."[32] The setbacks to the British during the Arras offensive of 1917 and during their defence against the German offensives of early 1918 were in part a result of the high command's failure to process and implement the lessons of the war, although aggressive and always evolving German tactics must be credited with ably finding the cracks in the British armour. The decision to attack at Passchendaele, however, rests squarely on the shoulders of the army commanders, and ultimately on Haig's, as no amount of training or advanced tactics would have delivered a breakthrough on that battlefield.

But part of the credit for the Hundred Days campaign—one of the most difficult and continuous series of interconnected battles ever fought by British armies in their centuries-long history—must also go to Haig. He had transformed the BEF from a junior partner of the French in early 1916 to a hard-fighting army that consistently drove back the Germans along the entire Western Front. The Canadians were able to avoid some of these problems experienced throughout the BEF because of their fine commanders and their homogeneous corps structure. But errors were still made, and Canadian soldiers paid for this at Festubert, the March 1, 1917 gas raid, the attack on Lens, and, during parts of the Somme and Hundred Days fighting, they paid for poor decisions that pushed the infantry beyond their endurance. But more often the Canadian generals fought for their men, trying to ration lives by substituting shells for bodies in battle. They followed a long and painful learning curve that was often jagged and uneven instead of gently rising towards progress and enlightenment.

The silent cities of the dead, marked by row upon row of white crosses, are indeed hard to see beyond, and seem to suggest failure and the need to assign blame for the use of archaic tactics. In contrast to the popular memory of the war, which often pegs the fighting as tactically stagnant—with long lines of men advancing a few metres at a time through muddy graves into the mouth of the guns—the reality is that soldiers first learned how to survive on the battlefield, and then they learned how to conquer the enemy.[33] Training, tactics, command and control, doctrine, weapons, and technology all evolved and improved to allow attacking forces to defeat the power of the defender, who held the inherent advantage of remaining strongly fortified behind barbed wire, protected by deep dugouts, defences-in-depth, artillery and sweeping small-arms fire, and reinforcements. Noel Birch, one of the British army's great gunners of the war, noted astutely: "We had to learn our lesson in the pitiless school of war."[34]

Mistakes were made, studied, acknowledged, and compensated for with new doctrine, and then different mistakes were made. Each time a new weapon was added to the arsenal—airplanes, tanks, poison gas, flame throwers—the other side adapted, overcame, or absorbed the devastating casualties, always finding ways to battle back. Both sides embarked upon learning how to master the battlefield—the Allies generally maximizing offensive power while the Germans sought to improve the power of the defensive. Moreover, the evolution in warfighting cannot be understood in the context of improvements in single arms, such as the infantry, artillery, or machine guns, but rather in terms of how they were welded together to create the combined-arms attack doctrine. The combined-arms battle, when employed within limited set-piece attacks, provided the foundation for victory. The sophisticated new attack doctrine, which led to the fighting soldiers' understanding of tactical limitations on the modern battlefield, was based on balanced infantry sections with flexible firepower, supported by devastating artillery fire; a robust logistical system that incorporated railways, light rail, trams, lorries, animals, load-carrying men, and even air drops; new technologies and weapons to weld the arms together; the ability of the soldiers to fight through the gas-saturated environment of the only continuous chemical battlefield in the history of warfare; and commanders who increasingly understood the need to decentralize control into the hands of those at the front. The learning process that both sides underwent speaks to the ingenuity of Great War soldiers and perhaps reinforces the adage that individuals do their best thinking on the eve of an execution. As inhumane as the conditions were, they were conducive to sharpening focus—to learning and improving. The alternative was little more than assisted suicide.

"THE SURVIVING MEMBERS of the Canadian Expeditionary Force belong to an army to which there come no recruits," wrote Sir Arthur Currie in 1932, a year before his death. "Every year our ranks grow less and the time will inevitably come when the Canadian corps will be but a memory."[35] By the first decade of the twenty-first century the number of veterans had been reduced to a few dozen, and as lived memory faded out, the field of Great War studies exploded. But no single memory or view of the war dominated the discourse, and the subject became increasingly contested territory. Scholars attacked and counterattacked, using the archives as their ammunition. Hard truths were uncovered as the myths of the war were systematically chewed over like gristle. Conferences, academic journals, and history books contained the newest scholarship, but almost all of it went completely unnoticed by non-academics. In popular memory, the Great War retained its unqualified image as the futile war of fetid ditches and slaughtered youth, fought incompetently and achieving nothing. But new television documentaries, new Hollywood films, and a new Canadian War Museum kept the war from disappearing into the No Man's Land of memory, even if at times the reality was necessarily oversimplified for public consumption. Canadians interested in their family history as it related to the war were ably supported by digitized material on the web, including essential official documents from the National Archives of Canada, such as attestation papers and war diaries. Letters, photographs, and memoirs were found and published, both in print and digital form; amateur historians offered tour-guide books of the Western Front; and even the academic historians were occasionally consulted in the mass media.

But even as the war took on new meaning, it was being wilfully forgotten by some. In Quebec, the connotations of the Great War are far different than in the rest of the country. Over successive decades, provincial governments have largely expunged the war from the province's curriculum, robbing those who have passed through the educational system of almost any knowledge of this crucial event in the country's history. And in those instances where it is covered in textbooks, instead of the focus being on Vimy, Currie, or even the French-Canadian 22nd Battalion, the memory passed on is one of conscription imposed on a largely francophone province by an English majority who had not yet learned what it meant to be Canadian, and who continued to bow before an Empire and feed men into the mouths of angry guns. The 1918 anti-conscription riots over Easter weekend in Quebec City left four dead after English militia units opened fire on a crowd that was throwing rocks and firing small arms. The memory of those martyrs has seemingly overshadowed the tens of thousands of Quebeckers who served and sacrificed overseas during the war.[36] But the process of forgetting the war has not been limited to this one province. The Dominion Institute, a privately run history organization, has periodically polled Canadians from across the country and has found some dismal results, including that, in 2006, when respondents were presented with a list of four famous military men, only thirty-one percent succeeded in identifying flying ace Billy Bishop and Sir Arthur Currie as Canadian Great War heroes (the other two being American generals Douglas MacArthur and Ulysses S. Grant).[37] However, another survey in 2007 found that sixty-three percent of respondents believed that

Vimy Ridge was an important milestone in the nation's history, and fifty-one percent passed a knowledge test on the war; but only a shocking eight percent of Quebeckers could identify Vimy Ridge as the name of a key battle during the war.[38] While different generations remember, forget, and shape their own stories of the war, it is worth recalling that most historical surveys tend to yield very low scores for fact-based questions. What is certain, however, is that the Great War has achieved importance over the last decade as a cultural and political event to be marked by the government and media in all the provinces save Quebec, especially in comparison to its almost complete marginalization in the middle decades of the twentieth century.

The important commemoration ceremonies around the time of the Second World War's fiftieth anniversary in 1994–1995 reminded Canadians about the epoch-changing role its veterans had played in shaping their country and the modern world, and of the courageous sacrifice made by all who took up arms for their country in any war. This perspective had a positive impact on the meaning of the Great War—a war that had forged Canada like no other event in the young country's history. A ceremony in 2000 marked the return to Canadian soil of the Unknown Soldier, one of Canada's 6,846 sons who fought in the Great War and whose remains were never identified. After a ceremony at the Vimy Ridge memorial, the soldier, who was disinterred from a cemetery near Vimy, was flown back to Ottawa, where tens of thousands paid their respects at his new permanent cenotaph in the nation's capital. In the early years of the new millennium, Remembrance Day ceremonies across the country, their attendance now greatly increased, still employed many of the Great War's symbols of remembrance, even though the war's few living veterans were no longer able to attend. In the present day, ongoing controversies, including the redress for interned Ukrainians, the periodic attacks against Billy Bishop's Victoria Cross–winning feat of June 1917, and the long campaign to obtain a pardon for the twenty-five Canadian soldiers executed during the war, periodically keep the Great War on the media's radar. A more identifiable signpost event was the rededication ceremony of the Vimy Memorial in April 2007, attended by the Queen, Prime Minister Stephen Harper, and several thousand Canadians (veterans and schoolchildren alike) who made a pilgrimage overseas, and watched by millions more on television. It was a day of ceremony, commemoration, and even celebration, which included traditional and non-traditional forms of remembrance ranging from poems to fiddle-playing, appreciated by a crowd wearing badges, ball caps, and T-shirts that proclaimed: "Vimy 1917: Birth of a Nation."

NINETY YEARS ON, the Great War continues to be fought and refought by each new generation. "The war will not last forever; but the memory of it, the suffering of it, the incalculable waste of it, will last for all that remains of our lives," declared Great War veteran Coningsby Dawson in 1919.[39] Indeed the memory of the war has outlived those who fought it, but what of the future? Whither the Great War? In what direction, to what end, to what place, will the Great War move within the constructed realm of individual and national memory? Will it fade from the public mind, like most historical events, to be dredged up in newspaper columns on anniversary days or reduced to curricular content force-fed to students and then largely forgotten? This will no doubt occur, but the war also seems to have a weightier presence in national, local, and personal memory. For despite the inability of many Canadians to draw upon facts and dates, the Great War still holds a resonance with many segments of Canadian society, who well know the brutal struggle that forever shaped the country. It captures the imagination of poets, writers, novelists, filmmakers, and historians, and is deeply intertwined with commemorative events such as those on November 11 and multiple sites of memory. The Great War will remain one of those events, like the French Revolution or the American Civil War, that will not easily wither away, swept into the dustbin of history.

Even when the last Great War veteran from Canada passes away, along with those around the world, the poignant legacy of the war will live on. The Great War continues to resonate; it continues to haunt us. The destruction of several empires, the rise of the United States and Soviet Union superpowers, the seeds of decolonization, the fermenting of modern conflicts in the Middle East, the birth of new nations, the loss of ten million battlefield dead, the many more millions of shattered lives of wives, children, and parents who lost their husbands, fathers, and sons, and the ushering in of the bloodiest century in human history: all this can be traced back to the Great War battlefields. The No Man's Land that divided the armies on the Western Front now separates the history of Western civilization like a wound refusing to heal,

Even when the last veteran of the Great War is swallowed by the mists of history, the war will continue to resonate as each new generation will remember the horror faced and heroism exhibited by a generation of ordinary Canadians forced to confront the extraordinary. They did, and Canada would never be the same.

forever marking the extreme sacrifice of a generation, and marking too a historical wedge between Victorian and Edwardian (and indeed earlier) times—which now seem almost impossibly quaint—and "our" brutal world of the twentieth century and beyond. The Great War for Civilization in fact destroyed the civilization that came before and created "modernity" in countless fields of human ideas, expression, and identity.

THE GREAT WAR was the first modern, industrial conflict in which machines seemed to rule men. Artillery, machine guns, rapid-firing bolt-action rifles, grenades, and mortars wreaked death and destruction alongside the new weapons of the tank, poison gas, liquid fire, airplanes, and submarines. The million-shell bombardments rendered the battlefield a moonscape of destruction, and sent soldiers burrowing into the ground for their lives. But despite the mechanical aspect of the war, which chewed up men at a fearsome rate, soldiers at the front were less cannon fodder than storm troops, even if the two realities, unfortunately, went hand in hand on the Western Front. The industrial, modern war could not have been fought without a loss of men. With the enormous shellfire bombardments, dense clouds of poison gas, and millions of small-arms bullets polluting and raking the battlefield, victories were never easy. In fact, the most shocking thing about the Great War was not the appalling hemorrhage of the armies, but that any of the soldiers were able to endure such a struggle.

By the war's end, the Canadian Corps was recognized by friend and foe as the most effective strike force in the Allied armies. Forward-thinking commanders, a robust corps structure, an ability to learn from errors and implement reforms, and the creation of a combined-arms battle system had led to victory. But none of this could have been achieved without the Canadian combat formations, largely civilian-soldiers, who gave so much during the war. "Infantry are shock troops: it is the personal conflict of the infantry which determines the fate of a battle," observed Sir Arthur Currie.[40] Medical officer and future parliamentarian R.J. Manion praised the men he served with:

> The ordinary common soldier, without any special qualifications, who, day in and day out, night in and night out, performs the dirty, rough, hard, monotonous, and often very dangerous tasks of the Tommy; who does his duty, grumbling perhaps, swearing often, but does it without cowardice, without hope of honor or emolument, except the honor of doing his duty and doing it like a man. When his work is done he comes back, if still alive and well, to sleep in wet clothes, on a mud floor, under a leaky roof or no roof, often hungry, or his appetite satisfied by bully beef and biscuit.

Manion was quite right to conclude his account of the fighting troops with this final thought, which rings forward over the ninety years since the last shell was fired: "The real hero of the war is the ordinary common soldier."[41] Despite the trials of shells and snipers, gas and mortars, mud and rats, unending trauma and loss, it was these citizen soldiers—from across Canada—who were forged into the shock troops of the Western Front, where they fought, endured, and finally delivered victory in the Great War.

NOTES ON SOURCES

Citations for sources are located within the endnotes linked to the text. A full bibliography is available at **www.canadaandthegreatwar.com**. However, this brief account provides an outline of available sources relating to the Canadian Corps and its operations. Readers should keep in mind that an enormous international literature exists on all facets of the subject, and a number of Canadian studies explore the impact of the war on the home front.

Owen Cooke's bibliography, *The Canadian Military Experience, 1867–1995*, provides a comprehensive list of books on the subject, and a bibliographic essay, "From Colony to Nation," also compiled by Cooke, is available on the Library and Archives Canada (LAC) website. Tim Cook's *Clio's Warriors* examines the historiographical trends and historical battles within the canon of war writing.[1]

Histories of the war have been published since the second year of the conflict, and while works by Lord Beaverbrook and other wartime journalists must be treated with caution, they contain unique information and contemporary observations.[2] These "instant" histories were later supplanted by regimental histories and the first official history, written by Colonel A.F. Duguid. While Duguid produced only one of eight projected volumes, the regimental histories remain an important source for readers to understand the inner workings of a battalion, battery, or other unit.[3] About half of the infantry battalions have some form of regimental history (although they are less common among the engineering and artillery units), and these works often contain first-hand testimonials, letters, and keen insight into the soldiers' experience at war. A one-volume essential official history of the Canadian Expeditionary Force was published in 1960 by G.W.L. Nicholson.[4] It has stood the test of time—although it documents the Canadian war experience from the high command to the battalion level, and rarely below that. In recent decades, a number of essential histories have been published in Canada—including those by A.M.J. Hyatt, Daniel Dancocks, Bill Rawling, Desmond Morton, Shane Schreiber,

Tim Cook, and J.L. Granatstein.[5] These works build upon early histories but are distinguished by their extensive use of archival records. The Great War also continues to attract scholarly study from graduate students, and some of the best works have remained unpublished.[6]

It is never easy to know what was happening on the "other side of the hill." German sources are sparse, but this study has benefited from access to translations of German documents held within the official Canadian records as well as intelligence reports compiled during the war. German official and regimental histories offer some insight into the German experience of battle against the Canadians, and these will soon be available through Mark Humphries's multi-volume series, *Germany's Western Front: Translations from the German Official History of the Great War.*

At the time of writing, only one Canadian Great War veteran is still living. While we will soon no longer be able to talk to the veterans, we can continue to "listen" to them. From the first years of the war to the present, Canadian soldiers' letters, memoirs, and diaries have been written. While the historian must be wary of men who wrote with an eye on history or to protect or destroy reputations, there are few better sources than the soldiers' own words, cross-referenced with archival records, to shed light on soldiering on the Western Front. Collections of first-hand accounts and oral histories also provide deep insight into the soldiers' experiences. The most important of these is the Canadian Broadcasting Corporation's (CBC's) interviews of some 600 veterans in the early 1960s for a multi-part radio program, *Flanders Fields.* The audio tapes and original interviews, as well as the transcripts of those interviews, are held at LAC, and they are an invaluable resource for any historian.[7] Putting aside the vagaries of memory and the occasional error of fact, these interviews provide searing accounts of men at war. This study has drawn on the interview transcripts and the tens of thousands of pages that formed the raw interviews. Other resources have become more accessible over the last decade as museums, universities, and archives have increasingly digitized their Great War collections, and readers should be aware of The Canadian Letters and Images Project, a valuable resource for writers, scholars, and students of Canadian military history that continues to expand monthly.[8]

While this volume builds upon a long tradition of historical writing, remarkable gaps remain in our understanding of the Great War. Throughout the book, I have returned to archival sources in order to better understand events, especially as they were first recorded—before they were filtered through the perspectives of historians or other writers. This is a history from the bottom up. Battles and engagements were reconstructed from the official archival records, including the daily war diaries, intelligence reports, battlefield maps, postbattle reports of operations, casualty lists, and dozens of other types of sources. Most of these are held at LAC, with the core of the records in Record Group (RG) 9 (Records of the Department of Militia and Defence), RG 24 (Records of the Department of National Defence), and RG 150 (Records of the Overseas Ministry), although Great War records can be found throughout most government collections. These archival sources, numbering in the millions of pages, are the bare bones of history, and they have been used extensively in this book. The maps in this volume have been based on the maps from G.W.L Nicholson, *Canadian Expeditionary Force, 1914–1919: Official History of the Canadian Army* (Ottawa, 1960).

Of these sources, the daily war diaries—kept at the battalion, brigade, division, and corps level—document decisions taken in the planning and execution of trench warfare or set-piece battles, as well as revealing the consequences of such actions. LAC has recently digitized these rich records, and they are now available to all Canadians. In this history, I cite not only the digitized sources but also the original paper copies, as the time frame for my research stretches back to the years before the war diaries were digitized. Moreover, tens of thousands of the subject files in RG 9 related to every aspect of the soldiers' experience remain available only in textual (undigitized) form, and these too must be examined to gain a full appreciation of the complexity of soldiers' experiences in battle. Additionally, valuable research files from the Department of National Defence's Army Historical Section contain statistical information and aggregate data.

Equally important are the private papers of Canadian soldiers, from the highest-ranking general to the lowest members of the rank and file. All contain valuable insight into the war, and serve to round out the official records that rarely document the human condition: fear and anxiety, grim humour and belief systems, and how soldiers dealt with the daily reality of the trenches are revealed in these private collections. Several hundred private collections were consulted at LAC, the Canadian War Museum (CWM), and in archives across this country and overseas. The contents of these collections range from a few letters to detailed memoirs, diaries, and even official or semi-official reports. Each collection furthers our understanding of the war and its effects upon ordinary Canadians dealing with extraordinary circumstances. While hundreds, perhaps thousands, of these collections exist in archives, museums, and other historical repositories across the country—and increasingly on the internet—thousands more lie abandoned in attics and basements, slowly succumbing to climate and time. They are all valuable and should be archived for future generations.

Finally, less conventional sources, such as photographs, maps, war art, postcards, ephemera, poetry, trench cartoons, material history artifacts, and study tours taken on the battlegrounds in Europe have provided additional perspectives on factors that shaped the combat efficiency of the Canadian Corps in the Great War.

ENDNOTES

INTRODUCTION: SHOCK TROOPS (PP. I–IO)

1. Canadian War Museum [hereafter CWM], 20020112-003, Harry Coombs papers, letter to brother, 25 July 1915.

2. David Lloyd George, *War Memoirs of David Lloyd George,* volume [hereafter v.] 6 (London: Ivor Nicholson and Watson, 1936) 3367.

3. See Brian Bond, *The Unquiet Western Front: Britain's Role in Literature and History* (Cambridge: Cambridge University Press, 2002); George W. Egerton, "The Lloyd George War Memoirs: A Study in the Politics of Memory," *Journal of Modern History* 60 (1988) 55–94.

4. For an examination of this uneven learning curve, see Tim Cook, *At the Sharp End: Canadians Fighting the Great War, Volume I: 1914–1916* (Toronto: Viking, 2007).

5. Jay Winter and Antoine Prost, *The Great War in History: Debates and Controversies, 1914 to the Present* (New York: Cambridge University Press, 2005) 1.

6. C.P. Stacey, *Canada and the Age of Conflict: A History of Canadian External Policies* (Toronto: Macmillan of Canada, 1977) 238.

7. CWM, 58A 1 193.3, Alexander Lightbourn papers, letter, 1 October 1915.

8. Library and Archives Canada [hereafter LAC], MG 30 E113, George Bell papers, unpublished memoir, Back to Blighty, preface.

CHAPTER I: DYING TO SURVIVE (PP. II–38)

1. Deborah Cowley (ed.), *Georges Vanier: Soldier. The Wartime Letters and Diaries, 1915–1919* (Toronto: Dundurn Press, 2000) 174.

2. Ollie Miller (ed.), *Letters Bridging Time: Tom Johnson's Letters* (self-published, 2007) 26.

3. CWM, 19810740-054, Charles Pearce papers, Pearce to Dad, 21 August 1915.

4. CWM, 20050153-001, Garnet Dobbs papers, Garnet to Millie, 10 September 1917.

5. Armine Norris, *Mainly for Mother* (Toronto: Ryerson Press, [1919]) 118.

6. Heinz Hagenlucke, "The German High Command," Peter Liddle (ed.), *Passchendaele in Perspective: The Third Battle of Ypres* (Barnsley, UK: Pen and Sword, 1997) 46.

7. Hew Strachan, *The First World War: A New Illustrated History* (London: Simon & Schuster, 2003) 227.

8. CWM, 19650038-014, William E.L. Coleman papers, diary, 14 November 1916.

9. LAC, MG 30 E16, W.H. Hewgill papers, diary, 30 December 1916.

10. CWM, 19920187-002, H.H. Burrell papers, diary, 27 December 1916.

11. Daniel Dancocks, *Gallant Canadians: The Story of the Tenth Canadian Infantry Battalion, 1914–1919* (Calgary: Calgary Highlanders Regimental Funds Foundation, 1990) 103.

12. Victor Wheeler, *The 50th Battalion in No Man's Land* (Ottawa: CEF Books, 2000) 66.

13. CWM, 19980050-005, Herbert Clemens papers, Herbert to family, 27 October 1916.

14. See the instructions for inquiry and suggestions for areas of study: LAC, Records of the Department of Militia and Defence [hererafter RG] 9, v. 4011, 17/1, G. 428, 3 November 1916.

15. Christopher Pugsley, "Learning from the Canadian Corps on the Western Front," *Canadian Military History* 15.1 (Winter 2006) 12.

16. Dan Todman, "The Grand Lamasery revisited: General Headquarters on the Western Front, 1914–1918," in Gary Sheffield and Dan Todman (eds.), *Command and Control on the Western Front: The British Army's Experience 1914–18* (London: Spellmount Limited, 2004) 49.

17. See LAC, RG 24, v. 1843, Canadian Generals; William Frederick Stewart, Attack Doctrine in the Canadian Corps, 1916–1918 (Master's thesis: University of New Brunswick, 1982) 74.

18. LAC, MG 30 E100, Sir Arthur Currie papers [hereafter CP], v. 35, file 159, Notes on French Attacks Northeast of Verdun in October and December, 1916.

19. A.M.J. Hyatt, *General Sir Arthur Currie: A Military Biography* (Toronto: University of Toronto Press in collaboration with Canadian War Museum, 1987) 64.

20. E.L.M. Burns, *General Mud: Memoirs of Two World Wars* (Toronto: Clarke, Irwin & Co. Ltd., 1970) 35.

21. LAC, RG 9, v. 4136, 24/3, Canadian Corps G. 340, 27 December 1916.

22. Ibid.

23. Currie noted this in his Verdun report: LAC, CP, v. 35, file 159, Notes on French Attacks Northeast of Verdun in October and December, 1916.

24. J.A. MacDonald, *Gun-Fire: An Historical Narrative of the 4th Bde. C.F.A. in the Great War* (4th Brigade Association, 1929) 56.

25. For information on artillery on the Somme, see Jonathan Bailey, "British Artillery in the Great War," in Paddy Griffith (ed.), *British Fighting Methods in the Great War* (London: Frank Cass, 1996) 28–35.

26. Robert F. Zubkowski, *As Long as Faith and Freedom Last: Stories from the Princess Patricia's Canadian Light Infantry from June 1914 to September 1919* (Calgary: Bunker to Bunker Publishing, 2003) 251.

27. "Editorial," *Canadian Defence Quarterly* 2.4 (July 1925) 322.

28. LAC, CP, v. 35, file 160, A.G.L. McNaughton, Some Artillery Impressions Gained during a Visit to the Verdun Battlefields—January 5th, 6th, 7th, 8th, 1917; John Swettenham, *McNaughton* (Toronto: Ryerson Press, 1968) I: 69.

29. Major General A.G.L. McNaughton, "The Development of Artillery in the Great War," *Canadian Defence Quarterly* 6.2 (January 1929).

30. Bill Freeman and Richard Nielsen, *Far from Home: Canadians in the First World War* (Toronto: McGraw-Hill Ryerson, 1999) 105.

31. Robin Prior and Trevor Wilson, *Command on the Western Front: The Military Career of Sir Henry Rawlinson, 1914–18* (Blackwell Publishers: Oxford, 1992) 40.

32. For more on the science behind these techniques, see J.S. Finan and W.J. Hurley, "McNaughton and Canadian Operational Research at Vimy," *Journal of the Operational Research Society* 48 (1997), 10–14.

33. For counter-battery intelligence gathering, see A.G.L. McNaughton, "Counter Battery Work," *Canadian Defence Quarterly* 3.4 (July 1926) 381–6; Albert Palazzo, "The British Army's Counter-Battery Staff Office and Control of the Enemy in World War I," *Journal of Military History* 63.1 (January 1999).

Chapter 2: From Amateurs to Professionals (pp. 39–54)

1. Pierre Berton, *Marching as to War: Canada's Turbulent Years, 1899–1953* (Toronto: Doubleday, 2001) 134.

2. Henry Borden (ed.), *Robert Laird Borden: His Memoirs*, v. 1 (Toronto: Macmillan, 1938) 457.

3. Berton, *Marching as to War*, 134.

4. Borden, *Robert Laird Borden*, 462–3, 523.

5. For a detailed discussion of the overseas ministry, see Desmond Morton, *A Peculiar Kind of Politics: Canada's Overseas Ministry in the First World War* (Toronto: University of Toronto Press, 1982).

6. LAC, MG 27 II G 1, Series E, Lord Beaverbrook papers, microfilm reel A-1764, Hughes to Aitken, 26 October 1916.

7. G.W.L. Nicholson, *Official History of the Canadian Army in the First World War: Canadian Expeditionary Force, 1914–1919* (Ottawa: Queen's Printer, 1964) 209.

8. For information on Beaverbrook, see Maria Tippett, *Art at the Service of War: Canada, Art and the Great War* (Toronto: University of Toronto Press, 1984) and Tim Cook, *Clio's Warriors: Canadian Historians and the Writing of the World Wars* (Vancouver: University of British Columbia Press, 2006) chapter 1.

9. See H.A. Bruce, *Politics and the Canadian Army Medical Corps* (London, 1919) and Sir Andrew Macphail, *The Medical Services, Official History of the Canadian Forces in the Great War, 1914–1919* (Ottawa: King's Printer, 1925) 156–69.

10. Hugh M. Urquhart, *Arthur Currie: The Biography of a Great Canadian* (Toronto: Dent, 1950) 140.

11. LAC, MG 30 E46, Sir Richard Turner Papers, v. 11, file 78, Turner to Perley, 30 November 1916.

12. Currie has three biographers; Turner has none. See Urquhart, *Arthur Currie* and Hyatt, *General Sir Arthur Currie*, as well as Daniel Dancocks, *Sir Arthur Currie: A Biography* (Toronto: Methuen, 1985).

13. LAC, MG 30 E241, D.E. Macintyre papers, diary, 4 February 1916 and 1 March 1916.

14. House of Commons, Debates, 21 August 1914, 56.

15. For quotation, see entry for "Argyll House," in David Bercuson and J.L. Granatstein, *Dictionary of Canadian Military History* (Toronto: Oxford University Press, 1992) 6.

16. Cowley (ed.), *Georges Vanier*, 38–9.

17. Nicholson, *CEF*, 224.

18. Peter G. Rogers (ed.), *Gunner Ferguson's Diary: The Diary of Gunner Frank Byron Ferguson, 1st Canadian Siege Battery, Canadian Expeditionary Force, 1915–1918* (Hantsport, N.S.: Lancelot Press, 1985) 19.

19. CWM, 19840484-001, W.D. Melvin papers, Willard to Father, 9 Dec 1915.

20. *The Letters of Spr. H. James Elliot, 1916–1919* (unpublished letters: Canadian War Museum library) 11 November 1916.

21. Paul Dickson, "The End of the Beginning: The Canadian Corps in 1917," in Geoffrey Hayes et al. (eds.), *Vimy Ridge: A Canadian Reassessment* (Waterloo: Wilfrid Laurier University Press, 2007) 34.

22. Canadian Letters and Images Project [hereafter CLIP], Herbert D'Alton Bolster, letter to Lloyd, 24 March 1918.

23. CWM, 20030153-001, J.W. McClung papers, diary, 11 June 1916.

24. CWM, 20020054-005, John Saywell papers, letter to parents, 2 August 1917.

25. Ernest Black, *I Want One Volunteer* (Toronto: Ryerson Press, 1965) 93.

26. Norris, *Mainly for Mother*, 47.

27. Daniel Dancocks, *Sir Arthur Currie: A Biography* (Toronto: Methuen, 1985) 80.

28. Morton, *A Peculiar Kind of Politics*, 93. Also see LAC, RG 24, v. 1840, 10–39, Shorncliffe Training Division, Inspection by Major-General Lessard, April 1916.

29. For Currie and Hughes quotations in paragraph, see Stewart, Attack Doctrine, 87–9.

30. For the training schools, see David Campbell, "Schooling for War: Canadian Infantry Training, 1914–1917," in Chris Bullock and Jillian Dowding (eds.), *Perspectives on War: Essays on Security, Society & the State* (Calgary: University of Calgary Press, 2001) 15–30.

31. W.F. Stewart, Attack Doctrine in the Canadian Corps, 1916–1918 (Master's thesis: University of New Brunswick, 1980), 100–1.

32. Morton, *A Peculiar Kind of Politics*, 55.

33. D.J. Corrigall, *The History of the Twentieth Canadian Battalion (Central Ontario Regiment) Canadian Expeditionary Force, in the Great War, 1914–1918* (Toronto: Stone & Cox, 1935) 7.

34. Alexander McClintock, *Best o' Luck: How a Fighting Kentuckian Won the Thanks of Britain's King* (Ottawa: CEF Books, 2000) 7.

35. Reginald Roy (ed.), *The Journal of Private Fraser* (Ottawa: CEF Books, 1998) 23.

36. On training for the 1st Division, see Andrew Iarocci, *Shoestring Soldiers: The 1st Canadian Division at War, 1914–1915* (Toronto: University of Toronto Press, 2008) chapters 1 to 3.

CHAPTER 3: RAIDING—THE LABORATORY OF BATTLE (PP. 55–72)

1. Louis Keene, *"Crumps": The Plain Story of a Canadian Who Went* (Boston: Houghton Mifflin Company, 1917) 110.

2. LAC, RG 24, v. 1826, GAQ 5–89, Raids, Canadian Corps, Summary of Raids.

3. For the value and danger of raids, see Nigel Dorrington, "'Live and Let Die': The British Army's Experience of Trench Raiding 1915–1918," *Journal of the Centre for First World War Studies* 3.1 (September 2007) 1–31.

4. For the preparation, see Andrew B. Godefroy, "A Lesson in Success: The Calonne Trench Raid, 17 January 1917," *Canadian Military History* 8.2 (Spring 1999) 25–9.

5. LAC, Digitized War Diary [hereafter WD], 4th Brigade, Appendix 68, Chronological Notes of Operations, 17 January 1917.

6. Corrigall, *The History of the Twentieth Canadian Battalion*, 102–3.

7. WD, 4th Brigade, Appendix 72, BM.661 – 26/1/17; Will Bird, *The Communication Trench* (Ottawa: CEF Books, 2000) 19.

8. WD, 4th Brigade, Appendix 62.

9. David Campbell, The Divisional Experience in the C.E.F.: A Social and Operational History of the 2nd Canadian Division, 1915–1918 (Ph.D. dissertation: University of Calgary, 2003) 332.

10. Lieutenant General Maurice A. Pope, *Letters from the Front, 1914–1919* (Toronto: Pope and Company, 1996) 79.

11. Urquhart, *Arthur Currie*, 145–6, 157.

12. LAC, MG 30, E300, Victor Odlum papers, v. 24, file Trench Discipline, BM.7-3-270, 6-1-1917.

13. LAC, MG 27 II G 1, Series E, Lord Beaverbrook papers, reel A-1764, Aitken to Hughes, 20 April 1916; Watson to Aitken, 12 October 1915.

14. Brian Bond, "Ironside," John Keegan (ed.), *Churchill's Generals* (London: Warner Books, 1991) 18.

15. For the role of the specialist companies, see Charles H. Foulkes, *Gas: The Story of the Special Brigade* (London: William B. Blackwood & Sons, 1936) and Donald Richter, *Chemical Soldiers: British Gas Warfare in World War I* (Kansas: University Press of Kansas, 1992).

16. LAC, RG 9, v. 3831, 14/3, Gas attack made in successive waves, in Champagne, 31 January 1917.

17. Joseph Hayes, *The Eighty-Fifth in France and Flanders* (Halifax: Royal Print, 1920) 44.

18. LAC, Records of the Canadian Broadcasting Corporation (RG 41), B-III-1, Transcripts to *Flanders Fields*, 1964 CBC Radio program, 54th Battalion, Alex W. Jack, v. 15, program 1/page 11 [hereafter 1/11].

19. LAC, MG 30 E300, Victor Odlum papers, v. 19, file Gas Attack, Vimy Ridge, Odlum to Ironsides, 20/2/17; LAC, RG 41, v. 20, J. Keiller MacKay, 2/11. Lieutenant E.L.M. Burns, a signaller at divisional headquarters, remembered "overhearing General Odlum arguing with division for cancellation of the raid, using very stiff, almost insubordinate language." Burns, *General Mud*, 40.

20. Pierre Berton, *Vimy* (Toronto: McClelland & Stewart, 1986) 128.

21. WD, 12th Brigade, 26 February 1917.

22. LAC, RG 9, v. 3858, 83/3, Operation Order No. 27.

23. The number of cylinders is listed in Richter, *Chemical Soldiers*, 175.

24. LAC, RG 9, v. 4814, Summary of Operations—German Translation of Extracts.

25. LAC, RG 41, v. 16, M. Young, 72nd Battalion, 1/8.

26. LAC, RG 9, v. 3858, 83/4, Messages, 4:44 A.M.

27. WD, 54th Battalion, 1 March 1917.

28. Jack Sheldon and Nigel Cave, *The Battle for Vimy Ridge, 1917* (Barnsley, U.K.: Pen and Sword, 2007) 136.

29. WD, 75th Battalion, 1 March 1917.

30. Alexander McKee, *Vimy Ridge* (London: Souvenir Press, 1966) 41.

31. WD, 73rd Battalion, 1 March 1917.

32. LAC, RG 41, v. 15, Stephen & MacDonald, 50th Battalion, 1/12.

33. WD, 75th Battalion, 1 March 1917.

34. LAC, RG 41, v. 15, Alex W. Jack, 54th Battalion, 1/13.

35. LAC, RG 41, v. 15, Stanley Baker, 54th Battalion, 1/12.

36. For the story of Quinnell, see Tim Cook, "A Proper Slaughter: The March 1917 Gas Raid," *Canadian Military History* 8.2 (Spring 1999) 7–23.

37. LAC, RG 9, v. 3858, 83/4, Preliminary Report on 4th Canadian Division Gas Raid, 1–2; Messages, 5:12 A.M.; LAC, RG 41, v. 16, M. Young, 72nd Battalion, 1/6.

38. LAC, RG 41, v. 16, M. Young, 72nd Battalion, 1/7.

39. LAC, RG 41, v. 15, Stanley Baker, 54th Battalion, 2/2.

40. WD, 73rd Battalion, 1 March 1917.

41. Sheldon and Cave, *The Battle for Vimy Ridge, 1917*, 126.

42. LAC, RG 9, v. 3858, folder 83, file 4, Incident which Occurred after the Gas Operation on the Morning of 1st March; LAC, RG 41, v. 11, 26th Battalion, 5/16–17; WD, 54th Battalion, 1 March 1917.

43. Nicholson, *CEF*, 234. The Canadian Corps' war diary minimizes the high casualties suffered by the raiders. Other units in the Canadian Corps got wind of the disastrous raid, and Lieutenant Stuart Tompkins of the 31st Battalion privately recorded in his diary that there were "bad rumours of the raid, hundreds of casualties. The cause not known but apparently the gas never reached the German lines." Stuart Ramsay Tompkins, *A Canadian's Road to Russia* (Edmonton: University of Alberta Press, 1989) 282.

44. WD, 54th Battalion, 1 March 1917.

45. LAC, RG 41, v. 15, 54th Battalion, Howard Green, 1/10.

CHAPTER 4: BUNGO AND THE BYNG BOYS (PP. 73–92)

1. CWM, 20030153-001, John Wesley McClung papers, diary, 8 April 1917.

2. Corrigal, *The 20th Battalion*, 109.

3. David Woodward, *Lloyd George and the Generals* (London: Associated University Press, 1983) 136.

4. Nicholson, *CEF*, 238.

5. John Turner, "Lloyd George, the War Cabinet and High Politics," in Peter Liddle (ed.), *Passchendaele in Perspective: The Third Battle of Ypres* (Barnsley, U.K.: Pen and Sword, 1997) 17.

6. Robert Blake, *The Private Papers of Douglas Haig, 1914–1919* (London: Eyre & Spottiswoode, 1952) 195.

7. H.F. Wood, *Vimy!* (Toronto: Macmillan of Canada, 1967) 22–3.

8. Michael Boire, "Vimy Ridge: The Battlefield before the Canadians, 1914–1916," in Geoffrey Hayes et al. (eds.), *Vimy Ridge: A Canadian Reassessment* (Waterloo: Wilfrid Laurier University Press, 2007) 59.

9. CWM, Military History Research Centre [hereafter MHRC], R.G. Kentner, *Some Recollections of the Battles of World War I* (self-published, 1995) 24.

10. CWM, MHRC, Ia/33703, Consideration as to the Defence and Construction of Positions, 3 February 1917.

11. R.C. Fetherstonhaugh, *The 24th Battalion, C.E.F., Victoria Rifles of Canada, 1914–1919, Regimental History* (Montreal: Gazette Printing Company, 1930) 142.

12. LAC, RG 9, v. 3846, 51/7, Notes on the Vimy Ridge Operation by General Radcliffe, 2.

13. For information on German unit strength, see Andrew Godefroy, "The German Army at Vimy Ridge," in Geoffrey Hayes et al. (eds.), *Vimy Ridge: A Canadian Reassessment* (Waterloo: Wilfrid Laurier University Press, 2007) 227; David Nash (ed.), *German Army Handbook, April 1918* (London: Arms and Armour Press, 1977) 33–5.

14. Heinz Hagenlucke, "The German High Command," in Peter Liddle (ed.), *Passchendaele in Perspective: The Third Battle of Ypres* (Barnsley, U.K.: Pen and Sword, 1997) 48.

15. LAC, MG 30 E300, Victor Odlum papers, v. 21, Odlum to Nelson, 4 November 1917.

16. LAC, RG 41, v. 16, 72nd Battalion, Harry Bond, 1/13–14.

17. D.E. Macintyre, *Canada at Vimy* (Toronto: Peter Martin, 1967) 100.

18. Captain Cyril Falls, *History of the Great War: Military Operations, France and Belgium, 1917*, v. 1 (London: Macmillan, 1940) 308.

19. Stephen Beames, untitled memoirs, 39. In author's possession; courtesy of Sarah Ross, and Martha and Miriam Beames.

20. Ron Corbett, "I am the last of my generation," Canada.com News, 12 November 2002.

21. Kim Beattie, *Dileas: History of the 48th Highlanders of Canada 1929–1956* (Toronto: 48th Highlanders of Canada, 1957) 211.

22. CWM, CP, 58A.1.59.4, Report of Operations Carried Out by the 1st Canadian Division, April 9th–May 5th, 1917.

23. LAC, CP, v. 35, file 159, Notes on French Attacks Northeast of Verdun in October and December 1916.

24. Jeffery Williams, *Byng of Vimy: General and Governor General* (London: Leo Cooper in association with Secker & Warburg, 1983) 152.

25. Robert England, M.C., *Recollections of a Nonagenarian of Service in the Royal Canadian Regiment (1916–19)* (self-published, 1983) 2.

26. LAC, RG 9, v. 3846, 51/7, Notes on the Vimy Ridge Operation by General Radcliffe, 19; Colonel A. Fortescue Duguid, "The Significance of Vimy," *Canadian Defence Quarterly* 12 (October 1934 to July 1935) 399.

27. LAC, MG 30 E15, W.A. Griesbach papers, v. 3, file 18 (B), B.M.R. 516, A.C. Macdonell to all battalions, 10 March 1917.

28. LAC, MG 30 E15, W.A. Griesbach papers, v. 3, file 16(a), The Book of Wisdom, 122-10, 1st Brigade to Battalion commanders, 24 March 1917.

29. Patrick Brennan, "Julian Byng and Leadership in the Canadian Corps," in Geoffrey Hayes et al. (eds.), *Vimy Ridge: A Canadian Reassessment* (Waterloo: Wilfrid Laurier University Press, 2007) 98–9.

30. Wilfred Bovey, "The Old Canadian Corps," *The Legionary* (March 1965) 9–10.

31. LAC, RG 9, v. 3846, 51/5, Report of Operations of Canadian Corps against Vimy Ridge, 5.

32. Falls, *Military Operations, France and Belgium, 1917*, v. 1, 306.

33. Trevor Wilson, *The Myriad Faces of War: Britain and the Great War 1914–1918* (Cambridge: Polity Press, 1986) 453.

34. For the corps' fire plan, see WD, Royal Artillery, Canadian Corps, April 1917, Canadian Corps, Artillery Instruction for the Capture of Vimy Ridge, Appendix G.1.

35. Wood, *Vimy!* 34.

36. CWM, 19730295-007, Walter Draycot papers, The Story of Vimy Ridge, 8.

37. Generalleutnant Alfred Dieterich, "The German 79th Reserve Infantry Division in the Battle of Vimy Ridge, April 1917," *Canadian Military History* 15.1 (Winter 2006) 74.

38. G.W.L. Nicholson, *The Gunners of Canada: The History of the Royal Regiment of Canadian Artillery. Volume I: 1534–1919* (Toronto: McClelland & Stewart, 1967) 282.

39. WD, Royal Artillery, Canadian Corps, April 1917, Canadian Corps, Artillery Instruction for the Capture of Vimy Ridge, G.4.

40. CWM, 19930041-002, Edouard Leprohon papers, diary, 7 April 1917.

41. See Tim Cook, "The Gunners at Vimy: 'We Are Hammering Fritz to Pieces,'" in Geoffrey Hayes et al. (eds.), *Vimy Ridge: A Canadian Reassessment* (Waterloo: Wilfrid Laurier University Press, 2007) 105–24.

42. LAC, RG 9, III, v. 3922, 8/4, Notes on Counter Battery Work in Connection with the Capture of Vimy Ridge.

43. CWM, 20020130-001, William Antliff papers, letter, 8 April 1917.

44. Peter Hart, *Bloody April: Slaughter over the Skies in Arras 1917* (London: McArthur & Co / Orion Con Trade, 2005).

45. Nicholson, *Gunners of Canada*, v. 1, 282; Dieterich, "The German 79th Reserve Infantry Division," 75.

46. Brennan, "Julian Byng and Leadership in the Canadian Corps," 91.

47. LAC, CP, v. 10, file 32 (L), Currie to Neville Lindsay, 11 July 1933.

48. A.F. Duguid, *History of the Canadian Grenadier Guards, 1760–1964* (Montreal: Gazette Print Co., 1965) 138–9; Godefroy, "The German Army at Vimy Ridge," in Geoffrey Hayes et al. (eds.), *Vimy Ridge: A Canadian Reassessment* (Waterloo: Wilfrid Laurier University Press, 2007) 230.

49. LAC, RG 9, v. 3922, 8/2, Administrative Arrangements—Vimy Ridge Operations, 7.

50. CWM, 19730295-007, Walter Draycot papers, The Story of Vimy Ridge, 4.

51. Jonathan Nicholls, *Cheerful Sacrifice: The Battle of Arras, 1917* (London: Cooper, 1993) 57.

52. WD, 4th Division, Appendix B, unnamed [Report of 4th Division at Vimy], 21.

53. Official records vary on the number of tunnels, but estimates range from eleven to thirteen. For a map of the thirteen tunnels, see Jack Sheldon and Nigel Cave, *The Battle for Vimy Ridge, 1917* (Barnsley, U.K.: Pen and Sword, 2007) 55.

54. WD, 4th Division, Appendix B, unnamed [Report of 4th Division at Vimy], 23.

55. Dieterich, "The German 79th Reserve Infantry Division," 75.

56. WD, 4th Division, Appendix B, unnamed [Report of 4th Division at Vimy], 21.

57. LAC, MG 30 E15, W.A. Griesbach papers, v. 2, file 12, Currie to GOC, 1st Brigade, 4 April 1917.

58. CWM, edited transcripts for *Flanders Fields*, series 9, page 5.

CHAPTER 5: "YOU LIVE LIKE PIGS, AND YOU KILL LIKE PIGS" (PP. 93–106)

1. LAC, MG 30 E50, Elmer Jones papers, Translation of "Battle of Arras, 1917" by the German General Staff.

2. Berton, *Vimy*, 158.

3. LAC, RG 24, v. 1821, file GAQ 5-17, Report of Operations of Canadian Corps against Vimy Ridge, 3.

4. James MacGregor, *MacGregor V.C.* (Victoria: Victoria Publishing Company, 2002) 66.

5. Stephen Beames, untitled memoirs, 30.

6. R.C. Fetherstonhaugh, *The Royal Montreal Regiment, 14th Battalion, C.E.F.* (Montreal: Gazette Printing Company, 1927) 239.

7. Donald Stuart Macpherson, *A Soldier's Diary: The WWI Diaries of Donald MacPherson* (St. Catharines: Vanwell, 2001) 57.

8. WD, 5th Battalion, 9 April 1917; and Summary of operations on 9 April.

9. LAC, RG 9, v. 3846, 51/2, 2nd Brigade Narrative of Events.

10. WD, 5th Battalion, Summary of operations on 9 April.

11. Foster, *Letters from the Front*, 206.

12. CWM, *Flanders Fields*, 9/14.

13. LAC, RG 9, v. 3846, 51/2, 2nd Brigade Narrative of Events.

14. LAC, RG 9, v. 4051, 19/2, 15th Battalion Summary of Operations, 9 to 20 April 1917.

15. CWM, *Flanders Fields*, 9/12, H. Campbell; Beattie, *48th Highlanders of Canada*, 225.

16. WD, 14th Battalion, Report of Operations on 9 April; CWM, CP, 58A.1.59.4, Report of Operations Carried Out by the 1st Canadian Division, April 9th–May 5th, 1917.

17. LAC, RG 24, v. 20409, 958.009 (D40), Interview transcript with Archie McWade, no date [hereafter n.d.] [ca. early 1960s].

18. McClintock, *Best o' Luck*, 96.

19. Andrew Iarocci, "The 1st Canadian Division: An Operational Mosaic," in Geoffrey Hayes et al. (eds.), *Vimy Ridge: A Canadian Reassessment* (Waterloo: Wilfrid Laurier University Press, 2007) 159.

20. WD, 16th Battalion, 11 April 1917.

21. LAC, MG 30 E430, William Green papers, memoir, 4.

22. LAC, RG 9, v. 3846, 51/1, 3rd Battalion, Report of Operations [for Vimy Operation].

CHAPTER 6: "EVEN IF ONE MAN [IS] LEFT ALIVE THE OBJECTIVE MUST BE TAKEN AND HELD" (PP. 107–116)

1. Nicholls, *Cheerful Sacrifice*, 68–9.

2. For Burstall, see Campbell, The Divisional Experience in the C.E.F.: A Social and Operational History of the 2nd Canadian Division, 1915–1918, chapter 6.

3. LAC, RG 9, v. 3827, 6/23–26, Minutes of Conference of Corps Commanders, 29 March 1917.

4. WD, Royal Artillery, Canadian Corps, April 1917, Artillery Instructions, No. 2.

5. Dieterich, "The German 79th Reserve Infantry Division," 76.

6. WD, 18th Battalion, 9 April 1917; WD, 19th Battalion, 10 April 1917.

7. Lieutenant R. Lewis, *Over the Top with the 25th* (Halifax: H.H. Marshall, 1918) 52.

8. David Campbell, "The 2nd Canadian Division: A 'Most Spectacular Battle," in Geoffrey Hayes et al. (eds.), *Vimy Ridge: A Canadian Reassessment* (Waterloo: Wilfrid Laurier University Press, 2007) 178.

9. WD, 25th Battalion, 9 April 1917; WD, 21st Battalion, 9 April 1917.

10. WD, 31st Battalion, Report of Operations, 9 April 1917.

11. Dieterich, "The German 79th Reserve Infantry Division," 77.

12. LAC, MG 30 E351, Claude Craig papers, diary, 9 April 1917.

13. Lewis, *Over the Top with the 25th*, 55.

14. D.J. Goodspeed, *The Road Past Vimy: The Canadian Corps 1914–1918* (Toronto: Macmillan, 1969) 90.

15. D.E. Macintyre, *Canada at Vimy* (Toronto: Peter Martin, 1967) 112.

16. LAC, RG 41, v. 11, 27th Battalion, W.J. Sheppard, 1/9–10.

17. WD, 27th Battalion, 9–12 April 1917.

18. W.W. Murray, *The History of the 2nd Canadian Battalion* (Ottawa: The Historical Committee, 1947) 168–9.

19. Roy (ed.), *The Journal of Private Fraser*, 268.

20. Casualties compiled in Campbell, "A Most Spectacular Battle," 185; and Iarocci, "The 1st Canadian Division: An Operational Mosaic," 166.

21. WD, 6th Brigade, Narrative of operations, 9–10 April 1917.

22. Macphail, *The Medical Services*, 99–100.

23. Berton, *Vimy*, 236.

CHAPTER 7: "THERE BEFORE US, FRIGHTFULLY CLOSE, WAS THE EDGE OF HELL" (PP. 117–138)

1. William Breckenridge, *From Vimy to Mons* (self-published, 1919) 19.

2. For an appreciation of Lipsett's skills as an instructor, see Anonymous, "Major-General Louis James Lipsett," *Canadian Defence Quarterly* 6 (1928–29) 293–300.

3. LAC, RG 9, v. 3846, 51/7, Notes on the Vimy Ridge Operation by General Radcliffe, 14.

4. WD, 3rd Division, Narrative of operations, 9–14 April 1917.

5. WD, 1st Canadian Mounted Rifles, 9 April 1917.

6. CWM, 19920187-002, H.H. Burrell papers, diary, 9 April 1917; Falls, *Military Operations, France and Belgium 1917*, v. 1, 325.

7. WD, 1st CMR, Report of Operations Carried Out by the 1st CMR on 9 April 1917.

8. WD, 1st CMR, 12 April 1917.

9. CWM, 19920187-002, H.H. Burrell papers, diary, 9 April 1917.

10. LAC, RG 24, v. 20409, 958.009 (D40), Burgess to Wood, 13 November 1963.

11. CWM, *Flanders Fields*, 9/16.

12. MacGregor, *MacGregor V.C.*, 66–7.

13. WD, 2nd CMR, Appendix B, Operations against Vimy Ridge.

14. LAC, R8258, Gregory Clark papers, memoirs, unpaginated [Vimy narrative].

15. S.G. Bennett, *The 4th Canadian Mounted Rifles, 1914–1919* (Toronto: Murray Printing, 1926) 55.

16. WD, 4th CMR, Report by Lt. Col. H.D.L. Gordon, 9 April 1917.

17. LAC, RG 9, v. 3846, 51/5, 8th Brigade, Summary of Operations.

18. N.M. Christie (ed.), *Letters of Agar Adamson, 1914 to 1919* (Ottawa: CEF Books, 1997) 274.

19. Zubkowski, *As Long as Faith and Freedom Last*, 270.

20. Brereton Greenhous and Stephen J. Harris, *Canada and the Battle of Vimy Ridge: 9–12 April 1917* (Ottawa: Department of National Defence, 1992) 99–102.

CHAPTER 8: "WE WILL TAKE IT OR NEVER COME BACK" (PP. 129–140)

1. WD, 72nd Battalion, Preliminary Report of operation, 9/4/17.

2. WD, 12th Brigade, Report of Operations [for Vimy Operation].

3. CWM, 58A 1.171.29, T.W. MacDowell, Notebook, 9 April 1917.

4. LAC, RG 41, v. 16, 78th Battalion, D.G. Anderson, 1/1.

5. LAC, RG 41, v. 16, 78th Battalion, Stewart Scott, 1/10.

6. WD, 102nd Battalion, 9 April 1917.

7. Sheldon and Cave, *The Battle for Vimy Ridge, 1917,* 151.

8. Wood, *Vimy!* 140–1.

9. Figures drawn from the war diaries of the 54th and 102nd Battalions.

10. William Gray, *More Letters from Billy* (Toronto: McClelland, Goodchild & Stewart, 1917) 31.

11. Who called off the barrage and why it was never reinstated has remained a minor controversy in Canadian military history. See Falls, *Military Operations, France and Belgium 1917*, v. 1, 328; and Andrew Godefroy, "The German Army at Vimy Ridge," in Geoffrey Hayes, et al. (eds.), *Vimy Ridge: A Canadian Reassessment* (Waterloo: Wilfrid Laurier University Press, 2007) 225–38.

12. WD, 4th Division, Appendix B, unnamed [Report of 4th Division at Vimy], 24, 26.

13. Hayes, *The Eighty-Fifth in France and Flanders*, 53.

14. WD, 85th Battalion, Appendix A, Operations covering 8-4-17 to 14-4-17.

15. The war diary states 50 dead and 122 wounded for the period of 9–12 April. WD, 85th Battalion, Appendix A, Operations covering 8-4-17 to 14-4-17.

16. CWM, 19730295-007, Walter Draycot papers, The Story of Vimy Ridge, 10.

17. Wheeler, *The 50th Battalion in No Man's Land*, 95–6.

18. Tom Edgett and Dave Beatty (eds.), *The World War I Diaries and Letters of Louis Stanley Edgett* (Riverview: J.T. Edgett, 2005) 228.

19. WD, 50th Battalion, 10 April 1917.

20. CWM, *Flanders Fields*, 9/26, D.M. Marshall.

21. Kentner, *Some Recollections of the Battles of World War I*, 41.

22. LAC, RG 24, v. 1825, file GAQ 5-65, 4th Canadian Division at Vimy, 9th to 13th April 1917.

23. Sheldon and Cave, *The Battle for Vimy Ridge, 1917*, 168.

24. WD, 50th Battalion, 12 April 1917.

25. Wheeler, *The 50th Battalion in No Man's Land*, 100–1.

26. Jeffrey Williams, *Byng of Vimy* (Toronto: University of Toronto Press, 1983, 1992) 165.

CHAPTER 9: A VICTORY TOO COSTLY? (PP. 141–148)

1. CWM, 19730295-007, Walter Draycot papers, The Story of Vimy Ridge, 1.

2. Dieterich, "The German 79th Reserve Infantry Division," 82.

3. CWM, 20020130-001, William Antliff papers, letter, 13 April 1917.

4. LAC, MG 30 E241, D.E. Macintyre papers, diary, 9 April 1917.

5. Nicholson, *CEF*, 265.

6. Wood, *Vimy!* 158.

7. LAC, RG 24, v. 20409, 958.009 (D40), Diary of A.F. Brayman.

8. Nicholson notes that the casualties sustained in capturing the ridge on April 9 and 10 were 7,707; General Radcliffe estimated 8,000 for the same time frame. Nicholson, *CEF*, 261; LAC, RG 9, v. 3846, 51/7, Notes on the Vimy Ridge Operation by General Radcliffe, 34.

9. Murray, *History of the 2nd Battalion*, 170.

10. Wood, *Vimy!* 160.

11. Nicholls, *Cheerful Sacrifice*, 210; John Terraine, *The Smoke and the Fire: Myths and Anti-Myths of War, 1861–1945* (London: Sidgwick and Jackson, 1980) 46.

12. Sir Frederick Maurice (ed.), *The Life of General Lord Rawlinson of Trent: from his journals and letters* (London: Cassell, 1928) 191–2.

13. Peter Simkins, *The First World War: The Western Front, 1917–1918* (Oxford: Osprey, 2002) 28.

14. For the mutinies, see Leonard Smith, *Between Mutiny and Obedience: The Case of the French Fifth Infantry Division during World War I* (Princeton: Princeton University Press, 1994).

15. Goodspeed, *The Road Past Vimy*, 92.

16. Gary Sheffield, "Vimy Ridge and the Battle of Arras: A British Perspective," in Geoffrey Hayes et al. (eds.), *Vimy Ridge: A Canadian Reassessment* (Waterloo: Wilfrid Laurier University Press, 2007) 22.

17. CWM, *Flanders Fields*, 9/30.

18. Cowley, *Georges Vanier*, 190.

19. Total strength of the BEF in April 1917 was 1,893,874, all arms and all ranks. Peter Scott, "Law and Orders: Discipline and Morale in the British Armies in France, 1917," in

Peter Liddle (ed.), *Passchendaele in Perspective: The Third Battle of Ypres* (Barnsley, U.K.: Pen and Sword, 1997) 349.

20. Brian D. Tenyson, "A Cape Bretoner at War: Letters from the Front, 1914–1919," *Canadian Military History* 11.1 (Winter 2002) 44.

21. CWM, 19950008-014, Samuel Honey papers, letter to parents, 18 April 1917.

22. Kevin Shackleton, *Second to None: The Fighting 58th Battalion of the Canadian Expeditionary Force* (Toronto: Dundurn Press, 2002) 131.

CHAPTER 10: "DO YOUR DUTY AND FIGHT TO THE FINISH" (PP. 149–168)

1. John Macfie, *Letters Home* (Parry Sound: J. Macfie, 1990) 120.

2. Nicholson, *CEF*, 240.

3. CLIP, John Ellis, Ellis to "Darling Kitty," 14 April 1917.

4. CWM, 58A 1 47.9, Courtney Tower papers, diary, 13 April 1917.

5. The Adjutant [E.P.S. Allen] *The 116th Battalion in France* (Toronto: Hunted Rose, 1921) 25.

6. Nicholson, *CEF*, 270.

7. Matthew Hughes, "Edmund Allenby, Third Army, 1915–1917," in Ian Beckett and Steven Corvi (eds.), *Haig's Generals* (Barnsley, U.K.: Pen and Sword, 2006) 26.

8. WD, 8th Battalion, Operational Order, 25 April 1917; WD, 1st Division, Battle of Arleux, 28 April 1917.

9. LAC, RG 9, v. 3922, 8/1, Expenditure during recent operations on wire, trenches and villages by CCDHA trench batteries, 11.5.17.

10. WD, 1st Division, 27 April 1917; also see the artillery appreciation, RG 9, v. 3906, 24/8, Artillery Order No. 16.

11. CWM, MHRC, Ia/32662A, Principles of Command in the Defensive Battle in Position Warfare.

12. WD, 10th Battalion, 2nd Infantry Brigade, Operational Order No. 192.

13. WD, 8th Battalion, 26–27 April 1917.

14. WD, 10th Battalion, 2nd Infantry Brigade, Instructions for the Attack, No. 2.

15. WD, 10th Battalion, Report of Operations, Attack on Arleux, 28 April 1917.

16. WD, 10th Battalion, Appendix B to Operations.

17. WD, 10th Battalion, 2nd Infantry Brigade, Operational Order No. 192.

18. WD, 10th Battalion, Report of Operations, Attack on Arleux, 28 April 1917; Casualties listed in WD, 5th Battalion, 28 May 1917.

19. LAC, RG 9, v. 3906, 24/8, Artillery Order No. 19.

20. WD, 1st Division, Battle of Arleux, 28 April 1917, 7:25 P.M.

21. WD, 2nd Brigade, Operational Order 194.

22. Falls, *Military Operations France and Belgium 1917*, v. 1, 426.

23. Gary Sheffield, "Vimy Ridge and the Battle of Arras," 26.

24. Falls, *Military Operations France and Belgium 1917*, v. 1, 424.

25. Urquhart, *Arthur Currie*, 157.

26. Mike Bechthold, "In the Shadow of Vimy Ridge: The Canadian Corps in April and May 1917," in Geoffrey Hayes et al. (eds.), *Vimy Ridge: A Canadian Reassessment* (Waterloo: Wilfrid Laurier University Press, 2007) 251.

27. CWM, 58A 1.8.5, William Woods papers, A Private's Own Story of the First World War, 10.

28. WD, 1st Division, Narrative of Events, 3 May 1917, 2:50 A.M.; Urquhart, *Arthur Currie*, 156.

29. Murray, *History of the 2nd Battalion*, 176.

30. LAC, MG 30 E15, William Griesbach papers, v. 2, file 12, Summary of Operations of the Second Stage of the Attack on the Arleux and Fresnoy Positions.

31. Karl Weatherbe, *From the Rideau to the Rhine: The 6th Field Company and Battalion, Canadian Engineers, in the Great War* (Toronto: Hunter, Rose & Company, 1928) 242.

32. LAC, MG 30 E15, William Griesbach papers, v. 2, file 12, Summary of Operations of the Second Stage of the Attack on the Arleux and Fresnoy Positions.

33. CWM, 19930041-002, Edouard Leprohon papers, diary, 3 May 1917.

34. CWM, 58A 1.8.5. William Woods papers, A Private's Own Story of the First World War, 11.

35. LAC, RG 9, v. 3847, 55/4, 1st Brigade Report of Fresnoy Operation; Nicholson, *CEF*, 277.

36. Bert Walker, *A Soldier's Story* (self-published, 1998) 64.

37. W.B. Kerr, *Shrieks and Crashes: Being Memories of Canada's Corps 1917* (Toronto: Hunter, Rose & Company, 1929) 45.

38. Roy (ed.), *The Journal of Private Fraser*, 281.

39. Bruce Cane (ed.), *It Made You Think of Home: The Haunting Journal of Deward Barnes, CEF 1916–1919* (Toronto: Dundurn Press, 2004) 79.

40. Cane, *It Made You Think of Home*, 82.

41. LAC, CP, v. 1, file A to F, Currie to Brewster, 31 May 1917.

42. *Hansard*, 6 July 1917, 3094.

43. CWM, CP, 58A 1.59.4, 1st Canadian Division's Report on Vimy and Subsequent Fighting, 9 April to 5 May 1917.

44. Edgett and Beatty (eds.), *The World War I Diaries and Letters of Louis Stanley Edgett*, 232.

CHAPTER 11: "GOOD TO BE BACK IN CIVILIZATION" (PP. 169–178)

1. CWM, 20000013-008, George Ormsby papers, George to Maggie, 28 January 1916.

2. CWM, 19810740-054, Charles Pearce papers, Pearce to Dad, 10 March 1916.

3. Jeff Keshen, *Propaganda and Censorship during Canada's Great War* (Edmonton: University of Alberta Press, 1996) 142.

4. William Ogilvie, *Umty-Iddy-Umty: The Story of a Canadian Signaller in the First World War* (Erin, Ontario: The Boston Mills Press, 1982) 45.

5. Herbert Rae, *Maple Leaves in Flanders Fields* (Toronto: William Briggs, 1916) 43.

6. Hugh Kay, *The History of the Forty-third Battery, C.F.A.* (self-published, 1916) 11.

7. J. Clinton Morrison, *Hell upon Earth: A Personal Account of Prince Edward Island Soldiers in the Great War, 1914–1918* (Summerside, P.E.I.: J.C. Morrison, 1995) 194.

8. O.C.S. Wallace (ed.), *From Montreal to Vimy Ridge and Beyond* (Toronto: McClelland & Stewart, 1917) 283.

9. Morrison, *Hell upon Earth*, 34.

10. For a theoretical discussion of soldier-tourists, see Richard White, "The Soldier as Tourist: The Australian Experience of the Great War," *War & Society* 5.1 (May 1987) 63–77.

11. CLIP, William (Bill) Hutchinson, 26 March 1916.

12. CWM, 19650038-014, William E.L. Coleman papers, Coleman to wife, 28 March 1916.

13. Pope, *Letters from the Front*, 98.

14. Kerr, *Shrieks and Crashes*, 2.

15. CWM, 58A 1.34.8, H.C. Mason papers, Mason to folks, 10 April 1918.

16. Herbert McBride, *A Rifleman Went to War* (South Carolina: Thomas Samworth, 1935) 243–4.

17. CWM, MHRC, Oswald C. J. Withrow, *Facts for Fighters* (Toronto: Military Service Department of the National Council of the Young Men's Christian Associations of Canada, Toronto, 1918) 5.

18. Roy (ed.), *The Journal of Private Fraser*, 72.

19. John Callan (ed.), *The Original WWI Diary of Herbert 'Bert' Cooke* (self-published, n.d.) 57.

20. CWM, 19950008-014, Samuel Honey papers, Sam to mother and father, 4 January 1916.

21. Dale McClare (ed.), *The Letters of a Young Canadian Soldier During World War I* (Kentville: Brook House Press, 2000) 64.

22. CWM, 20020130-001, W.S. Antliff papers, letter, 10 July 1918.

23. T.J. Mitchell and G.M. Smith, *Medical Services: Casualties and Medical Statistics of the Great War* (London: Imperial War Museum, reprint 1997, original 1931) 75–7.

24. Desmond Morton, "A Canadian Soldier in the Great War: The Experience of Frank Maheux," *Canadian Military History* 1.1 & 2 (Autumn 1992) 82.

25. Jay Cassel, *The Secret Plague: Venereal Disease in Canada, 1838–1939* (Toronto: University of Toronto Press, 1987) 123.

26. Cheryl Warsh, Moments of Unreason: The Homewood Retreat and the Practice of Early Canadian Psychiatry, 1883–1923 (Ph.D dissertation: Queen's University, 1987) 148.

27. CWM, 20010241-015, Hendershott brothers papers, Warren Hendershott to parents, 29 April 1918.

28. John Becker, *Silhouettes of the Great War: The Memoirs of John Harold Becker* (Ottawa: CEF Books, 2001) 144.

29. Macfie, *Letters Home*, 50.

30. CWM, 20000003-002, G.F. McFarland papers, memoirs, 3 December 1917.

CHAPTER 12: "SING ME TO SLEEP WHERE BULLETS FALL" (PP. 179–196)

1. LAC, CP, v. 13, file 40, Currie to Rochfort, 15 August 1922.

2. CWM, 20000013-008, George Ormsby papers, George to Maggie, 10 June 1915.

3. *Report of the Ministry, Overseas Military Forces of Canada, 1918* (London, 1919) 88.

4. CWM, 20040015-005, Lawrence Rogers papers, Lawrence to May, 10 June 1915.

5. Foster, *Letters from the Front*, 49.

6. Grace Morris Craig, *But This Is Our War* (Toronto: University of Toronto Press, 1981) 40.

7. Clifford Wells, *From Montreal to Vimy Ridge and Beyond: The Correspondence of Lieut. Clifford Almon Wells, B.A. of the 8th Battalion, Canadians, B.E.F., November, 1915–April 1917* (Toronto: McClelland, Goodchild & Stewart, 1917) 234.

8. CLIP, John Ellis, Ellis to "Darling Wifey," 11 February 1917.

9. Ken Tingley (ed.), *The Path of Duty: The Wartime Letters of Alwyn Bramley-Moore, 1914–1916* (Alberta: Historical Society of Alberta, 1998) 74; CWM, 19820183-026, Ronald Main papers, Ronald to father, 17 October 1916.

10. CWM, 19950008-014, Samuel Honey papers, Sam to parents, 14 November 1916.

11. CWM, 199000227-001, Alfred E. Baggs, Baggs to wife, 13 March 1916.

12. Kerr, *Shrieks and Crashes*, 145.

13. Morrison, *Hell upon Earth*, 84.

14. See Ian Miller, *Our Glory and Our Grief: Torontonians and the Great War* (Toronto: University of Toronto Press, 2001) for a discussion on the impact of letters published in Canada. Keshen's *Propaganda and Censorship* suggests there was stronger censorship.

15. Lieutenant Stanley Rutledge, *Pen Pictures from the Trenches* (Toronto: William Briggs, 1918) 117.

16. *The Listening Post* 29 (1 December 1917), 31. No full set of Canadian trench newspapers has survived, but large collections are archived at the Library and Archives Canada and the Canadian War Museum, both of which have been consulted for this book.

17. *The Listening Post* 29 (1 December 1917), 31.

18. David Clarke, "Rumours of Angels: A Legend of the First World War," *Folklore* 113/2 (2002) 151–75.

19. Arthur Machen, *The Bowmen and Other Legends of the War* (London: Simkin, Marshall, Hamilton & Kent, 1915).

20. Rutledge, *Pen Pictures from the Trenches*, 56.

21. Randal Marlin, *Propaganda and the Ethics of Persuasion* (Peterborough: Broadview Press, 2002) 71–4.

22. CWM, 19980050-005, Herbert Clemens papers, letter, 10 May 1917.

23. See David Clarke, *The Angel of Mons: Phantom Stories and Ghostly Guardians* (West Sussex: Wiley, 2004).

24. J.G. Fuller, *Troop Morale and Popular Culture in the British and Dominion Armies, 1914–1918* (Oxford: Clarendon Press, 1990) 15.

25. CWM, *R.M.R. Growler* 1 (1 January 1916) 1.

26. Corrigall, *The History of the Twentieth Canadian Battalion*, 7.

27. CWM, *The Brazier* 1 (15 February 1916) 5.

28. CWM, *Dead Horse Corner Gazette* 1 (October 1915) 5.

29. H.M. Urquhart, *History of the 16th Battalion (The Canadian Scottish), Canadian Expeditionary Force, in the Great War, 1914–1919* (Toronto: Macmillan Company of Canada, 1932) 344.

30. CLIP, Robert Hale, letter, 22 February 1915.

31. Wells, *From Montreal to Vimy Ridge and Beyond*, 197.

32. CWM, 19950008-014, Samuel Honey papers, Sam to parents, 6 September 1916.

33. R.J. Manion, *A Surgeon in Arms* (Toronto: McClelland, Goodchild & Stewart, 1918) 52–3.

34. Michael Gauvreau, "Baptist Religion and the Social Science of Harold Innis," *Canadian Historical Review* 76.2 (June 1995) 174.

35. Ogilvie, *Umty-Iddy-Umty*, 10.

36. L. McLeod Gould, *From B.C. to Baisieux: Being the Narrative of the 102nd Canadian Infantry Battalion* (Victoria: R. Cusack Presses, 1919) 107.

37. John Brophy and Eric Partridge, *The Long Trail: What the British Soldier Sang and Said in the Great War, 1914–18* (London: Andre Deutsch, 1965) 24.

38. Foster, *Letters from the Front*, 59.

39. For surviving lyrics and the importance of songs, see Roy Palmer *"What a Lovely War!" British Soldiers' Songs* (London: Joseph, 1990); Regina M. Sweeney, *Singing Our Way to Victory: French Cultural Politics and Music during the Great War* (Middletown: Wesleyan University Press, 2001).

40. Wheeler, *The 50th Battalion*, 47.

41. Wood, *Vimy!*, 49.

42. Manion, *A Surgeon in Arms*, 20.

CHAPTER 13: "CAMARADERIE OF THE DAMNED" (PP. 197–218)

1. Foster, *Letters from the Front*, 159.

2. LAC, MG 30 E113, George Bell papers, memoir, Back to Blighty, 11.

3. LAC, MG 30 E220, E.W. Russell papers, memoir, A Private Soldier's View of the Great War, 1914–1918, 37.

4. LAC, MG 30 E132, Thomas Dalton Johnston papers, Dearest Dyne, 8 March 1917.

5. Stephane Audoin-Rouzeau and Annette Becker, *1914–1918 Understanding the Great War* (London: L Profile, 2002) 25a.

6. Richard Holmes, *Firing Line* (London: Jonathan Cape, 1985) 215.

7. Cited in Major General Sir Archibald Montgomery, *The Story of the Fourth Army in the Battles of the Hundred Days, August 8th to November 11th, 1918* (London: Hodder and Stoughton, [1920]) 1.

8. LAC, MG 30 E15, W.A. Griesbach papers, v. 1, file 7: Memo, 1st Brigade, 2 January 1919.

9. LAC, RG 41, v. 13, 42nd Battalion, James Page, 2/4.

10. LAC, RG 41, v. 10, 18th Battalion, Cyril Searle, 1/6.

11. Morrison, *Hell upon Earth*, 196.

12. James Pedley, *Only This: A War Retrospect* (Ottawa: Graphic, 1927) 16.

13. Morton, *When Your Number's Up*, 73.

14. Coningsby Dawson, *Living Bayonets: A Record of the Last Push* (Toronto: Gundy, 1919) 191.

15. Harold Baldwin, *Holding the Line* (Toronto: G.J. McLeod, 1918) 6.

16. S.L.A. Marshall, *Men against Fire: The Problem of Battle Command* (Norman, OK: University of Oklahoma Press, 2000); Fuller, *Troop Morale*, chapter 2; Anthony Kellett, *Combat Motivation: The Behavior of Soldiers in Battle* (Boston: Kluwer, 1982).

17. LAC, MG 30 E50, Elmer Jones papers, v. 1, file 4, Canadian Corps Officers' School of Instruction, Notes on Leadership for Company Officers, n.d.

18. LAC, RG 41, v. 10, W.P. Doolan, 1/12.

19. Morton, *When Your Number's Up*, 111.

20. Stephen Beames, untitled memoirs, 39.

21. Hugh R. Kay, *Battery Action! The Story of the 43rd (Howitzer) Battery, Canadian Field Artillery, 1916–1919* (Ottawa: CEF Books, 2002) 107–8.

22. See G.D. Sheffield, *Leadership in the Trenches* (London: Macmillan, 2000).

23. CWM, 20020130-001, W.S. Antliff papers, 2–3 September 1918.

24. LAC, RG 9, v. 3751, P.G. Bell, diary, 23 December 1914.

25. Gordon Pimm (ed.), *Leo's War: From Gaspé to Vimy* (Ottawa: Partnership Publishers, 2007) 121.

26. LAC, CP, v. 1, file 1, Currie to Brewster, 31 May 1917.

27. See Ronald Haycock, "'The Stuff of Armies': The NCO throughout History," in Douglas L. Bland (ed.), *Backbone of the Army: Non-Commissioned Officers in the Future Army* (Montreal and Kingston: McGill-Queen's University Press, 2000).

28. E.S. Russenholt, *Six Thousand Canadian Men: Being the History of the 44th Battalion, Canadian Infantry, 1914–1919* (Winnipeg: Printed to the order of Forty-Fourth Battalion Association by the Montfort Press, 1932) 130.

29. LAC, MG 30 E220, E.W. Russell papers, memoir, A Private Soldier's View of the Great War, 1914–1918, 33.

30. LAC, MG 30 E50, Elmer Jones papers, v. 1, file 4, Canadian Corps Officers' School, Lecture, "The Duties and Responsibilities of an Officer," by Brigadier General, GS, 21 July 1916.

31. J.F.B. Livesay, *Canada's Hundred Days* (London: T. Allen, 1919) 10.

32. LAC, MG 30 E220, E.W. Russell papers, memoir, A Private Soldier's View of the Great War, 1914–1918, 44.

33. Dancocks, *Sir Arthur Currie*, 131.

34. Cane (ed.), *It Made You Think of Home*, 165.

35. Thomas P. Rowlett, *Memoirs of a Signaller, 1914–1918* (unpublished memoir, CWM library, n.d.) 32.

36. For scholarship on this issue, see Craig Leslie Mantle, "Loyal Mutineers: An Examination of the Connection between Leadership and Disobedience in the Canadian Army since 1885," in Craig Leslie Mantle (ed.), *The Unwilling and the Reluctant: Theoretical*

Perspectives on Disobedience in the Military (Kingston: CDA Press, 2006) 43–85; Leonard V. Smith, *Between Mutiny and Obedience: The Case of the French Fifth Infantry Division During World War I* (New Jersey: Princeton University Press, 1994); Gerald Oram, *Military Executions during World War I* (New York: Palgrave Macmillan, 2003); and David Englander, "Mutinies and Military Morale" in Hew Strachan (ed.), *The Oxford Illustrated History of the First World War* (London: Oxford University Press, 1998) 194–203.

37. Kay, *Battery Action!* 19.

38. LAC, MG 30 E239, Edward Hilliam papers, field message, 27 October 1915.

39. Will Bird, *The Communication Trench* (Ottawa: CEF Books, 2000) 128–9.

40. Wood, *Vimy!,* 50.

41. LAC, MG 30 E113, George Bell papers, memoir, Back to Blighty, 45.

42. LAC, RG 41, v. 9, George Eyles, 2/2.

43. Harold Peat, *Private Peat* (Indianapolis: Bobbs-Merrill, 1917) 180.

44. J. Alexander (Sandy) Bain, *A War Diary of a Canadian Signaller* (Moncton: J.D. Bain, 1986) 99.

45. Hugh Halliday, *Valour Reconsidered: Inquiries into the Victoria Cross and other Awards for Extreme Bravery* (Toronto: Robin Brass Studio, 2006).

46. LAC, RG 9, v. 4162, 7/7, First Army to 3rd Division, 1 October 1916.

47. David K. Riddle and Donald G. Mitchell, *The Military Cross Awarded to Members of the CEF, 1915–1921* (Winnipeg: Kirby-Marlton Press, 1991), 389.

48. Statistics on medals from Surgeon Commander F.J. Blatherwick, *Canadian Orders, Decorations, and Medals* (Toronto: The Unitrade Press, 1994).

49. Hugh A. Halliday, "Symbols of Honour: The Search for a National Canadian Honours System," *Material History Review* 42 (Fall 1995) 62–3.

50. LAC, RG 9, v. 4162, 7/7, First Army to all divisions, 2 November 1916.

51. CWM, 20020130-001, William Shaw Antliff papers, 29 January 1918.

52. LAC, MG 30 E23, H.W. MacPherson papers, diary, 17 January 1916.

53. Christie (ed.), *Letters of Agar Adamson*, 311.

54. LAC, RG 9, v. 4334, 6/23, DAAG to 1st Division, 17 January 1918.

55. LAC, MG 30 E15, W.A. Griesbach papers, v. 3, file 16 (B), Book of Wisdom III, G.167-11, 1st Brigade to 4th Battalion, 17 April 1918.

56. CWM, 19710147-001, R.E.W. Turner papers, diary, 12 May 1915 (page 55).

57. Edgett and Beatty (eds.), *The World War I Diaries and Letters of Louis Stanley Edgett*, 186.

58. Roy (ed.), *The Journal of Private Fraser*, 84–5.

59. CWM, 19740046-001, Allen Oliver paper, Oliver to Mother, 4 November 1916.

60. Fetherstonhaugh, *The Royal Montreal Regiment*, Appendix F.

61. Fetherstonhaugh, *The Royal Montreal Regiment*, Appendix B.

62. Heather Robertson, *A Terrible Beauty: The Art of Canada at War* (Ottawa: National Museum of Man, 1977) 81.

63. CWM, 19810740-054, Charles Pearce papers, Pearce to Dad, 24 May 1915.

64. CWM, 20000013-008, George Orsmby papers, George to Maggie, 8 May 1915.

65. CWM, 20020130-001, W.S. Antliff papers, 29 April 1918.
66. CWM, 20020130-001, W.S. Antliff papers, 22 April 1918.
67. Roy, *Private Fraser*, 307.

CHAPTER 14: SUPERNATURAL BATTLEFIELDS (PP. 219–234)

1. CWM, 20000148-001, Fred Robinson papers, letter to cousin Ruth Mercer, 1 June 1918.
2. LAC, MG 30 E297, v. 1, Frank Maheux papers, letter to wife, 16 October 1916.
3. Conn Smythe, *If You Can't Beat 'Em in the Alley* (Toronto: McClelland & Stewart, 1981) 42.
4. MacGregor, *MacGregor V.C.*, 73.
5. Tom Spear and Monte Stewart, *Carry On: Reaching Beyond 100* (Calgary: Falcon Press, 1999) 56–7.
6. Gould, *From B.C. to Baisieux*, 34.
7. Harold Adams Innis, The Returned Soldier (Master's thesis: McMaster University, 1918) 9. Also see Duff Crerar, *Padres in No Man's Land: Canadian Chaplains in the Great War* (Montreal: McGill-Queen's Press, 1995).
8. Morton, *When Your Number's Up*, 279.
9. CWM, 19920187-002, H.H. Burrell papers, diary, 6 May 1917.
10. Richard Schweitzer, *The Cross and the Trenches: Religious Faith and Doubt among British and American Great War Soldiers* (London: Praeger, 2003) 50–3.
11. Ralf F.L. Sheldon-Williams, *The Canadian Front in France and Flanders* (London: A. and C. Black, 1920) 44.
12. Kerr, *Shrieks and Crashes*, 144.
13. LAC, MG 30 E113, George V. Bell papers, memoir, Back to Blighty, 103.
14. For the concept of trivialization, see George Mosse, *Fallen Soldiers: Reshaping the Memory of the World Wars* (Oxford: Oxford University Press, 1991) 134; also see Samuel Hynes, *The Soldiers' Tale: Bearing Witness to Modern War* (New York: Allen Lane, The Penguin Press, 1997) 191–3.
15. Cited in Wood, *Vimy!*, 46.
16. LAC, RG 41, v. 16, Charles Roy Grose, 1/6.
17. Keene, *"Crumps": The Plain Story of a Canadian Who Went*, 109.
18. G.R. Stevens, *A City Goes to War* (Brampton: Charters, 1964) 48.
19. Foster, *Letters from the Front*, 58.
20. LAC, MG 30 E42, John McNab papers, memoirs, 5.
21. Sheldon-Williams, *The Canadian Front in France and Flanders*, 176.
22. LAC, RG 41, v. 16, John Cadenhead, 1/6.
23. CWM, 20040015-002, Lawrence Rogers papers, letter, 19 September 1917.
24. LAC, MG 30 E241, D.E. Macintyre papers, v. 2, Men of Valour, 46.
25. George Anderson Wells, *The Fighting Bishop* (Toronto: Cardwell House, 1971) 201.
26. J.C. Dunn, *The War the Infantry Knew, 1914–1919* (London: Jane's, 1987) 148–9.
27. Malcolm Brown, *Tommy Goes to War* (Charleston: Tempus Publishing, 2001) 95–6.

28. Paul Fussell, *The Great War and Modern Memory* (New York: Oxford University Press, 1975) 124.

29. Norma Hillyer Shepard, *Dear Harry: The Firsthand Account of a World War I Infantryman* (Burlington: Brigham Press, 2003) 76.

30. Cowley (ed.), *Georges Vanier*, 109.

31. CWM, AL 2007 054, 19th Battalion Association papers, Henderson, "Selections from Mail Bag," n.d.

32. LAC, R8258, Gregory Clark papers, file 2-3, undated memoir.

33. Philip Gibbs, *Now It Can Be Told* (New York: Garden City Publications, 1920) 398–9.

34. CWM, 20020112-003, Harry Coombs papers, letter to brother, 25 July 1915.

35. Hugh R. Kay, George Magee, and F. A. MacLennan, *Battery Action! The Story of the 43rd (Howitzer) Battery, Canadian Field Artillery, 1916–1919* (Ottawa: CEF Books, 2002) 118–9.

36. Corrigall, *The 20th Battalion*, 136.

37. James Hayward, *Myths & Legends of the First World War* (Oxford: Isis Large Print, 2005) 143.

38. On monster stories, I have been informed by Carolyn Podruchny, "Werewolves and Windigos: Narratives of Cannibal Monster in French-Canadian Voyageur Oral Tradition," *Ethnohistory* 51.4 (Fall 2004) 677–700.

39. Hayward, *Myths & Legends of the First World War*, 144.

40. Coningsby Dawson, *Khaki Courage: Letters in War-Time* (London: Bodley Head, 1917) 96.

41. LAC, MG 30 E430, William Green papers, memoir, 16.

42. Harold Baldwin, *Holding the Line* (Toronto: G.J. McLeod, [1918]) 8–9.

43. CWM, 19730066-001, Chester E. Routley papers, The Eighteenth Battalion, 64.

44. J.M. Winter, *Sites of Memory, Sites of Mourning: The Great War in European Cultural History* (Cambridge: Cambridge University Press, 1995) 66.

45. CLIP, Frederick Barnes, letter, 13 August 1918.

46. Will Bird, *Ghosts Have Warm Hands* (Ottawa: CEF Books, 1997), 27–8.

47. Stanley McMullin, *Anatomy of a Seance: A History of Spirit Communication in Central Canada* (Montreal and Kingston: McGill-Queen's University Press, 2004); Marina Warner, *Phantasmagoria: Spirit Visions, Metaphors, and Media into the Twenty-first Century* (Oxford: Oxford University Press, 2006).

48. Hereward Carrington, *Psychic Phenomena and the War* (New York: American Universities Publishing Company, 1919) 158–9.

49. Carrington, *Psychic Phenomena*, 173–5.

50. Fussell, *The Great War and Modern Memory*, 204.

51. CWM, 20050153-001, Garnet Dobbs papers, letter, 19 June 1918.

CHAPTER 15: THE BREAKING POINT (PP. 235–254)

1. Lewis, *Over the Top with the 25th*, 161.

2. McClintock, *Best o' Luck*, 96.

3. CLIP, William Curtis, letter to mother, 2 June 1915.

4. CLIP, Herbert Irwin, 20 February 1918.

5. Fred W. Bagnall, *Not Mentioned in Despatches: The Memoir of Sergeant Fred Bagnall* (Vancouver: North Shore Press, 1933) 62.

6. Lord Moran, *The Anatomy of Courage*, 1.

7. Keene, *"Crumps": The Plain Story of a Canadian Who Went*, 106.

8. William Gray, *A Sunny Subaltern: Billy's Letters from Flanders* (Toronto: McClelland, Goodchild & Stewart, 1916), 121–2.

9. LAC, MG 30 E113, George Bell papers, memoir, Back to Blighty, 103–4.

10. J.L. Granatstein, "Hume Wrong's Road to the Functional Principle," in Keith Neilson and Roy A. Prete (eds.), *Coalition Warfare: An Uneasy Accord* (Waterloo: Wilfrid Laurier University Press, 1983) 57–8.

11. LAC, MG 30 E241, D.E. Macintyre papers, diary, 20 November 1915.

12. Coningsby Dawson, *The Glory of the Trenches* (New York: John Lane Company, 1918) 32.

13. Foster, *Letters from the Front*, 187.

14. Christie (ed.), *Agar Adamson*, 242.

15. WD, Medical Officer, 25th Battalion, 30 April 1916.

16. Hayes, *The Eighty-Fifth in France and Flanders*, 66.

17. Lew Perry, *Pickinem-Up-n-Putinem Down* (self-published, 1932) 112.

18. LAC, MG 30 E297, Frank Maheux papers, 20 June 1916.

19. LAC, RG 41, 72nd Battalion, Private Archie Selwood, 1/11-12.

20. LAC, MG 30 E241, D.E. Macintyre papers, diary, 7 November 1915.

21. Bird, *Ghosts Have Warm Hands*, 59–61.

22. There is a deep and ever-growing literature on shell shock in Britain; see, for starters, Ben Shephard, *War of Nerves* (London: Jonathan Cape, 2000); Peter Leese, *Shell-Shock: Traumatic Neurosis and the British Soldiers of the First World* (London: Palgrave, Macmillan, 2002). Canada has been less well served by its historians, and very little is available other than Tom Brown, "Shell Shock and the Canadian Expeditionary Force, 1914–18: Canadian Psychiatry in the Great War" in *Health, Disease and Medicine: Essays in Canadian History*, Charles Roland (ed.), (Toronto: Hannah Institute, 1983).

23. Craig, *But This Is Our War*, 54.

24. Mark Humphries, "The Common Sense Cure: A Comparison of Canadian and British Shell Shock Treatment in the Great War," *War and Society* 27.2 (2008).

25. Macphail, *The Medical Services*, 276–8.

26. Bill Rawling, *Death Thine Enemy: Canadian Medical Practitioners and War* (Ottawa: self-published, 2001) 92.

27. A.O. Hickson, *As It Was Then: Recollections, 1896–1930* (Wolfville: Acadia University, 1988) 70–1.

28. LAC, RG 24, v. 1844, GAQ 11-11-E; J.P.S. Cathcart, "The Neuro-Psychiatric Branch of the Department of Soldiers' Civil Re-establishment," *The Ontario Journal of Neuro-Psychiatry* 8 (1928) 46.

29. Roy, *Private Fraser*, 80.

30. LAC, RG 9, III-B-1, v. 2246, file A-5-30, pt. III, Report of Accident, Pte. Joseph Renaud, 1105202.

31. See Joanna Bourke, *Dismembering the Male: Men's Bodies, Britain and the Great War* (London: Reaktion, 1999); Cook, *No Place to Run*, 159–62; Jay Cassel, *The Secret Plague*, 130–1.

32. LAC, MG 30 E113, George Bell papers, memoir, Back to Blighty, 113–14.

33. LAC, RG 24, v. 6992, file: chapter VII, v. 2, Notes on Self-Inflicted Injuries; Macphail, *The Medical Services*, 278–9.

34. LAC, RG 150, reel T-8671, court martial of J.E. Luxford, 30879.

35. CWM, 19920187-002, H.H. Burrell papers, diary, 31 August 1917.

36. Marjorie Barron Norris (ed.), *Medicine and Duty: The World War I Memoir of Captain Harold W. McGill, Medical Officer, 31st Battalion, C.E.F.* (Calgary: University of Calgary Press, 2006) 199.

37. CWM, 20000003-002, G.F. McFarland papers, memoirs, [1919] 9.

38. LAC, MG 30 E300, Victor Odlum papers, v. 18, file: 7th Battalion Orders, Battalion Orders, 28 January 1916.

39. Christie, *Agar Adamson*, 360.

40. See Richard Holmes, *Tommy: The British Soldier on the Western Front, 1914–1918* (London: HarperCollins, 2004) 555–6; David Campbell, "Military Discipline, Punishment, and Leadership in the First World War: The Case of the 2nd Canadian Division," in Craig Leslie Mantle (ed.), *The Apathetic and the Defiant: Case Studies of Canadian Mutiny and Disobedience, 1812–1919* (Toronto: The Dundurn Group, 2007) 297–342.

41. See Max Dagenais, 'Une permission! ... C'est bon pour une recrue:' Discipline and Illegal Absences in the 22nd (French-Canadian) Battalion, 1915–1919, (Master's thesis: University of Ottawa, 2006); Jean-Pierre Gagnon, *Le 22e Bataillon (Canadien-français), Étude socio-militaire* (Ottawa et Québec: Les Presses de l'Université Laval en collaboration avec le ministère de la Défense Nationale et le Centre d'édition du gouvernement du Canada, 1986), Chapter VIII.

42. CWM, 19920187-002, H.H. Burrell papers, diary, 4 September 1917.

43. Morton, *When Your Number's Up*, 83; Chris Madsen, *Another Kind of Justice: Canadian Military Law from Confederation to Somalia* (Vancouver: UBC Press, 1999) 3.

44. The War Office, *Statistics of the Military Effort of the British Empire during the Great War* (War Office, 1922) 643–70.

45. Imperial War Museum [hereafter IWM], 97/26/1, H.R. Butt papers, diary, 31 January 1917.

46. See WD, 2nd Canadian Division A.P.M., 7 December 1915 and 1 July 1916.

47. Christopher Pugsley, *On the Fringe of Hell: New Zealanders and Military Discipline in the First World War* (Auckland: Hodder, 1991) 93.

48. Dave Campbell, The Divisional Experience in the C.E.F.: A Social and Operational History of the 2nd Canadian Division, 1915–1918 (Ph.D. dissertation: University of Calgary, 2003) 449.

49. See Teresa Iacobelli, "Arbitrary Justice: A Comparative Analysis of Canadian Death Sentences Passed and Commuted During the First World War," *Canadian Military History* 16.1 (Winter 2007) 23–36; and Andrew Godefroy, *For Freedom and Honour?: The Story of the 25 Canadian Volunteers Executed in the First World War* (Ottawa: CEF Books, 1998) 4.

50. John Peaty, "Haig and Military Discipline," in Brian Bond and Nigel Cave (eds.), *Haig: A Reappraisal 70 Years On* (London: Leo Cooper, 1999) 203; DHH, 506.009 (D10), Trial of Canadian Soldiers, Memo for the Honourable Minister, 4 June 1918.

51. Godefroy, *For Freedom and Honour?,* 42.

52. CLIP, Kenneth Foster, memoir, not paginated.

53. Black, *I Want One Volunteer,* 28–9.

54. Morton, *When Your Number's Up,* 252.

55. Bagnall, *Not Mentioned in Despatches,* 34.

56. LAC, MG 30 E113, George Bell papers, memoir, Back to Blighty, 83.

CHAPTER 16: A CANADIAN CORPS COMMANDER (PP. 255–272)

1. For Horne's plan, see Trevor Harvey, The Battle of Hill: 15–25 August 1917 (Master's thesis: University of Birmingham, 2006) 30–31.

2. Pope, *Letters From the Front,* 79.

3. LAC, RG 24, v. 1813, GAQ 4-15K, W.A. Griesbach, "Lieut-Gen. Sir Edwin Alderson, KCB," *The Khaki Call* 12.1 (February 1928) 1.

4. John J. Pershing, *My Experiences in the World War,* v. 2 (New York: F.A. Stokes, 1931) 2.

5. Paddy Griffith, *Battle Tactics of the Western Front: The British Army's Art of Attack, 1916–18* (New Haven: Yale University Press, 1994) 5.

6. See the correspondence by several of his former officers in the McGill Archives, MG 4027, H.M Urquhart papers, box 1, file 12 and file 13. For published sources, see A.G.L. McNaughton, "The Development of Artillery in the Great War," *Canadian Defence Quarterly* 6.2 (January 1929) 164; A.M.J. Hyatt, "The Military Leadership of Sir Arthur Currie," in Lieutenant-Colonel Bernd Horn and Stephen Harris (eds.), *Warrior Chiefs: Perspectives on Senior Canadian Military Leaders* (Toronto: Dundurn Press, 2001) 43–56.

7. T.G. Roberts, "I remember Currie," *The Ottawa Journal,* 6 April 1940.

8. LAC, MG 26H, Sir Robert Borden papers, reel C4355, v. 136, Perley to Borden, 9 June 1917.

9. LAC, CP, v. 43, file 94, diary, 10 July 1917.

10. George Anderson Wells, *The Fighting Bishop* (Toronto: Cardwell House, 1971) 160.

11. LAC, MG 27 IID23, Sir Sam Hughes papers, 14/5, Currie to Garnet, 8 May 1917 and Garnet to Currie, 11 May 1917.

12. Perhaps an explanation for Currie's change of heart regarding Garnet was that the corps commander believed "the tactics are changing so rapidly, demanding that new tactics be devised to meet the changed conditions, that one who has not seen service here, or who has been away for some months, must necessarily become very much out of date." LAC, MG 27 IID23, Sir Sam Hughes Papers, 14/5, Currie to Garnet, 30 October 1917. For Currie's quote, see LAC, CP, v. 27, file 7, Currie to McGillicuddy, n.d. (First page is missing.)

13. Urquhart, *Arthur Currie*, 164; LAC, CP, v. 43, file 94, diary, 15 June 1917.

14. LAC, CP, v. 27, file 7, Currie to McGillicuddy, n.d. (First page is missing.)

15. For more details, see Craig Brown and Desmond Morton, "The Embarrassing Apotheosis of a Great Canadian: Sir Arthur Currie's Personal Crisis in 1917," *Canadian Historical Review* 60.1 (March 1979) 41–63.

16. John Swettenham, *McNaughton*, v. 1 (Toronto: Ryerson Press, 1968) 98.

17. LAC, CP, v. 13, file 39, Currie to Ralston, 9 February 1928.

18. Stewart, Attack Doctrine in the Canadian Corps, 1916–1918, 106; LAC, v. 3850, 61/2, First Army to Canadian Corps, 9 July 1917.

19. One of Byng's last major doctrinal documents, May 1917's "Notes on the Attack," had been issued throughout the senior command of the Canadian Corps. It urged the corps not only to plan for its role in the attack but also to prepare for the now nearly automatic German counterattack. LAC, RG 9, v. 4028, 17/20, Notes on the Attack.

20. LAC, CP, v. 15, file P–R, Currie to Rattray, 22 April 1920.

21. LAC, CP, v. 2, file M–R, Currie to Charles Swayne, 23 January 1918.

22. LAC, RG 9, v. 4693, 53/10, 25th Battalion report.

23. Fetherstonhaugh, *The Royal Montreal Regiment*, 166.

24. Geoff Jackson, Hill 70 and Lens, the Forgotten Battles (Master's thesis: University of Calgary, 2005) 22.

25. WD, 9th Brigade, Appendix 18, Raid Report, OC 116th Battalion.

26. Norris (ed.), *Medicine and Duty*, 312.

27. LAC, RG 9, v. 4066, 11/10, Extracts from German Wireless, August 1917.

28. Mitchell and Smith, *Medical Services*, 33.

29. WD, Canadian Corps, Appendix III/I–III/5, Summary of Operations, 2 August 1917.

30. Nicholson, *CEF*, 279.

31. LAC, RG 9, v. 3859, 61/4, Artillery Order No. 52.

32. LAC, RG 9, v. 4026, 11/10, German Wireless Extract, 20 August 1917.

33. LAC, RG 9, v. 3850, 61/4, Canadian Corps Artillery Order No. 63, 14 August 1917; Nicholson, *Gunners of Canada*, v. 1, 297.

34. Christopher Pugsley, "Learning from the Canadian Corps on the Western Front," *Canadian Military History* 15.1 (Winter 2006) 24.

35. LAC, RG 9, v. 4014, 25/2, Appreciation of the Enemy's Defences and Disposition around Hill 70, 19 July 1917.

36. Otto Fliess and Kurt Dittmar, *5 Honnoverisches Infanterie-Regiment Nr. 165 im Weltkriege* (Oldenburg: Gerhard Stalling, 1927) 149–57. Translation by Wilhelm Kiesselbach; courtesy of Mark Humphries.

37. Public Archives of Nova Scotia, MG 100, v. 263, part 8, A Soldier's Diary by Gunner Basil E. Courtney, 14 August 1917.

38. LAC, MG 30 E249, v. 1, "The Diary of the 20th Battery, CFA, by J.C.K. Mackay," 31.

39. LAC, RG 9, v. 3868, 109/6, G.869/14-3, 10 August 1917.

CHAPTER 17: OVER THE TOP (PP. 273–284)

1. Arthur Lapointe, *Soldier of Quebec, 1916–1919*, translated by R.C. Fetherstonhaugh (Montreal: Éditions Edouard Garand, 1931) 56.

2. On the subject of money, see John William Lynch, *Princess Patricia's Canadian Light Infantry, 1917–1919* (New York: Exposition Press, 1976) 152.

3. CWM, 19870197-001, Gurney Palling Little papers, Siege Battery Experiences in World War I, 109.

4. Fliess and Dittmar, *5 Honnoverisches*, 149–57.

5. Lapointe, *Soldier of Quebec, 1916–1919,* 57.

6. LAC, RG 24, v. 1501, HQ 683-1-28, Laplante to Duguid, 4 June 1939.

7. Fetherstonhaugh, *The Royal Montreal Regiment*, 162.

8. Urquhart, *History of the 16th Battalion*, 232.

9. Kim Beattie, *48th Highlanders of Canada* (Toronto: Highlanders of Canada, 1932) 247.

10. CWM, Alvin Kines, Waiting to Catch the General's Head, memoir edited by Clare Kines, 2003, [11].

11. Dancocks, *Gallant Canadians*, 128.

12. For Japanese Canadians in the Great War, see Lyle Dick, "Sergeant Masumi Mitsui and the Japanese Canadian War Memorial: Intersections of National, Cultural, and Personal Memory," unpublished paper presented at the 2007 Canadian Historical Association.

13. WD, 5th Battalion, Report of Operation, August 14th to 18th, 1917.

14. Stewart, Attack Doctrine, 114.

15. WD, 8th Battalion, Capture of Hill 70, 15 to 17th August 1917.

16. Dancocks, *Gallant Canadians*, 132.

17. Marcelle Cinq-Mars, "From Cadet to Brigadier-General: Thomas-Louis Tremblay and the 22nd Battalion (French-Canadian)," in Colonel Bernd Horn and Dr. Roch Legault, *Loyal Service: Perspectives of French-Canadian Military Leaders* (Kingston: Canadian Defence Academy Press, 2006) 230.

18. WD, 25th Battalion, Appendix D, Narrative of Events for Attack on Cité St. Laurent.

19. LAC, MG 30 E488, William Morgan papers, diary, 24 July 1917.

20. WD, 5th Brigade, Appendix 5, Report of Operations [Hill 70 operation].

21. WD, 24th Battalion, Summary of Operations at Lens, 15 August 1917.

22. WD, 4th Brigade, Summary of Information, 15 August 1917.

23. Cane, *It Made You Think of Home*, 114–15.

CHAPTER 18: BLEEDING THE GERMANS WHITE (PP. 285–296)

1. Major von Plehwe, *Geschichte des 2. Garde-Reserve-Regiments. II. Teil: Von Mitte Oktober 1915 bis Januar 1919.* (Berlin: Mar Galle, 1921), 171–2. Translation by Wilhelm Kiesselbach; courtesy of Mark Humphries.

2. LAC, RG 9, v. 3907, 27/7, "Forward Observation," 23 July 1917.

3. General Sir Martin Farndale, *History of the Royal Regiment of Artillery: Western Front*

1914–18 (London: The Royal Artillery Institution, 1986) 205; LAC, RG 9, v. 4014, 25/2, Report GOC 1 Brigade Royal Flying Corps.

4. J.A. MacDonald, *Gun-Fire: An Historical Narrative of The 4th Brigade, C.F.A.* (unknown publisher, 1929) 106.

5. WD, Canadian Corps, Appendix III-I-III/5, Summary of Operations, 9–16 August 1917.

6. Claus Piedmont and Hugo Pieper, *Geschichte des 5. rheinischen Infanterie-Regiments Nr. 65 während des Weltkrieges 1914–1918.* (Oldenburg: Gerhard Stalling, 1927) 250–1. Translation by Wilhelm Kiesselbach; courtesy of Mark Humphries.

7. Nicholson, *CEF*, 289.

8. CWM, CP, 58A 1.59.5, Canadian Corps, Summary of Intelligence, 17 August 1917.

9. CLIP, Kenneth Foster, memoir, no pagination.

10. LAC, CP, diary, 15 August 1917.

11. WD, Canadian Corps, Appendix III/I-III/5, Summary of Operations, 9–16 August 1917.

12. Fetherstonhaugh, *The Royal Montreal Regiment*, 169.

13. Foster, *Letters from the Front*, 232.

14. CWM, 20030140-005, J.R. Preston papers, diary, 15 August 1917.

15. David Beatty, "The landscape has changed; the nightmare of it all, has not: Fred Robichaud's memories of the Great War," *The New Brunswick READER*, 12 November 1994, 6.

16. Bain, *A War Diary*, 91.

17. Wheeler, *The 50th Battalion in No Man's Land*, 142.

18. Lapointe, *Soldier of Quebec, 1916–1919*, 65.

19. WD, 1st Brigade, CFA, 18 August 1917.

20. LAC, MG 30 E61, C.H. Mitchell papers, 2/6, S.S. 581, "Extracts No. 10 from German Documents."

21. E.W.B. Morrison, "Vimy and Hill 70," *Toronto Star Weekly*, 24 April 1928.

22. LAC, RG 9, v. 3907, 27/8, Artillery Order No. 52: Artillery Plan for the Capture of Hill 70; CWM, CP, 58A 1.59.5, Canadian Corps, Summary of Intelligence, 18 August 1917.

23. M, *The Story of the Development of the Chemical Warfare Service* (General Electric Company, 1920) 175.

24. See report by the Medical Research Committee, *The Symptoms and Treatment of the Late Effects of Gas Poisoning*, 10 April 1918 in LAC, RG 9, v. 3618, file 25-13-6.

25. Canon Frederick Scott, *The Great War as I Saw It* (Ottawa: CEF Books, 2000) 143.

26. LAC, RG 9, v. 3831, 14/8, Report on Gas Bombardment.

27. LAC, MG 30 E12, A.F. Duguid Papers, v. 2, The Canadian as a Soldier, 25; RG 9, v. 4872, 2nd Canadian Infantry Brigade War Diary, August 1917, Report: "Action of August 15th, 1917, Capture of the Enemy's Positions on Hill 70 and Subsequent Operations," 28.

28. LAC, RG 41, v. 20, K.B. Jackson, 2/3.

29. CWM, CP, 58A 1.59.5, Currie to GOCRA, 28 August 1917.

30. WD, 2nd Battalion, 18 August 1917.

31. LAC, CP, v. 52, diary, 18 August 1917.

32. CWM, CP, 58A 1.59.5, Canadian Corps, Summary of Intelligence, 19 August 1917.

33. Nicholson, *CEF*, 292.

CHAPTER 19: "SWALLOWED UP IN THE SWIRLING MURK OF THE BATTLE" (PP. 297–308)

1. Major von Plehwe, *Geschichte des 2. Garde-Reserve-Regiments. II. Teil: Von Mitte Oktober 1915 bis Januar 1919.* (Berlin: Mar Galle, 1921), 174. Translation by Wilhelm Kiesselbach; courtesy of Mark Humphries.

2. IWM, 87/51/1, J.S. Davis papers, diary, 19 August 1917.

3. H.R.N. Clyne, M.C., *Vancouver's 29th* (Vancouver: Tobin's Tigers Association, 1964) 46.

4. LAC, RG 9, v. 4933, 25th Battalion War Diary, 22 August 1917.

5. Fraser, *The Journal of Private Fraser*, 305.

6. LAC, MG 30 E6, Henry Burstall papers, 1/7, Narrative of Operations, 2nd Division, 15th to 22nd August 1917, G.22.

7. Wheeler, *The 50th Battalion in No Man's Land*, 139.

8. WD, 50th Battalion, Report of Operations from August 17th to August 26th, 1917.

9. Wheeler, *The 50th Battalion in No Man's Land*, 139.

10. Philip Gibbs, "The Frightfulness of the Battle of Lens," *Canada in Khaki* 2 (CWRO, 1918) 13.

11. Fliess and Dittmar, *5 Honnoverisches*, 149–57.

12. Nicholson, *CEF*, 295.

13. E.S. Russenholt, *Six Thousand Canadian Men: Being the History of the 44th Battalion Canadian Infantry 1914–1919* (Winnipeg: Printed to the order of Forty-Fourth Battalion Association by the Montfort Press, 1932) 109.

14. Geoff Jackson, "'Anything but Lovely': The Canadian Corps at Lens in the summer of 1917," *Canadian Military History* 17.1 (Winter 2006) 14.

15. LAC, RG 41, v. 13, Allen Hart, 44th Battalion, 1/10.

16. Russenholt, *Six Thousand Canadian Men*, 112.

17. Colonel Roderick Macleod (translator), "Great battles fought during the First World War, 1914–1918: Flanders 1917," translation of material from the German official history and General von Kuhl's account, *Der Weltkrieg, 1914–1918, Deutschen voike dargestelt,* 2 volumes (Berlin: W. Kolk, 1929). Woolwich: Library of the Royal Artillery Museum, 19. Courtesy of Mark Humphries.

18. Harvey, "The Battle of Hill 70," 53; James Edmonds, *History of the Great War: Military Operations: France and Belgium, 1917,* v. 2 (London: Imperial War Museum, 1991 reprint) 225–8; LAC, CP, v. 13, file 39, Currie to Ralston, 9 February 1928.

19. LAC, MG 27 IID23, Sir Sam Hughes papers, file 14-5, E.W.B. Morrison to Garnet Hughes, 21 August 1917.

20. LAC, CP, v. 13, file 39, Currie to Ralston, 9 February 1928.

21. Donn Farr, *The Silent General: Horne of the First Army* (West Midlands: Helion and Company, 2007) 173.

22. LAC, CP, v. 43, diary, 15–18 August 1917.

23. LAC, RG 24, v. 1844, Battle Casualties—Hill 70 August 1917; Nicholson, *CEF*, 297. I would like to thank Matthew Walthert for bringing to my attention the division of casualties at Hill 70 and along the Western Front.

24. CWM, 19920187-002, H.H. Burrell papers, diary, 25 August 1917.

25. Russenholt, *Six Thousand Canadian Men*, 114–15.

26. Corrigall, *The Twentieth Battalion*, 147.

CHAPTER 20: CALLED TO BATTLE (PP. 309–328)

1. See Geoffrey Till, "Passchendaele: The Maritime Dimension," in Peter Liddle (ed.), *Passchendaele in Perspective: The Third Battle of Ypres* (London: Pen and Sword, 1997), 73–87.

2. Lloyd George, *War Memoirs*, 3423.

3. John Terraine, *The Road to Passchendaele* (London: Leo Cooper, 1977) 137–8.

4. Dan Todman, "The Grand Lamasery revisited: General Headquarters on the Western Front, 1914–1918," in Gary Sheffield and Dan Todman (eds.), *Command and Control on the Western Front: The British Army's Experience 1914–18* (London: Spellmount Limited, 2004) 51.

5. Robin Prior and Trevor Wilson, *Passchendaele: The Untold Story* (London: Yale University Press, 1996) 84–7.

6. CWM, 20000003-002, G.F. McFarland papers, memoirs, 24 October 1917.

7. Tim Travers, *How the War Was Won: Command and Technology in the British Army on the Western Front, 1917–1918* (London: Routledge, 1992) 16.

8. LAC, RG 9, v. 4025, 7/5, Second Army, "Notes on Training and Preparation for Offensive Operations," 31 August 1917.

9. Nicholson, *CEF*, 307–8.

10. Philip Gibbs, *Now It Can Be Told* (New York: Harper, 1920) 485.

11.Daniel Dancocks, *Legacy of Valour: The Canadians at Passchendaele* (Edmonton: Hurtig, 1986) 96.

12. LAC, CP, v. 5, file P–R, Currie to Paterson, 8 March 1920.

13. Haig believed the French forces were still unreliable as late as 19 September 1917; see Gary Sheffield and John Bourne (eds.), *The Haig Diaries: The Diaries of Field Marshal Sir Douglas Haig: War Diaries & Letters 1914–1918*, (London: Weidenfeld & Nicolson, 2005) 329.

14. One of the finest staff officers of the war, Sir Charles Harrington, also came to this conclusion; the British needed to capture the ridge to avoid losing all they had gained since early August. Sir Charles Harrington, *Tim Harrington Looks Back* (London: John Murray, 1940) 63–4.

15. Simon Robbins, "Henry Horne: First Army, 1916–1918," in Ian Beckett and Steven Corvi (eds.), *Haig's Generals* (Barnsley, U.K.: Pen and Sword, 2006) 104.

16. Foster, *Letters from the Front*, 244.

17. IWM, 87/51/1, J.S. Davis papers, diary, 24 October 1917.

18. IWM, 97/26/1, J.M. Poucher papers, diary, 19 October 1917.

19. Nicholson, *CEF*, 313.

20. Macpherson, *A Soldier's Diary*, 88.

21. A.G.L. McNaughton, "The Development of Artillery in the Great War," p. 13. (Article originally published in *Canadian Defence Quarterly* 6.2 [January 1929], but brought together in an untitled publication containing five of McNaughton's articles. Copy of publication found in RG 24, v. 1821, GAQ 5-27.)

22. Nigel Hamilton, *Monty: The Making of a General, 1887–1942* (London: Hamish Hamilton, 1981) 129.

23. Arthur O. Hickson, *As It Was Then* (Nova Scotia: Acadia University, 1988) 58.

24. The Adjutant [E.P.S. Allen], *The 116th Battalion in France* (Toronto: Hunter, Rose & Company, 1921) 51.

25. LAC, RG 9, v. 3909, 31/2, Canadian Corps Artillery Report, 5; CWM, MHRC, S.S.701, Notes on the Construction of Positions on the Ypres Battle Front for the Coming Winter.

26. LAC, RG 9, v. 3853, 68/7, 3rd Canadian Division, Intelligence File, Passchendaele Sector, No. 2, Appendix 3/1.

27. CWM, MHRC, Translation of German Order, New Method of Defence for the Ypres Group, Ia/87084/88187.

28. LAC, RG 9, v. 3853, 68/7, 3rd Canadian Division, Intelligence File, Passchendaele Sector, No. 1.

29. Robert T. Foley, "The Other Side of the Wire: The German Army in 1917," in Peter Dennis and Jeffrey Grey (eds.), *1917: Tactics, Training and Technology* (Canberra: The Chief of the Army's Military History Conference 2007) 164.

30. CWM, MHRC, S.S. 712, Extracts No. 12 from German Documents and Correspondence.

31. LAC, RG 9, v. 3854, 71/7, Currie to Second Army, 20 November 1917.

32. CWM, MHRC, S.S. 749, The Principles of Command in the Defensive Battle in Position Warfare, 1 September 1917.

33. LAC, RG 9, v. 3859, 85/8, G.724/27-3, 20 November 1917.

34. LAC, RG 24, v. 1832, GAQ 8-15d, Canadian Corps Artillery Report, Passchendaele.

35. LAC, RG 9, v. 3909, 31/2, Canadian Corps Artillery Report, 1 and 24.

36. Dancocks, *Legacy of Valour*, 109.

37. Becker, *Silhouettes of the Great War*, 120.

38. LAC, MG 30 E50, Elmer Jones papers, v. 1, file 6, Extracts from Second Army Intelligence Summaries, October 1917.

39. C.E.W. Bean, *The Australian Imperial Force in France 1917*, v. 5 (Sydney: Angus and Robertson, 1929–42) 676.

40. Kerr, *Shrieks and Crashes*, 179.

41. LAC, RG 9, v. 3909, 31/1, Canadian Corps Artillery Report [typed, but unformatted], 33.

42. Black, *I Want One Volunteer*, 63.

CHAPTER 21: "I DON'T KNOW HOW THE HUMAN FRAME STOOD UP" (PP. 329–340)

1. LAC, RG 9, v. 3909, 31/2, Canadian Corps Artillery Report, 8.
2. Dancocks, *Legacy of Valour*, 126.
3. Bennett, *4th Canadian Mounted Rifles*, 79.
4. CWM, 20000003-002, G.F. McFarland papers, memoirs, 26 October 1917.
5. Sheldon, *The Germany Army at Passchendaele*, 255.
6. CWM, 20000003-002, G.F. McFarland papers, memoirs, 13 January 1918.
7. Jason Adair, "The Battle of Passchendaele: The Experiences of Lieutenant Tom Rutherford, 4th Battalion, Canadian Mounted Rifles," *Canadian Military History* 13.4 (Autumn 2004) 72–80.
8. Dan Jenkins, Winning Trench Warfare: Battlefield Intelligence in the Canadian Corps, 1914–1918, (Ph.D. dissertation: Carleton University, 1999) 312–3.
9. CWM, *Flanders Fields*, 10/13.
10. Shackleton, *Second to None*, 174–8.
11. WD, 46th Battalion, Report of Operations against Passchendaele Ridge, October 26th, 1917.
12. James L. McWilliams and R. James Steel, *The Suicide Battalion* (Edmonton: Hurtig, 1978) 114.
13. WD, 46th Battalion, handwritten report to OC Tadpole, 29 October 1917.
14. Wheeler, *The 50th Battalion in No Man's Land*, 167.
15. WD, 50th Battalion, 26 October 1917.
16. CWM, *Flanders Fields*, 10/14–15.
17. Sheldon, *The Germany Army at Passchendaele*, 259.
18. LAC, RG 9, v. 3909, 31/2, Canadian Corps Artillery Report, 11.
19. Russenholt, *Six Thousand Canadian Men*, 121.
20. Freeman and Nielsen, *Far from Home*, 128.
21. CWM, *Flanders Fields*, 10/23.
22. Cane (ed.), *It Made You Think of Home*, 131.
23. Lyn Macdonald, *They Called It Passchendaele: The Story of the Third Battle of Ypres and of the Men Who Fought in It* (London: Joseph, 1978) 219.
24. LAC, RG 24, v. 1810, file GAQ 1-6, Statement of Casualties at Passchendaele.
25. CWM, MHRC, 58A 1.59.7, G.293, 3rd Division, Report on the Passchendaele Ridge Operation.

CHAPTER 22: CRAWLING OUT OF THE MUD (PP. 341–352)

1. LAC, MG 30 E393, A.J. Foster papers, memoir, 10.
2. Stevens, *A City Goes to War*, 100.
3. C.B. Topp, *The 42nd Battalion, C.E.F. Royal Highlanders of Canada in the Great War* (Montreal: Gazette-Printing, 1931) 159.
4. Breckenridge, *From Vimy to Mons*, 78.

5. LAC, RG 9, v. 3859, 85/8, 3rd Division, Notes on Recent Operations (26th to 30th OCTR); quotes from WD, 85th Battalion, Appendix A report of operation, n.d. [ca. 1 November 1917].

6. WD, 85th Battalion, Appendix A, Report of Operations, n.d. [ca. 1 November 1917].

7. LAC, RG 41, 78th Battalion, Archie Brown, 2/5.

8. WD, 72nd Battalion, Operational Order 79.

9. LAC, RG 9, v. 3859, 85/2, G7-265, Report by 1st Division, 14 December 1917.

10. CWM, CP, 58A 1.59.6, Intelligence report, No. 12, Prisoners Statements, 1 November 1917.

11. CWM, CP, 58A 1.59.6, Intelligence report, No. 12, 1 November 1917.

12. WD, 72nd Battalion, Report of Operations, October 28th–November 3rd, 1917.

13. Ibid.

14. WD, 4th Battalion, Instructions for the Offensive 1, 4 November 1917.

15. Peter Chasseaud, "Field Survey in the Salient: Cartography and Artillery Survey in the Flanders Operation in 1917," in Peter Liddle (ed.), *Passchendaele in Perspective: The Third Battle of Ypres* (London: Pen and Sword, 1997) 136.

16. Bernard McEvoy and A.H. Finlay, *History of the 72nd Canadian Infantry Battalion, Seaforth Highlanders of Canada* (Vancouver: Cowan & Brookhouse, 1920) 79.

17. Cited in Morrison, *Hell upon Earth*, 111–12.

18. Robert Graves, *Good-bye to All That* (London: Penguin, 1960) 133.

19. Zubkowski, *As Long as Faith and Freedom Last*, 293.

20. Christie (ed.), *Agar Adamson*, 309.

21. Stevens, *A City Goes to War*, 104.

22. Reginald H. Roy, *For Most Conspicuous Bravery: A Bibliography of Major-General George R. Pearkes, V.C., through Two World Wars* (Vancouver: University of British Columbia Press, 1977) 63.

23. G.C. Johnston, *The 2nd Canadian Mounted Rifles (British Columbia Horse) in France and Flanders* (Vernon, B.C.: privately printed, 1932) 57.

24. CWM, MHRC, 58A 1.59.7, G.293, 3rd Division, Report on the Passchendaele Ridge Operation.

25. Nicholson, *CEF*, 323.

26. Sheldon, *The German Army at Passchendaele*, 274.

27. Hayes, *The Eighty-Fifth in France and Flanders*, 103.

CHAPTER 23: "THE DEVIL HIMSELF COULDN'T HAVE STOPPED US" (PP. 353–366)

1. Lapointe, *Soldier of Quebec*, 74.

2. R.H. Rabjohn, *A Canadian Soldier's Diary, 1914–1918* (Burlington: DCM, n.d.) no page [hereafter n.p.] [31 October 1917].

3. CWM, CP, 58A 1.59.6, Canadian Corps Summary of Intelligence, 2 November 1917.

4. Wheeler, *The 50th Battalion in No Man's Land*, 165.

5. Milly Cooke Walsh and Naomi Hubbard, *The Original WW1 Diary of Herbert 'Bert' Cooke*, manuscript deposited in CWM archives, 58.

6. LAC, RG 9, v. 3853, 68/3, 1st Canadian Division, Report on the Passchendaele Ridge Operations, 1.

7. CWM, 58A 1 131.11, Private Henry Savoie papers, letter to mother, 5 December 1917.

8. LAC, CP, 59A 1 59.6, Examination of 4 Prisoners, No. 12, 1 November 1917.

9. LAC, RG 9, v. 3853, 68/1, Report by Lt. E.D.P. Hardy on interrogation of German POWs, 7 November 1917.

10. Walker, *A Soldier's Story*, 68.

11. CWM, CP, 58A 1.59.7, Field Artillery Narrative, November 4–12, 1917.

12. CWM, CP, 58A 1.59.7, 1st Division report, Appendix: Statement of Ammunition Expenditure.

13. James Robert Johnston, *Riding into War: The Memoir of a Horse Transport Driver, 1916–1919* (Goose Lane Editions and The New Brunswick Military Heritage Project, 2004) 12, 80.

14. LAC, RG 9, v. 4816, Canadian Corps Summary of Intelligence, 7 November 1917.

15. Murray, *History of the 2nd Battalion*, 211.

16. CWM, CP, 58A 1.59.7, 1st Divisional Report of the Passchendaele Ridge Operations, November 4–12, 1917.

17. WD, 2nd Battalion, Report of Operations for 4–7 November 1917.

18. CWM, CP, 58A 1.59.7, 1st Canadian Division, Summary of Intelligence, 6 November 1917.

19. LAC, RG 9, v. 3853, 68/3, 1st Canadian Division, Report on the Passchendaele Ridge Operations, 8.

20. Sheldon, *The German Army at Passchendaele*, 295.

21. WD, 28th Battalion, Narrative for the Capture of Passchendaele, 6/7 November 1917.

22. WD, 31st Battalion, Narrative of operations, Passchendaele Attack, 4, 5, 6 November, 1917.

23. LAC, RG 9, III-B-1, v. 2226, file 2-28, Narrative Report of Operations for capture of Passchendaele, 6th Brigade, C.435.

24. Hickson, *As It Was Then*, 60.

25. CWM, CP, 58A 1.59.7, Daily Intelligence Summary, No. 573.

26. CWM, CP, 58A 1.59.7, Canadian Corps, Summary of Intelligence, 6 November 1917.

27. WD, 1st Battalion, 'B' Narrative, 6-7 November 1917.

28. CWM, CP, 58A 1.59.7, Canadian Corps, Summary of Intelligence, 6 November 1917.

29. Breckenridge, *From Vimy to Mons*, 96.

30. CWM, CP, 58A 1.59.6, Further Information from Prisoners of 38th Fusilier Regiment.

31. CWM, CP, 58A 1.59.6, Canadian Corps, Summary of Intelligence, 6 November 1917.

32. LAC, RG 24, v. 1831, file GAQ 8/7, Canadian Corps Ammunition Expenditure; LAC, RG 9, v. 3909, 31/2, Canadian Corps Artillery Report, Appendix B.

33. CWM, CP, 58A 1.59.6, Canadian Corps, Summary of Intelligence, 11 November 1917.

34. Percival Phillips, "'Hell All Alight': An Epic of Passchendaele," *Canada in Khaki* II (CWRO, 1918) 13.

35. Stewart, Attack Doctrine, 129–30.

36. Gould, *From B.C. to Baisieux*, 73.

37. CWM, *Flanders Fields*, Elmore Philpott and Tommy Adams, 10/28–9.

38. CWM, 20050153-011, Garnet Dobbs papers, 24 October 1917.

39. LAC, RG 9, v. 3854, 71/1, Reasons for Success and Failure, Passchendaele, 20 November 1917.

40. LAC, RG 24, v. 1825, GAQ 5-67, D.E. Macintyre, The Fight for the Craters, 1.

41. LAC, RG 24, v. 1822, Canadian Corps, Battle Casualties, 15 February 1946. It should be noted that Nicholson's official history lists the casualties as 15,654, which is at odds with those tabulated in the Battle Casualties file. Nicholson, *CEF*, 327.

42. Bird, *Ghosts Have Warm Hands*, 65; and Kerr, *Shrieks and Crashes*, 193.

43. For Churchill quote, see Churchill, *The World Crisis, 1914–1918*, v. 4, 1177. The casualty figures are unclear, ranging from 260,000 to 275,000 for the British and 202,000 to 220,000 for the Germans. For 275,000, see Frank E. Vandiver, "Field Marshal Sir Douglas Haig and Passchendaele," in Peter Liddle (ed.), *Passchendaele in Perspective: The Third Battle of Ypres* (London: Pen and Sword, 1997) 38. In the same volume, the Germans are listed as having 217,000 casualties: see Heinz Hagenlucke, "The German High Command," 54; and 216,000 in German Werth, "Flanders 1917 and the German Soldier," 329.

44. Prior & Wilson, *Passchendaele* (pg. 682, note 5).

45. Nicholson, *CEF*, 329.

46. Colonel Roderick Macleod (translator), "Great Battles Fought during the First World War, 1914–1918: Flanders 1917," translation from the German Official History and General von Kuhl's account, [*Der Weltkrieg, 1914–1918, Deutschen voike dargestelt*, 2 volumes (Berlin: W. Kolk, 1929)], Woolwich: Library of the Royal Artillery Museum, 21. Courtesy of Mark Humphries.

CHAPTER 24: "EDUCATED LARGELY BY OUR OWN MISTAKES" (PP. 367–382)

1. LAC, CP, v. 1, file 1, Currie to Sir William Hearst, 14 November 1917; also see LAC, RG 9, v. 3854, 71/7, Causes of Success and Failure—Passchendaele, report by Currie, 20 November 1917.

2. LAC, MG 30 E220, E.W. Russell papers, memoir, A Private Soldier's View of the Great War, 1914–1918, 15.

3. CWM, 58A 1 182.1, William Antliff papers, 2 December 1917.

4. Gibbs, *The War Dispatches*, 396.

5. J. Castell Hopkins, *Canada at War* (Toronto: The Canadian Annual Review Limited, 1919) 178.

6. LAC, RG 24, v. 1842, 10-44, Statement of the CEF in Canada and Overseas.

7. On conscription, see J.L. Granatstein and J.M. Hitsman, *Broken Promises: A History of Conscription in Canada* (Toronto: Oxford University Press, 1977).

8. LAC, MG 30 E65, Henry W. Baldwin papers, Baldwin to Will, 4 January 1918.

9. Wheeler, *The 50th Battalion in No Man's Land*, 175.

10. LAC, CP, v. 1, file, 1, Currie to Creelman, 30 November 1917.

11. See A.M.J. Hyatt, "Sir Arthur Currie and Conscription: A Soldier's View," *Canadian Historical Review* 50.3 (September 1969) 287; McGill Archives, MG 4027, H.M. Urquhart papers, box 1, file 13, Telegram from McInnes to Currie, 5 December 1917; Ibid., Currie to Oliver, 9 December 1917.

12. LAC, CP, v. 2, file M–R, Currie to Perley, 10 December 1917.

13. J.P. Harris, *Amiens to the Armistice: The BEF in the Hundred Days' Campaign, 8 August–11 November 1918* (London: Brassey's, 1998) 23.

14. Chris McCarthy, "Queen of the Battlefield: The Development of Command Organisation and Tactics in the British Infantry Battalion during the Great War," in Gary Sheffield and Dan Todman (eds.), *Command and Control on the Western Front: The British Army's Experience 1914–1918* (London: Spellmount, 2002) 185.

15. Dancocks, *Sir Arthur Currie*, 141–2.

16. For Currie's opinion, see LAC, CP, v. 1, file 2, Currie to F.O. Loomis, 27 January 1918.

17. McGill Archives, MG 4027, H.M. Urquhart papers, box 1, file 13, Currie to Loomis, 27 January 1918.

18. Urquhart, *Arthur Currie*, 205–6.

19. LAC, RG 24, v. 1833, file GAQ 8-16, Notes re. Organization of Canadian Machine Gun Sections, Brigade Machine Gun Companies, Machine Gun Companies, and Machine Gun Battalions; Michael Holden, Constantly Shifting and Constantly Adapting: The Tactical Exploits of the Canadian Motor Machine Gun Brigades, 1914–1918, (Master's thesis: University of New Brunswick, 2003) 52–3.

20. Stewart, Attack Doctrine in the Canadian Corps, 186–7; Rawling, *Surviving Trench Warfare*, 175–6; Kenneth Radley, *We Lead, Others Follow: First Canadian Division 1914–1918* (St. Catharines: Vanwell, 2006) 115.

21. Nicholson, *CEF*, 315.

22. Nicholson, *Gunners of Canada*, v. 1. 209.

23. Paul Dickson, *A Thoroughly Canadian General: A Biography of General H.D.G. Crerar* (Toronto: University of Toronto Press, 2007) 62–3.

24. Colonel A.J. Kerry and Major W.A. McDill, *The History of the Corps of Royal Canadian Engineers, Vol. 1: 1749–1939* (Ottawa: The Military Engineers Association of Canada, 1962) 161–4.

25. Shane Schreiber, *Shock Army of the British Empire: The Canadian Corps in the Last 100 Days of the Great War* (Westport: Praeger, 1997) 22.

26. LAC, MG 30 E75, H.M. Urquhart papers, v. 3, file 6, Currie to Turner, 3 November 1917.

27. Sheldon-Williams, *The Canadian Front*, 143.

28. Denis Winter, *Haig's Command: A Reassessment* (London: Penguin, 1992) 146–7.

29. LAC, CP, v. 10, file 29, undated note in file.

30. Pope, *Letters from the Front*, 106.

31. McGill Archives, MG 4027, H.M Urquhart papers, box 1, file 13, Response to Circular letter, Ox Webber, n.d. [ca. 1934].

32. A.M.J. Hyatt, "Sir Arthur Currie and Politicians: A Case Study of Civil-Military Relations in the First World War," in Richard Preston and Peter Dennis, *Swords and Covenants* (Croom Helm: Rowman and Littlefield, 1976) 156.

33. Cook, *Clio's Warriors,* chapter 1.

34. Becker, *Silhouettes of the Great War*, 167.

35. LAC, CP, v. 2, file 4, Currie to Swayne, 23 January 1918.

36. CLIP, Ronald MacKinnon, letter to father, 10 September 1916.

37. Arthur Hunt Chute, *The Real Front* (New York: Harper, 1918) 240.

38. Hugh Monaghan, *The Big Bombers of World War 1: A Canadian's Journal* (Burlington: Ray-Gentle/Communications, 1976) 44.

39. Herbert McBride, *The Emma Gees* (Indianapolis: Bobbs-Merrill, 1918) 98.

40. Wilfred Brenton Kerr, *Arms and the Maple Leaf: Memories of Canada's Corps, 1918* (Seaforth, Ontario: The Huron Expositor Press, 1943) 40.

41. Kerr, *Arms and the Maple Leaf,* 40–1.

42. LAC, CP, v. 2, file 4, Currie to Swayne, 23 January 1918.

CHAPTER 25: BACKS TO THE WALL (PP. 383–398)

1. Michael Neiberg, *Fighting the Great War: A Global History* (Cambridge: Harvard University Press, 2005) 225.

2. Martin Kitchen, *The German Offensives of 1918*, 16; Tim Travers, "Reply to John Hussey: The Movement of German Divisions to the Western Front, Winter 1917–1918," *War in History* 5.3 (1998) 368.

3. See David Zabecki, *The German 1918 Offensive: A Case Study in the Operational Level of War* (London: Routledge Press, 2006).

4. CWM, 58A 2 7.7, George McFarland papers, memoirs, 24 December 1917.

5. LAC, RG 9, v. 3751, diary of G.S. Strathy, 15 January 1918.

6. C.S. Grafton, *The Canadian "Emma Gees"* (London: The Canadian Machine Gun Corps Association, 1938) 104.

7. Macintyre, *Canada at Vimy*, 148.

8. CWM, 20030169, John Baird papers, diary, 9 January 1918.

9. For the administration of this program, and earlier leaves for compassionate leave, see RG 9, III, v. 2853, 9–33.

10. A.L. Barry, *Batman to Brigadier* (self-published, 1969) 36.

11. Breckenridge, *From Vimy to Mons*, 63.

12. Wheeler, *The 50th Battalion in No Man's Land*, 191.

13. CWM, 58A 2.7.7, George F. McFarland papers, memoirs, 4–5 September 1917.

14. CWM, MHRC, T/9, Notes on Recent Fighting – No. 16, issued 11 June 1918.

15. LAC, RG 9, v. 3980, 17/8, Secret Report from Chemical Advisor of the Canadian Corps. Total casualties from 1 December 1917 to 21 March 1918 were 3,552.

16. LAC, MG 30 E32, Albert West papers, diary, 5 March 1918.

17. Dancocks, *Legacy of Valour*, 6.

18. See Martin Kitchen, *The German Offensives of 1918* (Stroud: Tempus, 2005).

19. Travers, *How the War Was Won*, 54.

20. Kitchen, *The German Offensives of 1918*, 68.

21. Rudolf Binding, *A Fatalist at War* (London: G. Allen and Unwin, 1929) 204.

22. CWM, CP, 58A 1.60.1, Notes on Defensive Employment of Machine Guns, Lessons Learned in Recent Fighting, 4 April 1918; Ibid., 58A 1.60.2., Notes on Recent Fighting – No. 10, The Creeping Barrage.

23. CWM, CP, 58A 1.60.3, Experiences of the Recent Fighting (Translation of a German document), Ia/54064, 22.7.18.

24. CWM, CP, 58A 1.60.2, Iz/51186, Notes on the Conduct of the Infantry Attack, 23 April 1918.

25. Strachan, *The First World War*, 289.

26. LAC, RG 9, v. 4032, 1/11, Change in the Discipline and Morale of the German Army; Neiberg, *Fighting the Great War*, 317.

27. LAC, RG 9, III, v. 4245, 6/2, Harassing fire, 17 April 1918.

28. Morrison, *Hell upon Earth*, 146.

29. Russenholt, *Six Thousand Canadian Men*, 141.

30. Becker, *Silhouettes of the Great War*, 162–3.

31. John Marteinson, *We Stand on Guard: An Illustrated History of the Canadian Army* (Montreal: Orvale Publications, 1992) 183.

32. DHH, Narrative, Covering Operations of the 1st Canadian Motor Machine Gun Brigade, the Canadian Independent Force, the Composite Brigade and Brutinel's Brigade During 1918 (Army Historical Section, 1926) 7. I would like to thank Dwight Mercer and the CEF Study Group for sharing this document.

33. Cameron Pulsifer, "Death at Licourt: An Historical and Visual Record of Five Fatalities in the 1st Canadian Motor Machine Gun Brigade, 25 March 1918," *Canadian Military History* 11.3 (Summer 2002) 56.

34. Cameron Pulsifer, "Canada's First Armoured Unit," *Canadian Military History* 10.1 (Winter 2001) 51.

35. See Charles E. Connolly, "The Action of the Canadian Cavalry Brigade at Moreuil Wood," *Canadian Defence Quarterly* 3.1 (October 1925).

36. John Grodzinski and Michael McNorgan, "'It's a charge, boys, it's a charge!' Cavalry Action at Moreuil Wood, 30 March 1918," in Donald Graves (ed.), *Fighting for Canada: Seven Battles, 1758–1945* (Toronto: Robin Brass, 2000) 265.

37. S.H. Williams, *Stand to Your Horses: Through the First World War with Lord Strathcona's Horse (Royal Canadians)* (self-published, 1961) 206.

38. A.M.J. Hyatt, *General Sir Arthur Currie: A Military Biography* (Toronto: University of Toronto Press, in collaboration with the Canadian War Museum, 1987) 104–7; quote from Gary Sheffield and John Bourne (ed.), *Douglas Haig: War Diaries and Letters, 1914–1918* (London: Weidenfeld & Nicolson, 2005) 405.

39. Robert Blake, *The Private Papers of Douglas Haig, 1914–1919* (London: Eyre & Spottiswoode, 1952) 266.

40. Desmond Morton, "'Junior but Sovereign Allies:' The Transformation of the Canadian Expeditionary Force, 1914–1918," *Journal of Imperial & Commonwealth History* 8.1 (October 1979) 56–67.

41. CWM, Sir Arthur Currie, *Canadian Corps Operations during the Year 1918—Interim Report* (Ottawa, 1919) 19–20; LAC, CP, diary, 31 March 1918.

42. McGill Archives, MG 4027, H.M Urquhart papers, box 1, file 13, Brig-General Alexander Ross to Urquhart, n.d. [ca. 1934]; Jonathan Vance, *Death So Noble: Memory, Meaning and the First World War* (Vancouver: University of British Columbia Press, 1997) 101–2.

43. Zubkowski, *As Long as Faith and Freedom Last*, 313.

44. McGill Archives, MG 4027, H.M Urquhart papers, box 1, file 13, Response to Circular letter by Brigadier General Ox Webber, n.d. [ca. 1934]; Ibid., file 12, D.E. Macintyre to Urquhart, 20 November 1934; Griesbach to Urquhart, 26 October 1934.

45. LAC, RG 41, v. 9, H.W. Johnston, 1/14.

CHAPTER 26: "OUR NERVES GREW STEADIER; OUR TEMPERS IMPROVED" (PP. 399–408)

1. Travers, *How the War Was Won*, 45.

2. LAC, CP, v. 1, file 1, Currie to Borden, 26 November 1918.

3. WD, 2nd Canadian Division, digitized Narrative of Operations, 13 March to 11 November 1918, 2.

4. Robert E. Inglis, *Reminiscences of World War I* (self-published, 1967) 82.

5. LAC, RG 41, B-III-1, *Flanders Fields*, v. 11, C.J. Albon, 3/3.

6. Dave Campbell, The Divisional Experience in the C.E.F., 398.

7. LAC, 2nd Canadian Division, digitized Narrative of Operations, 13 March to 11 November 1918, 3.

8. McGill Archives, MG 4027, H.M. Urquhart papers, box 1, file 12, Currie to Macdonald, 5 March 1924.

9. CLIP, William (Bill) Hutchinson, 16 May 1918.

10. James McRandle and James Quirk, "The Blood Test Revisited: A New Look at German Casualty Counts in World War I," *Journal of Military History* 70 (July 2006) 686; Hew Strachan, "The Morale of the German Army," in Hugh Cecil and Peter Liddell, *Facing Armageddon: the First World War Experienced* (Barnsley, U.K.: Pen and Sword, 1996) 390.

11. Englander, "Mutinies and Military Morale,"198–9.

12. Harald Hoiback, *Command and Control in Military Crisis* (London: Frank Cass Publishers, 2003) 44.

13. S.L.A. Marshall, *World War I* (Boston: Houghton Mifflin Books, 2001) 301.

14. Strachan, *The First World War*, 303.

15. Neiberg, *Fighting the Great War*, 334.

16. Dancocks, *Sir Arthur Currie*, 148.

17. Morton, *When Your Number's Up*, 68; LAC, MG 30 E220, E.W. Russell papers, memoir, 29.

18. LAC, RG 24, v. 1824, file GAQ 5-42, The Growth and Control of the Overseas Military Forces of Canada, 2–16.

19. Urquhart, *History of the 16th Battalion*, 262.

20. For training, see Mark Osborne Humphries, "The Myth of the Learning Curve: Tactics and Training in the 12th Canadian Infantry Brigade, 1916-1918," *Canadian Military History* 14.4 (2005) 15–30.

21. LAC, CP, v. 2, file 4, Currie to Swayne, 23 January 1918.

22. Dinesen, *Merry Hell!*, 149.

23. LAC, MG 30 E15, W.A. Griesbach papers, v. 3, file 16 (B), Book of Wisdom III, G.874-8, 27 June 1918, 1st Brigade to all COs, Attacking M.G. Defences in Depth.

24. Quoted in Stewart, Attack Doctrine in the Canadian Corps, 197.

25. Gould, *From B.C. to Baisieux*, 88.

26. Pedley, *Only This*, 281.

27. Pope, *Letters from the Front*, 124.

28. LAC, MG 30 E65, Henry W. Baldwin papers, letter to mother, 18 June 1918.

CHAPTER 27: THE EMPIRE STRIKES BACK (PP. 409–418)

1. Michael Neiberg, "'What True Misery Is': France's Crisis of Morale 1917," in Peter Dennis and Jeffrey Grey (eds.), *1917: Tactics, Training and Technology* (Canberra: The Chief of the Army's Military History Conference 2007) 121.

2. Simkins, *The First World War*, 62.

3. Russenholt, *Six Thousand Canadian Men*, 153.

4. CWM, 19930034-018, Brooke Ferrar Gossage, diary, 2 August 1918.

5. On logistics, see Neal Porter, From Logistics to Open Warfare: The State of Logistics in the Canadian Corps, August to November 1918, (Master's thesis: University of Ottawa, 2002) 28–32; and Michael P. Ryan, Supplying the Materiel Battle: Combined Logistics in the Canadian Corps, 1915–1918 (Master's thesis: Carleton University, 2005).

6. WD, 26th Battalion, August 1918, Appendix B, Report of Operations, 5 to 15 August 1918.

7. Johnston, *The 2nd Canadian Mounted Rifles*, 18.

8. Livesay, *Canada's Hundred Days*, 21.

9. Brereton Greenhous, *The Battle of Amiens, 8–11 August, 1918* (Canadian War Museum Battle Series No. 15) 6.

10. LAC, MG 30 E6, Henry Burstall papers, 3/21, 2nd Canadian Division, Narrative of Operations, March 13th to November 11th, 1918.

11. LAC, RG 9, v. 3893, 56/4, Operations of Canadian Corps Artillery, 1918, 2.

12. LAC, RG 9, reel T-11120, 1st Division, Amiens Report, 8–20 August 1918.

13. Paul Dickson, "The End of the Beginning: The Canadian Corps in 1917," in Geoffrey Hayes et al. (eds.), *Vimy Ridge: A Canadian Reassessment* (Waterloo: Wilfrid Laurier University Press, 2007) 45.

14. Dean Chappelle, "The Canadian Attack at Amiens, 8–11 August 1918," *Canadian Military History* 2.2 (Autumn 1993) 89.

15. James McWilliams and R. James Steel, *Amiens: Dawn of Victory* (Toronto: Dundurn Press, 2001) 31.

16. LAC, RG 41, v. 10, R.H. Camp, 2/5.

17. LAC, CP, v. 1, file A to F, Currie to Harold, 26 October 1918.

CHAPTER 28: THE EIGHTH OF THE EIGHTH (PP. 419–436)

1. Zubkowski, *As Long as Faith and Freedom Last*, 324.

2. Kerr, *Arms and the Maple Leaf*, 51.

3. LAC, RG 9, v. 3910, 36/3, 2nd Divisional Artillery, Report of Operations.

4. WD, 2nd Canadian Division, digitized Narrative of Operations, 13 March to 11 November 1918, 7.

5. Cane (ed.), *It Made You Think of Home*, 226.

6. WD, 19th Battalion, Report of Capture of Marcelcave, 8 August 1918.

7. From the units' war diaries: all from 8 August 1918.

8. WD, 24th Battalion, 8 August 1918; WD, 5th Brigade, Narrative of Operations, 8–10 August 1918.

9. WD, 26th Battalion, "Short Story of Three Days Fighting."

10. S. Douglas MacGowan, et al., *New Brunswick's "Fighting 26th": A History of the 26th New Brunswick Battalion, C.E.F., 1914–1919*, (St. John, NB: Neptune Publishing, 1994) 262–3.

11. Fetherstonhaugh, *The 24th Battalion*, 228; for the 26th Battalion, see the WD, company report of operations in the August 1918 appendices.

12. Stevens, *A City Goes to War*, 119.

13. CWM, 19770669-043, Raymond Collishaw papers, memoirs.

14. See Wise, *Canadian Airmen and the First World War*, 523.

15. McWilliams and Steel, *Amiens*, 118.

16. CWM, CP, 58A 1.60.3, Translation of a German Document, Notes on Anti-Tank Defence.

17. F.W. Noyes, *Stretcher Bearers at the Double* (Toronto: Hunter, Rose & Company, 1937) 213–14.

18. WD, 14th Battalion, Report of operations for 8 August 1918.

19. WD, 16th Battalion, Narrative of Action in front of Amiens.

20. LAC, MG 30 E60, H.H. Matthews papers, 7/25, 1st Division to Canadian Corps, 17 August 1918.

21. Pedley, *Only This*, 345.

22. WD, 1st Brigade, 1st Canadian Infantry Brigade Report, 12 August 1918.

23. WD, 1st Brigade, 8 August 1918.

24. WD, 10th Battalion, Narrative of Phase 'A', 7–9.8.1918.

25. The Adjutant [E.P.S. Allen], *The 116th Battalion in France* (Toronto: Hunter, Rose & Company, 1921) 68.

26. Roy, *For Most Conspicuous Bravery*, 72–3.

27. Foster, *Letters from the Front*, 312.

28. WD, 58th Battalion, Narrative of the Operation, 8–17 August 1918.

29. WD, 1st Canadian Mounted Rifles, 8 August 1918.

30. LAC, RG 24, 1835, 9–16, Narrative Covering Operations of the 1st Canadian Motor Machine Gun Brigade (Historical Section, September 1926) 14.

31. LAC, RG 9, v. 3893, 56/5, Operations of Canadian M.G. Corps, 1918, 16.

32. For the armoured cars, see Pulsifer, "Canada's First Armoured Unit," 44–57.

33. LAC, RG 9, v. 3964, 30/14, Summary of Operations, Canadian Engineers.

34. Wheeler, *The 50th Battalion in No Man's Land*, 232.

35. WD, Royal Canadian Regiment, Narrative of Operations, 8 August 1918.

36. George A. Maxwell, *Swan Song of a Rustic Moralist* (New York: Exposition Press, 1975) 116–7.

37. Ibid.

38. G.D. Kilpatrick, *Odds and Ends from a Regimental Diary* (self-published, n.d.) 20.

39. WD, August 1918, 42nd Battalion, Report of Operations Carried out by 42nd Battalion.

40. LAC, RG 24, v. 1840, GAQ 10-27, Casualties to the Canadian Cavalry Brigade, Battle of Amiens.

41. LAC, RG 9, v. 4809, 189/19–20, 4th Canadian Infantry Brigade—Comments and Lessons.

42. Urquhart, *History of the 16th Battalion*, 261.

43. CWM, George McFarland, 58A 2 7.7, memoir, 6 June 1918.

44. Nicholson, *CEF*, 405.

45. CWM, 20030140-005, J.R. Preston, diary, 8 August 1918.

46. WD, 54th Battalion, Operations, August 1918.

47. WD, 54th Battalion, Operations, August 1918, Report by OC B Company.

48. Becker, *Silhouettes of the Great War,* 203.

49. WD, 75th Battalion, 8 August 1918.

CHAPTER 29: "I THINK THIS IS THE BEGINNING OF THE END" (PP. 437–452)

1. Erich Ludendorff, *My War Memories,* v. 2 (London: Hutchinson, 1919) 679; Erich Ludendorff, *The Concise Ludendorff Memoirs, 1914–1918* (London: Hutchinson, n.d.) 290.

2. Nicholson, *CEF*, 407.

3. C.E. Montague, *Disenchantment* (London: MacGibbon & Kee, 1968 [original, 1922]) 126–7.

4. Charles Carrington, *Soldiers from the War Returning* (London: Hutchinson, 1965) 233.

5. Black, *I Want One Volunteer*, 52–3.

6. LAC, MG 30 E14, Cecil French papers, draft history of the CAVC, Amiens chapter 1.

7. William Stewart, *Memories of a Gunner* (self-published, 1986) 25.

8. LAC, RG 24. v. 1825, file GAQ 5-56, translation of German official history, *Die Katastrophe des 8 August 1918.*

9. Charles Bean, *The Australian Imperial Force in France during the Allied Offensive, 1918,* v. 6 (Sydney: Angus and Robertson, 1942) 684.

10. Kerr, *Arms and the Maple Leaf,* 56.

11. WD, 75th Battalion, 9 August 1918.

12. NAC, MG 30 E6, Henry Burstall papers, v. 3, file 21, 2nd Canadian Division, Narrative of Operations from March 13th to Nov. 11th, 1918, 1.

13. H.R.N. Clyne, M.C., *Vancouver's 29th* (Vancouver: Tobin's Tigers Association, 1964) 63.

14. WD, 29th Battalion, Narrative of Operations for 8–9 August 1918; War Diary, 6th Brigade, Narrative of Operations, Amiens.

15. WD, 31st Battalion, 9 August 1918.

16. WD, 5th Brigade, Narrative of Operations, 8–10 August 1918.

17. WD, 25th Battalion, Narrative of Events of A Company, 8–9 August.

18. WD, 5th Brigade, Narrative of Operations, 8th, 9th, 10th August 1918.

19. WD, 22nd Battalion, 9 August 1918; War Diary, 25th Battalion, Narrative of Events of A Company, 8–9 August and Narrative of Events of B Company, 8–9 August.

20. WD, 5th Brigade, Narrative of Operations, 8th, 9th, 10th August 1918.

21. WD, 2nd Brigade Narrative, 8–9 August 1918.

22. CWM, 19810280-120, T.B. Philips papers, Philips to sweetheart, 11 August 1918.

23. CWM, 20020024-003, Badeu to Whitmore, 16 August 1918.

24. Casualties in RG 9, v. 3893, Medical Arrangements during the Second Battle of Amiens, August 8th to 20th.

25. RG 9, III, v. 4810, file Medical Arrangements, Records of Canadian Medical Services During Last Hundred Days; RG 9, v. 3893, Medical Arrangements during the Second Battle of Amiens, August 8th to 20th, 4.

26. Kentner, *Some Recollections of the Battles of World War I,* 99.

27. Dinesen, *Merry Hell!,* 229.

28. Pedley, *Only This,* 363.

29. Zubkowski, *As Long as Faith and Freedom Last,* 329.

30. James Robert Johnston, *Riding into War,* 86.

31. Nicholson, *CEF,* 414.

32. CWM, *Flanders Fields,* J.A. Clark, 14/19.

33. The number of tanks available on the British front dropped from 342 on August 8 to 145 on the 9th, to 85 on the 10th, down to only 6 on the 12th. John Terraine, *The Smoke and the Fire,* 154.

34. CWM, 20030140-005, J.R. Preston papers, diary, 11–12 August 1918.

35. Freeman and Nielsen, *Far from Home,* 191.

36. McGill Archives, MG 4027, H.M. Urquhart papers, box 1, file 12, T. Stewart Lyon to Urquhart, 15 August 1934; for the letter, see RG 9, v. 3854, 73/5, Currie to Rawlinson, 13 August 1918.

37. CWM, CP, 58A 1.60.3. C.E.323/6-45, 20 August 1918.

38. CWM, CP, 58A 1.60.3, Extract from G.H.Q. Summary of Information, 26 August 1918.

39. On German anti-tank tactics, see CWM, CP, 58A 1.60.3, Translation of a German Document, Notes on Anti-Tank Defence.

40. RG 9, v. 3893, 56/4, Operations of Canadian Corps Artillery, 1918, 3.

41. Jackson Hughes, The Monstrous Anger of the Guns: The Development of British Artillery Tactics, 1914–1918, (Ph.D. dissertation: University of Adelaide, 1994) 284.

42. CLIP, Frederick Barnes, letter, 13 August 1918.

43. LAC, RG 24, v. 1844, 11-5, Amiens; on prisoners, see CWM, CP, 58A 1 60.3, Special Order [by Currie], 12 August 1918.

44. Erich Ludendorff, *My War Memories,* v.2 (London: Hutchinson, 1929): 684; McWilliams and Steel, *Amiens,* 257.

45. Daniel Dancocks, *Spearhead to Victory: Canada and the Great War* (Edmonton: Hurtig Publishers, 1987) 43.

46. LAC, RG 24, v. 1844, 11-5, Amiens.

47. CWM, 19800957-010, George Anderson papers, Anderson to Mother, 22 August 1918.

CHAPTER 30: HARD POUNDING (PP. 453–466)

1. Winter, *Haig's Command,* 204.

2. Niall J.A. Barr, "The Elusive Victory: The BEF and the Operational Level of War," Geoffrey Jensen and Andrew Wiest (eds.), *War in the Age of Technology: Myriad Faces of Modern Armed Conflict* (New York: New York University Press, 2001) 216–7.

3. William Breckenridge, *From Vimy to Mons* (self-published, 1919) 201.

4. LAC, MG 30 E75, Hugh Urquhart papers, v. 3, file 7, manuscript of *Arthur Currie,* 243.

5. *Flanders Fields,* Raymond Brutinel, 14/20.

6. Pope, *Soldiers and Politicians: Memoirs* (Toronto: University of Toronto Press, 1962) 39.

7. Travers, *How the War Was Won,* 146.

8. *Report of the Ministry, Overseas Military Forces of Canada 1918* (London, 1919) 148.

9. WD, 9th Brigade, G.662, Instruction, No. 1.

10. LAC, RG 9, v. 3893, 56/4, Operations of Canadian Corps Artillery, 1918, 4.

11. T.W. L. MacDermot, *The Seventh* (Montreal: The Seventh Canadian Siege Battery Association, n.d. [after 1944] 12.

12. J.P. Harris, *Amiens to the Armistice: The BEF in the Hundred Days' Campaign, 8 August–11 November 1918* (London: Brassey's, 1998) 154.

13. John Swettenham, *Breaking the Hindenburg Line* (Canadian War Museum: Canadian Battle Series, 1985) 13.

14. Breckenridge, *From Vimy to Mons,* 216.

15. Ogilvie, *Umty-Iddy-Umty,* 51.

16. WD, 5th Canadian Mounted Rifles, Battle of Arras Narrative.

17. Lt. Col. G. Chalmers Johnston, *The 2nd Canadian Mounted Rifles in France and Flanders* (Vernon: Vernon News, 1932) 69.

18. WD, 42nd Battalion, Report of Operations, 26 August 1918.

19. *Flanders Fields*, T.T. Shields, 14/27.

20. WD, PPCLI, Narrative of Operations, 25th–28th August 1918.

21. WD, 49th Battalion, Report of Operations [Arras].

22. WD, 27th Battalion, Instructions for the Offensive, 25 August 1918; Narrative of Attack South-East of Arras.

23. WD, 19th Battalion, Operations by the 19th Canadian Battalion, 26–29 August 1918.

24. Steuer, *Unter-Elsässische Infanterie-Regiment Nr. 132 im Weltkriege*, 399.

25. CWM, 58A 1 67.6, R.C. Germain papers, Buster to mother and father, 29 August 1918.

26. WD, 21st Battalion, 26 August 1918; WD, 20th Battalion, 30 August 1918; WD, 4th Brigade, 31 August 1918.

27. Dancocks, *Spearhead to Victory*, 98.

CHAPTER 31: "HAMMER AND TONGS FIGHTING" (PP. 467–482)

1. Foster, *Letters from the Front*, 298.

2. WD, 52nd Battalion, Narrative of Events, August 26th to 29th.

3. WD, 43rd Battalion, Narrative of Operations, August 26th to 29th.

4. LAC, MG 30 E32, Albert West papers, diary, 28 August 1918.

5. Noyes, *Stretcher Bearers at the Double*, 220.

6. WD, 19th Battalion, Operations for 19th Battalion, 26–29th August, 1918.

7. Barry, *Batman to Brigadier*, 46.

8. *Flanders Fields*, J.I. Bickerton, 14/22.

9. Serge Bernier, *The Royal 22e Regiment, 1914–1999* (Montreal: Art Global, 2000) 69.

10. Armine Norris, *Mainly for Mother*, 115.

11. Fetherstonhaugh, *The 24th Battalion*, 239–40.

12. Livesay, *Canada's Hundred Days*, 138.

13. WD, 26th Battalion, C Company report, 26–28th August, 1918.

14. WD, 26th Battalion, A Company report, 26–28th August, 1918.

15. CWM, CP, 58A 1.60.3, Experiences of the Recent Fighting (Translation of a German document), Ia/54064, 22.7.18.

16. Steuer, *Unter-Elsässische Infanterie-Regiment Nr. 132 im Weltkriege*, 399.

17. David Jay Bercuson, *True Patriot: The Life of Brooke Claxton, 1898–1960* (Toronto: University of Toronto Press, 1993) 40.

18. Norris, *Mainly for Mother*, 212.

19. For casualties, see WD, 5th Brigade, Narrative of Operations, August 19th to 29th, 1918; and the individual WDs for each unit.

20. Peter Simkins, "'Building Blocks': Aspects of Command and Control at Brigade Level in the BEF's Offensive Operations, 1916–1918," in Gary Sheffield and Dan Todman (eds.),

Command and Control on the Western Front: The British Army's Experience 1914–18 (London: Spellmount Limited, 2004) 150–1.

21. WD, 9th Brigade, Report of Operations, [73rd Battalion].

22. Nicholson, *CEF*, 432.

23. Ibid., 433.

24. *Report of the Ministry, Overseas Military Forces of Canada 1918*, 153.

25. CWM, 19900072-004, Harvey Story Spencer papers, diary, 30 August 1918.

26. CWM, 20020140-001, Clifford Johnston papers, diary, 28 August 1918.

27. Ibid., 28 September 1918.

28. LAC, RG 9, v. 3893, 56/4, Operations of Canadian Corps Artillery, 1918, 4.

29. Kerr, *Arms and the Maple Leaf*, 59.

30. LAC, MG 30 E113, George Bell papers, memoir, Back to Blighty, 127.

31. LAC, MG 30 E15, W.A. Griesbach papers, v. 1, file 1, Griesbach to Macdonell, 2 February 1927.

32. WD, 1st Battalion, 30 August 1918.

33. WD, 2nd Battalion, 30 August 1918.

34. Both quotes from WD, 1st Battalion, 30 August 1918.

35. CWM, 58A 1 188.34, George McLean papers, George to sister, 12 September [1918].

36. Ibid.

37. WD, 1st Division, Arras Operations, 28 August to 5 September 1918, No. 35, Lessons Learned.

38. WD, 1st Brigade, Report of Operations, 31 August 1918.

39. CWM, CP, 58A 60.4, General Staff Report for 30 August to 6 September [1918].

40. Dancocks, *Spearhead to Victory*, 131.

41. WD, 1st Division, Arras Operations, 28 August to 5 September 1918, No. 27, Casualties.

42. Howard Graham, *Citizen and Soldier* (Toronto: McClelland & Stewart, 1987) 65.

43. Kentner, *Some Recollections of the Battles of World War I*, 116–7.

44. Nicholson, *Gunners of Canada*, v. 1, 352, 355.

CHAPTER 32: "IT WAS MURDER TO MOVE AND SUICIDE TO STAY PUT" (PP. 483–500)

1. CWM, CP, 58A 1.60.3, First Army, No. 2379, Summary of Information, 26 August 1918.

2. LAC MG 30 E69, David Watson papers, diary, 29 August 1918.

3. LAC, CP, v. 43, diary, 29 August 1918.

4. LAC, RG 24, 1835, 9–16, Narrative Covering Operations of the 1st Canadian Motor Machine Gun Brigade (Historical Section, September 1926) 30; CWM, CP, 58A 1.60.3, Canadian Corps Operation Order, No. 234, 31 August 1918.

5. LAC, MG 30 E150, R.A. MacKay papers, v. 10, diary, 2 September 1918.

6. WD, 3rd Infantry Brigade, Narrative of Events [Message Logs].

7. LAC, CP, v. 15, file 43, Currie to Urquhart, 8 October 1931; WD, 3rd Infantry Brigade, Report on the Drocourt-Quéant Line, September 2nd, 1918; Murray, *The 2nd Battalion*, 212.

8. Urquhart, *History of the 16th Battalion*, 294.

9. WD, 3rd Infantry Brigade, Drocourt-Quéant Operations, Instructions No. 1.

10. George McKean, *Scouting Thrills: The Memoir of a Scout Officer in the Great War* (Ottawa: CEF Books, 2003) 115.

11. Fetherstonhaugh, *The Royal Montreal Regiment*, 239.

12. WD, 3rd Infantry Brigade, Report on the Drocourt-Quéant Line, September 2nd, 1918

13. Quote from WD, 3rd Infantry Brigade, Report on the Drocourt-Quéant Line, September 2nd, 1918.

14. WD, 1st Infantry Brigade, Report of Operations, 6 September 1918.

15. LAC, RG 24, v. 1824, file GAQ 5-45, H.H. Matthews report, 2 September 1918.

16. Quote from WD, 3rd Infantry Brigade, Report on the Drocourt-Quéant Line, September 2nd, 1918.

17. WD, 3rd Battalion, untitled report [Narrative of Drocourt-Quéant Line battle, 2 September, 1918].

18. WD, 3rd Infantry Brigade, Report on the Drocourt-Quéant Line, September 2nd, 1918.

19. Kentner, *Some Recollections of the Battles of World War I*, 129.

20. McWilliams and Steel, *The Suicide Battalion*, 169; WD, 44th Battalion, Report of Operations, 1 to 4 September 1918.

21. WD, 50th Battalion, 2 September 1918.

22. WD, 10th Brigade, Message Logs, Narrative of Operations for Battle of Arras.

23. Wheeler, *The 50th Battalion in No Man's Land*, 251–2.

24. Ibid.

25. WD, 12th Brigade, Report of Scarpe Operations.

26. McEvoy and Finlay, *History of the 72nd Canadian Infantry Battalion*, 131–2.

27. Hayes, *The Eighty-Fifth in France and Flanders*, 139; WD, 4th Division, Report on the Scarpe Operations.

28. WD, 4th Division, Report on the Scarpe Operations.

29. WD, 38th Battalion, Report of Operations, as part of WD, 12th Brigade, Report of Scarpe Operations.

30. WD, 72nd Battalion, Report of Operations, as part of WD, 12th Brigade, Report of Scarpe Operations

31. WD, 2nd Canadian Motor Machine Gun Brigade, Canadian Independent Force.

32. WD, 12th Brigade, Report of Scarpe Operations.

33. Ibid.

34. LAC, MG 30 E113, George Bell papers, memoir, Back to Blighty, 135.

35. Nicholson, *CEF*, 440; WD, 4th Division, Narrative of Operations, 28 August to 4 September 1918.

36. Schreiber, *Shock Army*, 1.

37. Winter, *Haig's Command*, 2 and 271.

38. LAC, CP, v. 2, file M–R, Currie to Oliver, 2 September 1918.

39. LAC, CP, v. 2, file M–R, Currie to Morrison, 11 September 1918; WD, 4th Division, Report on the Scarpe Operations.

40. Steuer, *Unter-Elsässische Infanterie-Regiment Nr. 132 im Weltkriege*, 401.

41. LAC, RG 24, v. 1844, 11-5, Arras.

42. CWM, O.B./1919, Organization of the Infantry Battalion, September 1918; Manion, *A Surgeon in Arms*, 11–12.

43. WD, 12th Brigade, Report of Scarpe Operations, Comments.

44. LAC, CP, v. 1, file A to F, Currie to Alistair, 7 December 1918.

45. Livesay, *Canada's Hundred Days*, 187.

46. LAC, CP, v. 2, file M–R, Currie to Oliver, 2 September 1918.

CHAPTER 33: "BE BOLD—ALWAYS BOLD" (PP. 501–508)

1. Dancocks, *Spearhead to Victory*, 119.

2. Russenholt, *Six Thousand Canadian Men*, 180.

3. CWM, CP, 58A 60.4, 1st Division Report of Operations, [Canal du Nord operation], Strength Return.

4. CWM, CP, 58A 1.60.3, Experiences of the Recent Fighting (Translation of a German document), Ia/54064, 22.7.18.

5. Edmonds, *Military Operations: France and Belgium, 1918*, v. 5, 312.

6. Maxwell, *Swan Song of a Rustic Moralist*, 126.

7. CWM, CP, 58A1 60.4, Ia54327, Lessons Drawn by the German Higher Command from the Recent Offensives.

8. Bird, *Ghosts Have Warm Hands*, 139.

9. LAC, RG 9, v. 3978, 9/8, B.M. 50/126-1; RG 9, v. 3978, 11/9, Report on Hostile Gas Shell Bombardment on Canadian Corps Front for WEEK ending Saturday September 14th, 1918.

10. McGill Archives, MG 4027, H.M. Urquhart papers, box 1, file 12, Colonel C.D.H. MacAlphine, 12 November 1934.

11. LAC, CP, diary, 10 September 1918.

12. Major-General Sir W. Hastings Anderson, "The Crossing of the Canal du Nord," *Canadian Defence Quarterly* 2.1 (October 1924) 65.

13. LAC, MG 30 E15, W.A. Griesbach papers, v. 1, file 1, G.6-97, Lessons Learned from Recent Fighting, by 1st Division.

14. LAC, RG 41, 72nd Battalion, Harold Cline, 1/9.

15. John Terraine, *To Win a War: 1918, the Year of Victory* (London: Sidgwick & Jackson, 1978) 158.

16. Pope, *Soldiers and Politicians*, 40–1.

CHAPTER 34: SHOCK AND AWE (PP. 509–534)

1. *Report of the Ministry, Overseas Military Forces of Canada, 1918*, 157.

2. LAC, RG 9, v. 4807, file 176, Artillery Notes: Bourlon Wood, 27 September–1 October 1918.

3. LAC, RG 9, v. 3893, 56/4, Appendix B, Table of Batteries, Guns, Personnel.

4. Count Richard Rose, *Das Infanterie-Regiment 188 im Weltkriege*. (Eisleben: n.p., 1928), 308. Translation by Wilhelm Kiesselbach; courtesy of Mark Humphries.

5. CWM, 20010241-015, Hendershott brothers papers, Warren to mother, 27 September 1918.

6. CWM, CP, 58A 1.60.4, G.760-8, 1st Brigade Report of Operations.

7. Ibid.

8. WD, 3rd Canadian Division, Report on Cambrai Battle, digitized, The Engagement of German Divisions.

9. Nicholson, *CEF*, 446fn.

10. Fetherstonaugh, *The Royal Montreal Regiment*, 251.

11. WD, 50th Battalion, Report of Operations.

12. Wheeler, *The 50th Battalion in No Man's Land*, 265.

13. For the role of the engineers, see Bill Rawling, *Technicians of Battle* (Toronto: Military Engineering Institute of Canada, 2001) 40–4.

14. LAC, RG 9, v. 4807, file 174, Artillery Notes.

15. Sir Archibald Macdonell, "The Old Red Patch: The 1st Canadian Division at the Breaking of the Canal du Nord Line," *Canadian Defence Quarterly* 9.1 (October 1931) 3; also see CWM, CP, 58A1 60.4, Notes on Recent Fighting, No. 20.

16. WD, 2nd Battalion, Report of Operations.

17. WD, 2nd Brigade, Narrative of Operations, Bourlon Wood.

18. Dancocks, *Spearhead to Victory*, 144.

19. CWM, CP, 58A 1.60.4, G.760-8, 1st Brigade Report of Operations.

20. LAC, RG 41, 85th Battalion, Small and Cromwell, 2/3.

21. Hayes, *The Eighty-Fifth in France and Flanders*, 168–9.

22. LAC, RG 24, v. 1813, file 4-15E, biography of J.L. Ralston.

23. LAC, MG 30 E393, A.J. Foster papers, memoir, 27.

24. WD, 12th Brigade, Bourlon Wood operations, 72nd Battalion.

25. Dictionary of Canadian Biography Online, Fred Gaffen, "Samuel Honey"; CWM, 58 1 112.12, Samuel Honey papers, Semmens to Honey's parents, 7 October 1918.

26. Urquhart, *History of the 16th Battalion*, 240.

27. WD, 11th Brigade, Report of Operations, Bourlon Wood.

28. Ibid.

29. WD, Royal Canadian Regiment, Narrative of Operations.

30. Morrison, *Hell upon Earth*, 157.

31. Russenholt, *Six Thousand Canadian Men*, 199.

32. Foster, *Letters from the Front*, 301.

33. McWilliams and Steel, *The Suicide Battalion*, 181.

34. WD, 10th Battalion, Narrative of Operations, 4 October 1918.

35. Ibid.

36. WD, 2nd Brigade, Narrative of Operations, Bourlon Wood.

37. WD, 10th Battalion, Narrative of Operations, 4 October 1918.

38. CWM, 20020140-001, Clifford Johnston papers, diary, 29 September 1918.

39. Dancocks, *The Fighting Tenth*, 191.

CHAPTER 35: "EVERY TIME I LOOK AROUND FOR A FAMILIAR FACE, I FIND THEY HAVE GONE" (PP. 535–550)

1. CLIP, Bertram Cox, letter, 29 August 1918.

2. WD, 12th Brigade, October 1918, Appendix 10, Report of Operations, Canal du Nord and Cambrai.

3. McEvoy and Finlay, *History of the 72nd Canadian Infantry Battalion*, 149–50.

4. WD, 12th Brigade, Bourlon Wood operations, 72nd Battalion, Lessons.

5. WD, 9th Brigade, Narrative of Operations, 116th Battalion.

6. Topp, *The 42nd Battalion, CEF*, 269–70.

7. Breckenridge, *From Vimy to Mons*, 218.

8. Zubkowski, *As Long as Faith and Freedom Last*, 343.

9. *Report of the Ministry, Overseas Military Forces of Canada, 1918*, 162.

10. Travers, *How the War Was Won*, 156.

11. Schreiber, *Shock Army*, 106.

12. WD, 11th Brigade, Report of Operations, Bourlon Wood Attack [misfiled in WD, February 1919].

13. CWM, 20030140-005, J.R. Preston papers, diary, 2 October 1918.

14. *Report of the Ministry, Overseas Military Forces of Canada, 1918*, 162.

15. WD, 1st Brigade, Attack on Abancourt, 1 October 1918.

16. Ibid.

17. Ibid.

18. *Report of the Ministry, Overseas Military Forces of Canada, 1918*, 162.

19. CWM, CP, 58A 1.60.4, 1st Canadian Division, Report on Administrative Arrangements for Bourlon Wood and Cambrai Operations.

20. WD, 9th Brigade, Narrative of Operations, Identification.

21. WD, 9th Brigade, Narrative of Operations, Lessons.

22. WD, 9th Brigade, Narrative of Operations, Casualties.

23. MacDermot, *The Seventh*, 131.

24. WD, 3rd Canadian Division, Report on Cambrai Battle, The Engagement of German Divisions.

25. LAC, CP, v.1, file A to F, Currie to Borden, 26 November 1918.

26. CWM, CP, 58A 1.60.4, 1st Canadian Division Report on Administrative Arrangements for Bourlon Wood and Cambrai Operations.

27. WD, 3rd Canadian Division, Report on Cambrai Battle, Casualties.

28. WD, 4th Division, G.29/S734, Narrative of Operations, Enemy Order of Battle.

29. Barry, *Batman to Brigadier*, 58.

30. Lynch, *Princess Patricia's Canadian Light Infantry*, 182.

31. LAC, MG 30 E32, Albert West papers, diary, 9 September 1918.

32. Cane, *It Made You Think of Home*, 264.

33. WD, 9th Brigade, Narrative of Operations, Special Order of the Day, 3 October 1918.

34. Schreiber, *Shock Army*, 107.

35. Hastings Anderson, "Lord Horne as an Army Commander," *Journal of the Royal Artillery* 56.4 (January 1930) 416–17.

36. LAC, CP, v.2, file M–R, Currie to Miller, 4 October 1918.

CHAPTER 36: "WE STEELED OURSELVES NOT TO LET DOWN THE CORPS" (PP. 551–568)

1. LAC, CP, v.1, file A–F, Currie to Borden, 26 November 1918. Also see *Report of the Ministry, Overseas Military Forces of Canada*, 194.

2. LAC, CP, v. 2, file M–R, Currie to Oliver, 2 September 1918; LAC, v. 1, file 2, Currie to Kemp, 1 November 1918.

3. Figures compiled from Nicholson, *CEF*, 419 and 460.

4. Neiberg, *Fighting the Great War: A Global History*, 187.

5. Sheldon-Williams, *The Canadian Front*, 156.

6. WD, 3rd Canadian Division, Report of Operations, 1918/10/22 to 1918/11/11, Report of Operations, 3rd Brigade, Canadian Engineers.

7. CWM, 19800957-010, George Anderson papers, Anderson to Ruby, 1 November 1918.

8. WD, 3rd Canadian Division, Report of Operations, 1918/10/22 to 1918/11/11, Administration of Civilians.

9. Dancocks, *Sir Arthur Currie*, 169.

10. Robertson, *A Terrible Beauty*, 96.

11. James A. Elliot (compiler), *Book of Remembrance: A Record of the Men of Port Hope Who Participated in the Great War of 1914–1918* (1919, reprinted by the Port Hope Archives, 2007) 81.

12. LAC, MG 30 E32, Albert West papers, diary, 24 October 1918.

13. Schreiber, *Shock Army*, 121.

14. WD, 44th Battalion, Report of Operations, 29 October to 1 November 1918.

15. A.G.L. McNaughton, "Introduction," in J.A. MacDonald, *Gun-Fire: An Historical Narrative of The 4th Brigade, C.F.A.* (unknown publisher, 1929) 11.

16. DHH, unprocessed central registry files, box 7, file 1-6-6, pt. I, McNaughton to Nicholson, 4 May 1961.

17. LAC, RG 9, v. 3914, 46/13, Outline of Report … Mont Houy Operation; Bill Rawling, "A Resource Not to Be Squandered: The Canadian Corps on the Battlefield," in Peter Dennis and Jeffrey Grey (eds.), *1918: Defining Victory* (Canberra: Army Historical Unit, 1999) 66.

18. Kerr, *Arms and the Maple Leaf*, 80.

19. LAC, CP, v. 1, file 2, Currie to Kemp, 1 November 1918.

20. WD, 44th Battalion, Report of Operations, 29 October to 1 November 1918.

21. LAC, RG 9, v. 3914, 46/13, Report of Mont Houy Operations.

22. McWilliams and Steel, *The Suicide Battalion*, 198.

23. WD, 46th Battalion, Report of Operations, 1 November 1918.

24. On Cairns, see WD, 46th Battalion, 'A' Company report on Valenciennes battle, 1 November 1918; McWilliams and Steel, *The Suicide Battalion*, 200–1.

25. WD, 46th Battalion, Report of Operations, 1 November 1918.

26. McWilliams and Steel, *The Suicide Battalion*, 202.

27. WD, 47th Battalion, Report of Operations, 31 October to 1 November 1918.

28. LAC, RG 9, v. 3914, 46/13, Outline of Report … Mont Houy Operation.

29. WD, 38th Battalion, 1 November 1918.

30. WD, 72nd Battalion, Seaforth Highlanders of Canada, Report of Operations, 22 October to 6 November 1918.

31. LAC, RG 9, v. 3914, 46/13, Report of Mont Houy Operations; WD, 46th Battalion, Examination of prisoners, IG9/1.

32. Foster, *Letters from the Front*, 304.

33. WD, 50th Battalion, Report of Operations, Valenciennes.

34. LAC, CP, v. 13, file 38, Peck to Currie, 11 July 1931.

35. LAC, RG 9, v. 3914, 46/13, Report of Mont Houy Operations.

CHAPTER 37: "A BLOODY LONG WAY TO MONS" (PP. 569–580)

1. Ogilvie, *Umty-Iddy-Umty*, 53.

2. DHH, unprocessed central registry files, box 7, file 1-6-6, pt. I, J.L. Melville to Nicholson, 17 August 1961.

3. WD, 5th CMRs, Report of Operations, 2–9 November 1918.

4. LAC, RG 24, v. 1810, file GAQ 2-1, v. 1, 1st Canadian Division, Order of Battle, 11.11.18.

5. WD, 3rd Canadian Division, Report on Cambrai Battle, digitized, The Engagement of German Divisions.

6. WD, 3rd Canadian Division, Report of Operations, 22 October to 11 November, 1918, Canadian Corps order, I.G. 168.

7. CWM, 20000034-044, Letters to Daniel Smith from former pupils, Alton to Smith, 10 November 1918.

8. WD, 3rd Canadian Division, Report of Operations, 1918/10/12 to 1918/11/11.

9. Nicholson, *CEF*, 482.

10. CWM, CP, 58A 1 61.5, Currie to Mewburn, 17 March 1919.

11. Bird, *Ghosts Have Warm Hands*, 147.

12. LAC, CP, v. 18, file 61, W. Martin King to Currie, 30 March 1928.

13. Nicholson, *CEF*, 482.

14. CWM, 19880282-003, J. Mansfield papers, diary, 11 November 1918.

15. G.R. Stevens, *A City Goes to War* (Brampton: Charters Publishing Company, 1964) 140.

16. 3rd Canadian Division, Report of Operations, 1918/10/12 to 1918/11/11. See Report of Casualties. This figure is important as a decade later, during the 1928 Sir Arthur Currie defamation of character trial, it would be reported that only one Canadian was killed on 11 November.

17. LAC, RG 24, v. 448, HQC 54-21-1-210, Circumstances of Death, 18 November 1918; LAC, CP, v. 18, file 61, W.B. Pearson to Currie, 3 August 1931.

18. LAC, RG 24, v. 1844, file 11-5, Casualties, [Hundred Days]; Simkins, "'Building Blocks,'" 165.

CHAPTER 38: "I WANTED TO GET THE HELL HOME" (PP. 581–597)

1. CWM, 19800957-010, George Anderson papers, Anderson to mother, 11 November 1918.

2. Macpherson, *A Soldier's Diary*, 161.

3. LAC, RG 41, v. 10, 2/10-11, Bert Warren, 20th Battalion.

4. CWM, 20030142-001, William H. Hay papers, Hendrie to mother, 28 November 1918.

5. I.F.W. Beckett, *The Great War, 1914–1918* (New York: Longman, 2001) 387.

6. Craig, *But This Is Our War*, 140.

7. Murray, *The 2nd Battalion*, 328.

8. CWM, CP, file 58A 1 61.1, Griesbach to Macdonell, 22 December 1918.

9. Stevens, *A City Goes to War*, 144.

10. Cited in Rawling, *Death Thine Enemy*, 100.

11. CWM, 58A 1 141.3, A.O. White, Memories of World War I, November–December 1918.

12. McGill Archives, H.M. Urquhart papers, 4027, box 1, file 12, Griesbach to Urquhart, 26 October 1934.

13. CWM, 58A 1 217.1, Garnet Dobbs papers, letter, 4 January 1919.

14. LAC, MG 30 E241, D.E. Macintyre, diary, 13 December 1918.

15. CWM, MHRC, GOC, 2nd Army, A.G. 2981/P.S. [n.d., post-11 November 1918].

16. LAC, MG 30 E15, W.A. Griesbach papers, v. 1, file 5, diary, 10 December 1918.

17. Morrison, *Hell upon Earth*, 166.

18. Urquhart, *History of the 16th Battalion*, 328.

19. CWM, 58A 1.8.5, A Private's Own Story of the First World War, by William B. Woods, 22.

20. LAC, RG 9, III-C-3, v. 4024, 4/8, Order by Plumer, Second Army, to CEF, 27 Nov 1918.

21. Spear and Stewart, *Carry On*, 69.

22. CWM, CP, 58A 1 61.3, Currie to Mewburn, 1 January 1919.

23. LAC, RG 9, III A 1, v. 93, 10-12-50, pt. 2, case file of Pte. A.D. Norval, 1263356.

24. LAC, RG 9, III-C-5, v. 4389, file 19/1, Minutes of a Conference Held at [3rd] Divisional Hdqrs, 18 Dec. [1918].

25. LAC, MG 30 E15, W.A. Griesbach papers, v. 1, file 7: Memo, 1st Brigade, 2 January 1919.

26. Hyatt, *General Sir Arthur Currie*, 126.

27. Black, *I Want One Volunteer*, 48.

28. For the education program, see Tim Cook, "From Destruction to Construction: The Khaki University of Canada, 1917–1919," *Journal of Canadian Studies* 37.1 (Spring 2002) 109–43.

29. Quote from LAC, Henry Marshall Tory papers, 3/7, *General Survey of Canada's Repatriation Plans*, Repatriation Committee, Ottawa, Canada, 5. For the pivotal men policy, see Morton and Wright, *Winning the Second Battle,* 105–9; Nicholson, *CEF,* 530–3.

30. For Currie's wishes, see LAC, MG 30 E60, H.H. Mathews papers, 6/6, Demobilization Conference [6 December 1918]; LAC, CP, 1/2, Currie to Kemp, 6 November 1918.

31. LAC, RG 9, III, v. 1765, file U-1-13, pt. 16, report, 5 July 1918; Ferguson to HQ, Cdn Troops, Bramshott, 5 August 1918.

32. Tim Cook, "He was determined to go": Underage Soldiers in the Canadian Expeditionary Force," *Social History/histoire sociale* 41.81 (May 2008).

33. For the YSB riot, see LAC, RG 24, v. 1841, file GAQ 10-34F, Disturbances in Canadian Camps and Areas, 1918–1919.

34. The YSB was officially disbanded on 7 December 1918.

35. Rowlett, *Memoirs of a Signaller,* 63.

36. Howard G. Coombs, "Dimensions of Military Leadership: The Kinmel Park Mutiny of 4–5 March 1919," in Mantle, *The Apathetic and the Defiant,* 405–38.

37. Desmond Morton, "'Kicking and Complaining': Demobilization Riots in the Canadian Expeditionary Force, 1918–19," *Canadian Historical Review* 61 (1980) 346.

38. Ibid., 348.

39. Ibid., 355.

40. LAC, MG 30, D204, Frank Underhill papers, v. 16, file World War 1 Correspondence, 1919, Underhill to mother, 30 May 1919.

41. CWM, 19801226, CP, file 58A 1 61.5, Currie to Mewburn, 17 March 1919; LAC, MG 27 II-D-9, Mewburn papers, v. 154, file P-6, clippings, *Globe Toronto*, 16 March 1919.

42. LAC, CP, v. 39, file 175, Report: Canadian Troops Overseas and the British Press, 15 July 1919.

43. *Report of the Ministry, Overseas Military Forces of Canada*, 520–1.

44. Macphail, *The Medical Services*, 231 and 233.

45. Johnston, *Riding into War*, 26.

46. Macphail, *The Medical Services*, 233.

47. Morton and Granatstein, *Marching to Armageddon*, 253.

48. Vance, *Death So Noble*, 127.

CHAPTER 39: "LIFE TO ME CAN NEVER BE THE SAME" (PP. 599–610)

1. Noyes, *Stretcher Bearers at the Double*, 275.

2. Freeman and Nielsen, *Far from Home*, 234.

3. CWM, 19730066-001, Chester Routley papers, "Eighteenth Battalion," 159.

4. See Robin Brownlie, "Work Hard and Be Grateful: Native Soldier Settlers in Ontario after the First World War," in Franca Iacovetta and Wendy Mitchinson (eds.), *On the Case: Explorations in Social History* (Toronto: University of Toronto Press, 1998).

5. Lapointe, *Soldier of Quebec, 1916–1919*, preface.

6. CWM, Warren Hendershott to parents, 16 May 1918.

7. Edgett and Beatty (eds.), *The World War I Diaries and Letters of Louis Stanley Edgett*, 185–6.

8. Morton and Granatstein, *Marching to Armageddon*, 250.

9. Rawling, *Death Thine Enemy*, 106.

10. LAC, CP, v. 15, file 43, Currie to [unknown], 21 April 1927.

11. Morton and Wright, *Winning the Second Battle*, 9–10.

12. Ibid., 52.

13. Morton, *When Your Number's Up*, 265.

14. Morton, *When Your Number's Up*, 259.

15. CWM, 19820340-011, Proceeding of a Meeting of the Advisory Board to the Board of Pension Commissioners, 21 November 1916.

16. Morton and Wright, *Winning the Second Battle*, 77.

17. Jeffrey Keshen, *Propaganda and Censorship during Canada's Great War* (Edmonton: University of Alberta Press, 1996) 59.

18. Bird, *The Communication Trench*, 118.

19. For an exploration of the pension battle for non-visible wounds, see Tim Cook, *No Place to Run*, conclusion.

20. Stephen Beames, untitled memoirs, 35.

21. CWM, MHRC, *The Forty-Niner* (January 1935) 31.

22. Morton and Wright, *Winning the Second Battle*, 88.

23. LAC, MG 30 E113, George Bell papers, memoirs, introduction.

24. CWM, MHRC, *The Forty-Niner* (January 1937) 33.

25. Vance, *Death So Noble*, 89.

26. Foster, *Letters from the Front*, 219.

27. John Herd Thompson, *The Harvests of War: The Prairie West, 1914–1918* (Toronto: McClelland & Stewart, 1978) 9.

28. LAC, CP, v.9, file 27, Currie to Gibson, 29 November 1926.

29. L. James Dempsey, *Warriors of the King: Prairie Indians in World War I* (Regina: Canadian Plains Research Center, University of Regina, 1999) 72.

30. LAC, RG 41, 78th Battalion, Oscar Erickson, 2/3.

CHAPTER 40: THE BUTCHER'S BILL (PP. 611–620)

1. Niall Ferguson, *The Pity of War*, 295; Modris Eksteins, "Memory and the Great War," in Hew Strachan, *The Oxford Illustrated History of the First World War* (Oxford: Oxford University Press, 1998) 307.

2. Stéphane Audoin-Rouzeau and Annette Becker, *1914–1918: Understanding the Great War*, 21–2.

3. LAC, RG 24, 10-47E, v. 1843, Scott to Secretary, Office of the High Commissioner, 3 September 1930; C.A. Sharpe, "Enlistment in the Canadian Expeditionary Force 1914–1918: A Regional Analysis," *Journal of Canadian Studies* 18.4 (1983–84) 17–19.

4. LAC, RG 24, v. 1843, Scott to Ebbs, 31 March 1932.

5. See Wise, *Canadian Airmen and the First World War*, 645.

6. For the Newfoundlanders, see Nicholson, *The Fighting Newfoundlander: A History of the Royal Newfoundland Regiment* (St. John's: The Government of Newfoundland, 1964) 508–9 and David R. Facey-Crowther, *Lieutenant Owen William Steele of the Newfoundland Regiment* (Montreal: McGill-Queen's University Press, 2002) 13. The Books of Remembrance record the names of 1,656 dead from the Great War, but see the discussion later in this chapter for the nuances surrounding casualty figures, especially from the Books of Remembrance. Of the 60,932 dead, 2,919 died in Canada, presumably a combination of wounded Canadians coming back from overseas and succumbing to their wounds and Canadians dying in training camps in Canada. See Nicholson, *CEF*, 548.

7. This does not include 2,415 Newfoundlanders wounded or captured prisoner. The 172,950 figure includes 34,784 injuries and other non-fatal casualties not suffered in battle, of which 21,471 occurred in France and Belgium, as well as 13,313 suffered in other theatres, the majority occurring in England. See Nicholson, *CEF*, 548.

8. Morton, *When Your Number's Up*, 257.

9. Figures from LAC, RG 24, v. 1820, file GAQ 5-14, The Canadians in the Great War.

10. LAC, RG 24, v. 1821, file GAQ 5-16, Total and average number of other ranks who passed through the four divisions' infantry battalions.

11. Fuller, *Troop Morale*, 30.

12. LAC, RG 24, v. 1821, file GAQ 5-16, Statement showing the number of other ranks that passed through the fighting battalions of the Canadian Corps.

13. Bennett, *The 4th Canadian Mounted Rifles, 1914–1919*, 154–5.

14. RG 24, v. 1843, 10-47E, Duguid to Thompson, Board of Pension Commissioners, 19 April 1932, appendix, Statistics OMFC.

15. Edmonds, *Military Operations: France and Belgium, 1916*, v. 1, 282.

16. Mitchell and Smith, *Medical Services*, 40.

17. The figures come from Nicholson, *CEF*, 548. Of those casualties, 10,661 were suffered by infantry, artillery, engineers, and machine-gunners. There is no mention of how many of the gas casualties were fatal. Macphail incorrectly gives the total gas casualties as 11,356 (see *The Medical Services*).

18. Total casualties from Nicholson, *CEF*, 535.

19. Cook, *No Place to Run*, 229–30.

20. Macphail, *The Medical Services*, 396.

21. Morton, *When Your Number's Up*, 181.

22. Hayes, *The Eighty-Fifth in France and Flanders*, 205.

23. Figures compiled from the CWGC database. The author would also like to thank Dominique Boulais, deputy secretary-general of the Canadian Agency, Commonwealth War Graves Commission, for confirming statistics.

24. The author would like to thank Catherine Tremblay, senior officer for Canada Remembers Ottawa of the Department of Veterans Affairs, for sharing some research on the Books of Remembrance.

CHAPTER 41: WHITHER THE GREAT WAR? (PP. 621–648)

1. See Vance, *Death So Noble*; Suzanne Evans, *Mothers of Heroes, Mothers of Martyrs: World War I and the Politics of Grief* (Montreal: McGill-Queen's University Press, 2007).

2. David W. Lloyd, *Battlefield Tourism: Pilgrimage and the Commemoration of the Great War in Britain, Australia and Canada, 1919–1939* (Oxford: Berg, 1998).

3. Vance, *Death So Noble*, 51; for the importance of naming, see Thomas Laqueur, "Memory and Naming in the Great War," in J.R. Gillis (ed.), *Commemorations: The Politics of National Identity* (Princeton: Princeton University Press, 1994) 150–67.

4. Alan Young, "'We Throw the Torch': Canadian Memorials of the Great War and the Mythology of Heroic Sacrifice," *Journal of Canadian Studies* 24 (1989/90) 5–28.

5. Laura Brandon, *Art or Memorial?: The Forgotten History of Canada's War Art* (Calgary: University of Calgary Press, 2006) chapter 1.

6. Jacqueline Hucker, "After the Agony in Stony Places: The Meaning and Significance of the Vimy Monument," in Geoffrey Hayes et al. (eds.), *Vimy Ridge: A Canadian Reassessment* (Waterloo: Wilfrid Laurier University Press, 2007) 279–90.

7. LAC, CP, v. 11, file 33, Currie to A.C. Macdonell, 19 April 1922.

8. Desmond Morton, *A Military History of Canada: From Champlain to the Gulf War*, Third Edition (Toronto: McClelland & Stewart, 1992) 176.

9. Steve Harris, "From Subordinate to Ally," *Revue Internationale d'Historie Militaire* 51 (1982) 110.

10. Stevens, *A City Goes to War*, 145.

11. LAC, RG 41, 85th Battalion, A.Y. Jackson, 1/13.

12. House of Commons Debates, Session 1919, vol. 1, 3 March 1919, 207.

13. McGill Archives, H.M Urquhart papers, MG 4027, box 11, file 3, Currie to Margerie Currie, 26 December 1918.

14. For the best account of the trial, see Robert J. Sharpe, *The Last Day, the Last Hour: The Currie Libel Trial* (Toronto: The Osgoode Society, 1988).

15. LAC, CP, v. 7, file 20, Currie to Campbell, 28 September 1927.

16. Dancocks, *Sir Arthur Currie*, 280.

17. Noyes, *Stretcher Bearers at the Double*, 280.

18. See Brian Bond, *The Unquiet Western Front: Britain's Role in Literature and History* (New York: Cambridge University Press, 2002).

19. Jeffrey A. Keshen, *Propaganda and Censorship during Canada's Great War* (Edmonton:

University of Alberta Press, 1996) 195. Also see Dagmar Novak, *Dubious Glory: The Two World Wars and the Canadian Novel* (New York: Peter Lang Publishing, 2000).

20. Vance, *Death So Noble*, 127.

21. See Hynes, *The Soldiers' Tale*.

22. For the reception of Harrison's work, see Jonathan Vance, "The Soldier as Novelist: Literature, History, and the Great War," *Canadian Literature* 179 (Winter 2003).

23. Urquhart, *History of the 16th Battalion*, 342.

24. A.M.J. Hyatt, "Canadian Generals in the First World War and the Popular View of Military Leadership," *Social History/Histoire sociale* 12.24 (November 1979) 418–30.

25. LAC, CP, v. 11, file 33, A.C. Macdonell to Currie, 26 June 1930.

26. Jonathan Vance, "'Today they were alive again': The Canadian Corps Reunion of 1934," *Ontario History* 87, 4 (December 1995) 327–44. On soldiers' nostalgia, see Stephen Garton, "Longing for war: Nostalgia and the Australian returned soldiers after the First World War," in T.G. Ashplant et al. (eds.), *The Politics of War, Memory and Commemoration* (London: Routledge, 2000) 222–39.

27. Thomas P. Socknat, *Witness against War: Pacifism in Canada, 1900–1945* (Toronto: University of Toronto Press, 1987).

28. For the phrase, see William Kilbourn (ed.), *Canada: A Guide to the Peaceable Kingdom* (Toronto: Macmillan of Canada, 1970).

29. Colonel A.F. Duguid, *Official History of the Canadian Forces in the Great War, 1914–1919, General Series*, v. 1 (Ottawa: J.O. Patenaude, Printer to the King, 1938).

30. For the writing of the Great War in Canada, see Tim Cook, *Clio's Warriors*.

31. For the popular memory of the war, see Bond, *The Unquiet Western Front*; and Gary Sheffield, *Forgotten Victory. The First World War: Myth and Realities* (London: Headline Book Publishing, 2001); Dan Todman, *The Great War, Myth and Memory* (London: Hambledon, 2005).

32. Goodspeed, *The Road Past Vimy*, 123.

33. See notes 5 and 6 below.

34. Hughes, The Monstrous Anger of the Guns, 341.

35. LAC, CP, v. 13, file 38, Currie to H.E. Pense, 12 February 1932.

36. Desmond Morton, "La Guerre d'indépendance du Canada une perspective Anglophone," in Roch Legault and Jean Lamarre, *La Première Guerre mondiale et le Canada* (Montreal: Meridien, 1999) 11–34.

37. Rod Mickleburgh, "Remembrance Day being forgotten, poll finds," *The Globe and Mail*, 10 November 2006.

38. Dominion Institute, Vimy Ridge 2007 Survey.

39. Dawson, *Living Bayonets*, 182.

40. LAC, CP, v. 9, file 28, Currie to D.M. Goudy, 12 June 1925.

41. Manion, *A Surgeon in Arms*, 181.

NOTES ON SOURCES (PP. 649–652)

1. Owen A. Cooke, *The Canadian Military Experience, 1867–1995: A Bibliography* (Ottawa: Department of National Defence, 1997); "From Colony to Nation: A Reader's Guide to Canadian Military History": http://www.collectionscanada.ca/military/ 025002-6000-e.html; Tim Cook, *Clio's Warriors: Canadian Historians and the Writing of the World Wars* (Vancouver: UBC Press, 2006).

2. See, for example, Sir Max Aitken, *Canada in Flanders: The Official Story of the Canadian Expeditionary Force,* v. I. (London: Hodder and Stoughton, 1916); J.F.B. Livesay, *Canada's Hundred Days: With the Canadian Corps from Amiens to Mons, Aug. 8–Nov. 11, 1918* (Toronto: T. Allen, 1919).

3. Colonel A.F. Duguid, *Official History of the Canadian Forces in the Great War, 1914–1919, General Series,* v. I. (Ottawa: J.O. Patenaude, Printer to the King, 1938).

4. G.W.L. Nicholson, *CEF.*

5. For a sampling, see A.M.J. Hyatt, *General Sir Arthur Currie: A Military Biography* (Toronto: University of Toronto Press and Canadian War Museum, 1987); Daniel Dancocks, *Welcome to Flanders Fields: The First Canadian Battle of the Great War: Ypres, 1915* (Toronto: McClelland and Stewart, 1988); Bill Rawling, *Surviving Trench Warfare: Technology and the Canadian Corps* (Toronto: University of Toronto Press, 1992); Desmond Morton, *When Your Number's Up: The Canadian Soldier in the First World War* (Toronto: Random House of Canada, 1993); Shane B. Schreiber, *Shock Army of the British Empire: The Canadian Corps in the Last 100 Days of the Great War* (Wesport: Praeger, 1997); Tim Cook, *No Place To Run: The Canadian Corps and Gas Warfare in the First World War* (Vancouver: University of British Columbia Press, 1999); J.L. Granatstein, *Canada's Army: Waging War and Keeping the Peace* (Toronto: University of Toronto Press, 2002).

6. William Stewart, Attack Doctrine in the Canadian Corps, 1916–1918 (Master's thesis: University of New Brunswick, 1982); Ian M. McCulloch, The "Fighting Seventh": The Evolution and Devolution of Tactical Command and Control in a Canadian Infantry Brigade of the Great War (Master's thesis: Royal Military College of Canada, 1997); David Campbell, The Divisional Experience in the C.E.F.: A Social and Operational History of the 2nd Canadian Division, 1915–1918 (Ph.D.dissertation: University of Calgary, 2003); Andrew Iarocci, 1st Canadian Division at War, 1914–15: A Study of Training, Tactics and Leadership (Ph.D. dissertation: Wilfrid Laurier University, 2005).

7. The transcripts are held in the Records of the CBC (RG 41).

8. http://www.canadianletters.ca.

ACKNOWLEDGMENTS

This book marks the culmination of more than a decade of research and writing into the Great War. I have had wonderful opportunities to delve deeply into the official and unofficial archives and history of Canadians at war through my work as a former archivist at the National Archives of Canada and as the current First World War historian at the Canadian War Museum. Yet I could not have written these books without the veterans, writers, and historians who came before me, who created the rich history of the war over the last ninety years.

My goal in these two histories was to write an engaging study of the Canadian Corps that reached beyond academia but was still based in deep archival research and informed by the latest Canadian and international scholarship. My agent, Rick Broadhead, sold the idea to Penguin (Canada), which has been a model publisher. Editorial Director Diane Turbide has been a delight to work with, as her enthusiasm, dedication, and expertise made this a better book. The entire team at Penguin has been fully supportive, and special thanks go to Katie Hearn, Elizabeth McKay, and Debbie Gaudet. Editor Tara Tovell worked on volumes I and II, and her skill at line and copy editing has made this a far better book. I'm deeply grateful for her patience, thoroughness, and belief in the project.

I am a far better historian for having worked at the Canadian War Museum for the last six years. Senior managers Dr. Dean Oliver and Mark O'Neil have been fully supportive of this project. The opportunity to produce exciting exhibitions and projects, while working with brilliant and dedicated colleagues, has been an enriching experience. I would also like to thank the staff and students at Carleton University, who have offered an equally stimulating environment, allowing me to grow as an educator. I am especially indebted to the Carleton students, who have continually forced me to think about and formulate new ideas relating to all aspects of Canadian military history.

Two of my colleagues at the CWM—Dr. Peter MacLeod and Dr. Andrew Iarocci—read the manuscript in its entirety and have offered key observations that have strengthened the final book. A former Carleton student, Jennifer Lazuk, conducted some essential research into personnel files, for which I am grateful. As well, Mark Humphries of Western University and the Wilfrid Laurier Centre for Military Strategic and Disarmament Studies, shared research from his forthcoming multivolume series, *Germany's Western Front: Translations from the German Official History of the Great War,* which provides rare accounts of German forces who faced the Canadians. I'd also like to thank Professor Terry Copp, who made these translations available for the book. Terry has been a driving force in the study of Canadian military history and he and many other senior scholars in the field have been generous with their willingness to show younger colleagues how to engage the past in the present.

My parents, Drs. Sharon and Terry Cook, instilled in me a passion for history, but more importantly their generosity, kindness, and love have shaped and guided my brother Graham and me into productive members of society. It was touch and go for a few of our teenage years, but our parents were, and remain, always there for us.

Publishing three books in three years takes its toll, but Sarah, Chloe, and Emma have been a constant delight, and without them I could not have finished this project. They remind me daily that I am a husband and father first, and I would not want it any other way. To them this book is dedicated, along with my love, and also to baby number three, who will arrive in a few months and whom Chloe calls Piper-Paige. We think of her daily.

Finally, I am drawn to that generation of Canadians who sacrificed so much during the Great War. While I have studied and read about them for longer than I can remember, many aspects of their lives remain a mystery, although I hope these two volumes will help others to better understand those who lived and died fighting in what Canadians in the early twentieth century called the Great War for Civilization.

INDEX

CREDITS

Permission to reproduce the following copyrighted works is gratefully acknowledged.
Note: Canadian War Museum (CWM); Library and Archives Canada (LAC)

Photographs

Page 8: Library and Archives Canada (LAC), PA-002439

Page 12: LAC, PA-000868

Page 15: LAC, PA-001356

Page 20: Canadian War Museum, George Metcalf Archival Collection, 017-19900346-127(b)

Page 27: In author's possession

Page 32: LAC, PA-034180

Page 48: LAC, PA-001989

Page 56: CWM, Beaverbrook Collection of War Art, AN 19710261-0431

Page 60: *The War Illustrated*, 25 September 1916

Page 81: In author's possession

Page 89: LAC, PA-001133

Page 100: LAC, PA-197658

Page 113: LAC, PA-004388

Page 119: LAC, PA-001409

Page 125: LAC, PA-001079

Page 143: LAC, PA-002047

Page 164: LAC, PA-001168

Page 170: LAC, PA-000914

Page 180: City of Toronto Archives, Fonds 1244, Item 829

Page 223: LAC, PA-001211

Page 258: LAC, PA-002497

Page 274: LAC, PA-000732

Page 275: LAC, PA-001196

Page 277: LAC, PA-002444

Page 287: LAC, PA-002013

Page 294: LAC, PA-080027

Page 314: LAC, PA-002165

Page 320: LAC, PA-203266

Page 325: LAC, PA-002084

Page 326: LAC, PA-002137

Page 333: LAC, PA-002352

Page 339: LAC, PA-002107

Page 355: LAC, PA-002162

Page 364: LAC, PA-002195

Page 385: LAC, PA-000723

Page 412: LAC, PA-003235

Page 421: LAC, PA-002879

Page 448: LAC, PA-002853

Page 466: LAC, PA-003187

Page 485: LAC, PA-003130

Page 490: CWM, 19940001-412

Page 527: LAC, PA-003138

Page 537: LAC, PA-003202

Page 543: LAC, PA-002139

Page 554: LAC, PA003641

Page 566: LAC, PA-003377

Page 579: In author's possession

Page 618: Courtesy of Tristan Glen

Page 626: LAC, PA-083625

Page 647: CWM, George Metcalf Archival Collection, O.2265

Illustrations

Page 24: CWM, S.S. 182, page 40

Page 26 (top): CWM, *Instructions on the Lewis Automatic Machine Gun, 1917*, page 20

Page 26 (bottom): CWM, *Instructions on the Lewis Automatic Machine Gun, 1917*, page 20a

Page 29: CWM, *Field Entrenchments, 1916*, page 211

Page 94: In author's possession

Page 190: *The Listening Post*, Christmas Issue, 1917, page 15

Page 250: CWM, 20030054-001

Page 264: CWM, *Instructions on the Lewis Automatic Machine Gun, 1917*, page 121

Page 454: CWM, Sir Arthur Currie papers, 58A 1 60.2, Notes on recent fighting, No. 13

Page 471: CWM, S.S. 153, plate 1

Page 629: *Halifax Herald*